IMPORTANT

HERE IS YOUR REGISTRATION CODE TO ACCESS MCGRAW-HILL PREMIUM CONTENT AND MCGRAW-HILL ONLINE RESOURCES.

For key premium online resources you need THIS CODE to gain access. Once the code is entered, you will be able to use the web resources for the length of your course.

Access is provided only if you have purchased a new book.

If the registration code is missing from this book, the registration screen on our website, and within your WebCT or Blackboard course will tell you how to obtain your new code. Your registration code can be used only once to establish access. It is not transferable

To gain access to these online resources

1. USE your web browser to go to: **www.mhhe.com/degenova6**

2. CLICK on "First Time User"

3. ENTER the Registration Code printed on the tear-off bookmark on the right

4. After you have entered your registration code, click on "Register"

5. FOLLOW the instructions to setup your personal UserID and Password

6. WRITE your UserID and Password down for future reference. Keep it in a safe place.

If your course is using WebCT or Blackboard, you'll be able to use this code to access the McGraw-Hill content within your instructor's online course.

To gain access to the McGraw-Hill content in your instructor's WebCT or Blackboard course simply log into the course with the user ID and Password provided by your instructor. Enter the registration code exactly as it appears to the right when prompted by the system. You will only need to use this code the first time you click on McGraw-Hill content.

These instructions are specifically for student access. Instructors are not required to register via the above instructions.

The McGraw-Hill Companies

Mc Graw Hill Higher Education

Thank you, and welcome to your McGraw-Hill Online Resources.

0-07-296294-1 t/a
Degenova
Intimate Relationships, Marriages and Families, 6/e

REGISTRATION CODE

*Intimate Relationships,
Marriages, and Families*

Intimate Relationships, Marriages, and Families

SIXTH EDITION

Mary K. DeGenova

F. Philip Rice

McGraw Hill

Boston   Burr Ridge, IL   Dubuque, IA   Madison, WI   New York
San Francisco   St. Louis   Bangkok   Bogotá   Caracas   Kuala Lumpur
Lisbon   London   Madrid   Mexico City   Milan   Montreal   New Delhi
Santiago   Seoul   Singapore   Sydney   Taipei   Toronto

Higher Education

To Louis and Eleanor

INTIMATE RELATIONSHIPS, MARRIAGES, AND FAMILIES
Published by McGraw-Hill, a business unit of The McGraw-Hill Companies, Inc., 1221 Avenue of the
Americas, New York, NY, 10020. Copyright © 2005, 2002, 1999, 1996, 1993, 1990 by The McGraw-Hill
Companies, Inc. All rights reserved. No part of this publication may be reproduced or distributed in any
form or by any means, or stored in a database or retrieval system, without the prior written consent of The
McGraw-Hill Companies, Inc., including, but not limited to, in any network or other electronic storage or
transmission, or broadcast for distance learning.

Some ancillaries, including electronic and print components, may not be available to customers outside the
United States.

This book is printed on acid-free paper.

2 3 4 5 6 7 8 9 0 VNH/VNH 0 9 8 7 6 5

ISBN 0-07-287501-1

Publisher: *Phillip A. Butcher*
Senior sponsoring editor: *Carolyn Henderson Meier*
Senior marketing manager: *Daniel M. Loch*
Producer, Media technology: *Jessica Bodie*
Senior project manager: *Rebecca Nordbrock*
Lead production supervisor: *Randy L. Hurst*
Designer: *Preston Thomas*
Media project manager: *Kathleen Boylan*
Photo research coordinator: *Alexandra Ambrose*
Art editor: *Emma C. Ghiselli*
Photo researcher: *Toni Michaels*
Art director: *Jeanne Schreiber*
Permissions editor: *Marty Granahan*
Cover design: *Irene Morris*
Cover photo: *@Images.com/CORBIS*
Interior design: *Jean Mailander and Linda Robertson*
Typeface: *9.5/12 Palatino*
Compositor: *Thompson Type*
Printer: *Von Hoffmann Corporation*

Library of Congress Cataloging-in-Publication Data

DeGenova, Mary Kay.
    Intimate relationships, marriages, and families/Mary Kay DeGenova, F. Philip Rice.—6th ed.
        p. cm.
    Includes bibliographical references and index.
    ISBN 0-07-287501-1 (alk. paper)
    1. Family life education—United States. I. Rice, F. Philip. II. Title.
HQ10.5.U6R53 2005
306.8—dc22   2004044884

www.mhhe.com

Brief Contents

Contents

CHAPTER 2

Family Backgrounds and How They Influence Us   36

CHAPTER 5

Attraction and Dating   108

CHAPTER 6

CHAPTER 7

CHAPTER 8

CHAPTER 9

Work, Family Roles, and Material Resources   216

CHAPTER 10

Power, Decision Making, and Communication 246

CHAPTER 11

Family Planning and Parenting 266

CHAPTER 12

Pregnancy and Childbirth   298

CHAPTER 13

CHAPTER 14

Parents and Extended Family Relationships   346

CHAPTER 15

Conflict, Family Crises, and Crisis Management   366

CHAPTER 16

The Family and Divorce   394

CHAPTER 17

Coming Together: Remarriage and Stepparenting 422

Boxed Features

About the Authors

Mary Kay DeGenova received her Ph.D. in 1992 from Purdue University in Child Development and Family Studies. She was an associate professor of Family Studies at Central Michigan University and the University of New Hampshire and has taught various courses on marriage and the family. Her work on this text is a direct result of her experiences in the classroom and her experiences with diversity, including work as a Peace Corps Volunteer in West Africa and a Fulbright Scholar in Chile. In addition to her recent work on this text DeGenova has written *Families in Cultural Context: Strengths and Challenges in Diversity,* published by Mayfield Publishing Company. She is currently working from home on numerous writing projects while caring for her two children.

The late **F. Philip Rice** received his Ed.D. in Marriage and Family Relationships from Teachers College of Columbia University and taught courses in the field of Marriage and Family for many years at the University of Maine–Orono. In addition to *Intimate Relationships, Marriages and Families* he wrote more than twenty other texts on Marriage and Family, Stepparenting, Working Mothers, Human Sexuality, Human Development, and numerous others in related fields. His principal areas of research included Human Development, Child Development, Adolescent Development, Adult Development, and Marriage and Family Relations.

Preface

All people share a fundamental drive to form intimate relationships with other human beings, though these relationships may take a variety of forms. As you go through life, your needs for intimacy constantly change. A young infant needs to be fed and cuddled; a school-aged child needs to have friends; an adolescent begins exploring sexuality; most adult men and women seek a partner, marry, and have children; and many elderly people need assistance from family in the later years of life.

When people are in relationships, it is almost inevitable that there will be challenges. Very few long-term intimate relationships exist without some degree of friction and pain. For most people, it takes a lot of work to create and maintain healthy, fulfilling relationships; for others, it is a constant struggle. And while relationships can be a source of pain, they also can be our biggest source of joy in life, bringing happiness, satisfaction, even exhilaration. In the end, most people would agree that experiencing intimate and family relationships is the true essence of life and the abiding force that sustains and transforms them. The goal of this textbook—and most likely your course overall—is to help you learn to resolve interpersonal conflicts, develop social skills, and seek relationships that fulfill and enrich your lives.

Each of you has tremendous capacity to grow and change; and choices in regard to relationships are abundant today. To choose wisely, and to grow and change in ways that are best for you, you need a cognitive understanding of what is involved, what choices you have, and what the consequences of these choices may be. It is here that the information provided by the social and behavioral sciences can help. As a student using this text, you will have the opportunity to learn from thousands of research studies examining many facets of relationships. Objectively studying many different kinds of relationships can help you understand and make better choices in your own relationships as well as clarify your own personal attitudes and values.

The more you understand about the vast array of relationships and different kinds of challenges they present, the better able you are to be objective and tolerant of others. You will learn from this text that marriage and family patterns are tremendously diverse and that no one way can be considered the "right way" or the ideal for everyone. Also, as we study many different relationship patterns, we learn that some of our own quirks actually may be more widespread than we would have imagined.

It is also important to understand how your choices and actions as a citizen impact intimate relationships and families on a societal level. When you vote, you elect officials who write laws and policies that determine such things as who can get married or how much funding after-school programs receive. Many public policy issues such as these directly affect most families. Each chapter in this book explores a public policy issue and its relationship to families. These issues, like so many family issues, are often controversial. This text adopts neither a liberal nor conservative view, but rather it presents you with many different sides of an issue and challenges you to find your own individual values and answers to these important questions.

As you examine relationships over the life course, you will see that relationships are dynamic and constantly changing. One thing for sure is that change, while it is some people's biggest fear, is inevitable in life. People change, situations change, relationships change. The love you feel today may not be exactly the same as the love you will feel 10 years from now. The person you were in high school changed into the person you are today. At the same time there is also continuity to life, and what happens now greatly influences tomorrow. What happened in your families when you were children impacts what will happen in your families when you are adults. This book illustrates that there is similarity in the ways humans develop and cope with changes, but there is also diversity. To show students what may be expected at a particular life stage, how others have responded, and how those responses have affected the quality of their intimate relationships is an important aim of this book.

ORGANIZATION

One of the biggest changes in the sixth edition is its organization. The text was restructured to include 17 chapters—four fewer than the previous edition—to make it more practical for classroom use. Much of the material in the eliminated chapters is now covered in other places. For example, the text no longer has a chapter on cultural and ethnic diversity in families, but material on cultural diversity has been increased and is now woven throughout the text as opposed to being set aside in a separate chapter.

The text begins with an examination of the trends and changes taking place in marriage and family today and how different theoretical perspectives interpret those changes (Chapter 1). Chapter 2 describes ways that family background influences our attitudes toward intimate relationships, gender roles, marriage and divorce, parenthood, and communication within the family. The concepts of gender and

gender roles are examined and some of the influences on their development are described in Chapter 3.

Chapters 4 through 6 explore relationships before marriage ranging from singlehood to dating to partner selection. Marriage brings with it a new set of demands for growth and change. Chapter 7 considers first the qualities essential to happy and successful marriages, and Chapter 8 discusses changes in marital relationships over the life cycle. Chapters 9 and 10 explore work and family roles and the effect of economic status and power, decision making, and communication.

Chapters 11 to 14 focus on parenthood. The decisions involved in parenthood and family planning are discussed in Chapter 11, and Chapter 12 follows the birth process from conception through pregnancy and the preparations made by the family for a new baby. Chapter 13 examines parent–child relationships, While Chapter 14 considers relationships among members of the extended family, especially aging relatives.

Most families at one time or another experience some conflict or face a period of crisis. The text explores conflict and family crises in Chapter 15, the causes and effects of divorce in Chapter 16, and the special challenges of remarriage and stepparenting in Chapter 17.

NEW TO THE SIXTH EDITION

The sixth edition has changed in many ways. All chapters were carefully revised and updated to incorporate current research and statistics and newly emerging topics. Chapters have been streamlined and reorganized, as mentioned, to more closely match the way most instructors teach the course. Especially significant is the change we have made to our coverage of cultural diversity, which is no longer set aside in a separate chapter but is now integrated throughout the text. Research studies that included a culturally diverse sample are discussed wherever possible. And the chapter on gender identity was moved to the front of the text to precede a discussion on dating, love, and mate selection.

A thorough examination of the recent trends in marriage and families explains those trends using the most current U.S. statistics. Among the trends discussed are:

- the increase in cohabitation and its impact on family life
- increased life expectancy and its relationship to families
- grandparents raising their grandchildren
- sex outside of marriage
- marital delay
- gay and lesbian families
- oral sex and STDs
- changes in dating practices
- Internet dating and cybersex
- changing gender roles and identity
- changes in fertility, contraception, and childbirth
- the increase of cultural diversity in the United States

A careful review of literature was conducted that focused on positive aspects of family life and qualities of fulfilling and satisfying intimate relationships. Among the topics covered are:

- the importance of couples' rituals and family time
- qualities of a successful marriage
- sex and a happy marriage
- the impact of premarital education
- premarital predictors of marital quality
- the newlywed years as predictors of marital satisfaction
- the need for families to have more time together
- family happiness and material wealth
- causes and correlates of divorce
- healthy and happy stepfamilies

The sixth edition expands on and updates information on the relationship between family life and economics, and it also deals with the increase in the number of families struggling financially. Some of the subjects included are:

- the increase in consumer debt
- poverty, the working poor, and family life
- the widening gap between rich and poor
- work, stress, and the family
- characteristics of dual-earner families

- family-friendly policies in the workplace

PEDAGOGICAL AIDS

In addition to all the changes already mentioned, we include plentiful, current photographs to make the book even more inviting and relevant for students. Redesigned and carefully updated tables and figures highlight and amplify the text coverage. Chapter outlines, objectives, marginal definitions, and review sections combine with a comprehensive glossary to help students master the material. And to maintain student interest and spotlight important current issues, we also include a number of innovative features in this edition:

- *A Question of Policy*—This new end-of-chapter section, designed to foster debate and help develop students' critical thinking abilities, introduces the public or social policy implications of an emerging, often controversial family issue.
- *Cross-Cultural Perspectives*—In keeping with the text's emphasis on diversity, we have created this box to illuminate diversity research and issues—highlighting things like cultural conflict and acculturation, racism, family strengths across cultures, and more.
- *At Issue Today*—Another unique box, this one is designed to focus student attention on some of today's most pressing challenges—STDs, welfare and family, grandparents who parent their grandchildren, and more.

SUPPLEMENTS

As a full-service publisher of quality educational products, McGraw-Hill does much more than just sell textbooks. The company creates and publishes an extensive array of print, video, and digital supplements for students and instructors. This edition of *Intimate Relationships, Marriages, and Families* is accompanied by a complete supplements package.

For the Student

- *Reel Families CD-ROM*—This unique, interactive movie takes the concept of active learning to a whole new level, enabling students to take on the role of one of the story's characters and influence key plot turns by making choices for that character. The movie, centered on an assault that takes place in a college town, allows students to explore course concepts and terminology in a relevant and meaningful context. Movie segments are augmented by a robust array of review and assessment features. With this breakthrough learning tool, students can explore a wide variety of course topics firsthand— divorce, domestic violence, racial, ethnic, and class differences among families, and more—and master concepts more completely than they could by just reading any text.

- *Online Learning Center Website*—An innovative, text-specific website featuring PowerWeb— online access to articles from the popular and scholarly press, weekly updates, and daily newsfeeds—as well as flash cards that can be used to master vocabulary, quizzes with feedback that students can use to study for exams, and more.

For the Instructor

- *Instructor's Resource CD*—A single CD with an easy-to-use interface providing access to a wide array of important ancillaries.
  - *Instructor's Manual/Testbank*—Includes detailed chapter outlines, key terms, overviews, lecture notes, and a complete testbank.
  - *Computerized Testbank*—Easy-to-use computerized testing program for both Windows and Macintosh computers.
  - *Reel Families Instructor's Guide*—Teaching tips and notes that make it easy to integrate the *Reel Families* CD into your course.
  - *PowerPoint Slides*—Complete, chapter-by-chapter slideshows featuring text, art, and tables.
- *Reel Families Lecture Launcher Videotape*—Even if you can't require students to use the CD, you can use the movie footage to jump-start lectures in a unique and exciting fashion.
- *Online Learning Center Website*—Password-protected access to important instructor support materials and additional resources.

- *Course Management Systems*—Whether you use WebCT, Blackboard, e-College, or another course management system, McGraw-Hill will provide you with a cartridge that enables you to either conduct your course entirely online or to supplement your lectures with online material. And if your school does not yet have one of these course management systems, we can provide you with PageOut, an easy-to-use tool that allows you to create your own course Web page and access all material on the Online Learning Center.

ACKNOWLEDGMENTS

A special acknowledgment goes to the late F. Philip Rice for his years of hard work and commitment to writing this textbook. I thank him for his insight and valuable instruction on marriage and the family, and I am grateful his ideas and writings live on in this text.

This text would not have been possible without the assistance and cooperation of many people. I would like to thank my editor, Carolyn Henderson Meier, for her support, expertise, and valuable suggestions for improving this edition. I am grateful to senior project manager, Rebecca Nordbrock, for keeping this project on track. Photo researcher Toni Michaels did an excellent job providing new and interesting photos for selection, and the selection process was enjoyable because of her effort. Lastly, I would like to thank Joan Wilder Jordan, for her assistance in writing this edition and her numerous hours of library research with government documents and statistics. Her humor, wit, extraordinary capability, scrupulous eye for detail, and friendship made working together on this edition an enriching and cherished experience.

The authors thank the reviewers for their guidance and suggestions: For the first edition:

Jeanne H. Ballantine, Wright State University
Bruce L. Campbell, California State University at Los Angeles
Eugene W. Jacobs, Presbyterian College
Jeanne Kohl, University of Washington
Sherrill Richarz, Washington State University
Jay D. Schvaneveidt, Utah State University
Barbara H. Settles, University of Delaware
Benjamin Silliman, Louisiana Technical University

W. Fred Stultz,
    California Polytechnic State University

For the second edition:

Scott M. Allgood, Auburn University
Esther DeVall, New Mexico State University
Deborah Gentry, Illinois State University
Jeanne E. Kohl, University of Washington
Lowell J. Krokoff, Florida International University
Estella Martinez, University of New Mexico
Bernita Quoss, University of Wyoming
Kenrick S. Thompson, Northern Michigan
    University.

For the third edition:

Scott M. Allgood, Utah State University
Esther L. DeVall, New Mexico State University
Bernita Quoss, University of Wyoming
Kenrick S. Thompson, Northern Michigan
    University.

For the fourth edition:

Glee Absher, University of Central
    Oklahoma–Edmond
Scott M. Allgood, Utah State University
Elizabeth B. Carroll, East Carolina University
Patricia A. Levy, University of Southern
    Colorado

Thanks are also due to Jeanne Kohl-Welles, University of Washington, for her work on the study guide and test bank, both past and present editions; and to Kenrick Thompson, now of Arkansas State University, Mountain Home, for his updating of the test bank.

For the fifth edition:

Scott M. Allgood, Utah State University
Elizabeth B. Carroll, East Carolina University
Bryce Dickey, Western Michigan University
Patricia Gibbs, Foothill College
Joyce M. Johnson, Santa Rosa Junior College
Michael Traugot, Tennessee State University

Also, the authors thank Eileen Malone Beach, Amy Voege, and Laura J. Vogel for their support and assistance in revising the fifth edition of this text.

The authors wish to thank the following people who have reviewed and offered guidance and suggestions for the sixth edition:

Maria Lavooy, University of Central Florida
Theodore N. Greenstein, North Carolina
    State University
Jeffrey Rosenfeld, Nassau Community College
Denise A. Donnelly, Georgia State University
Robin Jarrett, University of Illinois
    at Urbana–Champaign
Beverly Stiles, Midwestern State University
Sylvia M. Asay, University of Nebraska
    at Kearney

*Intimate Relationships,
Marriages, and Families*

CHAPTER 1

LEARNING OBJECTIVES

After reading the chapter, you should be able to:

- Define *family* and describe various family forms.

- Explain the changes in family philosophy and emphasis: the change from institution to companionship and from patriarchy to democracy.

- Outline the basic trends in marriage rates, median age at first marriage, birthrates and family size, working mothers, one-parent families, cohabitation, and gay and lesbian families.

- Summarize the basic trends in divorce rates, remarriage, and blended families.

- Describe present trends in nonmarital sexual behavior and use of contraceptives.

- Define ethnicity and culture and describe the composition of U.S. population by race.

- Explain behavior and patterns in families using the seven different family theories.

Intimate Relationships, Marriages, and Families in the Twenty-First Century

Families are universal and yet each is unique. In an ever-changing world, families cannot remain static. Thus, families as we know them today are different from those of previous generations. They differ in structure, composition, size, and function. The reasons people marry and their marital expectations have changed. Changes have also occurred in how families are governed, in who supports families, and in how people behave sexually. An analysis of marriage rates and ages, birthrates, the percentages of working mothers, numbers of one-parent families, cohabitation rates, gay and lesbian families, grandparents as parents, divorce and remarriage rates, and the numbers of blended families, reveals some significant trends.

We are going to examine some of these changes and trends and their effects on society and the individual. In addition, it's important for each of us to consider: How have these changes affected me?

WHAT IS A FAMILY?

What makes a family? Do its members have to be related by blood? By marriage? Do they have to share the same household? We'll examine a few of the countless definitions of *family* that have been formulated in recent decades, and then we'll look at some of the variations in types of families that have been identified by psychologists, sociologists, and anthropologists.

Some Definitions

The U.S. Bureau of the Census (2000) defines a family as a group of two or more people (one of whom is the householder) related by birth, marriage, or adoption and residing together. In the census count, the number of families is equal to the number of family households. However, the count of family members differs from the count of household members because household members include any non-relatives living in the household. By this definition, the family may consist of two persons who are not necessarily of different genders: two brothers, two female cousins, a mother and daughter, and so on. They may also be of different genders: a husband and wife, a mother and son, a brother and sister, and so on. If the family includes two adults, they

may or may not have children. The common characteristics included in this definition are twofold: (1) The individuals must be related by blood or law, and (2) they must live together in one household. Thus, according to the Census Bureau, if adult children move out of their parents' household and establish families of their own, they are no longer considered a part of their parents' family.

Other definitions have been proposed. Winch (1971) defined the family as "a set of persons related to each other by blood, marriage, or adoption and whose basic societal function is replacement." But this definition seems to limit family functions to child rearing. Burgess and Locke (1953) defined the family as "a group of persons united by ties of marriage, blood, or adoption; constituting a single household; interacting and communicating with each other in their respective social roles (husband and wife, mother and father, son and daughter, brother and sister); and creating and maintaining a common culture." This definition would eliminate those cohabiting, though not legally related or married. It seems to assume as well that individuals in a family must conform to some sort of prescribed social roles.

None of these definitions seems to cover all types of family situations: particularly nonmarried cohabiting couples and gay and lesbian couples. It is understandable that many people, such as those in committed gay and lesbian relationships, omitted in the U.S. Bureau of the Census definition of the family would like to see a change in that definition. A more comprehensive and less stereotyped definition is used in this book: A **family** is any group of persons united by the ties of marriage, blood, or adoption, or any sexually expressive relationship, in which (1) the adults cooperate financially for their mutual support, (2) the people are committed to one another in an intimate, interpersonal relationship, and (3) the members see their individual identities as importantly attached to the group, and (4) the group has an identity of its own.

This definition has a number of advantages. It includes a variety of family structures: the traditional married couple with or without children, single-parent families, families consisting of blood relatives (such as two widowed sisters, a grandparent and grandchildren, and a multigenerational extended family). It also includes persons not related by marriage, blood, or adoption who have a sexual relationship: an unmarried cohabiting couple, a gay or lesbian couple. Because this definition insists that the persons be committed and in an intimate interpersonal relationship, it eliminates cohabiting couples who live together for practical reasons, without commitment, and those who have only a casual relationship even though they may have sex together. The members must see their individual identities as importantly attached to the group, and the group must have an identity of its own.

Family Forms

We can categorize families according to their structure and the relationships among the people in them.

A **voluntarily childless family** is a couple who decide not to have children. (Some people refer to this as a child-free family.)

A **single-parent family** consists of a parent (who may or may not have been married) and one or more children.

A **nuclear family** consists of a father, a mother, and their children. This type of family as a proportion of all families has been declining as the family form has become more diverse.

A **family of origin** is the family into which you are born and in which you are raised. The family consists of you, your parents, and your siblings.

A **family of procreation** is the family you establish if you have children of your own.

An **extended family** consists of you, possibly a partner, any children you might have, and other relatives who live in your household or nearby. It can also include grandparents who are helping to care for grandchildren.

A **blended, or reconstituted, family** is formed when a widowed or divorced person, with or without children, remarries another person who may or may not have been married before and who may or may not have children (Dowling, 1983). If either the husband or wife has children from a former marriage or previous relationship, a **stepfamily** is formed.

A **binuclear family** is an original family divided into two families by divorce. It consists of two nuclear families: (1) the maternal nuclear family headed by the mother and (2) the paternal family headed by the father. The families include whatever

children were in the original family and may be headed by a single parent or two parents if former spouses remarry (Ahrons and Rodgers, 1987).

A **polygamous family** is a single family unit based on the marriage of one person to two or more mates. If the man has more than one wife, a **polygynous family** is formed. If a woman has more than one husband, a **polyandrous family** is formed. Polyandry is rare, but polygyny is practiced in African and Asian countries. Both are illegal in the United States.

family Any group of people united by ties of marriage, blood, or adoption, or any sexually expressive relationship, in which (1) the adults cooperate financially for their mutual support, (2) the people are committed to one another in an intimate interpersonal relationship, (3) the members see their individual identities as importantly attached to the group, and (4) the group has an identity of its own.

voluntarily childless family A couple who decide not to have children.

single-parent family A parent (who may or may not have been married) and one or more children.

nuclear family A father, a mother, and their children.

family of origin The family into which you are born and in which you are raised.

family of procreation The family you establish if you have children of your own.

extended family An individual, possibly a partner, any children you might have, and other relatives who live in the household or nearby.

blended, or reconstituted, family A family formed when a widowed or divorced person, with or without children, marries another person who may or may not have been married before and who may or may not have children.

stepfamily A remarried man and/or woman plus children from a former marriage.

binuclear family An original family divided into two families by divorce.

polygamous family A single family unit based on the marriage of one person to two or more mates.

polygynous family A man married to more than one woman.

polyandrous family A woman married to more than one husband.

The conventional idea of a family is two parents and one or more children, but in reality, there are many varieties of family structure.

A **patriarchal family** is one in which the father is head of the household, with authority over other members of the family.

A **matriarchal family** is one in which the mother is head of the household, with authority over other members of the family.

A **gay or lesbian family** consists of a couple of the same sex who are living together and sharing sexual expression and commitment. Some gay or lesbian families include children, usually the offspring of one of the partners.

A **cohabiting family** consists of two people of the opposite sex who are living together and sharing sexual expression, and who are committed to their relationship without formal legal marriage.

When talking about the family, then, we need to understand which type we are referring to. With such a wide variety of family forms, we can no longer assume that the word *family* is synonymous with *nuclear family*.

CHANGES IN FAMILY PHILOSOPHY AND EMPHASIS

Both the structure and the function of the family have changed over the years. It is important to have a historical perspective on change in order to better understand the present and possible future charac-

teristics of the family. Two large changes that have influenced many characteristics of the family have been from institution to companionship and from patriarchy to democracy.

From Institution to Companionship

One of the most important changes in family function has been a shift in emphasis (Mancini and Orthner, 1988; Scanzoni, 1987). Traditional views emphasized the role of the family as an institution whose function was to meet the needs of society or the physical needs of family members; this is the **instrumental role** of the family. More modern views of the family tend to emphasize its role in fulfilling emotional and social needs of family members; this is the **expressive role** of the family (Edwards, 1987). One explanation for this shift is that U.S. society has become highly industrialized.

In an industrial society in which the majority of people live in urban areas, neighbors remain strangers, and it becomes harder for people to find friendship, companionship, and emotional support. Affectional needs may not be met; the individual feels isolated and alone even though surrounded by millions of people. In such an impersonal society, it becomes more important to find intimacy, a sense of belonging, and emotional security in the family itself. There is a universal longing to be attached, to relate, to belong, to be needed, to care.

Most humans need a profoundly reaffirming experience of genuine intimacy. Erik Erikson (1959) suggested that the achievement of intimacy is one of the major goals of life. In a highly impersonal society, in which emotional isolation is frequent, developing a close family relationship can be vital to one's identity and security.

There has been some shift, therefore, in family functions. In the 1800s, people openly admitted to marrying to obtain economic security, to provide goods and services for one another, to attain social status, to reproduce, and to raise children. By the 1970s, people professed to marry for love, companionship, and the satisfaction of emotional needs. Raising healthy and happy children and having economic security are still important reasons for marriage, but love and affection are people's primary expectations in marriage today (Barich and Bielby, 1996).

This shift has changed the family itself. When people establish a family for love, companionship, and emotional security but don't find fulfillment, they may become disappointed, frustrated, and full of feelings of failure. The higher their personal expectations, the greater the possibility of failure. Sometimes expectations are charged with so much romantic fantasy that fulfillment becomes impossible. Some couples begin to feel that their personal happiness no longer depends on their being married (Glenn and Weaver, 1988). This is one reason for the high rate of divorce. Rather than staying together, couples often separate if their personal needs and expectations are not met.

From Patriarchy to Democracy

Throughout most of our history, the American family was patriarchal. The father was considered head of the household, with authority over and responsibilities for other members of the family. He was the supreme authority in making decisions and settling disputes. He was entitled to the deference and respect of other family members, who were expected to be submissive and obedient.

As head of the household, he owned the property, which was passed to the next generation through the male line. This is known as **patrilineal descent.** The wife and children were expected to reside with the husband and with or near the husband's family, according to his choice. This is **patrilocal residence.** However, patriarchy is not seen in all families. As noted earlier, in the section on family forms, some families are matriarchal, meaning the mother is the head of the household. The terms that refer to female descent and residence are **matrilineal descent** and **matrilocal residence.** This practice was seen in traditional Iroquois society, in which men were expected to move to the female household, and important lines of descent were traced through the female.

Generally, in the 1950s and before, one characteristic of the traditional patriarchal family was a clear-cut distinction between the husband's and wife's roles in the family. The husband was the breadwinner and was usually responsible for clearly defined chores that were considered "man's work," such as making house repairs or mowing the lawn. The wife was responsible for "woman's work," including housecleaning, cooking, sewing and mending, and caring for the children.

With the cultural climate of activism of the civil rights movement of the 1950s and the women's rights movement of the 1960s, the ideals of the patriarchal family were challenged. The patriarchal family was

patriarchal family A family in which the father is head of the household with authority over other family members.

matriarchal family A family in which the mother is head of the household with authority over other family members.

gay or lesbian family Two people of the same sex who are living together, having sex, and being mutually committed.

cohabiting family Two people of the opposite sex who are living together and sharing sexual expression, and who are committed to their relationship without formal legal marriage.

instrumental role The role of the family in meeting the needs of society or the physical needs of family members.

expressive role The role of the family in meeting the emotional and social needs of family members.

patrilineal descent Inheritance that is traced through the male line.

patrilocal residence A residential pattern in which a newlywed couple resides with or near the man's family.

matrilineal descent Inheritance that is traced through the female line.

matrilocal residence A residential pattern in which newlyweds reside with or near the woman's family.

The family pictured here was once considered the ideal. The father was traditionally the head of the household, with authority over all the family members.

replaced by the democratic family, in which women were treated more as equals and demanded a greater voice in family governance (Vannoy, 1991).

This change had several causes. First, with the rise of the feminist movement, women gained some economic power and freedom. The feminist movement in the United States was launched at Seneca Falls, New York, in 1848, where the first women's rights convention was held. The delegates asserted that "men *and* women are created equal . . . endowed . . . with certain inalienable rights." Starting with almost no political leverage and no money, and with conventional morality against them, the suffragists won enactment of the Married Women's Property Act in the latter half of the nineteenth century and ratification of the Nineteenth Amendment to the Constitution in 1920, which gave women the right to vote. The Married Women's Property Act recognized the right of women to hold property and borrow money. As some economic power gradually shifted to women, they gained more power and authority in family governance as well. Property could now be passed on through **bilateral descent** (through both the father and the mother).

bilateral descent   Inheritance is passed through both the male and the female line.

neolocal residence   A residential pattern in which newlyweds leave their parents' home and reside in a new location of their choice rather than with either family.

Second, in the 1960s and 1970s, increasing educational opportunities for women and the gradual increase in the percentage of married women working outside the home encouraged the adoption of more egalitarian gender roles in the family. As more wives earned an income, more husbands were asked to bear equal responsibility for homemaking and child care. While a sharing of responsibilities was the developing ideal, it was not always followed in practice, and working wives continued to do most of the housework (Blumstein and Schwartz, 1983). The general trend, however, is toward a more equal voice in decision making and a more equitable and flexible distribution of family responsibilities; see Chapter 3 for a detailed discussion. Democratic, egalitarian, dual-career families, often prefer a **neolocal residence**—a place where both spouses choose to live, rather than living with either spouse's family.

Third, in the 1960s and 1970s, the demand for equality of sexual expression resulted from the recognition of the sexual needs of women. With such recognition, marriages could be based on the mutual exchange of love and affection. Development of efficient contraceptives also freed women from unwanted childbearing and enabled them to have a personal life of their own and a social life with their husband.

Fourth, the child study movement after World War II catalyzed the development of the child-centered family. No longer was it a matter of what children could do to serve the family; rather, it became a matter of what the family could contribute

After years of protest, in the latter half of the nineteenth century, women won the right to own property and borrow money with the enactment of the Married Women's Property Act. Women who fought for the right to own property may have been arrested for the cause.

to the total development of the child. The rights and needs of children as important members of the family were emphasized.

The net result of these and other changes has been the development of a democratic family ideal that emphasizes egalitarian rights and responsibilities in a group concerned with the welfare of all. This ideal has not always been achieved, but family philosophies, forms, and functions continue to change as new needs arise.

CHANGES IN MARRIAGE AND PARENTHOOD

As we will see, marriage and parenthood have undergone various changes in recent decades. The marriage rate has gone down, the age at which people marry has gone up, and the number of children per family has declined.

Marriage Rates

The marriage rate is the number of persons who marry during the preceding 12 months per 1,000 population. The rate depends on economic and political conditions, as well as on the percentage of persons of marriageable age in the population. The rate reached a peak of 12.2 per 1,000 population in 1945, the last year of World War II. The rate then declined very rapidly after the war, falling to 8.5 per 1,000 in 1960. The rate varied at a fairly high level for two decades and then began to fall again in 1980, after most of the baby boom babies had married (see Figure 1.1). Today the rate is 8.4 per 1,000 (U.S. Bureau of the Census, 2001).

Median Age

One of the most dramatic trends in marriage patterns over the decades has been the postponement of marriage to a later age. At the beginning of the twentieth century, the median age at first marriage started a decline that ended in the mid-1950s, reaching a low of 22.5 years for males and 20.1 years for females. Since then, the estimated median age has been rising, with especially rapid increases since 1980. In 2000, the median age was 26.8 for males and 25.1 for females. Figure 1.2 shows this trend. The gap between males and females has also narrowed over the years, but on average, men are still 1.7 years older than women the first time they marry.

A higher age at marriage is associated with economic prosperity and school enrollment. Today,

Figure 1.1   Marriage Rate per 1,000 Population (*Note:* From *Statistical Abstract of the United States, 2002* [Table 110] by U.S. Bureau of the Census, Washington, DC: U.S. Government Printing Office.)

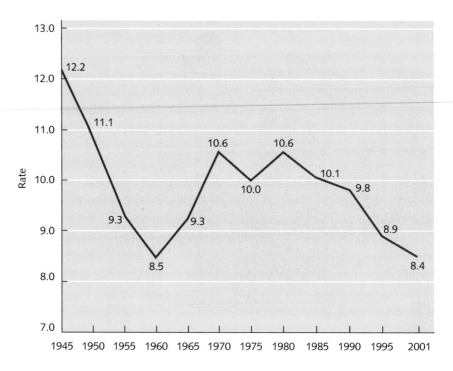

Figure 1.2   Median Age at First Marriage, by Sex: 1890 to 2000 (*Note:* Data from *Vital Statistics of the United States* by U.S. National Center for Health Statistics [U.S. Department of Health and Human Services], annual, 1890–2000, Washington, DC: U.S. Government Printing Office; *Monthly Vital Statistics Report* by U.S. National Center for Health Statistics, monthly, Washington, DC: U.S. Government Printing Office; and *Statistical Abstract of the United States, 2000,* by U.S. Bureau of the Census, 2000, Washington, DC: U.S. Government Printing Office.)

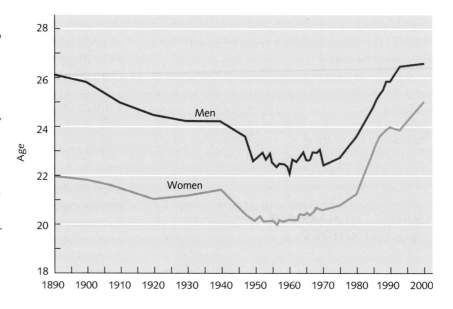

Americans are more educated than ever before. In 2000, 80% of American adults had a high school diploma, compared with 75.2% in 1990, and 15.5% had earned a bachelor's degree in 2000, compared with 13.1% in 1990 (U.S. Bureau of the Census, 2000). The delay in marriage is also associated with the decline in negative attitudes toward remaining single, a longer life expectancy, smaller families, and more career options for women. (See Chapter 4 for more discussion.)

Also, people today marry later and may experience a period of cohabitation prior to marriage (Barich and Bielby, 1996). The reasons for the trend toward marital delay probably include increased opportunities for nonmarital sexual intercourse and increased acceptance of nonmarital cohabitation (Cooney and Hogan, 1991; Miller and Heaton, 1991).

This trend is significant because those who wait until they are in their middle or late twenties to marry have a greater chance of marital success than do those who marry earlier. In fact, one of the strongest and most consistent predictors of the propensity to divorce is the age at which persons marry. Virtually every study of marital dissolution undertaken since the late 1960s has found both spouses' age at marriage to be statistically significant with respect to the probability of divorce (South, 1995). The delay of marriage also has resulted in a marked increase in unmarried young adults in the population. In 2000, 31% of men and 25% of women 15 years old and over had never married, up from 28% and 22% for men and women, respectively, in 1970. Also, in the past three decades, the proportion of women ages 20 to 24 who had never married doubled, going from 36% to 73%, and the proportion of men ages 30 to 34 who had never married more than tripled, going from 6% to 22% (see Figure 1.3) (U.S. Bureau of the Census, 2000). This is due to a decline in negative attitudes toward remaining single, a longer life expectancy, smaller families, and more career options for women. See Chapter 4 for a complete discussion.

Birthrates and Family Size

The birthrate in the United States climbed very rapidly after 1945 and stayed high for the next 20 years. This **cohort,** known as the baby boomers, was larger than any that had been born since the years before the 1910s and 1920s. At the present time, birthrates are on the decline. Birthrates for all groups have fallen to their lowest level since 1986. Declining birthrates since 1965 have resulted in smaller families. The average number of persons per family was 3.67 in 1960 and 2.62 in 2000. Figures 1.4 and 1.5 show the change in the average population per family from 1960 to 2000.

Between 1970 and 2000, households with five or more people decreased from 21% to 10% of all households. During the same period, the share of households with only one or two people increased from 46% to 59%. Overall, the growth in the number of households slowed dramatically in the 1990s; the percentage of people living alone grew from 17% in

1970 to more than 25% in 2000 (U.S. Bureau of the Census, 2000). The decline in family size can be attributed to several factors, including changes in fertility, marriage, and divorce patterns. For example, the numbers of single-parent families and child-free families have increased, resulting in fewer people per family. Increases in divorce generally reduce the size of households by separating one household into two smaller ones. In addition, the decline in the proportion of households with children under age 18 is an important component in the overall decline in household and family size over the last 30 years. Households with children under 18 dropped from 45 percent of all households in 1970 to 35 percent in 1990 and to 33 percent in 2000 (U.S. Bureau of the Census, 2001).

As you can see in Figure 1.5, 53% of White families in 2000 had no children of their own under 18 years of age at home. An additional 19% of White families had only one child of their own at home who was under 18 years of age. Higher percentages of both Black and Hispanic families had greater numbers of children. The birthrate continues to be higher for most minority groups because of cultural differences and different employment opportunities.

Seventy-two percent of White families had only one or no children under 18 at home. Among Black families, the figure was 69%. These figures reflect the fact that American women of all races are having fewer children. At the beginning of the twentieth century, the average married woman had five children. By the end of the century, the average number of total births to ever-married women between the ages of 15 and 55 had declined to 1.8.

The decline in family size can be attributed to several factors. Until the twentieth century, women were expected to "be fruitful and multiply." Large families were considered not only a blessing but also an economic asset: More hands were available to work the family farm. Furthermore, reliable birth control methods were largely unavailable. In fact, in 1873, Congress enacted the Comstock Law, which imposed heavy fines and long prison terms for

cohort A group of people born during the same period of time.

Figure 1.3   Marital Status of the Population 15 Years and Over by Sex: Selected Years, 1970 to 2000 (in percent) *(Note: From U.S. Bureau of the Census, Current Population Survey, March Supplements: 1970 to 2000.)*

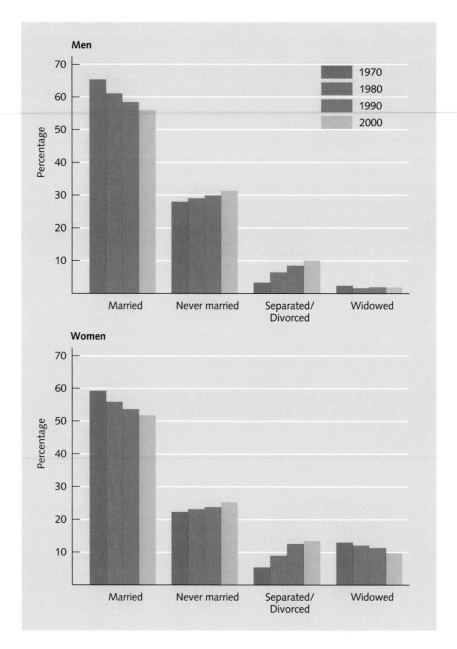

sending information on contraceptives through the mail. Twenty-four states passed additional statutes that banned advertisements for and the publication and distribution of information on contraceptives. Another 14 states made it illegal for anyone, including physicians, to provide information about contraception.

As families moved from farms to the city, having large numbers of children became financially

difficult, so it became economically expedient for women to have fewer children (Margolis, 1984). Also, women began to work in factories and offices and could not take care of large families. At the same time, more efficient means of contraception became available, and couples were more willing to use them. Federal and state laws prohibiting the dispensing of contraceptive information and methods were gradually repealed. When married women

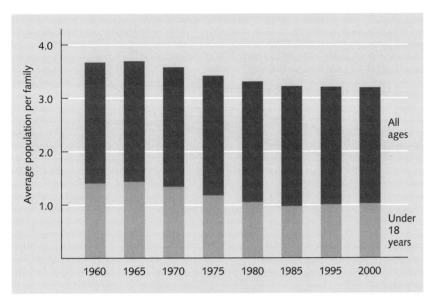

Figure 1.4 Average Population per Family, 1960–2000 (*Note:* Data from *Statistical Abstract of the United States, 2002* [Table 59, p. 51] by U.S. Bureau of the Census, 2002, Washington, DC: U.S. Government Printing Office.)

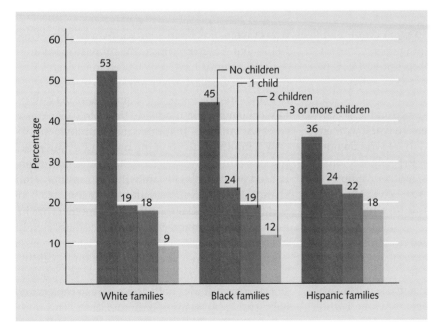

Figure 1.5 Percent Distribution of Families, by Number of Own Children Under 18 Years Old and by Ethnic Group, 2000 (*Note:* Data from *Statistical Abstract of the United States, 2000* [Table 58, p. 51] by U.S. Bureau of the Census, 2000, Washington, DC: U.S. Government Printing Office.)

began a massive movement into the world of work, the birthrate decreased even more.

Working Mothers

Another important change in family living has been the large influx of married women into the workforce (Floge, 1989). Until the early 1980s, married women with no children under age 18 had higher labor force participation rates than did those with children under age 6. This long-standing pattern began to change during the 1980s and has now reversed. In 1998, married women whose youngest child was between ages 6 and 17 had the highest labor force participation rates (80.6%; see Figure 1.6). Sixty-two percent of married women with the

Figure 1.6 Labor Force Participation Rates of Married Women, Age of Youngest Child, 2000 (*Note:* Data from *Statistical Abstract of the United States, 2001* [Table 577] by U.S. Bureau of the Census, 2001, Washington, DC: U.S. Government Printing Office.)

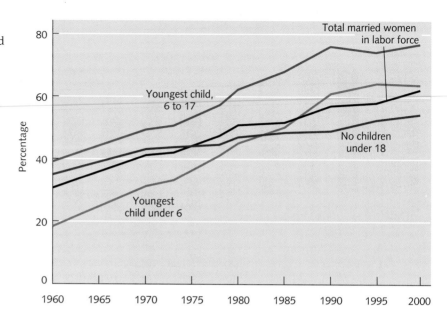

youngest child under age 6 also were employed. This represents a larger percentage than that of married women without children under 18 (U.S. Bureau of the Census, 2000). This trend will be discussed in more detail in Chapter 9.

Research has revealed some demographic, social, and attitudinal differences between married women who work outside the home and those who do not. Those who do not are more likely to hold traditional attitudes regarding marital roles, mothers' employment outside the home, and sexuality. Married women who are not employed full-time have more children and live in households with less income. Married women who are employed full-time are better educated and have fewer children and more income than married women who are not employed (Glass, 1992). There has also been a marked increase in the proportion of highly educated women who convert their professional training into paid employment (Cooney and Uhlenberg, 1991).

Mothers are entering the workforce for reasons both economic and noneconomic. The major reason is financial need: Many families simply can't make it financially without both parents working. Factors such as inflation, the high cost of living, and the desire for a higher standard of living pressure families to have two incomes. Employment opportunities for women have also increased. Noneconomic reasons for employment are important as well. Large num-

bers of women want to work for reasons of personal fulfillment. For many, this is the primary motive.

These trends have only added to women's burdens. Most working wives now try to meet the usual demands for housework and family care in addition to working full-time outside the home. Generally, research indicates that the wife's employment has only a minimal effect on the husband's household responsibilities. Women's satisfaction is greatly enhanced when husbands are willing to assume a fair share of the total responsibilities (Scanzoni, 1987). In addition, increased employment for mothers has intensified the demand for child care. Eighty-eight percent of mothers working 35 or more hours a week use nonparental child care for their children under 6 years of age (U.S. Bureau of the Census, 1999a). This includes both group care in centers and baby-sitting by relatives or nonrelatives. This trend will be discussed more in Chapter 9.

One-Parent Families

One of the most far-reaching changes since the 1970s has been the increase in the number of families that consist of a single parent maintaining a household with one or more children. The high rates of separation and divorce, as well as the increased number of births to single women, have contributed to the large increase in this family type.

In 2000, nearly 1 out of every 3 families (31.1%) with children under age 18 was a one-parent family, up from 1 in 10 in 1970. The number of one-parent families tripled between 1970 and 2000 (from 4 million to 12 million; U.S. Bureau of the Census, 2002). Among one-parent families, 2.2 million were headed by fathers, and 10 million were headed by mothers. Thus, eighty-three percent of one-parent families in 2000 were mother–child families. The older the parent (and the children), the more likely the father is to maintain a one-parent family with his children. Boys are more likely than girls to be living with fathers.

Single-parent families are increasing for all ethnicities, but single-parent families are disproportionately concentrated among Black families compared with other ethnicities. In 1970, one-third of Black children under age 18 lived in one-parent families; today approximately half of all Black children live in one-parent families. This is compared with 17% of all White children and 23% of Hispanic children under age 18 living in a single-parent family. The primary reason for this increase has been the high rate of births to unmarried women. In 1999, births to unmarried Black women accounted for 69% of all live births to Black women (U.S. Bureau of the Census, 2000).

However, researchers emphasize that the single-mother African American family is not a result of slavery or of welfare policies, nor is it a traditional African American family form; rather, it is the result of poverty, high rates of unprotected intercourse among teenagers, and Black male unemployment and underemployment. This trend reflects the greater difficulty that Black men have in finding employment to help support a family (Smith, 1993). Unmarried African American women are far less likely to marry if they become pregnant than are unmarried White women. This will be discussed more in Chapter 9, but we should note here that research suggests that the negative effects of illegitimacy tend to impact Whites more than they impact African Americans (Fine et al., 1992). One reason for this is that African American extended families often help single parents raise their children to a greater extent than do White extended families.

Another reason for the rise of one-parent Black families is the high divorce rate (Norton and Moorman, 1987). Two out of three Black marriages will eventually dissolve, and African American women are less likely to remarry than are White women. In general, African Americans are significantly less likely than Whites to feel that their marriages are harmonious, and African American women are less likely to be satisfied with their marriages (Broman, 1993).

The increase of births to unmarried women in general, and to Black women in particular, is problematic in that households headed by never-married mothers expereince more persistent poverty and longer spells of welfare receipt than do other types of households (Franklin, Smith, and McMiller, 1995). Of course, this puts children at a greater risk of growing up in poverty. The negative consequences of children growing up in poverty will be discussed in Chapter 9.

Statistics for a particular year fail to show the true extent of one-parent families (Hofferth, 1985). Cross-sectional studies show only the percentages of one-parent families during the year of the survey, not the total number that have ever been one-parent

Family life is an important source of life satisfaction for African Americans, especially if the family has a comfortable and steady income.

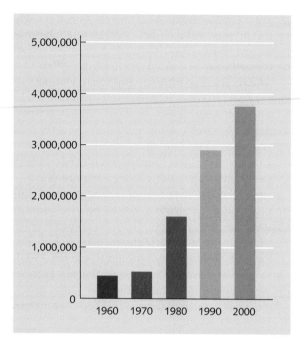

Figure 1.7   Number of Unmarried Couples Cohabiting, 1960–2000 (*Note:* Data from *Statistical Abstract of the United States, 2001,* by U.S. Bureau of the Census, 2001, Washington, DC: U.S. Government Printing Office.)

families. According to projections, nearly 60% of all children born in 1986 can expect to spend at least a large part of one year in a one-parent family before reaching the age of 18 (Norton and Glick, 1986). The effects on mothers and on children are discussed in detail in Chapter 13.

Cohabitation

People choosing to live together instead of legally marrying is one of the most dramatic changes in family form. Today more than 50% of opposite-sex couples who plan on getting married live together first, up from 10% in 1965. As Figure 1.7 shows, the number of live-in opposite-sex couples increased from less than half a million in 1960 to 3.8 million in 2000. About 60% of cohabitors are between 25 and 44 years old (U.S. Bureau of the Census, 2001).

Childbearing is becoming increasingly common within nonmarital unions. In 2000, 41% of unmarried partner households included children under 18 (U.S. Bureau of the Census, 2002). It is estimated that between one-fourth (Graefe and Lichter, 1999)

and one-half (Bumpass and Lu, 2000) of all children today will spend some time in a cohabiting household before age 16. The effect on these children depends a great deal on the quality and harmony of the cohabiting relationship—and on the quality of the relationship that nonparent as well as parent cohabitors establish with the children. Children need love, affection, security, and guidance in their lives. If the cohabiting relationship supplies these needs, children will likely benefit; if it does not, they will be affected negatively. Children in cohabiting households face a greater likelihood than children in married households that the couple will break up (W. D. Manning, 2002). After 5 to 7 years, 39% of all cohabiting couples have broken off their relationship (Casper and Bianchi, 2002).

Overall, controlling for relationship duration and demographic characteristics, cohabitors in general have poorer relationship quality than their married counterparts. Popenoe and Whitehead (2002a) conducted a comprehensive review of research on cohabitation and found that although most young people believe it is a good idea to live with a person before marrying, living together is not a good way to prepare for marriage or to avoid divorce. They specifically found that living together before marriage increases the risk of breaking up after marriage; that it increases the risk of domestic violence for women, and the risk of physical and sexual abuse for children; and that unmarried couples have lower levels of happiness and well-being than do married couples. Another study showed that couples who did not live together before marrying had a 31 percent chance of splitting up after 10 years, compared with a 40 percent chance for couples who cohabited before marriage (Bramlett and Mosher, 2002).

It is hard to know exactly why cohabitation increases the risk of breakup, but some researchers speculate that overall commitment in cohabiting relationships is less than that in marriages and that cohabitation offers less certainty of a lifetime partnership. It may not be the experience of cohabiting that increases the chances for divorce, but rather the personality of the people who choose to cohabit. People who live together before marriage may be the type who are more likely to consider getting a divorce than are people who marry without first cohabiting. However, cohabitors who report plans to marry their partner are involved in unions that are not significantly different from marriage (S. L. Brown and Booth, 1996). See Chapter 6 for more discussion on cohabitation.

An important financial difference between children of married parents and those of cohabiting parents is the entitlement to child support once the relationship has ended. Whereas married couples can file for child support under the federal Divorce Act, cohabiting couples must seek support under the Family Relations Act. The latter act entitles the child to support only until the age of 19, whereas under the Divorce Act child support is payable as long as the child remains a "child of the marriage" (Storey, 2000). This means that child support continues if the child is pursuing a higher education or if the child has a disability that keeps him or her from becoming independent. Both higher education and a disability can be an enormous financial burden for many families.

Gay and Lesbian Families

As in any family type, there is a wide diversity of gay and lesbian lifestyles. A large number of gays and lesbians have made long-term commitments in stable relationships. Although only a few states have legitimized same-sex unions, marriagelike liaisons are increasingly accepted by society.

In describing the union of a gay couple he performed, Reverend Philip Zwerling, a California clergyman, wrote:

> I had never married two people of the same sex. I finally realized that their sexual orientation did not lessen their commitment to each other, or their love for each other. I cannot now predict the future of their relationship, but I do believe that they freely chose what both believe best for them.
>
> Gay people have the same desire for happiness in our society as heterosexuals. And one of those desires is the chance . . . to create a marital relationship of depth and love. (Zwerling, 1989)

Gays and lesbians are fighting harder than ever before for the right to legally marry. Public support for marriage equality continues to grow, but many states and Congress have passed laws that allow them to refuse to honor gay marriages in the event that a state court permits them. By passing some form of antimarriage law, states have sanctioned public policy discriminating against lesbian and gay couples. However, some states have adopted more progressive policies regarding gay and lesbian marriages. For example, the Vermont Supreme Court in 2000 ordered the state legislature to extend to lesbian and gay couples the same rights, protections, benefits, and obligations available to nongay couples through marriage. While the court held that all the benefits and protections of marriage must be made equally available, the justices explicitly did not rule on whether to allow lesbian and gay couples access to civil marriage.

Many cities and businesses are now recognizing gay and lesbian couples as domestic partners and extending benefits commonly granted only to married couples. Although these laws and policies do not include all of the rights of marriage, they generally grant partners some of the recognition and benefits extended to married couples. The benefits vary depending on city and company but typically include the right to visit a sick or dying partner in the hospital, sick leave to care for a partner, bereavement leave to attend a partner's funeral, housing rights such as rent control, and health insurance.

Many gays and lesbians are parents of children who were born during previous heterosexual unions. In the 1990s, many gays and lesbians also used artificial insemination and adoption as avenues to parenthood. One of the problems in obtaining exact numbers is that discrimination still exists, and so many gay and lesbian parents keep their sexual identity relatively hidden. Child custody can be denied if a parent's homosexuality can be proved to adversely affect the child (Patterson and Redding, 1996). Indeed, fear of losing their children is often the biggest barrier to gays' and lesbians' openly declaring their sexual orientation. During custody cases, the courts often are concerned with several issues surrounding the social and psychological development of children being raised by gay or lesbian parents. These include concerns that the parents' homosexuality will adversely affect the child's gender and emotional development, that social stigma or peer rejection will result due to parental homosexuality, and that there is an increased likelihood of the child becoming homosexual (B. Fitzgerald, 1999). However, the studies that have been conducted on children who grow up in gay and lesbian families show that they develop in a positive manner psychologically, intellectually, behaviorally, and emotionally. They have no greater incidence of homosexuality than do children who grow up in a

Figure 1.8   Grandchildren in Grandparents' Homes by Presence of Parents, 1970–1997 (*Note:* Data from Bureau of the Census, 1970 and 1980, and "Marital Status and Living Arrangements: March 1994" [Table A-6] and "Marital Status and Living Arrangements: March 1997" [Table 4] and "From Birth to Seventeen: The Living Arrangements of Children, 2000," by U.S. Bureau of the Census, Current Population Surveys, Washington, DC: U.S. Government Printing Office.)

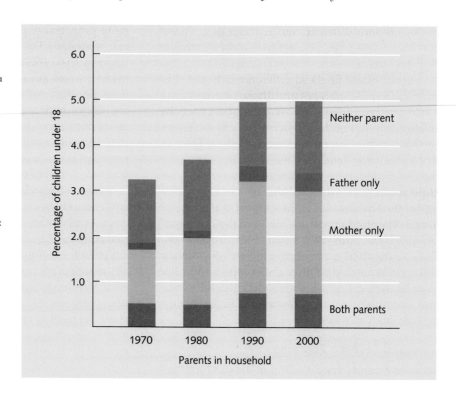

heterosexual family, and the presence of a heterosexual parent of each gender is not crucial to healthy child development (see B. Fitzgerald, 1999, for a review of the literature).

Because of the amount of research showing that the children of gay and lesbian parents develop as normally as children in other families, the American Academy of Pediatrics in 2002 called for state laws to allow for gays and lesbians to adopt their partner's children. This would allow for children to be covered under health insurance policies and receive survivor benefits. The American Academy of Child and Adolescent Psychiatry has similar views on adoption rights for gay and lesbian parents.

Grandparents as Parents

One notable trend in the evolution of the family in recent decades is the dramatic increase in the number of children living in grandparent-maintained households. In 1970, 2.2 million children under age 18 lived in their grandparents' home, with or without parents present; by 1998, that number had grown to almost 4 million (Casper and Bryson, 1998). When these households are categorized by the presence of parents, it becomes evident that the greatest increases have occurred in households in

which one parent is also residing in the home. Between 1970 and 1997, grandparent-maintained households in which the mother was present increased by 118 percent, and those in which the father was present increased by 217 percent (see Figure 1.8). Research has indicated that possible reasons for this trend include an increase in drug use among parents, higher rates of teen pregnancy or divorce, the rapid rise in single-parent households, AIDS, child abuse and neglect, and incarceration of parents (Minkler, 1998).

The arrangement of grandparent as caregiver has benefits and drawbacks, for both grandparents and children. Grandparents may experience a greater sense of purpose for living, a renewed vitality, and a feeling of rejuvenation (Kleiner, Hertzog, and Targ, 1998). They may relish the opportunity to raise a child differently or to nurture family relationships, and they may be rewarded with love and companionship they did not have previously with the grandchild (Burton, Dilworth-Anderson, and Merriwether-de-Vries, 1995).

Children may also benefit from living in grandparent-maintained households. Compared to children in single-parent households, children being raised solely by their grandparents are health-

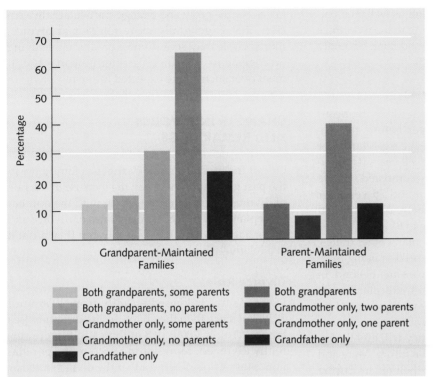

Figure 1.9 Percentage of Children in Different Family Types Who Are in Poverty, 1997 (*Note:* Data from "Coresident Grandparents and Grandchildren" [p. 8] by K. Bryson and L. M. Casper, 1999, Current Population Reports, Series P-20, No. 168, Washington, DC: U.S. Government Printing Office.)

ier, have fewer behavioral problems, and are better adapted socially (Solomon and Marx, 1995). And compared to children in foster care, those in grandparent-maintained households may be less traumatized, enjoy the continuation of family identity and culture or ethnicity, and maintain a connection to their siblings (W. Bell and Garner, 1996).

Much of the research, however, puts more emphasis on the apparent negative effects on grandparents and children in these households. Economic difficulties are prevalent in grandparent-maintained households. Twenty-seven percent of children who live with their grandparents are in poverty, and if the grandmother is raising the children alone, almost two-thirds of the children are living in poverty. Both numbers are significantly greater than the 19 percent of children in poverty who live with their parents (Casper and Bryson, 1998). Figure 1.9 shows the comparison. Grandparents may even be penalized for their willingness to care for their grandchildren, being denied foster-parent benefits because of their blood relation to the children (Kleiner et al., 1998).

Some grandparents also experience increased health problems and loss of stamina. Many report feeling emotionally and physically drained from having to care for their grandchildren (Kleiner et al., 1998). Other drawbacks include loss of time for themselves that they had rediscovered after their own children left home, isolation from their social networks, and resentment based on jealousy and role confusion on the part of other grandchildren and family members (Kleiner et al., 1998).

Aside from being poor, children living with their grandparents are more likely to be living with caregivers who have not graduated from high school: one-third of children in grandparent-headed households versus one-eighth of children in parent-headed households (Casper and Bryson, 1998). Another negative consequence for children in grandparent-maintained households is a lack of health insurance. Fifty-six percent of children residing with both grandparents, with no parent present, are uninsured, compared to 13% of children living with both parents (Bryson and Casper, 1999).

Given the increase in the number of grandparents raising their grandchildren and the impact this arrangement has on both caregiver and child, the government and the community likely are going to be called on to provide more support. Policies and programs intended for traditional and foster families could be extended to these families as well, and employers of grandparents remaining in the workforce will expect subsidized child care and family-friendly policies (Casper and Bryson, 1998).

Changes in Life Expectancy

Life expectancy has been rising for years. Americans are now living longer than ever before and are healthier in later life. Today, the life expectancy for men is 74 years, and for women, 80 years (U.S. Bureau of the Census, 2002). This is compared to a life expectancy of 68 years for men and 75 years for women in 1970. It is projected that by 2050, men and women will be living on average to 81 and 87 years, respectively. This means, among many other things, that one now has a greater potential of being married to the same person for 60 years and beyond. In comparison, in 1900 when the life expectancy was 46 years for men and 48 years for women, marriages lasted for a much shorter period of time.

This increase in life expectancy will greatly impact marriages and families in the future. More and more families will be caring for their elders during the same years that they are rearing their children. As people survive longer due to medical advances, the elders' care may become more complex and they may become dependent on their adult children. This puts a strain on families who already struggle to meet the demands of careers and children. It may be difficult to take time to nurture other family relationships under the circumstance of caring for numerous dependents, especially dependents with disparate needs.

The impact of longevity on duration of marriage is also a significant question to examine. For example, if a couple marries at age 25, it is very possible they will live to age 80, creating a 55-year marriage.

Yet as people grow and change, particularly in a society that is generally more tolerant of divorce, more people may seek divorce or alternative living arrangements to achieve greater personal fulfillment over such a long expected life span.

CHANGES IN DIVORCE AND REMARRIAGE

One of the most dramatic changes in family life in the past generation has been the increase in the rate of divorce and remarriage, along with the number of stepfamilies. In recent years, rates of divorce and remarriage have declined slightly, but they are still at a relatively high level.

Divorce Rates

Divorce rates increased steadily from 1958 until 1979, but since then they have declined slightly (see Figure 1.10). In 2000, 19.8 million adults were currently divorced, representing 9.8% of the population. Most scholars believe that the divorce rate has stabilized, with about 50% of new marriages likely to end in divorce. Certainly, there has been a decline in the belief in the ideal of marital permanence, which may have contributed to the increase in marital failure (Glenn, 1991).

Remarriage Trends

The majority of people who divorce eventually remarry. The National Center for Health Statistics estimates that 56% of women who get divorced will marry again within 5 years. Remarriage happens fairly quickly. The median number of years between divorce and remarriage is 3 years for women and 4 years for men (U.S. Bureau of the Census, 2000).

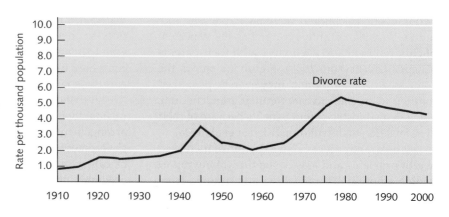

Figure 1.10   Divorce Rates, 1910–2000 (*Note:* Data from *Vital Statistics of the United States* by National Center for Health Statistics [U.S. Department of Health and Human Services], annual, 1910–1998, Washington, DC: U.S. Government Printing Office; and *National Vital Statistics Reports* 49, no. 6, August 22, 2001.)

Whites remarry more quickly than African Americans and Latinos. These remarriage rates will be discussed in subsequent chapters. However, since the early 1990s, the proportion who remarry appears to be declining.

Redivorce rates for remarried persons also show slight signs of decline from previous years, so future rates of redivorce may be quite similar to those of first divorce. This may be due to economic factors, as in the case of divorced men who are paying child support and are reluctant to assume financial responsibility for another family. Currently, the chance that a second marriage will end in divorce is 23% after 5 years and 39% after 10 years compared to 20% after 5 years and 33% after 10 years for people in their first marriage (Bramlett and Mosher, 2002).

However, the incidence of divorce in the United States remains among the highest in the world. The net effect of a high rate of divorce and remarriage is an increase in reconstituted, or blended, families.

Blended Families

Overall, about 46% of American marriages are remarriages for the husband, wife, or both (Clarke, 1995). When a parent remarries and brings children from a previous marriage into the new family unit, a blended, or reconstituted, family is formed. If the couple has children together, the blended family may consist of children from her previous marriage, children from his previous marriage, and children born to them since they married each other.

Family relationships in a blended family can become quite complicated, because each parent faces the challenge of forming new relationships with stepchildren, with the children of the new marriage, and perhaps with the spouse's ex-spouse. The children face the challenge of adjusting to stepparents and to stepsiblings, as well as maintaining relationships with natural parents both inside and outside their new family unit. If both their natural parents remarry, the children must adjust to two stepparents and to any stepsiblings in their newly constituted families. Also, both parents and children may have to form new relationships with other relatives on both sides of the families. In short, obviously, many adjustments are required. See Chapter 17 for a detailed discussion of remarriage and stepparenting.

CHANGES IN NONMARITAL SEXUAL BEHAVIOR

Sexual Activity

Researchers have reported significant changes in attitudes toward and behaviors associated with

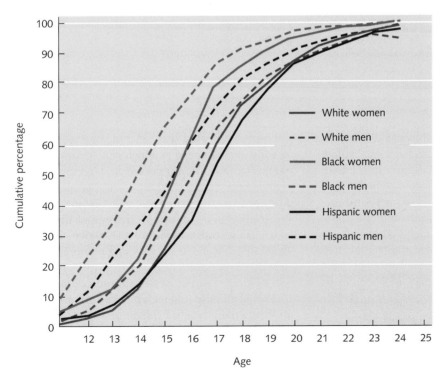

Figure 1.11 Age of First Intercourse, by Ethnic Group and Sex, 1992 (*Note:* From Robert T. Michael, J. H. Gagnon, E. O. Laumann, and G. Kolata, *Sex in America*, p. 91. Copyright © 1994 by CSG Enterprises, Inc., Edward O. Laumann, Robert T. Michael, J. H. Gagnon and Gina Kolata. By permission of Little, Brown and Company, Inc.)

Oral Sex and STDs

Studies now report that many teens, and even children as young as middle schoolers, who claim to be virgins are actually engaging in oral sex. Many teens do not see oral sex as "real" sex because of the lack of vaginal penetration, and experts believe that the type of oral sex practiced by young teenagers is primarily **fellatio** (stimulation of the male genitals with the mouth), not **cunnilingus** (stimulation of the female genitals with the mouth) (Remez, 2000). Teens also think that oral sex is safer than vaginal sex because the risk of pregnancy is not there. However, what is often not known is that sexually transmitted diseases (STDs) can be contracted through oral sex. For example, herpes simplex virus type 1, which is normally found in or around the mouth in the form of a cold sore, can be transmitted to the penis or vagina during oral sex. Likewise, STDs normally found in the genital tract can be transmitted to the mouth and throat during oral sex. STDs that can be transmitted orally include human papillomavirus, herpes simplex virus, hepatitis B, gonorrhea, syphilis, chlamydia, and chancroid. The human immunodeficiency virus (HIV), the virus that causes acquired immunodeficiency syndrome (AIDS), can also be transmitted through oral sex, although such transmission is relatively rare because saliva tends to inactivate HIV. Not surprisingly, some reports from family planning clinics and health care providers show increases in oral herpes and gonorrhea of the throat in teenagers. So although the risk of pregnancy is not there, the risk of STDs is certainly present.

Due to lack of prior reporting, it is difficult to conclude whether or not oral sex has increased, but one can definitely conclude from current reports that many adolescents are engaging in it. One study of 1,297 adolescent males found that 49% have received oral sex and 39% have given oral sex (Gates and Sonenstein, 2000). Another survey, conducted by the Kaiser Family Foundation, found that 23% of students questioned in 7th through 12th grades said they had had oral sex. When 11th and 12th grades were considered alone, the number increased to 42%. The survey also found that 38% of teens did not think oral sex was as big a deal as sexual intercourse. Thirty percent didn't know that a boy or girl could possibly become infected with HIV by having oral sex (Kaiser Family Foundation, 2001). In an online survey of more than 10,000 teenage girls, 18% said that oral sex was something that you did with your boyfriend before you were ready to have sex and that oral sex was a substitute for intercourse. Twenty-five percent of the respondents had had oral sex, and 27% described that act as something you do with a guy for fun (Birnbaum, 2000).

Most health care professionals and educators urge parents, teachers, and the community to initiate honest discussions about the health risks involved with oral sex. However, this is often met with reluctance because many adults and teens are not comfortable talking about sex. How to counsel adolescents about lowering risks is especially problematic when many young people consider oral sex itself to be a form of risk reduction and are probably already reluctant to discuss oral sex openly or to use dental dams or condoms (Remez, 2000).

nonmarital sexual activity over the past 40 years. A comprehensive survey conducted in 1992, called the National Health and Social Life Survey, is based on 3,432 interviews with people across the United States. These respondents answered a 90-minute questionnaire about their sexual behavior and other aspects of their sex lives (Michael, Gagnon, Laumann, and Kolata, 1994). One of the trends that

fellatio Stimulation of the male genitals with the mouth.
cunnilingus Stimulation of the female genitals with the mouth.

the results revealed was, with a few exceptions, a steadily declining age at which people first had sexual intercourse. Men reported first having sex at a younger age than did women, and Blacks reported doing so at a younger age than did Whites.

Another way to look at the age of first intercourse is illustrated in Figure 1.11, which shows the age at which teenagers and young adults first experienced sexual intercourse. The graph shows that half of all Black men have had intercourse by age 15, half of all Hispanic men by age 16½, and half of all White men by age 17. Half of all Black women have had intercourse by age 17, and half of all White and Hispanic women have had intercourse by about age 18. By age 22, about 90% of each group have had intercourse (Heaton and Jacobson, 1994).

When asked why they had intercourse the first time, 51% of the men said curiosity and readiness for sex, and 25% said affection for their partner. Among the women, it was the reverse: About half said affection for their partner, and about 25% said curiosity and readiness for sex. A very small percentage of both men and women said they had sex because of a desire for physical pleasure. Most of the men said they were not in love with their first sexual partner; most of the women, in contrast, said they were.

Today, American teenagers are having sex earlier than their parents did. About half of today's young adults begin having intercourse between the ages of 15 and 18, and at least four out of five have had intercourse by the time they are 21. Given that the average age of marriage is now the midtwenties, few Americans are waiting until they marry to have sex. But most sexually active young people show no signs of having large numbers of partners. More than half of the men and women between ages 18 and 24 in 1992 had had just one sex partner in the past year, and 11% had had none.

The National Health and Social Life Survey gives no support to the idea of a promiscuous society or of a dramatic sexual revolution in which large numbers of people have multiple, casual sex partners. Instead, the survey indicates that most people form partnerships and ultimately get married. And no matter how sexually active people are before and between marriages, and no matter whether they live with a sexual partner before marriage or they are virgins on their wedding day, the vast majority, once married, have no other sexual partner; their past is essentially erased. Marriage remains the great leveler (Michael et al., 1994).

The Use of Contraceptives

People in a high-risk category—those who have more than one partner, especially if they do not know them well, and those who have the most frequent sexual relationships—need to use condoms consistently to protect against sexually transmitted

Condom Use with Primary Partner

Respondent had two sex
partners in past 12 months

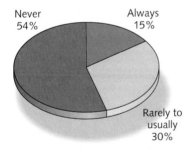

Never
54%

Always
15%

Rarely to
usually
30%

Condom Use with Secondary Partner

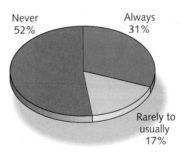

Never
52%

Always
31%

Rarely to
usually
17%

Respondent had three or more
sex partners in past 12 months

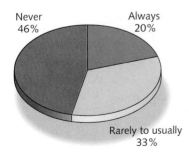

Never
46%

Always
20%

Rarely to usually
33%

Never
42%

Always
40%

Rarely to usually
18%

Figure 1.12 Frequency of Condom Use over the Past 12 Months with Primary and Secondary Sex Partners, 1992 (*Note:* From Robert T. Michael, J. H. Gagnon, E. O. Laumann, and G. Kolata, *Sex in America*, p. 197. Copyright © 1994 by CSG Enterprises, Inc., Edward O. Laumann, Robert T. Michael, J. H. Gagnon and Gina Kolata. By permission of Little, Brown and Company, Inc.)

diseases, especially AIDS. According to the National Health and Social Life Survey, nearly half the people in the high-risk category never use condoms during vaginal intercourse with their primary partner or a secondary partner (see Figure 1.12). Nevertheless, perhaps because they want to protect their spouse or lover from infection and because they recognize the riskiness of their behavior, people who have several sex partners in a year are more likely to use a condom with their primary partner and with their secondary partners than are people who have only one other partner.

CULTURAL DIVERSITY IN FAMILIES

One of the biggest changes in families in the United States in recent years has been the increase in cultural diversity. Cultural and ethnic backgrounds strongly affect family life, and the diversity of heritages in the United States is reflected in the variety of family styles. Figure 1.13 shows the composition of the U.S. population by race and Hispanic origin (U.S. Bureau of the Census, 2002). About 196 million people (69% of the population) are classified as White non-Hispanic; many of their family trees have roots in some European country that date back 200 or more years. Non-Hispanic African Americans number 33 million individuals (12% of the population). Lati-

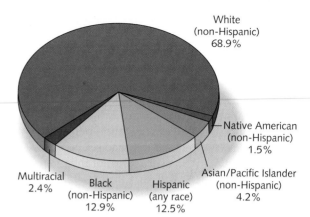

Figure 1.13   U.S. Population by Race and Hispanic Origin (*Note:* Data from "Resident Population by Race, Hispanic Origin: 2001" U.S. Bureau of the Census, Statistical Abstract 2002 Table 14.)

nos—whose family roots may be in Mexico, the Spanish-speaking Caribbean, or Central and South America—total about 31.3 million people (11.5% of the population). About 20.6 million, or 65% of the Latinos in the United States, hail from Mexico (U.S. Bureau of the Census, 2002). About 10 million people (3.6% of the population) identify themselves as Asians or Pacific Islanders. Non-Hispanic Native Americans from various tribes number about 2 million (0.74% of the population).

Chinese American families enjoy a higher standard of living than do most other minority groups and include a greater percentage of college-educated members.

Neither Real Americans nor Real Asians?

Asian Americans often find themselves caught between not being considered "real" Asians because they have adopted mainstream cultural habits and not being considered "real" Americans because of their looks. Consider the following quotations from the media:

> "You know, I'm tired of the Kristi Yamaguchis and the Michelle Kwans! They're not American . . . when I look at a box of Wheaties, I don't want to see eyes that are slanted and Oriental and almond shaped. I want to see American eyes looking at me."
>
> —Bill Handel, popular morning DJ for KFI-AM, one of the nation's most listened-to talk radio stations.

> "American beats Kwan."
>
> —MSNBC's erroneous headline after figure skater Tara Lipinski beat Michelle Kwan during the 1998 Winter Olympics. Both women are Americans.

Mia Tuan (1999) has explored what she called the "authenticity dilemma" confronting Asian Americans today. She interviewed 95 third-, fourth-, and fifth-generation Chinese and Japanese Americans living in northern and southern California to (1) determine the content, meaning, and salience of ethnicity in their lives; (2) explore the extent to which they felt that ethnicity was an optional rather than imposed facet of their identities; and (3) examine the role played by race in shaping life experiences. The following excerpts are from her interviews:

Q: How do you identify yourself?

A: *That's a really hard question actually. I guess as an Asian-American. I don't consider myself just Japanese, just Chinese. I don't consider myself just American. I don't know. I kinda like terminology like Asian-American and African-American because it's kinda messy. . . . By blood, I'm Chinese and Japanese. By culture, I don't know if I am so much of either. I don't know. . . . Mom would always tell me I used to get confused growing up. "How can I be Japanese and Chinese and American?" "Well, you are half Japanese, half Chinese, and all American." (p. 108)*

A: *I don't think I can be just American just for the fact that I look different from the typical American, white. (Why not just Japanese then?) Because I definitely am American-ized, an American raised in America. And I don't always agree with what Japanese, Japan stands for. (p. 109)*

A: *Usually I say Chinese-American because I realize I'm not Chinese. People from China come over here and*

like, whoa, they're like a foreign species. And I'm not American because just one look and I'm apart. I used to struggle with this question a lot and to make a long story short, Chinese-American is a hybrid of its own. It's kind of like Afro-Americans. Boy, they're not African and they're not American and it's just its own species and that's the way it is. (p. 116)

A: *Like my girlfriend, it's kinda funny because she's of Irish descent, but people would never think that or ask where are you from because they see her as being Caucasian. And if they look at me they would say, "Oh where are you from," because I'm perceived as being Asian first. It's like girl, an Asian girl, and anything that follows after that. For my girlfriend it would be like, she's white, she's of Irish descent but it doesn't really matter. It's like way down the list of whatever. (p. 112)*

These statements go to the heart of the dilemma many Asian Americans face: They have learned that others view them as outsiders in American society. Even though they are lifelong Americans, they are not perceived as such because they do not fit the image of a "real" American. About half the respondents reported having felt out of place or suddenly conscious of their racial background at some time. Reasons for this reaction included stares, comments, and even threats from others who looked upon them as strangers or intruders in a public place. European Americans see it as a matter of personal choice whether to identify along ethnic lines, but the respondents found that not identifying in ethnic or racial terms was problematic in their interactions with non-Asians. Complicating matters for many Asian Americans was that their foreign-born counterparts saw them as "too American" and not knowledgeable enough about Chinese or Japanese ways (Tuan, 1999).

Tuan (1999) summarizes:

Today, Asian ethnics exercise a great deal of choice regarding the elements of traditional ethnic culture they wish to incorporate or do away with in their personal lives. They befriend whom they please, date and marry whom they please, choose the careers they please, and pursue further knowledge about their cultural heritage if they please. In this sense, ethnicity has indeed become optional in my respondents' personal lives. But in another very real way, being ethnic remains a societal expectation for them despite how far removed they are from their immigrant roots or how much they differ from their foreign-born counterparts. (p. 123)

In fact, the United States contains people from virtually all the world's cultures. In a general sense, **ethnicity** can be thought of as the way people define themselves as part of a group through similarities in an ancestry and cultural heritage (race, relation, or national origin). **Culture** can be defined as the sum total of ways of living, including the values, beliefs, aesthetic standards, linguistic expressions, patterns of thinking, behavioral norms, and styles of communication a group of people has developed to ensure its survival in a particular physical and human environment (Hoopes, 1979). Ethnicity and culture are not always the same thing, as culture can encompass many different ethnicities. For example, American culture is a mixture of the arts, beliefs, customs, and other products of human endeavor and thought created by many different ethnic groups. If people take the time to learn about and benefit from this diversity, the cultural makeup of the nation becomes a significant strength.

Family life exhibits a wide range of patterns. Differences in families are characterized by differences in family structure, household composition, goals and philosophies, power structures, gender roles, spousal relationships, sexual values and behavior, and child-rearing patterns. Despite the differences, there are many similarities. All families are made up of people with needs, feelings, values, hopes, dreams, problems, and intense desires to love and to relate to others within the family context. Ironically, the more deeply we explore differences, the more we recognize how very much alike people are, no matter what their country of origin. Ultimately, if you look beyond surface differences, you will find far more similarities than differences with regard to family life and cultures.

As the United States continues to become more ethnically diverse, a multicultural perspective on the family is necessary if we are going to understand and appreciate different cultural patterns. It is a mistake for one group to judge another by its own set of values or to believe there is one single ideal family form. The challenge is for people to develop understanding of other groups while maintaining pride in their own group. The individual who is proud to be part of a particular cultural group, and who is respected by the rest of society, can contribute richly to a nation that prides itself on being the world's melting pot (F. P. Rice, 1993).

Throughout this text, you will be reading about many different family groups, forms, and cultures. Be aware that when you read about a particular group, you are reading generalizations. There is tremendous individual and family variation *within* groups as well as differences among those groups. For example, each cultural group has some distinctive features, but socioeconomic factors combine with cultural and ethnic characteristics to form particular family patterns. Any discussion of family diversity must take into account the differences within groups. Our goal is to help you develop a better understanding of your own family life as well as that of others.

THEORIES TO HELP EXPLAIN FAMILY BEHAVIOR

As rational creatures, we seek explanations. When a husband and wife divorce, for instance, family and friends look for answers to a variety of questions: What happened? Why are they getting a divorce? What agreements will be made? What will happen to them and the children after it's all over?

There are dozens of theories related to intimate relationships, marriages, and families. Theories have been formulated to explain why people are attracted to one another, why people fall in love, why people select the mates they do, how gender roles develop, how families make decisions, what causes sexual dysfunctions, how to raise children, and what causes divorce and remarriage.

Here we are interested in theories related to the family itself. According to scientific methods, theory building is a process of formulating a problem, collecting data to aid in solving the problem, developing a hypothesis, testing it, and then drawing conclusions, which are stated in the form of a

ethnicity The way people define themselves as part of a group through similarities in ancestry and cultural heritage.

culture The sum total of ways of living, including the values, beliefs, aesthetic standards, linguistic expressions, patterns of thinking, behavioral norms, and style of communication a group of people has developed to ensure its survival in a particular physical and human environment.

Families differ in may ways. In the United States, cultural and ethnic diversity is reflected in differences in family styles and philosophies of child rearing.

theory. A **theory** is a tentative explanation of facts and data that have been observed (Klein and White, 1996).

Psychologists and sociologists have formulated a number of theories about the family (Holman and Burr, 1980). Seven important ones have been selected for discussion here: structural-functional theory, family developmental theory, symbolic interaction theory, systems theory, exchange theory, conflict theory, and feminist theory. They are certainly not the only theories to help explain family behavior, but they are some of the ones most often used.

Structural-Functional Theory

Structural-functional theory looks at the family as a social institution and asks, How is the family organized, and what functions does it serve in meeting society's needs? When talking about the family, structural-functionalists usually refer to the nuclear family. From this point of view, the family is considered successful to the extent that it fulfills societal expectations and needs.

Family functions have been described in numerous ways. A generation ago, Murdock (1949) identified four basic functions of the nuclear family: providing a common residence, economic cooperation, reproduction, and sex. Since Murdock's time, the nuclear family has become much less common, and some of the functions he identified are not necessarily confined to the family. In an attempt to provide an even more basic definition of the family, sociologists and family theorists have proposed other functions. However, Murdock's four are a good place to start discussing the family's role in society.

Common Residence   In recent decades, changes in society have created many variations of the function of common residence. In commuter marriages, for example, spouses maintain separate residences for much of the time, seeing each other only on weekends or occasionally during the month. Today, family members may share a common residence only some of the time, but they still form a family.

Economic Cooperation   Economic cooperation is a broad concept that can include a wide range of activities, from cooking, to maintaining a household, to earning an income. It includes the production, allocation, distribution, and management of resources such as money, material goods, food, drink, services, skills, care, time, and space.

Historically, the family was almost a self-sufficient economic unit. The traditional rural family produced much of its own food, housing, and clothing. Family members cooperated in this production and depended on one another for goods and services.

During and after the industrial revolution, many families moved off the family farm and came to depend more on those outside the family for the production of goods and services. As families became consumers rather than producers, earning an income became even more necessary. Partly because of increasing demands for income, wives as well as husbands were enlisted in the task of providing a living. Thus, spouses become mutually dependent in fulfilling this task.

The economic functions of the family are still important, but the nuclear family has never been able to meet all of them. Some needs have been met by other groups. For example, insurance companies provide health and life insurance, and industries and the Social Security Administration provide pensions for the retired or disabled.

Reproduction   Although the reproductive function of the family has always been important, nonmarital reproduction is now common as well. Advances in reproductive technology—in vitro fertilization, for example—have made it possible for fertilization to take place without any sexual contact between a man and a woman.

Sexual Functions   Murdock's (1949) concept of sexuality was synonymous with heterosexual relationships within the family. Obviously, sexual expression, both heterosexual and homosexual, may take place between two people outside a family unit. Some gay and lesbian couples have children from previous heterosexual relationships or have been able to legally adopt children, and some lesbians have given birth.

Nurture and Socialization of Children   Sociologists have described other family functions. I. L. Reiss (1980) insists that the only universal function of the family (nuclear, extended, or otherwise) is the nurturance and socialization of children. According to this view, parents do not have to be biologically related to their children (the children may be adopted), but society insists that socialization is the responsibility of the family group (N. E. Moss and Abramowitz, 1982). Whether parents are single,

Families exist in a variety of forms, but the nuclear family is still much in evidence. Its most enduring function may be the care and guidance of children.

separated, divorced, married, or remarried, they are expected to be responsible for meeting their children's physical, emotional, social, intellectual, and moral needs. The family is not the only caregiving or socialization unit. Schools, churches, and social groups such as the Cub Scouts, Brownies, Girl and Boy Scouts, and YMCA participate in the socialization process (Hoge, Petrillo, and Smith, 1982). But society delegates to the family primary responsibility for this process. Failure to meet this function constitutes legal grounds for charges of child neglect or abuse. Additional information on the socialization of children may be found in Chapter 13, on parenting.

Family Developmental Theory

Family developmental theory includes two basic concepts. The first is that of the family life cycle, which divides the family experience into phases, or

stages, over the life span and describes changes in family structure and roles during each stage. The traditional family life cycle is an early marriage (with no children), years devoted to childbearing and child rearing, empty-nest years, retirement, and the death of one's spouse and widowhood. Chapter 8 discusses the family life cycle in more detail.

The second concept is that of developmental tasks, which Duvall (1977) defines as growth responsibilities that arise at certain stages in the life of the family. The successful completion of these tasks leads to immediate satisfaction and approval, as well as to success with later tasks. In contrast, failure leads to unhappiness in the family, disapproval of society, and difficulty with later developmental tasks. Examples of developmental tasks are the need to develop parenting skills when a child is born and the need to make adjustments at the time of retirement. For the family to continue to grow, biological requirements, cultural imperatives, and personal aspirations need to be satisfied during each stage of the family life cycle.

To be successful, family members need to adapt to the changing needs and demands of other family members and the changing expectations of the larger kin network, the community, and society. Family members also need to attend to tasks that are necessary to ensure family survival. Family tasks can be grouped into five categories: (1) physical maintenance, (2) socialization for roles inside and outside the family, (3) maintenance of family morale and motivation to perform tasks, (4) social control, and (5) the acquisition of family members (through birth or adoption) and their launching when mature (Mattessich and Hill, 1987). Chapter 8 provides a more detailed discussion of developmental tasks over the family life cycle.

theory A tentative explanation of facts and data that have been observed.

structural-functional theory A theory that emphasizes the function of the family as a social institution in meeting the needs of society.

family developmental theory A theory that divides the family life cycle into phases, or stages, over the life span and emphasizes the developmental tasks that need to be accomplished by family members at each stage.

Symbolic Interaction Theory

Symbolic interaction theory describes the family as a unity of interacting personalities (Stryker, 1972; R. H. Turner, 1970). It focuses attention on the way that family members interact through symbols: words, gestures, rules, and roles. People are socialized to understand the meaning of various symbols and to use them to communicate messages, feelings, intentions, and actions. Family members interact through symbols, and together they develop roles (such as father, husband, mother, wife, or daughter) and assign roles to others in the family, who "play" the assigned role. Each actor adjusts his or her behavior to what he or she thinks the other person is going to do.

Children derive much of their self-concept, or thoughts and feelings about themselves, from symbolic messages conveyed by their parents. These messages may be expressed in words: "David is a naughty boy," or "Joan is a very smart girl." Or they may be expressed in actions, such as withholding or bestowing rewards. From symbolic messages, children learn to enact expected roles and follow prescribed behavior.

But meanings are conveyed both ways. That is, children influence the way parents act as well. Parents will respond differently to a child who is rebellious and to a child who is a conformist, for example.

symbolic interaction theory A theory that describes the family as a unit of interacting personalities communicating through symbols.

systems theory A theory that emphasizes the interdependence of family members and how those members affect one another.

exchange theory The theory that people choose relationships in which they can maximize their benefits and minimize their costs.

equity theory A subcategory of exchange theory holding that people seek a fair and balanced exchange in which the partners can mutually give and receive what is needed.

conflict theory A theory that family conflict is normal and that the task is not to eliminate conflict but to learn to control it so that it becomes constructive.

feminist theory Theory (or perspective) that focuses on male dominance in families and society and examines how gender differences are related to power differentials between men and women.

The same principles of reciprocal interaction by means of symbols apply to the relationship between spouses and other family members.

Symbolic interaction is important because our actions and feelings are determined not just by what happens to us but also by how we interpret those events. For example, people define family violence differently. One woman may regard a slap by her husband as unacceptable violence and seek help from the police or a crisis center; another woman may view a couple of punches as a loss of temper not worth mentioning. Symbolic interaction theory is widely used in family therapy to help individuals understand how they perceive one another and how they can modify their perceptions and behavior to develop a more meaningful and harmonious relationship.

Systems Theory

Systems theory emphasizes the interdependence of family members (Broderick and Smith, 1979). Family members do not live in isolation; rather, what one does affects all the others. A person with deep-seated fears and anxieties and emotional instability, for example, may upset everyone else in the family. Interdependence may involve not only money, shelter, and food but also love, affection, companionship, socialization, and other nontangible needs.

There may be various subsystems within the total family unit. Three children may constitute one subsystem, and their two parents another. A husband and his mother may constitute a subsystem, a mother and her daughter another, a father and son still another. Knowing how one subsystem relates to others can be important to understanding the relationships within a particular family. For example, chronic conflict in the husband–wife subsystem may have a negative effect on children in the family. To help the children, a therapist has to assist the spouses in dealing with their conflict.

The concept of interdependency of family members has been useful in the treatment of dysfunctional families. Chronic alcoholism, for example, is considered a family illness. A woman who is married to an alcoholic but denies the problem and covers up for the husband is an "enabler" because she enables him to continue drinking without suffering more consequences. Family interactions may become habitual and therefore difficult to change, even when they are dysfunctional. By analyzing the patterns of response and behavior, therapists seek to motivate partners to rethink and restructure the way they relate to each other and to other family members (Papp, 1983).

Exchange Theory

Exchange theory is based on the principle that we enter into relationships in which we can maximize the benefits to us and minimize our costs (Nye, 1978). We form associations that we expect to be rewarding, and we tend to stay away from relationships that bring us pain. At the least, we hope that the rewards from a relationship will be proportional to the costs (Aldous, 1977).

People seek different things in relationships. For example, people marry for many different reasons: love and companionship, sex, procreation, status, prestige, power, and financial security. People are usually satisfied with relationships that at least partially fulfill their expectations and that do not exceed the price they expected to pay.

Some relationships are one-sided; one person does most of the giving, and the other the receiving. Over the long term, the giver is likely to become resentful and angry and to seek a more equal exchange.

Equity theory is a variation of exchange theory holding that exchanges between people have to be fair and balanced so that they mutually give and receive what is needed. People cooperate in finding mutual fulfillment rather than compete for rewards. They learn that they can depend on each other to meet needs, and their commitment involves strong motivations to please each other. Exchange theory is discussed in detail in Chapter 6, on love and mate selection, and in Chapter 10, on power, decision making, and communication.

Conflict Theory

Conflict theory has never achieved the same status in contemporary family life literature as have symbolic interaction theory, systems theory, and exchange theory. Nevertheless, conflict theory is useful in describing and understanding family conflict as members struggle for ascendancy and power (Sprey, 1988).

Conflict theory begins by asserting that conflict in families is the normal state of affairs and that family dynamics can be understood by identifying the sources of conflict and the sources of power. What do family members fight about? Who wins, and how

and why? What can be done about the conflict? The issue is not how to avoid conflict, but how to manage it, deal with it, and resolve it. When conflict is disruptive and negative, change is needed; resolving the conflict becomes the motivation for establishing a more rewarding and meaningful relationship. Solutions come through establishing better communication, developing empathy and understanding, and being motivated to change. Solutions come as well through bargaining, negotiation, and compromise.

Feminist Theory

Feminist theory is often called a perspective rather than a theory because it reflects thinking across the feminist movement and includes a variety of viewpoints that focus on the inequality of power between men and women in society, and especially in family life (MacDermid, Jurich, Myers-Walls, and Pelo, 1992). While there are many variations within the feminist perspective, at the heart of all of them is the issue of gender roles, particularly traditional gender roles. *Gender* is defined as the learned behaviors and characteristics associated with being male or female, and feminist theories examine how gender differences are related to power differences between men and women. Feminists assert that the female experience is just as important and valuable as the male experience in life but that women are exploited, devalued, and oppressed (Osmond and Thorne, 1993; Walker and Thompson, 1984). Feminist theory argues that family and gender roles have been constructed by society and do not derive from biological conditions, and that these roles were created in order for men to maintain power over women. Feminist theory is similar to conflict theory in that the conflict perspective focuses on the unequal power within groups or larger societies, while feminist theory focuses on the sex-gender system and the way male dominance in the family and society is oppressive to women.

Proponents of feminist theories have a common interest in understanding the subordination of women (Osmond and Thorne, 1993) and working to change conditions in society that promote barriers to opportunities for women (L. Thompson and Walker, 1995). Unique to the feminist perspective is the use of knowledge to raise the level of awareness of oppression and to end oppression and subordination based on social class, race/ethnicity, age, or sexual orientation. The feminist perspective is concerned with the overall oppression of all groups that are defined on the basis of age, class, race/ethnicity, disability, or sexual orientation (Baber and Allen, 1992).

In general, feminists have challenged the definition of family that is based on traditional roles. They see the family as a dynamic and diverse system whose members are constantly changing, a system that should not confine men or women to prescribed roles. While men and women may have been socialized to perform particular roles (for example, males as provider and decision maker, and females as passive and nurturing), feminists maintain that both can play various roles and be quite functional in all of them. This perspective provides couples with more flexibility, because both men and women can play roles based on their unique skills and interests, as opposed to the roles traditionally assigned based on their gender.

The feminist perspective is about choice and about equally valuing the choices individuals make. For example, if the man wants to stay home and take care of the children while the woman pursues a career, his choice should be valued as equally as a decision to pursue a career. Similarly, if the woman

chooses to stay home and be the primary caregiver for the children, her choice, as well as her experience in the home, should be valued as equally as her husband's career. Feminists do not object to the idea of women being traditional as long as it is a choice that they make, and not a role imposed on them. Women need to make their own choices about how to live their lives, and they need access to the same opportunities available to men. And those choices need to be supported and valued as equally as the choices men make in their lives.

Critique of Family Theories

No one family theory has a monopoly on the truth. Each time a new theory is introduced, it is described as the key to understanding family phenomena (Nye, 1978) or as the wave of the future (Broderick and Smith, 1979; Holman and Burr, 1980). Inevitably, however, each theory falls short of completely explaining family processes. This shortcoming does not detract from the usefulness of theories but rather motivates us to look for additional ways to understand changing families and the interaction of the people in them.

A QUESTION OF POLICY
GAY AND LESBIAN FAMILIES

As discussed in this chapter, gay and lesbian families are an increasingly common family form today. There will always be gay and lesbian families, regardless of the controversy. However, when gays or lesbians form families, legal issues emerge and policies can either help support gay and lesbian families or try to discourage them.

Three major policy issues for gay and lesbian families are adoption by a co-parent, child custody, and legal marriages. Entire books could be written on each of these topics, and many different scenarios and legal issues are possible. We choose to focus on lesbian couples becoming parents as most of the "gayby boom" is brought on by lesbians choosing to become parents through sperm donation. Typically, these women

strongly intend to become parents and raise a child with two mothers in a loving, committed relationship.

For many lesbian mothers, important legal issues are adoption and child custody if the relationship should end either through breakup or death. Many states' adoption policies discriminate against gay and lesbian couples and will not allow a child to be adopted by a lesbian. If the co-parents' relationship ends, the nonbiological co-parent and the child are at risk for losing their familial relationship. Let's assume that a lesbian couple has raised a child together for 15 years but that the relationship is ending. Currently, the nonbiological mother has no legal right to retain custody of the child and no visitation rights.

Many family rights and custody problems stem from the fact that gay and lesbian unions are not seen as legal and thus are not afforded the same legal rights as marriages. In 1993 the state supreme court of Hawaii issued a ruling that raised the prospect of legalizing same-sex marriage, but other states quickly passed legislation to refuse to recognize same-sex marriages performed in other states (Stacey, 2003). The backlash against same-sex marriages was so intense that in 1996 Republicans in Congress introduced a bill to define marriage in strictly heterosexual terms. This bill was passed by both the Senate and the House of Representatives and signed into law as the Defense of Marriage Act. However, some employers are choosing to grant spousal benefits, such as health insurance, to cohabiting couples regardless of gender or sexual orientation. Because such benefits are not mandated by law, gay and lesbian couples have no legal means to demand them for their partner or nonbiological child.

QUESTIONS TO CONSIDER:

In the event of the breakup of a relationship, should a lesbian co-mother have legal custody or visitation rights to a child she did not bear? Why or why not?

Should adoption or custody rights regarding lesbian couples take into consideration the amount of time the two partners co-parented? What would a reasonable amount of time be for a nonbiological parent to be able to adopt or have custody rights?

Should gay and lesbian couples be allowed to legally marry and have the same legal rights afforded to them as heterosexual couples? Why or why not?

You are the C.E.O. of a large corporation, why would you choose to grant benefits to gay and lesbian couples? Why would you choose not to?

SUMMARY

1. A family is any group of persons united by the ties of marriage, blood, or adoption, or any sexually expressive relationship, in which the adults cooperate financially for their mutual support; the people are committed to one another in an intimate interpersonal relationship; the members see their identity as importantly attached to the group; and the group has an identity of its own.

2. Different family forms are determined by their structural arrangement, the persons in them, and their relationship to one another.

3. Modern views of the family emphasize its role in fulfilling personal needs for emotional security and companionship.

4. Although historically the American family was patriarchal, there has been a gradual shift to a more democratic power structure.

5. The marriage rate is the number of persons who marry during the preceding 12 months per 1,000 population.

6. The median age at first marriage is increasing for both men and women, resulting in an increase in unmarried young adults in the population.

7. Declining birthrates since 1965 have resulted in smaller families.

8. The percentage of married women in the workforce has been increasing steadily. At present, greater percentages of women with either preschool or grade-school children are working outside the home than are women without children.

9. The number of one-parent families, especially mother–child families, has risen considerably in recent years.

10. One increasingly common family form is gay or lesbian families.

11. Large numbers of gays and lesbians live in stable couple relationships, some with children.

12. Divorce rates increased steadily from 1958 until 1979, at which time they leveled off and

even declined. At the present rate, it is predicted that about 50% of new marriages will end in divorce.

13. Three out of four divorced women and four out of five divorced men will eventually remarry, although those rates appear to be declining. The relatively high rates of divorce and remarriage have resulted in a large number of reconstituted, or blended, families.

14. Over the past 40 years, more adolescents have been engaging in sexual intercourse and at a younger age.

15. It is important to understand and appreciate the cultures and values of the many ethnic groups that make up the population of the United States. As you study families, it is important to be aware of how cultural diversity may affect them.

16. A theory is a tentative explanation of facts and data that have been observed.

17. Psychologists and sociologists have formulated a number of theories about the family. Seven main ones in helping to explain families are structural-functional theory, family developmental theory, symbolic interaction theory, systems theory, exchange theory, conflict theory, and feminist theory.

KEY TERMS

family

voluntarily childless family

single-parent family

nuclear family

family of origin

family of procreation

extended family

blended, or reconstituted, family

stepfamily

binuclear family

polygamous family

polygynous family

polyandrous family

patriarchal family

matriarchal family

gay or lesbian family

cohabiting family

instrumental role

expressive role

patrilineal descent

patrilocal residence

matrilineal descent

matrilocal residence

bilateral descent

neolocal residence

cohort

fellatio

cunnilingus

theory

structural-functional theory

family developmental theory

symbolic interaction theory

systems theory

exchange theory

equity theory

conflict theory

feminist theory

ethnicity

culture

QUESTIONS FOR THOUGHT

1. What is your definition of *family*? How is it similar to or different from the definition used in the text?

2. How well does your family of origin or your present family (if you are married) adhere to instrumental and/or expressive roles?

3. What are the various reasons for current trends in marriage rates, age at first marriage, birthrates and family size, percentage of working mothers, and one-parent families?

4. What are your thoughts about current trends in nonmarital sexual behavior? What measures do you believe should be taken, if any, to decrease the incidence of unmarried pregnancy?

5. The text suggests that family philosophy has changed from an emphasis on institution to an emphasis on companionship. If you were to follow this philosophy, what kind of marriage would you strive to have? Explain.

6. Which family theory makes the most sense to you? How would you use that theory to help explain the behaviors and patterns in your family?

SUGGESTED READINGS

Coontz, S. (1992). *The Way We Never Were: American Families and the Nostalgia Trap.* New York: Basic Books. Dispels myths about the traditional family.

Coontz, S. (1997). *The Way We Really Are: Ending the War over America's Changing Families.* New York: Basic Books. Examines "nontraditional" family life and the way changes in family structure have had both positive and negative effects.

Cott, N. F. (2000). *Public Vows: A History of Marriage and the Nation.* Cambridge, MA: Harvard University Press. Examines the public and private purposes of marriage throughout history.

Drucker, J. (1998). *Families of Value: Gay and Lesbian Parents and Their Children Speak Out.* New York: Insight Books/Plenum Press. Presents stories by and about gay fathers and lesbian mothers raising children in various settings and situations.

Ganong, L. H., and Coleman, M. (1999). *Changing Families, Changing Responsibilities: Family Obligations Following Divorce and Remarriage.* Mahwah, NJ: Lawrence Erlbaum. Explores responsibilities of members of stepfamilies.

Hawes, J. M., and Nybakken, E. I. (2001). *Family and Society in American History.* Urbana and Chicago: University of Illinois Press. Presents an interdisciplinary perspective on the history of the family.

Jagger, G., and Wright, C. (Eds.). (1999). *Changing Family Values.* London, New York: Routledge. Covers the backlash against single mothers, lesbian and gay families and the law, family and social policy, and the future of the nuclear family.

Laird, J., and Green, R. (Eds.). (1996). *Lesbians and Gays in Couples and Families: A Handbook for Therapists.* San Francisco: Jossey-Bass. Presents a series of readings.

McLanahan, S., and Sandefur, G. (1994). *Growing Up with a Single Parent: What Hurts, What Helps.* Cambridge, MA: Harvard University Press. Argues that the disadvantages for children living with single parents are substantial, occur across several important life domains, and persist long into adulthood.

Mulroy, E. A. (1995). *The New Uprooted: Single Mothers in Urban Life.* Westport, CT: Auburn House. Examines how single mothers from a diverse set of social and economic circumstances experience the dual roles of sole family breadwinner and sole resident parent in the changing urban environment.

Rouse, L. P. (2002). *Marital and Sexual Lifestyles in the United States: Attitudes, Behaviors, and Relationships in Social Context.* Binghamton, NY: Haworth Clinical Practice Press. Explores the diversity of contemporary U.S. marital and sexual lifestyles.

Slater, S. (1995). *The Lesbian's Family Life Cycle.* New York: The Prepress. Traces five stages of the lesbian family life cycle.

Wood, J. T., and Duck, S. (Eds.). (1995). *Under-studied Relationships: Off the Beaten Track.* Thousand Oaks, CA: Sage. Discusses seven different types of relationships that have been understudied.

CHAPTER 2

LEARNING OBJECTIVES

After reading the chapter, you should be able to:

- Explain why it is important to examine our family background.

- Describe and explain the relationships between parents' attitudes toward their children and children's attitudes toward themselves.

- Describe how attitudes toward intimate partners are formed partly by the relationships experienced in the family of origin.

- Show how attitudes toward intimacy and expression of affection are developed in the family.

- Describe the role of the family in developing attitudes toward sex.

- Explain how attitudes toward marriage and divorce are affected by one's family background.

- Describe the role of the family in gender-role socialization.

- Describe the role of the family in developing family values toward work and in developing work habits.

- Summarize the various patterns of communication in families and the way these carry over into marriage.

Family Backgrounds and How They Influence Us

The marital relationship neither exists nor evolves in isolation. It has a family in back of it and usually one in front of it (Klagsbrun, 1985). Every marriage is influenced by the family backgrounds the partners bring to the relationship. Each couple, in turn, influences the family relationships their children will establish after them.

The first purpose of this chapter is to examine a representative variety of family relationships to illustrate their possible effects on the family relationships of the next generation. The second purpose is to stimulate and facilitate the examination of our own family backgrounds to see how they have influenced us.

This chapter is based on the assumption that family backgrounds do have an influence on our lives. The purpose of the chapter is to help us gain self-understanding through understanding the different ways our families can affect us. But this chapter is also devoted to discussing how personal responsibility comes with self-understanding. Once we know how we became what we are, we have a responsibility to decide how we want to be in the future. Our personalities are not locked in concrete; they can be changed. If someone decides to become a more sociable individual and assumes personal responsibility for trying to achieve this, this is a way of overcoming a negative factor in her or his own life. We can't change what has happened to us, nor can we really change those who influence us. But we can change how we react to what has happened to us, and we can change ourselves if we are highly motivated to do so.

WHY EXAMINE FAMILY BACKGROUND?

Our values, attitudes, and habits are largely molded by our family, although the influence of parents is subject to a number of variables. By being conscious of the positive and negative aspects of our family background, we can make responsible choices about the kind of partner we want to be and, if we choose to become parents, the kind of parent we want to be. Without understanding what influences behavior, it is very difficult to work toward change.

Because children observe, imitate, and model the behavior of their parents, parents have the opportunity to exert both positive and negative influence over them.

Understanding the Socializing Influence of the Family

The family is the chief socializing influence on children. In other words, the family is the principal transmitter of knowledge, values, attitudes, roles, and habits from one generation to the next. Through word and example, the family shapes a child's personality and instills modes of thought and ways of acting that become habitual. This process is called **generational transmission** (G. W. Peterson and Rollins, 1987).

This learning takes place partly through the formal instruction that parents provide their children and partly through the system of rewards and punishments they use to control children. Learning also takes place through **reciprocal parent–child interaction,** as each influences and modifies the behavior of the other in an intense social process. And learning occurs through **observational modeling,** as children observe, imitate, and model the behavior of others around them (Bandura, 1976). What parents say is important, but what children perceive parents to believe and do influences them most. As adults, our attitudes toward marital and parental roles are strongly related to the marital and parental role attitudes of our parents (Snyder, Velasquez, and Clark, 1997).

Determining Differential Effects

Not all children are influenced to the same degree by their families. The degree of influence that parents exert depends partly on the frequency, duration, intensity, and priority of their social contacts with their children. Parents who are emotionally close to their children and who have long-term loving relationships with them exert more influence than do those who are not so close and who relate to their children less frequently. Moreover, family influence may be either modified or reinforced by influences outside the family: the school, church, other social organizations, peer groups, or the mass media. Here again, the extent of influence depends partly on the duration and intensity of the exposure.

Another important factor in determining the influence of the family is the differences among individual children. Not all children react in the same way to the same family environment because children differ in temperament, cognitive perception, developmental characteristics, and maturational levels. Because A happens does not mean that B will inevitably result. When children are brought up in an unhappy, conflicting family, it is more difficult for them to establish happy marriages themselves (Fine and Hovestadt, 1984), but some still do. A person's marital fate is not cast in concrete.

Developing Self-Understanding

Not all children are influenced by their families to the same degree, and not all react the same way to the same environment. However, background has an effect, whatever it might be. The first task in developing self-understanding is determining what effects our families have had on us and evaluating those effects and the dynamics of their development.

What we have learned in our family of origin may be either helpful or detrimental to subsequent group living. Thus, a family may instill qualities of truth or deceit, of kindness or cruelty, of cooperation or self-centeredness, or of tolerance or obstinancy (Elliot, 1986). In relation to marriage and family living itself, the family may teach flexible or rigid gender roles. It may exemplify and teach democratic or authoritarian power patterns. It may

teach rational communication skills or habits of destructive conflict. It may teach children how to express love and affection or how to withhold it. Parents may model responsibility or irresponsibility; they may teach that sex is healthy and pleasurable or that it is dirty and painful. The family helps children develop positive self-images and self-esteem or negative self-images. The family may teach the value of work and the wise management of money or ways to avoid work and mismanage money. The family may teach what a happy marriage can be like or how miserable marriage can be. By examining family background, we can determine how much influence our family of origin had and whether it was positive or negative.

Assuming Personal Responsibility

Another task in examining family background is to begin to choose the goals and directions we want to take and to assume responsibility for our own selves. We can't continue to blame our parents for our problems if these problems are ever to be solved (Caplan, 1986). Nor can we assume that everything will be all right just because we grew up in a happy home.

When grown children enter into intimate relationships, they bring with them the background of experiences from their own families. They tend to feel that the way they were brought up is either the right way (which they try to duplicate in their own families) or the wrong way (which they try to avoid). By examining our family background, we can develop insight into what our own attitudes, feelings, and habits are, how these might cause us to respond, and whether we need to change any of them. Consider this example:

---

generational transmission The process by which one generation passes knowledge, values, attitudes, roles, and habits on to the next generation.

reciprocal parent–child interaction The influence of the parent on the child and the child on the parent so that each modifies the behavior of the other.

observational modeling The process by which children observe, imitate, and model the behavior of others around them.

One couple in their middle fifties went to a marriage counselor after the wife announced she wanted to divorce her husband. The wife's chief complaint was her husband's authoritarian dominance over the family. The wife explained: "Everything has to be done his way. He never considers my wishes. Several years ago I wanted to remodel the kitchen. It was going to cost five thousand dollars, but I was going to pay for it out of my own salary. He said he didn't want the kitchen remodeled and that was that. Our relationship has always been like that. I never do anything I want to do. So I decided I couldn't stand it any longer. I'm leaving him."

In subsequent counseling sessions, the family backgrounds of the couple were explored. The husband pointed out that his father was a dictator in his family. "I really got so I couldn't stand my father," the husband explained.

"And you're just like him," the wife remarked.

It was difficult for the husband to accept this observation at first, but by talking about his experience with his dad compared to his present role as a father, he was able to determine that he needed to change himself.

He did, and the marriage survived. (Author's counseling notes)

Making Peace with the Past

Examining family background also enables us to "make peace with our past." For example, if we are afraid of marriage because our parents were unhappily married, examining background experiences helps us to face these anxieties honestly and to rid ourselves of them so that we can dare to marry. Similarly, spouses who become hostile toward their partner because of unhappy experiences with their own parents may have difficulty relating to a partner in a positive, warm way. For example, research has indicated that physical violence witnessed in one's family of origin is predictive of greater psychological distress in adulthood for men and women. Men's reports of symptoms of psychological distress, such as depression or mental illness, in their family of origin indicate that this distress was an important contributor to their own displays of physical and verbal aggression in their marriages (Julian, McKenry, Gavazzi, and Law, 1999). Facing the past squarely, talking about it, and releasing the anger will often help people to change their feelings and behaviors. Similar steps have helped adult children of alcoholics move beyond their damaging histories.

In this chapter, we look at a variety of family patterns and situations and discuss some of their possible effects on individuals. The family situations selected represent only a small fraction of the infinite variety that exists in real life.

PARENTAL ATTITUDES TOWARD CHILDREN

A child's self-concept is strongly influenced by her or his parents. Children who are encouraged and affirmed by their parents are more likely to develop into self-assured adults who feel good about themselves. Conversely, children who are constantly criticized or even rejected by their parents are likely to be insecure, self-doubting adults. For example, research has shown that mothers who are very dependent and self-critical relate to their daughters in ways that may foster dependency and self-criticism by thwarting their daughters' attempts at autonomy or by being punitive and controlling (R. Thompson and Zuroff, 1998).

Approval

The most important contribution that parents can make to their children's development is to let the children know that they adore them, love them, approve of them, like them, value them, care about them, and accept them. Parents communicate these attitudes through words of approval, praise, and encouragement; through the interest shown and the care given; and through actions that demonstrate positive feelings and trust. Children base their view of how healthy their family is on whether their parents trust them (Kerr, Stattin, and Trost, 1999). Parents also communicate love through guidance, by caring enough about their children to be concerned.

Children who grow up with approval and positive affirmation and acceptance develop good feelings about themselves, adequate self-concepts, and confidence in their own worth and abilities. Lau and Pun (1999) examined the relationships between parents' evaluation of their children and their children's self-concept in four domains: academic, physical, social, and general. They found significant correlations between parental (especially maternal) evaluations and children's self-concept. Across sex and grade, academic self-concept was most influenced by parents' evaluations. When parents thought their children

African American Family Strengths and Influences

Many of the problems that beset the Black family are due to racial discrimination and the difficult economic conditions under which a disproportionate number of African Americans live. Black families show a number of positive characteristics that have enabled them to function and survive (Gary, Beatty, and Berry, 1986). These characteristics include the following:

- **Strong kinship bonds.** Extended families are common, and family members rely on one another for care, strength, and mutual support (Chatters, Taylor, and Neighbors, 1989; R. J. Taylor, 1985, 1986). According to one study, relatives of African American mothers are almost twice as likely as members of Anglo-American families to provide child care when children are sick or out of school (Benin and Keith, 1995). Compared to those of Whites, Black kin networks are more intensive and extensive. Blacks are more likely to live with relatives, to contact kin, and to visit their mothers (Baley, 1995).

- **A favorable attitude toward the elderly.** At all socioeconomic levels, African Americans have a more favorable attitude toward the elderly than do Whites.

- **Flexible roles.** Spousal relationships in most middle-class Black families are egalitarian, with men sharing significantly in the performance of household tasks (R. J. Taylor, Chatters, Tucker, and Lewis, 1990). Although the women spend more time than the men as primary caregivers of children, the men appear to be accessible and involved with their children (Ahmeduzzaman and Roopnarine, 1992). Roles of all family members are flexible. An uncle or grandmother can assume the vacated position of an absent parent.

- **Strong achievement orientation.** The median number of years of schooling completed is nearly equal to that for Whites (U.S. Bureau of the Census, 1999a). Moreover, most African Americans are highly motivated to get ahead and have pride in their own accomplishments and those of Black people generally (Belsky, Youngblade, Rovine, and Volling, 1991).

- **Strong religious orientation.** Religion traditionally has been a source of solace for oppressed people, as well as a vehicle for rebellion and social advancement (Coke, 1992). Religiosity has been linked with higher levels of marital interaction and with lower levels of marital conflict. The church contributes to cohesion in the African American community by acting as an agent of moral guidance and the center of community life. The potential benefits of African Americans' religious participation are underscored by research indicating that religious belief and activity form an important coping mechanism for negotiating life's stresses (Barnes, 2001; G. H. Brody, Stoneman, Flor, and McCrary, 1994).

were bright, the children had a higher self-concept with regard to their intelligence. Feelings of self-worth make the children more likely to choose a suitable marital partner. High self-esteem gives them a greater capacity to develop positive relationships because they feel that they are lovable and expect to be loved. They feel they are capable spouses, able to fulfill the expected roles of marriage, and they are confident that they can be good parents to their children.

Criticism and Rejection

Some children are brought up in the opposite type of family situation, in which the parents constantly express their disapproval and criticize them. "You never approve of me and compliment me" and "You always find fault with everything I do" are frequent complaints from the children. Children who are ignored by one or both parents may feel emotionally rejected. Maternal coldness often leads to insecure attachment in the daughter, which leads to self-criticism (R. Thompson and Zuroff, 1999). If dependency needs are unfulfilled and the child is made to feel undervalued as a person, feelings of inferiority and unworthiness may be carried over into all areas of life. For example, sometimes a person marries because of a need for an affectionate parent figure rather than a marital partner.

Every marriage is influenced by the family backgrounds the partners bring to the relationship. Will these children be influenced by their grandparents? How much of what the parents learned as children will be passed on to the next generation?

When children grow up with emotional deprivation, they may transfer their needs for attention, love, recognition, and approval to the marriage relationship and expect their spouse to fulfill all the emotional needs that were not met in their own family during childhood. The most frequent example of marriage for neurotic reasons is that of the spouse with exaggerated dependency needs. Such spouses may become clinging, smothering, and insatiable in their demands for attention. Such people may need constant reassurance: "I won't be rejected by you as my parents rejected me" (Messer, 1983).

At the opposite extreme are spouses who won't let their mate love them. They really can't believe that anyone would want to love them, and they won't let anyone get close for fear of being hurt and rejected. Early experiences with parents have an impact on the well-being of both elderly and young people. When parental care is recalled as neither warm nor attentive, unattached elderly people experience lower self-esteem and more loneliness; unattached older men also experience worse subjective health and more anxiety and depression. Apparently, differences in well-being in old age can be at least partially explained by differences in early experiences and interaction with primary caregivers or parents. And individuals' early experiences with parents add to predictability about who will react well when faced with adversity. Those who have

learned early in life that their proximity- or support-seeking behavior is rewarded on a reliable basis are less prone to anxiety when an attachment figure is not available (Andersson and Stevens, 1993).

ATTITUDES TOWARD INTIMATE PARTNERS

How we feel toward intimate partners is determined partly by the relationships we have experienced in our family of origin. It has been well documented that current relationship problems often are simply repeated patterns from past relationships. Through case studies, Zimmerman and Cochran (1993) learned that people not only repeat family patterns in other relationships in their lives but also revise these patterns in ways that allow them to heal emotional wounds, switch roles, and strengthen loyalties. How individuals resolve family-of-origin relationship issues determines how they handle similar matters in all of their relationships (Williamson, 1991). Family of origin even affects the attitudes of engaged partners toward premarital counseling and the likelihood that they will attend (Silliman and Schumm, 1995). Thus, it is important to have a good understanding of one's own family patterns in order to avoid repeating dysfunctional patterns (Deacon, 1999).

A large body of research suggests that family-of-origin experiences are related to the quality of the offspring's romantic relationships. Most research suggests that individuals who experience poor relationships with their parents are more likely to have adjustment difficulties in their intimate relationships and that poor marital and parent–child relationships predict lower quality and stability in the offspring's long-term intimate relationships (Rodgers, 1996).

While relationship problems can be transmitted across generations, the mechanisms underlying these patterns are not fully understood (C. M. Feldman, 1997). Two theories are often used to try to explain them: (1) social learning theory and (2) attachment theory.

Social learning theory suggests that parents act as role models for their children and that children learn to imitate their parents' behavior, attitudes, and perceptions. For example, exposure to violence in the family of origin is a consistent predictor of later domestic violence as an adult (C. M. Feldman, 1997). Barclay Martin (1990) assessed links between marital conflict, parent–child conflict, and conflict between the offspring and their romantic partners. Marital conflict was related to aggressive and avoidant patterns of parent–child conflict, and these patterns were similar to those found in conflicts with romantic partners. Parents who consistently engage in coercion or withdrawal may provide powerful models of negative behaviors and may fail to provide models of positive behavior (for example, expressing affection) that are vital to relationship quality (Stafford and Canary, 1991). Consistent with this idea, young adults' attributions about relationships with parents (both positive and negative) have been linked to their attributions about intimate relationships (Benson, Arditti, Reguero DeAtiles, and Smith, 1992).

Attachment theory suggests that early interactions with parents lead to the formation of attachments that reflect children's perceptions of their self-worth and their expectations about intimate relationships. These ideas about attachment are carried forward into subsequent relationships, where they guide emotional, cognitive, and behavioral responses (N. L. Collins and Read, 1994). Several research findings support attachment theory as a means of explaining how family-of-origin experiences are related to romantic relationships. Feeney and Noller (1996) found that adults' attachment style

predicts the quality of their dating and marital relationships: Those with insecure attachment show less constructive interaction patterns, which tends to result in lower relationship satisfaction and stability. Janice Kennedy (1999) examined the connection between adult romantic attachment style and measures of psychological well-being, healthy self-concept, attachment to primary caregiver, and family environment in 225 college freshmen. Individuals with a secure attachment style were less likely to experience depression and were more likely to have a positive self-concept, to rate their primary caregivers as higher in encouraging them to be independent, and to rate their families as higher in expressiveness, cohesiveness, participation in family recreational activities, and provision of a stimulating environment than were individuals with insecure or fearful attachment styles. Attachment theory supports the idea that thoughts and behaviors learned from negative family experiences can change over time when individuals' negative expectations about intimate relationships are consistently not confirmed (Feeney and Noller, 1996).

Examples of both of these theories at work can be found in the research of Judith Feeney (1999b). She studied the links between young adults' romantic relationships and their experiences in the family of origin in both newly dating and long-term dating couples. The majority of participants in both groups reported positive and negative links between their family-of-origin experiences and the functioning of their dating relationship. One participant commented:

> I see him as a lot different to me, because of his relationship with his family. They are really close-knit and caring, and that's probably why he's always concerned about whether things are going to affect them. And that's why he's sensitive to me, and always takes

social learning theory A theory that suggests that parents act as role models for their children and that children learn to imitate their parents' behavior, attitudes, and perceptions.

attachment theory Theory suggesting that early interactions with parents lead to the formation of attachments that reflect children's perceptions of their own self-worth and their expectations about intimate relationships.

account of what I think and feel. I see him as really caring. He cares about what I'm thinking, and whether there are problems between him and me. (Feeney, 1999b, p. 31)

Another participant wrote about communication difficulties with his girlfriend and attributed them to a range of problems in her family of origin, including not only marital conflict and breakdown but also poor parent–child relationships:

> She's been through a lot in her early family life. Yes, she's been through a lot in terms of her family—she's had a very hard life. She's come out—not unscathed—she still has a lot of troubles. She doesn't express her feelings very well. That's because of her life early on. She's been through so much with that and trying to escape from it. Because from what I've seen and what I've heard about, she's got every right to hate the world. So she has a lot of trouble expressing herself. She's frightened of being—she's put a lot of barriers up, throughout her life. (Feeney, 1999b, p. 31)

This comment clearly illustrates the perspective of social learning theory that communication patterns are learned in the home. In contrast, in the following example, the boyfriend described the relationship's problems in attachment-related terms:

> She has a low opinion of herself, and she can't understand herself—and then I look at her mother and what she did to her! And then I see her as a person who really needs someone to help them, and to attach to. But at other times I look at her and I see this evil person who doesn't really want you for what you're worth, it's just using you for what she can get out of you at the moment. She's a very mixed-up person. . . . She doesn't know how to relate to her own emotions, and all that external show she puts on is just a way of hiding what she really thinks of herself. (Feeney, 1999b, p. 32)

FAMILY CLOSENESS: ATTITUDES TOWARD INTIMACY

Some families are huggers, and others limit physical contact to an occasional dutiful peck on the cheek or a handshake. But we all have an inborn need for affection and physical contact.

A common complaint of men and women in intimate relationships is that their partner is not affectionate enough. By affection, they don't always mean sexual intercourse. They mean touching, holding, hugging, cuddling, kissing, and caressing. Advice columnist Ann Landers (1985) asked female readers to reply to the question, "Would you be content to be held close and treated tenderly and forget about the act?" Seventy-two percent of 100,000 respondents answered yes. This survey revealed that these women wanted to feel cared for and to receive tender and loving embraces more than they wanted to have sexual intercourse with an inexpressive male. Other women have offered the same complaint: "I am so hungry for him to touch, hug, or hold me. He will not, or cannot touch—not in the bedroom or anywhere else" (Renshaw, 1984, p. 63). Husbands, too, complain of the need for physical expressions of affection. One husband complained because he and his wife slept on either side of a king-size bed with her poodle in between. He remarked, "I'm so jealous of the attention, loving, stroking, and petting she gives it. . . . I want to touch her, but she will not let me" (Renshaw, 1984, p. 64).

Children's need for physical contact with parents, for "contact comfort," has been well documented. The desire for physical closeness seems to be inborn. It is one way that children feel secure and develop positive self-esteem (Barber and Thomas, 1986). By being loved, children see themselves as

The importance of affection in enduring relationships is well established, but this does not always mean sexual intercourse. It can also mean touching, holding, hugging, and caressing.

both lovable and able to love. By being stroked, caressed, cuddled, and loved, children learn to stroke, caress, cuddle, and love others. Often there is perceived favoritism in a family by one of its members. In one study, children who felt disfavored in their family also reported lower family cohesion, higher family disengagement, and more family conflict than did the other members of the family. Children who perceived themselves to be disfavored also reported more frequent shame and more intense fear (L. Brody, Copeland, Sutton, Richardson, and Guyer, 1998). Receiving parental love and perceiving oneself to be loved are important in learning how to express affection.

Families vary considerably in the way they express love. Leo Buscaglia (1982), a popular lecturer on love, recalls the physical expressiveness of his large Italian family: "Everybody hugs everybody all the time. On holidays, everyone gets together, and it takes 45 minutes just to say hello, and 45 minutes to say goodbye. Babies, parents, dogs—everybody's got to be loved" (p. 116).

Children who grow up in families that do not show affection often have difficulty expressing affection as adults. They may sometimes feel insecure and have difficulty knowing how to give or receive affection. Males especially have difficulty because they generally receive less affection while growing up than do females. They are often brought up to feel that it is "sissy" or "unmanly" to express tender emotions (Carter and Sokol, 1987).

ATTITUDES TOWARD SEX

Just as their attitudes about physical intimacy influence their children's attitudes, parents' attitudes about sex and expressions of sexuality also leave a legacy. Research has shown that, from generation to generation, the guidance parents give their children about sexuality is very similar to the guidance their parents gave them (Kniveton and Day, 1999). Research has also shown that adolescents are most likely to adopt their parents' attitudes about appropriate sexual behavior if the parents often discuss sex-related topics and seem comfortable doing so. If parents do not discuss sexual behavior at home, children are not likely to have an accurate perception of their parents' sexual attitudes and are far less likely to discuss sex with their parents (Whitaker

and Miller, 2000). However, negative attitudes can be unlearned, and positive attitudes can be learned.

Positive Attitudes and Teachings

Certain attitudes about sex and sexual expression are developed at home from the time children are young. Some parents are very matter-of-fact about the body and nudity. They don't get upset if their preschool children see them nude or walk in on them while they are in the shower or going to the bathroom. Young children have no embarrassment at exposing their bodies or at seeing their siblings naked. Their interest in how other people look reflects a naive innocence and curiosity. Their interest soon turns to boredom when their curiosity is satisfied. Gradually, as children get older, they tend to want some privacy.

Parents who exhibit matter-of-fact attitudes toward bodily functions are helping their children develop a healthy sense of acceptance toward these things. We know, for example, that parents who prepare their daughters for menstruation in a positive way (Ruble and Brooks-Gunn, 1982) or their sons for nocturnal emissions minimize any negative emotional reactions that otherwise might accompany these natural consequences of puberty. Similarly, parents who try to give positive information about human reproduction, masturbation, and sexual response and expression help their children accept their sexuality as a positive part of their lives.

Negative Attitudes and Teachings

At the opposite extreme are parents who try to repress any interest in or thoughts and feelings about human sexuality. They never allow anyone in the family to see anyone else nude—not even the baby. Toileting always takes place behind closed doors, and dressing and undressing are strictly private, with the sexes separated. Children are brought up to believe that touching their genitals or playing with them is wrong or dirty. For example, when a baby boy innocently holds his penis, his father slaps his hand and shouts, "Don't do that; it's dirty." Or when a baby girl scratches her itchy pubic area, her mother pulls her hand away and warns, "Nice girls don't do that." Normal childhood curiosity about the facts of human reproduction is denied and repressed. The children may not ask any questions about sexual arousal, response, and expression.

Knowledge and attitudes about sex are developed from the time children are young. When and in what setting should children learn about sex and sexual expression?

Possible Effects on Sexual Behavior

Many parents who initiate sexual discussions with their children, especially with adolescents, do so primarily to try to prevent early sexual activity and pregnancy. They typically communicate with their sons about topics related to sexual exploration, while they discuss physiological and contraceptive issues with their daughters (Downie and Coates, 1999). One national survey of 15- and 16-year-olds revealed that daughters of traditional parents who had communicated with them about sex were less likely to have had intercourse than were those whose parents had not talked to them (Moore, Peterson, and Furstenberg, 1986). However, family communication about sex had little influence on discouraging early sexual activity of sons.

One study examined the relationship between 5,300 mothers and their teenagers (McNeely et al., 2002). The researchers found that young teens who felt a close connection to their mothers, and whose mothers clearly communicated their sexual values to their children, were more likely to delay having intercourse than teens without such a mother–child bond. The effect on girls of a bond with their mothers was strongest for eighth- and ninth-graders and weakened later in high school. When teens perceived that their mothers opposed teens having sex,

the teens were less likely to begin having sex. The study also found that only 51% of mothers whose teenager had had intercourse knew it. While children may pay attention to their parents' values on sex, the message does not always get through and many parents do not know what their children are doing sexually.

Similarly, other studies have found relationships between support and parental monitoring of adolescents with sexual activity. Longmore, Manning, and Giordano (2001) found that parents who monitored their children in the early years had teens who delayed the onset of sexual activity. They posit that adolescents' dating and sexual behaviors may vary as a function of parental socialization strategies and that parents play a very important role in the development of social competencies and in the primary socialization of children and adolescents.

ATTITUDES TOWARD MARRIAGE AND DIVORCE

Attitudes toward marriage and divorce are also profoundly affected by one's family background. Some people brought up in very unhappy homes develop very negative attitudes toward marriage itself. They do not want to duplicate the unhappiness that they experienced in their family of origin, so they are hesitant to marry. Some of them never marry, a greater proportion delay marriage, and a still greater proportion get married but have little idea how to make it work. The marriage that they knew as a child serves as a poor model for marital success. A lot of people who have been brought up in unhappy homes resolve that what happened to their parents will never happen to them. Nevertheless, they tend to duplicate the patterns of family relationships in their own marriage that they experienced in their family of origin while growing up.

What about people who come from divorced parents? What effect does divorce have on children's attitudes toward marriage and divorce? One study indicated that respondents from intact families were generally more likely than those with divorced parents to voice approval of marriage, but having been brought up in a divorced family had little impact on the timing of marriage. This suggests that parental divorce does not influence the perceived desirability of marriage (Trent and South, 1992). Children of divorced parents have goals for and attitudes toward marriage and family that are similar to those of children from intact families: They want long-term, loving, rewarding relationships with their spouses. However, adult children of divorced parents do express more accepting attitudes toward divorce than people who grew up with both biological parents, unless their family was conflictive (Amato and Booth, 1991).

Attitudes toward divorce and marriage have become more liberal as divorce, cohabitation, and never marrying have become more common. Societal disapproval of unmarried mothers also has diminished as their numbers have increased. As nontraditional family forms become more predominant, with successive cohorts, different family forms will gain increased acceptance (Trent and South, 1992).

GENDER-ROLE SOCIALIZATION IN THE FAMILY

The term **gender role** refers to a person's outward expression of maleness or femaleness in a social setting. Traits and behavior thought to be appropriate for a male are considered masculine; those thought to be appropriate for a female are considered feminine. However, gender roles vary according to cultural ex-

pectations and are influenced partly by environmental factors, the most important of which is the family. Children learn expected gender roles through identifying with parents and modeling their behavior.

Gender-role learning in the family can be divided into three categories:

1. **Personality traits.** Children are taught how men and women are supposed to look and act; they also learn the attitudes and values that their culture considers appropriate for their gender.
2. **Marriage and family living.** Gender roles in this category include decision-making roles, the division of household responsibilities, and parental responsibilities.
3. **Vocational roles.** Children learn what career and job activities men and women are expected to perform.

The extent to which identification and modeling take place depends on the amount of time parents spend with their child and the intimacy and intensity of the contact. It also depends on the relative influence that the parents exert. Of course, the gender concepts the child learns depend on the patterns of role models exemplified. Thus, a girl who closely identifies with a masculine mother may only weakly identify with a typically feminine personality. A girl brought up by a mother who is a professional career woman will have a less stereotypic concept of femininity than will a girl whose mother is primarily a homemaker. For example, research has found that mothers and early adolescent daughters in traditional, dual-work, and dual-career family environments held similar attitudes toward marriage, children, and careers (J. Bohannon and White, 1999). Similarly, a boy brought up by a father who represents very traditional ideas of masculinity and the role of the husband and father in the family will likely develop quite different concepts about the masculine gender role than will a boy brought up by an egalitarian father.

Gender-role expectations are in a state of flux, with many people advocating a more egalitarian

gender role A person's outward expression of maleness or femaleness in a social setting.

Values and Marital Satisfaction

Having an adequate income can contribute to marital satisfaction, but marital satisfaction is not always the greatest when income is the highest. Many spouses want love more than a lot of money. With regard to income, what is important is whether the partners agree that the level they have achieved is satisfactory. The real problem arises when spouses each have different values in relation to their standard of living and work ethic. If both spouses are workaholics, they may not have much time for leisure activities and a social life. But if they're happy with each other, there is no real problem. If their life goals and lifestyles are similar, they can both be content with the level at which they are living. If they both lack ambition, have poor work habits, and simply want to enjoy life without too much effort or without many material possessions, at least they're compatible. A problem may arise when they have been brought up with different value systems.

Orientations toward work and lifestyle are most influenced by the way we were brought up. Thus, it's helpful to explore our family backgrounds and philosophies in trying to evaluate compatibility.

distribution of income earning, homemaking, and child rearing. In actual practice, role performance has not kept up with ideology. Large numbers of people still hold to traditional concepts of the roles spouses play in the family. See Chapter 9 for a more detailed discussion.

VARIATIONS IN FAMILY VALUES AND WORK HABITS

Our parents are the primary role models for the kind of life we want to live as adults. If a man's father was a workaholic, he's more than likely to be one, too—he's never had a good look at any other way to be. If a woman grew up in a well-off family, she's not likely to be happy spending all her time trying to make ends meet.

Workaholic Families

Patterns of work and industry may be developed in one's family of origin. One married man described his family situation as a child:

> When I was growing up, all I ever did was work—from the time I was eight years old. My parents had a corner grocery store. I was expected to come right home from school and help my parents in the store. I never had time to play or have fun like other kids. When I was in high school, I never could join any clubs or participate in activities. I had to work. The store was open seven days a week from eight o'clock in the morning until nine at night. That's where I spent my childhood when I wasn't in school. (Author's counseling notes)

This man had never learned to play. When his spouse wanted him to take time off to enjoy social activities and have fun, he felt very guilty doing so. He could never relax and enjoy himself. His spouse, in turn, felt isolated and alone because she and her partner never had any companionship. She complained, "He gives everything to his job: all of his time and energy. By the time he works eighty hours a week he's exhausted. He has nothing left to give me" (Author's counseling notes).

Family Values

The work habits that people develop are related to family goals and values. Some people are never happy unless they reach a high level of material prosperity. They want to live in a large house, have fine clothes and luxury cars, and take expensive vacations. They are used to a certain standard of living in their family of origin and seek to duplicate this lifestyle in their own marriage. They are willing to work to achieve what they want. Other people want similar things but haven't developed the work habits and assumed the responsibilities necessary to fulfill their expectations. Still other people have more modest goals, which they're willing to work just hard enough to achieve. They are content with a modest lifestyle and income.

Parental Role Models

The role models parents provide are crucial in establishing life goals and work patterns in their children. Children whose parents have high expectations and standards of work performance tend to

This child is learning that doing laundry is a family job, not a "mommy" role. What children are taught about common tasks has a lot to do with their adult attitudes.

adopt these standards themselves. One man commented, "My father and mother both went to college and held good jobs when we were growing up. They always assumed that we would go to college too, and make something of ourselves. And we all did. They also taught us how to do physical labor around the house." In contrast to this family, some parents present lenient standards of performance, whether on a job or at home. They place less value on working hard, doing a good job, and getting ahead in life.

COMMUNICATIVE, NONCOMMUNICATIVE, AND CONFLICTIVE FAMILIES

Effective communication is one of the most important requirements in intimate relationships. Couples who are close usually have good verbal and nonverbal communication, talk enough and listen carefully, discuss important issues, understand each other, show sensitivity to each other's feelings, say positive things to each other, and keep open the channels of communication. Chapter 10 discusses communication in more detail.

The patterns of communication that exist in a family also influence communication patterns that the children establish in families of their own. These communication patterns may be divided into seven basic categories: (1) open, honest, tactful communication; (2) superficial communication; (3) one-sided communication; (4) false communication; (5) avoidance of communication; (6) noncommunication; and (7) angry communication.

Open, Honest, Tactful Communication

Family members are able to reveal what they think and how they really feel in a tactful, sensitive manner. They voice their concerns and worries and talk about important issues. They each can talk about themselves and their lives and know that others will listen and understand.

Superficial Communication

Sometimes family members talk a lot but never about anything important. They avoid disclosing themselves and discussing "gut" issues. Because of denial, fear, or distrust, they haven't learned to share their concerns. They are taught to be independent and strong and to handle their own problems. As a result, they avoid discussing feelings and problems. When someone asks, "How is everything?" the answer is usually "Just fine," even though it may not be true. As a result, no one really knows or understands what the others are thinking and feeling.

A family's pattern of communication is reflected in how it handles discussions of feelings and problems.

One-Sided Communication

In some families, one person does all the talking while the others listen. A woman may do all the talking and not give her spouse a chance to express his opinions. He either sits passively or tries to withdraw so that he won't have to hear it. A man's idea of talking to his spouse or children may be to give them lectures, to talk *to* them rather than *with* them. He wants to tell them something, but he doesn't really want to discuss anything. If others try to talk, they are criticized for interrupting or talking back, and so they learn to be quiet. When the children in such families marry and establish their own families, they often either repeat their passive roles in family interaction or model their behavior after their talkative parent and dominate the conversation in their own families.

False Communication

Communication patterns can be negative. Family members may learn to lie to keep out of trouble. If they are punished or ridiculed when they tell the truth, they learn to make up stories or to tell others what they think they want to hear. Sometimes they say just the opposite of what they really feel to give false impressions.

Avoidance of Communication

In some cases, family members learn not to talk about sensitive issues because such discussions lead to fights. They hate arguments and so avoid touchy, controversial subjects. They repress their own ideas and feelings for the sake of family harmony, and they try to deny problems and hope they will go away. They are taught to inhibit honest feelings and to keep everything in. It becomes very difficult to resolve problems, because they are never discussed.

Noncommunication

Some people are nonverbal. They may not have learned how to express themselves, so they seldom discuss anything. Or they may simply be shy or afraid that others won't like them or accept them, or will criticize them and think they are stupid. As a result, they keep quiet.

Here again, the important question is, What patterns of communication existed in an individual's family while he or she was growing up, and how have they affected that person?

Angry Communication

Some people are not able to talk about anything without becoming angry. They have a very low tolerance for frustration and experience more emotional arousal than most people when they are frustrated. They perceive more life situations as annoying, and they get angry more often, are more likely to express verbal and physical aggression when provoked, have higher general anxiety, and make less effort at constructive coping. Angry people describe their family environments while they were growing up as significantly less cohesive, less emotionally expressive—that is, less tolerant of self-expression—and more conflict-ridden and disorganized than those of less angry people. In families in which the expression of anger is a way of life, the children may carry that pattern into their own marital relationships (Lopez and Thurman, 1993).

In an impersonal world, the family becomes an even more important source of support and love. It is here that family members seek fulfillment of their basic human needs for affection and love. However, families are not perfect and many people come from negative family situations. It is important to try to understand one's family background in order to grow as a person and create relationships that are meaningful and fulfilling. Most of life's experiences are more enjoyable when we are in the company of someone else. Most of life's saddest moments are less difficult if we have someone else to help ease the burden. Family relationships change and grow over time, and difficult family situations can become important areas for personal growth.

A QUESTION OF POLICY

FAMILY ENVIRONMENT

We all want children to get a good start in life and be raised in healthy, loving environments. Unfortunately, that is not the case for many children. Public policy has an important place in families' lives, and most policymakers and politicians are indeed concerned about family well-being. It is important to understand how policies can either strengthen or weaken your own family life, and how important you think public policy is in helping families.

Research shows that families are better at raising and nurturing competent, happy children who in turn become productive, caring adults when they have such things as the support of close friends, good schools, a good job, health care, proper nutrition, caring communities, and responsive government. While many Americans may agree that raising children is primarily the responsibility of families, and not of government, they also believe that governments can shape the conditions that make it easier or harder for parents to do a good job (Bogenschneider, 2002). For example, federal policies have been enacted to address issues such as adoption, child abuse and neglect, child care, gun control, children's health insurance, child support, domestic violence, education, family leave, family preservation, family poverty, same-sex marriage, telecommunication reforms (e.g., V-chips for all new televisions), Head Start, welfare reform—the list goes go on and on. Also, many policies fall under state jurisdiction, which means states differ in what and how policies are implemented.

Some families need more assistance than others in creating a healthy environment in which to raise their children. Imagine the difficulties facing a family that has few or no resources to obtain a good education, high-quality child care, health care, safe schools and neighborhoods, or jobs that pay a living wage. Now imagine the same family with enough resources to obtain these things. While most people want to see families doing well, there are many questions regarding family policies: Who pays for services when parents are not able to pay for them? How and when should government intervene? Who is ultimately responsible for the well-being of families?

QUESTIONS TO CONSIDER:

Do the environments in which families operate (e.g., neighborhood, faith community, school) affect their ability to function? Explain.

What role, if any, should government play in shaping family environments?

Have social policies failed to keep pace with the changing circumstances of contemporary families? Explain.

How did (does) family policy affect you?

What one family policy, if any, do you feel strongly about? Why?

SUMMARY

1. The family is the chief socializing influence on children. Examining our own family background helps us understand how our family has affected us. This is necessary if we are to develop self-understanding, assume responsibility for our own behavior, and make peace with our past.

2. The most important contribution that parents can make to their children's development is to let children know that they are adored, loved, liked, approved of, valued, cared about, and accepted. This knowledge gives children positive self-esteem and self-acceptance.

3. Children who are criticized or rejected grow up with poor self-images and are starved for affection, which makes mature marriage relationships more difficult for them to establish.

4. Rather than blame parents for our problems, we need to gain self-understanding, assume personal responsibility, and strive to change ourselves.

5. Current relationship problems are often repeated patterns from past relationships. People not only repeat family patterns in other relationships but also revise these patterns in ways that allow them to heal emotional wounds, switch roles, and strengthen loyalties.

6. Family-of-origin experiences are related to the quality of an offspring's romantic relationships. Individuals who had poor relationships with their parents are more likely to have adjustment difficulties in their own intimate relationships.

7. Social learning theory suggests that parents act as role models for their children and that children learn to imitate their parents' behavior and adopt their attitudes and perceptions.

8. Attachment theory suggests that early interactions with parents lead to the formation of attachments that reflect children's perceptions of their self-worth and their expectations in intimate relationships.

9. People are born with a need for affection. Some adults need more expressions of affection than others, and spouses sometimes complain that their partner is not affectionate enough. Expressing affection is behavior that is learned in the family.

10. The family is also instrumental in instilling either positive or negative attitudes toward sex. Those attitudes influence sexual behavior during adolescence and adulthood.

11. Attitudes toward marriage and divorce are developed in relation to our family background. People become more accepting of divorce for themselves if they have grown up in a divorced family.

12. The family also influences gender-role socialization. This socialization includes developing masculine or feminine personality traits, learning masculine or feminine gender roles and responsibilities in marriage, and learning vocational roles of men and women.

13. The roles parents model are crucial in establishing the life goals and work patterns that adults take into their own marriages.

14. Communication patterns are also influenced by one's family of origin. Types of patterns include open, honest, tactful communication; superficial communication; one-sided communication; false communication; avoidance of communication; noncommunication; and angry communication.

KEY TERMS

generational transmission

reciprocal parent–child interaction

observational modeling

social learning theory

attachment theory

gender role

QUESTIONS FOR THOUGHT

1. How has your family of origin influenced you in each of the following areas?
   a. Your attitudes toward intimacy and the expression of affection
   b. Your attitude toward sex
   c. Your gender-role socialization
   d. Your basic values and habits in relation to work
2. What pattern of communication best reflects the pattern in your family of origin, and how has this pattern affected each member of your family?

SUGGESTED READINGS

Barber, N. (1998). *Parenting: Roles, Styles, and Outcomes.* Commack, NY: Nova Science. Discusses parenting in different settings and situations and its effects on children, exploring the theory that antisocial behavior is a response to low parental investment.

Freeman, J. (1989). *Women: A Feminist Perspective* (4th ed.). Palo Alto, CA: Mayfield. Represents a classic reader dealing with feminism.

Grigorenko, E. L., and Sternber, R. J. (2001). *Family Environment and Intellectual Functioning: A Life-Span Perspective.* Mahwah, NJ: Lawrence Erlbaum. Discusses the role of the family environment, particularly with regard to intellectual functioning.

Joselson, R. (1996). *The Space Between Us: Exploring the Dimensions of Human Relationships.* Thousand Oaks, CA: Sage. Focuses on the development of human relationships.

Lucyshyn, J. M., Dunlap, G., and Albin, R.W. (2002). *Families and Positive Behavior Support: Addressing Problem Behavior in Family Contexts.* Baltimore, MD: Paul H. Brookes. Presents current theory, practice, and research on positive behavior support with families of children and youth with developmental disabilities and problem behavior.

Noller, P. (1993). *Communication in Family Relationships.* Englewood Cliffs, NJ: Prentice-Hall. Covers communication in several types of relationships, including parent–child, sibling, nontraditional family, and troubled family ones.

Socha, T. J., and Rhunette, C. (Eds.). (1999). *Communication, Race, and Family: Exploring Communication in Black, White, and Biracial Families.* Mahwah, NJ: Lawrence Erlbaum. Offers a collection of works focusing on communication within and about ethnic and biracial families.

CHAPTER 3

LEARNING OBJECTIVES

After reading the chapter, you should be able to:

- Define sex, gender, gender identity, and gender role.

- Explain how concepts of masculinity and femininity vary by society and culture.

- Discuss how the following environmental influences mold masculinity and femininity: societal expectations, parents, television, and school.

- Discuss how different theoretical views have different ideas about the development of "maleness" and "femaleness."

- Describe masculine and feminine stereotypes and norms and the problems they create.

- Discuss gender-role influences in interpersonal relationships between men and women.

- Discuss gender roles in the family, differing expectations and attitudes of various ethnic groups, and the way they affect housework and child care in families.

- Discuss how gender roles tend to change over the family life cycle.

- Describe how marital quality can be influenced by gender-role expectations.

- Explain the meaning of androgyny and its advantages.

Gender: Identity and Roles

Sex describes who we are biologically—male or female. We also manifest **gender,** or personality traits and behavior that characterize us as men (masculine) or women (feminine). These psychosocial components that characterize us as masculine or feminine are largely acquired behaviors (Lips, 1997). As noted in Chapter 2, our outward manifestations and expressions of maleness or femaleness are our gender roles, which are influenced by cultural expectations of what is considered socially appropriate for males and for females. There is a trend, however, toward less rigid and more androgynous gender roles. Our personal, internal sense of maleness or femaleness is our **gender identity.** Most children accept cognitively their assigned sex as a boy or a girl and then strive to act according to the expectations of society and the group of which they are a part. Some children and adults, however, have difficulty establishing their gender identity. They may experience gender dysphoria, or the feeling that their biological sex does not match their gender identity. Such **transgendered people** may alter their gender identity occasionally or permanently by cross-dressing or by becoming **transsexuals** with the help of hormones and surgery. In this chapter, we examine the concepts of gender and gender roles and describe some of the influences on their development.

ENVIRONMENTAL INFLUENCES ON GENDER

Sex is determined by biological factors. Gender identities and gender roles are influenced by the environment. Certain qualities of maleness are defined as and become "masculine" because of society's view of what being male means. Society prescribes how a male ought to look and behave, what type of personality he ought to have, and what roles he should perform. Similarly, a female is created not only by genetic conception but also by those psychosocial forces that mold and influence her personality (Lopata, 1993). When we speak of a masculine man, we express a value judgment based on an assessment of the personality and behavioral characteristics of the male according to culturally defined standards of maleness. Similarly, we label a woman feminine according to culturally determined criteria

Concepts of masculinity and femininity have undergone considerable change over the centuries. Is this eighteenth-century regency beau similar to the contemporary image of the "true man"?

for femaleness. In this sense, the development of **masculinity** or **femininity** involves an education in what it means to be a man or a woman within the context of the culture in which one lives (McCandless, Lueptow, and McClendon, 1989). Gender is as much about a set of beliefs as it is about anatomical differences (Sheinberg and Penn, 1991).

Concepts of masculinity and femininity vary in different societies and cultures. For example, Margaret Mead (1950), in studying three different groups, discovered some interesting variations in conceptions of masculinity and femininity. Arapesh men and women displayed "feminine" personality traits. Both males and females were trained to be cooperative, unaggressive, and responsive to the needs and demands of others. In contrast, Mundugumor men and women developed "masculine" traits. They were ruthless and aggressive, with maternal, nurturant aspects of personality at a minimum. In the third group, the Tchambuli, the women were dominant and impersonal, while the men were less responsible and more emotionally dependent.

Conceptions of masculinity and femininity have undergone considerable change in the United States. For example, in colonial times, a "true man," especially a gentleman, could wear hose, a powdered wig, and a lace shirt without being considered unmanly. Today, such attire would be considered quite feminine. Thus, the judgments made about masculinity or the extent of manliness are subjective, based on the accepted standards of maleness as defined by the culture. These standards vary from culture to culture and from era to era in the same society.

Societal Expectations

Because society plays such an important role in the establishment of the criteria for masculinity and femininity and in the development of maleness or femaleness, it is important to understand how gender identification and gender-role learning take place. Almost as soon as a child is born, society expects him or her to begin thinking and acting like a boy or like a girl, according to its own definitions. For example, if the child is a girl, she is often dressed in pink and is given dolls and other toys considered appropriate for little girls. She may be expected to act like a "little lady" or be encouraged to play girls' games. And as she gets older, she likely will be expected to help her mother around the house doing traditionally feminine chores. Thus, what society expects the girl to be and do becomes the basic influence in molding her into a woman. She also observes her older sister, her mother, and other females acting like women, and so she begins to identify with them, to imitate them, and to model her behavior after theirs. In short, as soon as a girl is born, she is programmed to behave in acceptable, appropriate ways for a female.

The same process applies to boys: Once he is born, a boy is often expected to manifest masculine traits and to do masculine things. He is programmed to become a man. Because programming begins very early in life, gender stereotyping is very common

in early-elementary-age children (Trepanier-Street, Romatowski, and McNair, 1990).

Various social influences play a role in gender identity and gender-role development. Three of the most important influences will be discussed here: parents, television, and school.

Parental Influences

One of the ways in which children develop gender identities and appropriate gender roles is through identification with parents and modeling of their behavior. **Parental identification and modeling** is the process by which the child adopts and internalizes parental values, attitudes, behavioral traits, and personality characteristics. Identification begins soon after birth, because of children's early dependency on their parents. This dependency, in turn, normally leads to emotional attachment. Gender identification and gender-role learning take place almost unconsciously and indirectly in this intimate parent-child relationship. Children may learn that their mother is affectionate and nurturing and that their father is playful and strong. Not only does each child receive different care from each parent, but he or she also observes that each parent behaves, speaks, dresses, and acts differently

gender Personality traits and behavior that characterize one as masculine or feminine.

gender identity A person's personal, internal sense of maleness or femaleness, which is expressed in personality and behavior.

transgendered people People who feel that their biological sex does not match their gender identity.

transsexual A transgendered person who seeks to live as a member of the opposite sex with the help of hormones and surgery.

masculinity Personality and behavioral characteristics of a male according to culturally defined standards of maleness.

femininity Personality and behavioral characteristics of a female according to culturally defined standards of femaleness.

parental identification and modeling The process by which the child adopts and internalizes parental values.

Because gender roles have become more flexible, females today can now be found in a wide range of professions.

Giving children gender-specific toys may have considerable influence on vocational choices. Such toys influence boys to be scientists, astronauts, or football players and girls to be nurses, teachers, or day care providers. Publishers have made a concerted effort to remove gender stereotypes from reading materials. Without realizing it, however, many teachers still encourage traditional masculine/feminine stereotypical behavior in school.

Studies of teachers' relationships with boys and girls reveal that teachers encourage boys to be more assertive in the classroom. For example, when the teacher asks questions, the boys often call out comments without raising their hand, whereas most girls sit patiently with their hand raised (Sadker and Sadker, 1985). Somewhere along the way, these children have received this message: Boys should be assertive academically; girls should be quiet.

Research indicates that teachers also have different beliefs about male and female students' competencies (Li, 1999). For instance, teachers tend to stereotype mathematics as a male domain, which is reflected in their tendency to overrate male students' mathematics capability, to have higher expectations for male students, and to have more positive attitudes toward male students (Li, 1999).

This gender bias is also reflected in parents' attitudes toward and beliefs about their children's subject competency in kindergarten and elementary school. Parents perceive boys as more competent than girls in science, and they perceive science as more important for boys and have higher performance standards for them (Andre, Whigham, Hendrickson, and Chambers, 1999). Moreover, jobs related to math or science are seen as more male dominated. All this suggests that gender stereotypes related to subject competency have their roots in the early elementary school years.

However, things are changing. For example, as part of the Equal Opportunity Act of 1972, Congress enacted Title IX to provide more opportunities for girls and women to participate in high school and college athletics—a domain once reserved for males. It affects all schools that receive federal funding of any kind. To comply with Title IX, an athletic department must meet at least one of these requirements: (1) provide athletic opportunities for females and males substantially proportionate to their respective enrollments, (2) consistently expand programs for the underrepresented sex, or (3) show that it fully and effectively meets the interests of the underrepresented sex. Schools that violate

Title IX requirements risk losing federal funds. Universities and colleges were given until 1978 to comply with its provisions. Since that time, there have been numerous lawsuits from those trying to block Title IX in their schools, but there is little doubt that Title IX has impacted women athletes. More U.S. women than ever before now compete in the Olympics, and women's teams have won gold medals in gymnastics, basketball, soccer, hockey, and softball. There are now women's professional basketball, soccer, and softball leagues—and in 1999 the women's soccer team won the World Cup. Improvements continue from grade school through college in the area of female sports in large part because of Title IX.

Title IX is not just about sports. It is a federal law that prohibits sex discrimination in any educational program that receives federal money. This means that public schools are required to have career education programs that treat female students equally in recruiting, counseling, testing, and admissions. Schools are not allowed to treat males and females differently in access to education and in career development. While Title IX remains controversial, it has no doubt provided opportunities for women, as well as role models, that go beyond traditional gender expectations and behavior. For example, after 30 years of Title IX, more women are going to college, more women are on college faculties, and more women are college presidents than before. The American Council of Education shows that in 2001 women were presidents at 22% of the nation's colleges and universities. That's up from 19.3% in 2000 and 9.5% in 1986 (G. Brown, Van Ummersen, and Phair, 2002).

THEORIES OF GENDER ROLE AND IDENTITY

While no one theory adequately explains all aspects of gender roles and identities, the various theories do provide helpful ways in which to think about and discuss patterns of behavior. Each theory might hold some of the answer to the mysteries as to why females act one way and males another. Five common theories used to explain gender roles and identities are (1) the social learning theory of gender identity, (2) cognitive developmental theory, (3) gender schema theory, (4) social structure/cultural theories, and (5) evolutionary theories.

Social Learning Theory of Gender Identity

The **social learning theory of gender identity** emphasizes that boys develop "maleness" and girls "femaleness" through exposure to scores of influences—including parents, television, school, and peers—that teach them what it means to be a man or woman in the culture in which they are brought up. They are encouraged to assume the appropriate gender identity by being rewarded for some behaviors and punished for others. Thus, the gender-role concepts and gender stereotypes of a particular culture become self-fulfilling prophecies. Those who live up to societal expectations are accepted as normal; those who do not conform are criticized and pressured to comply.

According to this theory, parental models, particularly those offered by the same-sex parent, are the most influential in shaping gender behavior. Other socializing agents, such as television, teachers, and peers, distinguish and reinforce children's gender roles. By the first year of life, children begin to be aware of the differences in gender roles, and by the third year, it is quite evident how girls and boys have been socialized to behave, play, and dress. A great deal of evidence supports social learning theory, but by itself it is insufficient to explain the development of gender roles and gender identity (Lips, 1997).

Cognitive Developmental Theory

Cognitive developmental theory suggests that gender, like other things, cannot be learned until a child

social learning theory of gender identity A theory emphasizing that boys develop "maleness" and girls develop "femaleness" through exposure to scores of influences—including parents, peers, television, and schools—that teach them what it means to be a man or a woman in their culture.

cognitive developmental theory A theory suggesting that gender roles and identities cannot be learned until children reach a certain stage of intellectual development.

reaches a certain stage of intellectual development. This theory suggests that between the ages of 3 and 5 children acquire "gender constancy," a fixed concept of gender that cannot be altered by superficial things, such as clothing or appearance. Prior to the development of gender constancy, children may confuse gender classifications and believe that classifications can arbitrarily change. According to cognitive developmental theory, once children categorize themselves as female or male, they will use this self-categorization to figure out how to behave. In response to positive reinforcement, they will attach higher value to gender-appropriate behaviors than to gender-inappropriate behaviors, which receive negative reinforcement (Lips, 1997). As children develop a model for proper gender behavior, they enter a phase of great rigidity. Around the age of 6 or 7, their views of gender roles are oversimplified and inflexible, relying greatly on stereotypes. For example, at this age, children may pretend to give one another "boy shots" or "girl shots" to protect themselves from becoming like members of the other sex. But within a few years, children become secure in their gender identity and so are more comfortable with occasional departures from the stereotypical gender role.

Whereas social learning theory is based on gender typing, such as sex-appropriate activities or occupations, cognitive developmental theory is based on cognitive aspects, such as knowledge of stereotypes and flexibility in applying them. Although some support exists for both theories, neither one can fully explain the development and maintenance of gender roles and gender identity (Lips, 1997).

Gender Schema Theory

A schema is the framework of logic and ideas someone uses to organize information and make sense of things. We all hold a variety of schemas, such as how an older person should act, what behavior is polite, and what it means to dress appropriately. According to **gender schema theory,** a person with a strong gender schema has very definite ideas about how males and females should look and behave. For example, baby girls typically are dressed in pink, and baby boys in blue; there are some blue outfits for baby girls, but virtually no pink outfits for baby boys. In addition, girls are often dressed in

lace and bows, while boys are dressed in clothes imprinted with sports- or tool-related images. From the first days of life, individuals' gender schemas (and those of their parents) influence how males and females are thought of and treated.

Here is a hypothetical example of a gender schema at work in the mind of a 4-year-old boy and his friends:

> Philip's sister received a Barbie doll for her birthday. When Philip saw it, he wanted his own Barbie doll. After his parents explained that only girls play with Barbies, Philip was still not satisfied and continued his pleading for his own doll. His parents reluctantly conceded and bought him one. Philip was so happy that he took the doll to school the next day to show his friends. They greeted him with "You must be a girl because only girls play with Barbies" and began to make fun of him. Philip never played with a Barbie doll again.

Of course, people differ in the degree to which they use their gender schemas to process information about themselves and others, with strongly sex-typed individuals tending to have stronger gender schemas (Bem, 1985). Gender schemas are shaped through the socialization of children and the degree to which males and females are treated differently. Thus, gender schema theory builds on both cognitive developmental and social learning theories in suggesting that children both cognitively construct gender categories and learn to respond to environmental cues about gender roles (Lips, 1997).

Social Structure/Cultural Theories

If we accept that children learn or cognitively develop different ideas about appropriate gender behavior, then an important issue is why society supports the perpetuation of these differences. According to **social structure/cultural theories** of gender, most of the differences between male and female gender roles are established because of the status, power, and division of labor in a given society. Researchers have shown that gender differences occur more frequently (and in some cases only) when the sexes are in the typical male dominant/female subordinate relationship and that much so-called feminine behavior is actually powerless behavior (Lips, 1991). Cultural theorists argue that, if males and females were seen as equally powerful in society, many of the so-called gender differences would disappear. For example, gender differences in nonverbal communication, such as who touches whom during conversation, parallel those between less powerful and more powerful people. Also, both women and members of lower-status groups are characterized as more controlled and passive, whereas men and members of higher-status groups are characterized as more direct and opinionated (Henley and Freeman, 1995).

These power and status differences are related to the differences in the division of labor between the sexes that still exists. For example, there are still far more male executives and female secretaries than vice versa. However, it is almost impossible to determine if the division of labor by sex is a cause or a consequence of the status differences between women and men, and most likely the process is a kind of vicious cycle (Lips, 1997):

> The way work is divided between women and men in our own society practically guarantees that women will have less control over economic resources than men do. Men's greater control over economic resources, achieved through better jobs with higher salaries and through more continuous participation in the paid labor force, creates the expectation that women (and children) will depend on men for support. Under this set of expectations, which is communicated to children long before they understand the economic realities on which it is based, it is little wonder that girls and boys, women and men, tend to make choices that emphasize different aspects of these skills, aspirations, and preferences. These choices lead males and females into different types of work, and the cycle repeats itself. Whatever its source, the division of labor by sex and the parallel male-female difference in control over resources contribute to gender differences in behavior. (p. 55)

However, not all theories about gender differences focus on culture, cognition, or learning, and many people believe it is not nurture but rather nature that contributes the most to gender differences. Thus, no discussion of theoretical approaches to gender differences would be complete without a discussion of evolution and biology.

Evolutionary Theories: Sociobiology and Functionalism

Sociobiology and functionalism are two theories rooted in the concept that human genetics have evolved over time so that men and women are best adapted for their biological functions and reproductive success. According to **evolutionary theories** such as these, genetic heritage is more important than the influence of learning and culture for gender roles. Proponents of sociobiology believe that male and female genes have adapted over time to meet each sex's reproductive goals. The inclination for males to attempt to fertilize as many eggs as possible stems from the innate drive to guarantee survival of their own genes, enhanced by the production of millions of sperm with very little energy expenditure. In contrast, the tendency for females to selectively seek a monogamous partner relates to the amount of effort required to produce comparatively few eggs and to support the life of an embryo. Similarly, functionalism suggests that males and females evolved genetically to fulfill reproductive tasks. The presence of a "maternal instinct," according to this theory, is genetically linked to the biological functions of pregnancy, lactation, and childbirth—all of which require tremendous energy. Theorists in the late 1800s actually argued that women expend so much energy on reproductive functions that they have little left over for other pursuits, such as higher education (Lips, 1997).

There is little empirical evidence to support evolutionary theories of gender, but they are still the basis for many societal assumptions. No evidence

gender schema theory   A theory suggesting that people have very definite ideas about how males and females should look and behave, based on the framework of logic and ideas used to organize information and make sense of it.

social structure/cultural theories   Theories suggesting that most of the differences between male and female gender roles are established because of the status, power, and division of labor in a given society.

evolutionary theories   Theories suggesting that genetic heritage is more important than social learning in the development of gender roles.

has linked any of these gender behaviors to a specific gene, and the universality of a trait has not been proven to mean that the trait is necessarily genetic rather than learned. If males are biologically predisposed to be aggressive and females to be submissive, it is certainly also true that society reinforces and accentuates these differences.

TRADITIONAL MASCULINE AND FEMININE STEREOTYPES

Many people develop stereotyped concepts of masculinity and femininity. These **gender stereotypes** are assumed differences, norms, attitudes, and expectations about men and women.

Masculinity

According to traditional masculine stereotypes, men were supposed to be all of the following:

Aggressive	Adventurous
Dominant	Courageous
Strong	Independent
Forceful	Ambitious
Self-confident	Direct
Rugged	Logical
Virile	Unemotional
Instrumental	

These stereotypes of masculinity still are considered socially desirable by some people (but certainly not all) in our society today.

Traditionally, a "masculine" man was supposed to be a provider; he was successful, had status, and was looked up to. A man was supposed to be a sturdy rock with an air of toughness, confidence, and self-reliance. Stereotypic masculine heroes are Bruce Willis in *Die Hard,* Russell Crowe in *Gladiator,* and Mel Gibson in *Lethal Weapon.*

Typically, the assertive male was also supposed to be the initiator in relationships between the sexes, and the woman was expected to follow. He was expected to ask *her* out on a date and to decide where to go, what to do, and when to meet. He was expected to court *her* while she demurely but coquettishly responded. He was expected to ask for *her* hand in marriage. The woman who was too bold or forward was regarded as a threat to the tra-

ditional relationship. And after marriage, the male continued his dominant role as decision maker and initiator. He was supposed to have the last word over both his wife and his children.

Femininity

What are the traditional concepts of femininity as taught by our society? In the past, women were supposed to be all of the following:

Unaggressive	Sentimental
Submissive	Softhearted
Weak	Dependent
Sensitive	Aware of the feelings of others
Gentle and tender	
Kind	Emotional and excitable
Tactful	Somewhat frivolous, fickle, illogical, and talkative
Warm and affectionate	

A "feminine" woman was never aggressive, boisterous, loud, or vulgar in speech or behavior. She was expected to cry on occasion and sometimes to get upset over small events. It was all right for her to like laces, frills, and frivolous things. She was expected to be interested primarily in her home.

Along with these stereotyped concepts of femininity, society emphasized gender norms that all women were expected to follow. The primary gender norm was the motherhood mandate. Girls were expected to play with dolls because, in most people's minds, doll play prepared girls to become mothers. When they got older, girls were considered more capable of babysitting than boys. When a young woman got married, one of the first questions she would be asked was when she was going to have a baby. If she delayed too long, friends and family began to worry that she was not living up to her expected role. If she had the biological capability of having children, she was expected to use it. Then, when she had a baby, the motherhood mandate said that she should be a good mother by devoting a majority of her time to caring for her baby (Doyle, 1985).

The marriage mandate was second in importance to the motherhood mandate. Women were expected to get married, since it was the rite of passage to the adult world, the way to unlock the shackles of dependency on their parents and best fulfill the motherhood mandate.

Concepts of femininity vary, and they change with time. Strenuous, competitive activity, such as this women's hockey game, is no longer automatically assumed to be inconsistent with femininity.

As another consequence of stereotypic gender roles, women were taught that their role was to please men, regardless of their own needs and desires. Nowhere was this more evident than in intimate relationships. Some women went through years of marriage attending only to their husband's wants. Many became very dissatisfied and depressed as a result (Whisman and Jacobson, 1989).

Problems with Gender Stereotypes

One problem with gender stereotypes is that, whenever rigid gender standards are applied to all members of one sex, individual personalities can become distorted. Everyone is expected to conform, regardless of individual differences or inclinations. Furthermore, gender identity and gender-role stereotypes place serious limitations on the relationships that people are capable of forming and on career or personal achievements.

Another problem with gender stereotypes is that they lead to different expectations of employment and pay for males and females, even among children. Although the rate of participation in the labor force is not different for boys and girls, their type of work is segregated by gender early on. Girls are more likely to be employed by family and neighbors to perform "benevolent" jobs, such as babysitting,

whereas boys are more likely to do manual work in more formal work settings, such as bagging groceries, mowing lawns, and busing dishes (Desmarais and Curtis, 1999). Although boys and girls work the same number of hours per week, girls earn significantly lower hourly wages. This gender inequality in youth employment reflects what is occurring among adult workers. Interestingly, studies show that female college students have lower perceived income entitlement for two main reasons. First, women are socialized to value the social and interpersonal aspects of their work rather than pursue monetary rewards. Second, women learn to downplay their work efforts or contributions when examining whether they are being paid a fair wage and thus tend to compare themselves to other women, who are also underpaid, rather than to men (Desmarais and Curtis, 1999).

Findings from the National Opinion Research Center General Social Surveys show that traditional

---

gender stereotypes Assumed differences, norms, attitudes, and expectations about men and women.

My Life on the Boundaries of Gender

By **BETSY LUCAL,** *Department of Sociology, Indiana University, South Bend*

What does it mean to live on the boundaries of gender? It means being a woman who answers to "Sir" because it is entirely likely that the speaker is talking to me. It means being a woman who thinks twice about using a public restroom in order to avoid comments like "This is the *ladies'* room!" that make it clear someone thinks I'm in the wrong place. It means facing the possibility that someone will challenge my use of a credit card because they're convinced that a card with a woman's name on it could not possibly belong to me. On the other hand, it also means not being afraid to walk alone at night, feeling safer than most women because I'm fairly certain that a potential attacker would not choose someone who appears to be a (relatively big) man. It means being taken seriously in all-male environments, such as auto parts stores, by people who think I'm one of them, and therefore someone who possesses relevant knowledge, rather than a naive woman.

These are among the consequences I deal with every day of my life as a woman who does not conform to the conventions of femininity. However, despite outward appearances, I am female, and I identify as a woman (that is, I am not transgendered—I am not a person whose gender identity is different from my sex). My appearance simply defies the rule that says a person's sex and gender display must match. I am a living illustration of the distinction between sex and gender. I am a female (sex) who is, because of my appearance, regularly mistaken for a man (gender). The fact that this happens shows that gender, contrary to popular belief, is not natural but is instead socially constructed. If gender followed naturally from sex, it would be impossible for a female to display masculinity or for a male to display femininity.

Yet my experiences (and those of other people) show that such a thing *is* possible. They provide a vivid reminder that gender is a set of social characteristics and expectations assigned to men and women, not something biological. Though I possess the physical characteristics of a female,

people often see me as a man. This is not surprising, given my large size (six feet tall), short hair, lack of jewelry and makeup, and nonfeminine clothes (no dresses or skirts, simple pants/shorts and shirts). As a member of our society, I understand that these are masculine gender markers—aspects of my appearance that may be taken as evidence that I am a man (and, therefore, also male).

So, why don't I align my gender display with my sex? At first, I did not do this with any purpose in mind. Growing up, I simply appeared in a way that was comfortable to me. The fact that my appearance confused other people and/or made them uncomfortable was just something I learned to live with. But as I gained a sociological understanding of the world, I realized that my life on the boundaries of gender gave me an opportunity to show people how gender is socially constructed, how sex and gender are distinct from one another. Hoping that my life could help break down the inequality that accompanies gender, I not only continued this practice but also began to use it to help people understand the consequences of gender in our society.

As a person who lives on the boundaries of gender, I get to see both the oppression of women and the privilege of men firsthand. Because I am a woman, I face the prospect of earning less money than a man with comparable credentials. As a woman, I must endure the derogatory media images of women that are ubiquitous in our society. On the other hand, I need not worry about the public harassment many women experience as they move through the world. If men think I am also a man, they will not engage in catcalls, sexual remarks and other verbal harassment. When mistaken for a man, I am treated more respectfully than a woman might be.

Like other social constructions, gender has very real consequences. My experiences show that people are treated differently based on the gender they are perceived to be. My experiences make it clear that gender does matter in our interactions with other people. Life on the boundaries isn't always easy, but it is instructive.

---

gender-role ideology in both men and women contributes to lower observed earnings for females, independent of the influences of individual characteristics. More traditional women are more likely to choose female-dominated jobs, which have low av-

erage earnings, and men with traditional gender views are more likely to think women belong in low-paid, traditionally female jobs. If a man believes a woman's place is in the home and he is responsible for deciding a woman's promotional opportunities and salary, this may impact her earnings negatively. Traditional gender-role ideology can also impact men's earnings. Employers may view men with sexist views of women as "lacking in openness to diversity" or as open invitations to discrimination lawsuits, which may affect their career success (Firestone, Harris, and Lambert, 1999).

The traditionally unaggressive, submissive, weak female was not able to stand up for herself at home, so she was thought to be unsuitable to assume positions of leadership in government or business. (In spite of women's advances, still only a few of the Fortune 500 corporations are headed by women.) If our daughters are expected to be breadwinners, if many women remain single, or if some women are required to raise their children alone, then they need the same assertiveness, independence, and rational thinking that we seek to develop in our sons. If women are to succeed, new roles require acceptance of different traits to fit the many challenges they will face.

Trying to follow traditional male gender roles also can be harmful to many men. Adherence to the traditional male role is associated with higher levels of suicide, substance abuse, health problems, stress, and emotional illness (Good and Mintz, 1990). Being openly aggressive, dominant, independent, and unemotional is distinctly disadvantageous. The overaggressive male gets in trouble with friends, family, and society. Yet many of the toys boys are typically expected to play with, such as G.I. Joes and Star Wars figures, still display these aggressive traits.

GENDER ROLES AND BODY IMAGE

Gender roles define not only masculine and feminine behavior but also masculine and feminine ideals of appearance. Trying to live up to these prescribed roles can damage self-esteem and even endanger health.

"Body image" most often refers to positive or negative feelings about specific parts of the body and to overall appearance (Feingold and Mazzella, 1998). How people feel about their body depends on many factors, both external and internal. People's body image attitudes are purely subjective and personal, but specific attitudes tend to be common to each gender and based on societal cues.

Today many young girls worry about the shape, size, and muscle tone of their bodies because they are taught that the body is the ultimate expression of the self (Brumberg, 1997). In contrast to women of a century ago, who externally controlled their bodies with corsets and girdles, most of today's young women control their bodies internally, with diet and exercise. Nevertheless, the woman who goes to the gym every day for the sole sake of her looks isn't very different from the woman who wouldn't go out before struggling into a corset (Turkel, 1998). Both are overly concerned about outward appearance.

In contemporary society, both males and females, particularly on television and in the movies, are less modest about their bodies and are showing more skin than ever before. This openness has profound implications for how adolescents handle their bodies, and it is particularly problematic for girls, because their bodies, even more than the bodies of boys, are constantly being displayed and appraised (Brumberg, 1997). It is not surprising, then, that there are now fourth-grade girls who diet dangerously, that one-half of 9-year-old girls have dieted, and that eating disorders, usually acquired in adolescence, can be seen in girls as young as 7 (Turkel, 1998). It is estimated that while only about 6.5% of high school girls are overweight, approximately 35% of them think they are overweight (Centers for Disease Control and Prevention, 2001).

This preoccupation with weight, perfectionism, and fear of rejection stems from our cultural expectations for females, rather than from individual psychopathology (Turkel, 1998). As Mary Pipher (1994) has observed, females measure their bodies against cultural ideals and can't help but feel inferior when measured against today's standard of abnormal thinness, which is unattainable for most females. Thus, in recent decades, females' dissatisfaction with their bodies has increased along with the number of eating disorders. It is not surprising that the number of cosmetic procedures to improve appearance increased from 2.1 million in 1997 to 8.5 million in 2001 (American Society for Aesthetic Plastic Surgery, 2002).

Adolescents learn a lot about feminine and masculine gender roles through television and popular magazines. Typically, boys watch programs that are activity-driven, with lots of action and movement, and girls watch programs about friendship and relationships. These programs teach boys to be strong and in control; they teach girls to look good and to please others. One study looked at the portrayals of overweight characters from top-rated television shows during the 1999–2000 season. The researchers found that heavyset women and men had fewer romantic interactions than their thinner counterparts. They were less likely to date and less likely to talk about having sex or to be shown in sexual encounters. Large women were made fun of more often than thin women, and heavyset characters were more likely to be minorities, older, and unemployed. While only 3 out of 100 female characters on television were obese, in real life 25% of women are obese (Greenberg, Eastin, Hofschire, Lachlan, and Brownell, in press).

Although most data collected on gender and body image are female-focused, men also are affected by the media's portrayal of them. Research is now examining eating and body image disorders among men. One study of eating disorders in men found that 2% of men had anorexia or bulimia, compared with 4.8% of women. Men with eating disorders were very similar to women with eating disorders on most variables (Woodside, Garfinkel, Lin, Goering, and Kaplan, 2001). Given that attention is now being focused on males with body image disorders, it is not surprising that in the last decade there has been an increase of men being admitted to eating disorder programs.

Steroid use is also a growing problem among young men. Steroids are laboratory-made versions of the human hormone testosterone, which aids the growth of muscles, bones, and skin. Men on steroids often do increase their strength and muscle mass, but at the price of interfering with normal body development. Males potentially face premature balding, breast enlargement and shrunken testicles. Females also use steroids to build muscle mass, and this usage has consequences for their normal development too. Females can face changes in or cessation of their menstrual cycle, stunted height, and severe acne. In a national survey of adolescent drug abuse, Leshner (2000) found that 2.8% of 8th graders, 3.5% of 10th graders, and 3.7% of 12th graders have used steroids.

Because male portrayals in the media are more about status and success than physicality, males' body images are not so dependent on the images in magazines or popular culture. However, toys depicting males are changing in terms of body characteristics. Although the inappropriate thinness of female dolls has long been noted and criticized, male action figures now also depict inappropriate and most likely impossible ideals of muscularity. One study of the physiques of G.I. Joe and Star Wars figures showed that the action figures today, as well as pop culture icons like Tarzan, are much more muscular than those of 30 years ago (see Figure 3.1) (Pope, Olivardia, Gruber, and Borowiecki, 1999). Though it might be premature to conclude that boys develop body image disorders solely because they are exposed to these muscular ideals at a young age, such toys do have an impact on children.

Advertisements promote the idea that females' personal happiness is linked to physical appearance rather than good character and positive self-esteem. While such ads have boosted profits for manufacturers of skin, hair, and diet products, they sap the creativity of girls and threaten their mental and physical health (Brumberg, 1997). One study found that girls who watched 8 or more hours of television a week reported greater body dissatisfaction than did girls who were less exposed to television (J. K. Thompson and Heinberg, 1999). Another study found that women who viewed typical female model images in magazines had higher levels of anger and depression than did women who viewed only images of objects (Pinhas, Toner, Ali, Garfinkel, and Stuckless, 1999). Viewing images of models had an immediate and negative effect on women's moods, creating feelings of depression, guilt, low self-esteem, and failure.

In our culture, females feel more negatively about their body image than do males. Not surprisingly, a study of 21 popular women's and men's magazines found that 78% of the covers of women's magazines contained a message regarding appearance, while none of the men's magazines did. In addition, 25% of the women's magazine covers contained information on weight loss, perpetuating the idea of slimness as the only attractive ideal. And where the men's magazines focused on entertainment, hobbies, and activities, the women's magazines focused on improving one's life by changing one's appearance (Malkin, Wornian, and Chrisler, 1999).

Although magazine covers do not fully represent the media and their messages, they do reflect cultural standards and shape attitudes regarding

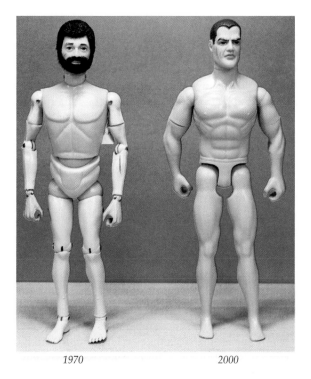

1970   2000

Tarzan of 2000

Figure 3.1 The Evolution of the Physiques of Action Figures and Traditional Heros (*Note:* From *Time*, April 24, 2000.)

Tarzan of 1930

gender behavior. Researchers have also analyzed the content of *Seventeen* magazine over a number of years to identify patterns in the concerns and interests of the modern teenage girl. Although minor changes have occurred in *Seventeen* over the years, its content still conveys the same message that it did when it was first published in 1944: that young women should be concerned only with improving their external appearance and pleasing a man (Schlenker, Caron, and Halteman, 1998). Even in the 1990s, this publication—the most widely distributed teenage magazine—still did not address most of the intellectual issues relevant to young women. Although more women than ever before are pursuing higher education, having careers, and delaying marriage, the content of their publications does not seem to reflect the aspirations and levels of achievement of which they are capable (Schlenker, Caron, and Halteman, 1998).

GENDER ROLES IN THE FAMILY

Beliefs about masculinity and femininity profoundly affect the roles men and women play in the family (Ferree, 1990). Some adults believe that gender roles are innate, that men and women are "born" to perform certain roles (Mirowsky and Ross, 1987). The male chauvinist, for example, considers women subordinate—lacking equal authority, destined to care for husbands and children, and not suited for many kinds of jobs because of their physical, emotional, and mental shortcomings. According to this view, if they are employed, women cannot expect equal pay for equal work, because men are meant to be the primary breadwinners.

Not surprisingly, men more often than women believe in innate gender roles. People who are older, less educated, and more conservative in their religious beliefs also hold more traditional beliefs about gender roles (Rogler and Procidano, 1986).

Most people believe that gender roles are a combination of both nature and nurture. While biology determines different genetic makeup of males and females, environment helps shape behavior. For example, research now shows that women's brains are wired both to feel and to recall emotions more keenly than the brains of men (Canli, Desmond, Zhao, and Gabrieli, 2002). However, the environment can certainly influence and exaggerate those

differences by expecting and grooming women to be the emotional caretakers of relationships. Girls may like to play with dolls and boys to play with trucks, but parents reinforce this behavior when they buy their boy child a pink baby doll and their girl child an action figure, but this goes against societal expectations of appropriate gender behavior. The issue of whether nature or nurture is more important in determining gender roles is a timeless argument most likely never to be resolved. One can think of gender roles on a continuum of scientific views with genetics on one end and environment on the other, with most people's beliefs falling somewhere in between.

One important goal of the women's movement has been to motivate women to achieve true egalitarian rights and roles. At the present time, however, there is still an incongruency between ideology and the practice of marital equality (Blaisure and Allen, 1995).

As long as sexist views persist, women will be placed in subordinate, inferior roles. Feminists' emphasis on equality does not mean they desire or expect women and men to be the same or to act identically (Margolin, Talovic, Fernandez, and Onorato, 1983). Rather, the goal has been freedom—the freedom to choose one's own destiny and status. This can mean the choice to be a stay-at-home mom or a CEO of a major company. With some conscious effort, partners can construct their own gender roles through the decisions they make concerning work, family, and marriage (Zvonkovic, Greaves, Schmiege, and Hall, 1996). The roles they choose can work for everyone in the family.

Ethnic Variations

The attitudes that men and women hold toward gender roles have a significant influence on many aspects of marital and family dynamics. As stated earlier, they also help perpetuate gender-differentiated opportunities in education, politics, employment, and other areas. A substantial body of literature has documented the formation of gender-role attitudes in women and girls. Far less attention has been focused on how the attitudes of men and boys are formed and change over time (Blee and Tickamyer, 1995), and researchers have only recently begun to look at differences in gender-role attitudes in different classes and ethnic groups.

Machismo

Historically, Mexican American families have been considered patriarchal (male-dominated). **Machismo** (the Spanish word for "manhood" that in English connotes masculinity) required that the male head of the household provide for and protect his family; protection included both the physical protection against aggressors and the protection of the family honor. In order to prove his masculinity, the male could have extramarital affairs; he could not, however, flaunt them, for that would demonstrate lack of respect for his wife. The sexual purity of women—the faithfulness of wives and the virginity of unmarried women—was symbolized by the Virgin Mary. The honor of a man was besmirched if his wife was unfaithful or his daughter was not a virgin at marriage. Girls were taught to be modest and were not supposed to learn about sexual relations through either conversation or experience. Males learned about sex from other males and from encounters with "bad" girls (Horowitz, 1983). The woman was thought to be the nurturer and caregiver for the family. In traditional families, these ideas about gender are still in place.

The most recent views of Mexican American families emphasize that machismo is still a persistent feature but that the fathers usually exercise their authority in a dignified and fair manner, showing honor and respect for other family members. The Mexican American family has been characterized as warm and nurturing, with cooperation among family members and with egalitarianism in decision making. Role relations range from patriarchal to completely egalitarian, with the most prevalent one being that the husband and wife share in decisions. While some studies indicate that Mexican American women follow the traditional roles of submission to their spouse's authority, more research rejects the notion that Mexican American women lack power within heterosexual relationships (Gutmann, 1996).

The research typically shows that young White women are at higher risk than young White men for depression, suicide attempts, eating disorders, substance abuse, academic underachievement, dropping out, and plummeting self-esteem and self-confidence (Brumberg, 1997). According to L. M. Brown and Gilligan (1992), White girls often struggle "against losing something which feels essential: their voice, their mind, their self" (p. 159). They begin "losing voice" and "abandoning self" around age 12, in various aspects of their lives, in exchange for being perceived as a "perfect" girl: passive, quiet, demure, and attractive to boys— qualities that make up the traditional female gender stereotype. They derive their worth from relationships rather than from their abilities and accomplishments.

Although such gender-role behaviors may be common among middle-class White girls, they are not universal. Today, a growing body of research is focused on female gender identity development among urban adolescents from different social class and ethnic backgrounds. In one sample of 362 girls from five different ethnic groups (Erkut, Fields, Sing, and Marx, 1996), almost half of the girls cited athletic abilities, rather than relationships, as the main thing that made them feel good about themselves. African American adolescent girls often are described not as "losing voice" but as being assertive, powerful, resilient, and resistant (Gibbs, 1996; J. Ward, 1996; Way, 1995). Among African American families, mothers socialize their daughters to be independent, strong, and self-confident rather than passive (Gayles, 1984). The most important message that African American adolescent girls receive from their mothers is to be self-reliant and resourceful (P. H. Collins, 1987).

Body image also seems to differ among different ethnic groups. In a study of 120 university men and women, African Americans reported greater body satisfaction and less overestimation of weight than their White counterparts. African American women also rated themselves as more sexually attractive than did Anglo-American women and had higher self-esteem regarding their weight. Hispanic women rated themselves as less sexually attractive than did African American women but more sexually attractive than did Anglo-American women.

machismo   Spanish for "manhood"; masculinity

Is cooking the family dinner a gender-typed role? The ability to perform any family task without concern for its gender appropriateness can make it easier for the child, when the time comes, to achieve an egalitarian marriage.

Males in all three groups demonstrated little difference (K. J. Miller, Gleaves, Hirsch, Green, Snow, and Corbett, 2000).

Recent scholarship about male attitudes toward gender roles has documented a variety of masculine standards that define manhood differently across ethnic, class, sexual, and regional boundaries. Men's attitudes toward female gender roles also vary. The idea that women's roles should be circumscribed by home and family may reflect only a narrow segment of White, middle-class heterosexual men. One study revealed that African American and White men differ in their attitudes about women's gender roles. Generally speaking, African American men are more liberal in their attitudes toward working wives than White men and are far more likely to have lived in a household with a working wife and/or mother (Blee and Tickamyer, 1995).

Housework and Child Care Roles

With over half of all married women employed outside the home, fairness demands a willingness on the part of husbands to assume shared responsibility for housework and child care. Some studies indicate that gender-role stereotypes, especially among college students, may be weakening, but most current research continues to find evidence of tradi-

tional gender roles (Ridgeway and Smith-Lovin, 1999). For example, although the gap between the amount of time women and men spend in family work is shrinking (Levine and Pittinsky, 1997), women are still doing more family work than most men are doing. Overwhelmingly, the evidence suggests that, even when women work as many hours outside the home as their spouses, they retain primary responsibility for home care and child care, although men do participate in domestic work more when their partner is employed (Pleck, 1997). However, men do relatively little domestic labor unless both they and their spouse are somewhat egalitarian in their beliefs about gender roles in marriage (Greenstein, 1996). In dual-earner families, fathers are more involved and engaged in activities with their children, and this involvement increases as the mother's work hours increase, but all other household chores continue to be gender segregated. Indoor work is predominantly completed by women, and outdoor work by men (Gottfried, Gottfried, Killian, and Bathurst, 1999).

Marital satisfaction depends partly on partners perceiving themselves and their spouses as each doing a fair share of family work (Deater-Deckard and Scarr, 1996; John, Shelton, and Luschen, 1995; Sanchez and Kane, 1996). When women work outside the home and also have to do most of the work

In families in which men help with child care and household responsibilities, working women report considerably less role conflict and stress.

more when they think they should, or perhaps that men who share more adjust their gender-role beliefs accordingly (Pyke and Coltrane, 1996). If the woman has egalitarian views and demands that the man share household tasks, his participation is more likely to increase (Hardesty and Bokemeier, 1989). Studies of married women indicate that egalitarian and full-time employed women perceive that their spouses give less support when domestic labor arrangements are more unequal. Women who perceive less support, in turn, experience lower marital and personal happiness than do those who perceive more equal household labor arrangements (Pina and Bengston, 1993).

Many studies have reported that men would like to spend more time doing family work, such as child care, but a number of factors affect their involvement, including gender-role flexibility and egalitarian views (Pleck, 1997). In some families, a barrier to men's involvement is maternal gatekeeping, which S. Allen and Hawkins (1999) define as

> the mother's reluctance to relinquish standards, wanting to be ultimately accountable for domestic labor to confirm to others and to herself that family work is truly a woman's domain. . . . [Maternal gatekeeping is] a collection of beliefs and behaviors that ultimately inhibit a collaborative effort between men and women in family work by limiting men's opportunities for learning and growing through caring for home and children. . . . [It is] a schema that builds, maintains, and reinforces the gate to home and family, which, if opened, could encourage more father involvement in housework and child care. (p. 200)

S. Allen and Hawkins (1999) studied specific gatekeeping beliefs and behaviors and found that 25% of the 1,500 women in their sample were gatekeepers. However, it is important to remember that maternal gatekeeping is just one of the many factors in men's involvement in domestic work.

Roles over the Family Life Cycle

The roles that people play depend partly on the family situation. For example, the adolescent who has a baby may be forced into a traditional mother role whether she wants to assume it or not (Krissman, 1990). Often, having or adopting a baby forces women into traditional domestic roles, at least for a

around the house and to care for the children, they experience considerable role conflict and strain. It is very difficult to combine multiple roles, do all of them well, and still have time to take care of oneself. Sharing domestic work is important, therefore, to individual well-being, to the marital relationship, and to quality parent–child relationships (L. Thompson, 1991). Greater paternal involvement in child care also increases the marital satisfaction of the woman (Harris and Morgan, 1991).

In sum, several studies—including ones of single- and dual-earner families and of upper-middle-class families—reveal that women still spend significantly more time doing housework and caring for children than do men (Berardo, Shehan, and Leslie, 1987; Ferree, 1991; Levant, Slattery, and Loiselle, 1987; Levine and Pittinsky, 1997). The man's gender ideology is the best single predictor of sharing housework. This suggests that men share

period of time (M. Hill, 1988). There's some evidence that women's satisfaction with the division of household labor rises and falls and rises again over the life cycle. Although women shoulder a disproportionate share of household labor, the disparity between their contribution and that of their spouses appears to be least in the preparental and postparental years and greatest in the early child-rearing years (Suitor, 1991). Men tend to spend more time performing domestic labor during periods of least occupational involvement—that is, early in their employment career and after retirement (Dorfman and Heckert, 1988; Rexroat and Shehan, 1987). Men's contributions to household labor rise when the woman is employed full-time (Pictman and Blanchard, 1996). The divisions of household labor are, in short, the result of multiple causes. Who does what around the house is shaped by time availability, relative resources, and ideology, and these three factors are intertwined and mutually reinforcing (Coltrane and Ishii-Kuntz, 1992).

In general, if spouses agree on gender-role expectations and performance, couples report higher marital quality than if there is disagreement (Bowen and Orthner, 1983). If a man does not fulfill the roles his spouse expects him to, she will not be completely satisfied with the relationship. Men, too, have certain preconceived expectations about the roles their spouses should fulfill; if the women do not live up to their expectations, their marital satisfaction is less (Bahr, Chappell, and Leigh, 1983). The need for **gender-role congruence**—that is, agreement between partners' gender-role expectations and their performance—is an important consideration in selecting a compatible partner (Bowen, 1989; Lueptow, Guss, and Hyden, 1989).

ANDROGYNY

What seems to be emerging in today's society is a gradual mixing of gender roles to produce **androg-**

gender-role congruence Agreement between partners' gender-role expectations and their performance.

androgyny A blending of male and female characteristics and roles; especially, a lack of gender-typing with respect to roles.

Androgyny expands the range of acceptable behavior. Clothes and hairstyles do not express either maleness or femaleness.

yny, a gender role that combines both the feminine and the masculine. Androgynous people are not gender-typed with respect to roles, although they are distinctly male or female in sex. They match their behavior to the situation, rather than being limited by what is culturally defined as male or female. For example, an androgynous male feels comfortable cuddling and caring for a young boy; an androgynous female feels comfortable changing the oil in her car. Androgyny expands the range of acceptable behavior, allowing individuals to cope effectively in a variety of situations.

The mixing of roles is advantageous to both sexes. Both sexes are restricted in their behavior and relationships by narrow gender-typed roles. Both masculine and androgynous people are more independent and less conforming than those identified with femininity, and both feminine and androgynous individuals are more nurturing than those who are traditionally masculine. Some men are beginning to realize that they can gain far more in their lives by caring, loving, and collaborating, and so they have less need to combat, compete with, and overpower one another (Freudenberger, 1987).

Historically, psychologists have taught that mental health depends on a clear-cut separation between male and female roles (E. P. Cook, 1985). Now, some studies reveal that androgynous individuals have better social relationships and are better adjusted than people who have more traditional gender identities. For example, a 6-month longitudinal study of college students found that individuals who showed more masculine and androgynous characteristics experienced less depression (Cheng, 1999). Another study revealed that more androgynous individuals possess adaptive capabilities and resources, such as effective coping techniques, emotional integration, communication skills, and a well-defined self-concept with a high level of ego strength (Small, Teagno, and Selz, 1980). Another study, this of 195 new mothers, showed that those classified as either androgynous or masculine scored lower on dimensions reflecting psychological distress than did their feminine or undifferentiated (having low scores on both masculine and feminine traits) counterparts (Bassoff, 1984). A study of adolescent females showed that those with androgynous or masculine gender-role orientation had higher self-esteem than did those classified as feminine or undifferentiated (Mullis and McKinley, 1989).

However, some people don't agree that androgyny should be a model for women and men. Rather, women's and men's biological, emotional, and psychological attributes should be valued equally. By emphasizing equal treatment for women and men, and nonsexist attitudes in general, one can also seek to acknowledge the fundamental difference between men and women and to equally value those differences.

Although researchers may use the categories of masculine, feminine, and androgynous, in reality, our gender self-concept probably changes across the various contexts in which we interact. The gender makeup of the group (that is, same-sex or mixed-sex) may influence the interactional style of the participants. Or the situation itself may influence the traits exhibited by individuals. For example, around her intimate partner, a woman may exhibit traditional feminine qualities, whereas at work she may exhibit more traditional masculine qualities. An analysis of national data by the National Center on Addiction and Substance Abuse found that girls who want to be one of the boys go drink-for-drink with them (Foster, Vaughan, Foster, and Califano, 2003). (This may be problematic for females, who metabolize alcohol more slowly, become intoxicated more quickly, and become alcohol-dependent faster than males.)

C. J. Smith, Noll, and Bryant (1999) examined the effect of social context on gender self-concept and challenged the assumption that it is static and consistent across contexts. They found that males are more likely to demonstrate feminine traits when they are with females and to avoid showing feminine characteristics when they are with other males. Being with other males seems to activate males' gender belief system (Deaux and Major, 1987). The females in the study were less likely to change their feminine self-concept across contexts. However, among unfamiliar people, both males and females are less likely to describe themselves according to gender-role stereotypes and are more likely to display androgynous characteristics. Overall, we seem to be developing more flexible and interchangeable gender roles.

A QUESTION OF POLICY

TITLE IX

As discussed in the chapter, Title IX is a federal law that prohibits discrimination on the basis of sex in federally funded educational institutions. While most people think of it as just pertaining to sports, that law actually applies to all aspects of education, including admissions, recruitment, counseling, financial assistance, student health, insurance benefits, housing, marital and parental student status, harrassment, educational programs and activities, employment, and physical education and athletics (Nelson, 2003). Much of the controversy of Title IX, however, does surround sports because some people believe that providing equal athletic access for women takes away opportunities for men.

Title IX is under federal review to see whether providing equal opportunity for women does discriminate against men. However, women do not have the same opportunity to participate in sports as do men even with Title IX. Even though it is a federal law, many universities do not comply with Title IX until a lawsuit is threatened; even so, the Office of Civil Rights has never withheld federal funds to a noncompliant institution. Nelson (2003) reports that high school boys still receive 1.1 million more opportunities than high school girls to participate in school-sponsored sports, male athletes still receive 58,000 more opportunities to play sports than women, men receive $133 million more in athletic scholarship assistance than women, and women's coaches earn approximately 35% less than men's coaches.

There is no doubt, though, that the opportunities for women have increased tremendously with Title IX. When funds are limited, which they typically are, schools may choose to reduce men's programs instead of increasing women's programs in order to achieve more equality. Some sports programs may get cut, such as men's wrestling, in order to pay for women's hockey. The opponents of Title IX say women are less interested in sports than men and universities should not be expected to provide equal opportunity because it does not reflect the interest of the students.

The office of President George W. Bush has created a commission to study Title IX and recommend whether it should be revised and, if so, how. Congress has proposed resolutions supporting Title IX as it was originally intended in the Education Amendments of 1972.

QUESTIONS TO CONSIDER:

Are schools discriminating against men by eliminating some men's sports in order to create opportunities for women? Give reasons and examples to back up your answer.

Does Title IX establish a quota system? Explain.

Do women want to participate in sports programs as much as men? Could a public policy be enforced that assumes that women don't care about sports as much as men do? It is acceptable to provide fewer opportunities for women because they are less interested, or would more women become interested if more opportunities were presented to them? Discuss.

If a survey found that women were not as interested in mathematics as men, would it be valid to limit their opportunities to study math? Or should we provide incentives to encourage women to study math? Discuss.

What are some of the consequences of having equality between men and women in educational programs?

SUMMARY

1. Sex refers to one's biological identity, male or female. Gender includes those psychosocial components that characterize one as masculine or feminine. Gender identity is an individual's personal, internal sense of maleness or femaleness that is expressed in personality and behavior. A gender role is the outward manifestation and expression of one's maleness or femaleness in a social setting.

2. Environmental influences are a major determinant of gender identities and gender roles. Society defines the qualities of maleness and femaleness expected of men and women. Three of the major influences on children's individual gender identities and roles are parents, television, and school.

3. The social learning theory of gender identity asserts that concepts of gender roles and ap-

propriate gender behavior are established through exposure to social influences such as parents, teachers, peers, and media.

4. Cognitive developmental theory suggests that children actively seek out cues and learn gender stereotypes at a particular stage of intellectual development—going through phases of rigidity and flexibility concerning gender behavior.

5. Gender schema theory combines elements of both cognitive developmental and social learning theories, suggesting that children cognitively determine gender categories in response to environmental cues.

6. Social structure and cultural theories directly relate power, status, and division of labor to concepts of gender identity. The view of women as subordinates in the workplace parallels the gender conception of women as less powerful and in need of support.

7. Evolutionary theories assert that gender roles have been established through genetic evolution, based on biological functions of the sexes and reproductive success.

8. People develop stereotyped concepts of masculinity and femininity. Traditionally, males were supposed to be aggressive, dominant, strong, forceful, self-confident, rugged, virile, instrumental, adventurous, courageous, independent, ambitious, direct, logical, and unemotional. To be a man, a male was supposed to be a big wheel, be successful, have status, and be looked up to.

9. Traditionally, females were supposed to be unaggressive, submissive, weak, sensitive, gentle, tender, kind, tactful, warm and affectionate, sentimental, softhearted, dependent, aware of the feelings of others, emotional and excitable, and somewhat frivolous, fickle, illogical, and talkative. Female gender norms included the marriage and motherhood mandates; that is, women were expected to get married and to have children.

10. The problem with stereotypes is that forcing everyone to conform to the same mold severely limits the development of individual personality and personal achievement. New gender roles encourage women to be more assertive and less passive, and men to be less ag-

gressive and more cooperative. Both sexes need the traditional female traits of tenderness, kindness, softheartedness, sensitivity, and awareness of the feelings of others in all types of human relationships. Cooperative sharing of roles results in greater contentment and companionship among family members.

11. Females are socialized to believe that the body is the ultimate expression of the self. Television, magazines, and advertisements influence the way women feel about themselves and their bodies and create unattainable standards for women to live up to, resulting in an increase in eating disorders and in negative self-image.

12. Beliefs about men and women profoundly affect the roles they play in the family. Those who believe that particular behaviors and attitudes are innate to each sex are more likely to subscribe to traditional conceptions of the subordination of women. Feminists have been working to achieve egalitarian rights and roles for women.

13. Gender-role expectations and attitudes have an effect on marital and family dynamics. African American men are more accepting of working wives than are White men.

14. Research on White adolescent girls has shown that, in addition to having increased rates of depression and suicide, they are more vulnerable to eating disorders, substance abuse, and low self-esteem. White girls also tend to "lose voice" and become more passive in order to fit the traditional gender stereotype. But recent research focusing on minority adolescent girls suggests that they have greater body satisfaction; specifically, African American girls are becoming more assertive and powerful, rather than "losing voice."

15. Egalitarian roles have not been achieved fully, even though marital satisfaction, individual psychological well-being, and child care quality are improved when spouses share in family tasks. Women still spend significantly more time than men doing housework and caring for children, even when they work full-time outside the home. This unequal division of labor is a source of resentment and anger for many women.

16. Roles tend to change over the family life cycle. Role segregation decreases after the husband retires.

17. Partners who agree on gender-role expectations and performance report higher marital quality than do those who disagree. Gender-role congruence is an important consideration, therefore, in selecting a mate with whom one will be compatible.

18. The present trend is toward androgyny, whereby people are not gender-typed with respect to roles. A mixing of roles is advantageous to both sexes. People may actually change gender roles depending on their social context.

KEY TERMS

gender

gender identity

transgendered people

transsexual

masculinity

femininity

parental identification and modeling

social learning theory of gender identity

cognitive developmental theory

gender schema theory

social structure/cultural theories

evolutionary theories

gender stereotypes

machismo

gender-role congruence

androgyny

QUESTIONS FOR THOUGHT

1. What are the traditional conceptions of a masculine person? What effects can such conceptions have on a man's life?

2. What are the traditional conceptions of a feminine person? What effects can such conceptions have on a woman's life?

3. What roles do you believe men and women should play in marriage and the family? Explain your views.

4. Write an essay on the role of television in influencing gender roles. Do you believe television is becoming more or less influential in children's development of gender roles? Explain.

SUGGESTED READINGS

Chira, S. (1998). *A Mother's Place: Taking the Debate About Working Mothers Beyond Guilt and Blame.* New York: Harper Perennial. Supports the argument that it is possible for women to be good mothers while working outside the home.

Deeghley, L. (1996). *What Does Your Wife Do? Gender and the Transformation of Family Life.* Boulder, CO: Rescue Press. Investigates how current rates of nonmarital sex, abortion, divorce, and women's employment affect family life.

Fausto-Sterling, A. (2000). *Sexing the Body: Gender Politics and the Construction of Sexuality.* New York: Basic Books. Discusses the argument that choosing to distinguish by gender is a social decision without a scientific basis.

Hunter, A. E., and Forden, C. (2002). *Readings in the Psychology of Gender: Exploring Our Differences and Commonalities.* Needham Heights, MA: Allyn & Bacon. Focuses on differences and similarities between males and females.

Lips, H. M. (2001). *Sex and Gender: An Introduction.* Mountain View, CA: Mayfield. Provides a comprehensive introduction to theories, research, and issues in gender studies.

Risman, B. J. (1998). *Gender Vertigo: American Families in Transition.* New Haven, CT; London: Yale University Press. Studies single fathers, married baby boom mothers, and heterosexual egalitarian couples and their children to discover how family relationships succeed without gender as a basis for family organization.

Satow, R. (2002). *Gender and Social Life.* Needham
Heights, MA: Allyn & Bacon. Offers a variety of ideas
about how gender structures our feelings about ourselves, expectations of ourselves and others, choices
we make, and the opportunities availabale to us.

Shields, S. A. (2002). *Speaking from the Heart: Gender and
the Social Meaning of Emotion.* New York: Cambridge
University Press. Examines how culturally shared
beliefs about emotion shape people's identities as
women and men.

CHAPTER 4

LEARNING OBJECTIVES

After reading the chapter, you should be able to:

- Identify in general terms the percentages of people in the U.S. population who are married, single, widowed, and divorced and point out cultural and ethnic differences.

- Explain the reasons for marital delay and the reasons some people remain permanently single.

- Understand the advantages and disadvantages of being single and discuss singles' health and well-being.

- Understand the need of singles for companionship, the difference between loneliness and alone-ness, and the differences between males and females in relation to companionship issues.

- Discuss the sexual behavior of singles.

- Describe the causes, symptoms, and treatments of the major sexually transmitted diseases, and explain in detail how AIDS is and is not transmitted and how one might protect oneself from AIDS infection and other sexually transmitted diseases.

- Compare singles with marrieds in terms of employment and level of income.

- Discuss the life situations of older, never-married adults.

Being Single

One of the choices adults face is whether to get married. In previous generations, adults had less choice: Society assumed that everyone who could do so would get married, and those who didn't marry faced social disapproval. Today, the number of never-married adults has increased dramatically, reflecting changing social conditions and attitudes.

The U.S. census of 2000 shows that more than 27 million Americans live by themselves, about one-fourth of all households and nearly 10% of the population. For the first time ever, one-person households now outnumber married couples with children, with more women being single than men. With the increase in the age at which people first get married, the increase in divorce rate, and the increase in longevity, the experience of being single is now one of the most widely shared experiences of adulthood (DePaulo, 2001). According to the American Association for Single People, an unmarried majority has emerged in many American cities.

Figures 4.1 and 4.2 illustrate the marital status of the U.S. population, 18 and older, in 2000. Overall, 59.5% were married, 23.9% were single (never married), 6.8% were widowed, and 9.8% were divorced. Obviously, the great majority of adults were married, and an additional number had been married at one time. Nevertheless, nearly one in four adults had never been married, but these were primarily in the youngest age groups.

When these figures are examined according to ethnic group, we find some variations. Only 42.1% of

Blacks age 18 or older were married. Over one-third had never been married. The percentage of Blacks widowed (7.1%) or divorced (11.7%) was slightly higher than for Whites. The statistics for Hispanics showed that about 28.0% had never been married, compared to 21.4% for Whites. Approximately the same percentage of both groups were married, and slightly fewer Hispanics than Whites were widowed or divorced. Marriage was more popular among White Americans than among other groups.

In this chapter, we examine the facts about being single and the reasons for the increase in those numbers. We examine why some people remain single and what some advantages and disadvantages of being single are. We discuss the lifestyles and living arrangements of singles, as well as factors such as social life and leisure time, loneliness and friendships, sexual behavior, sexually transmitted diseases, and employment and income. Finally, we examine the situations of single parents and of older, never-married adults.

CATEGORIES OF SINGLES

Several sociodemographic variables are related to the likelihood of never marrying—namely, age, race, and gender. First, age is negatively related to the likelihood of never marrying: the older one becomes, the greater the likelihood of remaining single. Approximately 74% of the never-married are younger than age 34 (U.S. Bureau of the Census, 2002). Between 1970 and 2000, the proportion of 25-

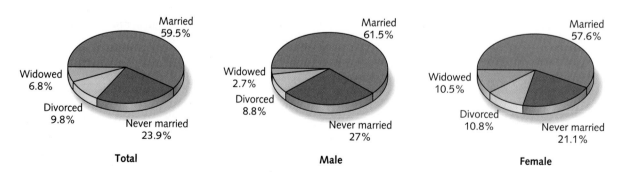

Figure 4.1 Marital Status of U.S. Population, Age 18 and Older, 2000 (*Note:* Adapted from *Statistical Abstract of the United States, 2002* [p. 47], by U.S. Bureau of the Census, 2002, Washington, DC: U.S. Government Printing Office.)

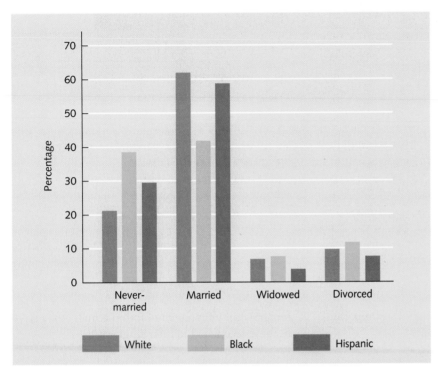

Figure 4.2 Marital Status of U.S. Population, Age 18 and Older, by Ethnic Origin, 2000
(*Note:* Adapted from *Statistical Abstract of the United States, 2002* [p. 47], by U.S. Bureau of the Census, 2002, Washington, DC: U.S. Government Printing Office.)

to 29-year-olds who were never married more than quadrupled, from 11% to 45% (U.S. Bureau of the Census, 2002). Although this reflects the trend toward delayed marriage, it also could indicate increasing societal acceptance of long-term singlehood (Barrett, 1999). If more people are choosing singlehood as a long-term status, it is reasonable to expect that the social resources and well-being of the never-married now include better social support in and higher satisfaction with their lives (Barrett, 1999).

Second, some research suggests that race is related to social support and well-being among the never-married. Non-White, never-married individuals have more frequent contact with relatives and are more likely to live with relatives other than their parents than are Whites (Raley, 1995). Research has shown that being never-married is associated with lower satisfaction among White women and men and non-White men, but no difference is observed between unmarried and married non-White women (Mookherjee, 1997). While only 21% of Whites have never married, 39% of African American and 28% of

Hispanics have never married (U.S. Bureau of the Census, 2000). The gap between Whites and African Americans appears to be widening, as the percentage of never-married African Americans is rising at a faster rate than that for Whites (Waite, 1995). It is possible that the higher proportion of never-marrieds among non-Whites makes the single status less stigmatizing (Barrett, 1999).

Third, some research associates being never-married with lower well-being and less social support for men than for women. Among the never-married, women interact more frequently with relatives than do men (Seccombe and Ishii-Kuntz, 1994). Studies on psychological health suggest that, among the never-married, men have more depression and anxiety (Davies, 1995) and a higher risk of suicide (Meehan, Saltzman, and Sattin, 1991) than women do. Much research supports the idea that never-married women are better off than their male counterparts.

There are various categories of single persons. P. Stein (1981) developed a typology of single persons based on whether their status is voluntary or

Table 4.1	Typology of Singles	
	Voluntary	**Involuntary**
Temporary	Never-marrieds and previously married who are not opposed to the idea of marriage but are not currently seeking mates	Those who have actively been seeking mates but have not found them
Stable (permanent)	All those (never-marrieds and former-marrieds) who choose to be single	Never-marrieds and former-marrieds who wanted to marry, who have not found a mate, and who have more or less accepted being single

Note: Adapted from Peter Stein, ed., *Single Life: Unmarried Adults in Social Context*, pp. 10–12. Copyright © 1981 Peter Stein.

involuntary. Table 4.1 shows the four major categories of singles according to Stein.

Voluntary Singles

The category **voluntary temporary singles** includes young people who have never been married and are not currently looking; they are postponing marriage even though they are not opposed to the idea of marriage. It includes cohabiters who will eventually marry each other or someone else. It includes recently divorced or widowed people who need time to be single, though they may eventually want to marry again. It also includes older never-marrieds who are not actively looking but who would marry if the right person came along.

The category **voluntary stable (permanent) singles** includes never-marrieds of all ages who have no intention of marrying, cohabiters who never intend to marry, and formerly married people who never want to marry again. It also includes those who have taken religious vows not to marry.

Involuntary Singles

The category **involuntary temporary singles** includes young adults who have never been married but are actively seeking a mate and divorced or widowed persons who want to remarry soon.

The category **involuntary stable (permanent) singles** includes never-married persons or widowed or divorced people who wanted to marry or

remarry but who have not found a mate; they have become reconciled to their single state.

MARITAL DELAY

Most singles are only temporarily unmarried, since by ages 45–54 only 8.9% of males and 7.2% of females have never married (see Figure 4.3). However, the trend is for adults to get married at older ages than they used to.

The reasons for delaying marriage are social, economic, and personal. One particular reason is the changing attitude toward single life. Societal disapproval of single people has diminished, and it is no longer unacceptable for those in their thirties to be unmarried, especially if they have a flourishing career and an active social life. However, often, both family and friends continue to expect that ultimately they will marry. Nevertheless, if they opt to remain single because this is their preferred lifestyle, family and friends come to accept their decision.

The lengthening of the period of education and economic dependency has greatly influenced the delay of marriage. Women who have career aspirations marry later in life than do those who planned to be homemakers. Lower-socioeconomic-status individuals, with lower educational and vocational aspirations, are more likely to marry at early ages.

The sexual revolution has also influenced the age at first marriage. The increasing acceptance of non-

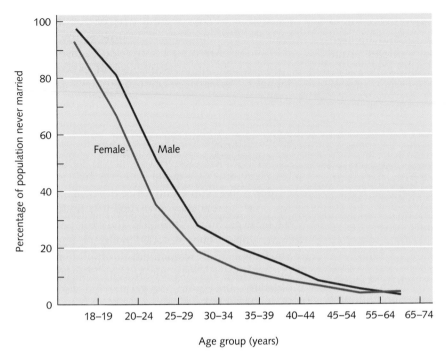

Figure 4.3 Never-Married People as a Percentage of Total Population, Age 18 and Older, by Age and Sex, 2000 (*Note:* Adapted from *Statistical Abstract of the United States, 2002* [p. 48] by U.S. Bureau of the Census, 2002, Washington, DC: U.S. Government Printing Office.)

marital sexual intercourse has made sexual expression possible at younger ages without necessitating marriage. The increased acceptance of nonmarital cohabitation also provides some benefits of marriage without the commitment—for example, companionship, sex, shared housing, and shared living expenses (Althaus, 1991).

The women's movement has also influenced views of marriage. Women are encouraged to seek their own identity, apart from marital identity and to find career fulfillment and economic self-sufficiency if that is what they desire. Most feminists are in no way opposed to marriage, but women are encouraged to explore opportunities in addition to or as alternatives to family fulfillment. At the least, this attitude has led to marital postponement as women explore other options.

WHY SOME PEOPLE REMAIN SINGLE

Just as marriage may be delayed for any of a number of reasons, there are also a number of reasons for never getting married. As we have seen, some people

remain single because of life circumstances and find singlehood to be the best lifestyle for themselves.

Deliberate Choice

Some people who never marry have deliberately chosen to stay single. They enjoy their single lifestyle and do not have a desire to be married. Some people perceive marriage as incompatible with their careers. Many people just prefer to live alone

voluntary temporary singles Never-marrieds and previously marrieds who are not opposed to the idea of marriage but are not currently seeking mates.

voluntary stable (permanent) singles Never-marrieds and previously marrieds who choose to be single.

involuntary temporary singles Never-marrieds and previously marrieds who have actively been seeking a mate but have not found one.

involuntary stable (permanent) singles Never-marrieds and previously marrieds who wanted to marry, who have not found a mate, and who have more or less accepted being single.

and are much better suited to do so. Today singles' groups do not necessarily focus on matchmaking and dating for lonely hearts. Many singles' groups are organized to support their members' chosen lifestyle and to address the political issues affecting them (DePaulo, 2001).

A survey of 3,000 single men and women from 36 states revealed that one-third of the men and one-fifth of the women were unmarried by choice (Simenauer and Carroll, 1982). For example, members of some religious orders take vows of chastity. Some people perceive marriage as incompatible with their careers. A minority of singles are gay or lesbian and do not share the legal right to marry.

Fear of Marriage

Fear of marriage is a powerful deterrent. Some singles who are afraid of marriage were brought up in unhappy homes in which their parents fought all the time. Others have been disappointed in love and are afraid to try again. Some have been married before and failed; they prefer not to remarry. Lutwak (1985) studied fear of intimacy among college women and found that, for some, emotional involvement was simply too risky. These women were so terrified of possible dependency that they could not conceive of healthy mutuality and inter-dependence. They were fearful of possible pain, vulnerability, and—most important—the possible loss of self. Many had a profound sense of insecurity about the consequences of caring. Many thought that marriage was a deception, a farce, and a trap.

Lack of Opportunity

At the other extreme are people who would prefer to marry but have never had the chance. In particular, some women are caught in the "marriage squeeze"; that is, they have difficulty finding eligible male partners. Until 1940, the male population in the United States exceeded the female population. Since then, adult women have outnumbered men; this is especially true for African Americans. The older the age group, the greater the discrepancy in numbers. Both the numbers of eligible men and their employment and education affect women's opportunity to select a partner (South and Lloyd, 1992).

Circumstances

For many people, remaining unmarried permanently is not necessarily a matter of deliberate choice, but rather a result of circumstances such as

A growing number of adults are delaying marriage or choosing to stay single throughout their lives.

family situations, geography, social isolation, or financial condition. Consider this case:

> Mary lived with her widowed father, who was very possessive and protective of her. He made her feel she had an obligation to take care of him. Her father was also very critical of every young man she dated or brought home. According to her father, no one was ever good enough for her. She had several chances to marry but was always dissuaded by her father. She vowed that she would marry after her father died, but the years slipped by. Her father lived until his mid-eighties. By this time, Mary was in her sixties and had remained single. (Author's counseling notes)

ADVANTAGES AND DISADVANTAGES OF BEING SINGLE

People find both advantages and disadvantages in being single. Some single people find advantages to include the following:

- **Greater opportunities for self-development and personal growth and fulfillment.** If singles want to take a course, go on to graduate school, or travel, they are freer to do so than are married people, who must consider their spouse's school and career plans and interests.

- **Opportunities to meet different people and to develop and enjoy different friendships.** Singles are free to pursue friendships with either men or women, according to their own preferences.

- **Economic independence and self-sufficiency.** As one single person said, "I don't have to depend on a spouse for money. I earn it myself and I can spend it as I want."

- **More varied sexual experiences.** Singles are free to seek experiences with more than one partner.

- **Freedom to control their own lives.** Singles are free to do what they want without having to consider a spouse's desires; they enjoy more psychological and social autonomy.

- **More opportunities for career change, development, and expansion.** Singles are not locked into family responsibilities and so can be more mobile and flexible in the climb up the career ladder.

Not all of these advantages apply to all singles. For example, not all singles have opportunities to meet different people, nor are all economically well off, nor are all free of family responsibilities. Nevertheless, most singles would list at least some of these items as advantages for them.

Those who are not in favor of remaining single describe a number of disadvantages, which include the following:

- **Loneliness and lack of companionship.** This is a pressing problem for some singles (Ponzetti, 1990).

- **Economic hardship.** This is especially true for single women. Single women earn less than single or married men and, because they do not have access to a spouse's income, have a lower standard of living than do married women. Also, top positions are more often given to married men than to single men or to women.

- **Feeling out of place in some social gatherings.** This may result because many people's social lives tend to be organized around married couples.

- **Sexual frustration.**

- **A lack of children or a family in which to bring up children.**

A consistent finding in research has been that for adults, the absence of a partner or prospective partner is associated with loneliness. However, loneliness occurs within marriage as well. Tornstam (1992) found that 40% of married people reported being lonely "often" or "sometimes," 16% said they felt lonely even when they were with others, and 7% said they were lonely all the time. In the same study, however, very few people reported having no friends at all. In addition, there appears to be gender differences in loneliness among married people. When asked about loneliness, women were more likely to indicate feeling lonely than were men, particularly married women ages 20–49. Women may simply be more willing to admit to feelings of loneliness, or they may have higher expectations for companionship within marriage that are not being met.

One study investigated the perceptions of being single among heterosexual single women ages 30–65. Some of these women had never been married; others were divorced. The most salient theme that emerged from the analysis is that single women have unresolved or unrecognized ambivalence about being single. This overarching theme was supported by three self-assertions: (1) Single women are aware of both the advantages and the disadvantages of being single; (2) single women are ambivalent about their single status; (3) although content with being single, many women simultaneously experience feelings of loss and grief (K. G. Lewis and Moon, 1997).

About half of the women interviewed said they wished to be married, and half said they did not. Some of the women blamed themselves for being single. These explanations fell primarily into four categories: (1) physical (overweight); (2) personality (shyness, independence or dependence, lack of social skills, lack of competency); (3) psychological (selfishness, low self-esteem, demanding nature, vulnerability, experience of sexual abuse as a child, codependency); and (4) cognitive (too much or too little intelligence, learning disability). An overwhelming majority of the women (including those who blamed themselves for being single) wrote comments that laid blame on men. Some women complained that the men they were meeting were not able to deal with their intelligence, confidence, assertiveness, and accomplishments. One woman remarked, "It scares them. Guys don't want women who are smarter than they unless they are looking for a mother." Another woman said, "I'm intelligent, have a responsible job and money. This makes me inappropriate for ninety-five percent of the men I meet."

The advantages of being single related to having increased freedom: freedom from having to take care of a man; freedom to do what they want, when they want, how they want; and freedom from having to answer to others in terms of time, decisions, and behaviors. The most frequently cited drawbacks to not being married were the absence of being special to a man, the lack of touch, the absence of children, the lack of ready companionship and someone with whom to share interests, and sadness about growing old alone.

Some of the women identified their primary loss in being single as not having children. Others felt that they had lost a lot by investing so much time and energy in previous years on relationships with men. Another major loss was not having assurances about the future. At no point did any of the women

know for certain whether marriage would occur in the future. As long as there was hope for marriage, the pain of ambiguity was present. As one woman said, "It'd be easier if I just knew for sure, then I could adjust fine." Another woman said, "If I knew for sure I would never meet a man, I could get on with my life" (K. G. Lewis and Moon, 1997).

THE HEALTH AND WELL-BEING OF SINGLES

For years, researchers have been investigating the effects of marriage and singlehood on people's health and sense of well-being (Mastekaasa, 1992). In general, the studies seemed to indicate that married people are healthier and happier than single people, so marriage may have a beneficial effect on well-being (G. R. Lee, Seccombe, and Shehan, 1991). Other research supports this idea. A national survey of more than 35,000 people indicated that, compared with those who never marry, and especially compared with those who have separated or divorced, married people report being happier and more satisfied with life (D. G. Myers, 2000). Although there are some indications that a bad marriage may be more depressing to a woman than to her husband, the myth that single women are generally happier than married women is not true (D. G. Myers, 2000). However, researchers are now concluding that marriage alone doesn't make the difference; rather, marriage is one of a number of variables that contribute to the quality of life.

In general, single people are less healthy than married people and have higher mortality rates (Trovato and Lauris, 1989). It may be, however, that singles simply *appear* to be less healthy because they go to their physicians more often than do married people; when singles live with other adults, their visits to physicians decrease, and they seem to be as healthy as married people (Anson, 1989). Another possible explanation for the better health and greater happiness of married people is that unhealthy and unhappy people are less likely to get married in the first place. In other words, those who have superior health and psychological well-being also have the highest probability of marrying. Or the stress of divorce, separation, or the death of a spouse may take a toll on one's health. In addition,

Are married people happier and healthier than single people? Recent research says not necessarily; marital status is just one of many variables affecting a person's well-being.

single people who were once married may be older on average than people who are married.

One study analyzed the impact of marriage on mental health. After taking into account premarital levels of mental health, the researchers found that young adults who get married and stay married report better mental health than do those who remain single (Horwitz, White, and Howell-White, 1996).

Many variables in addition to marital status determine life satisfaction and physical and mental well-being. Employment and socioeconomic status are especially important factors. It has been found that for women a good job and a high family income are positively correlated with good physical and psychological health (Ross, Mirowsky, and Goldstein, 1990). A study of the effects of women's marital status and employment showed that women who are married and have children and a high-prestige job have the highest level of well-being. But it was a high-prestige job rather than a spouse that was the best predictor of well-being. Being single in and of

itself was not associated with diminished well-being, but being single and having a low-level job was.

Barrett (1999) investigated social support and life satisfaction among the never-married by analyzing data collected from interviews with 3,178 respondents, age 30 and older. There were 266 never-married, 1,765 married, and 1,147 previously married respondents. She found that, compared with other marital groups, the never-married tended to be younger, better educated, and non-White. Females reported more hassles associated with never being married than did males, and non-Whites reported fewer hassles than did Whites. Women made up smaller proportions of the never-married and currently married than did the previously married. On average, the never-married had incomes between those of the married and the previously married, and they rated their health higher than did the previously married. The never-married reported less informal interaction, more hassles in arranging to go out with friends, and less likelihood of having a

Many single young adults would prefer to be independent but instead choose to live at home with their parents for financial reasons.

confidant than did members of the other groups. They had overall life satisfaction higher than that of the previously married but lower than that of the married. Among respondents ages 30–45, the never-married had more frequent interaction with friends, relatives, and neighbors than did members of the other groups. In those two groups, the pattern of informal interaction reversed, with the married and previously married reporting more interaction. Results indicated that the frequency of interaction increased with age among married and the previously married but decreased among the never-married. In addition, results showed that never being married or being previously married was negatively related to life satisfaction. Higher life satisfaction was associated with being older, female, White, married, and healthy.

Other research indicates that married women rate their health higher than do divorced, separated, widowed, or never-married women. The better economic circumstances of married women compared to the other groups may be the reason. Clearly, most married women have access to higher incomes than do most single women, and higher income is associated with better health. The married woman receives the material benefits that a higher family income provides, as well as a sense of security that her well-

being is not entirely dependent on her own earnings (B. A. Hahn, 1993).

LIVING ARRANGEMENTS

Most singles meet some of their needs for companionship and economic well-being by sharing a residence with friends or family. Singles who are still in school are most likely to live with their parents or with classmates; singles in their late twenties and early thirties are most likely to live with a roommate or by themselves; and older singles are most likely to live alone or with relatives.

Single elderly people often face worse housing problems than do other singles or elderly people in families. Single elderly people are likely to live in rental housing, where they face the risk of social isolation, and a disproportionate number are poor. In addition to having low fixed incomes, they are likely to lack any asset "cushion" in the form of home equity, and they may have little or no help available if they become impaired. Under these circumstances, subsidized housing is an important source of affordable housing and companionship for poor, single elderly people (Crystal and Beck, 1992).

Shared Living Spaces

Although large numbers of singles live in singles' complexes or apartment buildings, more live with the general population. The majority occupy individual apartments, usually with roommates. The usual pattern is to share an apartment and living expenses with one or more people who provide emotional support and companionship.

Living with Parents

The percentage of young adults (ages 18–29) who lived with parents reached a high in 1940, near the end of the Great Depression. The percentage bottomed out in 1960, near the end of the baby boom, and has risen modestly since then. In 2000, over 50% of 18- to 24-year-olds were living with their parents (U.S. Bureau of the Census, 2002). The increase has occurred because of marriage postponement and high rates of college enrollment, unemployment, divorce and separation, and birth to unmarried mothers. Most adults who live with their parents have a plan for achieving independence, such as saving enough money or getting more education. But while they are living at home, their parents still spend a lot of money on their food, clothes, cars, insurance, and other goods and services (Crispell, 1996). Table 4.2

shows the percentage of young adult men and women of different ages living at home with parents. Note that greater percentages of men than women of all ages live at home with their parents. Women who are married, separated, or divorced and have one or more children are more likely to live at home with their parents or relatives than are women who do not have any children.

Living Alone

Figure 4.4 shows the percentage of the population, by age and sex, living alone in 2000 (U.S. Bureau of the Census, 2002). This figure includes divorced, separated, and widowed people, as well as the never-married. As illustrated, greater percentages

Table 4.2 Percentage of Young Adults Living with Their Parents, by Age, 1998

	18–24 Years of Age	25–34 Years of Age
Total	53	11.5
Men	59	14.5
Women	48	8.5

Note: From *Statistical Abstract of the United States, 1999* (p. 57) by U.S. Bureau of the Census, 1999, Washington, DC: U.S. Government Printing Office.

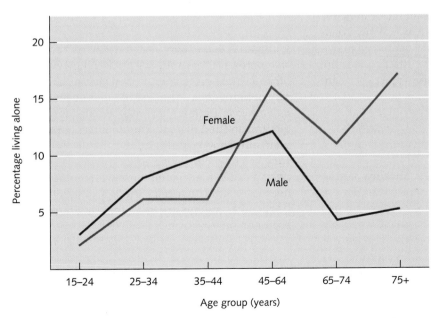

Figure 4.4 Percentage of Persons Living Alone, by Age and Sex, 2000 (*Note:* Data from *Statistical Abstract of the United States, 2002* [p. 53] by U.S. Bureau of the Census, 2002, Washington, DC: U.S. Government Printing Office.)

Loneliness is a common problem among single adults. The advantage of the increased freedom of being single is often outweighed by the lack of ready companionship. What are some other advantages and disadvantages of being single?

of males than females in the 15–44 age group live alone. With each succeeding age group (45–64, 65–74, and 75 and older), the percentage of females living alone increases rapidly. This is due to the greater numbers of older females in the population. Health status is the most important factor in determining how long they continue to live alone. When a move is necessary, many elderly people go to live with their children. Declining health increases the likelihood of institutionalization (Spitze, Logan, and Robinson, 1992).

SEXUAL BEHAVIOR

If we are to believe the media, all healthy young Americans are having a great deal of sex; if they are not, they are encouraged to do so as quickly as possible. The truth is far more complex. Americans, we find, are not having much sex at all—at least not much compared to what we are told is a normal and optimal amount. According to the National Health and Social Life Survey (NHSLS), as of 1994, 94–98% of men and women have had sexual intercourse by the time they reach age 25 (Michael, Gagnon,

Laumann, and Kolata, 1994). But when we inquire about the frequency of sex in the past 12 months, we get a completely different picture. According to the NHSLS, 23% of noncohabiting men and 32% of noncohabiting women have not had sex in the past 12 months. An additional 25% of men and 23% of women had sex only a few times during the past year. These figures certainly do not present a picture of frequent and promiscuous sex (Michael et al., 1994).

In light of the increase in HIV/AIDS and other sexually transmitted diseases, we are interested not only in the percentages of people having sexual intercourse but also in the number of sex partners they have had. According to the NHSLS, in 1994, 25% of never-married, noncohabiting men and women had no sex partners during the past 12 months, 38% had only one partner, and 28% had two to four. Only a small percentage of the population (9%) had as many as five sex partners during the past year; most of this group were young men who had never been married and were not living with anyone. These findings give no support to media images of a promiscuous society. Rather, they suggest that most people do in fact form partnerships and ultimately get married.

These findings, along with those from other studies, indicate, however, that a small percentage of young adults are still engaging in high-risk sexual behavior and thus risking contracting HIV/AIDS. A survey of 671 predominantly young, Black women living in 10 low-income housing developments in five cities revealed that 17% of the women had sex with multiple partners and that 22% had an exclusive partner. That exclusive partner, however, had other sexual partners in the past year or had a history of intravenous drug use. Of those women who had multiple partners, 26% were treated for a sexually transmitted disease. Condom use at previous intercourse and communication about condom use were less frequent among women with an exclusive, risky partner than among those with multiple partners. The more partners there are and the less frequently condoms are used, the riskier sexual behavior becomes (Wagstaff et al., 1995).

A 1991 study of a random sample of heterosexual undergraduates at a midwestern university yielded some disturbing figures, particularly in light of HIV/AIDS. During the 4 years since they first had vaginal intercourse, males reported an average of 8.5 vaginal-sex partners, and females reported an aver-

Cybersex

Methods of sexual expression continue to change with technological advances. With the introduction of the automobile came a new place for sexual exploits, with motion pictures came X-rated films, and with the telephone came phone sex. And so it follows, with cyberspace comes cybersex.

The Internet provides an anonymous environment in which people can participate in sexual activities with little risk of embarrassment or punishment. Lamb (1998) has suggested that cybersex might be harmless when adults use it to enhance one another's fantasies. The danger arises when adults contact children and solicit them to fulfill their fantasies and engage in deviant behavior. According to a survey on online victimization of children, one in five adolescents has been exposed to strangers who wanted cybersex (Finkelhor, Mitchell, and Wolak, 2000). It is estimated that as many as 24 million adolescents ages 10–17 were online regularly in 1999 and so were at risk for unwanted sexual solicitations and sexual materials, as well as threatening and offensive behavior directed at them.

Almost half of the 1,501 youths surveyed believed that the solicitations were from someone under the age of 18. A quarter of those seeking cybersex were perceived as being adults but were actually young adults ages 18–25. Thus, in teaching children about online safety, parents and others need to look beyond the stereotypic older male sexual predator (Finkelhor et al., 2000).

Other important data in the report included the following:

- One in 33 youths surveyed had received aggressive solicitation—someone asking to meet them, calling them on the phone, or sending regular mail, money, or gifts.
- One in four youths had received unwanted pictures of naked people or people having sex.
- Almost two-thirds of the incidents occurred in a chat room.
- Three-quarters of the advances were brushed off by the adolescent.
- About one-quarter of the youths who experienced a solicitation told a parent, and almost 40% who received sexual material told a parent.
- Only 17% of the youths and approximately 10% of the parents could identify an authority to whom they could report these incidents, such as police or social workers.
- One-third of the parents who had Internet access at home said they had filtering or blocking software on their computers.

As this report suggests, parents and other authority figures must constantly remind youths and teens that people have ulterior motives and hidden agendas, and any meetings with cyberfriends should be under supervision and in a public place.

---

age of 6.1 partners. In addition, 17% of the sexually experienced males and 18% of the sexually experienced females had engaged in heterosexual anal intercourse. Researchers concluded that a substantial number of college students had engaged in sexual behavior that placed them at risk for sexually transmitted diseases, including HIV/AIDS (Reinisch, Hill, Sanders, and Ziemba-Davis, 1995).

Data on substance use and sexual activity from a nationally representative probability-based sample of young adults ages 18–30 in 1990 indicated that those who had used marijuana in the past year and those who had consumed five or more drinks at a sitting were more likely than others to have had more than one sexual partner. Heavy drinkers were also less likely to use condoms, thus placing themselves at further risk (Graves and Leigh, 1995).

SEXUALLY TRANSMITTED DISEASES

Sexually transmitted diseases (STDs) are among the most common infections in the United States. An estimated 15 million Americans acquire an STD every year and more than 65 million are currently living with an incurable STD. Roughly one-quarter of new cases occurs among teenagers, and two-thirds of new cases occur in people under age 25 (Cates, 1999). At least one in three sexually active people will contract an STD by age 24. Yet, despite

sexually transmitted disease (STD) Disease transmitted through sexual contact.

their prevalence, STDs are the most unrecognized health problem in the United States today. Because the probability of multiple sex partners is greater when single, increasing a person's exposure to STDs, the topic of STDs is discussed in this chapter. However, STDs affect everyone who is sexually active.

Most Americans are unaware of the extent of the STD epidemic. One study found that most men and women of reproductive age (18–44) seriously underestimate the prevalence of STDs and their own risk for contracting an STD. Only 14% of men and 8% of women say they think they are at risk for STDs. Perhaps this is why so many couples do not use condoms consistently; two-thirds of single men and women say they do not always use condoms. The story is similar for teenagers ages 15–17: Approximately three-fourths of these girls and boys think the STD rate is 1 in 10 Americans over the lifetime, and only 1 in 5 teens think they are at risk of contracting an STD (Kaiser Family Foundation, 2001).

It is difficult to accurately gauge the number of STDs because many infections are asymptomatic and social stigma limits discussion of the problem. Many STDs can be detected only through testing, and many Americans do not discuss STDs with health care professionals. Thus, most STDs go undiagnosed. Of the STDs that are diagnosed, health care providers are required to report only cases of gonorrhea, syphilis, and chlamydia to state health departments. There is no national reporting requirement for the other STDs (Centers for Disease Control and Prevention [CDC], 2002b).

Infection rates for some STDs in the United States are the highest in the developed world; in some cases, they rival those reported in developing countries (C. Donovan, 1997). STDs can be grouped into three categories according to their cause:

1. Those caused by viruses: HIV/AIDS, herpes simplex, hepatitis B, and genital warts.
2. Those caused by bacteria: chlamydia, gonorrhea, syphilis, and various vaginal infections, including pelvic inflammatory disease (PID) and non-gonococcal urethritis.
3. Those caused by parasites: pubic lice and scabies.

Any of the STDs caused by viruses or bacteria can pose serious health problems if left undetected and untreated. Some, including AIDS, herpes, and hepatitis B, do not have a cure. About half the people

with an STD seek treatment. In one study, 49% of respondents who had contracted an STD went to a private practitioner for treatment, and 5% sought treatment at an STD clinic. Men were more likely than women to go to STD clinics, and respondents who were young, poor, or Black were more likely to use a family planning clinic for treatment than were those who were older, relatively wealthy, or White (Brackbill, Sternberg, and Fishbein, 1999).

An analysis of a representative national survey of households provided strong evidence that alcohol consumption exceeds illicit drug use as a risk factor for STDs. Men and women who report a history of an STD are significantly more likely to have a history of problem drinking, independent of high-risk sexual activity and demographic influences. A high rate of change in sexual partners over the past 5 years also increases the risk of STD infections. More than half of teens ages 15–19 have had sex, and these teens are at high risk for STDs. Women under the age of 24 may be at greater risk for acquiring an STD than older women because these diseases easily infect the immature cervix (National Women's Health Resource Center, 1998).

Sexually transmitted diseases are a serious health problem in the United States, but they are almost entirely preventable through choices in one's behavior. The expression of one's sexuality in an intimate relationship is vitally important, and so is mature and responsible behavior in order to have a safe, healthy, and satisfying sexual relationship.

HIV/AIDS

AIDS (acquired immunodeficiency syndrome) is a sexually transmitted disease characterized by virtually irreversible damage to the body's immune system and, eventually, death. An estimated 850,000–950,000 Americans are living with the human immunodeficiency virus (HIV), with 40,000 people becoming infected each year. The total number of reported AIDS cases in the United States at the end of 2001 was 816,149. New treatments have slowed the progression from HIV infection to AIDS and from AIDS to death. Consequently, rates of both AIDS cases and AIDS deaths have dropped dramatically, and an increasing number of people with HIV are living longer and healthier lives (CDC, 2003b).

A blood test measures the presence of HIV antibodies in the bloodstream. A person who tests positive for HIV antibodies has been exposed to the virus, is infected, and can transmit it to others. People may spread the virus without knowing they are infected. The incubation period may run from a few years to longer than 10 years. Several new drugs have been developed that, if used in combination, retard the development of the disease, but they are still being tested for their long-term effectiveness. One disadvantage is that these drugs cost thousands of dollars per year; another is their often serious side effects.

It is best to take the HIV antibody test at least 6 months after the last possible exposure to HIV. Almost everyone who is infected develops antibodies within 6 months, although there are rare cases of people who take longer. A negative test result within the first few months after exposure may mean only that the body has not had time to develop antibodies. Approximately two-thirds of Americans with HIV and AIDS have been tested confidentially (CDC, 2003b).

HIV is found in semen, blood, urine, vaginal secretions, saliva, tears, and breast milk and is transmitted from male to female, female to male, male to male, and female to female during the exchange of body fluids. HIV is transmitted through direct sexual contact or infected needles or syringes. HIV can also pass from mother to fetus during pregnancy and from mother to nursing infant through breast milk. Although HIV has been found in tears and saliva, no instances of transmission from these body fluids have been reported. HIV has, however, been transmitted via contaminated blood during a transfusion, and it has also been transmitted from health care worker to patient and from patient to health care worker through blood exchange. Some people fear that HIV might be transmitted in other ways, but there is no scientific evidence to support any of these fears. If HIV were being transmitted through other routes, such as through air, water, or insects, the pattern of reported AIDS cases would be much different from what has been observed. For example AIDS is *not* transmitted through casual, nonsexual social contact such as occurs at home or in offices, restaurants, or schools. Nor is it transmitted through touching, shaking hands, or playing together, unless a person with an open sore or wound comes into contact with the blood of a person who has AIDS. AIDS is also *not* transmitted by sneezing, breathing, or coughing, nor through food or insect bites, nor through door knobs, toilet seats, eating utensils, or water fountains (CDC, 2003b).

The more sex partners one has, male or female, the greater the risk of becoming infected (CDC, 2003b). In a study of college students seeking HIV testing at a private 4-year urban university, researchers sought to identify common characteristics of those who felt they were at risk for HIV. The 622 subjects completed surveys on initial and follow-up visits on three potential risk factors: multiple partners, condom use, and STDs. The results indicated that multiple partners was the only variable significantly related to getting tested for HIV (Fredericks, 1999). Many individuals infected with HIV do not know it. The Centers for Disease Control and Prevention (CDC) estimates that more than 75% of HIV-infected young gay and bisexual men are unaware they are infected, including 91% of infected African American men (CDC, 2003b). One study of 5,719 gay and bisexual men ages 15–29 found that 573 tested positive for HIV, but of those, 440 did not know they were infected. This study indicates that more work needs to be done to prompt at-risk groups to seek HIV counseling and testing.

In the United States, rates of HIV-related death are highest among young and middle-aged adults, particularly those in racial and ethnic minorities. HIV is the fifth leading cause of death for Americans ages 25–44. Among African American men and women in this age group, it is the leading cause of death. Many of these young adults were infected as teenagers. Scores of studies report that AIDS is an epidemic of the young, particularly women. Almost one-third of the estimated 40 million people worldwide who are infected with HIV are under 25, and half of new infections occur within this age group. In the United States this amounts to 20,000 infections a year, with one-third of these new infections occurring among women (CDC, 2003b).

The majority of young people are infected from heterosexual contact. Even though the number of new AIDS cases diagnosed each year is declining,

AIDS Acquired immunodeficiency syndrome; a sexually transmitted disease caused by the human immunodeficiency virus (HIV) and characterized by irreversible damage to the body's immune system and, eventually, death.

there has not been a comparable decline in the number of newly diagnosed HIV cases among youths. Obviously, there is a great need for AIDS education in schools and communities to prevent young people from being exposed to HIV. Research has shown that early, clear communication between parents and young people about sex is an important step in helping adolescents develop and maintain safe sexual behaviors (CDC, 2003a).

Herpes Simplex

Herpes simplex is caused by a virus that can produce cold sores or fever blisters on the mouth or face (oral herpes) and similar symptoms in the genital area (genital herpes). Herpes is different from other common viral infections because once it is introduced it lives in the body over a lifetime, often without symptoms or with periodic symptoms. Rates of infection have grown by 30% over the past two decades, and at least 50 million cases have been diagnosed. Genital herpes now affects more than one in five Americans over age 12, with a million new cases occurring each year. As many as 80–90% of those infected do not recognize the symptoms or have no symptoms at all, but they still transmit the virus ("New Survey," 2000). Although genital herpes is one of the nation's most prevalent STDs, one study showed that many adults in a high-risk category (those having multiple sex partners) saw themselves as having no risk of contracting genital herpes ("New Survey," 2000). In 1999, the estimated prevalence was 19 percent among the general U.S. population ages 14–49 (McQuillan, 2000).

Herpes is most easily spread during or a few days before an active outbreak. The virus can cause some discomfort, but it usually does not affect the immune system or lead to other health problems. It is important to remember that some symptoms are so mild that people don't notice them and that sometimes there are no symptoms at all. If symptoms do occur, they can include itching or tingling followed by a painful eruption of blisters and sores, headaches, flulike symptoms, swollen glands in the lymph nodes, and other breaks or irregularities in the skin, such as a cut, red bumps, or a rash. Signs and symptoms will vary from person to person and from one episode to the next ("Finding Answers," 1999).

Herpes is transmitted through anal or vaginal intercourse, oral-anal or oral-genital contact, genital-genital contact, and kissing. If a person gets the virus on his or her fingers and then touches his or her genitals or mouth, or someone else's, those areas may be infected. The best way to prevent the spread of genital herpes is to avoid sex during an active outbreak, to always use condoms between outbreaks, and to use suppressive antiviral therapy to reduce outbreaks ("Finding Answers," 1999). Genital herpes and cancer of the cervix and vulva appear to be associated, so periodic Pap smears and pelvic exams are especially advisable for women who have herpes. If a woman is pregnant and has herpes, it is important that she discuss this with her health care provider. While the spread of herpes to newborns is rare (less than 0.1%), an episode during late pregnancy and delivery can cause serious health problems for the newborn ("Finding Answers," 1999).

Hepatitis B

Hepatitis B is a highly contagious disease of the liver that can cause extreme illness and even death. Despite the availability of a vaccine, hepatitis B remains a leading STD, with 200,000 new cases a year transmitted through sexual contact (CDC, 2002b). Of these, it is believed that 120,000 infections are acquired through sexual transmission annually, mostly among young adults. An estimated 417,000 people are currently living with chronic sexually acquired hepatitis B infection (CDC, 2002b).

Many people show no symptoms and discover they have the virus only through blood tests. When symptoms occur, they include fever, nausea, loss of appetite, fatigue, muscular aches, headaches, jaundice, dark urine, abdominal swelling, light-colored feces, and a sweet odor to the breath.

The hepatitis B virus is present in seminal and vaginal fluids, saliva, urine, and blood, so it may be transmitted by contact with contaminated blood, or by vaginal and anal intercourse, oral-genital contact, and kissing. Having intercourse without a condom or performing oral sex without a moisture barrier increases one's risk of becoming infected. Infected needles, ear-piercing and tattooing tools, acupuncture needles, and medical or dental instruments that cut or puncture the skin may also transmit the virus. The virus can pass through defective latex condoms and lambskin condoms as well. A person may develop an immunity to the virus but still be a carrier and infect other people. Hepatitis B is potentially fatal and has no cure, but a vaccine has been developed that gives protection for 5 years. It may prevent infection even after exposure because of the virus's long incubation period (CDC, 2002b). Treatment consists of bed rest and careful attention to diet; antibiotics are not effective.

Human Papillomavirus (HPV)/Genital Warts

The term **human papillomavirus (HPV)** refers to a group of viruses that infect the skin. There are over 70 HPV types, with about 30 being sexually transmitted and causing genital warts. HPV is likely the most common STD among young, sexually active people, and it is of increasing concern with regard to public health. At any one time, an estimated 20 million people in the United States have genital HPV infections that can be transmitted to others, and every year about 5.5 million people acquire genital HPV infection (CDC, 2002b). One study among female college students found that an average of 14% became infected with genital HPV each year. About 43% of the women in the study were infected with HPV during the three-year study period (G. Ho, Bierman, and Beardsley, 1998). Based on a representative sample of 83 men who have sex with men, the CDC concluded that 38% of gay or bisexual men in the United States are infected with HPV type 16. That prevalence is nearly five times higher than the prevalence in heterosexual men and twice that in women. Anyone who has ever had sexual intercourse can be infected and not know it, because HPV often has no symptoms.

Genital HPV is spread through skin-to-skin contact, not through an exchange of bodily fluids, during vaginal, anal, or oral sex. When symptoms do occur, they can include growths or bumps on the vulva, in or around the vagina or anus, on the cervix, or on the penis, scrotum, or groin. Sometimes, HPV causes such tiny blemishes that they can be detected only with special instruments that magnify the lesions. Warts may appear months or even years after sex with an infected person. Thus, HPV can be contracted from one sex partner, remain dormant, and then later be unknowingly transmitted to another partner.

Concern about HPV has increased in recent years after studies showed that some types of HPV infection causes cancer. In women, HPV type 16 is associated with about half of all cervical cancer cases, and it's been linked to penile and anal cancer in men (CDC, 2002b). Although certain high-risk strains of HPV cause cervical lesions that, over time, can develop into cancer if untreated, most women with an HPV infection will not develop cervical cancer. However, HPV can put men at risk for anal and penile cancers (CDC, 2002b). Electrocautery, cryocautery (use of extreme cold), diathermy (use of heat), laser therapy, and surgery can be used to remove the warts.

Chlamydial Infections

Chlamydia is the most commonly reported infectious disease in the United States. The term refers to a family of infections caused by a bacterium; the infections are spread through sexual contact and may be one of the most dangerous STDs for women today. If left untreated, chlamydia can cause severe health consequences; men can develop nongonococcal urethritis and epididymitus, and women can develop cervical infections and pelvic inflammatory disease (PID). Up to 40% of women with untreated chlamydia will develop PID, and one in five women with PID becomes infertile. Moreover, women infected with chlamydia are three to five times more

herpes simplex   A sexually transmitted disease caused by a virus that can produce cold sores or fever blisters on the mouth or face (oral herpes) and similar symptoms in the genital area (genital herpes).

hepatitis B   A highly contagious sexually transmitted disease that affects the liver. It can cause extreme illness or even death.

human papillomavirus (HPV)   Any of a group of viruses that infect the skin. There are more than 70 types of HPV; 30 of these are sexually transmitted and cause genital warts.

chlamydia   A family of infections caused by a bacterium leading to nongonococcal urethritis and epididymitis in men, and cervical infections and pelvic inflammatory disease (PID) in women.

likely to become infected with HIV if exposed (CDC, 2002b). While the chlamydia infection can be cured with antibiotics, millions of cases go unrecognized, unreported, and untreated. One study found that nearly two-thirds of all people with chlamydia or gonorrhea, the top two reported sexually transmitted diseases, go untreated because they have no symptoms. An estimated 7.9% of the population ages 18–35 has either an untreated gonococcal or chlamydial infection, with the estimated prevalence substantially higher among Black women at 15% (C. F. Turner et al., 2002).

The number of new reported chlamydia cases has risen in recent years, but this is due mainly to improved screening. Overall, as more infections have been diagnosed and cured, the number of new cases has fallen from an estimated 4 million to about 3 million a year (American Social Health Association, 2000). The disease may be asymptomatic in 75% of women and 50% of men, so medical tests are important in detecting it (Nordenberg, 1999). Chlamydia must be treated early, or it can do permanent damage to the body (American Social Health Association, 2003).

Nongonococcal urethritis (NGU) is the most common chlamydial infection in men. Some men have no symptoms; others experience a burning sensation during urination and discharge a puslike fluid. If anal sexual contact was involved, rectal pain and soreness and rectal discharge may be present. A lab test is used to distinguish NGU from gonorrhea.

Epididymitis is an inflammation of the epididymis; it is most common in sexually active males under age 35. Symptoms include tenderness of the testicles and fever. Epididymitis may cause sterility if left untreated.

Chlamydial infections in women include oral, rectal, and cervical infections. As mentioned earlier, if left untreated, chlamydial infection can cause pelvic inflammatory disease (PID). Cervical smears are used in diagnosis. Tetracycline is used in treatment; pregnant women are given erythromycin. Some babies are exposed to the chlamydia bacterium when passing through the birth canal and are thus infected. Infected newborns are subject to lung, eye, and ear infections, as well as pneumonia and prematurity. However, pregnant women can take medicine to cure chlamydia and protect the baby.

PID is a general term for infections of the uterus, fallopian tubes, and ovaries, most often caused by untreated chlamydial or gonorrheal bacterium. Abdominal pain during intercourse is the most common symptom. Vaginal discharge, nausea, vomiting, high blood pressure, and fever may also occur. Long-term consequences are chronic pain, greater risk of ectopic pregnancy, and infertility from blocked fallopian tubes. Each year in the United States, more than 1 million women experience an episode of acute PID. More than 100,000 women become infertile each year as a result of PID, and a large proportion of the ectopic pregnancies occurring every year are due to the consequences of PID. More than 150 women die from this infection every year (CDC, 2002b).

Gonorrhea

Gonorrhea, also called the "drip" or "clap," is a highly contagious, sexually transmitted disease caused by the bacterium *Neisseria gonorrheae.* An estimated 650,000 cases of gonorrhea occur each year in the United States (Cates, 1999). The number of new cases had been declining since 1977, but since 1997 it has begun to increase. Rates of infection remain disproportionately high among persons under age 24 who have multiple sex partners and engage in unprotected sexual intercourse. Reported rates of gonorrhea among African Americans remain more than 30 times higher than rates among Whites and more than 11 times higher than rates among Hispanics. This trend likely reflects differences in access to prevention and treatment services. The reported gonorrhea rate in the United States remains the highest of any industrialized country and is roughly 50 times that of Sweden and eight times that of Canada (CDC, 2002b).

Gonorrhea is spread by oral, genital, or anal contact when the mucous membranes of the throat, genitals, or rectum come into contact with those of an infected person. Newborn infants of infected mothers may get gonorrhea of the eyes when passing through the birth canal. Treatment with silver nitrate or an antibiotic prevents blindness.

Many people who have gonorrhea have no obvious symptoms. Testing of discharge from the penis or vagina is important in detecting gonorrhea. When they do occur, symptoms in men appear from a few days to as long as a month after infection and may include a puslike penile discharge, blood in the urine, a burning sensation during urination, pressure or pain in the genitals, and enlarged lymph glands in the groin. The infection spreads through the urinary and reproductive systems if left untreated. If the disease spreads, it may cause chronic obstructions in the vas deferens and lead to infertility.

When they do occur, symptoms in women include a puslike vaginal discharge, which comes from cervical infection, and painful and frequent urination from infection of the urethra. The disease may spread to the ovaries, fallopian tubes, and uterus, causing PID. Infection may also occur in the mouth, throat, and rectum. Both men and women may develop gonorrheal arthritis. Treatment usually consists of a dose of antibiotics, although a strain has been discovered that is resistant to antibiotics. Gonorrhea can be easily cured, if detected early, and the long-term consequences can be prevented (CDC, 2002b).

Syphilis

Syphilis, caused by the spirochete (spiral-shaped) bacterium *Treponema pallidum,* is far more serious than gonorrhea because it can be fatal if not treated. Without a moist, warm environment, the spirochete dies within seconds outside the body. For this reason, it is transmitted exclusively by vaginal or anal intercourse or oral-genital contact. A fetus may contract congenital syphilis from the pregnant woman when the spirochete crosses the placental barrier. A fetus will not develop syphilis if the disease is diagnosed and treated before the fourth month of pregnancy (Dubroff and Papalian, 1982). If a woman is not treated in the early stages of the disease, the baby is likely to die before or shortly after birth. For these reasons, pregnant women should be tested for syphilis.

Syphilis develops in four stages: primary, secondary, latent, and tertiary. During the primary stages, a chancre, or sore, will develop at the site the spirochete entered. The chancre usually heals in 4–6 weeks, so the disease will seem to have disappeared. However, the spirochetes circulate in the blood, and secondary syphilis develops within 1–6 months. It is characterized by weight and hair loss, constipation, nausea, poor appetite, joint pain, swollen glands, headache, sore throat, fever, and a pinkish or red rash. The disease can be cured at this stage if treatment is initiated.

Without treatment, the symptoms disappear, but the disease enters the latent stage, during which the spirochetes burrow into the brain and spinal cord, blood vessels, bones, and other body tissues. The latent stage may last for years. After a year or two, the disease is no longer infectious except that a fetus may still contract congenital syphilis from a pregnant woman with latent syphilis.

Thirty to 50% of untreated infected people develop tertiary syphilis; the remainder remain in the latent stage the rest of their lives. Tertiary syphilis may damage the brain, spinal cord, nervous system, heart, and major blood vessels, causing paralysis or death. Syphilis causes genital ulcers, which increase the likelihood of sexual HIV transmission twofold to fivefold.

No blood test for syphilis is 100% accurate in the first 4–6 weeks following infection (during the primary stage), but all are 100% accurate during the secondary stage. Treatment usually consists of injections with penicillin (CDC, 2002b). Rates of syphilis in the United States are at the lowest levels in 20 years, with only about 6,657 new cases diagnosed annually. Because the levels are so low, the CDC has concluded it should be possible to eliminate syphilis in the United States (CDC, 2002b).

Parasitic Infections

Parasitic infections are not really diseases but rather infestations of parasites. **Pubic lice** (*Pediculosis pubis*), or "crabs," are wingless parasitic insects that suck blood from human hosts, causing itching. They may be identified with a magnifying glass. Permethrin or lindane creams, lotions, or hair shampoos are applied, and the nits removed with a fine-toothed comb (CDC, 2002b). Sexual partners should be treated simultaneously, and sheets, pillowcases, pajamas, and underclothing should be washed thoroughly in hot water.

gonorrhea A sexually transmitted disease caused by the bacterium *Neisseria gonorrheae.*

syphilis A sexually transmitted disease caused by the spirochete bacterium *Treponema pallidum.* It can be fatal if not treated.

pubic lice Parasitic insects occupying hairy regions of the body that suck blood from their human hosts, causing itching. Known informally as "crabs."

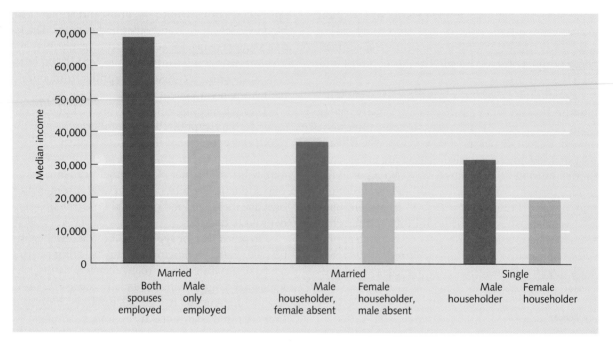

Figure 4.5   Median Income, by Household Type and Marital Status, 2000 (*Note:* Adapted from *Statistical Abstract of the United States, 2002*, by U.S. Bureau of the Census, 2002, Washington, DC: U.S. Government Printing Office.)

Scabies (*Sarcoptes scabiei*) is a parasitic infection that may be transmitted by contact with infected fabrics or through sexual contact. *Sarcoptes* mites burrow under the skin, lay eggs, and cause itching. Scabies is spread quickly among family members sharing the same living quarters. Treatment includes applying an antiscabies medication to the entire body and washing clothing and fabrics. All family members should be treated at once.

EMPLOYMENT AND INCOME

One stereotype holds that never-marrieds are richer than marrieds: They have no spouses or children to support, they do not require expensive homes, and

they can live more cheaply than marrieds. In fact, marrieds are better off financially than never-marrieds. In 2000, the median income of married householders with both spouses employed was $69,463; for married male householders with only the man employed, it was $39,735; and for single male householders it was $30,753. The median income for married female householders with the male absent was $25,794; for single female householders, it was $19,917. Figure 4.5 shows the comparison (U.S. Bureau of the Census, 2002). According to these figures, greater percentages of married householders are in high-income brackets than are never-married householders.

There are a number of reasons for these differences. Slightly more than half of all married women are employed outside the home, contributing substantially to the total household income. The combined income of two wage earners is likely to be greater than the income of one wage earner.

One reason is a practical one. Married people, especially those with families, have to earn more

scabies   A parasitic infection of mites that burrow into the skin, lay eggs, and cause itching.

money because their needs are greater, and they are more motivated to earn higher incomes. Despite many exceptions, this principle generally holds. Many married people are forced to work more than one job to provide sufficient incomes for their family.

In addition, the income discrepancies reflect deep-seated prejudices against women. Overall, the average woman with education and experience comparable to that of a man is paid only about 73% as much for the same work (U.S. Bureau of the Census, 2002).

SINGLE PARENTS

Single parents are becoming increasingly common. Statistics show that single-mother families increased from 3 million in 1970 to 10 million in 2000, while the number of single-father families grew from 393,000 to 2 million (Fields and Casper, 2001). A number of factors are related to the increase: prevalence of divorce; more women keeping their children as opposed to adoption; technology that allows a woman to become pregnant without a partner (e.g., sperm banks); and more acceptance of single people becoming parents.

Many single individuals become parents for the same reasons as do married people. Often a single person has the desire to nurture another human being and to share life in a full and intimate way with a child. Individuals may have reached their thirties without having a partner and still have a strong compulsion to raise a child. Many people learn of children in other countries who are abandoned or live in great poverty whom they could adopt and for whom they could provide a happy home. Also, many children with special needs live in foster care or institutions and would benefit greatly from a home with a devoted parent, regardless of marital status.

As can be seen from the statistics cited above, although the majority of single parents are mothers, a growing number of fathers are assuming primary care for their children. Most single-father families are a result of divorce as opposed to a man adopting a child. The increase stems from several societal and legal changes. In the past, fathers *only* assumed custody of their children when the mother

was proven unfit. Today, more gender-neutral custody criteria are in place, resulting in more fathers obtaining full or joint custody agreements. In addition, more mothers are choosing to pursue career or personal goals in favor of the father's custody, or mothers may not want to be full-time parents (Hamer and Marchioro, 2002). However, in the majority of divorce cases, custody still is awarded to the mother.

Men are adapting to parenting roles very well once they take custody (Hamer and Marchioro, 2002). Many fathers are motivated to fulfill a sense of duty and responsibility, to process and rework the effects of their own parent's deficiencies, and to provide a role model and further the already established bond with their children (Coles, 2002). Fathers can provide for social, physical, and emotional needs to the same extent that a mother can (Hamer and Marchioro, 2002), and they experience many of the same difficulties in single parenting as do mothers.

One distinction between single mothers and single fathers is that many single women choose to become mothers, whereas most single-father situations are a result of divorce. Births to unmarried women are no longer unusual. The birthrate among unmarried women rose almost 60% in the 1990s, with about one-third of unmarried women ages 15–44 becoming mothers (U.S. Bureau of the Census, 2002). Over half have never married. While teenage birthrates have declined by 22% since 1991, the overall number of births to unmarried women has risen by 3%, to over 1.3 million, the highest number ever recorded. Most of the increase is linked to the rise in the number of unmarried women of childbearing age (Ventura, Martin, Curtin, Mathews, and Park, 2000). Single White women in this age range have the most rapidly increasing birthrate. The birthrate doubled among never-married college-educated women and almost tripled among never-married women who work in a professional or managerial capacity.

Why are single women choosing to become mothers? Aside from the obvious, one answer is that the appeal of marriage may be diminishing for women. The rates of marriage for both men and women have declined. Women's increased options outside of marriage, including the ability to support themselves, are having a large effect on marriage patterns. The most significant of the options available to women is labor force participation. In ever

African American Single Mothers

As discussed in Chapter 1, single-parent families are disproportionately concentrated among African Americans. It must be noted, however, that single motherhood is not caused by any deficiency in ideology in relation to the family. African Americans believe strongly in the institution of the family. Single motherhood is related to the high rates of unemployment and underemployment of Black males. In sum, there is a shortage of African American males, especially those who are economically ready for marriage (Tucker and Taylor, 1989). For example, there are almost 1.9 million fewer Black men than women over age 14 (U.S. Bureau of the Census, 2002), and many of the unmarried men are underemployed, can't find jobs, or have dropped out of the labor force (Fossett and Kiecolt, 1993). Like people of many other ethnic or racial groups, African Americans tend to feel that a man's primary role is that of provider. However, in 2000, even if an African American man was working full-time, he earned on average only about 72% of the income of a White man (U.S. Bureau of the Census, 2000). Another factor in the shortage of eligible Black men is that, although the percentages are small, more African American men than women marry outside their race. The lack of eligible men for all the reasons listed here is one important factor in the increase in Black female-headed households (Joe and Yu, 1984).

The problem is especially acute for college-educated African American women. More Black women than Black men are enrolled in college, and the gap is widening. Not wanting to marry men with less education than they have, almost one-third of college-educated Black women remain unmarried past the age of 30 (U.S. Bureau of the Census, 1999a). Compared to White women, African American women place greater importance on having economic supports in place prior to marriage and are more resistant to marrying someone who has few resources (Bulcroft and Bulcroft, 1993). Overall, both Black men and Black women are significantly less likely to marry than are their White counterparts (South, 1993). African Americans also have strong kinship bonds, so the single mother is not necessarily left to raise her child on her own. Rather, she can rely on the assistance of members of her extended family (Hampson, Beavers, and Hulgus, 1990; Jackson and Berg-Cross, 1988; R. J. Taylor, Chatters, and Mays, 1988).

increasing proportions since the end of World War II, women have entered and remained in the labor force. Today, a greater percentage of women are able to support themselves and do not need a man's income in order to afford children. However, the most common reason for becoming a single mother is the basic desire to be a mother, regardless of economic resources. In the words of a single mother, "[I had a child] for the same reason I think any woman wants a child. I couldn't imagine not having a child. It's a greater passion than anything else" (Siegel, 1995, p. 202). Although they wanted a child, many single mothers were concerned about how their marital status would affect their ability to manage as a mother and how it would affect their child. One mother remarked, "I sorta felt bad but I thought there are so many kids today who grow up without a father. It wouldn't be like it was unique but I was concerned about a male role model and I still am" (Siegel, 1995, p. 202).

Stated very simply, some single women became mothers because they wanted to when it was time to do it. Some single mothers who are satisfied with their marital status tend either to put a low priority on marriage or to feel certain that marriage is not for them. A woman who became a mother by adoption, about 5 years after her divorce, reflected, "It [marriage] is not something that I care whether it happens or not. I think it is wonderful, being in love and finding someone to live with. But I'm not seeking it out. If it happens, it happens" (Siegel, 1995, p. 203). Family sociologists have observed a 30-year trend in American society toward an increasing separation of marriage and childbearing. Older single women who choose to become mothers are contributing to this trend.

Single mothers who do not marry often express a concern that they will not do well in marriage, either because they are not sure how to make marriage work or because they are not interested in doing what they think is necessary for marriage to work. One woman remarked, "I never wanted to be married. In actuality, I always thought I would be, but I have not wanted to be in the real way and am

Many older singles value their independence, rarely feel isolated, and are generally happy with their lives.

probably not well suited to it" (Siegel, 1995 p. 204). Some women who bore children have a fear of marriage because they reject their own parents' marriage. Their parents were miserable in marriage, and these women do not want to repeat the pattern in their own lives (Siegel, 1995).

The research on single versus married people needs to address the all-important factor of the effect of being single or married and having children. Single parents and married parents experience parenthood differently. Long-term single parenting, usually performed by employed women, is a chronic stressor. Compared with their married counterparts, most single mothers have little relief from the responsibilities and burdens of parenting. Marriage typically provides social integration, social support, and emotional support; spouses have someone to talk to, someone to listen, someone who cares about them as individuals and who cares about their problems. Research has shown that emotional support reduces depression, anxiety, and other psychological problems. Married parents also receive instrumental support from their spouses. If they have competing or conflicting demands, they can often rely on their spouses to help out. In contrast, single parents are often on their own.

It is important to remember that not all single-parent families are alike. The characteristics of single parents such as gender, age, ethnicity, and education all influence how a single-parent family functions. Resources such as income and stressors such as residential instability can help determine whether single parents and their children experience positive or negative outcomes in terms of psychological well-being, health, and parent-child relationships (Amato, 2000). Single parents will be discussed further in Chapters 16 and 17.

THE NEVER-MARRIED ADULT

One difference between older adults who have never married and younger ones is that many younger singles consider their status temporary, whereas older singles are often well adjusted to their situation. Older singles usually have an active social life and do a variety of things with a few close friends (Keith and Nauta, 1988), and their patterns of social support differ from those found in married groups. For example, the never-married interact more frequently with friends and less often with relatives than do married people (Stull and Scarisbrick-Hauser, 1989).

Substitution theory posits that the never-married use more remote family members or nonfamily individuals for support compared with the married or the previously married (Shanas, 1979). The nonkin relationships that form the social networks of never-marrieds are sometimes referred to as "constructed" ties (Rubinstein, Alexander, Goodman, and Luborsky, 1991). While these relationships resemble friendships, they involve role sets that are similar to those found in families. In support of substitution theory, research has shown that, compared with the other groups, never-marrieds see their relatives less frequently and interact more often with friends and neighbors (Stull and Scarisbrick-Hauser, 1989). However, despite higher levels of interaction with friends, the never-married report less satisfaction from friendships than do the married.

Barrett (1999) suggested that differences in dimensions of social support between the never-married and other marital groups may be greatest in later life. Compared with marrieds, older never-marrieds are at a disadvantage, in part due to their lower probability of having confidants and their lower levels of interaction and perceived support. Analyses of informal interactions indicate that younger never-marrieds (ages 30–45) have more frequent interaction with friends and relatives than do their currently or previously married peers. However, this pattern reverses in two older groups (45–60, 60 and older). It is possible that during middle and later adulthood never-marrieds, in anticipation of health declines in old age, learn to be more self-reliant and independent than do marrieds (Barrett, 1999). A possible explanation for the difference between marrieds and never-marrieds in terms of having confidants in later life could involve the potential differences in the identities of confidants among the groups. For example, never-marrieds are likely to have primary confidants who are significantly older than themselves (such as parents or older siblings), while marrieds tend to have similar-age confidants (such as spouses). A factor in the higher proportion of never-marrieds reporting having no confidants in later life may be the loss of close social ties due to death, a phenomenon that occurs somewhat later among married individuals (Barrett, 1999).

Overall, however, the happiness of single older adults is very dependent on satisfaction with their standard of living and with their level of activity, rather than merely the extent of their social contacts. Adequate financial resources permit mobility and reciprocation in developing and maintaining friendships. Also, people who are satisfied with their level of activity even though they are isolated from family or friends tend to express greater happiness. A life alone doesn't necessarily mean a lonely one, and most people do eventually form intimate, committed relationships with someone.

A QUESTION OF POLICY

SEX OUTSIDE OF MARRIAGE

As discussed in the chapter, many people in the United States are sexually active outside of a marital relationship. Currently, the federal government provides $50 million in grants each year to states for sex education programs that focus on abstinence until marriage. States are required to match every four dollars of federal money with three dollars of state money. California is the only state that does not take the federal government's grant for abstinence-only programs. The language of the current law requires programs to teach young people that "sexual activity outside the context of marriage is likely to have harmful psychological and physical effects," among other messages. Furthermore, programs are not required to be evaluated for effectiveness and are prohibited from discussing condoms and other means of contraception as effective ways to prevent unintended pregnancy and the spread of STDs. The only topic related to contraception that may be discussed is that of failure rates (Sexuality Information and Education Council of the United States, 2002).

Indiana introduced a bill that would add a requirement to current sexuality education law that any program must "include instruction on maintaining self-control, resisting peer pressure, and establishing positive relationships in preparation for marriage." Current law has three other requirements: (1) that the program teach abstinence from sexual activity outside of marriage as the expected standard of all school-age children; (2) that the program include that abstinence from sexual activity is the only certain way to avoid out-of-wedlock pregnancy, sexually transmitted diseases, and other associated health problems; and (3) that the program include that the best way to avoid sexually transmitted diseases and other associated health problems is to establish a mutually faithful monogamous relationship in the context of marriage.

QUESTIONS TO CONSIDER:

Do you think the government's policy emphasizing abstinence-only sex education programs will be effective? Why or why not?

How would an abstinence-only policy have influenced you when you were in high school?

What do you think are the best methods for preventing unwanted pregnancy and the spread of sexually transmitted diseases?

If you could design a policy to address these issues, what would it look like?

SUMMARY

1. Overall, the great majority of people in the United States marry.

2. Adult singles may be divided into four groups: voluntary temporary singles, voluntary stable (permanent) singles, involuntary temporary singles, and involuntary stable (permanent) singles.

3. Most adults who are single delay marriage rather than remain permanently single. By ages 45–54, only 8.9% of men and 7.2% of women have never married.

4. The reasons for marital delay are social, economic, and personal.

5. Reasons people remain single include deliberate choice, fear of marriage, lack of opportunity, circumstances, and lack of a good relationship with their parents.

6. There are both advantages and disadvantages to being single. Advantages include greater opportunities for self-development, personal growth, and fulfillment; opportunities to meet different people and enjoy different friendships; economic independence and self-sufficiency; more varied sexual experiences; freedom to control one's own life; and more opportunities for career change, development, and expansion.

7. Disadvantages include loneliness and lack of companionship, economic hardship, feeling out of place in social gatherings organized for couples, sexual frustration, and the absence of children.

8. Overall, single people are less healthy physically and mentally than married people and have a shorter life expectancy. The divorced,

CHAPTER 5

After reading the chapter, you should be able to:

- Discuss and evaluate the factors that contribute to attraction.

- Trace the history of courtship from colonial America to the present day.

- Summarize the reasons for dating.

- Explain how dating can be functional or dysfunctional as a means of partner selection, depending on the qualities looked for in a date.

- Discuss the problem of finding and meeting dates.

- Describe the changes in gender roles in dating.

- Understand some of the major problems in dating, such as achieving honesty and openness, maintaining extradyadic relationships, and getting too serious.

- Discuss the problem of sexual aggression in dating.

- Discuss the problem of violence in dating.

- Describe ways to minimize the pain of breaking up a relationship.

Attraction and Dating

In this chapter, we are concerned with attraction and dating. We explore what attracts us to others and what qualities men and women find attractive in one another. The subject of attraction has fascinated social scientists for years. We now have some of the answers—not all of them, to be sure, but enough to shed considerable light on the subject of interpersonal attraction and its role in relationships. Also, we examine the many issues associated with dating—from systems of dating and reasons for dating, to the process of obtaining dating partners, to problems and violence in dating.

ATTRACTION

The most obvious kind of attraction is physical; our first impression is based on how someone looks. But attraction, especially if the relationship is a lasting one, is also based on the less tangible factors of personality traits and even one's own past experiences and conditioning.

Physical Attractiveness

The most important element in attraction—at least in initial encounters—is physical attractiveness. We are attracted to those who are pleasing to look at, have good builds and well-proportioned bodies, and display other physical characteristics that appeal to our aesthetic sensibilities. Study after study finds physical appearance to be one of the chief ingredients in early attraction. In fact, one study of college students revealed that physical attractiveness was more important than relevant sexual history in making judgments about potential risks and probable future sexual activity with the person. This was especially true for males (Agocha and Cooper, 1999).

There is also something called couple attractiveness, which is the perception other people have of the couple and the quality of their relationship (Garcia and Khersonsky, 1997). Couples whose members differ in physical attractiveness are perceived differently. A currently dating opposite-sex couple in which both the man and the woman are physically attractive or in which the woman is attractive but the man is unattractive are perceived more favorably than are unattractive male/unattractive female couples and attractive male/unattractive female couples. They are also perceived as more satisfied with their current relationship than the others and as less likely to break up. In short, couples in which both members are physically attractive and in which the woman is attractive and the man is not are viewed as the most stable and happiest (Garcia and Khersonsky, 1997).

Standards of Attractiveness

Standards of attractiveness are culturally conditioned. In U.S. culture, slender women are considered more attractive than obese ones, tall men more attractive than short ones, and youthful men and women more attractive than the elderly. In contrast, in some cultures, obesity is synonymous with physical beauty.

Furthermore, in U.S. culture, standards of beauty have changed over time. For example, the mean bust-waist-hip measurements of Miss America contest winners in the 1920s were 32-25-35, with no winner having a larger bust than hips. In the 1940s, the mean measurements were 35-24-35, In this same era, Hollywood introduced the "sweater girl" Lana Turner and the buxom Jane Russell. Since 1950, the norm has been bust-hip symmetry, with an ideal measurement of 36-24-36.

As the 1950s progressed, the women featured as *Playboy* magazine's "Playmate of the Month" had increasingly larger breasts. This was a period of "mammary madness," with Hollywood and the fashion industry promoting large, cleaved bustlines, tiny waists, and wiggly-hipped walks (Mazur, 1986). Since that time, Playmates have become increasingly taller and leaner, but they still have large breasts in proportion to body size. At the same time, the idealized women shown in fashion magazines and on television often are far below the normal weight recommendations, bordering on the anorexic (Mann, 1994). It is interesting to note that Miss America contestants work out an average of 14 hours a week, and some as many as 35 hours a week, in order to achieve the current body ideal (Wilfley and Rodin, 1995). Thus, in the 1990s, the body size and shape of the average young adult became increasingly different from the underweight ideal being promoted by the media (Spitzer, Henderson, and Zivian, 1999).

Unfortunately, these standards of attractiveness do not make life easier for the average person. It is no wonder that the current standards of attractiveness for women promoted by the media lead women to rate their bodies negatively (Hamilton and Waller, 1993). Studies have reported body dissatisfaction greater than 60 percent for high school girls (Garner, 1997) and greater than 80 percent for college women (Silberstein, Striegel-Moore, Timko, and Rodin, 1998). A large percentage of young women feel that they are too heavy and are trying to lose weight even when their weight is within, or even below, the range that is considered healthy (K. L. Green et al., 1997). One of the most pervasive criticisms of advertising is that it promotes distorted body images by setting unrealistic standards of thinness and female beauty (Lavine, Sweeney, and Wagner, 1999), which only increases women's insecurities about and dissatisfaction with their bodies.

Personality and Social Factors

Factors other than physical appearance attract people to each other. In a study of mate selection standards, Regan (1998) found that women required higher levels of agreeableness (attentiveness to a partner's needs, kindness and understanding, honesty and trustworthiness) in a marriage partner than any other attribute, and they rated dominance as the least important trait. In a study of desired characteristics in a spouse, Regan and Berscheid (1997) found that women desired honesty, trustworthiness, and sensitivity above all other characteristics. However, they preferred a different characteristic—namely, physical attractiveness—for short-term and sexual partners (Regan, 1998; Regan and Berscheid, 1997). In contrast, some researchers have reported that women prefer dominant males characterized by high levels of assertiveness and confidence and high financial and social status. For example, Buss and Schmitt (1993) concluded that a man's ability to accrue resources was related to women's desire for either a short- or a long-term relationship. Ambition, industry, income, and status were all considered observable cues to a mate's potential value. Similarly, Botwin, Buss, and Shackelford (1997) reported that power, social ascendance, and resource acquisition were more prevalent in women's preferences for potential mates than in men's preferences. There is a discrepancy in the research findings, however. So-called nice guys, who are sensitive, patient, and nurturing, appear to be favored by many women, but men who are dominant, confident, and aggressive have reported the most sexual success with women (Reise and Wright, 1996).

The standards of beauty by which Miss America contestants are judged have changed over the years.

Other studies have confirmed that personality traits and the way people act are significant factors in whether others find them attractive. In general, people who are warm, kind, gregarious, intelligent, interesting, poised, confident, or humorous or who exhibit generally admired qualities are more attractive than those who are rude, insecure, clumsy, insensitive, unstable, or irresponsible or who manifest other negative traits.

Unconscious Influences

Sometimes people are not aware of why they find another person attractive. Unconscious factors are often at work. If, for example, we experienced love and security with our opposite-sex parent while we were growing up, we may seek to duplicate the

In eighteenth-century America, if a man desired the company of a woman, he had to meet her family, be formally introduced, and obtain permission to court her.

relationship and so be attracted to a dating partner or spouse who reminds us of that parent. Or we may be attracted to those who meet our needs and who make us feel good about ourselves. Some people are attracted to those who are helpless, alone, handicapped, or dependent; taking care of someone else makes them feel needed, important, and wanted. Other people are attracted to their "ego ideal," to someone who has all the qualities they wish they had. A smile, a glance, or a mannerism may trigger a positive response because of conditioning that took place years before.

THE DATING SYSTEM

Dating—defined as a courting practice in which two people meet and participate in activities together in order to get to know each other—is rare in most of the world. For example, it is uncommon in China and India, which together account for over half the world's population, as well as in most areas of Africa and South America and in some Mediterranean countries, such as Greece, Spain, and Portugal. It is forbidden by many families in Egypt, Saudi Arabia, Iran, Libya, and other Muslim countries.

Dating is widely practiced in most of western Europe and is most common in the United States, Great Britain, Canada, Australia, and New Zealand. In these countries, it is now recognized as *the* method by which young men and women get to know one another, learn to get along socially, and select partners by mutual choice.

Dating is a relatively recent phenomenon in the United States; it did not become firmly established until the years after World War I. Before that time, courtship consisted mainly of the young man paying formal visits to the young woman and her family. Dating evolved when marriage started to become an individual rather than a family decision and when love and mutual attraction started to become the basis for marriage.

Courtship in Early America

In the 1700s and 1800s, casual meetings at unsupervised social affairs were condemned. Parents carefully supervised the activities of their children, especially their daughters. Young women were not left alone to meet young men casually and indiscriminately. If a man desired the company of a woman, he had to meet her family, be formally introduced, and obtain permission to court her, as well as gain her permission to be courted, before they could "step out." Even after a couple had been formally introduced, they often were chaperoned (especially upper-class women) or attended social functions only in the company of friends or relatives. Parents exerted considerable influence, and even veto power, over whom a son or daughter might see or consider for marriage. Parents were concerned about the social standing and prestige, economic status, education, and family background of potential suitors. And if a young man wanted to marry a woman, he had to ask her father's permission for her hand.

At this time, marriage in Europe was arranged by parents, with little emphasis on romantic attraction. With some arranged marriages, parents sought to merge the property and good name of the families to ensure economic well-being and the perpetuation of family status and prestige. Only a few American marriages were parentally arranged. These were limited to the most aristocratic families, which sought to expand their financial empires through marriage. American courtship was controlled more by the participants, who exercised autonomy and freedom.

The Emergence of Dating

By the late nineteenth and early twentieth centuries, chaperonage and close supervision of courtship had declined. A new pattern of dating emerged whereby young people themselves arranged a time and place to meet. The primary purpose was to have fun and enjoy each other's company. Parents might have sought to maintain some control of dating partners, but the system usually allowed a high level of freedom from parental supervision.

In the years following World War I, the dating system was still comparatively stylized and formal. The man was expected to take the initiative in asking the woman for a date. Generally, he was expected to plan the activities, pay all the expenses, and exercise his masculine prerogatives as the leader. Over the years, however, the pattern became less structured and more informal, with greater equality between the sexes in initiating and planning dates. Today, couples frequently simply "get together" to do things or to "go out," without going through a specific ritual. "Going together" has replaced the formal patterns of courtship of previous generations.

The emergence of dating was due to numerous factors. The most important was the industrial revolution. Thousands of families moved from farms to crowded cities, where young people had increased opportunities for social contact. Lower-class women were employed in the mills and factories, where they met male workers. Some girls from farm families took up residence in boardinghouses away from home and so were separated from parental supervision. The invention of the telephone made regular contact much easier.

At the same time, the late 1800s saw the rise of free public high schools, where large numbers of physically mature youths were brought together for coeducational schooling (private academies had segregated the sexes). These schools offered activities that brought youths together for recreation and companionship and that promoted dating.

Increased affluence and leisure time allowed people to devote more time to their own pursuits and social lives. Having a date became a pleasant way to spend an evening. During and after World War I, middle-class women began to work in offices and stores and attained greater economic and personal freedom. For the first time, they were allowed to wear less restrictive clothing and to engage in strenuous sports. (They participated in the Olympic Games for the first time in 1920.) This new freedom allowed them to engage in many of these activities with men.

The invention and use of the automobile increased mobility and provided transportation to roadhouses, nightclubs, parties, dances, theaters, and restaurants. Dating couples could go from place to place or simply park.

The 1920s also witnessed an early surge in the women's equality movement. The women's movement encouraged women's rights politically, socially, and sexually and made it possible for young women to participate on a more equal basis with young men in the total life of the community. Liberated women with their bobbed hair and flapper dresses were now free to take a ride in their boyfriend's car and to engage in intimacy without being under the watchful eye of chaperones. As a result, dating emerged as an important part of the life of American youths, replacing the previous system of formalized courtship.

dating A courting practice in which two people meet and participate in activities together in order to get to know each other.

The Rating and Dating Complex of the 1930s

During the 1930s, Willard Waller (1937) observed dating behavior on the campus of Pennsylvania State University and published a paper titled "The Rating and Dating Complex." The report caused quite a stir because it described dating as a superficial, exploitative relationship rather than as a means of finding and selecting a future marriage partner. Men outnumbered women six to one on the campus, which resulted in much competition for dates. The fraternity system was flourishing. Men and women were rated according to their desirability as a date. Class A men belonged to one of the better fraternities, engaged in prestigious activities, had plenty of money and access to an automobile, were good conversationalists and dancers, were well dressed, and so were considered highly desirable dates. Men who did not rate in Class A were placed in a lower class: B, C, or D. Women with high ratings wore good clothes, were good conversationalists, could dance well, and were considered popular. Coeds tried to give the impression of being sought after even if they did not belong to Class A. Young women often allowed themselves to be paged several times in the dorm when the telephone rang for them. They were never supposed to make themselves available for last-minute dates. They avoided being seen too often with the same young man so as not to discourage others, and they tried to have many partners at dances. Above all, Class A women dated only Class A men, and so forth. The system emphasized emotional excitement. Pretending to be in love was an important part of the game, as each person wanted to feel more involved than he or she was.

Other research has substantiated part of Waller's description of campus life of the 1920s and 1930s, especially the role that fraternities and sororities played in creating social activities. According to Fass (1977), the University of Wisconsin hosted 30 college dances and 80 fraternity and sorority dances each month in 1925. However, other observers looked at campus life in the 1930s and reported that the rating game was already cooling in intensity (Gordon, 1981). Certainly, the Great Depression altered undergraduate culture. College enrollments dipped, and Greek letter societies declined and were less able to maintain their dominant role on

campuses. World War II completed the transformation. Automobile rides and partying declined for the duration.

Today, there are still some prestige dimensions to cross-sex socializing, but the rating and dating complex has virtually disappeared. Pluralistic dating has given way to exclusive dating, but not necessarily to relationships oriented toward choosing a partner.

Dating and Courtship from the 1940s to the 1960s

The most important dating pattern to emerge just prior to World War II was that of **steady dating**—dating one person exclusively. This pattern developed as an outgrowth of both romantic contacts at younger ages and the practice of group and random dating in junior high school and early high school. Steady dating was an intermediate form between casual dating and engagement, since it involved a transition between the lack of commitment of casual dating and the very high commitment of engagement. This intermediate stage was necessary for individuals who were allowed personal responsibility for the selection of partners.

One of the best descriptions of the dating and courtship system of the 1950s was given by LeMasters (1957) in his book *Modern Courtship and Marriage*. The six stages LeMasters identified are shown in Table 5.1. These stages represented an orderly progression from the first date in the junior high

Table 5.1   Stages in Dating and Courtship in the 1950s

Ages or Grades	Stage
7th, 8th grade	Group dating
9th, 10th grade	Random dating between "steadies"
11th, 12th grade	Steady dating
College years (earlier for women, later for men)	Pinning
College years, or post–high school years	Engagement
Ages 19–21 for women, 20–24 for men	Marriage

Note: Reprinted with the permission of Simon & Schuster Adult Publishing Group from *Modern Courtship and Marriage* by E. E. LeMasters. Copyright © 1957 by Macmillan Publishing Company.

In the 1930s, dating was often a way of gaining prestige rather than a means of finding a future marriage partner. What kinds of changes have occurred in dating and courtship since then?

school years until marriage in the late teens or early twenties. An adolescent girl usually had her first crush in junior high school; boys reached this stage 1 or 2 years later. At each stage, the relationship was excessively romantic, with other considerations subordinate to the fact that the two were madly in love. Each successive stage involved a progressively deeper commitment. Each stage also implied an appropriate degree of sexual intimacy: the more commitment, the greater the intimacy that was allowed. This led one young man to remark:

> I often had the uncomfortable feeling that the California coed dispensed passion by some sort of rule book. It had all been decided beforehand: the first date, so many kisses, the second date, lips apart, tongue enters, fifth date, three buttons, next time, one zipper. . . . (G. Green, 1964, p. 131)

"Steadies" frequently broke up and realigned themselves with others, but broken engagements were serious matters.

There was sense and logic to the system except when a couple moved too rapidly from the earliest stages to marriage. Speeding up the courtship process was more common among lower-class youths than among middle-class youths—resulting in an increasing number of marriages at younger ages—

until the trend began to be reversed in the early 1960s.

Dating at the End of the Twentieth Century

A major change in dating was the increase in opportunities for informal sexual contacts. For example, high schools and colleges that used to be exclusively for men or women became coeducational. Many college dormitories had become coed, academic programs that used to attract only one sex or the other now enrolled both men and women, and some fraternities became coeducational. Also, men and women shared apartments and houses. These changes represented a drastic departure from the days when college men and women ate and slept in different parts of the campus. With such segregation, it was more difficult to get together, and often a formal phone call was required to arrange a meeting or a date. Group or paired social activities developed as a natural result of daily informal contacts in residences, classrooms, and social centers.

steady dating Dating one person exclusively.

Another major change was the lack of any set pattern of progression of intimacy and commitment from initial meeting to marriage. Earlier generations followed a fairly consistent pattern: casual dating, steady dating, going steady, an understanding (engaged to be engaged), engagement, and marriage. Some partners in the last decades of the twentieth century did follow the traditional pattern; others decided to date each other exclusively and, after a period of time, to live together before getting married. There may have been no formal engagement, but marriage developed out of the cohabitation experience. In other words, not all couples worked up to a formal engagement and then marriage. Patterns of dating and courtship varied.

Dating became much less formal than in previous generations. It was not necessary for the man to make a formal request in order to arrange a date. This sometimes happened, but a date may have been arranged by mutual consent as a result of conversation about the evening activities. In addition, more women began taking the initiative in arranging a get-together. Dress became certainly more casual, and the activities became often less formal or more casually planned. Many times, a social evening was not really called a date. Couples simply went out together for an informal evening.

Dating Today

Dating and getting together have undergone many changes since they emerged as a social phenomenon. *Getting together* is a popular term used today by many adolescents to describe the practice of going out with a group of friends to get to know potential intimate partners rather than going out with one individual on a date. These meetings are usually informal and casual. This change in dating patterns may be due to the reduced pressure to marry. Many of today's teens will remain single throughout their twenties and engage in casual dating relationships during the 10 or more years before they possibly get married.

Many researchers who study dating today believe that it is not oriented to marriage, as the dating culture was in the past. Confusion surrounds dating because the rules have not merely changed—but some believe there are very few rules at all anymore. Cere (2000) believes that courtship no longer occupies a vital place in American culture, and that men

and women can no longer turn to socially prescribed forms of conduct to help them find their way to marriage.

One study based on telephone interviews with a nationally representative sample of 1,000 college women found that they were indeed confused about dating on campus (Glenn and Marquardt, 2001). The study revealed that women felt they have basically two options: hooking up briefly with a male for casual sex or being so seriously involved with a partner that most free time is spent with him. The study found that hookups were common, with about 40% of women having had one hookup, and 10% having had more than six. The definition of **hooking up** varies, but generally it means engaging in anything from kissing to having intercourse without emotional involvement. Frequently, partners are almost strangers, have been drinking, get together for a physical encounter, and don't expect anything else. Thus, hookups are often defined by alcohol, physical attraction, and a lack of expectations in the morning. Glenn and Marquardt (2001) found that women are ambivalent about hookups. Some reported feeling hurt and awkward afterward if they had hoped for something more out of a relationship, while other women reported feeling strong, desirable, and sexy. The other side of hookups is what the study called the "joined at the hip" relationship, which develops quickly and is very intense and exclusive.

The lack of ritualized dating appears to be no different among noncollege men and women. Popenoe and Whitehead (2002b) gathered descriptions of the contemporary dating scene from noncollege men and women to explore the reasoning behind their views on mate selection, cohabitation, and future marriage. They described the dating scene today as a low-commitment culture of "sex without strings and relationships without rings" (Popenoe and Whitehead, 2002b). They found that young men and women today want to marry a best friend and "soul mate" who will share and understand their most intimate feelings, needs and desires. However, despite the strongly held aspiration for marriage and the ideal of a lifelong soul mate, young people, and especially young women, were not confident that they would achieve this goal. The men and women in this study rarely used the word *love* or the phrase *falling in love*. Instead, they talked about sex and relationships, and they considered sex as being for fun. Most regarded casual sex as an expected part of the dating scene, and only a few took a moralistic stand against it. Both men and women also agreed that casual sex is no-strings-attached sex, as it requires no commitments beyond the sexual encounter itself and no ethical obligation beyond mutual consent. In addition, it was reported that when women and men hook up for sex, they assume that their partner is likely to lie about past sexual history (Popenoe and Whitehead, 2002b).

Although some women still demand that men ask them out, take them to dinner, and get to know them before the subject of sex comes up, there are a lot of people agreeing to quick, casual sex (Townsend, 1998). Cherlin (1996) believes that this change in dating has resulted in the loss of the ability to slow down the process of becoming intimate and choosing a partner and that many times intimacy just comes too fast. Thus, some social scientists and religious leaders are calling for a return to the rules of courtship. Popenoe and Whitehead (2002b) believe that the virtual disappearance of adult participation in, or even awareness of, how today's young people find and marry one another should be seen as a major social problem.

There are some signs of change, however. Some people are recognizing that something has been missing over the last decade, and women especially are increasingly fed up with the hookup culture (Kass and Kass, 2000). On the other hand, most social demographers predict a continuation of the current trends; they see these trends as being persistent and pervasive across advanced Western societies (Popenoe and Whitehead, 2002b). Thus, we are left with interesting questions: Who is right? What will dating look like in the next 50 years?

REASONS FOR DATING

One of the most significant changes in dating patterns is in the reasons for dating. Dating fulfills a number of important functions in the lives of today's youth.

First, dating is a form of recreation. One reason couples go out is simply to relax, enjoy themselves, and have fun. It is a form of entertainment and thereby an end in itself.

Second, dating provides companionship, friendship, and personal intimacy. Many young people

have an intense desire to develop close, intimate relationships through dating. One study found that those couples who were able to share their most important thoughts and feelings in an egalitarian relationship were those most likely to be compatible and in love (Rubin, Hill, Peplau, and Dunkel-Schetter, 1980).

Third, dating is a means of socialization. Dating helps people learn social skills, gain confidence and poise, and begin to master the arts of conversation, cooperation, and consideration for others.

Fourth, dating contributes to personality development. One way in which individuals can establish their own identity is in relationship to other people. Since individuals mature primarily through successful experiences with others and since an adequate self-concept is partly a result of successful human associations, an important part of personality development is successful dating experiences. One of the reasons young people date is that such associations give them security and feelings of individual worth.

Fifth, dating provides an opportunity to try out gender roles. Gender roles must be worked out in real-life situations with partners. Many women today find that they cannot accept a traditionally passive role; dating helps them discover this and learn what kinds of roles they find fulfilling in close relationships. Men also try out the roles they want to assume in relationships.

Sixth, dating is a means of fulfilling the need for love and affection. No matter how many casual friends people have, they meet their deepest emotional needs for love and affection in close relationships with other individuals. This need for affection is one of the major motives for dating.

Seventh, dating provides an opportunity for sexual experimentation and satisfaction. Dating has become more sex-oriented, with an increasing percentage of young people engaging in sexual intercourse (Michael et al., 1994).

Eighth, dating is a means of selecting a long-term partner. In our culture, dating is the method

hooking up Engaging in sexual behavior—from kissing to having intercourse—without emotional involvement.

and women perceived themselves as equally successful in initiating relationships, men initiated more romantic relationships than did women. Men were more confident and more likely to use the strategies of manipulating the setting and being direct. A greater percentage of men than women were seeking sexual intimacy in the beginning states of their romantic relationship. Women were more likely to rely on the man to initiate the relationship and were more likely to be concerned about the risk of an unsuccessful initiation attempt. Thus, they were less direct, less motivated, and less likely to initiate a relationship with a potential partner. Women described themselves, and men described them, as being passive and using indirect or subtle strategies in relationship initiation. These findings are consistent with the literature on gender differences in communication. They also coincide with the evolutionary perspective, according to which females are heavily invested in each reproductive act and must be more discriminating than males about the quality of their partners (Clark, Shaver, and Abrahams, 1999). Thus, the researchers concluded that females take a more tentative approach to relationship initiation, making sure to evaluate prospective partners more carefully.

PROBLEMS IN DATING

Some type of dating is usually an important part of the social life of young people. Yet some people haven't learned the social skills and developed the self-confidence for a meaningful relationship to develop. Problems surrounding dating usually involve issues of communication and intimacy; maturity and some intimacy skills are required to handle these inevitable problems. One study of adolescent boys found that those who started dating early often experienced a big emotional letdown because they found themselves in relationships before they were fully equipped to handle them. These emotional letdowns caused the boys to have negative feelings about themselves and to have a difficult time bouncing back when the relationship ended. The study suggested that this behavior can harm boys' self-esteem and that boys are more vulnerable in dating relationships than previously thought. Because girls tend to get more prac-

tice at disclosing their feelings (mostly with each other) than boys do, it could be that boys have less confidence in their skills for sharing intimate information and thus take more emotional risk when they do self-disclose (Darling, Dowdy, Van-Horn, and Caldwell, 1999). When people (whether male or female) lack emotional maturity, they create expectations that are harmful to the development of a satisfying relationship.

Honesty and Openness

Men and women both look for honesty and openness in relationships. Because men and women strive to be on their best behavior while dating, a certain amount of pretense or playacting, called **imaging,** is necessary for them to present themselves in the best possible manner.

Researchers have found that men tend to deceive dating partners about commitment levels and financial resources and that women tend to deceive dating partners about physical attributes (Tooke and Camire, 1991). In one study (Keenan, Gallup, Goulet, and Kulkarni, 1997), researchers surveyed 60 undergraduate students about deception in dating strategies by members of the opposite sex and rated the responses according to financial, commitment, and physical dimensions of deception. For example, on the commitment subscale, one item read, "On a date, a person of the opposite gender would portray themselves as more interested in having a long-term relationship than they actually are." The survey revealed that women expect significantly more deception on financial characteristics from men than men expect from women. Women also expect more deception from men on variables related to commitment than men expect from women. However, men do not anticipate significantly more deception from women about physical characteristics than women expect from men. Overall, women expect significantly more deception from men than men expect from women. Women are especially suspicious of claims made by males who are sexually interested in them. These findings support the idea that women, who bear the greater cost for procreation and thus greater corresponding reproductive risk, are more selective and cautious at choosing a partner than are men (Keenan et al., 1997).

Extradyadic Relationships

One of the considerations in dating is whether to have sexual relationships outside the dating dyad. Certainly, there is ample evidence that both men and women most desire and experience sexual intercourse within a caring relationship (Sherwin and Corbett, 1985). The more involvement, the more men and women both desire and experience intercourse (McCabe, 1987).

The real question, however, is: To what extent do couples in committed dating relationships engage in **extradyadic sexual activity,** and with what effect? Hansen (1987) asked 215 college students who had ever been in a committed dating relationship to respond to the following question: "While in a committed dating relationship, have you ever engaged in the following with someone other than your dating partner?" Erotic kissing, intimate touching, and sexual intercourse were listed. Thirty-five percent of the men and 12% of the women reported having sexual intercourse with someone else while involved in a committed dating relationship. A little more than 40% of men and women were certain or fairly sure their dating partner knew about it. About 40% of both men and women felt their own extradyadic relations had hurt their dating relationships. But when their partner had had extradyadic relations, more than 70% of both men and women felt it had hurt their dating relationship. Apparently, the students were more accepting of their own extradyadic sexual relations than they were of their partner's.

In another study, Wiederman and Hurd (1999) asked 621 college students about their experiences with extradyadic dating and sexual activity. Despite general disapproval of extradyadic involvement, a majority of the respondents reported having had such an involvement. There were no gender differences in the incidence of extradyadic dating, but men were more likely than women to experience extradyadic fondling, oral sex, and intercourse. In general, extradyadic dating was related to less adherence to the belief that sex, love, and marriage should be associated, to increased sexual sensation seeking, and to a self-perceived ability to deceive one's partner.

Getting Too Serious

Another of the dating problems people face is the situation of one person getting more serious than the other person desires. A University of Maine student wrote:

> I am not ready for and have no immediate intentions of getting married—for the next five to ten years anyway. Through my dates I have made some very close personal male friends. But for the past three years the situations have ended abruptly because each time my partner decided the relationship was more serious than I wanted. How can I keep my enjoyable and good contacts without leading them on? (From a student paper)

Another student complained, "No matter what we're talking about, my partner always gets around to hinting about marriage, but I'm not ready to settle down. I have two more years of college and then grad school ahead of me."

Sometimes couples make a premature commitment; then one of them has second thoughts and wants to discontinue the relationship. People in new romances tend to expect that their relationship will last longer than it actually does (R. Buehler, Griffin, and Ross, 1995). Individuals who have made the decision to enter a dating relationship may focus on its present strengths and on their positive feelings and fail to consider the potential challenges to the relationship (T. MacDonald and Ross, 1999). Women are more likely than men to have second thoughts. One man wrote:

> My current girlfriend is very serious about getting married, but I'm not at all sure about the relationship now. How do I explain this to her (a very sensitive person), especially after I expressed a sincere desire to marry her at one time? (From a student paper)

Sometimes both people begin to realize that something is wrong in the relationship, but each is afraid to tell the other. In most instances, each partner needs to express the doubts, inquire about the other person's feelings, and discuss viewpoints

imaging The process of playacting to present oneself in the best possible manner.

extradyadic sexual activity Sexual activity outside the dyadic, or couple, relationship.

tactfully but openly. Most problems can be dealt with only by honest and sensitive communication.

Closeness and Distance in Relationships

Closeness and distance are both important needs in a dating relationship, and much research has focused on individuals' strategies for balancing closeness and distance (Feeney, 1999a). Romantic relationships involve many such "contradictions," and the need for a balance between autonomy and connection is one of the central ones (Baxter and Simon, 1993). Although any romantic relationship requires each individual to give up some autonomy in order to develop a couple identity, giving up too much of one's own identity can be problematic. This contradiction has been called the "me–we pull," because the individual has a desire both to be true to his or her self and to be flexible enough to make the relationship work (Baxter, 1990). Baxter and Montgomery (1997) suggested that romantic partners deal with these issues over the course of the relationship but never fully resolve them, as the needs for autonomy and distance are constantly changing.

It is important to remember that every individual is unique and has different needs for distance and closeness in a relationship. In general, men and women differ in their interaction patterns in dating relationships. Researchers have found that women want more closeness in their intimate relationships than men do and that these needs are related to differences in patterns of communication. Women push for active discussion of relationship issues, whereas men tend to withdraw from such discussions (A. Christensen and Heavey, 1990). These differences are related to gender-role socialization whereby women are taught to be caretakers of relationships and men are taught to be independent and self-reliant. Unfortunately, these patterns tend to cause conflicts over intimacy levels in romantic relationships (Baxter and Montgomery, 1997).

People's attachment styles, which are developed early in life, also affect their need for closeness and distance in dating relationships. Studies of adult romantic attachment styles have consistently revealed two major dimensions: (1) comfort with closeness and (2) anxiety over relationships (see Feeney and Noller, 1996, for a review). Individuals who are comfortable with closeness prefer a balanced type of relationship, characterized by high levels of openness and closeness but also by a certain amount of independence. Individuals who are highly anxious about their relationships typically seek extreme closeness to partners and become overdependent on them. Avoidant individuals want the most distance in their relationships and so limit closeness, dependence, and affection (Feeney and Noller, 1991).

In a study of distance regulation in established dating relationships, the overwhelming majority (92%) of participants referred to issues of closeness and distance, such as partners' needs for autonomy and connection, the amount of time spent together versus apart, and involvement in individual versus joint activities (Feeney, 1999a). Couples with two secure partners were less likely to report problems with distance regulation than were couples in which one or both partners were insecure. The following statements highlight the importance of considering the attachment styles of both partners:

> I've never let anybody get really close to me. I think it's just like a self-defense mechanism that I have, to not get hurt. I always keep, you know—there's always a thin distance that I don't let people come near me; not a physical touch, but I think, spiritual. To me this is important, my own space. To have someone invade that space that is special to me, I feel violated. I get angry, I get irritated, I get very irritated. (Feeney, 1999a, p. 579)

> If they don't want to be with you . . ., you wonder what you've done wrong. Or you wonder why; if they don't love you anymore, or if they don't find you attractive anymore, or if they're bored with you, or if it's the end of the road. That's the hardest thing; if S doesn't want to be with me emotionally or doesn't want to be with me, there's nothing to look forward to [sniffling]. There's nothing at all, nothing I can do. It makes me quite miserable, quite alone and quite neglected; ugly, fat, boring, uninteresting; like a nothing. (Feeney, 1999a, p. 579)

SEXUAL AGGRESSION AND DATING VIOLENCE

Sexual aggression can take many forms. It may be limited to verbal coercion in order to obtain sex, or it may include physical attempts as well. Sometimes those attempts take the form of date rape, which has become an increasingly reported problem. Sometimes conflict on dates escalates into other forms of violence, such as physical abuse. Dating violence may be defined as the perpetration or threat of an act of violence by at least one member of an unmarried couple on the other member within the context of dating or courtship (D. B. Sugarman and Hotaling, 1989).

Violence is, unfortunately, not rare in dating relationships. Estimates vary because studies and surveys use different methods and definitions of violence and because many violent acts go unreported. The term *hidden rape* has emerged because many studies find that sexual assaults are not reported to the police, and some estimates indicate that fewer than 50% of all rapes are reported (Dupre, Hampton, Morrison, and Meeks, 1993). Thus, the incidence of violence in intimate relationships is probably much higher than the data indicate.

The National Center for Injury Prevention and Control (2002) estimates that nonsexual dating violence occurs in anywhere from 9% to 65% of dating relationships; the broad range is due in part to whether threats and emotional or verbal aggression are included in the definition. Evidence from a variety of studies indicates that physical violence occurs in at least 20% of dating relationships, and that from 80% to 95% of the rapes that occur on college campuses are committed by someone known to the victim (Abbey, Ross, Mcduffie, and Mcauslan, 1996).

In a study of eighth- and ninth-grade male and female students, it was found that 25% had been victims of nonsexual dating violence and 8% had been victims of sexual dating violence (Foshee et al., 1996). Among college students, a study revealed that, of those who had ever dated, 36.4% of the females and 37.1% of the males reported physical violence in a dating relationship (Molder and Tolman, 1998). In another study of more than 1,000 female students at a large urban university, over half had experienced some form of unwanted sex, with 12% of these acts being perpetrated by casual dates and 43% by steady dating partners (Abbey et al., 1996).

While both women and men report aggression and violence in dating relationships, the type of violence experienced is very different. A study of 857 undergraduate and graduate students indicated that women were more likely to experience sexual victimization, whereas men were more often the victims of psychological aggression (Harned, 2001). While both genders experience aggressive acts from dating partners, the impact of such violence is more severe for women than men (Harned, 2001). Because of this, much of the discussion in this section focuses on dating violence against women, but this is not to discount that men are also the victims of violence.

Psychological and Emotional Effects of Dating Violence

Violence can have a devastating effect on many aspects of a victim's life. An act of violence is not an isolated incident that only invokes physical harm—it affects the whole person. Research is now reporting that adolescents who endure either sexual or physical violence on a date are more likely than other adolescents to engage in subsequent behavior that threatens their health.

One study asked thousands of high school girls if they had ever been hit, slapped, shoved, or forced into sexual activity. Approximately 20% of the girls reported an abusive dating experience. Experiences with date violence and rape were associated with binge drinking, cocaine use, heavy smoking, multiple sexual partners, unhealthy weight control, and suicide attempts (Silverman, Raj, Mucci, and Hathaway, 2001). High school girls who were exposed to dating violence were four to six times more likely than their peers who were not abused to have been pregnant and eight to nine times more likely to have tried suicide in the previous year. The researchers concluded that dating violence is extremely prevalent in high school, and adolescent girls who report a history of experiencing dating violence are more likely to exhibit other serious health risk behaviors. However, the study did not address the question of whether dating violence causes teens to engage in unhealthy behaviors or whether already-troubled girls are more likely to date violent partners.

Dating violence has also been linked with eating problems. In a survey of 81,247 9th- and 12th-graders, Ackard and Neumark-Sztainer (2002) found that 1 in 10 girls and 1 in 20 boys had been raped and/or violently assaulted on dates, and that they were far more likely than other teens to develop serious eating disorders. The study found that 9% of girls and 6% of boys experienced violence and/or rape on dates. Girls who had been raped or physically assaulted were about twice as likely as other girls to binge or fast. Boys who experienced violent attacks were three times more likely to fast. The study also found poorer mental health overall among youths assaulted on dates. Ackard and Neumark-Sztainer believe that abusive experiences during dating relationships may disrupt normal developmental processes of thought, feeling, and behavior, including the development of a stable self-concept and integrated body image during adolescence.

In another study, 5,414 high school students were asked to complete the Youth Risk Behavior Survey, in which date violence was assessed with the following question: "During the last 12 months, how many times were you physically beaten up by the person you date or go out with?" Being physically beaten up was defined as being hit, kicked, or thrown down. Approximately 9% of females and 5% of males reported being the victim of violence on a date. Experience with date violence was associated with poorer quality of life, overall dissatisfaction with life and with friends, and thoughts and attempts of suicide for adolescent females. For adolescent males, dating violence was associated with dissatisfaction with life, poor perceived physical health, and suicidal ideas (Coker, McKeown et al., 2000).

The Youth Risk Behavior Survey was also used to collect data on 2,629 high school females. Date violence was assessed by asking, "Have you ever had a dating situation become violent with hitting or force used?" Approximately 14% of girls in the study reported violence on a date. Females who reported a violent dating situation were three times as likely to engage in purging behavior, and nearly two times as likely to use diet pills for weight control than females who did not report a violent dating experience (Thompson, Wonderlich, Crosby, and Mitchell, 2001).

Verbal Sexual Coercion

Men are more likely than women to use verbal coercion to obtain sex, but not all men use verbal coercion. A study of 194 undergraduate males at a large state university grouped subjects into three levels of sexual experience (Craig, Kalichman, and Follingstad, 1989). Twelve percent were classified

as being sexually inexperienced, 46% had had only consensual sexual relations, and 42% had used verbal coercion to obtain sex. Those in the first two groups approached relationships with women in terms of a broad spectrum of possibilities, including friendship, companionship, and enjoyment. Those in the third group saw relationships with women in terms of sexual possibilities. They placed a great deal of emphasis on the value of sex, devalued—but did not hate—women, and used a wide range of manipulative techniques: They said things they really didn't mean, made promises, and tried to talk women into having sex. The coercive men reported feeling aroused and in need of sex, and they believed they had accomplished a goal when they seduced a woman who was a stranger or acquaintance, particularly on a first or second date. Some admitted trying to get their dates to drink excessively.

Date Rape

Date rape is the forcing of involuntary sexual compliance on a person during a voluntary, prearranged date or after a couple meets informally in a social setting. Date rape and other types of sexual aggression are very common.

Women are told frequently, "Don't go out with a man whom you don't know. If you do, you're taking a big chance." This is probably sound advice, but one of the purposes of dating is to get to know other people. And no matter how well you know an individual, problems can arise. Date rapes can occur in relationships in which two people have been going out together for a long time. As familiarity grows, the sexually aggressive male may become more insistent and try to coerce his partner into sexual activity that she finds objectionable.

This coercion may reflect a lack of communication and understanding in the relationship. In particular, sexual aggression may occur in a long-term relationship in which there is a lack of disclosure about sexual feelings, attitudes, and desires (Herold and Way, 1988). Some men are brought up to believe that when a woman says no she really means yes and that it's up to the man to do what she really wants him to do. This reflects the same myth that exists in relation to other types of rape: that women want to be forced. It also reflects the social leaning in our culture: that men are supposed to be the sexual aggressors and overcome the reluctance and hesitancy of

date rape   The forcing of involuntary sexual compliance on a person during a voluntary, prearranged date or after a couple meets informally in a social setting.

The Date Rape Drug

Gamma hydroxybutyrate (GHB)—also known as G, Liquid X, Saltwater, Scoop, and Easy Lay—is a highly addictive depressant that causes quick sedation. Its effects include drowsiness, nausea, vomiting, headaches dizziness, coma, and even death. Much of the United States first took notice of GHB in the mid-1990s, when dozens of women across the nation reported waking up naked, bruised, and with no memory of what had happened the night before. Police learned that men had spiked their drinks with GHB and then raped the women after they lost consciousness. Death from taking GHB usually occurs when victims fall on their face and smother or aspirate on their own vomit. Drug abuse agencies nationwide have placed more emphasis on the dangers of GHB as treatment centers across the country have reported increases in GHB addiction and overdose.

women. Of course, some men rape their dates out of anger and hostility, and many of these men engage repeatedly in acts of sexual aggression with a series of partners (Heilbrun and Loftus, 1986).

Malamuth (1989a) reported that some men are more attracted to sexual aggression and less attracted to conventional sex. Men who are most attracted to rape are highly aroused by media portrayals of forced sex, are less sensitive to the victims when exposed to sexually violent materials (Byers, 1988; Linz, 1989), and have hostility toward women, the desire to dominate women, and antisocial personality characteristics (Malamuth, 1989b).

Many date rapes are never reported. People might not realize that such incidents qualify as rape; they sometimes feel ashamed and don't want anyone to know; they might hesitate to report someone they know; and they sometimes feel partially responsible.

According to a study of college men's perceptions of acquaintance rape and date rape scenarios, when a woman engages in some sexual activity but refuses sexual intercourse, perceptions of her accountability for the rape increase dramatically and perceptions of the perpetrator's accountability decrease dramatically (Yescavage, 1999). Women who say no to all sexual activity are not perceived to be as accountable for their victimization. Duration of the relationship also has an impact on perceptions of accountability: If the couple has been together a while and is sexually active, the victim is perceived as more accountable and the perpetrator as less accountable. This pattern of responses suggests that a woman is judged to have given up her right to say no to sex if she allowed sexual activity to reach a certain point, somewhere between light and heavy intimate touching (Yescavage, 1999).

A study that surveyed the prevalence of sexual assault on one college campus found that unwanted sexual experiences of some kind were common among the women respondents (Ward, Chapman, Cohn, White, and Williams, 1991). The experiences typically occurred in residences (university and community), were party related, and involved alcohol use. A range of types of relationships was reported, from "stranger" to "boyfriend." The men commonly ignored the women's protests and used verbal coercion; physical force was less frequent, although it did occur. The resulting psychological damage to the women was high, yet the women did not report the damaging experiences to university or criminal justice officials.

The women were also asked, "In what ways did you show that you did not want the experience?" Verbal protests were common; 91% of the women said no to attempted intercourse, which may explain why some attempts were not completed. Some women also resisted physically, with 28% struggling unsuccessfully against completed intercourse. Altogether, 73% of the instances of unwanted intercourse occurred in spite of the woman's verbal or physical protests.

Eighteen percent of the women reported being psychologically injured as a result of unwanted sexual contact, and 30% as a result of attempted intercourse. Psychological harm from unwanted sexual intercourse appeared to be high, with 51% of the women sustaining harm from the experience. Physical injury was less common but did occur in 10% of the completed intercourse instances.

127

Many instances of date rape go un-reported. Help is becoming more available for women who have experienced sexual aggression, although reluctance to report it continues.

Unwanted sexual activity continues to be a dilemma for many young people and adults. Many don't know how to cope with unwanted sex but blame themselves if they experience it. Clearly, more education is needed.

The Progression of Violence

Often, violence begins with verbal aggression, which becomes the seed of physical aggression (Stets and Henderson, 1991). Aggression may occur for the first time in a relationship when disagreement over some issue (for example, when to have sex) results in an uncontrollable, emotionally charged response. The response may come as a surprise to both perpetrator and victim. If it is negatively sanctioned by either or both partners, the perpetrator of the aggressive act may make a commitment never to respond that way in the future. If the act is immediately challenged, it may not recur.

Recurring aggression may be the result of persistent, long-term interaction patterns instead of a sensitive issue. An individual's tendency to repeatedly neglect the needs, wishes, and concerns of the other partner, and instead to put his or her wants and desires ahead of the partner's by controlling him or her, may contribute to repeated acts of aggression. In essence, refusal to meet the needs of the other person, together with a desire to maintain control over him or her, so that his or her perspectives and desires are neglected and the wishes are focused more on the self, creates excessive tension and may be a motivation for violence. When aggression occurs more than once, it may be not so much an expression of how one partner feels as an instrument to get what he or she wants. In such cases the aggression may be deliberate. If the conduct is not challenged, it may quickly enter one's repertoire of behavior as a means to one's own ends. The more time spent with a partner, the greater the likelihood that he or she will be severely hurt. Spending more time with each other may mean a greater likelihood that more sensitive issues will emerge, thus increasing the possibility of severe aggression (Stets, 1992). Therapeutic intervention is often necessary in helping women get out of violent dating relationships (Rosen and Stith, 1993).

BREAKING UP A RELATIONSHIP

Breaking up a relationship can be very painful, especially if the breakup is unilateral, with only one person wanting to end the affair. Contrary to popular belief, however, women more often break off relationships than do men—perhaps because men fall in love more readily than do women (Baumeister, Wotman, and Stillwell, 1993). Men are also more likely to report that they feel depressed, lonely, unhappy, and less free than are women who have broken up. Apparently, the women take a practical approach to the situation. They cannot allow themselves to fall in love too quickly, nor can they afford to stay in a relationship with the wrong person. After carefully evaluating their partner's strengths and weaknesses and comparing them to other potential partners, they make a decision about whether to continue the relationship.

Although not all breakups follow the same course, researchers have developed several theories and models of relationship dissolution. One such model is the process theory of relationship trajectories (Baxter, 1984), which outlines a series of relationship decisions and their possible outcomes. The various courses that the relationship may follow are based on six crucial factors: (1) gradual versus sudden onset of problems, (2) unilateral (one partner's) versus bilateral (both partners') desire to end the relationship, (3) use of direct versus indirect methods to dissolve the relationship, (4) rapid versus protracted disengagement negotiations, (5) the presence versus the absence of attempts to resolve the issues surrounding the breakup, and (6) relationship termination versus relationship survival as the final outcome (Baxter, 1984). The decisions made at each of these intervals will determine the relationship dissolution trajectory.

Another breakup model is based on social exchange theory. The premise of this model is that a relationship will be dissolved when the rewards of staying in the relationship no longer outweigh the costs. The variables used to make this determination are people's personal expectations for and feelings about the current relationship and the value they place on the costs and rewards of alternatives to the relationship (H. H. Kelley and Thibaut, 1978). Thus, if someone believes that he or she is receiving more from the relationship than any alternatives might offer, the tendency will be toward reconciliation. But if the current relationship seems to offer less than the alternatives, the tendency will be toward dissolution.

Some theories on relationship dissolution describe a sequential process, suggesting phases of a breakup. One such model involves four phases: the intrapsychic, the dyadic, the social, and the grave-dressing (Duck, 1982). In the intrapsychic phase, each partner privately assesses his or her satisfaction with the relationship and the possible alternatives should the relationship be dissolved. The next phase, the dyadic, begins when the thoughts of dissolution become public; this phase features both attempts at relationship repair and dissolution behaviors. The social phase occurs when the couple reach the decision to break up and begin to accept the societal response. Finally, the grave-dressing phase is characterized by each individual's analysis of what went wrong and eventual recovery (Duck, 1982).

Another sequential process theory is the cascade model for breaking up (Gottman and Levenson, 1992). The elements in this process are the behaviors individuals display when dissolving a close relationship. This process is initiated when one partner begins to complain about and criticize the other partner, resulting in mutual feelings of contempt. As these feelings intensify, first the partner being criticized becomes defensive, and then both partners react defensively; eventually, one partner, usually the male, stonewalls, or avoids interaction. These four phases of this cascade model—complaints/criticism, contempt, defensiveness, and stonewalling—have been referred to as the Four Horsemen of the Apocalypse (Gottman, 1994).

Based on the hypothesis that such relationship dissolution models could indicate a cultural script for breakups, a study was conducted involving 80 undergraduate students who completed questionnaires (Battaglia, Datteri, and Lord, 1998). The resulting information was compiled to create an ordered script that traced the cyclical process of breaking up.

Breaking up a relationship—and perhaps making someone you care for unhappy or perhaps angry—can be very uncomfortable. The best way to minimize the pain is through mutual discussion rather than unilateral action, which is the course many are tempted to take. Following are some guidelines to consider when you are thinking of breaking up a relationship:

1. Think very clearly about why you want to end the relationship; weigh the pros and cons very carefully before you make your decision.

In this chapter, we are concerned with love and the process by which mate selection, nonmarital cohabitation, and the period of transition to marriage can be used to make marriage successful and satisfying. Because the responsibility for mate selection in our culture is an individual one, we need to better understand the process so that we can make wise choices.

WHAT IS LOVE?

Love is a central part of most of our lives. Not only is it the single most prevalent focus of literature, drama, poetry, song and the popular media, but most people are highly involved in it (Bergner, 2000). Each person defines *love* according to his or her background and experiences. One person may describe love in terms of emotions and strong feelings. Another may describe it as a biological attraction or as a way of acting toward and treating others. Another may frame love in terms of liking and friendship or in terms of care or concern for someone else. Still another may say that there is no such thing as love, that it is just a myth or a delusion. Figure 6.1 shows the results of one poll on the possibility of love at first sight.

In fact, there are many different definitions of love. Although, in a sense, love is what each person thinks it is, this subjective view is not always helpful. It leads to misunderstandings between two people who say they love each other but have entirely different concepts of what they mean. When we talk about love, therefore, we need to know what kind of love we mean. The point of view reflected here is that love is not a single concept but has different dimensions. Let's start with a five-dimensional view of love: romantic love, erotic love, dependent love, friendship love, and altruistic love.

ROMANTIC LOVE

Romantic love has been defined as a profoundly tender or passionate affection for another person. Its chief characteristic is strong emotion, marked by intensity of feelings. A glance, a smile, a brushing of the hand of one's beloved may arouse powerful feelings of warmth and affection. Individuals in romantic love report that they become "alive again"

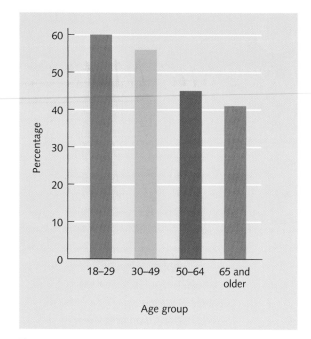

Figure 6.1 Percentage of Adults Who Believe in Love at First Sight, by Age, 1999 (*Note:* From *USA Today,* February 14, 2000.)

and start "to really feel for the first time in years." If the love is mutual and fulfilling, there is a strong sense of joy, exhilaration, and well-being.

Romantic lovers have a strong desire to be together so that they can continue to enjoy the pleasure of love. When apart, these lovers can become obsessed with thoughts of each other. It is also common for romantic love to result in physiological changes and manifestations: palpitations of the heart, a quickening pulse, breathlessness, trembling, a tightness in the chest, or halting speech. Loss of love can be so upsetting that the person can't eat or sleep. The literary portrayal of a debilitated and unhappy person as someone suffering from unrequited or lost love has some basis in fact.

The primary component of romantic love is strong emotion, but current research has indicated that a host of negative emotions, including anxiety and fear, may also be related to increased romantic love. Thus, romantic love appears to be derived from both positive and negative emotions, just as sexual desire may be enhanced by feelings of both intimacy and fear.

There is also a strong feeling of sexual attraction and a desire for physical contact in romantic love. In such a state of passion, romantic love is sometimes accompanied by idealization and adoration whereby the lovers focus on those physical traits and qualities of character that embody their ideal of womanhood or manhood. Theodore Reik (1957) theorized that individuals fall in love with people who manifest the characteristics of their ego ideal, and they project these characteristics onto the other person. This is **narcissistic love** in that it really represents love of the self, as reflected in the other person.

But romantic love can also involve altruism and unselfishness, with the lovers filled with feelings of generosity and wanting to shower each other with gifts. The sense of devotion and willingness to serve and to sacrifice is often astounding. Along with this desire to give up much for the sake of love comes a renewed feeling of self-confidence that one is beautiful and capable and can do the impossible.

These feelings have been substantiated by Dorothy Tennov (1979). She found that when the passion is strong the relationship eclipses all else. The lovers are in a wildly emotional state, seesawing between bliss and despair. They are obsessed with their loved one: When their loved one responds, they walk on air; when there is no response, they are crushed. Tennov labeled these feelings **limerence.** She reported that people can be this passionately involved with only one person at a time. For a while at least, the lovers may be completely out of control, and the emotional ups and downs can interfere with their work, study, sleep, and peace of mind.

Is Romantic Love a Sound Basis for Marriage?

An interesting issue regarding romantic love is whether it is a sound basis for marriage. There is no question that romance plays a significant role in attraction and the decision to marry. Romance brings individuals into serious sexual associations that may eventually lead to marriage. In this sense, romantic love is very functional.

However, if romantic love is taken as the only criterion for marriage, love can become very problematic. People can fall romantically in love with individuals who are completely unsuitable prospective partners and who will make their lives miserable. Having romantic feelings is not an accurate indication of suitability for marriage.

The idealism of romantic love is functional if it approaches reality. Strong, Wilson, Robbins, and Johns (1981) called rational love **conscious love.** They wrote, "When we love someone consciously, we are aware of who that person really is. We do not relate to their image, but to their reality" (p. 201). Romantic love becomes problematic if it blinds us to reality.

In addition, passion, which fuels romantic love, generally fades over time and is a function of a rapid increase in intimacy, which cannot be sustained over the lifetime of a marriage (Baumeister and Bratslavsky, 1999). Sharing new experiences, finding out that the other person cares for one deeply, and learning new things about the other person can all increase passion. In contrast, when people reach a point at which they understand each other completely, know all there is to know about each other, and do not share new experiences together, passion fades. Thus, partners in long-term relationships may have to deal with decreased passion even when intimacy and commitment remain high (Baumeister and Bratslavsky, 1999).

Emotional arousal, even from a frightening source, facilitates attraction. Perhaps this is why lovers who meet under dangerous conditions or who risk discovery experience greater excitement and passion than those who meet under more secure conditions. Perhaps this is why forbidden or secret love can be so intense.

The fear-breeds-passion principle was documented in research in Vancouver, British Columbia. Dutton and Aron (1974) conducted their experiment on two footbridges that cross the Capilano River. One bridge was a narrow, shaky walkway that swayed in the wind 230 feet above the stream. The other was a solid structure only 10 feet above the water. Near the end of each bridge, an attractive female experimenter approached men who were crossing and asked if

romantic love A profoundly tender or passionate affection for another person, characterized by intense feelings and emotion.

narcissistic love Love of self; selfish, self-centered love.

limerence A term used by Tennov (1979) to describe the intense, wildly emotional highs and lows of being in love.

conscious love Rational, reasoning love.

Love and Attachment

Several investigators have made significant breakthroughs in the development of a theory of romantic love. First, attachment theory, originally used to explain an infant's bonding with a parent, has been applied to the formation and maintenance of attachment bonds in adult love relationships. For example, the three styles of infant attachment—secure, anxious/ambivalent, and avoidant—have been applied to romantic relationships. The reaction of children to others is similar to the dynamics of romantic love in that they appear to experience both ecstasy and misery in response to closeness and distance, respectively. Changes in romantic love over time appear to be similar to the process of maintaining a secure attachment in a child when the child begins to take the parent for granted.

Support for attachment theory is found in research on romantic love. For example, people with lasting relationships tend to be secure, those who fall in love often tend to be anxious/ambivalent, and those doubtful of the existence of romantic love tend to be avoidant. In addition, love histories are different for individuals depending on whether they are secure, anxious/ambivalent, or avoidant. Secure individuals view their mothers as dependable; anxious individuals remember them in both positive and negative ways; and avoidant individuals remember them as domineering and cold (T. W. Roberts, 1992).

Longitudinal studies support the proposed relationship between childhood and adolescent/adult attachment styles (Mc-Carthy, 1999; McCarthy and Taylor, 1999). For example, Collins and Sroufe (1999) found that early attachment was associated with skills in social relationships in primary and secondary school. Adolescents who were securely attached as infants were more likely to have strong friendship groups, be dating, and have closer and more sustained relationships with their dating partners than those from the avoidant or anxious/ambivalent groups (Collins and Sroufe, 1999).

In another study of attachment theory, Moore and Leung (2002) examined the relationships between romantic attachment styles, romantic attitudes, and well-being among 461 students ages 17–21. Those who exhibited secure romantic attachment styles were more likely to be satisfied with their academic progress, less stressed, and less lonely than those in other attachment-style groups. The researchers found that secure young people, whether in or out of a relationship, were coping best with academic, social, and daily stress demands of university life. They believe that the link between romantic attachment style and well-being may occur through a link between romantic attachment style and some more basic adjustment variable associated with childhood attachment, such as the ability of those with a secure style to obtain social support and/or to have relatively problem-free relationships.

they would take part in an experiment on "the effects of exposure to scenic attractions on creative expression." They were asked to write down their associations to a picture she showed them. That the men on the narrow suspension bridge were more sexually aroused than the men on the low, solid bridge was inferred from the amount of sexual imagery in their associations. The men on the suspension bridge also were more likely to call the researcher afterward "to get more information about the study."

Sexual arousal produces intense physiological changes in the body, and these changes facilitate attraction. For example, in looking at photographs of different women, men will tend to label as most attractive seminude women who arouse them sexually; if there is no arousal, the women will be seen as less attractive.

There have been efforts to show the relationship between specific changes in the autonomic nervous system and various types of emotions (Ekman, Levenson, and Friesen, 1983). Liebowitz (1983) stated that the excitement and arousal of romantic love are a result of increased levels of **dopamine** and **norepinephrine** in the bloodstream. These neurotransmitters are activated by visual cues (by observing an attractive nude, for example), and they then bathe the pleasure center of the brain in a sea of chemical messages. Liebowitz also argued that romantic love stimulates the secretion of a chemical called **serotonin,** which can produce a feeling of intense pleasure. **Companionate love,** however, defined by Walster and Walster (1978) as "a more low-key emotion with feelings of friendly affection and deep attachment," results in the brain producing narcoticlike substances called **endorphins,** which give a sense of tranquillity.

These timeless studies emphasize the importance of emotional excitement as a component of attraction and of romantic love. The more positive excitement a relationship generates, the more likely the participants are to report that they are in love. However, since intense emotional arousal and excitement cannot be sustained, love that is to endure in a marriage must include components other than emotional excitement.

EROTIC LOVE

Erotic love is sensual love. This type of love can be defined as sexual attraction to another person. It is the biological, sensual component of love relationships. What is the relationship between love and sex?

Are Love and Sex the Same?

According to Sigmund Freud, love and sex are really one and the same thing. Freud (1953) defined love as "aim inhibited sex," as a yearning for a "love object"—for another person who could meet one's own sexual needs. Love, to Freud, was narcissistic in that it was measured by the extent to which the love object could satisfy someone's sexual aims.

Freud emphasized two important elements of the sexual aims of adults. One element is physical and sensual. In both men and women, this element consists of the desire for physical pleasure such as the release of sexual tension through orgasm.

The second element of the sexual aims in adults is psychical; it is the affectionate component—the desire for emotional satisfaction. Freud emphasized that a normal sexual life is assured when there is a convergence of the affectionate and sensual components. The desire for true affection and the desire for the release of sexual tension are the needs that motivate individuals to seek love objects. Freud (1953) also claimed that, once an appropriate love object was found, sexual strivings diminished. In turn, diminished yearnings resulted in a search for only one love object at a time.

While Freud emphasized that love and sex are the same thing, other writers would say that love and sex are two separate entities, that they are not identical, and that a distinction must be made between them. Reik (1957) argued that love and sex are different in origin and nature. Sex, according to Reik, is a biological function whose aim is the release of physical tension. Love stems from psychic needs and provides affection and emotional satisfaction. More

recent research indicates only a low correlation between sexual desire and love. This means that many individuals tend to separate the two things—that they can be in love without having sexual desire or they can have sexual desire without being in love (J. C. Beck, Bozman, and Qualtrough, 1991).

Still other writers have suggested that romantic love arises when sexual expression is denied. This "sexual blockage" theory emphasizes that romantic love is felt most strongly for those who play "hard to get." Once sexual involvement begins, romantic love declines.

A common manifestation of the separation of love and sex today is casual sex, as discussed in Chapter 5. This is sex for its own sake, because it is pleasurable and fun, without the necessity of love and commitment. As one student remarked, "What's wrong with just enjoying one another's bodies? Do people have to be in love to do that?" Commonly cited motives for casual sex are sexual desire, spontaneous urges, interest in sexual exploration and experimentation, and use of alcohol or drugs (Regan and Dreyer, 1999). In general, men and women have similar motives for engaging in short-term sexual relationships, which challenges the idea that sexual desire is an inherent aspect of the male but not the female experience (Regan and Dreyer, 1999). However, more women than men reported having entered a casual sexual encounter to increase their chances of obtaining a long-term commitment from the sex partner. Even though sex is a popular form of adult play, with the rise of sexually transmitted diseases (STDs), casual sex can be potentially hazardous.

dopamine A neurotransmitter that functions in the parts of the brain that control emotions and bodily movement.

norepinephrine A hormone secreted by the adrenal glands that has a stimulating effect on blood pressure and acts as a neurotransmitter.

serotonin A chemical neurotransmitter that has a stimulating effect on the body and can produce a feeling of intense pleasure.

companionate love A low-key emotion with feelings of affection and deep attachment.

endorphins Chemical neurotransmitters that have a sedative effect on the body and can give a sense of tranquillity.

erotic love Sexual, sensuous love.

Is physical attraction more than skin deep? Freud defined love as "a yearning for a 'love object.'" It's possible that, for some, the appearance of one of these men satisfies Freud's definition of a love object, although another of these friends might satisfy that definition for someone else.

Sex as an Expression of Love

Many couples can't separate sex from all other aspects of their relationship, at least in the long term. One woman summed up her feelings:

> I like sex a lot. But it can only supplement a warm, affectionate, mutually respecting, full personhood relationship. It can't be a relationship. It can't prove love. It can't prove anything. I have found sex with people I don't really like, or who I'm not certain will really like me, or with people I don't feel I know well, to be very shallow and uncomfortable and physically unsatisfying. I don't believe you have to be "in love" and married "till death do us part." But mind and body are one organism and all tied up together, and it isn't even physically fun unless the people involved really like each other. (Hite, 1981, p. 48)

In modern Western society, there has been considerable fusion between love and sex (Weis, Slosnerick, Cate, and Sollie, 1986). Some maintain that love increases the pleasure of sex and that erotic pleasure is reduced when love is at a minimum. Sex can be important as a confirmation of the love relationship; it says to the other person, "I love you." In this view, sex can be both a physical and an emotional expression of deep feeling. But many adults disagree completely with this point of view, arguing that it simply is not true that sexual pleasure is less when the partners do not love each other. Whichever view an individual holds, many people want sex with affection, not without it, and insist that love and sex should go together.

DEPENDENT LOVE

One of the components of a durable love is dependency. **Dependent love** develops when someone's needs are fulfilled by another person. In its simplest form, it works like this: "I have important needs. You fulfill those needs; therefore, I love you." This is the type of love the dependent child feels for the mother who feeds, clothes, and cares for him or her: "You give me my bottle; you keep me warm; you hold me, cuddle me, and talk to me. That's why I love you."

But it is also the kind of love that develops when the intense psychological needs of adults that have been denied in the past are now fulfilled by a lover. For example, a lover who has a strong need for approval may be getting that need met through a partner who is full of compliments and praise.

Maslow's Theory of Love as Need

Abraham Maslow (1970) is one of the chief exponents of love as dependency and need fulfillment. According to him, human needs may be arranged in a hierarchy, ascending from physiological to psychological, as shown in Figure 6.2.

Maslow referred to the first four levels of need as D-needs, or Deficiency-needs, and to the last three levels as B-needs, or Being-needs. He emphasized that the needs at each level must be met before a person can move up to the next level. An individual develops Deficiency-love for a person who meets D-needs and Being-love for the person who fulfills B-needs.

Maslow emphasized that in marriage **D-love** refers to all forms of self-centered love whereby two people love each other because the needs of each are met by the other. It is a sort of bookkeeping arrangement, with the man meeting certain needs of the woman even as she meets certain needs of his, and vice versa. Since the focus of attention is on the fulfillment of self and personal needs, D-love may be fragmented. For example, a woman may enjoy her spouse as a sexual partner because he meets her biological and emotional needs but dislike him in some other ways because of his sense of values.

This fragmentation cannot happen in **B-love**, because it is love for the very existence and uniqueness of the other person. The sexual impulse is anchored in the deep love of the qualities of one's mate. With this type of love, neither person feels insecure and threatened, because each feels accepted by the other and is comfortable in the other's presence. The love is not conditioned by the extent to which the other person fills one's needs. It is not possessive, nor is it motivated by any desire to fulfill some personal need or some selfish aim. It is unconditional and offers the kind of relationship in which each person can develop the best that is in him or her.

It is important that need fulfillment be mutual and that partners strive to meet each other's D-needs. This assumes the needs are reasonable and capable of fulfillment. However, difficulty can arise if an individual's D-needs were not met while growing up; he or she may become possessive, domineering, and overly dependent and manipulate the other person only for self-satisfaction. In such a situation, self-actualization and B-love are impossible. There is no room for growth, freedom, and fulfillment, because the partner is only being used. One woman explained:

My husband says that if I really loved him, I would want to be together with him all the time. He didn't

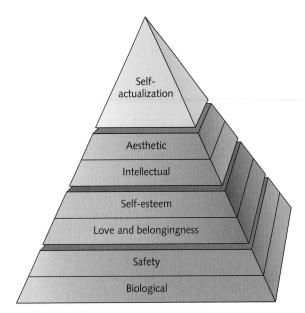

Figure 6.2 Maslow's Hierarchy of Needs (*Note:* From Abraham Maslow, *Motivation and Personality*, 3d ed. Copyright © 2000. Reprinted by permission of Pearson Education, Inc., Upper Saddle River, NJ.)

want me to go to work (we don't have any children), but I did anyhow. He calls me several times during the day to talk to me. I'd like to go to lunch with the girls once in a while, but he insists on having lunch with me every day. When we're home, he follows me around the house. I can't even go to the bathroom without his following me. If I don't feel like sex, he feels hurt, starts to pout, and starts drinking beer. Sometimes he'll drink the whole weekend because I turned him down (I do so very seldom, however).

In a counseling session, the husband revealed that he had felt very rejected and unloved by his mother when he was growing up, that she was never home for him. Unconsciously, he expected his wife to make up for all the love he had never received as a

dependent love Love that one develops for someone who fulfills one's needs.

D-love Term used by Maslow for Deficiency-love, which develops when another person meets one's needs.

B-love Term used by Maslow for Being-love, which is love for the very being and uniqueness of another person.

child. His demands were unreasonable, and the more he expected, the more she came to resent and shun him (Author's counseling notes).

If, however, D-needs have been met as one is growing up, the individual does not need to strive for their fulfillment and thus can show an active concern for the life and growth of the loved one. Maslow (1962) recognized that there is some mixture of D-love and B-love in every relationship (see Figure 6.3).

People differ regarding their need for emotional closeness and distance in their family relationships. If they experience excessive emotional distance, their anxiety increases because of fears of rejection and abandonment. They then attempt to reduce the anxiety by seeking increased togetherness. However, if people experience excessive togetherness in their family, they may become anxious over perceived threats to their autonomy and independence. Anxiety about excessive closeness prompts them to increase the emotional distance from other family members.

Functional, or healthy, families have ample tolerance for normal variations in closeness and distance, and low levels of anxiety are sufficient to return the family to a balance between closeness and distance. In dysfunctional families, however, minor variations in closeness or distance frequently provoke intense anxiety. Moreover, intense anxiety and persistent reliance on anxiety to regulate closeness and distance result in chronic anxiety within the family (Benson, Larson, Wilson, and Demo, 1993).

FRIENDSHIP LOVE

Another important element of love is **friendship love,** similar to what is called companionate love. This implies a type of love between individuals with common concerns. This type of love may exist between good companions because of similar interests; it may arise out of respect for the personality or character of another. Research has shown that the most comprehensive and profound relationships are between two lovers whose involvement includes friendship. While romance may exist without friendship, love becomes more complete and enduring with it.

Loving and Liking

There is some evidence to show that loving and liking are separate phenomena and may be measured separately (K. E. Davis, 1985). But this research defines love only in romantic terms. Other research emphasizes that as love matures over the years, it contains more and more elements of friendship. This means that partners grow to like each other. In fact, liking has been called the key to loving. Liking in a relationship brings relaxation in the presence of the beloved; it is a stimulus for two people to want to be with each other. It is friendship in the simplest, most direct terms.

Friendship love is certainly more relaxed and less tense than romantic love. It is less possessive

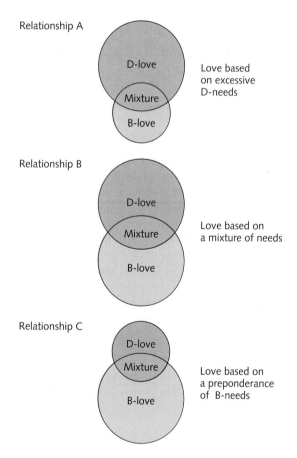

A reciprocal relationship (Relationship B) involves a balanced and mutual give-and-take of D-love and B-love.

Figure 6.3   Degrees of Dominance of D-Love and B-Love in Relationships (*Note:* From F. Philip Rice, *Marriage and Parenthood*, p. 106. Copyright © 1979 by F. Philip Rice. Used with permission.)

and less emotional, and it affords more security without anxiety. In such a secure environment, partners are free to live, work, and go about their lives supported by their friendship.

ALTRUISTIC LOVE

Altruistic love reflects unselfish concern for the well-being of another. It is the investment of someone's psychic energies and abilities in caring for another individual and in seeking what is best for the other person. By nurturing someone else and doing all one can to make that person happy, the individual finds meaning and satisfaction in his or her own life.

Fromm's View of Altruistic Love

One of the chief exponents of altruistic love was Erich Fromm (1956). Fromm saw love as an activity, not a passive affection; it is a "standing in," not a "falling for." In the most general terms, the active character of love can be described as primarily giving, not receiving. To Fromm, giving did not mean "giving up" something, not being deprived of or sacrificing. Rather, it involved giving of oneself—one's joy, interest, understanding, knowledge, humor, even sadness. Thus, when one gives of one's life, the person one loves is enriched.

In addition to the element of giving, Fromm emphasized four basic components of love: care, responsibility, respect, and knowledge. Fromm used the illustration of a woman who says she loves flowers but forgets to water them; it would be difficult to believe she really loves her flowers. As Fromm (1956) put it, "Love is the active concern for the life and growth of that which we love" (p. 22). Where concern is lacking, there is no love. Care and concern also imply responsibility, not as a duty imposed from the outside, but as a voluntary act in which one responds to the needs (primarily psychic) of the other person. Love also depends on respect, which involves not fear and awe, but an awareness of the unique individuality of the other person and a concern that he or she grow and unfold as he or she is. Respect is possible only where freedom and independence are granted. It is the opposite of domination. Finally, love also requires knowledge of the other person, in order to see his or her reality and overcome any irrational, distorted image.

Research shows that lovers whose involvement includes friendship maintain more enduring relationships.

The love that Fromm described is an unselfish, caring, giving love. But, ideally, this type of love, like dependent love, should be mutual. If it is not, the relationship will certainly have problems and may not survive.

COMPONENTS OF LOVE

Western culture emphasizes romantic love as the basis for partner selection. Because it is so highly regarded, it cannot be ignored. When based on reality

friendship love   A love based on common concerns and interests, companionship, and respect for the partner's personality and character.

altruistic love   Unselfish concern for the welfare of another.

instead of an idealization of the partner, romantic love provides a functional basis for marriage.

Erotic love is an important part of love. Certainly, sexual attraction is an important factor in relationship building, and sexual satisfaction strengthens the bond between two people. Ordinarily, love and sex are interdependent. A loving relationship becomes a firm foundation for a happy sex life, and a fulfilling sexual relationship reinforces the total love of the partners for each other.

Dependent love is an important basis for a strong relationship when it involves mutual dependency. Integration in the relationship takes place to the extent that each person meets the needs of the other. Difficulty arises if the needs of one person are so excessive that neurotic, possessive dependency becomes the basis for the relationship. Most people need to receive as well as give if they are to remain emotionally healthy. Those who enjoy giving without receiving become either martyrs or masochists.

Friendship love, based on companionship, is an enduring bond between two people who like each other and enjoy each other's company. It can endure over many years. For most people, friendship alone is not enough for marriage, but it is an important ingredient in loving relationships.

Finally, altruistic love adds genuine concern and care to the total relationship. Behavior, rather than feelings, is the active means by which the individual shows care. As in dependent love, giving and receiving must be mutual. Altruistic love allows the person expressing it to gain satisfaction through caring for another. It allows the receiving person to be cared for and loved for his or her own sake.

Research on the Components of Love

Research findings support the idea that the most complete love has a number of components. Robert Sternberg (1986, 1998) asked subjects to describe their relationships with lovers, parents, siblings, and friends. Analysis of the results revealed three components of close relationships: intimacy, passion, and decision/commitment to maintain the relationships (see Figure 6.4).

Intimacy involves sharing feelings and providing emotional support. It usually involves high levels of self-disclosure through the sharing of personal information not ordinarily revealed because of the risk involved. Intimacy gradually increases as the relationship matures and deepens.

The passion component refers to sexuality, attraction, and romance in a relationship.

The decision/commitment component involves both short- and long-term factors. The short-term factor is the decision, made consciously and unconsciously, to love another person. The long-term factor is the commitment to maintain the love. Sometimes people fall in love but do nothing afterward to maintain it.

Figure 6.4 The Triangle of Love (*Note:* From Robert Sternberg, "A Triangular Theory of Love," *Psychological Review*, 1986, Vol. 93, pp. 119–135. Copyright © 1986 Robert Sternberg. Used with permission.)

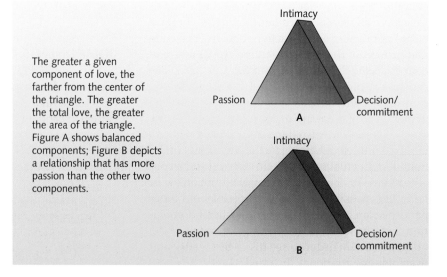

The greater a given component of love, the farther from the center of the triangle. The greater the total love, the greater the area of the triangle. Figure A shows balanced components; Figure B depicts a relationship that has more passion than the other two components.

Sternberg and Barnes (1988) described eight different combinations of these three components of love:

1. **Absence of intimacy, passion, and commitment**—no love.
2. **Intimacy only**—liking (but no passion or commitment).
3. **Passion only**—infatuation (but little intimacy or commitment).
4. **Decision/commitment only**—empty love (with no passion or intimacy).
5. **Intimacy and passion**—romantic love (no commitment).
6. **Intimacy and commitment**—companionate love (without passion).
7. **Passion and commitment**—fatuous love (foolish love, without real intimacy).
8. **Intimacy, passion, and commitment**—consummate love (the most complete love).

Sternberg emphasizes that the most complete love, **consummate love,** results from a combination of all three components (Trotter, 1986). The love relationship is balanced when all three elements are present in relatively equal degrees. People are more likely to be satisfied with their relationship if their love triangles match—that is, if they have fairly equal amounts of the same components of love (Sternberg, 1998; Sternberg and Barnes, 1985).

A study that examined the relationship between personality and the three components of love proposed by Sternberg attempted to determine what fundamental personality characteristics were associated with love and whether personality variables were differentially related to intimacy, passion, and commitment (Engel, Olson, and Patrick, 2002). The researchers found that conscientiousness was a significant predictor of love for both males and females in close opposite-sex relationships. This study implied that conscientious people tend to be motivated workers in their love relationships and are willing to work at the relationship, just as they are in jobs and academics. The connection between conscientiousness and the components of love in Sternberg's triangular theory is commitment. Commitment is largely a cognitive component that involves a decision to engage in a relationship and maintain the relationship over time (Engel et al.,

2002). "Commitment is the extent to which a person is likely to stick with something or someone and persist until the goal underlying the commitment is achieved" (Sternberg, 1998, p. 12). Persons high in conscientiousness are reliable, persistent, and oriented to fulfilling obligations that would likely lead to greater commitment in the relationship (Engel et al., 2002).

K. E. Davis (1985) described love relationships in terms of three categories that differ somewhat from Sternberg's: passion, caring, and friendship. Each of these, in turn, features a cluster of characteristics. The passion cluster includes fascination with each other, a desire for exclusiveness, and sexual desire. The caring cluster includes giving the utmost of oneself, being a champion and advocate of the partner's interests, and making sure that the partner succeeds. The friendship cluster involves enjoyment, acceptance, trust, respect, mutual assistance, self-disclosure, understanding, and spontaneity.

B. F. Moss and Schwebel (1993) described the multidimensional nature of love with a related set of components. They saw intimacy in enduring romantic relationships as depending on the level of commitment and positive affective, cognitive, and physical closeness in a reciprocal (although not necessarily symmetrical) relationship. Their definition specified five components of intimacy: commitment, affective intimacy, cognitive intimacy, physical intimacy, and mutuality. Most people strive to achieve intimacy in their lives.

CHANGES OVER TIME

Some researchers feel that love changes over time, with romantic love becoming more rational and less emotional. Couples' ideas of love may change over the years, with fewer components of romance and more components of friendship, trust, cooperation, dependability, and acceptance.

Montgomery and Sorell (1997) measured differences in love attitudes across family life stages. Their sample included 250 adults in four groups:

consummate love A term used by Sternberg to describe love as a combination of intimacy, passion, and commitment.

(1) college-age single young adults; (2) young, childless married adults; (3) married adults with children living at home; and (4) married adults with grown children living on their own. Contrary to expectations, the researchers did not find a smooth developmental progression of love attitudes over the course of the life span involving the peaking of erotic, romantic love early in life and the rising valuation of friendship in midlife. Although a developmental model that includes the rising and falling of different love attitudes throughout the family life course was not evident, a number of differences were found between young singles and older married adults, regardless of family life stage. Possessive, playful love attitudes were held more strongly by young singles than by any of the married adult groups, and unmarried youths were lowest in altruistic love attitudes. Playful as well as obsessive and possessive attitudes are characteristic of courtship. Marriage, in contrast, may encourage self-giving love and altruism. A rational, "shopping-list" attitude was understandably prevalent in younger adulthood because of the emphasis on partner selection.

In this study, child rearing did not appear to be associated with differences in love attitude. The older married adults had practical attitudes reflecting generational pressures to form socially and economically viable partnerships. Consistent with previous research, the erotic and altruistic styles of love were associated with high relationship satisfaction for all the groups. Erotic, altruistic, and friendship types of love seemed to have enhanced importance when children were living in the home. Strategies that maintained eroticism were likely to increase a couple's satisfaction with the relationship, no matter the stage of the life cycle. Exclusive commitment to a partner, partner-supportive attitudes, sexual intimacy, and the passionate valuing of the partner and the relationship were most likely to enhance the partners' satisfaction.

These findings suggest that men and women are quite similar in their love attitudes across adulthood. At all stages of the life course, adults value passion, friendship, and self-giving love attitudes. This research indicates that there are far more similarities than differences between the love attitudes of men and women. Friendship/companionship love attitudes are important for all groups and do not differ by family life stage. The results of this study also indicate that passion and friendship/companionship do not occur consecutively in a romantic relationship after all. Rather, they appear to exist concurrently in both dating and married life stage groups (Montgomery and Sorell, 1997).

THEORIES OF MATE SELECTION

Selecting a mate is one of the most important decisions we make during our lifetime. We are concerned here with theories of mate selection and their applicability to real life. What factors influence mate selection? How important is family background? What are the possibilities for intermarriage between people of different socioeconomic classes, educational levels, ethnic groups, and religions? How important is consensus of attitudes and values? How do you know if you are compatible? Is it necessary to have similar role concepts and personal habits?

This section presents the results of years of study by researchers of the mate selection process. If you aren't already married, perhaps the section will help you choose your mate wisely.

Theories of mate selection attempt to explain the process and dynamics by which people select mates. Some theories have proved more valid than others, and no one theory tells the whole story; but together they provide some explanation of what happens (Surra, 1990). The major theories discussed here can be divided into four groups: (1) psychodynamic theories, (2) needs theories, (3) exchange theories, and (4) developmental process theories.

Psychodynamic Theories

Psychodynamic theories of mate selection emphasize the influence of childhood experiences and family background on one's choice of mate.

Parent Image Theory   The **parent image theory** is based on Freud's psychoanalytic concepts of the Oedipus complex and Electra complex and states that a man will likely marry someone resembling his mother and that a woman will likely marry someone resembling her father. Jedlicka (1984) tested this theory and found that the resemblance between a man's wife and his mother and between a woman's husband and her father occurred more frequently than expected by chance. In general, the data supported the theory of indirect parental influence on mate choice.

Ideal Mate Theory　　The **ideal mate theory** states that people form a fantasy of what an ideal mate should be like, based partly on early childhood experiences. R. Schwartz and Schwartz (1980) wrote:

> Somewhere we "remember" how it felt to have another human being take care of us. We take this memory with us as we mature. Ultimately, it becomes our model, our expectation of a loving relationship. (p. 4)

There is little doubt that many people form fantasies of an ideal mate. The problem occurs when people hold unrealistic fantasies and their mate never fulfills them. If they pressure their mate to do so, rather than accept him or her as is, it places a strain on the marriage.

Needs Theories

Needs theories of mate selection are based on the idea that we select a partner who will fill our needs. Various theorists have offered descriptions of how needs influence mate selection. For example, the complementary needs theory, which was originated by Robert Winch (1958), states that people tend to select mates whose needs are opposite but complementary to their own. According to this theory, a nurturant person who likes to care for others would seek out a succorant mate who likes to be cared for. A dominant person would select a submissive person. Winch later (1967) added a third aspect of complementariness: achievement/vicariousness. The person who has a need to achieve tends to select a person whose need is to find vicarious recognition through attainment of a spouse. The individual selects a mate who gives the greatest promise of providing maximum need gratification. This is the person whose needs are complementary to one's own.

Since Winch's formulation, subsequent research has provided either no support or only partial support for this theory (Murstein, 1980). In fact, similarity of need may be more functional than complementarity in mate selection.

Exchange Theories

Exchange theories are a sort of cost-benefit analysis of relationships. These theories are based on the notion that we enter into relationships with those who possess resources (both tangible ones, such as a good income, and intangible ones, such as attractiveness, intelligence, or good humor) that we particularly value. If the emotional costs of the relationship begin to outweigh its benefits, we will probably end the relationship.

Traditional exchange theory (discussed in Chapter 1) holds that the basis for a continuing relationship between two partners is that each believes he or she will get at least as much from the relationship as it will cost (Filsinger and Thoma, 1988). Each person tries to maximize her or his chances for a rewarding marriage. Sometimes, the partners end up being equal in their abilities to reward each other. Other times, however, those who are motivated primarily to maximize their own benefits may exploit their partner, which is not conducive to a loving relationship.

An improvement over exchange theory, equity theory (also discussed in Chapter 1) insists on fairness, on the assumption that people should obtain benefits from a relationship in proportion to what they give. The exchanged benefits might not be the same. People may desire different things, but they are attracted by a deal that is fair to them. Some people are attracted to others not primarily for what they can get, but for what they can give to a relationship. Judging equity, then, is an individual matter.

Developmental Process Theories

Developmental process theories describe mate selection as a process of filtering and weeding out ineligible and incompatible people until one person is selected. These theories describe various factors that are used in the selection process.

The Field of Eligibles　　The first factor to be considered in the mate selection process is the field of eligibles. For women, shortages of potential mates affect not only the likelihood of marriage but also the quality of the spouse in the event of marriage. A favorable marriage market (measured in terms of the relative number of men to women) increases the likelihood of

---

parent image theory　A theory of mate selection that a person is likely to marry someone resembling his or her parent of the opposite sex.

ideal mate theory　A theory that people tend to marry someone who fulfills their fantasy of what an ideal mate should be like, based partly on early childhood experiences.

needs theories　Theories of mate selection proposing that we select partners who will fulfill our own needs—both complementary and instrumental.

The ideal mate theory states that people form fantasies of what a mate should be like, but sometimes such fantasy images are not realistic.

marrying a high-status man rather than a low-status man (measured in terms of education and occupation) (Lichter, Anderson, and Hayward, 1995). At the same time, it decreases the number of eligible women from whom men can choose.

Propinquity   Another factor in mate sorting is **propinquity** (Davis-Brown, Salamon, and Surra, 1987). That is, geographic nearness is a major factor influencing mate selection. However, this does not mean simply residential propinquity; institutional propinquity is equally important. In other words, people meet in places of business, schools, social organizations, and churches.

Attraction   People are drawn to those whom they find attractive (see Chapter 5). This includes physical attraction and attraction because of specific personality traits. Many mate preferences are thought to be sex-linked; in other words, men and women look for different characteristics in potential mates. Women have been shown to look for mates with attributes related to their ability to provide for future offspring, such as intelligence, extroversion, and ambition. Men who possess these characteristics are seen as better providers for offspring. Men, conversely, look for physical signs of health in mates, most often represented in terms of physical attractiveness. While everyone has specific and different

needs when choosing a mate, many of these sources of attraction fall within this biological framework (Botwin, Buss, and Shackelford, 1997).

Homogamy and Heterogamy   People tend to choose mates who share personal and social characteristics, such as age, race, ethnicity, education, socioeconomic class, and religion (Dressel, 1980; Rogler and Procidano, 1989b; Stevens and Schoen, 1988). This tendency to choose a mate similar to oneself is called **homogamy.** Choosing a mate different from oneself is called **heterogamy.** Homogamous marriages tend to be more stable than heterogamous marriages, although there are exceptions. Various types of heterogamy and homogamy will be explored in detail in later sections of this chapter.

The major reason that marriages are generally homogamous is that we tend to prefer people who are like us and to feel uncomfortable around those who are different. Another important factor, however, is social pressure toward **endogamy,** or marrying within one's group. People who marry someone who is much older or younger or who belongs to a different ethnic group, religion, or social class may meet with overt or subtle disapproval. Conversely, people are generally prohibited from marrying someone who is too much like them, such as a sibling or a first cousin. This is social pressure for **exogamy,** or marrying outside one's kin group.

Compatibility   The concept of **compatibility** refers to peoples' capability of living together in harmony. Compatibility may be evaluated according to temperament, attitudes and values, needs, role conceptions and enactment, and personal habits. In the process of mate selection, individuals strive to sort out those with whom they are compatible in these various areas.

The Filtering Process   Figure 6.5 shows a schematic representation of the **filtering process.** The figure is based on numerous theories and research studies. Rather than relying on any one narrow view, the diagram represents a composite of various theories to show the process in detail.

As the figure shows, we begin the process of filtering with a very wide field of eligibles. This group goes through a series of filters, each of which eliminates ineligibles, so that the numbers are reduced before we pass on to the next filter. Before making a final decision, two people may go through a final

propinquity   In mate selection, the tendency to choose someone who is geographically near.

homogamy   The selection of a partner who is similar to oneself.

heterogamy   The selection of a partner who is different from oneself.

endogamy   Marriage within a particular group.

exogamy   Marriage outside of a particular group.

compatibility   The capability of living together in harmony.

filtering process   A process by which mates are sorted by filtering out ineligibles according to various standards.

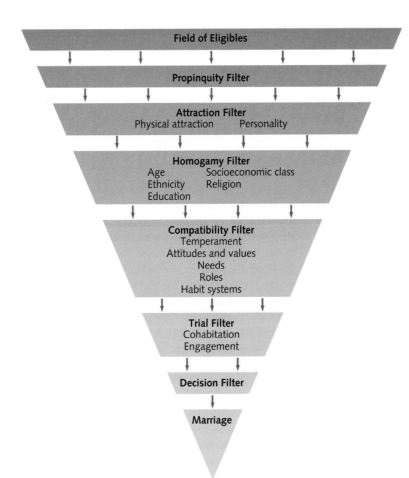

Figure 6.5   The Filtering Process of Mate Selection

trial period, either through cohabitation or formal engagement or both. If they survive this filtering process, the final filter is the decision to marry.

The order is approximate. Obviously, partners are selected according to propinquity first, and physical attraction plays a significant role early in the relationship, followed by attraction based on other personality traits. Gradually, people begin to sort out homogamous mates according to sociocultural factors: age, ethnicity, education, socioeconomic class, and religion. As the relationship develops, they find out if they are compatible according to temperament, attitudes and values, needs, role concepts, and personal habits. Some couples place more emphasis on some factors than on others. Some may explore compatibility without regard for homogamy. Others are more interested in selecting someone with the same socioeconomic background. Generally, both homogamous factors and compatibility factors are important. A testing of the relationship provides further evidence of whether the choice is a wise one.

As you can see, mate selection is a complex process by which people sort out a variety of social, psychological, and personal factors prior to making a final choice. Unfortunately, some people are not this thorough. They move from physical attraction to marriage without going through the intervening filters. Or situational factors, such as pregnancy, pressure them into a marriage that is unwise. The remainder of this chapter discusses factors in mate selection.

FAMILY BACKGROUND FACTORS IN MATE SELECTION

Family background influences everything that people are, want to become, or do. A detailed discussion of family background and its influences may be found in Chapter 2. But we need to look at it from the point of view of mate selection. How people are brought up influences how they view marriage, how they want to bring up their children, and what their gender-role preferences are. It influences their personalities, traits, attitudes, values, and feelings. There is probably no area of living that is unrelated to family background.

For these reasons, it is helpful in mate selection to learn about the family background of a potential marriage partner. There is an old saying: "I'm not marrying his or her family." But that is not completely true. We marry a son or daughter, a person who is the product of his or her family experiences. When we marry someone, we marry everything the family has been able to impart to that individual. Knowing something about the family helps us to know the person who grew up in that family.

When both spouses have been exposed to healthy family-of-origin experiences, they more often achieve greater marital satisfaction than do spouses who have not been exposed to healthy experiences (Wilcoxon and Hovestadt, 1983). If we discover troubling things about a person's background, we can discuss those things to find out how our partner feels or has been affected. These problems may be thought of as caution signals influencing us to slow down while we examine them. Strong feelings about unresolved issues may require professional premarital counseling to see if they can be worked out. If not, they may be reasons to discontinue the relationship.

Socioeconomic Class

The possibilities of marital satisfaction are greater if people marry within their own socioeconomic class. Interclass unions do take place, but partners experience more stress in heterogamous unions. Moreover, the spouses who marry down are more stressed than the ones who marry up, if status is important to them. That is, if the spouses from a higher class are class-conscious, they are more aware of the lower background of their spouse, and the relationship with their spouse is less affectionate, less emotionally supportive, and subject to less consensus.

Overall, women are less willing than men to marry someone with low earnings or unstable employment. But economic considerations are not irrelevant to men's preferences, either; men are less willing to marry a woman lacking steady employment than one having steady employment. Both men and women with high earnings and education are less willing to marry a formerly married person with children or a person with low socioeconomic status. Among African Americans, both men and women report less willingness than their White counterparts to marry someone of low status (South, 1991). The increasing reliance of couples and fami-

Marriage brings together two families, not just two individuals. Knowing something about a marriage partner's family experiences can be important to successful marital adjustment.

lies on two incomes might well be altering the field of eligibles. As the tradition of the man as the family's sole source of income disappears, men increasingly are considering the economic characteristics of potential wives in the mate selection process.

Education and Intelligence

There is a tendency for couples to enter into homogamous marriages with respect to education. Overall, women with 4 years of college tend to marry men who are also 4-year college graduates or who have more education than they do. However, Black women are significantly more likely than White women to marry men who are less educated than they are (Shehan, Berardo, Bera, and Carley, 1991), primarily because the pool of eligible well-educated Black males is less than the pool of well-educated White males.

What about the compatibility of spouses who are mixed with respect to education? As a general principle, educationally homogamous marriages tend to be slightly more compatible than educationally heterogamous marriages. In fact, the risk of marital instability is highest among couples who are heterogamous with respect to education (Tzeng, 1992). Among couples with unequal levels of education, the risk of marital disruption is about twice as high if the woman is more educated (Bumpass, Martin, and Sweet, 1991). **Hypergamous unions** (woman marries upward) have lower divorce rates than **hypogamous unions** (woman marries downward).

Obviously, however, educational attainment is not the only important factor. People who lack the advantages of a formal education but who are quite intelligent may be very happily married to those who

hypergamous union Marriage in which the woman marries upward on the social ladder.

hypogamous union Marriage in which the woman marries beneath herself on the social ladder.

Declining social barriers between individuals of different ethnic and cultural backgrounds reflect a general decline in prejudice against intergroup marriage.

Consensus and Similarity of Attitudes and Values

Marital compatibility is enhanced if spouses develop a high degree of consensus and similar attitudes and values about things that are important to them. Two people can never agree on everything, but ordinarily the greater the consensus, the easier it is to adjust to each other in marriage. People who share attitudes and values usually feel more comfortable with each other. There is less friction and stress in adjusting to each other.

Consensus develops slowly in a relationship. A dating couple may not even get around to talking about important values until after the partners have been together for some time. The more intimate the two people become, the more likely they are to express agreement in a number of important areas. There may be two reasons for this: (1) Being together may create greater understanding and agree-

ment, and (2) those who disagree too much may not progress to the next stage of intimacy. Whichever reason is more valid, value consensus in a couple is related to satisfaction and to progress toward permanence in the relationship.

From this point of view, compatibility may be described partly in terms of the extent of agreement or disagreement about key issues such as employment, residence, money matters, relationships with parents and in-laws, social life and friends, religion and philosophy of life, sex, manners and living habits, children, and gender roles.

Gender Roles and Personal Habits

Compatibility is based not only on attitudes and values but also on behavior. A couple will have a more satisfying and successful life together if the partners share common expectations about gender roles and if they can tolerate each other's personal habits.

Compatible Role Concepts   One measure of compatibility in marriage is the similarity of male and female role expectations. Every man has certain concepts of the kind of roles he should perform as a husband and certain expectations of what roles his spouse should perform. Every woman has certain concepts of what roles she should perform as a wife and certain expectations of what roles her spouse should perform. What the two people expect and what they find, however, may be different. The following examples illustrate instances where role expectations were never realized in marriage:

> **A young husband:** I always wanted a wife who was interested in a home and family. My wife doesn't like housework, hates to cook, and doesn't even want children.

> **A new bride:** In my family, my father always used to help my mother. My husband never lifts a finger to help me. (Author's counseling notes)

Leigh, Holman, and Burr (1984) found that individuals who had been dating their partner for a year were no more likely to have role compatibility than when they first started dating. This indicates that role compatibility is not very important for continuing dating relationships. However, it becomes very important after marriage. Spouses often assume their partner will enact the roles they expect, only to find out afterward that they have very different ideas and expectations. Data collected from 168 couples married for the first time showed that individuals' role preferences and leisure interests were highly related to the quality of their marriage and to their subjective evaluations of their relationship (Houts, Robins, and Huston, 1996). Role expectations should be discussed before marriage.

Habits   Advice columns in newspapers are filled with letters from people complaining about the annoying habits of their mate. Their spouse has terrible table manners, is careless about personal cleanliness, smokes or drinks too much, snores too loudly, goes to bed too late, won't get up in the morning, leaves dirty dishes scattered all over the house, never replaces the cap on the toothpaste, or has other habits the partner finds irritating. The writers have either tried to get their mate to change or tried

One measure of compatibility in marriage is the similarity of male and female role expectations and the degree to which these are being fulfilled in the relationship. Many partners agree that the male can be a nurturing parent and the woman can have a satisfying professional career.

to learn to accept the habit, often without success. Over the years, some of the habits become serious obstacles to marital harmony. Most personal habits that were annoying before marriage become exasperating in the closer and more continuous shared life of marriage. Most problems can be worked out, however, if people are caring, flexible, and willing to assume responsibility for changing themselves.

NONMARITAL COHABITATION

As stated in Chapter 1, cohabitation has become common, with between 50% and 60% of new marriages now involving couples who have lived together first (Bramlett and Mosher, 2002). In 2000, 7.6 million men and women were cohabiting, representing 3.8 million unmarried-partner households. It is estimated that about a quarter of unmarried women between the ages of 25 and 39 are currently living with a partner and that about half have lived at some time with an unmarried partner. Cohabitation is usually a short-term arrangement, with most couples either splitting up or marrying within 18 months.

Patterns of Relationships

One of the most important considerations is what the relationship means to the couple involved. No single pattern and no set meaning can be applied to all cohabitors. Any one relationship may fall along a continuum from friendship to long-term commitment to a substitute for marriage. For purposes of analysis, the relationships may be grouped into five basic types (Tanfer, 1987): (1) utilitarian arrangement, (2) intimate involvement with emotional commitment, (3) trial marriage, (4) prelude to marriage, or (5) alternative to marriage.

In order to avoid misunderstanding, those contemplating cohabitation would be wise to discuss their feelings ahead of time to ascertain the meaning each person associates with the decision to live together. If one partner considers cohabitation paramount to engagement and the other is participating without love and commitment, hard feelings and emotional pain result.

Utilitarian Arrangement   A good number of adults live together for utilitarian reasons. They save money by sharing living quarters and expenses, and they also share the work of housekeeping, laundry, and general maintenance. Some adults don't want to get married because they will lose some financial benefits: alimony, welfare, pension payments, or tax breaks. In such cases, they may or may not have an intimate relationship. They may be lovers or only friends.

Intimate Involvement with Emotional Commitment
This group includes those who love each other, want to have sex together, and want to be together in a monogamous relationship. They usually have a strong commitment to each other but are not planning marriage. They do not consider themselves married and are content to wait and see what happens. There is no statistically significant association between cohabitation and the type of relation that eventually evolves—that is, whether the couple marries.

Trial Marriage   Some adults want to live together to test their compatibility, to help them decide if they are meant for each other and if they want to get married. The arrangement is considered a "little marriage" to see if a "big marriage" will last.

Prelude to Marriage   A number of adults move in together before they get married. They have already committed themselves to marriage and see no reason to be apart in the meantime.

Alternative to Marriage   Those in this category are cohabiting not as a prelude to marriage but as a substitute for it. This includes those who are married to someone else and separated but not divorced and those who have been unhappily married and have become skeptical about the viability of legal marriage. Others have witnessed their friends' unhappy marriages and have concluded that legal marriage is not for them. People have numerous philosophical, legal, and ideological arguments about why they decide not to marry.

The Effect on Marriage

An important issue is the extent to which cohabitation results in greater satisfaction in subsequent marriage. There is no evidence that cohabitation weeds out incompatible couples and prepares people for successful marriage. One reason is that the kind of person an individual chooses to cohabit with is not necessarily the kind of person he or she would

choose to marry (Schoen and Weinick, 1993). For example, in a recent study, those who cohabited with rather than married their partner were found to be less selective with regard to education level and race. There was also less economic egalitarianism among cohabitors, and women were less upwardly selective of partners when they were planning to cohabit rather than marry (Blackwell and Lichter, 2000).

The divorce rate among those who cohabited before getting married is higher than among those who have not. Some experts say that is often because those who choose to cohabit are not great believers in marriage in the first place. While cohabiting relationships can look like marriages, they often differ in levels of commitment and autonomy, with people who cohabit possibly being less committed to marriage and more committed to autonomy (Popenoe and Whitehead, 2002a). Popenoe and Whitehead (2002a) explained that it is possible that once a low-commitment, high-autonomy pattern of relating is learned, it becomes difficult to unlearn and presents problems in maintaining the commitment to marriage. Cohan and Kleinbaum (2002) found that cohabitation before marriage was associated with more negative and less positive problem-solving support and behavior during the marriage. They explain that because long-term commitment can be less certain with couples who cohabit, it is possible that those who choose to cohabit are not as motivated to develop the necessary conflict resolution and support skills needed for a healthy marriage.

However, it is important to remember that the type of cohabitation is important to the future success of the relationship. Many people choose to cohabit after they have made plans to get married in the near future. These types of cohabitation are seen as prenuptial and appear not to have negative effects on the future marriage (S. L. Brown and Booth, 1996). Approximately 46% of all couples who cohabit are planning to get married (Casper and Bianchi, 2002).

THE TRANSITION TO MARRIAGE

How do two people know if they are ready for marriage? What legal requirements must they fulfill? What can the couple do to prepare for marriage ahead of time? What kinds of marital education, as-

Nonmarital cohabitation increased rapidly in the 1980s and 1990s, reflecting changes in social norms. One factor associated with the increase in cohabitation may be the increase in the average age at first marriage.

sessment, and counseling might be considered? How can engagement become a constructive period of preparation? This section attempts to answer these questions.

Marital Readiness

A number of important factors in the transition to marriage determine marital readiness (T. D. Holman and Dao Li, 1997). Based on the research information we have, the following considerations may be significant:

- Age at the time of marriage.
- The level of maturity of the couple.
- The timing of marriage.
- Motives for getting married.

- Readiness for sexual exclusiveness.
- Emotional emancipation from parents.
- The level of education and vocational aspirations and the degree of their fulfillment.

Age and Maturity　Age and level of maturity are important considerations in evaluating marital readiness. Teti, Lamb, and Elster (1987) found that males who married before they turned 19 were more likely to divorce or separate than were those who married later. Booth and Edwards (1985) found that marital instability was higher for men and women who married while in their teens.

There are a number of reasons for the greater instability of teenage marriages (Teti and Lamb, 1989). Teenagers are usually emotionally immature and not able to deal with the problems and stresses of early marriage. They do not have the social skills necessary to deal with a sustained intimate relationship. Their lack of skills leads to dissatisfaction with the way the spouse fulfills certain marital obligations, which leads, in turn, to friction and marital instability. Booth and Edwards (1985) found that the principal sources of marital dissatisfaction among spouses who married young are lack of faithfulness, the presence of jealousy, and the lack of understanding, agreement, and communication. Attempts to dominate or refusal to talk makes communication difficult.

Early marriages often are precipitated by pregnancies and result in couples abandoning educational pursuits in favor of parenthood, or full-time (and lower-status) employment, or both (Haggstrom, Kanouse, and Morrison, 1986). The results include low income and increased stress from trying to deal with the strains of adolescence, marriage, and parenthood. Long-term consequences are especially negative for women, who more frequently are compelled by circumstances to make a career-inhibiting life choice (Lowe and Witt, 1984).

The Timing of Marriage　Another factor in marital readiness is the extent to which people really choose to get married at the particular time they do. One husband explained:

> Margie and I could not have picked a worse time to get married. I was laid off work a week before we got married. Her mother was sick and later diagnosed as having terminal cancer. Margie and I didn't really

Age and level of maturity at the time of marriage are important factors that determine marital readiness. What other considerations might be significant?

give ourselves time enough to know one another well. (Author's counseling notes)

One wife felt she and her husband got off to a bad start because she let him talk her into marriage before she was ready. Such people become disenchanted, not because they are not in love or because they don't want to get married eventually, but because they simply are not ready when they do marry.

Motives for Marriage The motives for marriage are also important to marital success or failure. Most people in our culture get married for positive reasons, such as love, companionship, and security. Other people get married for essentially negative reasons, such as an attempt to escape from unhappy situations or relationships, to get even with others, to heal a damaged ego on the rebound, or to prove worth and attractiveness. Some people mistake gratitude for love. Very paternal or maternal people are attracted to those who seem to need to be cared for or nurtured. In a society that overromanticizes marriage, some people find it hard to resist the temptation.

Readiness for Sexual Exclusiveness Ordinarily, monogamous marriage in our society means that spouses desire sexual exclusiveness. Although many adults are quite tolerant of nonmarital sexual intercourse, most insist on the marital fidelity of their mate. Marital readiness for the majority of couples requires an attitude of sexual exclusiveness.

Emotional Emancipation from Parents Another indication of marital readiness and maturity is emotional emancipation from parents. Individuals who still seek emotional fulfillment primarily from their parents are not yet ready to give their primary loyalty and affection to their spouse, as is necessary for a successful marriage. No spouse, male or female, wants to play second fiddle to an in-law. Overall, young adults today stay single longer and live with their parents until later in life than did those in the 1960s ("Young U.S. Adults," 1988). However, the reasons are usually economic, not social.

Educational and Vocational Readiness There is a significant relationship between educational and vocational aspirations and the time of marriage. The lower the educational and vocational aspirations of youths, the more likely they will marry early. Youths with no post–high school educational plans are likely to feel that, since they have completed their education, marriage is the next step. The higher their educational aspirations, the longer young people wait after graduating from college before they marry. Once married, the higher their educational level, the longer after graduation they wait before beginning their families. Women who are in their twenties and have career aspirations tend to marry later in life than do those who plan to stay home and raise families.

Marriage and the Law

All people who get legally married enter into a civil contract. This means that their marriage is not just a personal affair. It is also of social concern, and each state has set up laws defining people's eligibility to marry and the procedures by which a contract may be established, as well as laws governing the maintenance of the contract once it is made.

Because marital regulation is the responsibility of individual states rather than the federal government, marital laws differ from state to state. However, the following discussion covers most of the major legal requirements regulating getting married.

Age   In most states and territories, males and females may marry without parental consent at age 18. The minimum age for marriage with parental consent in most states is 16 for females and males, although marriages at even younger ages are possible in some states with the parents' and a judge's consent.

Consanguinity   The term **consanguinity** refers to a blood relationship or descent from a common ancestor. Because of the belief in the increased possibility of genetic defects in the offspring of people who share some of the same genetic makeup, states forbid marriage to one's consanguineous son, daughter, mother, father, grandmother, grandfather, sister, brother, aunt, uncle, niece, or nephew. About half the states forbid marriages to first cousins. Some states also forbid marriages of second cousins or marriage to a grandniece or grandnephew.

Affinity   The term **affinity** refers to a relationship resulting from marriage. Some states forbid marriage to one's stepparent, stepchild, mother- or father-in-law, son- or daughter-in-law, or aunt- or uncle-in-law. But critics argue that the law has gone overboard in forbidding such marriages, since no biological harm can result from them.

Mental Deficiency   Because some severely developmentally delayed people are not able to meet the responsibilities of marriage, a number of states forbid

their marrying. Other states have no clear definition of mental deficiency and so cannot prevent such marriages. In other instances, sterilization or placement in institutions prevents mentally deficient people from reproducing.

Insanity   Most states prohibit marriages of the legally insane for the reason that an insane person cannot give his or her consent. Additionally, such a marriage could create severe problems for both family and society.

Procedural Requirements   Couples must obtain the legal permission of the state before marrying. This is accomplished through issuance of the marriage license, but the couple must fulfill certain requirements before getting the license. Some states will issue the license the same day the couple applies, but the rest have a waiting period of from 24 hours to 5 days. All but about a dozen states also require marriage within a specified period of time after issuance of the license for the license to be valid.

Some states also require a blood test for sexually transmitted diseases. A few states also require women to be tested for rubella, some states may require sickle cell anemia tests, and some give AIDS tests or information to marriage license applicants.

Common-Law Marriages   A **common-law marriage** is marriage by mutual consent, without a license. About 12 states still permit common-law marriages. The basic requirements to create a common-law marriage are that the partners must (1) have legal capacity (of age, opposite sex, with sufficient mental capacity) to marry; (2) intend to marry and have a current agreement to enter a marital relationship; (3) cohabit as husband and wife; and (4) represent themselves to the world as husband and wife (which means, for example, having the mail delivered to "Mr. and Mrs.," filing joint tax returns, and referring

consanguinuity   The state of being related by blood; having descent from a common ancestor.

affinity   A relationship formed by marriage without ties of blood.

common-law marriage   A marriage by mutual consent, without a license, recognized as legal under certain conditions by some states.

to themselves as husband and wife). With the rising numbers of couples who are opting for cohabitation rather than marriage, it is important to clarify what constitutes a common-law marriage and to point out that cohabiting without meeting the requirements just listed will not result in a common-law marriage. Although common-law marriages are recognized in some states and the District of Columbia, a common-law marriage validly created in one of those jurisdictions may not be recognized in a state that does not normally recognize common-law marriages.

Void or Voidable Marriages   If the legal requirements have not been met, a marriage may be defined as void or voidable. A **void marriage** is never considered valid in the first place, so a court decree is not necessary to set it aside. Marriages may be considered void in cases in which a prior marriage exists (bigamy), the marriage partners are related to each other within certain prohibited degrees, or either party is judged mentally ill.

Voidable marriages require an act of annulment to set them aside, after legal action has been instituted by one party. Only one spouse needs to take steps to void the marriage, and action must be brought during the lifetime of both spouses. The most common grounds for voiding a marriage are if either party is under the age of consent, either party is physically incapable of having intercourse, either party consents to the marriage through fraud or duress, or either party lacks the mental capacity to consent to the marriage.

Preparing for Marriage

The need for marriage preparation has long been recognized by professionals. Studies of high school and college students indicate a need for and interest in marriage preparation programs. There also is evidence that marriage preparation programs are effective; however, such programs are notoriously underattended (Duncan, Box, and Silliman, 1996). It seems ironic that couples will spend months and months planning their wedding but scarcely any time preparing for their marriage. One young man revealed different priorities: "We aren't going to have much of a wedding, but we're going to have a wonderful marriage" (Author's counseling notes). To this young man, marriage was more important than the wedding. Why spend thousands of dollars

Individual counselors or community agencies and organizations may offer classes and workshops in premarital education.

and many hours planning a wedding, only to have the marriage founder shortly after?

The basic theme here is that couples can prepare themselves for marriage in a way that will improve their chances for marital success. There are no guarantees, of course. But why do we often feel that vocational preparation is important and possible, and marital preparation is not? People aren't born knowing how to be good spouses and how to succeed in marriage any more than they are born knowing how to design a bridge. These things must be learned. But how?

We have mentioned elsewhere in this book, especially in Chapter 2, that much of what we know about marriage and family living was learned as we grew up in our family of origin. This is the most important means of learning. But there are other, more formal ways of preparing for marriage. Here we will discuss premarital education, premarital assessment, and premarital counseling.

Premarital Education Premarital education takes many forms (Mace, 1987). It may include a college-level course in marriage and family living (Sollie and Kaetz, 1992). It may include short courses offered by counselors or by community agencies and organizations such as child and family service agencies, mental health clinics, community counseling centers, women's clubs, service organizations, churches, or schools.

Over the past decade, a vast assortment of premarital and marital enrichment programs have been developed and partially evaluated. These programs are of special interest because of their focus on teaching couples specific communication skills related to individual and couple functioning. In general, research tends to support the claim that these programs have a positive effect on the participants. The most often reported finding is that couples do, in fact, learn the communication skills taught in the programs.

Some clergy and churches require couples to come for instruction before weddings are performed. Such programs are most often designed to interpret the religious meaning of marriage, but they may also include discussion of sexual, emotional, economic, social, and familial aspects of marriage.

Hospitals do an excellent job of offering childbirth education classes to expectant mothers and their partners. Concerned community leaders might well consider doing as thorough a job by offering marriage preparation programs to couples on a regular basis.

Premarital Assessment and Counseling Marriage preparation includes an evaluation of the extent to which the couple is fit and ready for marriage (T. D. Holman, Larson, and Harmer, 1994). The most common form of assessment is health assessment: a physical examination and blood tests for sexually transmitted diseases. In addition to the usual blood test for syphilis, many couples are now tested for AIDS, gonorrhea, and herpes. Certainly, if either partner has a sexually transmitted disease, the other needs to know about it.

Premarital assessment involves more than a health assessment, however. It may profitably include an assessment of a couple's overall relationship. Such an assessment is difficult for the partners to complete themselves because it's hard for them to be objective. A couple can go to a marriage counselor for the express purpose of exploring important areas of the relationship and determining the level of adjustment and any possible unresolved difficulties. Premarital counseling also helps couples, individually or in groups, to address difficulties that have been revealed.

One well-known instrument for predicting marital success is a premarital inventory called PREPARE (Fowers and Olson, 1989; Olson, Fournier, and Druckman, 1982). PREPARE is a 125-item inventory designed to identify relationship strengths and weaknesses in 11 relationship areas: realistic expectations, personality issues, communication, conflict resolution, financial management, leisure activities, sexual relationship, children and parenting, family and friends, equalitarian roles, and religious orientation. Additionally, the instrument contains an Idealistic Distortion Scale (Fowers and Olson, 1986). For each scale, an individual score is provided for each spouse. In addition, a Positive Couple Agreement (PCA) score is provided for each category; it measures the couple's consensus on issues in that area (Fowers, Montel, and Olson, 1996; Fowers and Olson, 1986).

Validity tests of PREPARE have shown that the inventory can correctly predict in 80–85% of cases whether partners will be happily married or will end up divorcing, in 79% of cases whether partners will be happily or unhappily married, and in 78% of cases whether partners will be happily married or will cancel marriage plans (Fowers and Olson, 1986; Larsen and Olson, 1989). This high predictive accuracy is exciting news, since it gives counselors a very useful tool for premarital and marital counseling.

Another widely used premarital inventory is FOCCUS (Facilitating Open Couple Communication, Understanding, and Study). FOCCUS has replaced the Pre-Marital Inventory (PMI) as the predominant premarital inventory used in marriage

void marriage A marriage considered invalid in the first place because it was illegal.

voidable marriage A marriage that can be set aside by annulment under certain prescribed legal circumstances.

Chinese Wedding Ceremonies

All cultures have rituals surrounding weddings. The traditional Chinese wedding ceremony has many rituals that differ from those of the traditional Western wedding. In a traditional Chinese wedding, the color red is very important. Red symbolizes happiness and prosperity for the Chinese, and often gifts are wrapped in red paper or money is placed in a red envelope. The color white is associated with death and is not used for gift giving in traditional families.

Historically, gift giving began about a week before the actual wedding. The family of the groom would go to the house of the bride and give her family gifts placed in red baskets or wrapped in red paper. The baskets were carried by male members of the groom's family and contained various items such as fruit, jewels, linens, and money. The bride opened the gifts with her family and typically returned about half of them to the member of the groom's family who brought them. Three days before the wedding, the bride's family brought gifts in red baskets or red paper to the groom's family. The baskets were carried by females of the bride's family and, again, about half were returned to the bride's family. While most of the gifts were for the groom, some contained personal items of the bride such as her clothing and jewelry. By accepting these gifts, the groom's family was welcoming the bride to their family. On her wedding day, when the bride moved into the groom's home, all her personal belongings would already be in place.

Many of the ethnic Chinese customs are being combined with Western customs or being ignored all together, but in traditional and many rural families they are still in place and are important family rituals. One wedding ritual that is still practiced and seen as very important in Chinese families is a special tea ceremony. On the day of the wedding, the bride and groom serve tea to both sets of parents while kneeling down in front of them. This symbolizes paying respect to their parents and asking permission to get married. The couple also serve tea to other older relatives, such as aunts and uncles, as a sign of respect. In return, they are presented with jewelry or money wrapped in red paper as a sign of wishing the couple much happiness and prosperity together.

preparation by the Catholic Church. FOCCUS is used by approximately two-thirds of the Roman Catholic dioceses in the United States as well as by over 500 Protestant churches of various denominations (L. Williams and Jurich, 1995).

Results indicate that FOCCUS and PREPARE are roughly comparable in terms of their predictive validity. FOCCUS scores during engagement predict a couple's future marital success 4–5 years later and indicate with 67.6–73.9% accuracy (depending on the scoring method used) whether the couples will have a high-quality or low-quality marriage. FOCCUS scores are able to identify 75% of the couples who later develop distressed marriages. Yet the fact that FOCCUS is not 100% accurate in its predictions is an important reminder that it should not be used as the single, infallible predictor of future marital success.

RITES OF PASSAGE

Rites of passage are ceremonies or rituals by which people pass from one social status to another. In our culture, the rites of passage from a single to a married status include the engagement, the wedding ceremony, and the wedding reception.

Engagement

An engagement to be married is an intermediate stage between courtship and marriage after a couple has announced the intention to marry. Engagement may be informal, at least for a while, during which time the two people have an understanding to marry. Marriage may still be too far off to make a formal announcement, or the couple may want to further test their relationship. Because many engagements are broken, a couple is probably wise to be very certain before making a formal announcement. Some couples move from informal engagement to marriage without ever formalizing the engagement period.

Engagement also becomes a final testing of compatibility and an opportunity to make additional adjustments. Some problems, such as planning finances or making housing arrangements, are difficult to resolve unless a date has been set for the wedding. One woman commented:

While wedding practices vary among different religious groups, all have certain things in common. Four parties are normally represented in the religious wedding rite: the couple, the religious group, the state (witnesses), and the family.

Sam owns a lot of property. I didn't feel free to bring up anything about ownership until after we were engaged. As it happens, he's going to put my name on all of it too. But I can see how the whole subject could have caused a lot of problems. (Author's counseling notes)

If any problems that have arisen in the couple's relationship have not been worked out before engagement, this period allows an additional opportunity to address them. The more things are worked out prior to marriage, the fewer adjustments and surprises arise afterward.

The engagement period also involves preparation for marriage itself. A most important part of this period, but one often neglected, is premarital education. A couple may choose to take advantage of premarital assessment and counseling. Marriage preparation also involves applying for a marriage license and having a physical examination and blood tests for sexually transmitted diseases.

The Wedding as a Religious and Civil Rite

Most marriages are performed under the auspices of a religious group that treats the wedding as a sa-

cred rite. The Catholic Church considers marriage a sacrament, with special graces bestowed by God through the church to the couple. The marriage bond is considered sacred and indissoluble. Both Judaism and Protestantism consider marriage a covenant of divine significance, sanctified by God and contracted between the spouses and the religious group with God as an unseen partner. While lifelong marriage is considered ideal, divorce and remarriage are allowed under certain circumstances.

Any religious rite is rich in meaning and symbolism. Although the rites vary among different religious groups, they have certain things in common. Four parties are represented in the service: the couple, the religious group (clergy), the state (witnesses), and the parents (usually through the father of the bride). Each party to the marriage rite enters into an agreement, or covenant, with the other parties to fulfill his or her obligations so that the marriage will be blessed "according to the ordinances

rites of passage Ceremonies by which people pass from one social status to another.

of God and the laws of the state." The denomination, through the clergy, pledges God's grace, love, and blessing. The man and woman make vows to each other "in the presence of God and these witnesses." The state grants the marriage license once the requirements of the law have been fulfilled.

In the wedding rite, the two people must indicate their complete willingness to be married; they must make certain pledges to each other; they indicate to the clergy their agreement to abide by divine ordinance and civil law. They join hands together as a symbol of their new union. Rings are a sign of eternity (having neither beginning nor end) and so symbolize the eternal nature of love. They are also a sign, seal, and reminder of the vows taken. The license is signed and witnessed as evidence that state law has been fulfilled.

Different religious groups have different rules and customs regarding weddings, but more and more clergy of all faiths are giving couples an opportunity to share in some of the decisions and even to help design their own service if they so desire.

A QUESTION OF POLICY

MARRIAGE INCENTIVES

In the United States today, there is a focus on policy to help promote marriages. The underlying beliefs behind this are that children are better off in two-parent families than in single-parent families and that policy can help encourage more two-parent families. In Chapter 9 we discuss the dramatic changes in welfare policies over the past 10 years. Some believe the traditional welfare policy could be construed as having disincentives for marriage. For example, in some states a two-parent family on welfare could not work more than 100 hours a month, but a single-parent family did not have that restriction. This led to the idea that some welfare recipients may have chosen to divorce or to remain unmarried in order to maintain welfare benefits. Congress decided that welfare needed to be reformed to reflect a more pro-marriage policy.

In 2003, Congress passed the Personal Responsibility, Work, and Family Promotion Act, which called for equitable treatment of married, two-parent families and awarded grants to states for the promotion of healthy marriages. Funds could be used to support any of the following programs and activities: public advertising campaigns on the value of marriage; education in high schools on the value of marriage, relationship skills, and budgeting; marriage education, including parenting skills, financial management, and conflict resolution for unmarried expectant parents; premarital education for engaged couples; marriage enhancement training for married couples; divorce reduction programs that teach relationship skills; marriage mentoring programs that use married couples as role models; and programs to reduce the disincentives to marriage that may be inherent in welfare rules if offered in conjunction with the other programs mentioned above.

QUESTIONS TO CONSIDER:

What if a state offered a monthly payment—of, say $100—to encourage couples to get married or stay married? What might be the consequences of that policy? (One state actually implemented this policy in the late 1990s.)

To what extent should taxpayers fund marriage initiatives?

Who should decide what information is included in a marriage enhancement program?

Should a marriage enhancement program be offered to anyone or just to low-income families on public assistance? Explain.

Why might someone be opposed to the policy of marriage promotion?

SUMMARY

1. Love is not a single concept, but has different dimensions. The five dimensions of love discussed here are romantic (emotional), erotic (sensual), dependent (need), friendship (companionship), and altruistic (unselfish).

2. The five elements of love discussed in this chapter are all important in the most complete love.

3. Researchers have identified various components of love. Sternberg revealed three components—intimacy, passion, and commitment—that he linked together as consummate love. Davis included three categories of love: passion, caring, and friendship. Moss and Schwebel specified five components of intimacy: commitment, affective intimacy, cognitive intimacy, physical intimacy, and mutuality.

4. Psychological intimacy involves two people, with each disclosing, listening, and developing attachment to the other. Intimacy lays the groundwork for making love; sex alone cannot substitute for intimacy.

5. At all stages of life, adults endorse passion, friendship, and self-giving love as highly important. There are far more similarities than differences between the love attitudes of men and women.

6. Selecting a mate is one of the most important decisions we make during our lifetime. Various theories have been developed to explain the process: psychodynamic theories, needs theories, exchange theories, and developmental process theories.

7. Family background factors are important influences in a person's life and so need to be investigated when choosing a mate. Marriages tend to be homogamous with respect to socioeconomic class, education, intelligence, and race. Divorce rates are higher in interracial marriages than in racially homogamous marriages.

8. Religious heterogamy produces no negative effects on women's evaluation of their marriage, but men are more likely to evaluate their marriage negatively if they are in a religiously heterogamous relationship. Parents' religious influence on their children depends on the parents' religiosity and not on whether the marriage is religiously homogamous.

9. Research on individual traits focuses on physical, personality, and mental health factors. Physical illness puts stress on a relationship, making it less satisfying and less stable. Certain personality traits make it difficult for people to have a happy marriage. Neurotic behavior, mental illness, depression, and impulsivity have been shown to weaken marital stability and quality. High self-esteem and adequate self-concept are positively related to marital satisfaction.

10. Sociocultural and background factors that influence marital quality include age at marriage, education, income, occupation, social class, and ethnicity.

11. Individual personal characteristics that influence the quality of marriage include physical and mental health, self-esteem and self-concept, interpersonal skills, unconventionality, and sociability. Age differentials are not a significant factor in marital quality, but marriage at a very young age is.

12. Marital compatibility is enhanced if spouses develop a high degree of consensus and similar attitudes and values about things that are important to them. A measure of marital compatibility is similarity of male and female role expectations. It is also helpful if the spouses have compatible personal habits.

13. Danger signals in the choice of a mate include a substance abuse problem, personality and character flaws, family problems, inability to get along with other people, lack of social skills, a lack of friends, and an unstable job history.

14. Rates of nonmarital cohabitation have increased greatly in recent years.

15. Cohabitation may mean different things to different people. A relationship may be a utilitarian arrangement, an intimate involvement with emotional commitment, a trial marriage, a prelude to marriage, or an alternative to marriage.

16. The transition from singlehood to marriage ordinarily takes place over several years. The

CHAPTER 7

LEARNING OBJECTIVES

After reading the chapter, you should be able to:

- Discuss various criteria of a successful marriage, including durability, approximation of ideals, fulfillment of needs, and satisfaction.

- Identify what makes some marriages happy and others miserable, according to John Gottman.

- Discuss the relationship between sex and a happy marriage and what factors account for sexual satisfaction in a marriage.

- Identify and explain the 12 qualities of successful marriages that are described in the textbook: communication; admiration and respect; com-

panionship; spirituality and values; commitment; affection; the ability to deal with crises and stress; responsibility; unselfishness; empathy and sensitivity; honesty, trust, and fidelity; and adaptability, flexibility, and tolerance.

- Describe potential problems in marriages that often can be seen before the couple actually gets married.

- Discuss how and why the newlywed years are important predictors of marital satisfaction.

- Explain why some people regret their choice of mate.

Qualities of a Successful Marriage

This book is about relationships: marital relationships, family relationships, and intimate relationships between unmarried persons. We begin here on a positive note by discussing how we can get along with other people and live together in a harmonious, fulfilling way. Living together happily is an art, requiring important qualities of character, a high degree of motivation, and finely tuned personal and social skills.

The focus in this chapter is on the marital relationship. However, most of the principles discussed here can be applied to all intimate relationships and to interpersonal relationships in the larger family unit.

CRITERIA FOR EVALUATING MARITAL SUCCESS

Before we look at the various characteristics of a successful marriage, we need to consider what defines a successful marriage. Four different criteria of a successful marriage are discussed here—durability, approximation of ideals, fulfillment of needs, and satisfaction—but no one alone seems adequate. Instead of adopting a single criterion, we discuss 12 different characteristics of successful marriage in the next section.

Durability

What constitutes a successful marriage? One measure that has been used is durability. Many people would say that the marriage that lasts is more successful than the one that is broken (Heaton and Albrecht, 1991). In many cases, marital stability and marital quality do go together. However, some marriages last a lifetime and are filled with hatred, conflict, and frustration (P. Bohannan, 1984). Some spouses haven't spoken to each other, except through the children, for decades. For many of us, marital success involves criteria more important than the number of years a couple stays together, regardless of other aspects of the relationship.

Approximation of Ideals

Another way of evaluating marital success is the extent to which the marriage approximates a couple's ideals or fulfills their expectations. Both partners have their own concept of an ideal relationship.

When asked, "What is your concept of a good marriage?" one student replied:

> A good marriage is one in which two people love one another, get along well together, in which they think alike on important issues, share common goals and interests, enjoy each other's company and have fun together, in which they are really good friends, are able to talk to one another to work out problems together.

Other students add to this fairly typical reply, describing a good marriage in these terms:

> One that allows you to be yourself and to be completely honest with one another.

> Fifty-fifty, where partners share everything.

> One that allows you freedom to do your own thing and to grow.

> One where your partner is your best friend.

Other students add different characteristics that are important to them. Marital success, in their view, is determined by the extent to which idealistic expectations are fulfilled.

One problem with this way of assessing the success of a marriage is that some people have very unrealistic expectations in the first place. The standards by which they judge their marriage are impossible to achieve. To be met, expectations need to be realistic, not just romantic fantasy.

Fulfillment of Needs

Another criterion of marital success is whether the marriage makes a sufficient contribution to individual needs, including the following:

- **Psychological needs**—for love, affection, approval, and self-fulfillment.
- **Social needs**—for friendship, companionship, and new experiences.
- **Sexual needs**—for both physical and psychological sexual fulfillment.
- **Material needs**—for "room and board" and physical maintenance and services.

This view assumes that partners are aware of each other's needs and willing and at least partly able to fulfill them (Tiggle, Peters, Kelley, and Vincent, 1982). Note the emphasis here on partial fulfillment. Marriage can never meet every need. Some needs will always have to be met apart from the marriage itself. One's job, friendships, hobbies, and recreational pursuits all contribute to need fulfillment. However, a successful marriage makes an acceptable contribution; any marriage that doesn't has failed in the eyes of most couples.

Two cautions need to be added. First, it is helpful if need fulfillment is mutual (Fowler, 1982). In relationships in which one person does all the giving and the other all the receiving, the giver often becomes exhausted. Second, mutual need fulfillment is most possible if needs fall within the limits of realistic expectations. A highly dependent, possessive person, for example, may demand so much love and approval that no one could possibly fulfill those needs. In this case, the marriage might fail, not because of the unwillingness of the giving person to fulfill needs, but because of the unreasonable demands of the insatiable partner.

Satisfaction

Much of the research on marriage success measures marital satisfaction: the extent to which couples are content and fulfilled in their relationship. According to this view, marital success is defined as the extent to which both partners in the relationship are satisfied that it has fulfilled reasonable expectations and mutual needs (Hunsley, Pinsent, Lefedvre, James-Tanner, and Vito, 1995). This definition rec-

ognizes that there are individual differences in expectations and need requirements, so that what satisfies one couple might not satisfy another. Marital satisfaction includes marital quality, marital adjustments, and marital happiness (Heyman, Sayers, and Bellack, 1994). Marital satisfaction is a comprehensive concept and is the one accepted here as the criterion for marital success. It is important that *both* partners be satisfied. Sometimes one partner is very content with a relationship while the other is ready to file for divorce.

Obviously, there are degrees of success. Few marriages live up to *all* expectations and fulfill *all* needs all the time. Furthermore, successful couples strive for improvement. Their marriages are in the process of becoming, and few ever feel they have completely arrived. However, if they are satisfied with the progress they have made, they judge their effort as successful. We will discuss growth and fulfillment further in Chapter 8.

HAPPY VERSUS UNHAPPY MARRIAGES

What makes some marriages happy and others miserable? John Gottman has been studying this question for decades and has found the pattern of communication in couples to be very important in

The number of years a couple stays together is not the most important indicator of marital success. Qualities such as empathy, respect, companionship, and affection are but a few of the characteristics of a successful marriage.

marital happiness. In happy couples, when one partner makes a positive statement, it is reciprocated in a positive manner; in unhappy couples, partners often have no immediate response to a positive statement. In happy couples, after one partner makes a negative statement, the other offers no immediate response; in unhappy couples, both partners continue to reciprocate negatively. This **negative affect reciprocity** is a consistent characteristic of distressed couples (Gottman, 1998).

Some messages can be interpreted either positively or negatively. For example, the statement "Stop interrupting me" may be an attempt to repair an interaction, but it may also be said with irritation. Gottman believes that in a happy marriage there is a greater probability that the listener will focus on the repair aspect of the message and respond by saying, "Sorry, what were you saying?" In an unhappy marriage, there is a greater probability that the listener will respond only to the irritation in the message and say something like, "I wouldn't have to interrupt if I could get a word in edgewise." In this case, the message does not repair any part of the communication pattern, and the negativity bounces back and forth (Gottman, 1998).

Gottman also sees differences in how spouses in happy and unhappy marriages view positive and negative actions of their partner. In a happy marriage, if one partner does something negative, the other partner tends to think that the negativity is fleeting and situational. For example, negative behavior may be attributed to a tough day at work or a bad mood, as opposed to a fixed characteristic of the individual. Thus, the negativity is viewed as temporary and the cause as situational. In an unhappy marriage, however, the same behavior is likely to be interpreted as a sign of inconsideration, selfishness, and indifference and as internal to the partner. The same pattern exists for positive behavior. Happy couples interpret positive behavior as internal to the partner, whereas unhappy couples are likely to interpret the same positive behavior as a fluke and to not believe that it will last (Gottman, 1998).

The "demand–withdraw" (or "pursuer–distancer") pattern is another characteristic of unhappy marriages. With this pattern, it is usually the woman who raises and pursues the issues and the man who attempts to avoid the discussion and tends to withdraw. Research suggests that in unhappy marriages with high negative affect men withdraw emotionally and women do not (Gottman and Levenson, 1988).

Agreement about what needs to be done in the household and by whom directly contributes to a successful marriage.

Furthermore, in two longitudinal studies, Gottman (1994) found that it was not anger that led to unhappy marriages and reliably predicted divorce, but rather four processes that he called "the Four Horsemen of the Apocalypse": criticism; defensiveness; contempt; and stonewalling, or listener withdrawal. Other researchers added belligerence—a behavior that is provocative and is designed to escalate the conflict ("What can you do if I do go out tonight? What are you gonna do about it? Just try to stop me")—as a likely predictor of divorce. These findings were replicated in a recent study which found that contempt, belligerence, and defensiveness are common negative behaviors during conflict and lead to unhappy marriages (Gottman, Coan, Carrere, and Swanson, 1998).

In a national study of 21,501 married couples, family science researcher David Olson (2000) found that happy and unhappy couples differ in five key areas: (1) how well partners communicate, (2) how flexible they are as a couple, (3) how emotionally close they are, (4) how compatible their personalities are, and (5) how they handle conflict. When given Olson's 165-question inventory, happy couples identified those five areas (communication, flexibility, emotional closeness, compatibility, and conflict resolution) as strengths; unhappy ones did not. For example, about 75% of happy couples agreed on the high quality of their communication, whereas only 11% of unhappy couples did. Similarly, 75% of happy couples agreed that they can change and adapt when necessary, whereas only 20% of unhappy couples believed this to be true. Olson believes that spouses must feel they can adapt to change and feel close and connected in order to have a happy marriage.

He also identified five other areas that affect a couple's happiness: (1) the sexual relationship, (2) the choice of leisure activities, (3) the influence of family and friends, (4) the ability to manage finances, and (5) agreement on spiritual beliefs. He advises that, in order to build strength as a couple, partners should pay the same sort of attention to the relationship that they did when they were dating and praise the other partner for the positive things, instead of focusing on what bothers them about the partner (Olson, 2000).

SEX AND A HAPPY MARRIAGE

What is the relationship between sex and a happy marriage? Can people be happily married without a satisfying sex life? Certainly, the positive expression of sexuality contributes to marital satisfaction in particular and to life satisfaction in general (Maddock, 1989). Healthy sexuality is meant to be a blessing, not a problem (Dyk, 1990). However, what is satisfying to one couple may not be acceptable to another. Human beings differ in their sexual needs, preferences, habits and aims. Some couples want intercourse every day; others would find this frequency unacceptable. If both partners are satisfied with their sex life, it can contribute in a positive way to their overall happiness; but if the partners disagree, or if one or both are frustrated or unhappy with their sex life, it can significantly reduce or even destroy relationship satisfaction.

Questions often asked are "How frequently do couples have intercourse?" and "What is the relationship between frequency and sexual satisfaction?" It is always dangerous to play the numbers game, because any figure mentioned is going to be disappointing to someone. But, as a starter, let's examine what some couples do.

In general, men experience sexual desire somewhat more frequently than do women, although there is a considerable variation among individuals (Beck, Bozman, and Qualthrough, 1991). One study of women in the early years of marriage showed that the frequency of intercourse declined from an average of almost 15 times per month during the first years of marriage to about 6 times per month during the sixth year (Greenblat, 1983). However, there was a wide range of frequency: from 4 to 45 times per month for couples married under 1 year. Another study consisted of interviews regarding a variety of attitudes and experiences of Americans and showed that married respondents engaged in sexual intercourse an average of 67 times per year, or slightly over once a week. The frequency rates were highest among the young and those married less than 3 years (T. W. Smith, 1994).

Typically, most couples start out marriage engaging frequently in intercourse, but then the incidence begins to decline and they settle into their own individual patterns. However, couples report that affection, love, tenderness, companionship, and physical closeness continue to be strong needs.

Declining health may be an issue for some older men and women with regard to their sexual activity, but for many individuals 60 and older, sexuality remains an important part of their lives. A 1999 survey conducted by American Association of Retired Persons revealed a relatively sexually active population of individuals 60 and older. It found that among 60- through 74-year-olds, 30% of men and 24% of women were having sex at least once per week, and 25% of those 75 years old and older were having sex at least once per week. While frequency drops with age, more than 60% of surveyed men and women who have regular partners are sexually active enough to have intercourse at least once or twice a month. Americans 60 and older believe that better health would do more to enhance their sexual pleasure than any other life change, but more

negative affect reciprocity   A pattern of communication in unhappy couples whereby partners respond negatively to each other's statements.

and support each other in their respective endeavors, who are proud of each other's achievements, who openly express appreciation of each other, and who build each other's self-esteem are fulfilling their emotional needs and building a satisfying relationship (R. A. Bell, Daly, and Gonzalez, 1987; J. Lauer and Lauer, 1985). Respect in marriage encompasses respect for individual differences and respect for the other person as an important human being (Curran, 1983).

Partners who are able to meet these needs are usually emotionally secure people themselves. They don't have to criticize each other or put each other down to build themselves up. They like expressing appreciation and giving compliments. Their approval is not conditional, requiring the partner to do certain things before it is granted. Rather, their approval is what psychologists call **noncontingent reinforcement.** It is **unconditional positive regard.** They don't try to change their spouse but are able to accept him or her as he or she is. If they have any complaints, they voice them in private, not in front of other people. They are not threatened by a competent, high-achieving spouse and so avoid destructive competition. They like themselves and each other and express their approval in word and deed.

Companionship

One important reason for getting married is companionship. Successful married couples spend sufficient time together—and quality time. The partners enjoy each other's company, share common interests and activities, and have a lot of laughs together. They are interested in each other's hobbies and leisure-time preferences. Furthermore, they try to be interesting companions to each other.

Research indicates that partners who share interests, who do things together, and who share some of the same friends and social groups derive more satisfaction from their relationship than do partners who are not mutually involved. However, it's not just the amount of time spouses spend together that is related to marital satisfaction but also the quality of the relationship they enjoy when they are together. Marital satisfaction increases when communication is high during shared leisure time (T. B. Holman and Jacquart, 1988). Research shows that attending to relationships—that is, putting effort into them—is important in maintaining satisfaction. Women often attend to relationships by thinking and talking about them, whereas men often attend to relationships by sharing activities and spending time together (Acitelli, 2001).

It is unrealistic to expect partners to do everything together or to have all their interests in common. Most people want some separateness in their togetherness; they want to be able to do some things with their own friends. But it is helpful to have interests and friends in common. Problems arise when partners continue to enjoy most of their social life with friends they knew before marriage rather than spend time together. Some couples drift apart simply because the partners seldom see each other. Curran (1983) goes so far as to state, "Lack of time together may be the most pervasive enemy the healthy family has." Marital interaction and happiness seem to go together. An acceptable degree of interaction contributes to marital happiness, and marital happiness tends to increase the amount of interaction (Zuo, 1992).

People also differ on how close a companion they want their spouse to be. When one wants close companionship and the other doesn't, it can become a source of tension and conflict. Mace and Mace (1974) likened the marriage relationship to the dilemma of two porcupines settling down to sleep on a cold night. If the porcupines get too close, their quills prick each other. If they move too far apart, they can't benefit from each other's body heat. So the porcupines shift back and forth, first together and then apart, until they arrive at a position in which they can achieve the maximum amount of warmth with a minimum amount of hurt.

Friendship, like companionship, is very important in marriage. John Gottman has studied more than 2,000 couples by conducting extensive interviews and videotaping couple interactions. In a recent study (Gottman, 2000a) of 100 married couples, he found that for women, the vital ingredient in improving sex, romance, and passion in marriage was to increase the sense of friendship. Women need a deep sense of connection to feel passionate, which means that the husband must get to know who his wife is on a profound level and must express genuine affection toward her. Examples of this type of connection or friendship are being able to define a spouse's life dreams; showing respect, affection, and small gestures of appreciation rather than criticizing; and attempting to connect through jokes or playful comments. For men, the key to im-

Successful married couples share common interests and activities; they enjoy each other's company.

proving sex, romance, and passion was found to be conflict reduction; arguing activated men's "fight or flight" response and left them feeling threatened and not eager for sex.

However, P. Schwartz (2000) cautions that the goal of having your spouse be your best friend is very difficult to achieve and isn't appropriate for everyone. As wonderful as friendship is, most people do not select a partner the same way they select a friend, and marriage does not work the same as friendship does. Most people do not spend nearly as much time with their friends as they do with their spouses, nor do mere friends negotiate such daily challenges as living together, maintaining a sexual relationship, rearing childen, and sharing finances. It is great when couples are friends, but you do not need a best friend to have a good marriage.

As with most friendships, having fun together is also an important component of good marriages. It is important to have fun in a marriage, along with confidence that the marriage will last and persistence in the commitment (Arp, Arp, Stanley, Markman, and Blumberg, 2000). Fun has been understudied and underestimated in its ability to increase passion and overall satisfaction in a long-term relationship. In addition, research has shown that the pursuit of

novel, exciting activities together serves to enhance relationship satisfaction in marriage by helping couples grow both individually and relationally (Aron, Norman, Aron, McKenna, and Heyman, 2000).

Spirituality and Values

Another factor that contributes to successful marriage is shared spirituality and values (R. C. Hatch, James, and Schumm, 1986). Successful couples share spiritual activities; the partners have a high degree of religious orientation and similar beliefs and values that are manifested in religious behavior.

Religious couples indicate that their religion contributes to their marriage in a number of ways. They derive social, emotional, and spiritual support from their faith. In some cases, church involvement provides friends and activities for the couples to

noncontingent reinforcement   Unconditional approval of another person.

unconditional positive regard   Acceptance of another person as he or she is.

Successful couples commonly share spiritual activities and similar beliefs. Studies find such shared values to be a consistent predictor of marital adjustment, regardless of how liberal or conservative the couple's beliefs are.

share. Religious faith also encourages marital commitment through the value that is placed on the marital bond and through spiritual support in times of difficulties. Some people point to the increased intimacy that results in sharing such an intimate thing as one's religious faith. Many married couples turn to their faith for moral guidance in making decisions and dealing with conflict (L. C. Robinson and Blanton, 1993).

Commitment

Successful marriage requires a high degree of motivation: the desire to make the marriage work and the willingness to expend time and effort to ensure that it does. Some couples encounter so many serious problems in their relationship that one wonders how the marriage will ever succeed. But, through extraordinary motivation and determination, they overcome their obstacles, solve their problems, and emerge with a satisfactory relationship. Other couples give up after very little effort; some of these people really didn't want to be married in the first place, so they never worked at the marriage (Nock, 1995a; Surra and Hughes, 1997).

Commitment, rather than satisfaction or investment, is the strongest predictor of relationship persistence (Rusbult, Olsen, Davis, and Hannon, 2001). Commitment is regarded as having three components: intention to persist, psychological attach-

ment, and a cognitive orientation to being in the relationship for the long term. Many couples' interventions include components that focus on these cognitive and affective dimensions (Rusbult et al., 2001). Sahlstein and Baxter (2001) made the important point that relationships change over time, often encompassing a number of contradictory elements. Periodically defining levels of commitment and trust in close relationships contributes to marriage maintenance and enhancement.

Marital success is more attainable if the commitment is mutual. One person can't build a relationship or save a marriage, no matter how much he or she tries. In their research on 301 married persons, Sabatelli and Cecil-Pigo (1985) found that partners who were participating equally in the relationship and who experienced maximum interdependence were also the most committed. People aren't going to put forth their best effort if their partner is not equally involved.

One of the important questions is, To whom and to what is the commitment? The commitment is really threefold:

1. **The commitment is of the self, to the self.** This involves the desire to grow, to change, and to be a good marriage partner. Some people who come for marriage counseling want their partner to change, but they are unwilling to change themselves or to assume any personal responsi-

bility for making things better. None of us can really change other people if they don't want to change, but we can change ourselves if we need to. It's not easy, but it can be done.

2. **The commitment is to each other.** When people say "I do" in a marriage ceremony, they make a personal promise or pledge to each other.

3. **The commitment is to the relationship, the marriage, and the family.** Mace and Mace (1980) define commitment as a willingness to support "ongoing growth in their relationship." When children are involved, the commitment goes beyond the couple relationship to include the whole family unit.

Stanley and Markman (1992) make a distinction between personal dedication and constraint commitment. *Personal dedication* refers to the desire of an individual to maintain or improve the quality of his or her relationship for the joint benefit of the couple. It is evidenced by a desire not only to continue in the relationship but also to improve it, to sacrifice for it, to invest in it, to link personal goals to it, and to benefit the partner as well as oneself.

In contrast, *constraint commitment* refers to forces that compel individuals to maintain relationships regardless of their personal dedication to them. Constraints may arise from either external or internal pressures, and they promote relationship stability by making termination of the relationship more costly economically, socially, personally, and psychologically.

But what happens if there is conflict between commitments? Is the commitment to the marriage and the family or to one's partner more important? Mae West famously described marriage as an institution but asked, "Who wants to live in an institution?" Indeed, who does, unless it serves the needs of those in it? Some people are able to work out troubled relationships because marriage is sacred to them and they want to preserve the family unit. In so doing, they may find individual and couple fulfillment. For other people, however, commitment to save the marriage may come at great cost to themselves and the children.

One of the most basic challenges is maintaining a sense of autonomy while also experiencing a sense of relatedness to one's partner (Rankin-Esquer, Burnett, Baucom, and Epstein, 1997). Partners in successful marriages have mastered the art of losing themselves in their relationship without losing their sense of self. This requires a well-developed identity and high self-esteem. Figure 7.1 depicts three types of relationships. In A, two people maintain their individual identities but make little effort to achieve oneness as a married couple. In B, two people lose their separate identities, which become swallowed up in the relationship. In C, there is sufficient commitment to form a union, but enough separateness for each to maintain a sense of self.

Marital Rituals   Most married people need privacy and time to pursue their own interests as individuals. They also need time together as a married couple, and they need time to be with their children as a whole family. Keeping a family healthy is not easy, especially with young children. When the children are young, it's easy to become absorbed in taking care of them and thus neglect the marital relationship, but a marriage relationship has to be nurtured to stay alive.

Couple rituals can play an important role in nurturing a relationship. Families have long been engaged in rituals that help them define who they are

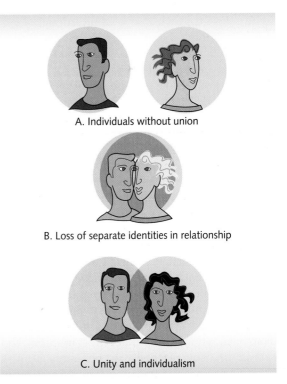

A. Individuals without union

B. Loss of separate identities in relationship

C. Unity and individualism

Figure 7.1   Different Types of Relationships

and provide a sense of cohesion. Rituals for couples are just as important as family rituals and contribute to the success of the marital relationship. Doherty (2001) defines *marital rituals* as social interactions that are scheduled moments that are mutually decided on, repeated, and coordinated and that have positive emotional significance. These rituals include things such as a loving greeting, a routinely planned "date night," 20 minutes of together time after the evening meal during which both spouses work on their connection. Such marital rituals help maintain connection between partners, which in turn helps hold marriages together in times of stress. When couples do not make time for their relationship amid the hectic and busy schedule of everyday life, the marital relationship often gets neglected. Marriage, like most things, needs a commitment of time to help maintain its well-being. A mindfully maintained ritual can bring that needed element of time together to keep marriages operating successfully.

Affection

One important expectation of most married partners is they will meet each other's need for love and affection. This need varies from couple to couple, depending on the way the partners are socialized. Some people have a higher need for emotional intimacy than others. But most expect their needs to be met in their marriage (Dandeneau and Johnson, 1994; Kenny and Acitelli, 1994).

Several related factors are important. J. Lauer and Lauer (1985) stress the importance of spouses' agreeing on how to show affection and how often. Some people want a lot of physical contact: hugging, kissing, cuddling, touching, caressing. Others are satisfied with an occasional kiss. Some people are very uninhibited in sexual expression and desire playful sex. Others are more restrained. There also may be differences in the desired frequency of intercourse. In successful marriages, couples are able to work out such differences.

In their research, R. A. Bell, Daly, and Gonzalez (1987) found that both physical and verbal affection were important to successful marriage. As one wife put it, "I know he loves me, but I want him to tell me." Words that express warmth, appreciation, endearment, and approval, that raise low spirits, and that boost damaged egos can be as essential as physical contact and sexual intimacy. Spouses involved in long-term happy marriages often point to each other's admirable qualities, as opposed to

their negative qualities, and appreciate the pleasure they find in their relationship without taking it for granted (Wallerstein and Blakeslee, 1995).

Interestingly, even though fulfillment of affectional and sexual needs is important to marital success, strong feelings of romantic love are not a requirement. Romantic love is one of the most important factors in emotional attraction and in motivating couples to want to be together. In successful marriages, love may continue to grow, but it changes over the years, with fewer components of romance and stronger bonds of attachment and affection. Emotional bonding and affective expression are important ingredients in successful marriages (S. A. Anderson, 1986; Carstensen, Gottman, and Levenson, 1995; Kinston, Loader, and Miller, 1987).

The Ability to Deal with Crises and Stress

All couples, both those who achieve marital success and those who do not, experience problems and stress in and outside their relationship. One of the factors that distinguishes the two groups is that spouses who have successful marriages are able to solve their problems and manage stress in a creative fashion. Stinnett and DeFrain (1985) found that successful couples are "able to weather the storms of life." These partners expect problems as a normal part of life and develop problem-solving skills so that they can cope (Curran, 1983). They often interpret crises as an opportunity to move in a positive direction. They feel they have grown from struggling through and coping with the crisis. In one study of strong families, 77% felt that something positive had developed as a result of coping with a crisis (Stinnett, Knorr, DeFrain, and Rowe, 1981). One of the characteristics of strong families is that family members turn to one another for strength and assistance. This enhances family unity, cohesiveness, and commitment.

Successful couples also have a greater tolerance for frustration than do unsuccessful couples. In this sense, the partners are more emotionally mature and stable. They have learned healthy, constructive ways of dealing with anger, rather than taking it out on other family members (Hardy, Orzek, and Heistad, 1984). Similarly, spouses who have a positive attitude toward life are more likely to maintain satisfying marriages (Veroff, Douvan, Orbuch, and Acitelli, 1998), whereas moodiness, abrasivenenss, and nervousness are associated with relatively high levels of interpersonal negativity and with low levels of marital satisfaction (Caughlin, Huston, & Houts, 2000).

Research evidence also suggests that the degree of depression is a strong predictor of marital quality. Depression both arises from and creates marital dissatisfaction. Persons who are unhappy in their marriage report relatively high levels of depression, and depressed persons and their spouses report stressful, unsatisfying marriages (J. D. McLeod and Eckberg, 1993).

Responsibility

Responsibility involves being accountable for one's own behavior within the context of the family. It also means assuming responsibility for family maintenance (Fincham and Bradbury, 1992). Successful marriage depends on the mutual assumption, sharing, and division of responsibility in the family. Typical complaints brought to marriage counselors include the following:

My partner is completely irresponsible.

My partner never does anything around the house. I do everything, inside and outside work both.

My partner is irresponsible in handling money.

My spouse doesn't like to work. He'd rather be out with friends partying and having a good time.

My spouse doesn't take enough responsibility for cleaning the house. She knows that if she doesn't do it, eventually I'll get it done.

My partner doesn't show any interest in taking care of the children. He feels that because he brings home a paycheck, that is the end of his responsibilities. He leaves everything else to me.

I have to make all the decisions and plans for our social life. I wish my spouse would assume some of this responsibility. (Author's counseling notes)

In marriages in which couples report a high degree of satisfaction, two conditions exist in relation to the division of responsibility. First, the partners feel there is a fairly equal division of labor. In situations in which one partner is working 100 hours a week and the other works little, the working spouse rightfully resents the uneven distribution of responsibility. Women in particular are dissatisfied when they perceive unfairness in the performance of household chores and in the spending of money (Blair, 1993). Consider this account:

Ed worked hard all his life building up a cleaning business. He was very successful and decided to retire at age 60. He spends his time playing golf at the country club and playing cards at the Elks club. Since the family needs the money and the business needs attention, his wife Edith spends her days managing the company. She resents deeply the fact that she is still working and her husband isn't. (Author's counseling notes)

Numerous studies reveal that an inequitable division of household and child care responsibilities causes conflict in families. Despite changes in gender attitudes and the increased participation of women in the workforce, women still do the majority of the housework (Shelton, 1992). The research on household task performance provides little evidence of egalitarianism in marriage when it comes to housework, as employed women do nearly twice as much as men. This lack of equity is a major source of dissatisfaction for many women.

Second, in successful marriages, gender-role performance matches gender-role expectations. Many couples have set ideas about who should perform what tasks. Thus, if a man expects his spouse to perform traditional feminine roles in the family—caring for children, taking care of the home, attending to his needs—but she's more interested in pursuing her career, conflict develops. If the woman expects her spouse to be the primary breadwinner and an all-around handyman at home and he doesn't live up to her expectations, she may become very dissatisfied with the relationship.

Unselfishness

Ours is an age of individualism in which many try to find happiness through self-gratification and narcissistic **selfism.** Selfism in marriage lessens each partner's responsibility for the success of the relationship. Social exchange theory emphasizes that people seek relationships in which the cost–benefit ratio is satisfactory and fair. From this perspective, decreased investment on the part of one spouse decreases the likelihood that the other will receive the

selfism A personal value system that emphasizes that the way to find happiness is through self-gratification and narcissism.

rewards deemed sufficient to continue the relationship. The result is marital instability, because associations are continued only if each partner feels he or she is receiving what is deserved and expected.

It is not surprising, therefore, that the most successful marriages are based on a spirit of mutual helpfulness, with each partner unselfishly attending to the needs of the other, as well as to his or her own (R. A. Bell, Daly, and Gonzalez, 1987). One woman explained:

> My husband is the most generous, giving man I have ever known. He will give you the shirt off his back. Every day he does so many little things for me. When we go out, he always makes sure that I'm having a good time. He insists on bringing my coffee while I'm in bed in the morning. He helps me around the house all the time. He never seems to think about himself. He's too busy thinking about the rest of us. (Author's counseling notes)

It is not evident in the quotation, but the woman was just as giving and unselfish as her spouse. They had a wonderful marriage, primarily because the unselfishness was reciprocal.

Empathy and Sensitivity

Empathy refers to the ability to identify with the feelings, thoughts, and attitudes of another person (Wampler and Powell, 1982). It is the vicarious sharing of the experiences of another person. Kagan and Schneider (1987) call this ability **affective sensitivity** and describe its development in five phases:

- **Phase 1: Perception.** Developing empathy begins with contact and interaction during which someone perceives the thoughts, feelings, memories, anticipations, and aspirations of another person and the emotional tones associated with them.
- **Phase 2: Experiencing.** The observer resonates to, or vicariously experiences, the emotions of the other.
- **Phase 3: Awareness.** Awareness is the process of acknowledging to oneself that one has perceived and resonated to the emotions of another individual.
- **Phase 4: Labeling.** Awareness is acknowledged verbally; the observer speaks of having sensitivity to what another person has communicated.

- **Phase 5: Stating.** Empathy requires a person to communicate verbally or by some other means that he or she has perceived another person's message. Communication may be nonverbal, such as touching. The purpose of this final phase is to let the other person know that one understands.

According to the research, empathy is an important ingredient in a successful marriage (Long, Angera, and Carter, 1999). An empathetic person is someone who listens, understands, and cares (Sprecher, Metts, Burleson, Hapfield, and Thompson, 1995).

Simpson, Ickes, and Orina (2001) describe empathic accuracy as a relationship maintenance strategy in which one partner accurately identifies the thoughts and feelings of his or her partner. One study examined 48 romantically involved couples who voluntarily participated in a 10-hour empathy training program (Long, Angera, and Carter, 1999). The purpose of the program was to increase the expression of empathy among romantic partners. The researchers found not only that couples increased their self-reported expression of empathy with a partner but also that the change in empathic expression with a partner was positively related to relationship satisfaction. That is, when individuals improve their abilities to express empathy in their relationship, the partners' satisfaction with the relationship improves.

Honesty, Trust, and Fidelity

According to the research of R. A. Bell, Daly, and Gonzalez (1987), the old-fashioned virtues of honesty, trust, and fidelity are important ingredients in contemporary successful marriages. Sincerity, truthfulness, faithfulness, and trust are the cement that bind people together. Partners know they can accept each other's word, believe in each other, and depend on each other to keep promises and to be faithful to commitments that are made. One young woman comments:

> I never have to worry about my husband. When he tells me something I know it's true. He's a very sincere, up-front person. I know just where I stand with him all the time. He always keeps his word. If he promises the kids something, he never disappoints them. He travels a lot, but I trust him completely. I

No Time for Love

Although people say they choose to marry for companionship, marriage counselors hear couples complaining over and over, "We never spend any time together," or "We don't talk to each other," or "We don't have any interests in common," or "We've drifted apart." These comments come from couples who in the beginning of their marriages said the primary reasons for getting married were companionship and love.

Obviously, something has gone wrong. Usually, one of several things has happened:

- One or both spouses spend most of their time on the job, with little left over for the family. It's easy under these circumstances to drift apart.

- One or both spouses have separate friends and spend most of their leisure time with their own friends rather than with joint friends as a couple.

- One or both spouses have individual hobbies and leisure time activities that they pursue separately rather than together. If these activities take up most of the leisure time, the couple are separated during leisure hours. One man described his situation: "My wife is a marathon runner. She works out several hours a day and works full-time in addition. It doesn't leave us any time together as a couple" (Author's counseling notes).

- The spouses spend most of their free time attending movies, concerts, or athletic events, and they spend little time alone together just talking. They are in each other's company, but they are not finding real intimacy based on emotional closeness.

- One or both spouses spend their free time with the children rather than devoting some of it to being together as a couple. One man complained, "Since the baby was born, my wife's whole life has been wrapped up in Sarah. My wife has no time for me" (Author's counseling notes).

- One or both spouses don't enjoy being together. They are embarrassed by what the other person does when they do go out, and often argue when in each other's company. One man explained, "When we go to another couple's house, my wife totally monopolizes the conversation. She interrupts. She turns the conversation around to talk about something she's interested in. It's very embarrassing" (Author's counseling notes).

In each of these situations, the couple doesn't spend enough quality time together. When the partners are together, their activities are not conducive to companionship, which doesn't help to strengthen their relationship. Although people in intimate relationships need time for themselves, they also need to set time aside for the "we" in the relationship. Planning ahead and scheduling this time in advance, as one often does with other priorities, can help ensure that companionship needs in a marriage will be met. For example, some couples hire a babysitter at regular intervals in order to go out on a "date." These dates can even be set up several months in advance to make sure that both partners' schedules are clear, as opposed to being together as a couple only in whatever time is left at the end of the day.

know he's faithful to me. He isn't the kind of man to sneak around. If two people can't believe in one another, or depend on one another, they don't have much of a relationship in my opinion. (Student comments to author)

When two people first start going out together, one of the things each seeks to discover is whether the other is honest and sincere about the relationship. In marriage itself, once one spouse begins to doubt the honesty, sincerity, and faithfulness of the other, he or she will feel increasingly insecure and vulnerable. In fact, the future of the relationship may be threatened. Once trust is broken, develop-

ing it again involves a willingness to forgive. When one partner does something that hurts the other but is truly sorry for what has happened, the relationship can be rebuilt only if the person who has been hurt is willing to forgive the other (Hargrave and Sells, 1997).

affective sensitivity Empathy, or the ability to identify with the feelings, thoughts, and attitudes of another person.

Adaptability, Flexibility, and Tolerance

Spouses whose marriages are successful are usually adaptable and flexible (Wilcoxon, 1985). They recognize that people differ in their attitudes, values, habits, thought processes, and ways of doing things. They recognize that their own preferences are not necessarily the only viable ones, so they accept individual and group differences. They don't insist that everyone they live with be a carbon copy of themselves.

They recognize as well that life is not static, that situations and circumstances change as we go through various stages of the life cycle. They are able to accept change as the norm and are willing to adjust to varying circumstances (deTurck and Miller, 1986). They also are willing to grow with the relationship as time passes (S. A. Anderson, 1986).

Adaptability and flexibility require a high degree of emotional maturity. People have to be secure enough to let go of old thoughts and habits that are no longer functional or appropriate. But to let go requires some confidence that the new will work as well as the old. Flexible people are not threatened by change. In fact, they welcome new challenges because they offer a chance to grow and develop. Marcus (1983) wrote:

> One person's capacity to adapt to another requires a degree of security. . . . Instead of feeling threatened by flexibility, they . . . feel proud of their capacity to be flexible. Because marriage requires a series of adaptations, it is of itself a stimulus toward achieving mature adult status. (p. 120)

The most difficult people to deal with are perfectionists, who have only one rigid standard by which they judge everyone and everything. Perfectionists have no tolerance for imperfection. They have impossibly high standards for themselves and others and are completely inflexible in the way they think. Since they believe that they are always right and others wrong, they insist that any changes in a relationship have to be made by someone else. As one man said, "When my wife and I discuss anything, I'm right ninety-nine percent of the time, and she's wrong" (author's counseling notes). Certainly, it's very difficult to work out problems with a person who is so arrogant and rigid in his thinking. (Barrow and Moore, 1983).

PREMARITAL PREDICTORS OF MARITAL QUALITY

Potential problems in marriages can often be seen before the couple actually gets married. What happens in the premarital relationship is often a good predictor of what will happen in a marriage. In an extensive review of more than 60 years of research on premarital predictors of marital quality, T. D. Holman, Larson, Stahmann, and Carroll (2001) presented the following conclusions: (1) Premarital background, beliefs, and behaviors have a continuing influence on marital functioning, even after several years of marriage. (2) Multiple premarital factors such as family of origin, characteristics of the individual, social connections, and couple interactional processes are prominent in influencing later marital quality, either directly or indirectly. (3) Some premarital predictors are more important than others and have a more lasting influence, with family-of-origin background factors (e.g., parent–child relationships) being perhaps the most important.

Teaching and intervention should occur before people get married in order to improve the likelihood of having a high-quality marriage. Several intervention principles can help practitioners work with couples to this end. Such interventions can help people (1) restructure, come to terms with, or let go of unpleasant issues from the family-of-origin experiences; (2) improve their emotional health and self-esteem and their valuing of marriage and family life; (3) revise negative values, attitudes, and beliefs about marriage; (4) increase social network support, such as the premarital support of the marriage from parents and friends, which can provide support during tough times; and (5) improve communication and conflict resolution skills in their relationship and increase perceived similarity and consensus. Intervention strategies such as these will help increase the probability of marital success (T. D. Holman et al., 2001).

Of all the family-of-origin issues that could be addressed, the parent–child relationship, the parents' marriage, and the parents' mental health and/or dysfunctional behavior are the most important. Improving these will tend to lead to the most improvement in the probability of adult children's marital success. Thus, the most important things parents can do for the future marital happiness of their children are to maintain a strong marriage;

create a pleasant, happy home environment; and be involved in their children's lives. Practitioners need to help more parents understand what is happening in their own marriage, in their home, and in their relationship with their children (T. D. Holman et al., 2001).

Gender differences need to be taken into account in premarital interventions if later marital quality is to be optimally strengthened. For example, family-of-origin factors play a greater role in predicting marital satisfaction 6 years into marriage for females than for males. A woman's family-of-origin experience has more impact on a man's marital satisfaction than does the man's own family-of-origin experience. However, husbands' family-of-origin experience has no significant effect on females' marital satisfaction (T. B. Holman et al., 2001).

Many more intervention principles and a variety of methods for teaching these principles to individuals can be found in the book *Premarital Prediction of Marital Quality or Breakup* (T. D. Holman et al., 2001). In addition, examples of some programs and materials that teach about marital preparation have been cataloged by the Coalition of Marriage, Family, and Couples Education. A description of these programs and materials can be found on the Internet at www.smartmarriages.com.

THE NEWLYWED YEARS AS PREDICTORS OF MARITAL SATISFACTION

What happens in the first 2 years of marriage is important in predicting marital satisfaction over the long run. Huston, Caughlin, Houts, Smith, and George (2001) examined connections between the first 2 years of marriage and marital satisfaction and stability after 13 or more years of marriage. They examined whether newlyweds who are highly affectionate were more likely than other couples to sustain a satisfying marriage, and whether newlyweds who bicker were likely to overcome their initial difficulties or were destined for an unhappy marriage.

In examining these questions among newlywed couples, they found that changes in the marriage over the first 2 years influenced the fate of the marriage after 13 years. For those who stayed married, differences in the intensity of newlyweds' romance,

as well as the extent to which they expressed negative feelings toward each other predicted whether or not couples were happy 13 years later. For those who divorced, intensity of romance and expression of negative feelings toward each other influenced how long their marriage lasted prior to separation. The study showed that an abatement of love, a decline in overt affection, a lessening of the belief that one's spouse is responsive, and an increase in ambivalence about the relationship distinguished couples headed for divorce from those who established a stable marital bond. The researchers found that most of the differences between couples who stay married, but differed in marital happiness, existed at the outset of marriage rather than developing during the first 2 years of their marriage. The spouses who were not happy 13 years into marriage were less in love, viewed each other as less responsive, were more ambivalent, and were more negative than were spouses who stayed married and were happy (Huston et al., 2001).

WHY SOME PEOPLE REGRET THEIR CHOICE OF MATE

As discussed in Chapter 2, all couples are influenced by the characteristics of their own family of origin. In general, the higher the marital quality in the parents' marriage, the higher the marital quality in their children's marriages. Parental divorce, parental mental illness, and family dysfunction have a negative influence on the children's marital success. Support from parents and in-laws after marriage has a positive influence on marital success.

Several sociocultural factors influence marital quality, including age at marriage, education, income, occupation, social class, and ethnicity. The relationship between young age at marriage and marital instability is among the strongest and most consistently documented in the research literature. Individuals who marry as teenagers are especially likely to separate or divorce.

There are a number of reasons people regret their choice of mate. One reason is they don't really get to know the other person (Stafford and Reske, 1990). People who are in too much of a hurry to get married may not give the relationship enough time to develop. Getting to know another person usually takes several years of being together under varying circumstances. Even then, the knowledge is incomplete. Sometimes, the types of activities a couple share are not conducive to developing rapport and communication. The partners may participate in a whirl of social activities, spending all their time with other people or going to movies, concerts, or sporting events. The activities are fun, but the relationship remains superficial because of minimal interpersonal interaction.

Some people choose the wrong mate because they live in a fantasy world. Their concept of marriage has been gleaned from romantic movies and the media, and marriage represents an escape from their own humdrum existence. Their parents may have a troubled marriage, but they are sure it won't happen to them. They completely overlook the faults of their partner and the problems in their relationship. Love will conquer all, and they will live happily ever after. Their views of marriage and their relationship are completely unrealistic.

Other people choose the wrong mate because they look for the wrong qualities in a person. They emphasize physical characteristics and attractiveness without regard for important personal qualities. They don't stop to think about whether their partner is a good person. They are also looking for the wrong things in their relationship—perhaps for excitement instead of stability. They are thrilled with new relationships that are emotionally arousing, forgetting that the high level of emotions will subside and that only more permanent qualities will sustain the relationship.

Some people make the wrong choice because they confuse sex with love. They enjoy each other sexually and have intercourse whenever they are together. Their relationship focuses primarily on sexual passion, and so they assume they are much in love. But, as explained in Chapter 5, theirs is an incomplete love. Other components, such as friendship and care, are needed to sustain the relationship over a period of time.

Another common reason for marrying the wrong person is a poor self-image and lack of self-esteem. Such people can't believe that anyone desirable would really love them and accept them, so they settle for less than they might. They court rejection and unhappiness because they believe they are unworthy of support, love, and nurturance (Abramson, 1983).

Some people succumb to pressures to marry. One pressure is from their biological clock. One woman remarked, "I'm thirty-two years old and I want to have children. I'm marrying Charlie because I'm afraid I might not find someone else in time. I don't really love him, but I can't wait any longer" (author's counseling notes). Other people have a now-or-never attitude. They are afraid if they don't get married to this person, they may never get another opportunity to marry.

Another pressure is that of pregnancy. The number one reason for marrying while still in school is pregnancy. Yet the prognosis of success for the marriage, particularly if the partners are in their teens, is poor. Most such marriages simply don't work out. Or a couple is cohabiting and the parents pressure them to marry. Parental intervention in the process of choosing a mate is more often indirect than direct (Davis-Brown, Salomon, and Surra, 1987). Instead of actively expressing approval or disapproval, parents try to arrange conditions so that their children will meet and marry suitable partners. Pressure to marry can also come from relatives and friends. When two people have gone together for some time, friends begin to ask, "When are you two going to get married?"

There are also unconscious, neurotic needs that people try to fulfill by marrying. For example, women who have an unconscious need to feel needed marry men they can mother. They may marry men who are immature, who have problems with alcohol or drug abuse, or who can't hold a job. In other situations, people feel uncomfortable with successful, desirable people, so they marry someone to whom they can feel superior as a means of boosting their own ego. Others boost their ego by choosing a mate they feel will enhance their image in others' eyes—for example, a "trophy wife."

Neurotic people may be drawn together to enable them to play roles in each other's games and transactions. Such role combinations include father–daughter, sadist–masochist, pursuer–pursued, beater–battered, and rescuer–victim (Hoyt, 1986). These unconscious feelings and needs may be very powerful motives to marry a particular person.

A QUESTION OF POLICY

COVENANT MARRIAGES

There is a growing movement in the United States to help make marriages stronger and divorce less common. Some states have created what is called a covenant marriage, which legally binds the couple to stricter legal standards for divorce than ordinary marriages do. For example, covenant marriages require all couples to have premarital counseling and fully disclose to one another everything that could adversely affect the decision to marry. Grounds for divorce under covenant marriage laws require proof that there was abuse, adultery, addiction, or felony imprisonment. Before a divorce can be granted, couples are required to take reasonable steps to resolve problems such as going to marital counseling or separating for at least two years. Already-married couples may at any time change their original marriage to a covenant marriage (Hawkins, Nock, Wilson, Sanchez, and Wright, 2002).

QUESTIONS TO CONSIDER:

What benefits does the covenant marriage hold over a standard marriage? Consider the viewpoint of the husband, the wife, the children.

What reasons might impel a couple to form a legally binding covenant marriage? What reasons might another couple have for deciding against a covenant marriage?

To what extent is covenant marriage a reasonable matter for public policy? Could couples privately commit to this higher standard, as many do, without laws governing it? Explain.

Who benefits the most from a covenant marriage?

Would you consider a covenant marriage for yourself? Why or why not?

SUMMARY

1. A successful marriage has been defined as one that endures, approximates ideals, fulfills mutual needs, and satisfies both partners.

2. Marital success reflects the extent to which both partners in a relationship are satisfied that it has fulfilled reasonable expectations and mutual needs.

3. In happy marriages, after one partner makes a negative statement, the other partner is likely not to respond immediately, whereas in unhappy marriages, both partners continue to reciprocate negatively.

4. In happy marriages, if one partner does something negative, the other partner tends to think that the negativity is fleeting and situational. In unhappy marriages, however, the same behavior is likely to be interpreted in terms of overall inconsideration, selfishness, and indifference.

5. The "demand–withdraw" pattern is characteristic of unhappy marriages. In this pattern, it is usually the woman who raises and pursues the issues and the man who attempts to avoid the discussion and to withdraw.

6. The presence of criticism, defensiveness, contempt, and stonewalling on the part of one or both partners is characteristic of unhappy marriages.

7. The positive expression of sexuality contributes to marital satisfaction. Typically, most couples start out marriage engaging frequently in intercourse, but then the incidence begins to decline and they settle into their own individual patterns. If both partners are satisfied with their sex life, it can contribute in a positive way to their overall happiness; but if the partners disagree, or if one or both are frustrated or unhappy with

their sex life, it can significantly reduce or even destroy relationship satisfaction.

8. Twelve characteristics of successful marriage are communication; admiration and respect; companionship; spirituality and common values; commitment; affection; the ability to deal with crises and stress; responsibility; unselfishness; empathy and sensitivity; honesty, trust, and fidelity; and adaptability, flexibility, and tolerance.

9. Potential problems in marriages can often be seen before the couple actually gets married. What happens in the premarital relationship is often a good predictor of what will happen in a marriage.

10. What happens in the first 2 years of marriage is important in predicting marital satisfaction

over the long run. An abatement of love, a decline in overt affection, a lessening of the belief that one's spouse is responsive, and an increase in ambivalence about the relationship has been shown to distinguish couples headed for divorce from those who establish a stable marital bond.

11. People regret their choice of mate for a number of reasons: They don't get to know the other person; they live in a fantasy world; they look for the wrong qualities in a person; they confuse sex with love; they have a poor self-image and low self-esteem; they succumb to pressures to marry; or they have unconscious, neurotic needs that they are trying to fulfill by marrying.

KEY TERMS

negative affect reciprocity	unconditional positive regard	affective sensitivity
noncontingent reinforcement	selfism	

QUESTIONS FOR THOUGHT

1. How would you describe a successful marriage, and how does this description differ from, or how is it similar to, the definitions discussed in the textbook?

2. For single students brought up in two-parent families: Did your parents have a successful marriage according to your views? Why or why not?

3. For single students brought up in a one-parent family: Select a married couple that you know

well. Is this a successful marriage according to your views? Why or why not?

4. For married students: Would you define your marriage as successful? Why or why not?

5. Select the four most important qualities for a successful marriage according to your views, discuss them, and tell why you feel they are so important.

SUGGESTED READINGS

Cutrona, C. E. (1996). *Social Support in Couples: Marriage as a Resource in Times of Stress*. Thousand Oaks, CA: Sage. Surveys theoretical issues confronting researchers in studying social support in the context of marital relationships.

Doherty, W., and Carlson, B. (2002). *Putting Family First: Successful Strategies for Reclaiming Family Life in a Hurry-Up World*. New York: Henry Holt. Focuses on strategies to help families spend more quality time together.

Golden, L. B. (2000). *Case Studies in Marriage and Family Therapy*. Upper Saddle River, NJ: Merrill. Utilizes actual cases to discuss therapy practices for couples and families.

Gottman, J., and Silver, N. (2000). *Why Marriages Succeed or Fail*. New York: Simon & Schuster. Argues that marital stability and satisfaction result from teachable conflict management skills.

Gottman, J., and Silver, N. (1997). *The 7 Principles for Making Marriage Work.* London: Weidenfield & Nicolson. Provides a research-based guide to revitalizing and strengthening marriages.

Gray, J. (1999). *Mars and Venus: 365 Ways to Keep Passion Alive.* London: Vermilion. Gives practical advice for maintaining an exciting and intimate relationship.

Gray, J. (2000). *Mars and Venus in Touch.* New York: HarperCollins. Explores how communication between men and women can increase passion and intimacy in a relationship.

Harvey, J. H., and Wenzel A. (2001) (Eds.). *Close Romantic Relationships: Maintenance and Enhancement.* Mahwah, NJ: Erlbaum. Focuses on strategies to improve intimate relationships.

Mackey, R. A., and O'Brien, B. A. (1995). *Lasting Marriages: Men and Women Growing Together.* Westport, CT: Praeger. Explores why some marriages last while others fail.

Olsen, D., and Stephens, D. (2001). *The Couple's Survival Workbook: What You Can Do to Reconnect with Your Partner and Make Your Marriage Work.* Oakland CA: New Harbinger. Intends to help individuals change the interactions with their partners.

LEARNING OBJECTIVES

After reading the chapter, you should be able to:

- Understand the basic stages of the family life cycle in an intact marriage and in a family in which there is divorce and remarriage.

- Describe the various trends in marital satisfaction, from the honeymoon stage to late adulthood.

- Summarize the major marital adjustment tasks and problems early in marriage.

- Describe how gay and lesbian families are different from and similar to other types of families.

- Describe the adjustments to parenthood.

- Discuss the major adjustments during middle adulthood, including the postparental years.

- Summarize the major adjustments during late adulthood, including divorce.

- Discuss problems of family relationships for the elderly and the widowed, including alternatives for caring for the elderly.

Marital Relationships over the Family Life Cycle

Marriage relationships are never static but rather are constantly changing, developing, and growing. Sometimes relationships are frustrating, unsatisfying, and troublesome; other times they are fulfilling and vital.

The adjustments that people face early in marriage are unique because the relationship is so new. The adjustments during parenthood and middle age relate to the aging process and to children growing older and leaving home. Late adulthood requires establishment of new roles in the family as a couple, as older parents of adult children, and as grandparents. The elderly have to make peace with their past and be able to accept their life as they have lived it.

Most people face the prospect of separation from their spouse for some part of their lives. A small percentage of older people get divorced at this stage of life (which will be discussed in Chapter 16); more live out their lives as widows or widowers. Being alone requires special adjustments that couples do not face.

The extent to which the elderly are able to overcome their problems and make the adjustments that life requires will determine their levels of well-being and life satisfaction during this stage of life. Each phase of life has its own joys and its own problems. Knowing what some of these are helps everyone pass through each stage more successfully.

MARRIAGE AND PERSONAL HAPPINESS

The positive link between satisfaction with marriage and family life and psychological well-being is well established (Mills, Grasmick, Morgan, and Wenk, 1992). Few married people would disagree with the idea that the quality of their marriage has a strong effect on their happiness and satisfaction with life (Zollar and Williams, 1987). An unhappy marriage can have a negative effect on life satisfaction and subjective well-being (Haring-Hidore, Stock, Okun, and Witler, 1985). People who are having severe

family life cycle The phases, or stages, of the family life span, each of which is characterized by changes in family structure, composition, and functions.

marital problems may not be able to eat properly or to sleep; and so they can become quite debilitated.

Marital relationships are seldom static. Partners may report a period of harmony during which everything seems fine, only to have "all hell break loose" to the point at which the couple is talking about divorce. The more unstable the couple, the more variable the relationship. Most couples have some ups and downs in their relationship. What is important, however, is the general quality of the relationship over time and the extent to which partners report satisfaction with it.

THE FAMILY LIFE CYCLE

One of the most helpful ways of examining marital relationships over time is in terms of various phases of the family life cycle. The **family life cycle** consists of the phases, or stages, over the life span and seeks to describe changes in family structure and function during each stage. The cycle can also be used to show the challenges, tasks, and problems that people face during each stage, as well as the satisfactions derived.

Data on Family Life Cycles

Figure 8.1 shows the traditional family life cycle of spouses in an intact marriage. The ages of the spouses are median ages for the U.S. population. Thus, the man is married at 27, the woman at 25. They wait 2 years before having the first of two children. The man is 51 and the woman 48 when the youngest child is 20 and leaves home. The empty-nest years until retirement are from age 51 to 65 for the man and age 49 to 65 for the woman. The man dies at age 74 while the woman lives to age 79, spending her last years as a widow (U.S. Bureau of the Census, 2001).

The family life cycle is different for divorced couples. Figure 8.2 shows separate cycles of spouses who marry, have two children, and divorce; each remarries a spouse with two children. The children reside with their mother after the divorce. Note that the median age of first marriage for couples who divorce is 2 years younger than for couples who never divorce. The man is 32 and the woman 30 when they divorce. Their children are 3 and 5 years old. The father remarries 4 years later, at age 36, to a woman who is 33, with two children 6 and 8 years old who reside with her and her new spouse. The father is 50

The quality of marriage has a strong effect on personal happiness and life satisfaction. Since the marital relationship is seldom static, most couples will experience periods of both instability and harmony.

when his youngest stepchild is 20 and moves out of the house. He and his spouse have 15 empty-nest years until he retires at age 65 and an additional 8 years together before he dies at age 74.

The woman is 30 when she divorces. Her two children are ages 3 and 5. She remarries 3 years later, when her children are 6 and 8. She is 47 years old when her youngest child is 20 and moves out of the house. She spends 18 empty-nest years with her spouse until she retires at age 65 and has 9 more

years with him until he dies at age 74. She spends the last 8 years of her life, from age 71 to 79, as a widow (U.S. Bureau of the Census, 2001).

Of course, the family life cycle is different for everyone, and these graphs do not represent the life cycle of all types of families. However, they do give us a sense of what happens to the majority of people in the United States. Exceptions to the two basic life cycles include those who remarry more than once, those who have much larger families, gay

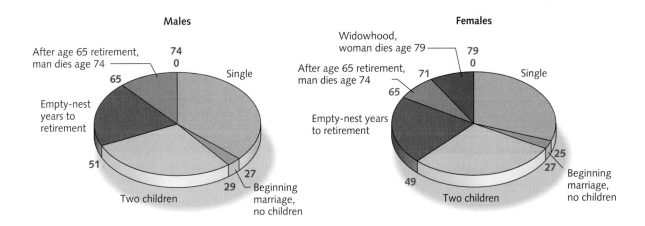

Numbers around circumferences are ages in years.

Figure 8.1 Family Life Cycle—Intact Marriage (*Note:* Data from *Statistical Abstract of the United States, 2000,* by U.S. Bureau of the Census, 2001, Washington, DC: U.S. Government Printing Office.)

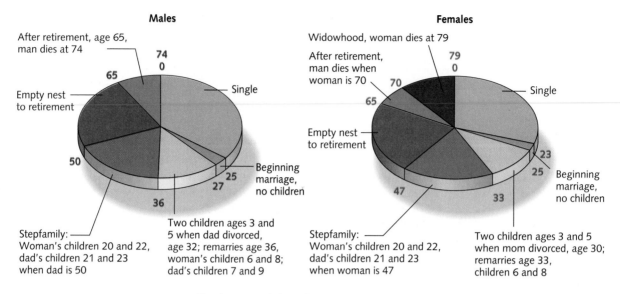

Numbers around circumferences are ages in years.

Figure 8.2   Family Life Cycle—Marriage, Divorce, Remarriage; Children Reside with Wife (*Note:* Data from *Statistical Abstract of the United States, 2000,* by U.S. Bureau of the Census, 2001, Washington, DC: U.S. Government Printing Office.)

and lesbian families, and single-parent families. Twenty-two percent of White families, 29% of Hispanic families, and 56% of African American families are one-parent families (U.S. Bureau of the Census, 2001). In general, African Americans are less likely to marry than Whites, and those who marry do so at an older age than Whites. Greater percentages of African Americans than Whites get divorced. Divorce takes place after about the same length of marriage as for Whites, but Blacks typically wait longer to remarry, so Black stepparents begin the postparental stage at a later age than White stepparents. On average, African Americans live 7 years less than Whites: men to age 68 and women to age 75 (U.S. Bureau of the Census, 2001).

Changes in Marital Satisfaction

How does marital satisfaction change over various phases of the family life cycle? The answer depends on the particular family. Family patterns differ. The most helpful model of what happens over long-term marriage has been outlined by Weishaus and Field (1988), who describe six different types of long-term marriage:

1. **Stable/positive.** These partners have stable but not static marriages, maintaining moderately high to high satisfaction and generally positive affection and interaction throughout the years.

2. **Stable/neutral.** These partners never experience emotional closeness but marry for other reasons. They are generally comfortable with each other and are without excessive conflict.

3. **Stable/negative.** These partners experience primarily negative emotions throughout marriage, manifested as hostility or indifference. Lack of any positive feeling is apparent. There is little joy, only the feeling that duty has been performed.

4. **Curvilinear.** For these partners, satisfaction is high early in marriage, drops during the middle years, and rises again after the children have left home.

5. **Continuous decline.** These partners experience gradual and more or less continuous eroding of marital satisfaction.

6. **Continuous increase.** These partners derive increasing satisfaction as the years pass.

The Curvilinear Pattern

The most common pattern of change in marital satisfaction is curvilinear: high satisfaction at the time of marriage, lower during the child-rearing years, and higher again after the youngest child has passed beyond the teens (S. A. Anderson, Russell, and Schumm, 1983). Marital happiness has been found to decrease as the newness of the relationship wears off (D. R. Johnson, Amoloza, and Booth, 1992). Some studies show the decline in satisfaction lasting only until all the children have started school (Belsky and Rovine, 1990). However, these studies are based on cross-sectional or retrospective data. Other longitudinal studies show no U-curved change in marital satisfaction over the life course. They do show some deterioration in the woman's reported marital satisfaction during the 31st to 45th years of marriage (Vaillant and Vaillant, 1993).

The common assumption that spouses, particularly women, are affected negatively by the children's leaving home cannot be substantiated by research. In fact, data from six U.S. national surveys indicate that women whose children have left home are happier, enjoy life more, and have greater marital satisfaction than do women whose children are still at home (Glenn and McLanahan, 1982).

The most plausible explanation for why marital satisfaction is at an ebb when the children are of school age seems to be that the demands placed on the couple during these years are at their greatest. The couple is under increased financial pressure because of the needs of a growing family. Usually, job

Some couples breathe a sigh of relief when the last child leaves home, and many couples report a noticeable increase in marital satisfaction.

responsibilities outside the home are at a maximum. The children make increasing demands as they get older, and community responsibilities also increase during the middle years of marriage. Specifically, the intensity and number of social roles gradually increase until the middle years. As a result, the partners experience greater role strain because they cannot perform all these roles as well as they and others might expect. This role discrepancy results in less satisfaction with the marital relationship. After the children are grown, however, role expectations and strain decrease, with a concomitant increase in marital satisfaction (D. H. Olson et al., 1983).

The increased satisfaction continues for a while, but as the problems of growing older increase, marital satisfaction begins to decline again. In spite of the decrease in marital satisfaction, however, divorce rates are not higher late in marriage. The lower divorce rate for older marriages occurs because couples have more barriers and fewer alternatives from which to choose.

Gay and Lesbian Families

Most of the research and discussion of gay and lesbian families has focused on how they differ from other, more traditional family forms. However, they share many similarities with other family types and in most respects are like all other families. As Laird (1993) observed:

> They must negotiate their relationships with the larger community and their families of origin, forging social networks and establishing boundaries between themselves and the outside world, as well as negotiating relationships and roles, developing problem-solving strategies, mediating conflicts, and marking boundaries inside the family. They must decide who will do what, when, where, and how in order to meet the particular needs of the family as a whole and of individual family members, whose interests at times may conflict or compete. Like all families, they face possibilities for conflict over divisions of labor, the use of money, space, and time, their sexual and intimate relationships, issues of closeness and distance, dominance and subordination, child-rearing ideologies, and so on. (p. 308)

However, Laird went on to point out that gay and lesbian families differ from others in at least two important ways. First, most families are headed by same-sex couples, although some are headed by single gay or lesbian parents and others by multiple parenting figures. Second, these families are often stigmatized as inappropriate family forms, which presents them with unique challenges. For example, although gay and lesbian single parents face the same issues of finances, time constraints, and dating as most heterosexual single parents, the prospect of forming new long-term relationships and families is complicated by society's judgment of gay and lesbian families. Two-parent gay and lesbian families with children from previous marriages often share similar situations and deal with similar important issues as stepfamilies. However, there have been child custody cases in which custody or visitation rights were not granted to a parent on the sole basis of his or her sexual orientation. This kind of discrimination can have a powerful influence on the decision-making process of gay and lesbian individuals and families. Imagine the stress of living with the fear of losing your children due to your sexual orientation or of having your children ridiculed because of your family form. Unfortunately, that is a reality for many gay and lesbian parents and often causes them to be more private and secretive than they would like to be.

Some researchers believe that gay and lesbian families go through different life stages than other families because of their sexual orientation and the discrimination they face. For example, the "coming out" process is a unique experience to gays and lesbians. Minton and McDonald (1983/1984) suggested that this is a developmental process that often covers the life span and eventually leads to personal acceptance and management of a positive gay self-image. In fact, the whole identity of being gay appears to represent a relatively new and unique cultural category in history (Herdt, 1992), particularly gay and lesbian families. While there are many socially prescribed roles for males/fathers and females/mothers in families, same-sex couples lack clear traditions or guidelines for role and task decision making. This has its benefits in that it allows for tremendous role flexibility for members of gay and lesbian families. However, it also introduces more uncertainty and complexity into role negotiation, and it can be frustrating to continually challenge prevailing notions of family structure and function.

Traditionally, gay and lesbian families were not child-centered if one or both partners had not been previously married. This is changing somewhat

with what has been labeled the "lesbian baby boom," or "gayby boom" (see Chapter 1), as more lesbians are opting to have children through known or unknown donor insemination. In some cases, both women in the relationship are choosing to bear children. For gay couples, adoption is still difficult because some states have enacted prohibitive agency policies to discourage gays and lesbians from adopting children. Florida remains the only state that bans same-sex couples from adopting, after New Hampshire repealed a similar law in 1999. However, research consistently has shown that gay and lesbian families are just as successful at carrying out normal family roles and tasks and raising healthy children as other types of families (see Patterson, 1992, for a review of this literature).

As in all family types, there is tremendous diversity within gay and lesbian families in terms of family patterns, forms, and membership. No two families are ever alike, however similar they may seem superficially. Much of the literature to date on gay and lesbian families has chosen to stress the differences between them and heterosexual families and has emphasized each's commonalities as a group rather then their diversity (Laird, 1993). Certainly, gay and lesbian families have special strengths, raising families so well despite oppression and discrimination. As Laird (1993) stated, this suggests that we need to know more about their secrets to success and their ways of overcoming the lack of socially sanctioned rituals such as marriage, as well as the lack of other social and legal sanctions such as spousal rights and benefits. Boxer and Cohler (1989) observed that, in order to understand the life course of gays and lesbians, it is crucial to understand how gay and lesbian families remain strong and resilient in the face of so much discrimination.

ADJUSTMENTS EARLY IN MARRIAGE

Most partners discover that marriage does not live up to all of their expectations. As a result, they go through a series of adjustments in which they try to modify their behavior and relationship to achieve the greatest degree of satisfaction with a minimum degree of frustration.

Marital adjustment may be defined as the process of modifying, adapting, and altering individ-

Individualism versus Familism

Family duty and obligation, as opposed to the pursuit of individualism, varies across cultures. For example, studies consistently show stronger levels of obligation, more frequent social interaction, more support exchanged, and a greater likelihood of shared living arrangements with elders in Mexican American families than in European American families (Holmes and Holmes, 1995). It is important for the individual to be committed to the welfare of the family system, as opposed to their own individualism, while the family remains the center and focus of all endeavors (Garcia, 2001). **Familism** among Mexican Americans means that they emphasize the needs of the family above those of the individual. For example, either a parent or the older children may stay home from school or work to care for a sick family member or visit a relative who is bedridden. Individuals find their identity and sense of belonging in family groups, and Mexican Americans are much more likely than European Americans to believe that the younger generation should support and provide living accommodations for the older generation if needed (J. Burr and Mutchler, 1999). One study examined the attitudes toward family obligations among more than 800 Mexi-

can American adolescents and found that they possessed stronger values and greater expectations regarding their duty to assist, respect, and support their families than did their peers with European backgrounds (Fuligni et al., 1999).

Chinese Americans also place a great deal of emphasis on intergenerational ties and the extended family being the most important societal unit (Feldman, Mont-Reynaud, and Rosenthal, 1992). Children have a high sense of duty to parents and of filial responsibility, and parents blame themselves when a young person fails to live up to expectations. A child who misbehaves can bring shame to the family name (Ishii-Kuntz, 1997). Thus, an individual's shame can bring loss of face to both himself and his extended family which is a major concern in many families (Wu, 2001). Because of the emphasis Chinese Americans place on family as opposed to the individual, they see education not just for the advancement of the individual, but for the family enhancement as a whole. It is thought that conforming to the group is more important than fulfilling one's own needs and that conformity helps both a family and a society function better (Sue, 1997).

---

ual and couple patterns of behavior and interaction to achieve maximum satisfaction in the relationship. According to this definition, adjustment is not an end in and of itself, but a means to an end: satisfaction in and with the marriage. It is quite possible for spouses to adjust to each other but still be quite unhappy and dissatisfied with the relationship. For example, people who like sex may come to accept the fact that their mate seldom wants to have intercourse with them. They learn to adjust to this situation, but this does not mean that they really like it or are satisfied with this accommodation. Or people may learn to adjust to a mate's bad temper and try to overlook it, but this does not mean they approve. They have learned how to avoid overt conflict, but this adjustment gives them very little real comfort or joy. The goal of adjustment is to achieve the greatest degree of marital satisfaction and success.

Sometimes a particular adjustment may not be the best that one would like, but it may be said to be successful to the extent that it provides the highest satisfaction possible under the circumstances. Obviously, adjustment is not static, not a step taken

just once. It is a dynamic, ongoing process that takes place throughout a couple's married life.

Marital Adjustment Tasks

Most couples discover that they have to make adjustments in order to live together harmoniously. The areas of adjustment might be called **marital adjustment tasks;** 12 categories are shown in Table 8.1. The extent to which couples need to make adjustments after marriage will depend partially on the extent to which some of these tasks are confronted during courtship.

---

marital adjustment The process of modifying, adapting, and altering individual and couple patterns of behavior and interaction to achieve maximum satisfaction in the relationship.

familism Emphasis on the needs of the family above those of the individual.

marital adjustment tasks Areas of concern in marriage in which adjustments need to be made.

Table 8.1 Marital Adjustment Tasks

Emotional fulfillment and support

Learning to give and receive affection and love

Developing sensitivity, empathy, closeness

Giving emotional support, building morale, fulfilling ego needs

Sexual adjustment

Learning to satisfy, fulfill each other sexually

Working out mode, manner, timing of sexual expression

Finding, using acceptable means of birth control

Personal habits

Adjusting to each other's personal habits, speech, cleanliness, grooming, manners, eating, sleeping, promptness (J. H. Larson, Crane, and Smith, 1991)

Reconciling differences in smoking, drinking, drug habits

Eliminating or modifying personal habits that annoy each other

Adjusting to differences in body rhythms, schedules

Learning to share space, time, belongings, work

Gender roles

Establishing spousal roles in and outside the home

Working out gender roles in relation to income production, housekeeping, household maintenance, homemaking, child care

Agreeing on division of labor

Material concerns, finances (F. P. Rice, 1986)

Finding, selecting a residence: geographic area, neighborhood, type of housing

Equipping, maintaining a household

Earning adequate income, managing money

Work, employment, achievement

Finding, selecting, maintaining employment

Adjusting to type, place, hours, conditions of employment

Working out schedules when one or both are working

Arranging for child care when one or both are working

Social life, friends, recreation

Learning to visit, entertain as a couple

Deciding on type, frequency of social activities as individuals and as a couple

Selecting, relating to friends

Family, relatives (J. L. Fischer, Sollie, Sorell, and Green, 1989)

Establishing relationships with parents, in-laws, relatives

Learning how to deal with families

Communication

Learning to disclose and communicate ideas, worries, concerns, needs

Learning to listen to each other and to talk to each other in constructive ways

Power, decision making

Achieving desired balance of status, power

Learning to make, execute decisions

Learning cooperation, accommodation, compromise

Conflict, problem solving

Learning to identify conflict causes, circumstances

Learning to cope with conflict constructively

Learning to solve problems

Learning where, when, how to obtain help if needed

Morals, values, ideology

Understanding, adjusting to individual morals, values, ethics, beliefs, philosophies, life goals

Establishing mutual values, goals, philosophies

Accepting each other's religious beliefs, practices

Making decisions in relation to religious affiliation, participation

Most couples who enter into a serious relationship are faced with most of the adjustments listed in Table 8.1. Some couples make many of them before marriage and so have fairly smooth sailing afterward. Other couples make few adjustments ahead of time and so are faced with nearly all of these marital adjustment tasks after marriage. These tasks can be overwhelming if encountered all at once. This situation often leads to a period of disillusionment and disenchantment in couples who have not realized what marriage involves.

Problems during Three Early Stages

One longitudinal study investigated the problems of 131 couples during three stages of the early years of their relationship (Storaasli and Markman, 1990): (1) before marriage, (2) during the first year of mar-

Table 8.2 Relationship Problems during Three Early Stages

		Mean Problem Intensity*			
Before Marriage		**First Year of Marriage**		**After Birth of First Child**	
Money	48.6	Money	42.3	Money	39.0
Jealousy	25.0	Communication	21.2	Sex	33.5
Relatives	22.7	Sex	19.8	Communication	32.4
Friends	18.5	Relatives	19.7	Relatives	23.9
Communication	17.8	Friends	16.7	Recreation	13.7
Sex	14.2	Children	15.3	Children	12.8
Religion	13.8	Jealousy	13.2	Friends	12.5
Recreation	12.8	Recreation	11.3	Jealousy	9.1
Children	11.8	Alcohol/drugs	8.8	Religion	7.6
Alcohol/drugs	11.8	Religion	6.4	Alcohol/drugs	6.5

*0 indicates no problem; 100 indicates a severe problem.

Note: Data from "Relationship Problems in the Early Stages of Marriage" by R. D. Storaasli and H. J. Markman, 1990, *Journal of Family Psychology, 4,* pp. 80–98.

riage, and (3) after the birth of their first child. Table 8.2 shows the results.

Note that money was the number one problem at all three stages of the relationship. Jealousy was a big problem before marriage but declined thereafter. Relatives were a problem before marriage and again after the first child was born. Communication and sex became greater problems after marriage and after the first child was born. Relationships with friends, religion, and alcohol and drugs were more of a problem before marriage. Problems having to do with recreation declined in importance after marriage and then rose after the first child was born.

ADJUSTMENTS TO PARENTHOOD

"First pregnancy," says one psychiatrist, "is a nine-month crisis. Thank God it takes nine months, because a child's coming requires enormous changes in a couple's ways of adjusting to each other" (Maynard, 1974, p. 139). Getting used to living with another adult in a committed relationship is challenging, but adding a third member to the family, an infant who is totally dependent, is a stressful transition in the family life cycle—and one of the most rewarding (Hackel and Ruble, 1992).

Parenthood as Stress

In recent years, there has been a tendency to refer to the addition of a first child less as a crisis and more as a period of stress and transition. The more stress-ful a couple's marriage before parenthood, the more likely it is that they will have difficulty in adjusting to the first child. Changes in marital quality and marital conflicts were explored in a longitudinal study of White and African American couples who made the transition to parenthood within the first 2 years of marriage. All the couples, regardless of ethnic group, reported lower marital happiness and more frequent conflicts after the transition than before (Crohan, 1996).

Sometimes stress arises if the pregnancy was not planned (Snowden, Schott, Awalt, and Gillis-Knox, 1988). Part of the stress comes from the fact that most couples are inadequately prepared for parenthood. As one mother stated, "We knew where babies came from, but we didn't know what they were like." Many new parents have no experience in caring for infants. Couples who prepare for parenthood by attending classes, reading books, and so forth find greater satisfaction in being a parent than do those who do not prepare. In addition, the level of stress during the transition to parenthood is reduced for couples who are socialized for their roles as parents by attending parenting classes (Gage and Christensen, 1991).

Part of the stress arises because of the abrupt transition to parenthood. Stress will vary from child to child depending on each child's temperament and how easy each child is to care for. Some children never give any trouble. Others, such as hyperactive or sickly children, require an abnormal amount of care.

The birth of a first child is a period of transition and stress, but successful adjustments are measures of parenting readiness.

Stress is greater if parents are young and immature. Almost half a million teenagers become parents each year. Eighty-six percent of teenage fathers have female partners ages 15–19. Twelve percent of all babies born have at least one teenage parent; 4% have parents who are both under 20 (U.S. Bureau of the Census, 2001). A majority of these parents have not even finished high school. It is highly unlikely that significant numbers of these teenagers are ready for parenthood (Landry and Forrest, 1995).

The economic status of the family also has been found to be a factor in parents' level of distress. It affects both spouses' parenting-related stress, as well as their psychological well-being. Parents who are struggling to make ends meet feel higher levels of stress in raising their children than do parents with greater economic resources (Lavee, Sharlin, and Katz, 1996).

The transition to parenthood ushers in many life changes and adjustments, as well as new patterns, responsibilities, and routines. Much research has focused on the transition to parenthood and on what concurrent variables in a parent's life are associated with competent parenting. Many variables, including social support from family and spouse, are associated with the degree of warmth and sensitivity a parent exhibits toward the infant. Social support is associated with the adaptation to parenthood and with positive parent–infant interactions. For example, women who receive support during pregnancy experience more positive mental and physical health outcomes during labor, delivery, and the postpartum period than do women who do not receive support (L. H. Goldstein, Diener, and Mangelsdorf, 1996).

Parenthood and Psychological Well-Being

The research shows that children may have a positive effect on marital adjustment and the well-being of parents (Umberson, 1987), or a negative impact (Ross and Huber, 1985), or a minimal impact (McLanahan and Adams, 1987; Menaghan, 1989; Umberson and Gove, 1989). Wallace and Gotlib (1990) found that marital satisfaction for couples increased from the middle of pregnancy to 1 month postpartum but decreased rapidly over the next 5 months. (Assessment was not made after 6 months.) In other words, after the initial excitement of having a baby wore off, marital satisfaction declined. Other research has found that the transition to parenthood is not an inescapable detriment to marital quality, but it does require a realignment of men's and women's marital roles. Any mismatch between marital-role expectations and enactment following parenthood may cause conflict and erode feelings of love between spouses (Crnic and Booth, 1991; MacDermid, Huston, and McHale, 1990).

In terms of psychological well-being, much depends on the individual parent's situation (McLanahan and Adams, 1987; Menaghan, 1989; Umberson and Gove, 1989). Being a single parent, for example, may be more emotionally taxing than being one of two parents taking care of a child (Garfinkel and McLanahan, 1986; Hughes, 1989). Other research has shown that women experience greater parental strain than men because of their greater responsibilities (Scott and Alwin, 1989; Wethington and Kessler, 1989). Also, the greater the number of children, the greater the strain on the parents while the children are young (Goldsteen and Ross, 1989).

ADJUSTMENTS DURING MIDDLE ADULTHOOD

The most noticeable changes of middle adulthood are physical ones. These changes are gradual, but increasing wrinkles, graying hair, and balding heads remind us of the aging process. Muscle tone declines, weight typically increases, and strength and endurance ebb. "Body monitoring" increases as individuals concern themselves with the dimensions of their middle-aged bodies. Physical exercise becomes more necessary to keep in shape and to offset the decrease in the body's metabolism, which results in the tendency to put on weight (Poehlman, Melby, and Badylak, 1991).

Health concerns become increasingly related to life satisfaction (Willits and Crider, 1988). Perhaps for the first time, adults are confronted with their own mortality (Kercher, Kosloski, and Normoyle, 1988). Previously, they have counted the years past, but now they begin to count the years ahead. The midlife transformation is precipitated by the awareness that one's years are numbered. Paradoxically, people are entering the prime of life and the period of greatest life fulfillment. In any case, the physical reminders of aging pale when compared to the dramatic confrontation with one's own mortality, as parents and even peers begin to die.

This personalization of mortality leads to an awareness that time is finite, that life is a race against time; there is a sense of urgency to accomplish all that one wants to achieve. Oles (1999) created a model of midlife transition in men and suggested that during midlife a man begins to examine his unrealized goals and strivings and begins to wonder about the meaning of his life. There are both similarities and differences between men in midlife crises and people with depression (Oles, 1999). Both groups have a similar depressed mode, but people with depression have a decrease in productivity and activity, whereas middle-aged men show an increase, possibly caused by a new sense of urgency. Thus, many middle-aged men, and

women, intensify efforts to live life while they can, before it is too late.

This crucial shift of time orientation in the life cycle may lead to introspection, self-analysis, and self-appraisal. Middle-aged people engage in an existential questioning of self, values, and life itself. They ask, Who am I? What have I done with my life? Where is my life going? What is the purpose of life? What am I here for? Is there anything else for me? These identity issues are an important source of marital dissatisfaction during the middle years (Steinberg and Silverberg, 1987).

This assessment of self extends to an examination of responsibilities, career, and marriage. As one middle-aged individual put it, "I'm tired of doing what is expected, what I'm supposed to do. I'd like to find out what I want to do, and start thinking of me for a change" (author's counseling notes). Financial responsibilities tend to be heavy in middle age. Some men at midlife become obsessed with financial security for themselves and their family in retirement. Family income becomes an important contributor to feelings of mastery and power over one's life.

Many middle-aged people are under considerable stress. This is the time of heaviest responsibilities at work and in the community. The main stresses for men are related to work and finances (D. J. Levinson, 1978), and job burnout may occur during this time (Arthur, 1990). Middle-aged women typically feel stress over the lack of companionship with their spouses, their own work, and the possibility of their young adult children making poor personal and professional choices. As far as work is concerned, however, employment of middle-aged women is also a buffer against other stresses in their lives.

Thus, midlife is a time when personal, practical, and existential issues are all in focus. It can become a time for reexamination, a time to chart new courses in life.

Marital Adjustments

As we have discussed, marital satisfaction tends to be at its lowest ebb when the children are of school age or in their teenage years. On average, the woman is 41 and the man 43 when the youngest child is 13 (see again Figure 8.1). If the partners have been busy working and raising children and being active in community affairs, they may have drifted apart, spending less time communicating, playing, and simply being together. It is easy for spouses to get so absorbed with other activities that the marriage suffers from lack of attention. Parents who stay together until their children are grown now feel freer to dissolve their relationship—and some do.

For others, however, middle age can become a time for revitalizing a tired marriage, for rethinking the relationship, and for deciding that they want to share many things in life together. It has been suggested that there are three cycles in most marriages—falling in love, falling out of love, and falling back in love—and that the last cycle is both the most difficult and the most rewarding. If spouses can learn to communicate and express tender feelings, especially feelings of love and affection that they have neglected, they can develop greater intimacy than they have experienced in a long time. This improved communication can also uncover and resolve troublesome issues and lead to improved companionship and togetherness.

Middle-aged people differ greatly in their ability to make necessary changes during this period of life. Researchers talk about **ego resiliency (ER),** or the generalized capacity for flexible and resourceful adaptation to stressors. It is an important personality resource that enables individuals to competently and adaptively negotiate their life under changing conditions such as those of the midlife transition. Adults entering midlife with high levels of ER are likely to view midlife as an opportunity for change and growth, whereas individuals with lower levels of ER are likely to experience it as a time of stagnation or decline (Klohnen, Vandewater, and Young, 1996).

Some middle-aged people are called on to assume another role—that of caregiver to an impaired parent or parent-in-law (Dwyer and Coward, 1991; Seccombe and Ishii-Kuntz, 1991). Over 40% of people in their late fifties have at least one parent still alive (Seccombe and Ishii-Kuntz, 1991). Although the elderly today are less likely to live with their children than they were 40 years ago, grown children, especially daughters or daughters-in-law, still bear primary responsibility for aged parents (Dwyer and Coward, 1991). Thus, many women are called on to assist or supervise elderly relatives in shopping, preparing meals, and so on. The majority of these women assuming the caregiving role also work and face their own family responsibilities. The role strain is often considerable, as women juggle the demands of the competing roles of worker, wife, homemaker, mother, grandmother, and caregiving daughter or daughter-in-law.

One study stressed both the rewards and the stresses of assuming this caregiver role (Stephens, Franks, and Townsend, 1994). Rewards included knowing that the care recipient was well cared for. The caregiver usually received a great deal of satisfaction from assuming this role if the care recipient showed affection or appreciation, if the relationship became closer and the care recipient's health improved, if he or she was cooperative and not demanding, and if his or her good side came through despite illness.

But caregiving also created a number of stresses, especially if the care recipient was critical or com-

When the last child leaves home, the postparental years begin. Although most couples report a noticeable increase in marital satisfaction, today's empty nest doesn't always stay empty. What effect might a returning child have on marital satisfaction?

plained, was unresponsive or uncooperative, was agitated, was in declining health, asked repetitive questions, or was forgetful. All of these conditions were sources of stress. If caregivers did not receive help from family or friends or if considerable extra expenses were involved in the caregiving, these factors became additional sources of stress.

Because they are caught between caregiving responsibilities for their children and for their elderly parents, middle-aged adults are sometimes called the **sandwich generation.** One study investigated whether multigenerational caregiving roles adversely affected middle-aged caregivers' marital quality, psychological well-being, financial resources, satisfaction with leisure time pursuits, and perceived fairness of the household division of labor (Loomis and Booth, 1995). Drawing on a national sample of married persons, the researchers found, perhaps surprisingly, that the change in family responsibilities had little or no effect on caregivers' well-being. The researchers concluded that there is probably a selection effect whereby those most able to take on the responsibilities of caregiving do so. Those who have strong marriages tend to assume multigenerational caregiving responsibilities and are probably generous caregivers in their own marriage. Also, individuals who take on additional care responsibilities may be more proficient at balancing time allocations for family, work, and personal needs. People who take on such responsibilities place a high value on caring for others. Meeting the additional obligations may be a source of fulfillment that offsets any negative effects on well-being imposed on the caregiver.

The researchers explained that they do not wish to imply that caring for an elderly parent, particularly one who is disabled or in very poor health, does not sometimes adversely affect family caregivers. In general, however, the effects of assuming significant obligations to parents appear to be minimal. They conclude that assuming multigenerational responsibilities does not develop into an especially difficult situation for most middle-aged adults (Loomis and Booth, 1995).

The Postparental Years

The term **postparental years** usually refers to the period between the last child's leaving home and the parents' retirement. Some writers prefer the term the *empty-nest years*, because once children are born, one is always a parent (Raup and Myers,

1989). As shown in Figure 8.1, if the woman gets married at the median age of 25 and has two children, she will be 49 when the last child leaves home. The man who marries at age 27 and has two children will be 51 when the last child leaves.

Many parents find it especially upsetting when the last child leaves home (R. A. Lewis, Volk, and Duncan, 1989). However, there is considerable evidence that adults in the postparental period are happier than are those earlier or later in life (G. R. Lee, 1988b). The period has been described as a time of freedom.

One postscript needs to be added: Unmarried children continue living with their parents for a longer period of time than they used to. This is due partly to the delay of marriage (Goldscheider and Goldscheider, 1989). Moreover, once the children leave, the empty nest may not stay that way; that is, grown children may return to the nest. High divorce rates and financial need have resulted in increasing numbers of adult children returning home to live with their parents. Today's generation of young adults has been referred to as the "boomerang kids" since they may leave home and return several times (Mitchell and Gee, 1996).

This has important ramifications for parents, their adult children, and the grandchildren. Many parents do not welcome the return of their children and view their stay as a short-term arrangement (Clemens and Axelson, 1985). The sources of potential conflict include everyday maintenance of self and clothing, the upkeep of house and yard, the use of the family car, and the lifestyle of the child, including sexual expression, drinking, drugs, and friends. Furthermore, although most grandparents love their grandchildren, they find it difficult to assume the role of frequent babysitter while the parent goes out to work or play. Sometimes the adult child reverts to the role of dependent child, and the parents return to superordinate roles of earlier times. Increasing evidence points

ego resiliency (ER) The generalized capacity for flexible and resourceful adaptation to stressors.

sandwich generation Middle-aged adults caught between caregiving for their children and for their elderly parents.

postparental years The period between the last child leaving home and the spouses' retirement; also called the empty-nest years.

to a lessening of life satisfaction for all parties involved (Clemens and Axelson, 1985).

ADJUSTMENTS DURING LATE ADULTHOOD

Late adulthood brings a number of major life changes. These changes affect not only the aging individual but also his or her spouse and other family members. Because late adulthood can extend over a 30-year period and dramatic physiological, psychological, and sociological changes can take place during these years, late adulthood is often divided into three stages. People ages 65–74 are sometimes referred to as the young-old, those 75–84 are the middle-old, and those 85 and over are the oldest-old. The developmental tasks these three groups face may be quite different. For example, people age 85 and over are more likely than people under 85 to be in poor health; to need assistance in dressing, bathing, eating, and other activities of daily living; and to need home health care (Seccombe and Ishii-Kuntz, 1991).

Late adulthood involves some major transitions: from marriage to widowhood, from living with a family member to living alone, and from physical independence to physical dependence. The transitions in marital status and household structure are likely to occur around the midseventies, usually some years before the onset of any disabilities. The timing of these transitions is significant for long-term survivors. By the time they reach the age when their family would be an important source of assistance, they are unlikely to have a surviving spouse, and a large proportion live alone. As many as one-third of the very old have no live-in family members who can respond to their needs (C. L. Johnson and Troll, 1996).

Developmental Tasks

The major **developmental tasks,** or adjustments, facing elderly people can be grouped into nine categories: (1) staying physically healthy and adjusting to limitations, (2) maintaining adequate income and means of support, (3) adjusting to revised work roles, (4) establishing acceptable housing and living conditions, (5) maintaining identity and social status, (6) finding companionship and friendship, (7) learning to use leisure time pleasurably, (8) establishing new roles in the family, and (9) achieving integrity through acceptance of one's life. We'll discuss each of these tasks briefly before turning to a

Older people dread physical problems that impair mobility and independence. One of the developmental tasks of late adulthood is to stay physically healthy.

more detailed discussion of the marriage and family relationships of the elderly.

Staying Physically Healthy and Adjusting to Limitations   The task of staying physically healthy becomes more difficult as people age. It requires good health habits and the practice of preventive medicine. Getting enough exercise and proper nutrition is especially important for maintaining health in old age. Older people dread physical problems that impair their mobility, their senses, and their ability to care for themselves (W. H. Quinn, 1983). As a consequence, maintaining good health is one of the most important predictors of life satisfaction in the elderly (Baur and Okun, 1983; Heidrich and Ryff, 1993).

Maintaining Adequate Income and Means of Support   Many adults face the problem of having inadequate income in their old age. Socioeconomic resources vary tremendously among the elderly, with age itself being an important correlate of resource level. In 2001, 10.1% of people 65 and over lived below the poverty level. The older the people were, the greater the percentage who lived in poverty. There is also a difference in economic resources according to gender. Seven percent of males but 12% of females 65 and over live below the poverty level (U.S. Bureau of the Census, 2001). There are also differences according to ethnicity. Among African Americans, 22% of those 65 and over live below the poverty level, as opposed to only 9% of older White people.

One study revealed that elderly people who felt they were better off financially than their relatives reported higher life satisfaction than did those who were not as well off (Usui, Keil, and Durig, 1985). Those with financial problems experience diminished feelings of control over their lives. Financial strain and diminished feelings of control are related to increased stress (Krause and Baker, 1992). Most older adults want financial independence, but this requires careful long-term planning (Strate and Dubnoff, 1986).

Adjusting to Revised Work Roles   Retirement at age 65 is no longer compulsory, but many workers must retire at 70. Forced retirement has been ranked among the top 10 crises in terms of the amount of stress it causes the individual (Sarason, 1981). People who elect retirement, plan for it, and look forward to it feel they have directed their own lives and are not being pushed or manipulated (Kilty and Behling, 1985, 1986). This is not the case for the many people who must delay retirement because they do not have the means to finance it (Richardson and Kilty, 1992), or for those who are forced to retire before they intended because of health limitations (Henretta, Chan, and O'Rand, 1992). Those most satisfied with retirement are those who have been preparing for it for a number of years. This is an important point, since the quality of the retirement experience influences marital satisfaction after retirement (Higginbottom, Barling, and Kelloway, 1993). Chronological age, health, and self-perception of the ability to adjust to retirement are all important influences on planned retirement age (M. A. Taylor and Shore, 1995).

One study listed four primary reasons for retirement: (1) job stress, (2) pressure from employer, (3) desire to pursue one's own interests, and (4) circumstances, such as age or health. Those who retired to escape job stress found relatively greater rewards

from the reduced stress in retirement. Those who were pressured by their employer to retire were more likely to report a difficult transition, less satisfaction with retirement, fewer sources of enjoyment in retirement, and poor function in physical, social, and leisure activities than were people who retired voluntarily. Voluntary retirees who retired to pursue their own interests reported an easier transition to retirement and higher satisfaction with, more sources of enjoyment in, and positive adjustment to retirement. The reaction to retirement of those who retired because of circumstances, for example, age or health, depended on whether they really wanted to retire (Floyd et al., 1992). Certainly, retirement should be retirement to, not from, something. Retirees who are most satisfied seem to be those most involved in meaningful activity following retirement.

Employment serves as an important power resource for many spouses. Retirement can therefore undermine a spouse's status in the marriage and alter both spouses' relative power in the relationship. The effect of retirement is partly dependent on the employment status of the other spouse, as well as on both spouses' gender-role attitudes. The man's loss of a provider role undermines his status in the marriage and makes him more dependent on the marriage itself. The woman's employment status, by contrast, seems to have little impact on dependence perception. For example, women whose spouse has retired see themselves as relatively less dependent on the marriage regardless of whether they themselves are employed or retired (Szinovacz and Harpster, 1993).

Using longitudinal data from a national sample of married couples, one study (S. M. Myers and Booth, 1996) explored a wide range of contextual factors that influenced the effect of retirement on marital quality. Characteristics of the man's job, the division of labor within the marriage, social support, health, and marital quality are preretirement factors that affect the influence of retirement on marital quality. Leaving a high-stress job improves marital quality, whereas gender-role reversals, declines in health, and reduced social support associated with the retirement adversely affect marital quality. Furthermore,

developmental tasks   Growth responsibilities that arise at various stages of life.

the effects of retirement vary according to the number of changes that accompany retirement.

Other findings of the study suggest that the division of labor within and outside the household is one of the most troubling areas. Given that a substantial number of women are in the labor force and are younger than their spouses, it follows that men increasingly find themselves retiring before their mate does. Men's persistent resistance to performing housework, coupled with feeling threatened by their spouse's occupational success, suggests that couples in which men retire first will have poorer quality marriages (S. M. Myers and Booth, 1996).

Establishing Acceptable Housing and Living Conditions   For some older people, being able to keep their own home is of great importance. It allows them independence and usually more satisfactory relationships with their children. However, they may experience difficulty in home maintenance. Income has a marked effect on the quality and quantity of home upkeep (Reschobsky and Newman, 1991).

Statistics from 2000 reveal that almost 80% of houses maintained by people age 65 and older were owned by them. In the remaining houses, the elderly were renting. Of course, many older people (about 1 out of 10 men and 1 out of 5 women 65 and older) are not heads of households, since they live with their children. Forty-two percent of people age 75 and older live with their spouse (U.S. Bureau of the Census, 2001).

Maintaining Identity and Social Status   The aged have high status and prestige in many societies because they possess the greatest knowledge of skills, traditions, and ceremonies considered essential for group survival. For example, the elderly have had high status in agricultural societies because they controlled the property, had the greatest knowledge of farming skills, were able to perform useful tasks, and were the leaders of the extended family. But as our society became more industrialized and modern, the elderly lost their economic advantages and their leadership roles both in industry and in the extended family. Consequently, they lost their status and prestige (Ishii-Kuntz and Lee, 1987).

Part of the loss of status comes when people retire, because many people find status through their occupation (Hurst and Guldin, 1981). When they leave that role, they have the feeling that they have lost their main identity. For example, a former mechanic is no longer a mechanic—occupationally, he or she is nothing. Those who are able to develop a meaningful identity through avocations, social life, marriage, children, or other activities adjust more easily than those whose identity is inseparable from their occupation.

Finding Companionship and Friendship   Loneliness is one of the most frequent complaints of older people, especially of the formerly married (Essex and Nam, 1987). Their challenge is to find meaningful relationships with others (Hatch and Bulcroft, 1992). Developing and maintaining friendships with peers seems to be more important to the emotional well-being of the elderly than does interaction with kin. The elderly who are able to find dating partners can likely satisfy their need for companionship and emotional fulfillment (Adams, 1985). One 73-year-old woman stated:

> It was a lot harder when my boyfriend, Ted, died than when my husband of forty years passed away. I needed Ted in a way I never needed my husband. Ted and I spent so much time together; he was all I had. And at my age I know it will be hard to find someone else. . . . I would like to date someone like Ted again . . . but, well, let's face it; how many men want a seventy-three-year-old woman? (Bulcroft and O'Connor, 1986, p. 401)

Field (1999) studied older adults to try to understand how friendships change in old age. Participants were interviewed twice, once as young-old adults ages 60–74, and again when they were at least 75. The study found that acquaintances and casual friends became less and less important in old age but that close friends and relatives remained very important. Casual friends were no longer as useful, and so contact with them decreased. However, there were gender differences in older-generation friendships. Women were more involved in friendships than were men, while men had less desire to make new friends and had less intimate contact with friends. These gender differences were less pronounced at the young-old age and more pronounced at the older stage.

Learning to Use Leisure Time Pleasurably   Late adulthood offers most people an opportunity to enjoy themselves. As work roles decline, more leisure time is available for preferred pursuits. Life satisfaction in late adulthood is very much dependent on social activity. People need worthwhile, pleasurable activities to help them feel good about themselves and about life in general.

Establishing New Roles in the Family   Several events bring about the adjustment of family roles: children marrying and moving away, grandparenthood, retirement, the death of a spouse, or dependence on one's children. All of these circumstances require major adjustments and a realignment of family roles and responsibilities (Brubaker, 1990). Family relationships during late adulthood will be discussed in more detail later in this chapter.

There is some reversal of gender roles in relation to authority in the family as people get older. The man who retires loses some status and authority in family governance, and the woman often assumes a more dominant role as an authority figure (Liang, 1982). This is especially true in relation to planning activities for herself and her mate and to assuming a nurturing role that has not been possible since the children left home.

Late adulthood offers an opportunity to pursue leisure activities. Enjoying pleasurable activities is key to life satisfaction for older people.

Achieving Integrity Through Acceptance of One's Life
Erikson (1959) stated that the development of ego integrity is the chief psychosocial task of the final stage of life. This includes reviewing one's life, being able to accept the facts of one's life without regret, and being able to face death without great fear. It entails appreciating one's own individuality, accomplishments, and satisfactions, as well as accepting the hardships, failures, and disappointments one has experienced. Ultimately, it means contentment with one's life as it is and has been (Reker, Peacock, and Wong, 1987).

Marital Satisfaction

As the health and longevity of the elderly increase, an increasing proportion of adults over age 65 are still married and living with their spouse. In 2000, 80% of men ages 65–74 and 69% of men 75 and older were married. Figures for women of comparable ages were 56% and 31%, respectively. Obviously, there are far greater numbers of widowed women than men. Table 8.3 shows the figures (U.S. Bureau of the Census, 2001).

For many older adults, marriage continues to be a major source of life satisfaction. Marital happiness and satisfaction usually increase during a second honeymoon stage after the children leave home and after retirement. The spouses usually have more leisure time to spend with each other and with adult children and grandchildren, and they depend more on each other for companionship. As one wife remarked, "I feel closer to Bill than I have for years. We had forgotten what it meant to have real companionship" (author's counseling notes). Marital satisfaction tends to be high among those whose spouse is also the most important confidant (G. R. Lee, 1988a).

At some point, declining physical health and financial resources usually begin to take their toll. Spouses often find it harder to cope with their life situation as they grow older. Declining status and involuntary disengagement from society result in increasing discontent. Spouses may have fewer physical, social, and emotional resources with which to reward each other in mutual marital exchange, and marital satisfaction may decline.

Divorce

Divorce at any time of life is a distressing experience. If it comes during late adulthood, it is even more difficult. Chiriboga (1982) found that the proportion of

Table 8.3 Marital Status of Older Americans, by Age and Gender, in Percentages, 1998

Marital Status	Male			Female		
	55–64	65–74	75+	55–64	65–74	75+
Never-married	5.5	4.3	4.1	4.6	3.7	3.5
Married	79.1	79.6	69.3	68.0	55.6	31.1
Widowed	3.0	8.3	22.7	11.8	31.3	60.5
Divorced	12.5	7.8	3.9	15.3	9.3	4.9

Note: From Statistical Abstract of the United States, 2000, by U.S. Bureau of the Census, 2001, Washington, DC: U.S. Government Printing Office.

divorced adults who are unhappy increases steadily with age. In comparison to those who are middle-aged at the time of divorce, adults who are over 60 are lower in morale and overall happiness. They exhibit more symptoms of psychological disturbance and report they are troubled by the separation.

The effects of later-life parental divorce on the relations between parents and young adult children were explored in a sample of 3,281 young adults who had grown up in intact families. Family dissolution that occurred after children were grown had sizable effects on parent–adult child relations. Later-life parental divorce lowered the relationship quality and level of contact between adult children and parents, especially between fathers and children. The effects of later-life marital dissolution on the exchange of health-related support and financial assistance differed by sex of the child and parent. Divorce disrupted parent–son support exchange more than parent–daughter (Aquilino, 1994).

Parent–Adult Child Relationships

The image of parents growing older without contact with their adult children does not coincide with the facts. Most older people are *not* isolated from their children (Dorfman and Mertens, 1990).

Aldous (1987) examined the relationships between 124 older couples and their adult children. The couples were in their early and midsixties; some were retired, and some were not. On average, the couples had been married 30 years or more. About a third of the fathers had professional, technical, or managerial careers. The parents had an average of 3.6 children, most of whom had left home and lived, on average, 487 miles away. The parents' relationships with their children exhibited certain common characteristics.

First, contacts were frequent. Parents and children kept in touch with one another by letter or telephone more than weekly in the previous year. They visited in one another's homes more than once a month and celebrated holidays together at least once every 2 months.

Second, they helped one another. Because parents had greater resources than children, parents had made loans, given gifts, or paid bills for each child about once every 2 months. They also provided child care, house care, shopping, transportation, and help in times of illness. Parents were most in touch with adult children who were most in need. For example, the never-married and divorced were of special concern to parents. Divorced daughters with children most often received household help and child care from parents.

Third, the children reciprocated as they were able. They provided gifts and financial aid of $50 or less in value about four times a year. They were most able to provide help requiring physical energy, giving assistance with house and yard work six times a year.

Fourth, both mothers and fathers reported some disagreement with their adult children over the rearing of grandchildren, treatment of siblings, treatment of themselves, and frequency of get-togethers. Generally, however, both parents and adult children were very satisfied with their relationship.

Other studies have reported the following important factors in parent–adult child relationships:

- Frequency of contact is not the key factor in satisfactory relationships.

- Emotional support is important and can be more significant than whether adult children provide financial support (Houser and Berkman, 1984).

- The morale of the elderly is higher if they feel they can reciprocate some of the help their children or friends give them (Roberto and Scott, 1986; Stoller, 1985).

Most older people have strong ties to their children and grandchildren. Becoming a grandparent brings about a welcome new status.

- Although moderate amounts of intergenerational support are beneficial to older adults, excessive support received from adult children actually may do harm by eroding feelings of competence and imposing excessive demands on the older person. In the beginning, support from children is much appreciated by older parents, but as time passes, greater support begins to depress them and make them feel bad about their situation (Silverstein, Chen, and Heller, 1996).

- Providing extensive care for severely functionally impaired parents causes extreme stress and hardship for the caregivers. Community personal care services, day care, home nursing, and homemakers' services are often needed. Nevertheless, the most important resource an elderly person can have is responsible and caring children (Matthews and Rosner, 1988; Walker, Shin, and Bird, 1990).

WIDOWHOOD

The death of a spouse is one of life's most traumatic events at any age. Loss of a loving partner is a painful and stressful human experience. A deeply felt loss is intrinsically linked to the disruption of personal identity. The survivor often confronts emotional, economic, and physical problems precipitated by a spouse's death.

Couples who married and had children in the 1990s and whose marriages are not broken by divorce or separation can expect to live together for 45 years. From birth, the female's life expectancy is 79 and the male's is 74, but the man is 2 years older than the woman when they marry, so she can expect to be a widow for 7 years (U.S. Bureau of the Census, 2001). The greater longevity of women means that the number of widows exceeds that of widowers at all age levels. Table 8.4 shows the ratios at different ages (U.S. Bureau of the Census, 2001). Partly as a result of these ratios, the remarriage rate for widows is lower than for widowers. The older a person is when a mate dies, the lower the chances of remarriage.

Older people, especially widows, have a consistently high degree of contact with other family members, including married children. Usually, the elderly woman is closer to her children, especially daughters, than is the elderly man. However, the woman is more likely to depend on them for material aid. The more dependent elderly people become and the more helping roles are reversed, the lower their morale. All research findings stress the importance of peer support in helping widows and widowers adjust. Morale is positively associated with involvement with friends.

In addition to the psychological stress of spousal loss and the need to reconstruct a new sense of self, widows have to solve some practical, everyday problems of living (DeGarmo and Kipson, 1996).

as central to their psychological and physical well-being. Research shows that strong commitment to one role does not necessarily preclude strong commitment to the other role (Barnett and Hyde, 2001).

Galinsky (1999) found that most parents with children under 18 reported being at least somewhat successful in managing work and family, and maternal employment in and of itself has very little impact on children. Any impact on the child depends on a number of factors. For example, the benefits of multiple roles depend on the number of roles, the demands of each role, and role quality (Voydanoff, 2002). Everyone has limits, and when overloaded individuals reach their upper limits, distress occurs (Voydanoff and Donnelly, 1999). On the one hand, work that is satisfying and rewarding can have positive effects on level of stress in a person's life. On the other hand, work that is not satisfying or that brings with it discrimination or sexual harassment is not an experience that contributes to life satisfaction and feelings of success (Voydanoff and Donnelly, 1999; Barnett and Hyde, 2001).

Haddock and her colleagues (2001) studied adaptive strategies from successful families for balancing work and family. They found 10 adaptive strategies:

1. **Valuing family:** The highest priority for successful couples was a commitment to family. Couples worked hard at maintaining family time and family rituals such as bedtime stories every evening and "pizza night" every Friday.
2. **Striving for partnership**: Trying to have equality and partnership in the marital relationship was vital to the success of balancing work and family. Important issues of equality and partnership surrounded division of household chores and child care, decision making, respect, and appreciation and support on an interpersonal level.
3. **Deriving meaning from work:** Couples who liked their work and experienced enjoyment and fulfillment from it felt that it brought energy and enthusiasm to their lives and helped in the balance of work and family.
4. **Maintaining work boundaries:** Couples who put limits on work and did not allow work to control their lives were better able to balance work and family.
5. **Focusing and producing at work:** Being productive at work helped people put family as a

top priority and still feel good about their job performance.
6. **Prioritizing family fun:** Given that many dual-earner families have fewer hours to play, successful families made a point to enjoy playtime together and used it as a way to de-stress from a busy day in the workforce.
7. **Taking pride in dual earning.** Most of the successful couples felt that being a dual-earner family was positive for all members of the family. They did not experience guilt for working and felt it was the right choice for them as family.
8. **Living simply:** Successful couples felt they needed to maintain a simplified life. This included limiting activities that restrict family time such as TV and children's extracurricular activities, controlling their finances, developing realistic expectations about housework, and finding strategies that were efficient and simple in managing the household.
9. **Making decisions proactively:** Successful couples took control of their life through decision making rather than allowing the pace of their life and work to take control. The priority to their family shaped their decisions, and they were consciously making decisions together that reflected this commitment to family and marriage.
10. **Valuing time:** Successful couples stated that they were aware of the value of time and attempted to maximize their use of time. They were protective and thought about how they were going to use time. They thought about ways to spend meaningful and rewarding time together.

Needed: More Time

Clarkberg and Moen (2001) indicated from their research that there is a considerable disparity between couples' self-reports of how much they would like to work and how much they are working. They found that long workweeks generally do not reflect employee preferences but rather result from constraints and demands imposed by the workplace. The rising sense of a time squeeze in American society may stem from all-or-nothing assumptions about the nature and structure of work and the pressure to put in long hours to be seen as committed, productive, and able to advance.

Indeed, American parents are working more hours away from home than they did 20 years ago, and working more hours than parents in other countries (Coontz, 2000). The Economic Policy Institute reported that while an average middle-class family's income rose by 9.2% after inflation from 1989 to 1998, the family also spent 6.8% more time at work. Government figures show that while the average full-time employee's workweek has remained fairly steady, at about 43 hours, the share of married women working full-time rose to 46% in 1998 from 41% in 1989. The study also found that middle-class Black families work an average of 9.4 hours more per week than their White counterparts and that Blacks work more hours than Whites at every income level. Hispanic families work 5 hours more per week than their White counterparts. Upper-income Hispanic families work the most of any group in any economic class, putting in 12.9 hours more per week than White families (Mishel, Bernstein, and Boushey, 2003). It is therefore no surprise that people report feeling more rushed today than they did 30 years ago (Jacobs and Gerson, 1998) or that more than 60% of American workers report wanting to work fewer hours (Bond, Galinsky, and Swanberg, 1998). In most cases, couples are trying to find more time to be together and still provide economically for their families.

Much research has documented that long work hours may have negative consequences for families who struggle to balance the demands of work and home life (Crouter, Bumpus, Head, and McHale, 2001; Major, Klein, and Ehrhart, 2002). In a study of 513 employees in a Fortune 500 company, long work hours were associated with increased work–family conflict and psychological distress (Major, Klein, and Ehrhart, 2002). People worked longer hours when they had strong career identity, had too much to do in too little time on the job, perceived that their supervisors expected them to work extra hours as needed, had fewer responsibilities away from work, and believed that they had relatively great financial needs. Regardless of how flexible employees' schedules were or how much responsibility they bore for home and family duties, the more hours a week they worked, the more work interference with family they reported.

Crouter and her colleagues (2001) examined how long work hours and role overload affected the quality of men's relationships with their spouse and children. They found that the more hours men

worked, the less time they spent with their spouse. Long work hours did not relate to spouses' love, perspective taking, or conflict, but role overload consistently predicted less-positive marital relationships. When fathers had both long hours and high overload, they developed less-positive father–adolescent relationships.

Another barrier to family togetherness is a job schedule that makes it difficult for members to be together. Hattery (2001) explored the costs and benefits of utilizing nonoverlapping shift work as a way of balancing work and family when couples have children. She found that nonoverlapping shift work allowed the parents of young children to provide all of the child care themselves and thus save on child care costs. However, when couples work different shifts, little time is left over for the marital relationship and one parent is often caring for the children alone, which can be stressful.

If a couple has to work shifts, working the same shift can be important in maintaining a relationship. One study found that divorce is common among couples in which one spouse works nights (Presser, 2000). Fathers who work nights are six times more likely to divorce than are fathers who work days, and mothers who work nights triple their odds of divorce. Other jobs, such as that of a police officer, are very stressful in and of themselves and require a lot of work on weekends and holidays. Some work, such as serving in the armed services and merchant marines, requires long periods of separation. This can cause conflict between family and job demands and become a source of individual and family stress.

Many couples are trying to scale back to have more time for family (Becker and Moen, 1999). Some choose a one-job, one-career marriage, and others trade off overtime for family time. Time is a precious commodity, and people need to sort out their priorities and ask themselves if their job is worth sacrificing their family for. Marriages and family relationships, like anything else worthwhile, require time and attention to maintain.

The Parents' Child Care Role

The decisions that parents make about work and family, especially about how they care for their children, help shape their children's intellectual development, social behavior, and personalities. In everything they do, from the jobs they choose to the way they allocate household chores, parents provide powerful models of male and female behavior for their children. Parents, inadvertently or intentionally, prepare their children for similar future roles in the workplace and the family.

Today, most fathers are expected to share in the responsibilities of child care, especially in dual-earner families. Several researchers have found that men contribute more to household and child care responsibilities than they did in the past, but they still do not contribute as much as their wives do (J. Williams, 2000).

Both parents benefit from fathers' participation in raising children. Fathers who assume responsibility for child care ease the burden of employed mothers and reduce the maternal stress associated with work overload, anxiety, and a shortage of time

Increasing numbers of fathers participate in child care as part of their family responsibilities. A father's involvement in child rearing benefits his children's academic achievement, social competence, and self-esteem.

for rest and leisure. Fathers who are actively involved in caring for their children enjoy the positive effects of multiple roles, which include enhanced marital relations and closer father–child bonds. Men—like women—who combine different life roles such as parent, worker, and spouse may be better off emotionally than individuals with fewer life roles (Voydanoff and Donnelly, 1999).

While fathers are assuming more child care responsibility, it does not alleviate the challenge for many parents of finding appropriate child care during the workday. As stated before, some parents have opted to work different shifts from their spouses to meet the child care challenge. Yet conflicting work schedules often contribute to marital stress and dissatisfaction, and spending time in child care may come at the expense of time with a spouse (Brayfield, 1995). Thus, most couples do not want to live their lives working different shifts in order to meet child care demands.

The challenge of child care is even more pressing for couples who do not work the day shift. Parents who work evenings, late afternoons, or weekends often find it very difficult to find child care centers or other formal arrangements that are available during those hours. Parents who are employed at odd hours have fewer choices in caring for their children and may have to select child care they feel is less than adequate because of what is available.

The availability of different types of child care will be discussed in more detail in Chapter 13. However, regardless of the type of care, most dual-earner families admit they have to budget their time very carefully around child care issues. Most centers have strict hours of operation, and dropping off a child early or picking up a child late is not feasible. Many employers also require employees to work strict hours of business. However, if parents have some flexibility in controlling their work schedules, it is easier to mesh job and child care responsibilities. Some companies have recognized the struggles many of their employees face with child care and have **flextime** that allows workers to choose the hours during the day when they will work (Meer, 1985).

Research shows that job flexibility does play an important role in family life. One study indicated that job flexibility is associated with increased work satisfaction and increased family well-being (S. C. Clark, 2001). Another study indicated that perceived job flexibility is related to improved work–family balance and appears to be beneficial to both the individuals and to businesses. For example, employees with perceived job flexibility were better able to work longer hours before workload negatively impacted their work–family balance (E. J. Hill et al., 2001). Employees with flextime have been found to be more satisfied with their jobs and more likely to want to remain on the job than those without flextime (Galinsky and Johnson, 1998).

However, many companies still don't offer job sharing, telecommuting, flexplace, or other arrangements that may help working parents meet the demands of their families (E. J. Hill et al., 2001). According to a study by the Society for Human Resource Management (2001), just 24% of companies allow employees to bring children to work in an emergency, and just 5% have on-site child care. Another study of more than 1,000 U.S. companies showed that 68% had flexible starting and stopping times, but only 24% allowed this change on a daily basis (Galinsky and Bond, 1998). The study also showed that more companies allow flexplace than flextime: 55% of the companies allowed employees to work at home occasionally. However, many workers do not take advantage of flexplace because they believe that time in the office is related to promotion (Bond et al., 1998); some research supports this idea (Judiesch and Lyness, 1999).

Because of the challenges with child care, many spouses also try to arrange their schedules so that one or the other is available to care for children and so that they can spend time together as a couple. As stated earlier, some couples work different shifts so that one partner or the other is always available to care for children. Most couples admit that they have to give up a number of activities just to have time for necessary things. Dual-earner couples may not entertain as often as they would like. Nor is there as much time for involvement in community activities or for such pastimes as gardening or reading.

One study found that many middle-class dual-earner couples cope with the dual demands of work and family by "scaling back" (Becker, 1999). That is, the partners place limits on the number of hours they work, reduce expectations for career advancement, decide to have a one-job/one-career marriage, or trade family and job responsibilities over the life course. Women, however, do the most scaling back. In 2000, only 3% of married-couple families with

children younger than 6 had a father who was not employed while the mother worked, according to the U.S. Department of Labor. This is in contrast to the 38% or so of families with young children that have a father employed but not the mother. While both parents may agree that having the mother stay home with the children is the most practical plan for child care, there are important consequences to consider. Research shows that, compared to their employed counterparts, women who leave the labor force, even for a short time, have more difficulty with career advancement and salary gains if they decide to return to the labor force. This needs to be considered against the fact that about half of first marriages end in divorce; a stay-at-home mother who is dependent on her husband, particularly for a long time, may face a financial challenge if the couple divorces and she becomes a single parent.

EMPLOYED MOTHERS AND THE FAMILY

Women report that their experience of mothering is altered significantly when they work outside the home, and they often must address new variations of problems concerning time pressures and conflicting role demands. Mothers who are employed not only have less time to spend with their children but also spend fewer hours on household chores such as meal preparation and cleaning. For example, in 1965, the average woman spent 27 hours a week on cooking and cleaning; in 1995, she spent only 15½ hours a week (J. P. Robinson, Godbey, and Jacobson, 1999). Since 1965, the number of hours spent in domestic labor (excluding child care and shopping) has steadily declined. A study of time diaries showed that since the 1960s, women have cut their housework hours by almost 50% (from 24 hours per week to 12 hours per week). Men, by contrast, have almost doubled their housework time since the 1960s from a few hours per week to slightly over 5 hours per week. Men today are responsible for almost a third

flextime A company policy that allows employees to choose the most convenient hours for them to work during the day, selected from hours designated by the employer.

of the housework. (Bianchi, Milkie, Sayer, and Robinson, 2000).

All women have experienced a decrease in time spent on housework, whether they were employed or unemployed, single or married, or young or old. Although modern conveniences have reduced the time needed for housework, much of the decrease is attributed to the fact that working women simply have less time available to maintain the household.

Like women who remain at home, however, employed mothers perform most of the household chores and care activities. Women employed full-time may reduce the amount of time they spend on household tasks, but not the range of their responsibilities. This led some researchers to refer to employed mothers as "supermoms"—mothers who remain heavily involved with family responsibilities while also meeting the demands of paid employment (DeMeis and Perkins, 1996).

But what about the impact of paid employment on women's lives? Are employed mothers more fulfilled, more satisfied with life, and just plain happier than stay-at-home moms? Work has been described as an alienating force in the lives of men, but it is sometimes transformed into a liberating force in the lives of women. This position assumes that any sort of paid employment is preferable to full-time homemaking. The research on life satisfaction of mothers who work outside the home versus those who do not shows slightly greater satisfaction among those working outside the home, but the results depend on a number of variables (Tiedje et al., 1990).

Ethics and Value Systems

Part of the effect of the women's employment on the marriage depends on the ethics and value systems of the couple. Many couples find themselves torn between two ethics: the ethic of equity, defined as a relatively fair division of household labor, and the ethic of care, defined as the desire to be attentive and responsive to the needs of individual family members. Many women's satisfaction with the division of labor appears contingent on the time spent and the number of tasks performed by them and by their spouse. Women often complain about imbalances in the division of household labor and feel that the divisions are unfair. Many women put the ethic of

care—being sensitive to the needs of various family members—first. This ethic is demonstrated through preparing meals, shopping for food, cleaning house, washing clothes, and caring for children. Employed women with this ethic routinely perform a proportionately greater share of daily household tasks than do their partners (Stohs, 1994).

Role Conflict and Strain

One important consideration in the life satisfaction of working mothers is whether they have been able to integrate their work life with their home life. A number of factors influence the role strain of working women. Basically, there are three major sources of strain: (1) individual (those that originate within the individual), (2) family-related (those that come from the family), and (3) work-related (those that originate from the work situation; R. F. Kelly and Voydanoff, 1985). The combination of family structure and responsibilities, work time, and job demands is related to the degree of role strain (Voydanoff, 1988).

One individual source of role strain is the woman's own conflict over the fact that she is working (Greenberger and O'Neil, 1990). If she prefers being at home but has to work for various reasons, her ambiguous feelings become a source of internal conflict and tension. Conversely, women who have nontraditional gender-role attitudes but who fill a traditional homemaker role evaluate their situation more negatively than do other women (McHale and Crouter, 1992). One mother remarked, "I hate working. I'd rather be home, but George and I can't make it financially unless I do, so I have no choice" (Author's counseling notes).

A family-related source of strain for working mothers is the presence of young children in the family (Eggebeen, 1988). The more young children in the family, the more stress is introduced. Some women feel guilty about leaving their children, especially when the children are small. However, mothers feel less stress if they are satisfied with the quality of substitute child care. The maternal leave law, which allows pregnant women to take a leave of absence from work to have their baby, is a help for some in eliminating the conflict between having to work and wanting to stay home and care for a newborn (Trzcinski and Finn-Stevenson, 1991). Hyde, Essex, Clark, and Klein (2001) investigated the relationship

Although balancing commitments to children, partner, and career can often be demanding and difficult, many working mothers would not choose anything less.

between the length of women's maternity leave and marital incompatibility. They examined variables such as the woman's employment, her dissatisfaction with the division of household labor, and her sense of role overload. They found that a short maternity leave is a risk factor for personal and marital distress. Women who took longer leaves were less dissatisfied with the division of household labor, and this was particularly true for women who worked longer hours. The combination of short leave and child care that did not match the woman's preferences was associated with the greatest increases in marital incompatibility. These results indicate that short maternity leave can be conceptualized as a risk factor that exacerbates the effects of other risk factors in creating psychological and marital distress. The level of the mother's stress also depends partially on the willingness of the father to become involved during infancy in caring for his child (Nugent, 1991; Volling and Belsky, 1991).

Another source of conflict is the strain of having to fulfill too many roles at once (Voydanoff and Donnelly, 1989b). Most working mothers recognize that they do not have as much time for child care, housework, and leisure time activities as they would if they were not working (Firestone and Shelton, 1988). If a mother works full-time, is raising one or more children, and tries to be a good spouse, she has taken on the responsibility of at least two and a half full-time jobs. If her job is demanding and her spouse is not very sympathetic and helpful at home, or if he, along with the children, demands a lot from her, she is under constant pressure to give and give. If she feels she can't fulfill her own or her family's expectations, she may become upset or depressed (Keith and Schafer, 1985).

The job itself may also be a source of stress and strain. One study found that changes in job-role quality were significantly associated with psychological distress (Barnett, Marshall, and Singer, 1992). Difficult job demands and assignments, inconvenient schedules, long hours, and pressures to produce all create strain (Wethington and Kessler, 1989). If a boss or coworkers are hard to get along with or if the job requires unreasonable hours and has a lot of responsibilities, the woman is exhausted by the time she gets home. The last thing she needs is to have to spend the rest of her waking hours trying to satisfy the demands of spouse and children. This is why assistance from a partner, older children, or hired help is so important. One woman remarked, "I'd love to be able to come home from work and have someone have *my* supper on the table for *me*" (Author's counseling notes).

For many women, however, working outside the home enhances their lives, especially if they love their job and have a spouse and children who help or are able to hire some assistance. Some women are more relaxed at work than at home and may even go to work to get away from their families. One mother remarked, "I can't wait to get out of the house in the morning. Work is the only place I have any peace and quiet. I'd go absolutely crazy if I had to stay home all day. My children could drive me crazy" (Author's counseling notes). One study of middle-aged and older Black women revealed that employment contributed significantly to their well-being (Coleman, Antonucci, Adelmann, and Crohan, 1987). Many women return to work after their children have left home, and they find their employment fulfilling (Moen, 1991).

There are all kinds of people and all kinds of needs. Some women are far better wives and mothers because they go to work. They're more patient, more giving, and more attentive during the time they are home than they would be if they were not working outside the home (Menaghan and Parcel, 1991).

Marital Adjustment

Social science has devoted considerable effort to comparing employed and nonemployed mothers to determine effects on spousal relationships. Some investigators report a positive relationship between women's employment and marital adjustment. For example, one study found that increases in women's income do not significantly affect marital discord, but, interestingly, marital discord increases women's income by increasing the likelihood that the women will enter the workforce (Rogers, 1999).

In many families, wives' employment has a positive effect on marital quality through increased family income, particularly when the husband's income is low and the wife's income can reduce financial strain. When families experience economic hardship, psychological distress and marital conflict often arise (Brennan, Barnett, and Gareis, 2001). Two incomes in a family can reduce the strain of one person having to provide all the financial resources. Wilkie, Ferree, and Ratcliff (1998) found that when both partners take responsibility for supporting the family, there were benefits to marital satisfaction for both husbands and wives, but the benefits were greater for husbands. In addition, a decline in men being solely responsible for supporting the family promotes a more egalitarian ideology among both men and women (Zuo and Tang, 2000).

However, the effect of women's employment on marital quality depends partially on the number of children in the household. One study found that, as the number of children in the household increases, so do their demands, and full-time employment of the mother thus is associated with less marital happiness and more marital conflict. Robinson, Flowers, and Carroll (2001) examined the relationship of work stress and marital cohesion and found that when work stress increases, marital cohesion decreases. These findings are consistent with previous research

reporting that work–family role strain was heightened for employed mothers and that marital interaction and quality were compromised when dual-earner families had children (S. J. Rogers, 1996).

In mother–stepfather families, the relationship between maternal employment and marital quality is more complicated. When the family is small, the mother's full-time employment is associated with less marital happiness and more marital conflict. This suggests that combining the demands of full-time employment and family has negative effects on the marital relationship that outweigh the potential benefits. When family size increases, however, the mother's full-time employment is associated with greater marital happiness and less marital conflict. The mother's contributions to the family income are likely to ease economic strain and increase marital quality.

A comprehensive review of findings from 27 studies summarized 2,018 comparisons between spouses of employed and nonemployed women and 2,584 comparisons between employed and nonemployed women to determine the degrees of marital adjustment (D. S. Smith, 1985). Marital adjustment was divided into five categories: physical, companionship, communication, tensions and regrets, and a global (overall) measure. Most of the comparisons showed no difference in adjustment between male groups and female groups. The very few differences tended to favor the nonemployed groups. However, when the results were controlled according to women's educational level, family income, and social class, the presence and age of children in various stages of the life cycle, and their spouse's education, the basic finding of little difference between employed and nonemployed groups remained.

What this means is that the mother's employment status alone appears to have little or no effect on marital adjustment (Spitze, 1988). This does not mean there aren't problems in dual-earner families. Certainly, there may be. For example, as stated earlier, a stressful job seems to be correlated with higher levels of stress and lower levels of marital adjustment (Sears and Galambos, 1992). But it does mean that whether the woman works is not *the* key to marital adjustment. Other factors are more significant. For example, one study found that a couple's belief in their ability to resolve disagreements, not the woman's work status, is the best predictor of marital adjustment (Meeks, Arnkoff, Glass, and Notarius, 1986). Another study found that an equitable relationship—that is, one in which there is a fair balance of rewards and constraints for both spouses—is the key factor in marital adjustment (Rachlin, 1987). Thus, both single-earner and dual-career couples may have either poor or good marriages.

Gender-role attitudes and role expectations may be much more important in determining the quality of a marriage than is the woman's employment status. The man's attitudes are more important to the experience of marital quality for both spouses than are the attitudes of the woman. His role expectations, gender-role identity, and support are important, as are his spouse's perceptions of his expectations and support. The marital quality experienced by both spouses is also strongly affected by the ability to give and receive support. Men with sensitive personalities produce a higher quality of marriage for their spouse. Women also experience higher marital quality the more egalitarian they believe their spouse's expectations to be (Vannoy and Philliber, 1992).

In a longitudinal study that examined salary gap in dual-earner couples, husbands experienced lower marital quality if their spouses earned more than they earned (Brennan et al., 2001). However, in analyzing marital power according to gender, Tichenor (1999) concluded that the dynamics of power within a marriage may not necessarily be tied to earnings. Even when the woman earns more than her spouse, he still usually holds more power in the relationship, and her actions often serve to reinforce the pattern of male dominance in the relationship. This finding suggests that marital power is tied more to gender than to status or income.

DUAL-CAREER FAMILIES

Earlier in this chapter, *dual-earner family* was defined as a family in which both spouses are involved in the paid labor force (Rachlin, 1987). Ordinarily, having a job does not involve as extensive a commitment, as much continuity of employment, or as much responsibility as the pursuit of a career.

The **dual-career family,** also called a dual-professional family (Hiller and Dyehouse, 1987), is a specific subtype of the broader category of dual-earner families (Rachlin, 1987). The dual-career

dual-career family Also called dual-professional family; a subtype of the dual-earner family in which there are two career-committed partners, both of whom are trying to fulfill professional roles that require continuous development.

If both members of a couple are career-committed individuals, they will face special challenges in trying to balance professional and family roles.

For the dual-earner family, finding quality child care can be a big problem. Ensuring the availability of quality day care for children is becoming recognized as a national concern.

family has two career-committed individuals, both of whom are trying to fulfill professional and family roles. But the pursuit of a career requires a high degree of commitment and continuous development. Individuals pursue careers by undergoing extensive education and preparation and then moving upward from one job level to another. A career ordinarily requires full-time employment, especially if one is working for someone else. The greater the responsibility and the higher the position achieved, the greater the commitment required of the individual—leaving less time to devote to spouse and child. The dual-career marriage is actually a minority pattern and, from a strictly managerial standpoint, is difficult to achieve. It is difficult to balance husband–wife and father–mother role relationships and responsibilities, to find adequate child care help in a society that expects parents to assume the major burden, and to maintain the expected spousal intimacy and companionship so that the marriage itself remains a viable relationship. Nevertheless, many couples succeed in pursuing careers and in being good spouses and parents. Other couples try to succeed at all three roles but find it too difficult to manage.

Issues for Dual-Career Couples

There are some real satisfactions and benefits in a dual-career marriage, as well as many added stresses. The financial rewards in a dual-career marriage can be considerable, especially if both spouses are earning salaries as professionals. One frequently mentioned reason any highly qualified person wants a career in addition to a family is the need for creativity, self-expression, achievement, and recognition. However, the stress in balancing both career and family responsibilities can be overwhelming. The most successful dual-career marriages are those in which the spouses treat each other as equal partners and share in the responsibility of child care and household tasks. In particular, women are far less satisfied and under more strain in marriages in which the responsibility for homemaking tasks and child care rests primarily on their shoulders.

Role Strain The strains of a dual-career marriage are considerable (Galambos and Silbereisen, 1989). One source of strain is overwork. The demands of the marriage, children, career, and home are great and often leave couples tense and exhausted. Factors related to role strain include flexibility of work schedule, the age of the youngest child, and the number of children. Flexibility of work schedule is significantly correlated with role strain, especially for men. The number of hours worked has no significant relationship to stress, provided there is a high level of marital equality for both men and women. In such marriages, the partners do favors for each other, listen and offer advice, and alter habits and ways of doing things to please each other. Both men and women report that the number of children is the most critical factor in stress levels. Both men and women with larger families report higher levels of distress (Guelzow, Bird, and Koball, 1991).

When spouses each have a career in addition to home responsibilities, they often need to work out difficult compromises. If one spouse is offered a promotion that means moving to another town, what will be the effect on the other spouse's career? The pressure to move frequently while one's career is becoming established can present difficulty for the two-career family (Kilpatrick, 1982).

Travel   The issue of travel arises in dual-career marriages because professionals often attend out-of-town meetings or conferences or consult with others in different locales. Professionals are frequently expected to go on business trips, usually from 2 to 10 days. Some have to travel monthly or more often; a few have to make extended trips abroad.

How does each spouse feel about the other traveling far from home on business trips? What child care arrangements work out best? What is the minimum level of housekeeping that both partners can live with? How can they best budget their time? These are some important issues.

Child Care   The difficulties involved in combining a career with parenthood become apparent after the first child is born. In the nuclear family, the spouses and children live in their own household separate from their relatives, so there is no other family member available to care for the children while the parents are working. This fact, added to job pressures and work loads, encourages the couple to make alternative arrangements for child care (R. R. Peterson and Gerson, 1992).

Parents can send their child to a day care center if one is available, but care is generally provided only during the day. The child must still be taken to the center and brought back home each day, an arrangement that further complicates the lives of two busy career people, especially if they have to drive miles each way. What happens when one parent is out of town? Usually, one or the other parent is available, but providing transportation is only part of the problem. The parent who is home must still get the child ready for day care and care for him or her after the center has closed. What if a child is sick or the parent has an important evening meeting?

MATERIAL RESOURCES

While some families are dual-earner for personal fulfillment and satisfaction (Cotton, Antill, and Cunningham, 1989), in most cases, financial necessity and the desire to improve the family's standard of living remain the most important motives for working (Eggebeen and Hawkins, 1990).

Financial Needs

The financial needs of today's families are great. Figure 9.1 shows the percentage of families at different income levels; the figures represent gross income (before deductions). The median family income level was $51,751 in 2000, meaning that 50% of all families were above and 50% were below that figure (U.S. Bureau of the Census, 2000).

In spite of the rise in family income over the years, however, real income, or purchasing power, has remained fairly constant (Aldous, Ganey, Trees, and Marsh, 1991). Because of inflation, the cost of living has increased as much as wages have increased during the past 15 years, so families are no better off now than they were 15 years ago (U.S. Bureau of the Census, 2000).

Various estimates have been given of how much it costs to bear and rear a child to maturity. In 2000, the cost of raising a child to age 18 in a middle-class family was about $165,600, according to the U.S. Department of Agriculture's annual report, *Expenditures on Children by Families* (see Figure 9.2; Lino, 2001). This figure was up 13 percent from 1960, after adjusting for inflation. Higher-income urban families (household income above $64,000 annually) spend an average of $242,600 to raise a child from birth to age 18 (Lino, 2001). In 2000, a family with two children could expect to spend over $320,000 to rear them to age 18. If college costs are added, the total will be much more.

A report from the Advisory Committee of Student Financial Assistance warns that a lack of financial aid is making college unreachable for even qualified high school students from families with low to moderate incomes. It is estimated that over the next decade, 4.4 million qualified students won't be able to attend a four-year college and 2 million won't be able to attend any college due to financial reasons (Horn, Chang Wei, and Berker, 2002). In the report "Unequal Opportunity: Disparities in College Access Among the 50 States," Kipp, Price, and

Figure 9.1 Gross Income Distribution of Families in the United States (*Note:* From *Statistical Abstract of the United States, 2001* [p. 69] by U.S. Bureau of the Census, 2001, Washington, DC: U.S. Government Printing Office.)

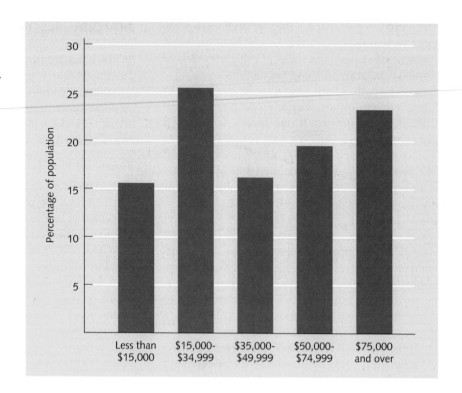

Figure 9.2 The Average Costs of Raising a Child to Age 18 (*Note:* From *Expenditures on Children by Families, 2001* [Miscellaneous Publication No. 1528-1999] by Mark Lino, 2001, Washington, DC: U.S. Department of Agriculture, Center for Nutrition Policy and Promotion.)

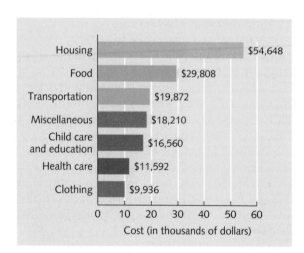

students—that is, traditionally aged students (18–22) who still rely on their parents' income. In 33 states, fewer than half of all institutions are accessible to low-income independent students, defined as those who are 24 years old or older.

Today, full-time college students are working longer hours than five years ago, and almost half of those who work more than 25 hours a week report that work is interfering with their academic achievement. Of all full-time students, 74% work while attending school and 84% identify themselves primarily as students working to meet college expenses (as opposed to employees who take classes). Moreover, 46% of full-time students work 25 or more hours a week, and 20% work 35 or more (T. King and Bannon, 2002).

Housing still ranks as the biggest expense for families, accounting for about one-third of expenses, just as it did 40 years ago. In some cities, families earning as much as $70,000 a year can't afford decent housing without spending more than half their income (Stegman, Quercia, and McCarthy, 2000). For example, in Boston in 1998, almost 31,000 families could afford to buy a $100,000–$125,000 home, but only 1,255 homes in that price range were available.

Wohlford (2002) reported that one-fourth of public colleges and universities in 16 states are considered inaccessible for low- and median-income dependent

Nationally, in 1997, 3 million moderate-income families had critical housing needs, which was 17% more than in 1995. Of these 3 million families, 76% spent more than half their income on housing, and the rest lived in substandard housing (Stegman et al., 2000).

The Gender Wage Gap

Although President John F. Kennedy signed the Equal Pay Act in 1963, outlawing wage discrimination based on gender, women in the United States still only earn 76¢, on average, for every dollar a man earns (U.S. Bureau of the Census, 2002). Title VII of the Civil Rights Act of 1964 was an even broader attempt to correct the inequity. However, women still consistently earn lower wages than men, many times even when doing the same work. The 2000 census data showed that the median income for a male living alone was $31,267, whereas for a female living alone the median income was $20,929. A 2002 analysis of census data found that, even during women's and men's peak earning years (ages 45–54), women earned 69% of what men earned. So why is it that the phenomenon continues?

Some would suggest that the wage gap is partly a result of differences in education. But the data show that when education levels are taken into account there is still an inequity in salaries (see Figure 9.3). In 2000, on average, women with professional degrees earned $60,560 less than men with professional degrees, and female college graduates earned $25,160 less than male college graduates.

Work experience is also cited as a determining factor in the gender wage gap, but again the argument is weakened by specific examples in which equal qualifications do not mean equal pay. Surveys conducted by the National Committee on Pay Equity (1998) show that in the field of public relations women with less than 5 years of experience make $29,726 a year,

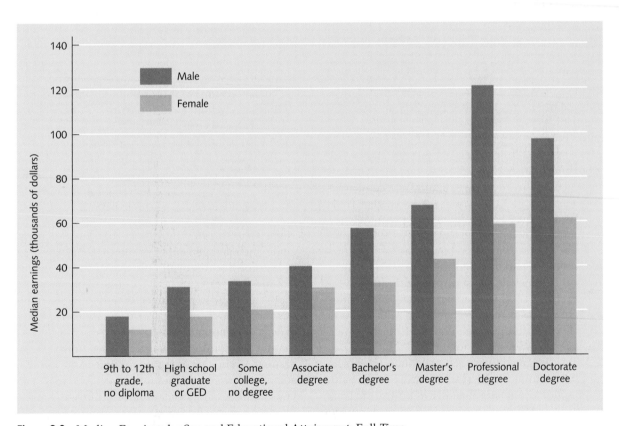

Figure 9.3 Median Earnings by Sex and Educational Attainment, Full-Time, Year-Round Workers, Age 18 and Older (*Note:* From Current Population Survey, 2001 [Table 218], by U.S. Bureau of the Census, 2001, Washington, DC: U.S. Government Printing Office.)

while men with the same amount of experience make $48,162. And when the experience level increases to 15–20 years, women average $49,270 and men average $69,120. A similar example can be found in the field of purchasing: Professional purchasers with 3 or fewer years of experience make $35,900 if they are women and $47,700 if they are men.

Evidently, other factors are at least partly responsible for the continued gender wage gap. Three reasons can be attributed to women themselves: (1) They choose to work in lower-paying industries, (2) they don't work as many hours per week as men, and (3) they don't "fight" for their own pay. Whole sections of the economy are traditionally women's jobs and have always been paid less—for example, nursing, secretarial work, and teaching. A study released by the National Bureau of Economic Research showed that a "sizable fraction" of the gender pay gap is caused by women's concentration in lower-paying industries and in lower-paying jobs within higher-paying industries (Krotz, 1999). Because women typically take on more family responsibilities than men, such as picking the children up from school or day care, they tend to put in less overtime and are less willing to travel on business. Some argue that men advance more quickly in companies because of their willingness to work longer hours, particularly if they have a spouse who assumes responsibility for child care. It is also well known among corporate headhunters that women aren't always prepared for compensation negotiations and, more often than not, take the offer on the table. That is, they often sell themselves short—and companies know it.

Various equal-pay measures have been debated in Congress, including the Fair Pay Act, which prohibits wage discrimination on the basis of race, national origin, and sex, and the Paycheck Fairness Act, which goes one step further and forbids employers to penalize workers who share salary information. Several companies have paid settlements in recent years after government audits or their own investigations revealed violations of the Equal Pay Act. Texaco agreed to pay $3.1 million to 186 female employees found to be systematically underpaid. Trigon Blue Cross Blue Shield gave $264,901 in back pay to 34 female managers, and US Airways agreed to give $390,000 in back pay and salary adjustments to 30 female managers (National Committee on Pay Equity, 1998). Experts, including economists, acade-

mics, and Labor Department officials, have varying opinions on how soon the wage gap will close—with answers varying from 1 year to never. Pay consultant James Brennan has tracked women's compensation for three decades and, using current and past rate extrapolations, has calculated that the wage gap will close in 2050 (Krotz, 1999).

Money and Marital Satisfaction

Family income has a close relationship to marital satisfaction (Schaninger and Buss, 1986). Financial complaints are consistently cited as a major problem by couples seeking divorce. However, marital satisfaction is not always greatest when income is highest. For most couples, marital satisfaction is dependent on partners' feelings that income is adequate (Berry and Williams, 1987). A study of the marital quality of Black couples expands on this observation: Subjective indices such as perceived economic adequacy are more closely related to all aspects of marital quality than are objective measures such as income, education, or occupation (Clark-Nicolas and Gray-Little, 1991). That is, if spouses are not earning as much as they feel they need, and if they feel their earnings aren't adequate, their marital satisfaction is lessened because of financial pressures and tensions over money.

Income is important for both marital and individual satisfaction. High incomes within marriage can increase security and provide the necessary means for healthy lifestyles. Income affects mortality through its effects on the physical, social, and psychological environment. High incomes improve people's housing, health behavior, and access to quality health care (S. J. Rogers, 1996).

Harmony or Discord Even more than the level of income, the management of money is a major source of harmony or discord in the marital relationship. Couples who can agree on handling finances report more satisfactory marriages than do couples who have conflict over money (Berry and Williams, 1987). When conflict occurs, it usually arises because of immature attitudes or unrealistic expectations toward earning, saving, or spending money. Money is also sometimes used as a tool for personal attacks. The emotional use of money to control or punish a spouse or to compensate for inadequacies, guilt, or an inability to give love also causes difficulty. Money can be a valuable resource for the marital system, but it can also be a source of irritation.

Reasons People Go into Debt   No matter how much money they make, some people are always in debt. They estimate that if they had a little more each month they would be able to balance their budget, but when that "little more" is obtained, they still can't make do. They never seem able to meet all their obligations. The more their income increases, the greater indebtedness they incur.

The families that are most in debt are not the poor but those in middle-income brackets. The poor less frequently have mortgages, charge accounts, or large installment debts, although they might if they were able to establish credit. Level of income is not the major reason couples do or do not go into debt. The reasons relate more to the lifestyle of the partners and their ability to manage their money wisely.

Couples go into debt for various reasons. For example, many people go into debt because of excessive and unwise use of credit. Credit can be helpful: Few couples can afford to pay cash for a home, automobile, or other large purchases. But habitual and unthinking use of credit often leads to excessive indebtedness.

Many people go into debt because of crisis spending. Unexpected events can throw the family budget off completely and force people to go into debt to meet the emergency. Unemployment is the most common crisis; illness is another one. Some couples, such as farm couples, have variable incomes; they never know from one year to the next what their earnings will be, so it is very hard to plan ahead.

Many people go into debt because they buy things carelessly or impulsively. As a possible consequence, they pay more than is necessary, get merchandise of inferior quality that doesn't last as long as it should, or purchase things they don't really need. Some people buy things without stopping to think whether they can afford them. One woman reported:

> My husband loves to go to auctions. Whenever he reads about someone selling the contents of their home in an auction, he always shows up. He loves the crowds and the excitement, but he gets carried away. Once he brought home a cement mermaid. I don't know what he expected to do with it since we don't have a fish pond or swimming pool. But he likes it. It's still down in the family room where he put it. (Author's counseling notes)

Some people are compulsive buyers. Their buying habits may be an expression of their emotional insecurity; they can't say no to a salesperson for fear of hurting that person's feelings or are afraid that person won't like them. Or they buy to try to gain status and recognition. Another woman reported:

Although a high income makes it easier for a family to weather life's crises, satisfaction with family life also depends on whether people feel that the family's income is adequate.

My husband Frank is a compulsive collector. He spends a fortune on his coin collection, will travel hundreds of miles to see a rare coin, and will always end up outbidding everyone else to buy it. He shows his collection to everyone who comes into the house and derives great satisfaction from owning a coin that other collectors have never seen. (Author's counseling notes)

The habit of living in debt can start early. A report in 2001 by the General Accounting Office, an arm of Congress, revealed that about half of college graduates leave school with about $19,400 in student loans (U.S. General Accounting Office, 2001). Forty-three percent of full-time undergraduates relied on federal student loans in 2000 to pay college costs—up from 30% in 1993. The average size of a student loan was $4,750 in 2000, up from $3,887 in 1993. Credit-card debt averaged $1,533 for freshmen and gradually increased to $3,262 for seniors. Nellie Mae, a student-loan agency, found that its customers carried an average credit-card debt of $2,748 in 2000, up from $1,879 in 1998. (Nellie Mae, 2000).

Debt is also a problem for many older Americans. Many live on little more than their Social Security check, which is often not enough to pay for housing, food, medical bills, and prescription drugs. Between 1989 and 1998, total debt approximately doubled for people 50 and older. While many people who lived through the Great Depression carefully avoided debt, the "new" seniors, ages 50 to 64, who are the earliest baby boomers, are accustomed to living with debt. They are more likely than their elders to use credit cards to cover everyday expenses. While credit cards can offer a safety net, high interest charges can sink a person further into debt. The aggregate debt burden, which is the ratio of family debt burden to family income, increased throughout the 1990s for older Americans; those at the lowest income level had the highest aggregate debt burden (Gist and Figueiredo, 2002; R. D. Manning, 2000).

Money Management   There is no right or wrong money management system. The best system is what works for the individual couple. Who actually manages the money is not as important as how well the task is done and the extent of the responsibility and agreement of both spouses. The person who has the most interest and skill in money manage-

ment might be the one to exercise the most control, as long as the other person is in agreement. Marital adjustment is smoother when couples adopt a "we" attitude in relation to making financial decisions.

POVERTY AND FAMILY LIFE

In 2000, the median income for all family households was $51,751 and the poverty line for a family of four was $18,104. Breaking it down by head of household, median income was $59,751 for married-couple households; $28,116 for female households, no husband present; and $42,129 for male households, no wife present (U.S. Bureau of the Census, 2001). Approximately 10% of the population ages 18–64 (32.9 million people) live below the poverty line. Of those under 18, approximately 16% live below the poverty line. Breaking it down among ethnic groups, the poverty rate for non-Hispanic Whites was 8%; for Blacks, 23%; for Asian/Pacific Islanders, 10%; and for Hispanics, 21%. For these families, daily life is a struggle merely to pay rent and to buy groceries, a pair of shoes, or a TV set. One study found that by the age of 70, 55% of Americans have lived below the poverty rate for at least 1 year of their life (Rank and Hirschl, 1999). Among the elderly, 26% of Blacks and 21% of Hispanics are living in poverty, compared with 8% of Whites (U.S. Bureau of the Census, 2001).

The Poverty Line

The poverty line was originally intended to establish the household income that a family required to afford basic necessities. The first threshold was tied to the spending of the average American family in 1955, starting with the proportion of the budget spent on food. In 1955, that proportion was about one-third. The formulation of the poverty line was based on the smallest amount of money necessary to provide adequate nutrition for one family member, multiplied by three, since food was considered to be one-third of a family's expenses. In 1964, the poverty line was adjusted due to a rise in food costs, and it has been adjusted for inflation every year since.

Critics of the current poverty line argue that the costs of many necessities have outpaced inflation and that many of the common expenses families incur today were not part of family life in 1955. Although food prices have risen since 1955 at practically the same rate as inflation, food today accounts for barely

Race and Economics

As discussed in Chapter 1, tremendous diversity exists within racial groups. Stereotypical thinking often prevents people from recognizing that diversity. One of the most significant differences within any racial group has to do with economics. We illustrate this point by focusing on the African American family as an example of how economic factors influence family patterns and of how variations within cultural groups often stem from differences in socioeconomic status. Wilkinson (1997) described four classes among Black families: (1) families in poverty, (2) the nonpoor working class, (3) the upwardly mobile middle class, and (4) the established upper class.

Impoverished families have very different histories, parenting behaviors, and expectations from those of families in other classes. Black American families are disproportionately represented in poverty. Almost one-fourth (22.7%) of African American families were below the poverty level in 2001, compared to 10% of the White population (U.S. Bureau of the Census, 2002). Poor families experience endless complications in trying to meet basic needs, such as finding safe, affordable housing. Proper attention to children's optimal development is difficult when parents are in constant economic distress, and many children of poverty end up on the streets or in the juvenile justice system. In any culture, daily financial and psychological distress can reduce the quality of parenting (Conger et al., 1992), and research has consistently shown that, compared with well-off parents, parents who experience economic stress display less nurturance and more harshness in their responses to their children (McLoyd and Wilson, 1992). Understandably, in families living in poverty because of a lack of education, job market segregation, and struggles with a welfare existence, the parents may be unable to participate in children's schooling or take an active role in community affairs (Wilkinson, 1997). Thus, one may perceive a difference in values, exemplified by behavior, between two different racial or ethnic groups. But in reality, it isn't values but rather economics that account for the difference.

African American working-class families usually have an annual income of $15,000–$35,000 and differ in composition and functioning from impoverished families. Spouses in these working-class families (about 30% of African American families in 2000) generally do not have the educational achievements of middle-class families, but they desire more education for their children than they have achieved themselves. Solidarity and internal strength are central to the nonpoor working class, and family life is characterized by a constant effort to maintain economic security. This preoccupation with the family's financial condition affects the opportunities for and aspirations of children (Wilkinson, 1997).

Increased educational and economic opportunities have contributed to the growth of a well-educated and economically secure African American middle class (Giles, 1994); in 1999, about 30% of African American families had an income between $35,000 and $75,000 (U.S. Bureau of the Census, 2000). Mothers in the middle class are more likely to be married, to have come from intact nuclear families, and to hold values that are more compatible with a nuclear family rather than an extended family. Fathers are effective authority figures, and discipline and decision making are joint parental responsibilities. These middle-class families tend to live in suburban areas and participate in various church and community activities. One of the primary expectations of both parents is that their children will attend college and obtain secure professional positions. Essentially, African American middle-class families are characterized by (1) a sufficient family income, (2) conformity to prevailing norms of morality, (3) close supervision of children, (4) dual employment of spouses, (5) at least one spouse with a college education, (6) a belief in upward mobility, (7) a close attachment to and involvement with their children's lives, and (8) the expectation that children will look to their parents as role models (Wilkinson, 1997).

The number of upper-class African American families is small but growing. In 2000, 15.8% of Black families had incomes over $75,000 (compared with 29.3% of White families; U.S. Bureau of the Census, 2000). Dual career marriages are common in the upper class. Although egalitarianism is an expectation in spousal relationships, child rearing is still a key dimension of the mother's role, and kinship bonds are essential. The majority of women have earned professional degrees, and the children often attend private schools, which usually have few Blacks. Intimate relationships in African American upper-middle-class and upper-class families are based on gender-role specificity, conservative attitudes toward nonmarital sex, and a strong belief in the value of monogamous relationships. These families are characterized by enduring values, a belief in higher education, exceptional parental role-modeling behaviors, and children's ambitions. Other characteristics of this group include inherited wealth or ample financial security, home ownership, a history of intergenerational family stability, and a middle-class or upper-class background for both spouses (Wilkinson, 1997).

If one controls for socioeconomic status, African Americans and White families are very similar and share similar mainstream values (Fine, McKenry, Donnelly, and Voydanoff, 1992).

(continued)

Research has shown that Black parents teach their children to be honest, to value education, and to act responsibly. Most Black children grow up in loving families, being cared for by an extended kin unit and taught values including strong family, cooperation, respect for the elderly, shared household work and child rearing, practical skills, racial pride, and flexible gen-

der roles (E. J. Hill et al., 2001; Nobles, 1985). Proponents of new models to study families suggest that more value be placed on factors such as support, caring, loyalty, religion, and spirituality than on socioeconomic factors to assess family stability (Barnes, 2001).

---

one-sixth of the average family budget, rather than the third on which the original poverty line was based. J. E. Schwarz (1998) offered the following outline of annual expenses for a family of four, providing for no more than the barest necessities:

Food	$4,576
Two-bedroom apartment (government-approved, low-cost) including minimum utilities and phone	$6,144
10-year-old car (operating, insuring, maintaining)	$3,700
Clothing	$250/family member
Medical, pharmaceutical, dental	$2,000
Personal/household (ranging from toothpaste to repairs)	$3,900
Taxes (federal, state, Social Security)	$3,270
Total	$24,590

Note that this budget does not include child care, emergency funds, or savings and that the food budget is only $88 per week, which comes to $1.05 per person per meal. Then compare the total to the 1998 poverty threshold for a family of four: $16,660. Today the poverty line doesn't measure the poor, but rather the very poor (J. E. Schwarz, 1998).

Not only has the poverty line become distorted, but the minimum wage that many people living below the poverty line rely on has also lost its value. The minimum wage in 1950 paid about 110% of the amount required for a family of four with two full-time workers and two children to survive (J. E. Schwarz, 1998). This used to be enough to raise a family into the middle class, but by the 1970s, the minimum wage for two full-time workers had fallen to 90% of necessary income, and it now stands at

70%. Today, the poorest families are likely to be the largest ones, ones headed by women alone, or ones in which the father has little education.

In 2002, the federal minimum wage was $5.15. If you worked full-time at minimum wage your yearly earnings would be $10,712. Different states have increased their minimum-wage level, with Connecticut being one of the highest, at $6.70. In recent years, there has been a campaign to pay people a living wage, rather than a minimum wage. Typically, the living wage is what it would take to bring a family of four out of poverty. With a living wage, workers would generally receive more than $8 an hour. Some states have passed living-wage ordinances that require certain employers to pay wages higher than federal or state minimum wages. Those employers covered by the ordinances are firms that receive local government contracts or that get tax breaks or government subsidies.

The Effects of Poverty

The effects of poverty on the family include (1) increased tension and unhappiness in the marital relationship; (2) high rates of children born to single mothers; (3) desertion, separation, and divorce; and (4) children brought up without a stable father figure in the home (Booth and Edwards, 1985). Low income results in cultural and social deprivation, with accompanying lower aspirations and educational levels (Rank, 1987). Limited resources also leave few opportunities for contacts with the outside world, resulting in isolation. Increased problems and the lack of resources result in much higher rates of mental and physical illness. Limited alternatives and feelings of helplessness and powerlessness leave little hope for the future or few prospects for getting ahead. And the poor are at the mercy of life's unpredictable happenings: sickness, injury, job loss, legal problems, and school difficulties (Spencer, Dobbs, and Swanson, 1988). These situations may arise because of factors

Spouses who have been able to agree about earning, saving, and spending patterns have overcome one of the biggest obstacles to a harmonious, happy marriage.

over which those affected have no control: problems in the economy, the changing nature of jobs, political trends and government policies, business practices, and racism and sexism in society (Chilman, 1991). Family members living in poverty strive for security because they never feel certain about their lives (Rank, 1987). Coping is especially difficult for parents with very low income; many are never able to free themselves from their situation. The task is made even more difficult when they are forced to raise their children in crime-ridden, dangerous neighborhoods (Bowen and Chapman, 1996).

Many families of low socioeconomic status live in America's inner cities. Since the 1970s, people with low incomes in search of jobs and affordable housing have become increasingly likely to live in metropolitan areas and in neighborhoods with a high concentration of low-income people (Klebanov, Brooks-Gunn, and Duncan, 1994). Neighborhood poverty is associated with a poorer home environment. Other poor families live in rural areas or are migrant workers, moving from place to place in search of seasonal employment (D. R. Morrison and Lichter, 1988).

A growing number of poor families are homeless, living on the streets or staying temporarily in homeless shelters (Axelson and Dail, 1988; Bode, 1987). According to the Urban Institute, 1 of every 100 Americans used a homeless service (such as an emergency shelter or soup kitchen) during 1996 (Burt et al., 1999). And the number of homeless nearly doubled over 10 years, from 1.4–1.8 million in 1987 to 2.3–3.5 million in 1996. Nearly 25% of homeless people who receive services are children, up from about 15% in 1987. Over the course of a given year, at least 38% of the entire homeless population are children. Researchers at the Urban Institute believe that rising housing costs are the main reason for the increase in homelessness.

The Feminization of Poverty

The population living in poverty in the United States increasingly is becoming one of women, irrespective of ethnicity or age. This process is known as the **feminization of poverty.** Women have higher poverty rates than men for two main reasons: (1) Women's economic resources do not approach parity with those of men, and (2) women are more likely than men to be single custodial parents during their working lives and to be unmarried and living alone in their later years. For these reasons, poverty is more likely to be a chronic problem among female-householder families (Starrels, Bould, and Nicholas, 1994). Figure 9.4 compares the income

feminization of poverty   The trend toward increasing proportions of women, regardless of ethnicity or age, living in poverty.

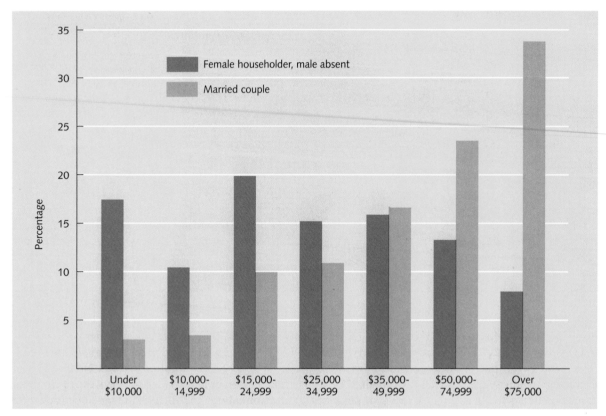

Figure 9.4   Income Distribution of Selected Household Types (*Note:* From *Statistical Abstract of the United States, 2001* [Table 663] by U.S. Bureau of the Census, 2001, Washington, DC: U.S. Government Printing Office.)

levels of households headed by women with those of households headed by married couples.

Many female-headed households are forced into poverty when the father defaults on child support payments. The failure of absent fathers to support their children economically has long-term consequences because mothers have fewer material resources to invest in their children (Paasch and Teachman, 1991). Large numbers of these mothers work, leaving their children under the care of relatives, friends, or whomever they can afford. Lack of adequate and affordable child care is one of the major reasons more mothers do not work outside the home (Joesch, 1991).

Opportunities for economic advancement are limited for people living in poverty. For single mothers, poverty reduces their chances of completing school, decreases their opportunities for marriage, and increases the likelihood that they will need public assistance to feed and house their family (Orth-

ner and Neenan, 1996). Single mothers with little education are often under severe economic pressure and are prone to experience negative life events (poor schooling for children, more stress, illness, and crime victimization) and low social support, which, in turn, are associated with psychological distress and ineffectual parenting practices (Simons, Beaman, Conger, and Chao, 1993b). Their sons in particular are at greater risk for antisocial behavior problems (Bank, Forgatch, Patterson, and Fetrow, 1993). In addition, low-income single mothers of young children are exposed to especially high levels of daily stress and, not surprisingly, are prone to depression and feelings of hopelessness (S. L. Olson and Banyard, 1993).

The Effects of Poverty on Children

Millions of American children are being raised in poverty, and the number is growing. For children, poverty is associated with poor school performance, higher school dropout rates, more teen pregnancies, and a greater likelihood of remaining in poverty when they are adults. Emancipation from family comes early and is often psychologically premature. These youths frequently are not ready to take their place in the adult world, and many turn to peers to replace family ties.

Dropout rates from school are high among low-socioeconomic-status (SES) youths (F. P. Rice, 1993). Although parents usually want their children to have more education than they did, there is often pressure on adolescents to get a job to help support the family; this pressure may contribute to some adolescents' decision to drop out of school after they reach the legal age to do so. Furthermore, many low-SES youths feel the prejudices of middle-class society and so experience isolation from mainstream school activities. If they are doing poorly academically, they often can't wait to quit school entirely. Of course, doing so perpetuates the cycle of poverty and cultural deprivation.

Low-SES families tend to be larger than average, and sometimes little attention is paid to the older children because the younger ones require immediate care. Guidance and discipline may take the form of orders, absolutes, and physical punishment. Child-rearing patterns tend to emphasize obedience, respect for parents, conformity to externally imposed standards, and avoidance of trouble rather than personal growth and the development of creativity, curiosity, independence, and self-direction. Some families exercise greater control over daughters than sons, so the daughters may use early marriage to escape from home (Abell, Clawson, Washington, Bost, and Vaughn, 1996).

Fathers of low-SES families are often less emotionally and behaviorally involved with their adolescent children than are fathers who are better off financially. However, a father's involvement, when it exists, can enhance youths' achievements and emotional well-being, and reduce delinquency (K. F. Harris and Marmer, 1996).

Research generally supports the concept that parental reasoning complexity is an important predictor of parents' behavior in interactions with their children. Reasoning complexity and behavior are significantly related to educational level and occupation, with more complex reasoning corresponding to higher educational levels. More complex reasoning also is related to an authoritative style of child rear-

ing, to the use of indirect positive controls, and to parental warmth, acceptance, and support. Less complex reasoning is typically expressed through authoritarian patterns and restrictiveness. Thus, how parents interpret the parent–child relationship and resolve the tasks of parenting depends to a large degree on the complexity of their reasoning (Dekovic and Gerris, 1992).

The Widening Gap between the Rich and the Poor

The late 1990s were characterized by economic growth, a booming stock market, and the lowest unemployment rate in decades. Median earnings rose by 10% from 1998 to 2001 and were up 41% from 1992 (U.S. Bureau of Labor Statistics, 2002). But a closer look reveals a problem that clouds this image—income inequality. On average, women earned $473 a week in 1999, while men earned $618. Salaries increased 10–20% in the information technology sector but only 4–5% in traditional industries. Numerous reports, cited by the Economic Policy Institute, concluded that the gap between the rich and the poor was greater than ever at the end of the century.

Research by the Congressional Budget Office supports this conclusion; the top 20% of households showed a 43% increase in after-tax income between 1977 and 1999, while the middle 20% had only an 8% increase, and the bottom 20% had a 9% drop (see Figure 9.5). In fact, income disparity has widened to the degree that in 1999 the richest 1% of the population were projected to receive as much after-tax income as the bottom 38%. In other words, the earnings of the 2.7 million richest Americans would equal those of the poorest 100 million combined.

The Federal Reserve reported in 2003 that the gap in wealth between the rich and the poor and between Whites and minorities continues to grow. In 2001, the median net wealth for the 20% of families with the lowest incomes was $7,900, compared to $833,600 for the 10% of families with the highest incomes. From 1998 to 2001, the gap between the poorest and richest Americans jumped 70% and the gap between Whites and minorities jumped 21% (Aizcorbe, Kinnickell, and Moore, 2003).

There are other indicators of the increasing disparity. For instance, in 1989, there were 66 billionaires and 31.5 million people living below the poverty line; by 1999, there were 268 billionaires and 34.5 million people living below the poverty

Figure 9.5 Change in After-Tax Family Income, 1977–1999 (*Note:* From *The Widening Income Gulf* by Center on Budget and Policy Priorities, September 4, 1999, Washington, DC: Congressional Budget Office.)

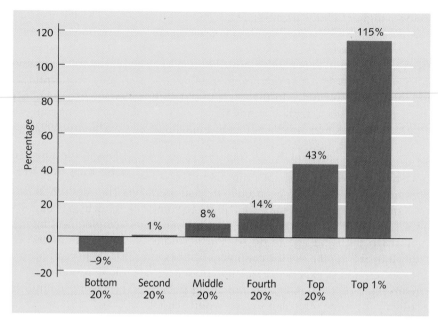

line. The disparity can also be seen when comparing the pay of CEOs to that of workers. This pay gap quintupled from the early 1990s to the end of the decade—making it 10 times wider than it had been in the early 1980s. In 1998, CEOs made 419 times as much as workers (Collins, Hartman, and Sklar, 1999). Table 9.1 lists representative salaries for a cross-section of occupations.

This growing disparity in income is relevant for several reasons and affects society as a whole. According to a recent survey by the Fannie Mae Foundation, urban historians, planners, and architects identified the income gap as the single most important factor influencing the shape of American metropolitan areas over the next 50 years. Disparity in income is related to the achievement gap between White and minority students, with a greater percentage of minority students living in poverty than their White counterparts. Our democratic institutions are also influenced by the income gap, with 80% of all political contributions coming from less than 1% of the population.

Many experts believe that the gap will continue to widen, with the rich getting richer and the poor getting poorer. It is a challenging situation to address, and there is much disagreement as to how to remedy the problem. One approach, suggested by the organization United for a Fair Economy, is an "asset-building agenda," which recommends actions that could help close the gap. Examples in-

Table 9.1 What People Earn	
Job	**Salary**
CEO, Major technical company	$90,000,000
University president	325,000
Vice president, Internet company	125,000
Architect	90,000
Trucker	65,000
Psychologist	60,000
Information technology specialist	55,000
Restaurant manager	45,000
Massage therapist	40,000
Children's book author/lecturer	40,000
Owner, home day care	37,000
Director, nonprofit agency	35,000
Website designer	34,000
High school teacher	33,000
Radio show host	30,000
Personal fitness trainer	28,000
Accountant	26,000
Bartender	16,000
Private, U.S. Army	13,404

Note: From "What People Earn," February 27, 2000, *Parade.*

clude tax-exempt savings programs, expanded earned-income credits, a higher minimum wage, increased access to homeownership, and a higher capital gains tax. Others believe that changes in the

Welfare and the Family

When people hear the word *welfare*, they show different reactions. People who are on welfare or who have been on it find it demeaning (Jarrett, 1996), but they admit that they are very glad to get it because the financial assistance is much needed. When people who have never been on welfare hear the word, they often assume recipients are lazy and do not want to work or look for a job since they're able to live off the state and the federal government.

The important question we will consider here is how the present welfare system affects the family. In 1996, the welfare system in the United States changed dramatically with the passage of the Personal Responsibility and Work Opportunity Reconciliation Act. The bipartisan welfare reform plan requires work in exchange for time-limited assistance. The new Temporary Assistance to Needy Families (TANF) program replaced the Aid to Families with Dependent Children (AFDC) and Job Opportunities and Basic Skills Training (JOBS) programs.

TANF brought an end to entitlement to federal assistance, allowing states, territories, and tribes to operate their own assistance programs. The federal government provides block grants to cover the costs of benefits, administrative expenses, and services, but the states determine eligibility and benefit levels. States, territories, and tribes are given enormous flexibility, provided that the programs they design accomplish the purposes of TANF, which are (1) to provide assistance to needy families so that children may be cared for in their own homes; (2) to reduce dependency by promoting job preparation, work, and marriage; (3) to prevent out-of-wedlock pregnancies; and (4) to encourage the formation and maintenance of two-parent families. Basic stipulations of TANF include the following: (1) Recipients must work after 2 years on assistance; (2) recipients who are not working must participate in community service 2 months after they start receiving benefits;

(3) recipients must participate in unsubsidized or subsidized employment, on-the-job training, community service, or vocational training, or they must provide child care for individuals participating in community service; and (4) families who have received assistance for 5 cumulative years are ineligible for cash aid.

All states offer basic health services to certain very poor people: individuals who are pregnant, aged, disabled, or blind and families with dependent children. One of these programs is Medicaid. Medicaid eligibility is automatic for almost all cash welfare recipients in the United States. Many people who are eligible go on welfare simply because they need some kind of medical insurance and services and cannot afford private health insurance. Some states extend Medicaid to certain other persons who qualify, such as people with medical expenses that when subtracted from their income reach a "medically needy" level. Within federal guidelines, each state determines its own Medicaid eligibility criteria and the health services to be provided under Medicaid. The cost of providing Medicaid services is jointly shared by the federal government and the states.

The federal Supplemental Security Income (SSI) program administered by the Social Security Administration provides benefits to the aged, the blind, and the disabled. The SSI program provides a minimum income for these persons and establishes uniform national basic eligibility requirements and payment standards. Most states supplement the basic SSI payments.

Data reported by the U.S. Department of Health and Human Services in 2001 showed a 53% drop in the number of families receiving assistance, with 6.5 million fewer recipients in 2001 than in 1996 (see Figure 9.6). The percentage of decline ranged from 94% in Idaho to 21% in Rhode Island.

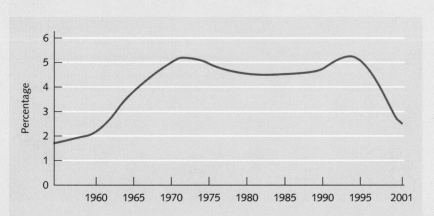

Figure 9.6 Percentage of U.S. Families on Welfare, 1960–2001 (*Note:* From U.S. Welfare Caseloads Information, by U.S. Department of Health and Human Services, the Administration for Children and Families, 2001.)

(continued)

But some researchers and welfare reform critics point to failings in the system and distortion in these statistics. Mary Jo Bane, former secretary for Children and Families in the Department of Health and Human Services, resigned from her position when President Clinton signed the welfare bill because of her concerns for the well-being of needy children. Her concerns mainly stemmed from Title IV of the act, which barred most legal immigrants from most federal benefit programs, and from Title VIII, which provided across-the-board cuts in food stamp benefits. Bane (1997) reported:

> Analyses produced by the Department of Health and Human Services and by the Urban Institute before the bill was enacted predicted that upward of a million children would be pushed into poverty as a result of the bill, and that some eight million families with children would lose income. The poverty effects result mostly from the cuts in food stamps, supplemental security income, and immigrant benefits, since many families potentially affected by the cuts have incomes right on the edge of poverty.

The Children's Defense Fund released findings from its analysis of government data in 1999 that showed an increase of almost half a million children living in extreme poverty just 1 year after enactment of the welfare reform act (Sherman, 1999). The report defined "extreme poverty" as households in which income was below half of the poverty line. Among single-mother families, the group hardest hit by welfare reform, the number of children living in extreme poverty jumped 26% between 1996 and 1997.

Sheldon Danziger, professor of social work and public policy at the University of Michigan, addressed the issue of whether the caseload is a false indicator of the act's success during a 1999 congressional briefing, "Is Welfare Reform Working? The Impact of Economic Growth and Policy Changes" (Consortium of Social Science Associations, 1999). Danziger argued that more attention should be focused on how recipients are faring and less on the declining number of cases. One example he cited is the number of cases in West Virginia that have been eliminated because SSI benefits have made them ineligible for TANF, not because the recipients have found employment. Danziger noted that research has shown that even during good economic times approximately one-third of those no longer receiving welfare are not working and that many who go off welfare do not earn more than they did while receiving aid, thus dooming a large group of children to live in poverty. For the current welfare system to protect children in poverty, more research is needed to determine the true reasons for current caseload decline.

The population in poverty in the United States is becoming increasingly composed of women. Food stamps enable many women and children to buy groceries that they would otherwise not be able to afford.

welfare program will help families out of poverty and that the prosperity of the rich has a positive effect on other aspects of the economy that directly benefit poor and working-class families. They believe that a higher minimum wage and increased capital gains taxes would only hurt the economy and ultimately take its toll on poor and working-class families. However, regardless of political ideology, no one disagrees that living in poverty is detrimental to the health and well-being of families, particularly children.

A QUESTION OF POLICY

EARNED INCOME TAX CREDIT

As discussed in the text, many families are struggling economically to provide for their families. In 1975, Congress created the earned income tax credit (EITC) to help families make the transition from welfare to work and to make work more attractive than welfare. The policy was originally intended just for families on welfare but has changed over the years and now includes low-income families. It also applies to working grandparents, foster parents, stepgrandparents, and other relatives caring for children if the children live in the household all year and are cared for as members of the family (Friedman, 2000).

Only families that work are eligible to receive the credit, and the amount of the credit depends on the family's labor market earnings. For example, in 2000, families with more than one child and an income of less than $31,152 received a credit of up to $3,888. The credit is flat for a range of earnings and is then phased out as earnings increase. The credit can offset taxes for families who make enough to pay taxes, or it can provide additional income for those who did not make enough to pay taxes. The idea is that by reducing the tax burden on families, the EITC strengthens their self-sufficiency and provides them with more disposable income (Friedman, 2000).

QUESTIONS TO CONSIDER:

Should low-income families without children be eligible for the EITC? Why or why not?

Should the credit be adjusted to account for family size so that families with more children get more credit? Why or why not?

To what extent is it the role of government to help alleviate economic stress in low-income families? What about in middle-income families?

If a policy provides additional income to families to help make ends meet, should there be any restrictions on how that money is spent? Explain.

Why might a qualified family choose not to take the EITC?

SUMMARY

1. Job stressors negatively affect the emotional health of families.

2. Some types of work are particularly stressful for the family, including work that is difficult, work that requires periods of separation from the family, and work that is too demanding of a person's time.

3. Sometimes the demand to work long hours comes from an employer who has a callous disregard for the employee's mental health and personal life. One of the barriers to family closeness is a job schedule that makes it difficult for family members to be together.

The marital ideology among educated, middle-class people in the United States emphasizes an egalitarian exercise of family power. That is, partners are equal and should share everything 50–50. But exactly what does this mean in relation to making decisions, influencing each other, and governing the family? In fact, this ideology isn't often worked out in practice. Some people want more power and control than others. Even when partners are equals, they usually don't share all decisions and control.

We are concerned here with patterns of power and with what gives some people power over others. We are concerned as well with the applications of power, the processes of power, and the ways power is applied in intimate relationships. And we are concerned with the outcomes of power: the effects of various power patterns on individuals and on marital satisfaction.

One of the most important requirements for a satisfying relationship is the ability to communicate. We aren't born with this ability; rather communication is a fine art that must be learned. Thus, in this chapter, we are also concerned with improving communication skills.

THE MEANING OF POWER

In perhaps the most popular conceptualization among social scientists, **power** in intimate relationships is defined as the ability to influence one's partner to get what one wants (Beckman, Harvey, Satre, and Walker, 1999). Power may be exercised in social groups and organizations and in all kinds of interpersonal relationships. We are concerned here only with family power. The power exerted by various family members is partly derived from social power—that which society exerts or delegates. Power within the family can be marital power,

parental power, offspring power, sibling power, or kinship power. There can also be combinations of power units, such as father–son, mother–daughter, or mother–son (S. S. Feldman, Wentzel, and Gehring, 1989). We are especially interested in marital power—the power relationship in the marital dyad—and to a lesser extent in power exercised by children over parents.

WHY PEOPLE WANT POWER

Some people always seem to need to be in control, whereas others always seem to avoid taking charge. What causes these differences in people's desire for power?

Self-Actualization

Most people want to feel that they have some control over their own life, that they have the power to change, influence, or direct what happens to them personally. People who are unwilling or unable to use power often lead a life of frustration. They never get to do what they really want to do, to realize their own desires, or to carry out their own plans. Indeed, hundreds of seminars and classes are conducted yearly to teach people how to become more assertive or empowered.

The person who asserts him- or herself eventually will lock horns with someone else who has other ideas, and a power struggle may ensue to see whose wishes are carried out. Even people who are not ordinarily combative find that they sometimes have to exert power over other people to be able to fulfill themselves. Without some personal power, it's difficult to survive as an independent individual. Even toddlers need to learn how to say no and how to influence parents if they are to grow up to be autonomous adults.

Social Expectations

Often people exert power because that is what they feel they are supposed to do, and they want to avoid criticism for not fulfilling expectations. Each society has its own institutionalized norms that prescribe domains of authority. This kind of power is referred to as **legitimate power,** or power bestowed by society on men and women as their right according to social prescription. What society prescribes may not always be fair, but it still may exert considerable influence on the behavior of individuals.

Family-of-Origin Influences

Patterns of power can often be traced to experiences in one's family of origin. Children tend to model their behavior after their parents'. For example, a son growing up under the influence of a dominant father may adopt the same pattern of behavior and have difficulty establishing a more democratic relationship with his spouse. Galvin and Brommel (1986) quoted one man:

> My German father and my Irish mother both exercised power over us in different ways. My father used to beat us whenever we got out of line, and that power move was very obvious. On the other hand, my mother never touched us, but she probably exercised greater power through her use of silence. Whenever we did something she did not approve of, she just stopped talking to us—it was as if we did not exist. Most of the time the silent treatment lasted for a few hours, but sometimes it would last for a few days. My brother used to say it was so quiet that "you could hear a mouse pee on a cotton ball." I hated the silence worse than the beatings. (p. 135)

The family of origin serves as the first power base from which the child learns to function. Methods used there are often repeated in the child's adult life. Certain types of power applications, such as physical violence and abuse, may be passed from generation to generation. Even techniques of control, such as silence, are learned behavior.

Psychological Need

Sometimes the need for power and the way it is expressed go far beyond ordinary limits. People who have deep-seated feelings of insecurity and inferiority may try to hide them or to compensate for them by becoming autocratic and dictatorial. They can't let their partner win an argument or get her or his way, for fear of feeling weak and ineffective. Their facade of power depends on not letting any cracks develop in their armor.

Three theoretical frameworks are often used to explain the need for power: attachment theory, social control theory, and feminist theory (Ehrensaft, Langhinrichsen-Rohling, Heyman, O'Leary, and Lawrence, 1999). According to attachment theory, aggression against an attachment figure, at any age, is a control strategy for regaining either emotional or physical closeness to a person when the bond with that person is perceived to be endangered. Individuals who are insecurely attached to their primary attachment figure are more likely to perceive subjective threats to the bond with that person than are individuals who are securely attached (Bowlby, 1977; Hazan and Shaver, 1987). This could explain why some partners are intensely jealous of their partner's interactions with others and try to limit and control those interactions.

According to social control theory, using power (or violence) as a response to an upsetting behavior by others serves three functions: (1) a means to manage conflict in a relationship, (2) an expression of grievances, and (3) a form of social control. Consistent with this theory, most marital assaults occur in the context of a disagreement (O'Leary et al., 1989). Social control theory can help explain why male batterers sometimes suggest that their partner deserved to be beaten for perceived offenses such as attempts at autonomy, failure to perform household chores, or disrespectful behavior (Ehrensaft et al., 1999).

According to feminist theory, the patriarchal hierarchy in families allows the use of male–female violence as a way of maintaining male power within the marriage. Consistent with this theory, rates of spouse abuse are lower in societies in which women have economic power within the marriage than in those in which women have little or no economic power (D. Levinson, 1988). Family violence is also lower in families in which men expect to share power with their spouse (O'Kelly and Carney, 1986).

SOURCES OF POWER

Various efforts have been made to sort out the origins of power (Sexton and Perlman, 1989). What gives husbands and wives power in the marital relationship? Various sources have been identified, including cultural norms, gender norms, economic resources, education and knowledge, personality differences, communication ability, emotional factors, physical stature and strength, and life circumstances. We will examine each of these bases of power as they relate to marriage partners. We will

Wearing a Veil

There are many Muslim women in the United States who wear a veil (hijab) when out in public. The veil can cover just the head or the entire body and the meaning and reasons for wearing a veil vary among women and cultures. Some Muslim women veil to express their strongly held convictions about gender differences and the importance of distinguishing men from women. Others wear a veil as a sign of solidarity with other Muslims, a sign of disapproval for the immodest Western culture, or to protect themselves from the unwanted sexual advances of men. However, the most prominent justification for veiling given is that it is believed to be commanded in the Koran and is thus a symbol of devotion to Islam (Read and Bartkowski, 2000).

Read and Bartkowski (2000) interviewed Muslim women living in the United States about their motivation for wearing a veil. They found that, aside from their devotion to Islam, many chose to wear a veil because it actually liberated them from men's sexual advances and made possible the pursuit of work outside the home. Many of the women interviewed believed the veil is the great equalizer between men and women because it prevents women from being judged solely on their appearance. They felt liberated from the sexual objectification that so many Western women face at work and could

thus work more comfortably alongside men and feel more respected. One of the women interviewed by Read and Bartkowski stated, "Women who wear the hijab are not excluded from society. They are freer to move around in society because of it . . . and if you're in hijab, then someone sees you and treats you accordingly. I feel more free. Especially men, they don't look at your appearance—they appreciate your intellectual abilities. They respect you" (p. 407).

also briefly look at ways children may exercise power over their parents.

Cultural Norms

The power structure in families varies among cultures. People in some cultures consider males to be the ultimate authority and power figure in the family and believe that women should be submissive to men. People in other cultures adopt a more egalitarian view of the sexes; men and women in these cultures have equal opportunity and power in economic and social life. Culture may instruct families on appropriate and acceptable modes of conduct, but the way in which families interpret and incorporate those modes into their lives varies widely. For example, the Mormon family is traditionally patriarchal, yet the Mormon church teaches that neither the husband nor the wife is more important, and both share in the family responsibilities. The church also teaches that the father's responsibility

is to serve as the head of his home and family with key roles being that of a leader, provider, and role model. He should assume financial responsibility for the family and lead the family through kindness and humility, not force or arrogance. A woman's expectation is to be a mother, teacher, and role model (Lambert and Thomasson, 1997). While this is seen as the model patriarchal family structure in the Mormon family, individual Mormon families may operate very differently. Culture certainly influences how families behave, but there is tremendous variation among families within any given culture.

Traditionally, the African American family has been considered matriarchal, with women dominant. But recent research tends to contradict this view. African American marriages tend to be more egalitarian than White marriages, with middle-class Black families more egalitarian than middle-class White families. However, African American marriages cannot be stereotyped any more than White marriages can. African American couples show variations in power structure within each socioeconomic level, just as White couples do.

Puerto Rican and Mexican American families have traditionally been considered patriarchal. The Mexican American male was expected to prove his machismo (manhood) by being dominant over his spouse and children. Mexican American families do emphasize male dominance, but the most prevalent pattern is one in which the partners share in decision making as equals.

Gender Norms

Power relationships are also influenced by stereotyped gender norms (Enns, 1988). Gender-role socialization that emphasizes women's passivity, submissiveness, and dependence reinforces patriarchal power structures and reduces women's authority. Traditional gender norms often specified a rigid division of responsibility. The man made financial decisions, while the woman cared for the children; the man did heavy outdoor chores, while the woman did maintenance inside the house. As more egalitarian gender norms develop and as interest spheres and power domains overlap, more family issues become subject to negotiation and compromise.

P. Smith and Beaujot (1999) examined three groups of men (traditional, intermediate, and liberal) and asked them open-ended questions about the woman's place in the family and whether women prefer to stay at home or be in the workforce. The traditional respondents unanimously thought that women prefer to stay at home cooking, cleaning, and caring for the children and that men should be in the workforce and should discipline the children. All of the traditional men believed that, if a sacrifice was needed in the family, the woman's career should go first because it was secondary to her job as wife and mother. The intermediate group was split on the issue of whether women prefer to stay at home or go to work. This group still held many of the beliefs of the traditional group, including the idea that women are more nurturing and should therefore be more responsible for the children and that men should be more responsible for the finances. Most of the liberal respondents believed that women were split between the ideas of staying at home and working outside the home. These men believed that household

work, marital power, and important decisions should be shared.

In general, in male-dominated societies, more men than women possess power in the form of resources, social status, respect, positive self-regard, and physical authority (Pratto, 1996). Researchers have found females to be less likely to have access to valued resources across the life span. Girls are even less likely than boys to gain access to scarce resources in a play situation in the absence of adults (Powlishta and Maccoby, 1990). This gender gap is carried over to the intimate relationships between men and women (Galliher, Rostosky, Welsh, and Kawaguchi, 1999).

Economic Resources

According to resource theory, those who control valued resources needed by other family members hold power over them (deTurck and Miller, 1986). Money and property are two valued economic resources. Some men who are the primary breadwinner feel they have a right to dictate family decisions. One man remarked, "It's my money, I earned it; therefore, I have the right to spend it as I please" (Author's counseling notes).

Women who have no independent source of income may not have equal power in their marriage if power is not relegated by their spouse and if they don't demand it (Klagsbrun, 1985). When the woman is gainfully employed, she usually gains more power in decision making in the family.

Tichenor (1999) examined the power differences between traditional families, in which the man made more money than the woman, and status-reversal families, in which the woman earned significantly more than the man. Status-reversal women did receive more help around the house, yet they still were responsible for a larger part of domestic labor than the men in traditional families. In fact, no man in either group who was employed full-time did over half of the domestic labor. One sentiment common to most of the status-reversal women was that they were not doing enough. Although these women earned the bulk of the money—and sometimes all of the money—they constantly felt that they were not helping out enough around the home. Many of these women spoke with awe of the great job that their partner was doing in raising the children and getting work done around the house. In contrast, none of the

The greater the woman's education and earnings, the more likely she is to share decision-making power with her partner.

men in traditional families spoke this way about their spouse. These findings suggest that power in families has more to do with gender than money. The status-reversal women often tried to downplay the amount of money they earned and emphasized that all money was shared. None of these women claimed that because they made more money they deserved more power, as is often the case in traditional families.

Education and Knowledge

In a society in which education is valued, a person who has superior education has an important source of power. This type of power is referred to as **expert power,** whereby a person is acknowledged as generally superior in intelligence. The influence of education on power depends partly on the cultural context and partly on the relative difference between the man and the woman.

Knowledge is also a source of power. One man commented, "My wife decorates the house. She knows much more about these things than I do" (Author's counseling notes). This type of power is referred to as **informational power** because it involves superior knowledge of a specific area.

According to the **theory of primary interest and presumed competence,** the person who is most interested in and involved with a particular choice and who is most qualified to make a specific decision will be more likely to do so. These two aspects, interest and competence, often go together. For example, if the woman will be using the kitchen utensils more than her partner, is more interested in which ones to buy, and has had more experience in the use of different utensils, presumably she will be the one who will exert the most influence on buying utensils. If the man does most of the barbecuing, presumably he will take more interest in and exert more influence on choosing what barbecue equipment to buy.

Personality Differences

Personality characteristics also influence power. A considerable age difference between spouses affects power, with the older spouse exerting power over the younger one. Regardless of age, some people seem to be more domineering and forceful than others, exerting considerable influence on all with whom they come in contact.

The degree of power depends partly on how motivated people are to gain strength and control. Some people strive for power to overcome inner feelings of weakness and insecurity. The converse also occurs: Those with the greatest relational power also report higher levels of self-esteem (deTurck and Miller, 1986). The two seem to go together. Then, too, charming people with a great deal of charisma may be natural leaders whom others follow readily.

Communication Ability

Some people are better talkers than others. They have superior verbal skills and are able to explain their ideas clearly and to convince others through the power of their words. Males seem to take more active control over conversation than do females. Some men, however, are relatively nonverbal, sometimes because they have been brought up in a home in which problems were never discussed. Some people do all the talking and complain that their partner doesn't talk to them.

Emotional Factors

Partners have an important source of psychological power: the ability to bestow or withhold affection. Some spouses use sex as a source of power, withholding it if their partner does not do what they want. For example, one woman would delay going to bed until her partner had fallen asleep in order to send the message that she was not interested in sexual intimacy with him until he became less distant with her.

Of course, love or sex must be valued before it can become a power source. When love dies, so does its power. According to social exchange theory, those with the greatest love and emotional need have the least power. Because they are so dependent, they have the most to lose if the relationship ends. They are so afraid of losing love that they often do everything possible to please their partner (Warner, Lee, and Lee, 1986).

Physical Stature and Strength

Coercive power is based on the belief that one spouse can punish the other for noncompliance. One type of coercion is the threat of physical punishment. One woman commented:

> My husband is a big man, and very strong. When he gets mad I never know what he's going to do. I'm afraid he'll hurt me. He once threw me down the front steps. (Author's counseling notes)

This woman realized what her spouse could do to her if he decided to strike her. Some people use physical violence as a way to punish or control their partner.

Life Circumstances

The more limited their alternatives, the less power people have in relationships. If a man feels that his partner can't leave because she has no one to turn to, no place to go, and no money to support herself, he has more power in the relationship than he would otherwise. The stage in the family life cycle

is an important consideration. Women who have the most dependent children or who are the most dependent economically and socially have less power over their situation than do women who are not yet parents or whose children are grown.

Circumstances may change power balances, or a crisis may result in a realignment of power in a relationship. Physical incapacitation or illness of one spouse may force an otherwise submissive partner to take a more dominant role. Egalitarian couples, because they are more fluid and flexible, are able to shift and exchange roles in order to meet the demands of a stressful situation.

Children

Children themselves have sources of power. That is, children exert considerable influence over their parents and other family members. Even the cry of a baby has considerable influence. An older child can render parents powerless if he or she can get them to disagree. For this reason, therapist Jay Haley (1982) emphasized the need for parents to discuss issues with each other and to present a united front to avoid confusion.

MARITAL POWER PATTERNS

Marital power patterns can be divided into four types: egalitarian, male-dominant, female-dominant, and anarchic. In an egalitarian power pattern, power is distributed equally between the partners. In a male-dominant pattern, the man has more power than the woman; in a female-dominant pattern, the pattern is reversed. In an anarchic power pattern, both partners have power and seek to exercise it in a

---

expert power   Power that is given because a person is considered superior in knowledge of a particular subject.

informational power   Power acquired because of extensive knowledge of a specific area.

theory of primary interest and presumed competence   The theory that the person who is most interested in, most involved with, and best qualified to make a particular choice will be more likely to do so.

coercive power   The threat of physical force or other types of punishment to force compliance.

random manner, disregarding all rules in governing the total family. Male-dominant couples are congruent with a traditional norm, while egalitarian couples are congruent with a more modern norm of balanced power between the spouses.

Most research on family power focuses on the distribution of power between spouses and examines the association between power distribution and marital adjustment. Studies of the relationship between power and marriage satisfaction have consistently shown two results: (1) Shared power (an egalitarian power pattern) is associated with the highest level of reported marital satisfaction, and (2) female-dominant couples are, on the whole, less satisfied than egalitarian or male-dominant couples. Egalitarian couples have a higher level of agreement on the desired distribution of power than couples with hierarchical relationships. Violence occurs least often in marriages in which power is shared.

High rates of dissatisfaction have been found in female-dominant relationships. Most spouses in such relationships view dominance by the woman as undesirable. Some argue the level of satisfaction in such marriages is low because the man cannot adequately exercise power, leaving the woman to assume more authority than desired by either spouse and causing dissatisfaction in both. The woman in a female-dominant marriage may be especially demanding because of a wish to force her spouse to take on a leadership role. When she confronts his unwillingness and resistance, she may use more control tactics than both a couple in which partners share power and a dominant man with role expectations and tradition on his side. The high-power woman may more frequently resort to demanding, negative communication, which may lead to marital dissatisfaction. Interestingly, therapy appears to be more successful for female-dominated couples than for couples with other power patterns (Gray-Little, Baucom, and Hamby, 1996).

An association between negative behaviors—such as complaints, hostile comments, and whining—and low marital satisfaction is one of the best-established findings in the literature on marital interaction. There is also a greater incidence of minor violence in both male- and female-dominant marriages than in egalitarian ones. And unhappy partners are more likely to disagree with each other about who has responsibility for what decisions.

Any kind of functional authority pattern may be better than none. Couples with little agreement will have different points of view, resulting in interactions that are anarchic. Anarchic couples exhibit more negative behavior than either male- or female-dominant couples. The lack of decision-making structure is detrimental to marital functioning. Partners who share power can reach mutually acceptable decisions based on compromise. When an anarchic couple is faced with a decision, however, there is neither an expressed norm nor an implicit understanding of who will exercise control. Each spouse contests the other's authority. As a result, the anarchic couple is caught up in a struggle in

Coercive power is based on the belief that one spouse can punish the other for noncompliance. An economically dependent spouse is more likely to stay in a severely abusive situation.

which each partner tries to control the other while resisting the other's influence.

Spouses who are able to negotiate compromises or who are willing to make accommodations to their partner's position seem to have higher levels of marital adjustment than spouses who are habitually confrontational (Gray-Little et al., 1996).

POWER PROCESSES

We have discussed power bases, that is, the sources of power and power patterns. **Power processes** are the ways in which power is applied. A distinction needs to be made between orchestration power and implementation power. **Orchestration power** is the power to make the important decisions that determine family lifestyles and the major characteristics and features of the family. **Implementation power** sets these decisions in motion. For example, one spouse may decide how much money can be spent on a new appliance, but the other spouse is the one who actually makes the purchase. Conflicts arise when the implementing spouse tries to modify the guidelines and boundaries established by the orchestrating spouse.

Power Tactics That Help

Power tactics are the means that people use to get others to do what they want them to do. Some tactics help build better relationships.

Discussing, Explaining, Asking, or Telling Discussing, explaining, asking, and telling are positive methods of power implementation. Partners who can explain things in a rational, intelligent way, or who ask questions directly and clearly, are using a gentle, or soft, form of power that is effective. It also builds positive feelings of satisfaction in the relationship (Kipnis, 1984).

Bargaining and Negotiating **Bargaining** is the process by which two parties decide what each will give and receive in arriving at a decision. The process involves quid pro quo, which means "something for something." The purpose of bargaining is to reach an agreement or compromise solution to a problem. Bargaining is a process of position modification and convergence.

Power Tactics That Can Help or Harm

Some power tactics are helpful under some circumstances but harmful in others.

Persuading Persuasion is stronger than discussion. Its purpose is to try to convince the other person to believe or do something that he or she is reluctant to. Sometimes, the person is genuinely convinced and accepts willingly; at other times, the person acquiesces, but against his or her inclinations. Consider this example:

> Bill wanted to go to Hawaii on his vacation. Sally was reluctant because she did not want to go so far away. Bill got all the brochures and for months talked to his wife about how wonderful it would be to go to Hawaii. He finally convinced her that Hawaii was *the* place to go. Sally went to Hawaii, but resented Bill for not considering her feelings. (Author's counseling notes)

Being Nice Being exceptionally attentive and considerate when one wants something may put people in a good mood and make them feel so grateful that they can't refuse a request. Some spouses are better than others at buttering up their partner. Sincere flattery and consideration are appreciated, but false efforts to win favors are deceitful and create distrust.

Power Tactics That Harm

When power tactics are used to maintain or increase the imbalance of power in a relationship, they are destructive.

Acting Helpless or Dependent Some people try to exert control by acting helpless or dependent. If they present themselves as powerless or unable to do something, they may evoke the sympathy of the other person, who is glad to show off his or her expertise. Some spouses play the weak, helpless role to evade responsibility, as this example shows:

---

power processes The ways in which power is applied.

orchestration power The power to make the important decisions that determine family lifestyle.

implementation power Power that sets decisions in motion.

bargaining The process by which two parties decide what each will give and receive in arriving at a decision.

Don hates yard work, house repairs, painting, and every kind of physical chore in and outside the house. Several times, his wife asked him to do something. He was all thumbs, completely inept, and did such a terrible job that his wife took over and did it herself. Don explained, "If she knows I'll do a terrible job, she doesn't ask me." (Author's counseling notes)

But this role has its downside. For instance, some women have no respect for a man who is not capable in many areas, especially in doing traditional men's chores.

Some men are flattered by requests for help from dependent females. For this reason, some women have been brought up to pretend to be helpless. Other women find such tactics demeaning to themselves and to all women.

Overprotecting   The overprotective man or woman does not allow his or her spouse to mature or become independent, thus rendering the spouse powerless. An example is the woman who plays mother hen to her spouse, treating him like a helpless child so she can rule the roost.

Deceiving, Lying, or Outwitting   Some people seek to control others by deceiving them, lying to them, or outwitting them. They make promises they don't intend to keep in exchange for concessions. They pretend to be what they are not. They become habitual liars to try to avoid responsibilities. For example, "Harry told Sylvia that he didn't want to discontinue their affair and that he would divorce his wife and marry her. Five years have passed, and he has never filed divorce papers" (Author's counseling notes).

Criticizing   One of the most personally destructive ways of gaining power is the constant use of criticism to undermine and demean the other person. Some spouses wait until other family members or company are present and then point out the wrong-doings and failures of their spouse. It's difficult for the criticized spouse to defend him- or herself without creating an embarrassing scene. One woman complained, "According to my husband, I never do anything right. It doesn't matter how hard I try, or what I do, he finds fault. He's beaten me down so I don't have any self-respect or self-confidence at all anymore" (Author's counseling notes). Comparing one person with another—with a friend or a sibling,

for example—is another way of making someone feel inept and inadequate.

Scapegoating   **Scapegoating** is a way of blaming someone else for every bad thing that happens. The goal is to make the other person feel responsible and guilty so that the controller doesn't have to accept the blame. For example, "Mary is married to an insensitive, cruel husband. When she decides to leave, he blames her for separating him from his infant daughter. He insists it's all her fault that she is leaving" (Author's counseling notes).

Gaslighting   The term **gaslighting** comes from the movie *Gaslight,* in which the husband attempts to drive his wife insane by turning down the gaslights and then telling her she's imagining things when she says they are growing dimmer. In gaslighting, one partner denies the truth of what the other is saying, sarcastically criticizes the other for his or her feelings or opinions, or turns things around to make the other partner feel guilty for having any doubts. Consider this example:

> A husband is having an affair that the wife suspects. He stays away all night Friday and has become very indifferent toward his wife. When she questions him, he accuses her of imagining things and claims that the only thing wrong with their marriage is that she doesn't trust him. He tells his wife that she is too jealous, too suspicious, and tries to possess him and run his life, and that if she gives him more freedom maybe things would work out. He insists she's imagining things and that the affair is all in her mind. (Author's counseling notes)

Punishing   Some spouses use a variety of punishments to influence the behavior of the other. For example, using the silent treatment can be very punishing. Some couples live in silence for days as tension continues. Silence, however, prevents reconciliation and perpetuates misunderstandings (Galvin and Brommel, 1986).

Blackmailing   Threatening blackmail is a coercive tactic that creates fear and anger, as this example suggests:

> Bill's parents hated alcoholic beverages and told him and their other children that if they ever drank they would disown them. Bill wanted to divorce his wife

Shirley, but she threatened to tell his parents about his drinking if he ever left her. (Author's counseling notes)

Expressing Anger   Emotionally unstable people may become violent, throw temper tantrums, punch out walls, break furniture, or use other power tactics to try to get their own way. For example, When Dick found out that his wife wanted to divorce him, he started throwing furniture around the house. "If you leave me, there won't be anything left of this house. You'll get nothing," he threatened' (Author's counseling notes).

Acting Cruel or Abusive   The most extreme form of control is cruel and abusive treatment. The man who beats up his spouse terrorizes her so that he can maintain control over her. It takes a strong woman to separate herself from such treatment, especially if her partner tries to make her believe that it is all her fault and that she deserves it. Sometimes it is the woman who is cruel and abusive to her spouse.

CONSEQUENCES OF POWER STRUGGLES

One of the most important considerations in evaluating patterns of power in the family is the effect that different patterns have on individuals and their relationships. Some people strive to gain control, but at what cost? If they gain the upper hand at the cost of alienating their partner, provoking anger and hostility, or destroying their relationship, what's the point? Some spouses are so intent on winning the battle that they lose the marriage.

Generally, extreme imbalances of power between two people tend to have a negative effect. Lack of power is associated with psychological distress for both men and women. At the other extreme, high levels of power can also be destructive, because power can corrupt. This means that power produces strong psychological changes in power holders, and they start to exploit those they control. They can become self-centered and selfish, as well as unfeeling and abusive. The person dominated becomes an "it" to use rather than a person to cherish.

One of the consequences of power imbalances in relationships is that the person who feels coerced or manipulated and who often gives in becomes frustrated and resentful. A person may accept coercion

for a while, but as frustrations and hostility increase, the relationship worsens. Couples who habitually deal with decisions on a win-or-lose basis often discover that a victory in a marital conflict is illusory. The victory turns into a loss for both partners when feelings of anger and hurt develop between them.

Marital satisfaction is maximized when couples achieve a balance of power that is acceptable to both partners. This balance varies with different couples (Henggeler, Edwards, Hanson, and Okwumabua, 1988; Whisman and Jacobson, 1990). Although dominance by one partner works for some couples, an extreme imbalance of power usually causes dissatisfaction.

Social science research emphasizes that equitable relations tend to be more stable and satisfying. In a study of Puerto Rican families, marital satisfaction of the women was closely associated with egalitarian gender roles (Rogler and Procidano, 1989a). Women who feel they have power to control the outcome of marital conflicts are more satisfied with their marriages than are women who have little control. If women blame their spouse for the conflict and have little control over the situation, they find their marriage very unsatisfying. Exchange theorists suggest that satisfaction in marriage hinges on the perception of fairness or equity in exchanges, rather than on the existence of a particular power structure.

COMMUNICATION

Sharing control is an important element in marital satisfaction (Honeycutt, 1986). Satisfaction also depends on the extent and nature of the communication between the partners (A. Allen and Thompson, 1984). Many authorities contend that good communication is the key to intimacy and to family interaction and is the lifeblood of the marital relationship (Stephen, 1985). One couple wrote:

---

scapegoating   Blaming someone else for every bad thing that happens.

gaslighting   The process by which one person destroys the self-confidence, perception, and sense of reality of another person.

There is no area of our married life that isn't affected by communication: our bed, our job, our children, our social life, our leisure time, our relationship with relatives and friends. All could become potential areas of discontent and friction when there isn't good communication between us. (Herrigan and Herrigan, 1973, p. 149)

Communication between human beings may be defined as a message one person sends and another receives. It involves both content and process (Boland and Follingstad, 1987). Content is what is communicated; process is the means by which feelings, attitudes, facts, beliefs, and ideas are transmitted between people. Communication is not limited to words but also occurs through listening, silence, glances, facial expressions, gestures, touch, body stance, and all other nonlanguage symbols and cues used to give and transmit meaning. In short, it may include all the messages sent and received and all the means by which people exchange feelings and meanings as they try to understand and influence one another.

One study examined 30 nondistressed couples and 30 distressed couples with respect to differences in communication skills and marital satisfaction. They found that distressed and nondistressed couples had the same communication skills level; however, the partners in the distressed couples used their skills with more negative intentions and ill will. In other words, it is not always a lack of communication skills that makes a marriage go awry. Rather, it can be the intentions of a partner that cause a marriage to be distressed (Burleson and Denton, 1997).

Verbal and Nonverbal Communication

Nonverbal communication comes in many forms. **Body language** involves physical reactions such as posture, facial expression, still or tense muscles, blushing, movement, panting, tears, sweating, shivering or quivering, an increased pulse rate, and a thumping heart. The message "I love you" may be communicated by facial expression (pleasant), touch (gentle and caring), eyes (attentive), speed of speech (slow), tone of voice (soft), and gesture (outstretched arms). The manner of dressing and the use of cosmetics are also forms of communication.

Both verbal and nonverbal communication are strongly associated with good marital adjustment.

However, nonverbal communication, the language of signs and signals, is more subject to misinterpretation. One study found that when men were able to read their spouse's nonverbal cues, the women were more satisfied with their marriage than when the men were not able to interpret them (Gottman and Porterfield, 1981).

Direct actions are another form of communication; that's why florists remind us, "Say it with flowers." Some nonverbal communication is symbolic communication. A surprise gift can send a message of care and love.

One of the most important uses of words is what has been called the stroking function. This refers to words that soothe; that give recognition, acceptance, and reassurance; and that fulfill emotional needs. Words can heal hurt egos and satisfy deep longings. What man is immune to the words "I think you're a handsome, wonderful person"? Words are also used to solve problems, to convey information, or to reveal emotions. One of the most important functions of words is to provide companionship; as the poet John Milton wrote, "In God's intention, a meet and happy conversation is the chiefest and the noblest end of marriage."

Sometimes the verbal and nonverbal messages are contradictory. A woman may say to her partner, "I'm listening, I'm listening," but she's sitting in front of the television set and paying close attention to it. Or a man may tell his partner "I love you" over and over, but she wonders if he means it because he seldom makes love to her, never wants to spend time with her, and refuses to do little things to help her. Inconsistent words and actions, often referred to as **double-bind communication,** cause stress between partners to increase as anxiety grows (Roy and Sawyers, 1986).

Barriers to Communication

Barriers to communication may be grouped under four categories: physical and environmental, situational, psychological, and gender.

Physical and Environmental Barriers   There is a close relationship between physical proximity and social interaction. In general, closer physical distances are associated with more intimate relationships. This means that factors such as the size and arrangement of living spaces and the location of furniture in those spaces influence interaction. The closer people sit

Female Empowerment

The traditional concept of power is described as a struggle of individuals or groups for control over another person or group. Any increase in power for one of the parties leads to a decrease in power for the other. This usually results in inequality, and in dominance and submission, with the stronger prevailing over the weaker. Such inequality is often the case in intimate relationships, with men typically having power over women and women being submissive to men.

Women handle power inequalities in different ways. Research has shown that gender inequality in the family does increase women's anger, and that some women express their anger while others do not (Ross and Van Willigen, 1996). Some women strive for equity—equality and fairness—in an attempt to make both parties satisfied. Others strive for personal power—empowerment—to improve their capacities and develop their own abilities. Personal power does not require submission or domination. For this reason, it can benefit both the empowered person and his or her partner. Feeling powerful in this sense implies the freedom and ability to direct one's energies outward in creative effort rather than being forced to express it in the struggle to dominate.

Carolyn Knapp (2003) presents another solution in her book *Appetites;* she describes how she sees the culture of power and inequalities for women today and writes in terms of the what ifs:

If only we lived in a culture in which internal measures of satisfaction and success—a capacity for joy and caring, an ability to laugh, a sense of connection to other, a belief in social justice—were as highly valued as external measures. If only we lived in a culture that made ambition compatible with motherhood and family life, that presented models of women who were integrated and whole: strong, sexual, ambitious, cued into their own varied appetites and demands, and equipped with the freedom and resources to explore all of them. If only women felt less isolated in their frustration and fatigue, less torn between competing hungers, less compelled to keep nine balls in the air at once, and less prone to blame themselves when those balls come crashing to the floor. If only we exercised our own power, which is considerable but woefully underused; if only we defined desire on our own terms. (p. 154)

To be able to do this, women need to be freed from the burden of inferiority, to recognize that the feminine qualities of sensitivity and understanding—which have caused women to be labeled as the weaker sex—are strengths that enable them to relate to others and to solve important problems in relationships and society.

---

around a table, the more likely they are to be friendly, talkative, and intimate. Whether couples sleep together in the same bed or in separate bedrooms influences the extent of their interaction.

Physical confinement is associated with accelerated self-disclosure, particularly in intimate areas of exchange. This means that the closer couples are physically, the greater the possibility that intimacy will develop. Of course, there is also the possibility that conflict and tension will arise.

Situational Barriers Situations can also enhance communication or make it more difficult. If employment separates couples frequently or for long periods of time, the tendency is for communication to break down, with a resultant loss of intimacy. When couples live together with others, lack of privacy becomes a major factor in making intimate communication more difficult. The situational context changes during different periods of marriage and affects communication. For example, men may make great efforts to give emotional support to their spouse during pregnancy; following childbirth, however, they may feel that their spouse does not require the same special support. The closeness reported during

communication A message one person sends and another receives.

body language Posture, facial expression, still or tense muscles, blushing, panting, tears, sweating, shivering, increased pulse rate, thumping heart, and other bodily reactions that convey feelings and reactions.

double-bind communication Conflicting messages sent when verbal messages and body language don't agree.

Good communication is the key to intimacy and family interaction and is the lifeblood of the marital relationship.

pregnancy then declines, resulting in the increased dissatisfaction that some women feel after childbirth.

Psychological Barriers   The most important barriers to communication are psychological: fear of rejection, ridicule, failure, or alienation and lack of trust between two people. Partners will not share experiences that are unrewarding, threatening, or painful if they are not sure of an empathetic reply.

Gender Barriers   Some barriers to communication are a result of socialized masculine–feminine differences. Gender differences in communication and power can be seen across the life span. In general, research on peer interactions in childhood has shown that girls and boys have different behaviors related to exerting power. For example, boys tend to use more aggressive conversational tactics, such as initiation and attention-getting devices, which are associated with higher status in our society; girls tend to use more subtle strategies, such as reinforcing what was already said (Berghout-Austin, Salehi, and Leffler, 1987). The same pattern can be seen in classroom settings, with boys using more direct attempts to influence their interaction partners and being more successful than girls in getting their way (Serbin, Sprafkin, Elman, and Doyle, 1982). By adolescence, girls in mixed-sex pairs are more likely to relinquish decision-making control to their male partner in problem-solving tasks (Lind and Connole, 1985). Not

surprisingly, similar patterns persist in adult intimate relationships.

Deborah Tannen (1982, 1994) has written many books on conversation styles and their relationship to gender. According to Tannen, men and women grow up in sex-separated cultures and learn different styles of interacting, which they practice and which are reinforced. Specifically, men inhabit a hierarchical social order in which conversation serves as a negotiating device that they use to maintain their independence and avoid failure. Women, in contrast, communicate for the central purpose of building connections with others and providing mutual support.

Although there may be hierarchies in women's communities, Tannen observed, their collectives are designed to sustain intimacy and to ward off social isolation. Thus, men and women have different perceptions of and assumptions about communication and use distinctively different ways to communicate. Men tend to perceive social relations in a hierarchical fashion, employing conversational styles that are competitive and fact-oriented. Women perceive social relations as egalitarian and often use conversation as a means of sharing feelings and promote intimacy. Women, for example, are inclined to express their preferences in the form of questions ("Would you like to go see a movie?"), whereas men tend to express their feelings in the form of definitive statements ("Let's go see a movie").

Tannen also identified gender differences related to the meaning given to verbal behavior. For example, when one woman offers to help another, she is likely to perceive the offer as a gesture of friendship and support. In contrast, when men offer help to one another, the one being offered help is more likely to perceive it as an act of condescension or a message that he is incompetent and thus needs help. Tannen did not draw conclusions about the origins of these gender distinctions. She suggested environmental origins but did not argue for them in any detail, noting only that differences in conversational styles can be seen in very young children (Franzwa and Lockhart, 1998).

IMPROVING COMMUNICATION SKILLS

Skill in communication has four requirements: (1) a positive feeling between partners who value and care for each other and are motivated to want to develop sympathetic understanding; (2) a willingness to disclose one's own attitudes, feelings, and ideas; (3) an ability to reveal attitudes, feelings, and ideas clearly and accurately; and (4) a reciprocal relationship in which disclosure and feedback originate with both partners, who listen carefully and attentively to each other. Successful communicators also know how to argue constructively.

Motivation and Concern

Communication is most possible when partners really show they care about each other and when they are motivated to try to understand each other. It is not just the communication itself that is important but also the spirit behind the message and the partners' feelings for each other. The tone of voice used and the words selected are important as well. Most researchers also talk about the importance of empathy—experiencing the feelings, thoughts, and attitudes of another person. Some people are sensitive to the feelings and wishes of others and try to understand them and act accordingly (Floyd, 1988). Partners who frequently make positive statements about each other have much higher marital satisfaction than do those who are very negative or disparaging in what they say. In addition, supportive communication stimulates reciprocal supportiveness, increasing the degree of marital integration.

Self-Disclosure

Communication depends partly on people's willingness to disclose their real feelings, ideas, and attitudes. People cannot really get to know others unless they are willing to talk about themselves. Some people can be classified as high revealers, and others as low revealers. High revealers are more prone to disclose intimate facets of their personalities and to do so earlier in their relationships than are low revealers. They are also able to more accurately assess the intimate attitudes and values of their friends than are low revealers. In general, dyads in which both persons are high revealers are more compatible than are pairs of low revealers or pairs that differ in the level of disclosure.

However, it's not just the amount of disclosure that is important, but also what is said, when, and how (Schumm, Barnes, Bollman, Jurich, and Bugaighis, 1986). People who are feeling hostile may be wise not to talk until they can discuss the situation more rationally. Satisfied partners infrequently discuss negative feelings pertaining to their mate. Feelings about their partner are usually positive and pleasant.

Clarity

Partners differ in their ability to convey messages clearly and accurately. Some people have few verbal skills and so make greater use of nonverbal techniques. You can learn to say what you mean and to accurately interpret what others say by doing the following:

1. Avoid "double-level" messages in which words say one thing and actions and innuendos another.
2. Speak clearly and to the point, and say what you really mean; avoid vagueness, ambiguity, and indirect approaches.
3. Avoid both exaggeration and understatement.
4. Avoid flippant, kidding remarks that mask your true feelings and opinions. How many times have you heard, "I didn't really mean that. I was only joking. Don't take everything so literally"?
5. Ask the other person to repeat what was said if there is any doubt about it or if it may have been misinterpreted.
6. Talk about important things when there is a minimum of distraction and when you both can focus your attention completely on what is being said.

Feedback and Reciprocity

Feedback involves responding to what the other person has said, as well as disclosing one's own feelings and ideas. This type of marital interaction has been correlated with marital satisfaction. In technical terms, feedback means receiving the output of a computer and feeding it additional information to correct its errors (Sollie and Scott, 1983). In human communication, feedback means paraphrasing the other person's statement to make sure it is understood, asking clarifying questions, and then giving one's own input or response. Accurate feedback also requires open listening and hearing, and giving one's undivided attention to what is said.

Arguing Constructively

Many couples repeatedly argue about the same issues without ever resolving them. At the heart of these quarrels may be issues of closeness and control (A. Christensen and Jacobson, 2000). For many people, these issues define the relationship, affirm their self-image, and determine in large part their satisfaction with the relationship. When issues of control and closeness arise, partners tend to overreact, and quarrels erupt.

A. Christensen and Jacobson (2000) endorsed something called "acceptance therapy" for couples in conflict. According to their research, a partner is not likely to change, and some conflicts simply can't be resolved. Thus, people need to learn to accept a partner, give up trying to change him or her, and instead work on changing themselves. Gottman (2000) reported that many quarrels in relationships are the same fight over and over again and that in these situations partners would do better to stop trying to solve that problem and come to accept both it and each other. Such problems may have their roots in childhood and different family backgrounds. These differences may never be resolved, and even if they are, the behavior is often not easy to change. For example, a couple may argue over and over again about closeness and intimacy issues. The man may have been raised in an unemotional household, while the woman was raised in one that was bois-terous and filled with laughter. The difference creates conflict in their relationship. The two partners may both move to the middle, but it is unlikely that one can shift entirely to the other's point of view. Acceptance of a partner's different traits does not mean giving in due to fear or intimidation, but rather being strongly committed to a more fulfilling and satisfying relationship.

Arguing is also an important part of communication. Since all couples argue from time to time, arguing per se is not a sign of a poor relationship. A. Christensen and Jacobson (2000) suggested several guidelines for arguing constructively:

1. Develop a "third side" of the argument that incorporates both your own and your partner's view; this can help the two of you see the problem more objectively.

2. See the problem as a difficulty the two of you have, rather than as something your partner does to you.

3. Demonstrate that you have heard your partner by summarizing what he or she has to say; ask your partner to do the same.

4. While arguing, do something positive for your partner with no strings attached.

5. Focus on one problem at a time, not a parade of them.

6. Focus on the painful reactions each of you experiences rather than on your partner's negative actions.

7. Recognize that your partner's hurtful actions may be a defense mechanism to mask pain.

8. Don't insist that yours is the only way.

9. Remember that the only person you can change is yourself.

10. Rather than arguing the same way every time, do something different, such as sending an e-mail, making a cassette tape, or writing a letter, which can help prevent you from getting caught up in the argument, escalating it, or raising your voice.

feedback   Response to the message another has sent and disclosure of one's own feelings and ideas.

A QUESTION OF POLICY

THE POWER OF FEDERAL JUDGES

Many people do not realize the power contained within the U.S. federal judicial system and its implications for family life. Rulings by federal judges on thousands of cases each year affect public policy on such things as environmental issues, abortion, worker and consumer safety, and employment discrimination. All of these issues have tremendous implications for families.

Many people today consider the appointment of Supreme Court justices of utmost importance, but in reality all federal court judges are very important. These judges are appointed for a life term in the interest of impartiality; not having to worry about being reappointed means that they can rule free from political influences or popular issues. Formerly, judges were appointed primarily according to their ability to objectively uphold the law; today, more emphasis is placed on political ideology (S. B. Goldberg, 2003) and appointing judges to advance a party's own political agenda. This has increased controversy regarding lifelong judicial appointments.

While citizens do not vote directly for federal judges, votes for a senator or a president influence who is appointed as a federal judge. The process of selecting a judge begins with a nomination by senators or congressional representatives who are members of the president's political party. The Senate Judiciary Committee holds hearings to confirm or deny judges. Senators will question the candidates on their past judgments; attitudes toward equity, poverty, and other social issues; and personal and professional practices. Once the committee approves a nominee, the whole Senate votes to approve or deny the candidate. The balance in the Senate between Democrats and Republicans is important because votes for judges can go strictly along party lines.

QUESTIONS TO CONSIDER:

Should judges be representative of the population at large? For example, should judges be of different races, religions, and genders? Discuss.

What are the consequences of not having a certain interest group represented in the judiciary or having the majority of people in one particular interest group sitting as judges?

Employment discrimination cases, including sexual harassment, fall under federal law. Consider the example of a woman who feels she is inappropriately touched by a male boss at work. After failing to remedy the situation through company policies and procedures, she files a formal complaint with the Equal Employment Opportunity Commission. Her case is presented to a federal judge. What differences might the background of the judge (e.g., the judge's race, sex, sexual orientation, age, education, income level, or disability) make on the outcome of the case?

SUMMARY

1. Power has been defined as the ability of an individual within a social relationship to carry out his or her will, even in the face of resistance by others.

2. People desire power for a variety of reasons: because they want to have control over their life, because society expects them to have it, because they are following the pattern modeled by their parents, or because of a psycho-logical need to compensate for feelings of inferiority and insecurity. Three theoretical frameworks explain the need for power: attachment theory, social control theory, and feminist theory.

3. Power is based on cultural norms, gender norms, economic resources, education and knowledge, personality differences, communication ability, emotional factors, physical

LEARNING OBJECTIVES

After reading the chapter, you should be able to:

- Outline the reasons for family planning.
- Discuss basic facts about oral contraceptives: how they prevent conception; types and administration; effectiveness, advantages, and health benefits; risks; and side effects.
- Discuss basic facts about other forms of hormonal contraceptives, such as progestin implants and injections and RU-486 (Mifepristone).
- Understand basic facts about the use of vaginal spermicides as contraceptives.
- Describe the use of IUDs and other mechanical devices or barrier methods: condoms, female condoms, diaphragms, and cervical caps.
- Describe the processes of male and female sterilization: vasectomy and tubal ligation.

- Discuss methods of birth control without the use of devices, including fertility awareness methods, coitus interruptus, and noncoital stimulation.
- Summarize the considerations in choosing which method to use.
- Discuss the legal, moral, social and realistic, and psychological and personal considerations in relation to abortion.
- Summarize the basic facts about infertility: causes, infertility and subjective well-being, treatments, and alternative means of conception.
- Discuss basic issues in relation to adoption.
- Discuss the basic issues and trends in relation to childlessness, smaller families, and delayed parenthood.
- Summarize the reasons for having or not having children.

Family Planning and Parenthood

We are fortunate to live at a time when efficient and safe methods of contraception are available. Without birth control, couples would have to resign themselves to having one child after another or to avoiding sexual relations after they'd had the number of children they desired. A walk through an old cemetery reveals the difference that family planning has made. Dozens of tombstones contain the names of women who died at young ages from bearing one child after another. Beside them are the names of many of their children who also did not get a chance at life.

Contraception has improved the lives of millions of people. Most important, it helps them to plan the number of children they want and to have them at the time that is best for all concerned. An additional option for couples is to have no children.

To acquaint couples with the options available, this chapter includes an overview of contraceptive methods and their use and discusses special treatments available to couples who have problems with fertility. The chapter also examines abortion and the decision of whether to parent. But first, we explore the importance of family planning.

THE IMPORTANCE OF FAMILY PLANNING

There are several reasons why individuals use **family planning**—defined as having children by choice and not by chance, and having the number of children wanted at the time planned. One reason is health. Births to females who are too young or too old and births that are close together pose increased health risks for both mothers and children (Wineberg and McCarthy, 1989). For example, getting pregnant beyond the age of 35 increases the risk of giving birth to a low-weight baby who may be at risk of serious medical and learning problems. One study found that babies born to women 35 and older are 20% to 40% more likely than newborns overall to have a low birth weight, 20% more likely to be born prematurely, and 20% more likely to be a twin to triplet (Tough et al., 2002). Similarly, infants conceived within a few months of a preceding birth have a higher-than-average risk of low birth weight, preterm birth, and neonatal death. Many family planning experts suggest that birth intervals be at least 2 years (J. E. Miller, 1991). Economics is also a major reason for family planning. As noted in Chapter 9, it costs about $164,000 to raise a child to age 18, and college will cost an additional $60,000–$145,000. It doesn't take much imagination to realize that having a large number of children places a great strain on the family budget. Family planning is often necessary to give children the best possible start in life.

Timing is an important issue in family planning and a major determinant of childbirth's effect on a family. For example, many teenagers are sexually active but have no desire to become parents at such a young age. In the United States alone, an estimated 1.65 million pregnancies among females ages 15–19 were avoided through the use of contraceptives in 1995 (J. G. Kahn, Brindis, and Glei, 1999). Women often want to wait to have a child until they finish their education or are situated in their careers. They have a plan for their lives, and the timing of motherhood is part of that plan.

The timing of fatherhood affects the way men fill the role of father (Cooney, Pedersen, Indelicato, and Palkovitz, 1993). Older fathers are more likely to be positively involved in their children's upbringing than younger fathers are. By delaying parenthood, men evidently are able to invest themselves more readily in the role and to feel good about their involvement. Also, delaying parenthood can promote marital satisfaction for men and women.

Family planning is often necessary for the good of the marriage and the family. The potential negative psychological impact on the mother and father is lessened considerably if parenthood is chosen and welcomed. Having children imposes strains on the marriage; having children early in a relationship adds additional stress. Because both premarital pregnancy and early postmarital pregnancy are associated with a higher-than-average divorce rate, many of these children grow up in a single-parent household. Furthermore, women whose pregnancy is unwanted or mistimed are four times as likely as women with an intentional pregnancy to be physically assaulted by their partner (Gazmararian et al., 1995).

In recent years, much emphasis has been placed on the humanitarian and ecological importance of family planning. At the present rate of population growth, the world will have 7.5 billion people by the year 2020. World population could reach 10.9 billion by 2050 if women do not gain better access

Training programs and community support have helped many teenagers adjust to their roles as new parents.

to education and health care, according to a report by the United Nations. The world now has more than 6 billion people, and population in the world's 49 least-developed countries is forecast to triple in the next 50 years. Can the world's resources support this many people? More than half of the people in the world already live in poverty. Family planning thus has become an important issue for many humanitarian groups.

HORMONAL CONTROL

The invention of birth control pills, or oral contraceptives, in the 1960s was a major advancement in contraceptive technology. The pill was more effective than any previous method in preventing pregnancy, and it was a no-mess, no-fuss alternative to condoms and diaphragms. Other forms of hormonal birth control have now been developed and tested, and some have become available to the public.

Oral Contraceptives

Oral contraceptives contain two synthetically produced female sex hormones that are chemically similar to ones the woman already produces in her body to regulate ovulation and the menstrual cycle. The natural hormones are estrogen and progesterone (progestin is the artificially produced equivalent). By manipulating the amount of these two

hormones in the woman's bloodstream, birth control pills prevent conception in three ways:

1. Ovulation is prevented in about 90% of the menstrual cycles.
2. The cervical mucus remains thick and sticky throughout the month, blocking the entrance to the uterus and making penetration by the sperm difficult.
3. The endometrium, the inner lining of the uterus, is altered so that successful implantation and nourishment of a fertilized ovum are difficult (Guttmacher, 1983).

Types of Oral Contraceptives There are several types of pills. **Combination pills** contain both estrogen and progestin. Because the pill is a prescription drug, it should never be taken without a prior physical examination and a doctor's prescription and guidance. A woman takes the pill for 21 days and

family planning Having children by choice and not by chance; having the number of children wanted at the time planned.

oral contraceptives Birth control pills taken orally (by mouth).

combination pills Oral contraceptives containing both estrogen and progestin.

then stops doing so for 7 days. Some brands have a different-colored pill, a **placebo** (a pill that has no pharmacological effect), which the woman takes for 7 days before recommencing the 21-day regimen. (The placebos serve merely as placeholders, though some do contain iron as a nutritional supplement.)

If a woman forgets to take a single pill, she should make it up by taking it as soon as she remembers. If she misses two pills, she should either take both at once or take one additional pill each of the next two days, depending on the type of pill. (The manufacturer's insert in each package contains directions.) If she misses more than two pills, it is generally recommended that a backup method be used for a month or so, until the hormone-regulated menstrual cycle is reestablished (Williams-Deane and Potter, 1992).

Another form of pill, called the **minipill** because it contains only progestin, is also available. This pill is taken daily with no break. The minipill does not prevent either ovulation or menstruation, but it greatly reduces the likelihood of impregnation by maintaining a mucous barrier in the cervix, altering the sperm cells within the tubes, or interfering with the passage of the egg down the tube. Although minipills have fewer side effects, they have a slightly higher failure rate than the combination pills. They are prescribed infrequently at present.

Some kinds of oral contraceptives are prescribed as **emergency contraceptives** to prevent pregnancy following unprotected sexual intercourse. A woman may require emergency contraception because the contraceptive method she was using failed (for example, a condom broke or a diaphragm slipped), she neglected to use a contraceptive method, or she was sexually assaulted.

Emergency contraception is used extensively in some countries. In the United States, however, emergency contraception is prescribed primarily for rape victims treated in emergency rooms, college health centers, or family planning clinics (Grossman and Grossman, 1994). Emergency contraception may be the best kept contraceptive secret in America. Students remark on how seldom emergency contraception is discussed and call for routine education about the method. Low utilization of emergency contraception is partly attributable to health care providers' lack of knowledge about the method. In a survey of 167 physicians with expertise in adolescent health, 84% said they prescribed contraceptives to adolescents, but only 80% of these prescribed

emergency contraception, generally a few times a year at most (Gold, Schein, and Coupey, 1997). One survey of 235 women who had received emergency contraceptives found that 91% were satisfied with the treatment. More than two-thirds of the women were using contraceptives before receiving emergency treatment, with 45% reporting problems with the condom and 23% reporting having unplanned sex. Twenty-nine percent of the sample believed that emergency contraceptives should be made available over the counter. As this study suggests, emergency contraceptives are options for women, but they should not be a substitute for regular contraceptive use (Harvey, Beckman, Sherman, and Petitti, 1999).

The most common method, the Yuzpe method, involves taking four combined estrogen/progestin pills: two tablets within 72 hours of unprotected coitus (preferably as soon as possible) and two more 12 hours later. Use of these emergency contraceptive pills (ECPs) reduces the expected number of pregnancies by more than 75%. However, repeated use of ECPs is not recommended because ECPs are not 100% effective and repeated use may pose health risks and cause unpleasant side effects. Another postcoital therapy less frequently used is insertion of a copper-releasing IUD (Hatcher et al., 1998).

Advantages of Oral Contraceptives   The combination birth control pill is one of the most effective contraceptives. Since some users are careless, however, the estimated typical user's failure rate is 3.8% (Kost, Forrest, and Harlap, 1991). The failure rate is the percentage of users (ages 15–44) who get pregnant during the first year of use. The pill is convenient and easy to use; all that is required is remembering to take a pill every day.

The birth control pill is a reversible contraceptive; that is, after the woman stops taking it, her fertility returns. However, some women who stop taking the pill because they want to become pregnant take slightly longer to conceive than do those who haven't been on the pill (R. Turner, 1990). A minority of women who have been on the pill become more fertile after ceasing to take it, usually because of more regular menstruation and ovulation.

There are also some noncontraceptive health benefits associated with oral contraceptives. Too often these beneficial effects have been ignored, especially by the media, which seem to emphasize the negative. The pill's positive effects on the following health problems are well documented:

- **Benign breast disease.** Oral contraceptives reduce benign breast disease. The longer the pill is used, the lower the incidence of the disease.

- **Cysts of the ovary.** The combination pills suppress ovarian activity and reduce ovarian cysts.

- **Iron-deficiency anemia.** Oral contraceptive users suffer approximately 45% less iron-deficiency anemia than do nonusers.

- **Pelvic inflammatory disease (PID).** Pill users have only half the risk of developing pelvic inflammatory disease. When the pill is used for 1 year or longer, the rate is 70% (Witwer, 1990c).

- **Ectopic pregnancy.** Current users of oral contraceptives have nearly complete protection against this condition.

The pill also seems to offer protection against rheumatoid arthritis, endometriosis, and osteoporosis (Hatcher et al., 1998). Although the evidence is not yet conclusive, pill users appear to be only half as likely to develop these conditions. Women who have used oral contraceptives appear to be about half as likely to develop ovarian and endometrial cancer as are women who have never used the pill (Kost et al., 1991). The protective effects of the pill against two of the most common cancers in American women appear to be long-lasting (Coker, Harlap, and Fortney, 1993).

Disadvantages of Oral Contraceptives　Birth control pills do not protect against sexually transmitted diseases (STDs), including AIDS, although they do lower the risk of pelvic inflammatory diseases (Hatcher et al., 1998). Regular use of condoms is recommended for women taking oral contraceptives unless they are in a monogamous relationship with an uninfected partner. One of the most serious concerns associated with the birth control pill is that it may cause blood clots (thrombosis). There is a slight increase in risk with age (Klitsch, 1996). Pill users who are younger than 50, do not smoke, and have no history of hypertension have a very low risk of blood clots, which cause strokes (Hatcher et al., 1998). For women who smoke heavily (more than 25 cigarettes per day), the risk of death from thromboembolism is nine times greater than for nonsmokers. If women who use the pill did not smoke, most of the deaths could be averted (Kost et al., 1991).

Many people believe that another drawback of the combination pill is the possible increased risk of breast cancer. However, the current consensus is that the risk is small and that the tumors spread less aggressively than they would in women who were not on the pill (Hatcher et al., 1998). A recent study of 9,200 women ages 35–64 found no increased risk of breast cancer in pill users. Neither race, age, weight, length of time on the pill nor type of pill used made any difference (Marchbanks et al., 2002). In fact, the increased risk may be due not to the pill but to the greater likelihood that women taking the pill will have their tumor diagnosed. However, women who have a family history of breast cancer may wish to discuss alternative contraceptives with their doctor. All women, whether they use oral contraceptives or not, are urged to get annual breast examinations (Coker et al., 1993) and to perform self-exams monthly.

There may be an increase in the risk of cervical cancer among pill users, especially among long-term users who started having sex early and have had multiple sex partners (C. Donovan and Klitsch, 1995; Hatcher et al., 1998). It is difficult to sort out variables. Those women who have been sexually active the longest and have sex the most frequently and with the most partners have increased risk. But it has also been shown that pill users have intercourse more frequently than those who don't use the pill, so which is the cause of cervical cancer—the pill or the sexual activity? This is why it is necessary for researchers to consider the sexual histories of the women in their research population (Lincoln, 1984). Doctors still recommend that women receive annual examinations, including Pap smears, to help detect cervical cancer.

The effect of taking the pill on sexual drive and frequency of intercourse is variable. There seems to be some evidence that for some women the pill alters vaginal secretions and decreases levels of free testosterone, which may decrease sexual drive (Hatcher et al., 1998). However, women who feel more comfortable and secure in their sexual relationships are more likely to make the commitment to an ongoing sexual relationship that is implied by oral contraceptive use (Bancroft, Sherwin, Alexander, Davidson, and Walker, 1991).

placebo　A pill that has no pharmacological effect.

minipill　An oral contraceptive containing progestin only.

emergency contraceptives　Oral contraceptives taken after intercourse to prevent unwanted pregnancy.

Other side effects of the pill, depending on the particular combination of ingredients, can include nausea, weight gain, swollen breasts, headaches, and nervousness. Many of the unpleasant side effects disappear after a woman's metabolism adjusts to the pill or after her doctor alters brands or dosage.

Other Forms of Hormonal Contraceptives

In recent years, scientists have been working to improve hormonal contraception. Since the main reason for the pill's failure as a contraceptive is failure to take it every day, one of the main focuses of this research has been on methods of safely delivering the hormones in longer-lasting doses. One method is the **progestin implant,** which is inserted under the skin of the upper arm (Weisman, Plichta, Tirado, and Dana, 1993). Flexible, nonbiodegradable tubes filled with hormones and placed under the skin release regular doses of synthetic progestin (Tanfer, 1994). Progestin implants come in various forms. Norplant, which was approved by the U.S. Food and Drug Administration in December 1990, provides sustained release of progestin directly into the bloodstream for 5 years (Darney, 1990). It is free of estrogen, and because it is administered subcutaneously rather than orally, it avoids possible liver damage and side effects such as nausea (Potts, 1988). It is a highly convenient method; once it is inserted, the user does not have to remember to do anything else, as she does if she is on the pill (Frank, Poindexter, Johnson, and Bateman, 1992).

The failure rate of implants is less than 0.1% for women in general. Adolescent mothers who choose hormonal implants such as Norplant as their contraceptive method are less likely to have a subsequent pregnancy than are their counterparts who use oral contraceptives (Hollander, 1995b).

Implants' apparent disadvantages include the fact that, like the pill, they provide no protection against sexually transmitted diseases. Insertion and removal must be done by a doctor in a minor surgical procedure; removal can be difficult if the implants were placed too far beneath the skin. Some users experience inflammation or infection of the insertion site and thus need to have the implants removed (Remez, 1996). Side effects can include an irregular menstrual pattern, breast tenderness, and depression.

A **progestin injection** has also been developed (Westfall, Main, and Barnard, 1996). Depo-Provera is the one most commonly used in the United States. There are two types of injectable contraceptives: One is injected at 1-month intervals, and the other is injected at 3-month intervals. The 1-month injection contains an estrogen and a progestin, while the 3-month injection contains only progestin. Injectable contraceptives are very effective; the probability of pregnancy among typical users is only 0.3%. Side effects, including menstrual irregularity, are similar to those of Norplant; weight gain seems to be somewhat greater than with Norplant. Disadvantages include lack of protection against sexually transmitted diseases, significant drops in high-density lipoprotein (HDL) cholesterol levels, and decreases in bone density for long-term users, especially if they smoke. Although there was once a concern that Depo-Provera might increase the risk of breast and other cancers, a number of international studies have found the risk to be minimal or nonexistent (Hatcher et al., 1998).

In a study of 965 university students on their knowledge of Norplant and Depo-Provera, researchers found that most knew little about the implants and injections. Higher levels of knowledge coincided with the greater likelihood of future use of both methods of contraceptives. Overall, the study revealed a need to educate the public on the benefits of these contraceptive devices, which are largely underutilized (Sawyer and Pinciaro, 1998).

A **vaginal contraceptive ring** is a flexible, transparent ring about 2.1 inches in diameter that is inserted into the vagina. It contains a combination of estrogen and progestin and releases these continuously at a low dose for 1 month. A woman must insert a new ring every month. A vaginal ring is about 98% effective against pregnancy, but it offers no protection against STDs. Side effects can include vaginal discharge, vaginitis, and irritation. Vaginal rings are similar to oral contraceptives with regard to increased risk factors, and thus a woman must have a prescription to obtain one.

The **contraceptive patch** is a patch applied weekly to either the buttocks, abdomen, upper torso, back, or outer upper arm. It releases hormones every 24 hours and must be reapplied on the same day of each week for three consecutive weeks. The fourth week is patch-free. The patch has a 99% effectiveness rate but, like other hormonal contraceptives, does not protect against STDs. The most common side effects are breast tenderness, headache, patch-site irri-

The Abortion Pill

After first being approved for use by the French in 1988, the drug formerly known as RU-486 was approved for use in the United States by the Food and Drug Administration (FDA) in 2000. Mifepristone, marketed as Mifeprex, is a drug used for the termination of early pregnancy, defined as 49 days or less from the beginning of the last menstrual period. It has not been approved for use as a "morning-after pill" or as a means to end pregnancy after 49 days (or 7 weeks after the start of the last period).

Mifeprex works by blocking production of the hormone progesterone, which is necessary to maintain a pregnancy. The FDA-approved regimen requires three visits to a doctor's office; they can begin as soon as the woman becomes pregnant. During the first visit, she takes three tablets of Mifeprex. Two days later, she visits the doctor to take two pills of a prostaglandin called misoprostol, which helps the uterus expel the embryo. A third visit to the doctor's office or clinic is required 12 days later to confirm that the pregnancy has been terminated (U.S. Department of Health and Human Services, 2000).

Nearly all women using Mifeprex experience at least one of its side effects, which include bleeding, cramps, and nausea. Bleeding and spotting usually occur for 9 to 16 days, and about 1 in 100 women experiences bleeding heavy enough to require a surgical procedure to stop it (U.S. Department of Health and Human Services, 2000).

Mifeprex can be distributed only through qualified doctors and will not be available through pharmacies (Center for Drug Evaluation and Research, 2000). To be qualified, doctors must be able to accurately determine the duration of a pregnancy, detect whether it is an ectopic (tubal) pregnancy, and verify that they will be able to provide surgical intervention in case of an incomplete abortion or severe bleeding.

More than 620,000 European woman have used mifepristone since its approval in France. It has also been approved in the United Kingdom and Sweden (U.S. Department of Health and Human Services, 2000).

---

tation, and nausea. Because hormonal contraceptives are not suited for everyone and risks are elevated for certain individuals, a doctor must prescribe a contraceptive patch.

The **intrauterine system (IUS)** is inserted into the uterus and releases very small amounts of progestin continuously for up to 5 years. When a woman has an IUS, her cervical mucus becomes thicker, which makes it more difficult for sperm to enter the uterine cavity. An IUS also suppresses the cyclic growth of the endometrium and, even if an ovum became fertilized, it would not be able to implant in the endometrium. The effectiveness of the IUS is similar to that of the pill. Side effects include bleeding between periods, headaches, breast tenderness, and nausea. These typically occur only during the first months of use. A broader description of how intrauterine devices operate in general is presented later in this chapter.

VAGINAL SPERMICIDES

Spermicides, or chemicals that kill sperm, come in the form of contraceptive foam, suppository, cream, jelly, and, most recently, film. They work in two ways: (1) by blocking the entrance to the uterus and (2) by immobilizing the sperm. To be most effective, they must be inserted in the very back of the vagina,

progestin implant   A capsule containing progestin that is implanted under the skin and can remain in place for several years to prevent pregnancy.

progestin injection   An injection of progestin to prevent pregnancy.

vaginal contraceptive ring   A flexible, transparent ring that is inserted into the vagina and releases a combination of estrogen and progestin continuously at a low dose for 1 month.

contraceptive patch   A patch applied weekly to either the buttocks, abdomen, upper torso, back, or outer upper arm that releases hormones every 24 hours to prevent pregnancy.

Intrauterine system (IUS)   A contraceptive device that is inserted into the uterus and releases very small amounts of progestin continuously for up to 5 years.

spermicides   Chemicals that are toxic to sperm and used as a contraceptive in the form of foam, suppository, cream, jelly, or film.

over the cervix, not more than 5–15 minutes before ejaculation. Spermicides lose their effectiveness within about an hour, so they must be reapplied each time intercourse is repeated.

The effectiveness of spermicides varies greatly; it has been estimated that the average failure rate is 26% for typical use and 6% for correct use at every act of intercourse over the course of a year (Hatcher et al., 1998). Foam can be used alone because it spreads more evenly and blocks the cervix more adequately than other spermicides. Creams and jellies are usually used in conjunction with a diaphragm, cervical cap, or condom.

Vaginal contraceptive film (VCF) is a newer product; once the transparent 2-inch square is inserted, it dissolves into a gel over the cervix. It is less messy than foams and jellies, which usually create some vaginal discharge, and it seems less irritating for those people who have an allergic reaction to other forms of spermicides.

In addition to being available without a prescription, spermicides, especially those with nonoxynol-9, have the benefit of providing moderate protection against some bacterial STDs. However, they do not protect against HIV and, because they can irritate vaginal tissues, may even increase the risk (Hatcher et al., 1998). Both men and women may experience burning or other adverse reactions to the chemicals, including urinary tract infections in some women, especially if the spermicide is used with a diaphragm. Allergic responses can sometimes be alleviated by switching to another type or brand of spermicide.

INTRAUTERINE DEVICES

The **intrauterine device (IUD),** is made of plastic and sometimes metal; it is placed in the uterus to prevent pregnancy. IUDs alter the chemical environment in the uterus and inhibit fertilization; they also interfere with the implantation of fertilized eggs.

The IUD must be inserted by a physician. He or she loads the IUD in an inserter that resembles a plastic straw and threads it through the cervical canal and into the uterine cavity. The IUD is unwound into a straight line while in the inserter but resumes its former shape when released in the uterus. A thin plastic thread extends from the lower end of the IUD through the cervical canal and into

the upper vagina. The physician trims the thread to about 1 or 1.5 inches long. Periodically, the woman checks the length of the thread to make sure that the IUD is still in place.

IUDs were quite popular in the United States in the late 1960s and early 1970s. In the mid-1970s, however, information began to appear about a high incidence of pelvic infections and infertility and even some deaths among users of a type of IUD called the Dalkon Shield. A number of lawsuits were filed against the manufacturer, and the Dalkon Shield was withdrawn from the market. Other types of IUDs, such as the Lippes Loop, the Copper 7, and the Copper T, had much better safety records, but because of the widespread publicity about the Dalkon Shield, as well as occasional medical problems with other IUDs, women became increasingly apprehensive.

IUD manufacturers were concerned about expensive lawsuits and insurance costs and withdrew all but one type, the hormone-releasing Progestasert, from the market (Forrest, 1986). In 1989, another IUD, the Copper-T 380A, or ParaGard, was approved for use. It has more copper than the earlier Copper 7 or Copper T, which increases its effectiveness (Klitsch, 1988b). A copper-containing IUD is also sometimes used as a form of emergency contraception by women who have had unprotected sexual intercourse (Grossman and Grossman, 1994). Researchers have found that copper IUDs are not associated with an increased risk of tubal infertility and may in fact be among the safest, most effective, and least expensive reversible contraceptives available (Hubacher, Lara-Ricalde, Taylor, Guerra-Infante, and Guzman-Rodriguez, 2001).

IUDs are more reliable than the pill; they have a failure rate of 2.5% for women who can retain them (Kost et al., 1991; Reinisch and Beasley, 1990). Once an IUD is inserted, it requires no attention except periodic checking of the string to make sure it has not been expelled. The hormone-releasing Progestasert has to be replaced every year; the Copper-T 380A can remain in the uterus for 10 years (Hatcher et al., 1999).

The spontaneous expulsion rate is about 7% for women who have never been pregnant and about 3% for women who have had children (Reinisch and Beasley, 1990). Other potential disadvantages of IUDs include a heavier menstrual flow, stronger cramps, and a slightly increased risk of pelvic inflammatory disease (PID). In addition, IUDs do not protect against STDs. The risk of serious PID might be lowered by careful selection of users, meticulousness in insertion of the device, and close monitoring for early signs of infection (Petitti, 1992). If an IUD is in place when a pregnancy is diagnosed, there is a significant chance of spontaneous abortion.

BARRIER METHODS

Some of the earliest forms of contraception were barrier methods designed to prevent the meeting of sperm and ovum. The condom was in use as early as the sixteenth century in Italy, primarily to provide protection against syphilis. Reusable diaphragms and cervical caps were in use in Europe in the 1800s (Hatcher et al., 1998).

Although condoms used with vaginal spermicides are more effective than other barrier methods in preventing pregnancy, all barrier methods are less effective than hormonal methods or IUDs. However, they have few adverse side effects, and they offer some protection against STDs, especially when used with vaginal spermicides. When used correctly, latex condoms can provide protection against HIV (Hatcher et al., 1998). Barrier methods may increase the risk of urinary tract infections in women (Althaus, 1997; Hollander, 1996a).

Condoms

The **condom** is usually made of thin, strong latex rubber or, less frequently, of polyurethane or natural membranes. It is placed over the end of the erect penis and then unrolled to enclose the penile shaft. Condoms come in different styles and colors. Some have a teat on the end to receive the ejaculate. If the condom doesn't have this feature, it can be unrolled on the penis so as to leave a half-inch space at the end to receive the semen. One style has an adhesive to seal the top of the condom to the penis, thus preventing leakage of semen. Other models come packaged singly in fluid, which provides lubrication and allows the penis to be inserted into the vagina easily. If a condom is not lubricated, a contraceptive jelly or cream may be used to aid penetration and to prevent the condom from tearing on insertion. Vaseline, baby oil, and other petroleum- or oil-based products should never be used, because they cause the condom to deteriorate.

The failure rate of condoms used alone as a contraceptive has been calculated at about 14% (Hatcher et al., 1999). When failure occurs, it is due to one or more of several reasons: (1) The condom has a hole in it, (2) it ruptures, or (3) it slips off. The most common reason for failure of condoms is slipping off the shaft of the penis during either intercourse or withdrawal, allowing the semen to leak out (Althaus, 1992). Slippage is more likely when additional lubrication is used (Trussell, Warner, and Hatcher, 1992). To prevent leakage or the condom's slipping off, users should hold on to the top of the condom when the penis is withdrawn. Educational programs would help ensure that more people know how to use a condom correctly (D. Cohen, Dent, and MacKinnon, 1991).

If a condom and a spermicidal foam, jelly, or cream are used together, the failure rate among typical users is about 2.5%. This level of efficacy compares favorably with the failure rate among typical users of oral contraceptives (Kestelman and Trussell, 1991).

Since the onset of the AIDS epidemic, the use of condoms has increased significantly, especially among young men (Sonenstein, Pleck, and Ku, 1989). Condoms are sometimes used in addition to other methods of birth control to prevent the spread of AIDS (Santelli, Davis, Celentano, Crump, and Burwell, 1995). Usage rates are still much too low, however. Recent findings show that women adopting long-term hormonal contraceptive methods decrease their use of condoms and increase their risk of contracting HIV/AIDS and other STDs (Cushman et al., 1998). A national AIDS behavioral survey in 1991 indicated that only 17% of men with multiple sex partners and 13% with high-risk sexual partners use condoms all the time (R. Turner, 1993). In another study of patients at an STD clinic in Baltimore, men who had had more than four partners in the previous year were less likely to use condoms than those who had had fewer partners, and women age 20 or

intrauterine device (IUD) A device that is inserted into the uterus and worn there as a means of preventing pregnancy.

condom A latex rubber sheath worn over the penis to prevent sperm from being ejaculated into the vagina; also prevents venereal disease.

older were less likely to use condoms than were women younger than 20. Only 17% of the men and 15% of the women had used condoms during their last sexual intercourse (S. Edwards, 1992a). A study of 210 undergraduate men and women on the association between dating relationships and condom use found that the length of the relationship was the only factor that independently predicted condom use. More serious and committed relationships and higher levels of love were associated with less condom use and a higher risk of contracting STDs (Civic, 1999).

Condoms have been widely promoted as the best method, except abstinence, of preventing the spread of STDs. The type and quality of the condom used are important. For example, lambskin condoms, often preferred for their sensitivity, allow the leakage of AIDS, herpes, and hepatitis B viruses through the membrane itself. Syphilis and gonorrhea bacteria are too large to pass through. A latex condom does not allow leakage of small viral organisms unless the condom is torn or improperly used. According to findings from a New Zealand study involving family planning clinic clients, condoms break, slip, or leak during active intercourse 11% of the time. All told, 40% of the clients reported at least one instance of a condom break, slip, or leak. These problems were more common among couples who were young or relatively inexperienced in using condoms. Oral and anal sex were 4.2 times more likely than vaginal intercourse to result in a condom break and 2.6 times more likely to result in a slip. Vigorous sex was perceived by respondents to have been the cause of some condom breaks. Vaginal dryness was mentioned as a cause of breakage in some cases, and tearing by fingernails was the cause in other instances. Leaving the condom on too long was the most frequently mentioned explanation for a condom slip. A condom was more likely to break or slip if the respondent reported that it was either too small or too large (P. Donovan, 1994). Dr. Gerald Bernstein, who worked on a government-funded condom evaluation, said, "Using condoms is not what people are talking about when they say 'safe sex.' It may be safer sex, but I think it's a misnomer to say condoms are 'safe' sex" (Parachini, 1987).

A female condom is somewhat like a polyurethane plastic bag with a flexible ring at the closed end and another at the open end. The upper ring helps with insertion and keeps the upper end of the condom in place over the cervix; the lower ring keeps the condom from being pushed inside the vagina and also covers part of the vulva, thus protecting a larger genital area from STDs than does the male condom. A female condom (marketed under the brand name Reality) was approved by the FDA in 1993 to reduce the risk of unwanted pregnancy and the transmission of STDs, including HIV. Effectiveness rates for the female condom range from 79% to 95%. Worldwide acceptability data indicate that women are often eager to try a device that is under their control. The vast majority of studies report that partners have acquiesced to its use and sometimes have preferred the device to a male condom (Gollub, Stein, and El-Sadr, 1995).

Diaphragms

The **diaphragm** is a thick, dome-shaped rubber latex, cap stretched over a collapsible metal ring, designed to cover the cervical opening. It comes in a variety of sizes and must be fitted to each woman by a physician. A snug fit is especially important, since the diaphragm's effectiveness as a contraceptive depends on its forming an impenetrable shield over the entrance to the uterus. If the fit is not right, the sperm can get around the edges of the diaphragm and enter the cervix. For this reason, the largest diaphragm a woman can wear comfortably is advised, since sexual excitement causes the back portion of the vagina to enlarge (Masters and Johnson, 1966). After childbirth, a woman always requires a larger diaphragm. Also, a size change may be in order whenever a woman gains or loses 15 pounds.

To add to the diaphragm's effectiveness as a contraceptive, a spoonful of spermicidal cream or jelly is smeared in the cup fitting against the cervix and about the rim to create a protective seal. For additional protection, foam may be inserted into the vagina after the diaphragm is in place and before each act of intercourse (Tyrer, 1984). When fitted and placed correctly, and when used in conjunction with a spermicide, the failure rate is 6% (Hatcher et al., 1999). Overall, however, the actual failure rate for typical users is 20% (due primarily to incorrect placement or dislodgement during intercourse). The diaphragm should not be removed until at least 6 hours after intercourse.

Cervical Caps

After nearly a decade-long delay, the FDA finally approved use of the **cervical cap** in 1988 (Klitsch, 1988a). The cervical cap is a small, thimble-shaped rubber barrier that fits tightly across the cervix and prevents sperm from entering the uterus. Like the diaphragm, it is used with a spermicide and inserted shortly before intercourse. It is approximately as effective as the diaphragm for women who have not had children, with a 9% failure rate for correct use and a 20% failure rate for typical use. For women who have had children, the failure rate is higher: 26% for correct use and 40% for typical use (Hatcher et al., 1999). Because initial use may cause changes in cervical cells, wearers should get a Pap smear after the first 3 months. The cap is recommended only for women with a normal Pap smear.

STERILIZATION

An estimated 15 million women ages 15–44 in the United States have chosen **sterilization** as their means of birth control. This is 1.4 times the number

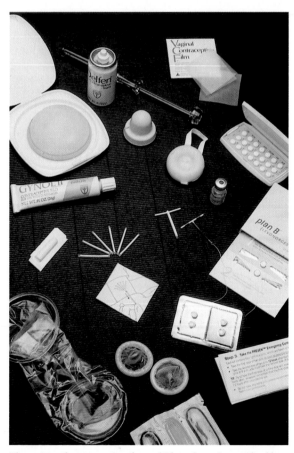

The variety of contraceptives from which to choose is considerable. How does one make the best choice? What are the risks of pregnancy and the health risks associated with each type of contraception?

that had chosen the pill (U.S. Bureau of the Census, 1999a). More women have been sterilized than men, although the acceptance of vasectomy is increasing.

Vasectomy

Male sterilization, or **vasectomy,** has become increasingly popular as a means of birth control. It is a simple operation, requiring only 15–30 minutes in a doctor's office, is relatively inexpensive, and is effective in 90% of cases (Hatcher et al., 1999). It involves either cutting and tying or cauterizing the vas deferens and is performed under local anesthetic (Althaus, 1995).

When failure occurs, it is due to (1) a spontaneous rejoining of the two severed ends of the vas deferens (the duct that carries sperm from the testicle to the penis), (2) a failure on the part of the doctor to tie an accessory vas (some men have three or four), or (3) intercourse without using other contraceptives while there are still residual sperm in the tubes. As a means of fertility control, vasectomy is usually effective, is less costly and less complicated than tubal ligation (female sterilization), and has fewer long-term health risks. Yet U.S. men are less likely than women to seek sterilization (Forste, Tanfer, and Tedrow, 1995).

There are a number of misconceptions regarding vasectomies. A vasectomy does not involve **castration,** which is the removal of the testicles. With a vasectomy, the man continues to ejaculate semen, but it contains no sperm. His physical ability to have sexual relations is in no way affected; he still has erections, orgasms, and ejaculation as usual. In addition, his voice, body hair, musculature, beard growth, and so on remain unchanged. And he still produces male

diaphragm   A thick, dome-shaped rubber latex cap that is stretched over a collapsible metal ring, designed to cover the cervical opening to prevent sperm from entering the uterus.

cervical cap   A small thimble-shaped rubber barrier that fits over the cervix and prevents the sperm from entering the uterus.

sterilization   The process of rendering a person infertile, by performing either a vasectomy in the male or tubal ligation in the female.

vasectomy   Male sterilization whereby the vas deferens is cut and tied to prevent the sperm from being ejaculated out of the penis.

castration   Removal of the testicles.

hormones that are released by the testicles into the bloodstream. Research indicates no adverse health consequences of vasectomy. It appears unlikely to raise men's chances of developing either prostate or testicular cancer (Hatcher et al., 1999).

Vasectomy should be considered permanent, since the chances of rejoining the vas deferens through surgery (vasovasostomy) are uncertain. The effectiveness of microsurgery to reverse the vasectomy depends on the type of vasectomy and the skill of the surgeon, but it can result in pregnancy rates of at least 50% and in the return of sperm to the ejaculate of 90% of the men (Hatcher et al., 1999). Some men who decide to have a vasectomy have some of their sperm frozen in a sperm bank. An overwhelming majority of males who have had vasectomies report they are glad they did and would recommend it to others.

Tubal Ligation

Tubal ligation is female sterilization by severing or closing the fallopian tubes, or both, so that mature egg cells and sperm cannot pass through the tube. Since the ovaries and the secretion of female hormones are in no way disturbed, there is no change in the woman's physique, menstrual cycle, sexual interest, or sexual capacity. In most cases, her interest in sex and her sexual responsiveness improve because the fear of unwanted pregnancy has been removed. Women who have undergone tubal ligation also have a reduced risk of contracting ovarian cancer (S. Edwards, 1994; Rind, 1992c).

Depending on the method of ligation and the surgeon's skill, tubal ligation is reversible in 60–80% of cases, but reversal is not easily accomplished since it requires a second major operation (Hatcher et al., 1999). Most women who request re-

versal were sterilized young and subsequently divorced and remarried ("Requests," 1984).

The most widely used method of tubal ligation is **laparoscopy.** With this method, the physician introduces a tubular instrument through the abdominal wall, usually through the navel, and closes the fallopian tubes with tubal rings or a spring-locked clip, or through electrocautery.

Existing literature indicates that approximately 0.8–3.7% of women will get pregnant during the first year after the operation, depending on the method of ligation (Hatcher et al., 1999). When pregnancy occurs, it is due to one of three reasons: (1) The woman had an undetected pregnancy at the time of the operation, (2) the surgery was performed improperly, or (3) the tubes reopen as a result of the body's healing process. Younger women have higher failure rates (Hatcher et al., 1999).

Women in the United States who are sterilized at age 30 or younger and those who obtain the procedure postpartum are twice as likely as others to regret the decision over the next 14 years. While this represents a significant portion of those sterilized, the majority are happy with the outcome and have few regrets about their decision (Hillis, 1999).

BIRTH CONTROL WITHOUT DEVICES

Some people, for religious or philosophical reasons, do not want to use artificial means of birth control. Some advantages of "natural" methods are that they are free and do not require a trip to the drugstore or the doctor's office. However, they are much less reliable than any other method of birth control, and they provide no protection against STDs.

Fertility Awareness Methods

The **rhythm method,** or calendar method, of birth control relies on timing coitus so that it occurs only during the so-called safe period of the month—that period when the woman is most likely to be infertile. Although authorities differ in their time estimates, we can say with reasonable certainty that the ovum can be fertilized up until 48 hours after it is released and that the sperm can fertilize an ovum up until 48 hours after being ejaculated. However, to be safe, we should add an extra 24 hours to these figures. The average woman ovulates 14 days before her next menstrual period, with a common

tubal ligation Female sterilization by severing and/or closing the fallopian tubes so that the ovum cannot pass down the tube.

laparoscopy Sterilization procedure whereby a tubular instrument is passed through the abdominal wall and the fallopian tubes are severed and/or closed.

rhythm method A method of birth control whereby the couple have intercourse only during those times of the menstrual cycle when the woman is least likely to get pregnant.

range of 12–16 days. A few women ovulate regularly outside of this common range; other women ovulate outside of this range occasionally. Some have very irregular ovulation. For these reasons, for some women, it is difficult to detect a completely "safe period" of the month when pregnancy can't occur. The failure rate during any 1 year is estimated at around 26% (E. F. Jones and Forrest, 1992).

A woman can use a variety of physical signs (such as consistency of cervical mucus or body temperature) and the calendar (after recording six menstrual cycles) to determine when she ovulates. Careful attention to one's individual cycle, by whatever means, can only minimize the possibility of pregnancy. Figure 11.1 illustrates the schedules of fertile and infertile periods of women on regular 26- and 31-day cycles and the schedule of a woman whose cycle varies from 26 to 31 days. Since the woman whose schedule is irregular never knows

exactly when ovulation occurs or when her next period will be, she is safer to abstain for 15 days instead of the usual 10. A woman whose cycle is irregular from 24 to 33 days can never find any safe period except during menstruation. Of course, these are only statistical calculations. As has been mentioned, one can't really be sure of any infertile period during any cycle. As can be seen in Figure 11.1, possible times for intercourse are limited, especially on the irregular cycle.

There are, however, two principal methods by which couples can improve on the rhythm method. One is the basal body temperature method. This method relies on the fact that body temperature rises a fraction of a degree at the time of ovulation and remains higher for the rest of the cycle. The woman records her temperature daily, looking for the rise. However, such a temperature rise can occur 72 hours prior to ovulation and up to 72 hours

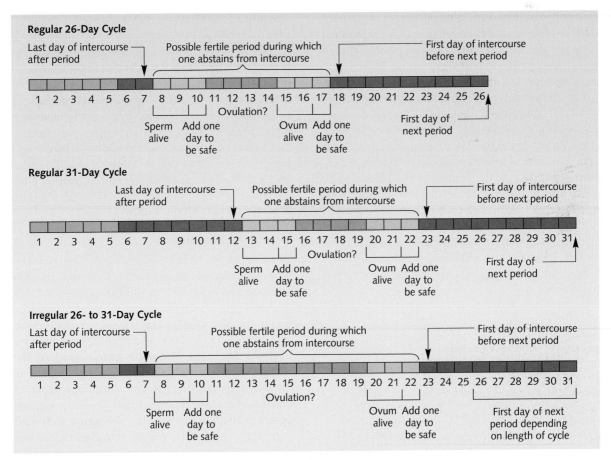

Figure 11.1 Fertile and Infertile Periods During a 26-Day, 31-Day, and Irregular (26- to 31-Day) Cycle

afterward. This method is not specific in pinpointing ovulation, but it indicates that ovulation is in process and that, by the third sustained day of the rise, it is in fact complete.

The cervical mucus ovulation detection method relies on cervical mucus as the predictor of ovulation. Sometime before the middle of the menstrual cycle, cervical mucus becomes detectable at the vulva when follicular estrogen rises. At this point, the mucus is sticky and gummy and appears yellow or white. With progressive ripening of the follicle, the mucus becomes increasingly slippery, clear, and stringy, like raw egg white. The vagina becomes increasingly lubricated. The last day of lubrication is called the "peak" and is followed no more than 24 hours later by ovulation. Abstinence is required from the first day of mucus discharge until the fourth day after the peak (H. Klaus, 1984). There are also a number of ovulation predictor kits on the market that attempt to pinpoint the time of ovulation. The possibility of intercourse and the risk of pregnancy during unsafe times is so great that the method cannot be considered ideal for most couples who want reliable contraception (Trussell and Grummer-Strawn, 1990).

These fertility awareness methods can be helpful as contraceptive techniques, and they can be helpful in conceiving. Physicians often advise couples who are having difficulty conceiving to use a combination of the basal body temperature method and the cervical mucus method. By having intercourse daily when the woman is most likely to be ovulating, a couple can greatly enhance the likelihood of conception. The probability of conception is highest on the day of ovulation and drops sharply immediately thereafter. Because it is difficult to determine exactly when ovulation takes place, the possibility of conception is increased when intercourse occurs daily during the most probable times (Hollander, 1996d).

Some people think that sperm can be flushed from the vagina by **douching** with water or some other liquid. However, douching is not effective as a means of contraception, because (1) sperm move very quickly and have probably already entered the cervix by the time the woman begins douching and (2) the jet of water may propel sperm still in the vagina up into the cervix.

Coitus Interruptus

Coitus interruptus refers to the practice of withdrawing the penis from the vagina before ejaculation occurs. Although this method is better than nothing, its success depends on a high degree of self-control on the part of the man. When sexually aroused, the normal man reaches a point beyond which ejaculatory control is impossible. If he doesn't withdraw in time, he will ejaculate whether he wants to or not. Also, before orgasm, the male discharges a small amount of lubrication fluid that has been secreted by the Cowper's glands, although he is not aware of when this preejaculate is discharged. Because this fluid often contains sperm cells that have been residing in the urethra, the sperm may be deposited before the man withdraws. Even though the sperm count is low and fertilization is less likely than with actual orgasm, it can occur. Depending on the care and timing of the man, withdrawal has a failure rate ranging from 4% to 19% (Hatcher et al., 1999). The greatest disadvantage to coitus interruptus is its interference with the sexual satisfaction and pleasure of both the man and the woman.

Noncoital Stimulation

Couples can use techniques of stimulation to orgasm other than intercourse. Mutual masturbation has been used for years as a substitute for intercourse. If the man gets semen on his fingers and introduces sperm into the vaginal canal, however, conception can occur. Interfemoral stimulation is a method whereby the man places his penis between the woman's closed thighs and rubs back and forth along the length of the clitoris. Climax may be reached in this way, but if the male ejaculates near the vaginal opening, there is a possibility the sperm may find their way inside. Oral-genital stimulation is sometimes used, not only as a method of precoital love play but also as a technique of arousal to orgasm.

douching Squirting liquid containing vinegar or another substance into the vagina; sometimes used to try to wash out sperm after intercourse.

coitus interruptus Withdrawal of the penis from the vagina prior to ejaculation; used as an attempt at birth control.

abortion The expulsion of the fetus. Can be either spontaneous or induced.

CHOOSING A METHOD OF CONTRACEPTION

The ideal contraceptive would be (1) 100% effective; (2) inexpensive; (3) convenient to use, without interfering with lovemaking; and (4) without any risk or adverse side effects. Currently, no one method meets all these criteria. Even with contraceptive use, about 1 in 10 women experience an accidental pregnancy. Inconsistent and incorrect use are the main reasons for this high level (Tew and Kirchgaessner, 1999). In deciding on a method, couples might consult their physician, weigh all factors, and make an informed decision.

What contraceptive methods are currently in use among women in the United States? The National Center for Health Statistics collected nationally representative data on contraceptive practices among women ages 15–44. The results of the survey are shown in Table 11.1. Sterilization was the most popular contraceptive method among married women and their husbands. The pill was the second most popular method, and the condom was third (U.S. Bureau of the Census, 1999a).

Contraceptive status and method of choice of never-married and previously married women differed sharply from those of married women. Sexually active, never-married women were less likely than married women to practice contraception and were more likely to choose the pill when they did. Previously married women were also less likely than married women to practice contraception but, when using a method, were more likely than either married or never-married women to use an IUD.

Table 11.1 Number and Percentage Distribution of Women Ages 15–44 Practicing Contraception, by Current Method, According to Marital Status

	Number (in Thousands) and Percentage			
Method	**Total**	**Never Married**	**Currently Married**	**Formerly Married**
	60,201	**22,679**	**29,673**	**7,849**
Sterilization (male and female)	24.8	4.8	37.0	36.7
Total sterile	29.7	6.9	43.2	45.1
Pill	17.3	20.4	15.6	14.6
IUD	0.5	0.3	0.7	0.4
Diaphragm	1.2	0.5	1.8	0.9
Condom	13.1	13.9	13.3	10.1
Rhythm/periodic abstinence	1.5	0.6	2.3	0.7
Other methods*	3.9	4.6	3.3	3.9
Seeking pregnancy	4.0	1.5	6.4	2.1
Nonsurgically sterile	1.7	1.1	2.0	2.2
Nonusers				
Never had intercourse	10.9	28.9		
No intercourse in past month	6.2	11.5	0.5	12.7
Had intercourse in past month	5.2	6.4	4.2	5.7
Pregnant, postpartum	4.6	3.1	6.4	1.9
Withdrawal	2.0	1.5	2.3	1.8

Note: Data from *Statistical Abstract of the United States, 1999* (p. 84) by U.S. Bureau of the Census, 1999, Washington, DC: U.S. Government Printing Office.

*Includes implants, injectables, morning-after pill, suppository, and less frequently used methods.

ABORTION

If contraceptives are not used or a given method fails, then a woman or a couple is faced with an unplanned pregnancy. One of the alternatives is **abortion.** Abortion raises some difficult questions to which there are no simple answers. Abortion issues may be divided into four categories, which are discussed in the following sections: (1) legal, (2) moral, (3) social and realistic, and (4) psychological and personal.

Legal Considerations

Abortion law is rather complex in the United States. On January 22, 1973, the U.S. Supreme Court ruled that a state could not inhibit or restrict a woman's right to obtain an abortion during the first trimester of pregnancy (the first 12 weeks) and that the decision to have an abortion was the woman's own in consultation with her doctor (*Doe v. Bolton*, 1973; *Roe v. Wade*, 1973; Sarvis and Rodman, 1974). The major ground for the Court's decision was the woman's right to privacy.

The Court further declared that during the second trimester of pregnancy (weeks 13–26)—when abortion is more dangerous—"a state may regulate the abortion procedure to the extent that the regulation relates to the preservation and protection of maternal health" (*Roe v. Wade*, 1973). Reasonable regulation might include outlining the qualifications or licensure of the person who performs abortions or the licensing of the facility where the abortion is performed. The Court went on to say that the state's interest in protecting the life of the fetus arises only after viability (after 24–28 weeks, when the fetus is potentially capable of living outside the mother's womb). However, the state "may go so far as to proscribe [forbid] abortion during that period except when it is necessary to preserve the life or health of the mother" (J. P. Reed, 1975, p. 205). The reasons the Court rejected the state's interest in protecting human life from the moment of conception were (1) that the "unborn have never been recognized in the law as persons in the whole sense" and (2) that the rights extended to the unborn, in law, are contingent upon live birth, so (3) a state's interest in protecting fetal life cannot override the woman's right to privacy (Sarvis and Rodman, 1974).

In 1997, Congress passed the Hyde Amendment, sharply restricting the use of federal Medicaid funding to pay for abortions for low-income women. This ban on federal funding of abortions has been renewed every year since. The Supreme Court has also ruled that a state may require an unmarried minor who seeks an abortion to notify or obtain the consent of her parents; if she does not wish to do so, she must be able to obtain permission from a judge ("The Supreme Court," 1990). The judge's authorization is based on a determination either that the minor is mature enough to make her own decision or that it is in the minor's best interest to have the abortion without informing her parents (Rodman, 1991).

This decision, which took effect in 1982 and was upheld in 1990, has had wide-ranging implications. Ideally, all unmarried minors should get parental advice about their pregnancy. But it is precisely because of the lack of good family relationships that minors refuse to talk to their parents. Agencies in three states report that 20–55% of their minor patients are going to court rather than confiding in their parents ("The Supreme Court," 1990). In Minnesota, which requires minors to notify both parents or to get permission of a judge to have an abortion, 43% of minors used the court bypass rather than tell their parents (Blum, Resnick, and Stark, 1990). This puts these minors through an emotionally difficult and sometimes traumatic experience.

Based on a nationally representative sample of more than 1,500 unmarried minors who had gotten an abortion, the most common reasons given for not telling their parents were wanting to preserve their relationship with their parents and wanting to protect the parents from stress and conflict. Of those who did not tell their parents, 30% had experienced violence in their family, feared that violence would occur, or were afraid of being forced to leave home (Henshaw and Kost, 1992). Another study, this one of Black urban teenagers, revealed that most adolescents voluntarily told one or both of their parents, usually their mother, when they became pregnant, and most involved their mother in their decisions. Even when a young woman did not confide in either parent, she generally sought support from a specific person, usually an adult who had served as a parent surrogate. If the respondent did not turn to her mother, it was often because they did not live together (Zabin, Hirsch, Emerson, and Raymond, 1992). Even if an adolescent did not confide in an important adult in her life as soon as she suspected she was pregnant, she was likely to do so at some time between the pregnancy test and her final decision.

In 1989, the U.S. Supreme Court agreed to hear a case brought to it by the state of Missouri (*Webster v. Reproductive Health Services,* 1989). The Court was asked to rule on four sections of a 1986 act passed by the Missouri legislature:

1. A preamble stating that "the life of each human begins at conception" and that state laws be interpreted to provide unborn children "with all the rights, privileges, and immunities available to other persons, citizens, and residents of this state," subject to the Constitution and the Court's precedents.

2. A prohibition on the use of public facilities or employees to perform abortions.

3. A prohibition on public funding of abortion counseling.

4. A requirement that physicians conduct viability tests prior to performing abortions.

In a 5–4 decision, the Court upheld the constitutionality of sections 2 and 4 of the Missouri act and returned to the states the right to place restrictions on abortion. The Court refused to acknowledge the constitutionality of the preamble and contended that it represented only a value judgment of the state of Missouri that did not restrict abortions in any way.

According to the Supreme Court, Missouri and other states may pass laws ensuring that public hospitals or other taxpayer-supported facilities not be "used for the purpose of performing or assisting an abortion not necessary to save the life of the mother." In addition, states may make it "unlawful for any public employee within the scope of his employment to perform or assist an abortion, not necessary to save the life of the mother." This latter ruling is not intended to direct the conduct of any physician or health care provider, private or public, but "is directed solely at those persons responsible for expending public funds" (*Webster v. Reproductive Health Services*, 1989). The Court did not declare illegal, as such, the performance of abortions in privately supported facilities by physicians who are paid privately. However, critics do point out that the decision severely restricts the availability of abortions to the poor.

One of the most controversial parts of the *Webster* decision is the rejection of the trimester provisions of *Roe v. Wade* (1973) and the acceptance of medical tests for viability as one possible substitute. According to the Court, a state may make it mandatory for medical tests to be performed on any fetus thought to be at least 20 weeks old to determine its viability before an abortion can be performed. The Court reaffirmed the provision in *Roe v. Wade* that states may pass laws regulating or proscribing abortion after viability "except where it is necessary . . . for the preservation of the life or health of the mother."

This decision has been criticized because, according to some, determination of viability is expensive, can be unreliable and inaccurate, and may pose significant health risks for both the pregnant woman and the fetus. Various tests can be done to find gestational age, fetal weight, and lung maturity. However, at 20 weeks of age, no fetus is viable or can be made viable. Tests of lung maturity cannot provide the necessary information until a fetus is 28–30 weeks old in gestational age; tests before this age are imprecise ("The Court Edges Away," 1989). Furthermore, the standard measure used by physicians to calculate the length of pregnancies is based on the woman's report of the onset of her last menstrual period. But using the first day of the last menstrual period as the beginning marker for terminated pregnancies is misleading because the calculations then include the 2 weeks that precede fertilization. Hence, the length of pregnancy is estimated by physicians as always 2 weeks more than the actual developmental age of the fetus (Santee and Henshaw, 1992).

In defending its position, the majority of the Court said, "We are satisfied that the requirement of these tests permissibly furthers the State's interest in protecting potential human life" (*Webster v. Reproductive Health Services*, 1989). Opponents argue that regardless of the tests' outcome the decision eliminates the woman's right to choose whether she will have an abortion.

Both right-to-choose and right-to-life advocates predicted that the Court's decision would lead to a 50-state battle to determine whether additional restrictions will be enacted. Faye Wattleton, then president of the Planned Parenthood Federation of America, commented, "Now a woman's access to abortion will become hostage to geography as states enact a patchwork of laws and regulations aimed at blocking abortions" (Dionne, 1989, p. 1). Archbishop John May, president of the National Conference of Catholic Bishops, observed, "The biggest winners today are the tiniest people of all—children within the womb" (Dionne, 1989, p. 1).

Another case heard by the U.S. Supreme Court was *Planned Parenthood of Southeastern Pennsylvania v. Casey* (1992). The Court reaffirmed the essential holding in *Roe v. Wade* that prior to fetal viability a woman has a constitutional right to obtain an abortion. After viability, a state may prohibit an abortion, but only if it provides exceptions when the woman's life or health is at risk. At the same time, however, the Court discarded *Roe*'s trimester framework, which severely restricted a state's power to regulate abortion in the early stages of pregnancy, stating that the trimester framework "undervalues" the state's interest in potential life, which exists throughout pregnancy. The Court held that the state may regulate abortion throughout pregnancy as long as it does not impose an "undue burden" on a woman's right to terminate her pregnancy. The Court defined "undue burden" as a regulation that "has the purpose or effect of placing a substantial obstacle in the path of a woman seeking an abortion of a nonviable fetus."

Applying the undue burden standard, the Court upheld several provisions of the Pennsylvania abortion law, including a 24-hour waiting period that follows completion of specific informed-consent requirements and reporting and record-keeping rules—provisions that were virtually identical to conditions the Court had declared unconstitutional just a few years earlier. The Court upheld the law's parental consent provision but struck down, as an undue burden, the requirement that a married woman notify her spouse of her intent to have an abortion ("Court Reaffirms *Roe* but Upholds Restrictions," 1992). The U.S. Supreme Court has agreed to hear other cases, so the stage has been set for further battles.

The most recent controversy in abortion law has been over late-term or partial-birth abortions. *Late-term* refers only to the time the abortion takes place, after week 26 and in the third trimester of pregnancy; *partial-birth* refers to the method used in aborting the fetus. Partial-birth abortions are performed in the second and third trimesters of pregnancy, through a procedure known as intact dilation and extraction, which involves inducing a breech delivery with a forceps (Abortion Law Homepage, 2000). In November of 2003, President George W. Bush signed into law a ban on partial-birth and late-term abortions. It permits no exceptions when a woman's health is at risk or a fetus has life-threatening disabilities. Supporters of the law have argued that this procedure is not so much abortion as infanticide, which is illegal. If the partial-birth delivery used in the procedure is indeed a "birth," then a person exists and has constitutional rights. Opponents of the law reject this idea and focus on the fact that other abortion procedures traditionally upheld by the Court can involve the delivery or partial delivery of a live but nonviable fetus that dies as a result of the procedure. They argue that these laws only serve to restrict a woman's right to an abortion (Sykes, 2000).

In sum, according to current Supreme Court rulings, states can regulate abortion in five ways: (1) ban elective abortions after the fetus is viable, (2) require parental consent or notice or a judge's bypass before a minor can obtain an abortion, (3) require informed consent or counseling before an abortion, (4) require certain kinds of record keeping for each state, and (5) require waiting periods, usually 24–48 hours, before an abortion.

Moral Considerations

Much of the controversy about abortion has centered on moral issues. For many individuals and religious denominations, abortion is wrong because it represents the murder of a human being. According to this point of view, the soul enters the body at the moment of conception, so the new life is immediately a human. The Christian Church in the centuries after Christ forbade abortion under all conditions from the beginning of pregnancy.

Opponents of this view argue that to say that a group of human cells, however highly differentiated at the early stages of growth, is a person is to stretch the point. These cells have neither consciousness nor any distinctly human characteristics and traits. Advocates of this view point to the teachings of the thirteenth-century theologian and philosopher Thomas Aquinas, who said that there was neither life nor ensoulment until the fetus moved, so abortion was not sinful in the first 16 weeks of pregnancy. Three centuries later, the Catholic Church fixed ensoulment at 40 days after conception, following Aristotle's teaching. Abortion during the first 40 days of pregnancy was not considered sinful until the First Vatican Council in 1869, when it was once more ruled that life begins at the time of conception and that abortion at any time is a grave sin. This view was reaffirmed by the Second Vatican Council and made official Catholic doctrine by Pope Paul VI in 1965.

Members of the right-to-life movement and others emphasize the right to life of the fetus and say that no individual or state should deprive the fetus of its constitutional and moral right to live. Legally, of course, the Supreme Court has never established the fact that the fetus is a person, enjoying full protection under the Constitution and the Bill of Rights. Right-to-choose proponents emphasize that the moral and legal rights of other parties must also be considered, not just those of the fetus. What about the rights of the mother, the father, and other family members (Finlay, 1981)? Should these lives be sacrificed for the sake of the fetus?

The Supreme Court ruling establishes the legal principle that the mother's rights take precedence, at least before viability. Obviously, the moral dilemmas raised by the abortion issue are not easy to solve (Allgeier, Allgeier, and Rywick, 1981; Silber, 1980).

Social Considerations

Those advocating the right to choose emphasize the fact that strict laws against abortion, such as those that permit abortion only when the mother's physical life is threatened, have never worked. A current example can be found in Ireland, where abortion law is very restrictive. The law forbids information about access to abortion and permits abortion only when a woman's life is threatened (directly or indirectly) by a pregnancy. Nonetheless, thousands of Irish women

The Supreme Court has repeatedly been asked to consider when life begins. Who has the right to decide when and if a pregnancy can be terminated? The dilemmas raised by the abortion issue are not easily solved by anyone.

travel to England, where abortion law is less restrictive, for abortions each year (Francome, 1992).

If a woman is determined not to have her baby, she may attempt, however foolishly (and sometimes futilely), to abort her own fetus. Or she may go to an unqualified person and get an illegal abortion that may threaten her life. Various estimates place the number of illegal abortions before 1967 at around 1 million per year, or about 20% of total pregnancies. Maternal death rates from illegal abortions in New York City were about 19 times higher than those from legal abortions. Legalized abortion, therefore, saves lives by reducing the number of illegal attempts (Guttmacher, 1983).

In reply to these social considerations, right-to-life groups emphasize their fears that without any restriction, except the individual woman and her conscience, an "abortion mentality" develops so that abortions become too commonplace. The majority of abortions today are not for medical reasons, but for personal, social, and economic reasons (Belsky, 1992). The highest abortion rate occurs among White women ages 18–19, followed by White women ages 20–24 (Henshaw, 1992). Women who live with a partner outside of marriage or who have no religious identification are 3½ to 4 times as

likely as women in the general population to have an abortion (Henshaw and Kost, 1996).

Most thoughtful advocates of abortion agree that it should be only a backup measure, not the primary method of birth control. They urge fuller use of contraceptives among all sexually active people.

Psychological and Personal Considerations

Right-to-life proponents have often pointed to the negative psychological effects on the woman who has had an abortion. But the incidence of psychological aftereffects is a major subject of dispute. Both sides cite facts to support their views. Those advocating the right to choose point to the fact that many women are far more depressed before the abortion is performed than they are afterward. One study found that depression and anxiety decreased after abortion (Rind, 1991). When abortions were illegal, much of the anxiety was over the illegality of the act, so these feelings have been eliminated. Other studies have shown that an abortion does not appear to have an adverse effect on women's self-esteem or psychological well-being (Klitsch, 1992a).

In contrast, right-to-life proponents point to the fact that some women do suffer psychological scars

A Preference for Males

The sex ratio among humans has consistently shown that slightly more males are born than females (the average being about 105 males to 100 females). However, several Asian countries show a significantly higher than average number of male births to female births. The cause of this disparity has been heavily debated, but many people believe the unusually high number of male births is due to a preference for male children over female children. Gender selection of a baby is made possible with technologies such as ultrasound, which reveals the gender of the fetus, followed by selective abortion. This gives humans the ability to change the natural sex ratio to favor males over females.

The debate over the reasons for the high male-to-female ratio has been very controversial in China, where the institution of a one-child policy at the end of the 1970s is believed by many to have caused an increase in female fetus abortions and female infanticide in order to assure that their one child is a boy (Secondi, 2002). Because of the perceived selective abortion problem, the government of China passed a law that bans gender identification before birth unless necessary for medical reasons. However, because the technology for gender identification of the fetus and abortion are both easily accessible, it is a difficult law to enforce. In addition, traditional values make it very important to many families to have a male child. For example, in traditional Chinese culture, family membership and economic cooperation, inheritance of property, and lines of authority were defined through males; even today, only a male child can continue the family line and fulfill duties in regards to ancestor worship; aging parents expect to be supported by male offspring, and male labor may be perceived as more valuable for agricultural families (Secondi, 2002). These values become more pressing when parents are only allowed one child.

Secondi (2002) examined the determinants of the biased sex ratio in rural China, with a focus on investigating whether the economic status of the parents affects the ratio of sons to daughters. He found that selective abortion and different treatment of boys and girls (e.g., boys getting more to eat) are likely to be the main sources of biased sex ratios, and that the unusually high ratio of boys to girls in China can be explained by parental behavior aimed at producing more male offspring than biologically normal. He found that first-born surviving children of lower-income parents were significantly more likely to be boys than girls. The desire to have sons (whether due to preferences or to financial considerations) seems equally widespread among rich and poor families, but first-born girls appear to be a luxury that higher-income parents are able to afford.

in the aftermath of an abortion. For this reason, abortion counseling, which assists the woman in working through her feelings ahead of time (and afterward if needed), is important. For some, abortion provides great relief with little if any disturbance; for others, the experience is upsetting. The key factor seems to be whether the woman wants an abortion or is reluctant to obtain one. Being refused an abortion and forced to bear an unwanted child can lead to psychological problems such as depression. But the woman who has health problems and has to have an abortion, or who is persuaded to have an abortion against her better judgment, is also likely to have negative psychological reactions. If the decision is the woman's, adverse psychological reactions are minimized.

INFERTILITY

It is estimated that over 9 million couples use infertility services (Centers for Disease Control and Prevention, 2002). For many couples, infertility treatment will be successful and they will be able to conceive and have a child.

Causes of Infertility

About 40% of infertility is a result of the male having problems. For a male to impregnate a woman, he must (1) be able to maintain an erection long enough to ejaculate sperm within the vagina, (2) have an unobstructed pathway through the vas deferens and the urethra, allowing the sperm and semen to pass through, (3) secrete semen in adequate amounts and with the right chemical composition to keep sperm alive and healthy and to transport it to the ovum, and (4) produce healthy sperm in sufficient numbers. Male infertility is caused by a number of psychological as well as physiological factors. The most common factor is impaired sperm production due to environmental toxins, heat, undescended testes, abnormal veins in the scrotum (varicocele), testicular atrophy, drugs (alcohol abuse, chronic marijuana use, and others), prolonged fever, and endocrine disorders affecting the production of sex hormones. Sometimes antibodies in the male or female are detrimental to sperm, or there is an obstruction in the seminal tract preventing the sperm from passing through. Defective delivery of sperm into the vagina may be due to functional or organic impotence or to premature ejaculation before penetration, or it may result from surgery to the bladder or prostate.

About 40% of infertility cases involve the woman. There are a number of causes of infertility in women (Ansbacher and Adler, 1988; Malinak and Wheeler, 1985), including the following: (1) disorders of the reproductive organs (ovaries, fallopian tubes, uterus, cervix); (2) vaginitis; (3) sexually transmitted diseases; (4) endocrine disorders of the pituitary, thyroid, ovaries, and adrenals; (5) systemic diseases such as diabetes mellitus; (6) genetic disorders; and (7) immunologic causes such as formation of antibodies detrimental to sperm. Women who smoke cigarettes also may have difficulty becoming pregnant when they wish to; the amount that they smoke appears to be related to the waiting time until conception. Research indicates that the median waiting time to achieve conception is approximately 1 month longer for women who smoke more than 10 cigarettes a day than for women who do not smoke (Hollander, 1996b). Age is also important to fertility: Fertility decreases gradually after age 35 and ceases at menopause.

About 20% of infertility is caused by factors that involve both partners. Negative factors include too frequent or infrequent intercourse, the use of petroleum jelly or another lubricant that damages the sperm, intercourse only during infertile periods of the month, and advanced age or poor health.

Infertility and Subjective Well-Being

Infertility causes stress and negatively affects women's and men's subjective well-being. The greater the stress, the lower the partners' self-esteem and inter-

nal control and the greater their interpersonal conflict (Abbey, Andrews, and Halman, 1994). They may feel they have failed, they may blame each other for their infertility, and they may experience considerable anxiety when they are striving to conceive. In addition, visits to the doctor can interfere with their ability to fulfill their job responsibilities. Uncertainty about future parenting makes it difficult for people to initiate endeavors such as a new job or additional schooling. The cost of fertility treatment can create a financial burden as well. Relationships with friends and family frequently are strained, either because the partners keep their situation a secret or because others' reactions to their problem are not helpful. Thus, infertility affects a variety of different aspects of men's and women's well-being, and this is reflected in its strong negative relationship to life quality (F. M. Andrews and Halman, 1992).

One study found that the great stress associated with infertility undermines the marital adjustment of both spouses. A man is better able to adjust to an involuntarily childless marriage if his partner is employed or has high earnings. A woman's marital adjustment diminishes with the length of marriage and the course of treatment for infertility. The stress women experience as a result of infertility influences the perception of their marriage and may undermine their ability to get the support they need in adjusting to nonparenthood (Ulbrich, Coyle, and Llabre, 1990).

In another study, significant increases in stress and decreases in marital functioning were experienced by subjects as the treatment progressed. Furthermore, greater levels of marital stress were observed in couples who did not conceive. Nonpregnant women experienced a substantially higher level of stress and lower levels of sexual satisfaction than women who became pregnant. In general, the women experienced greater stress than the men as treatment progressed (Benazon, Wright, and Sabourin, 1992). Another study found that infertility treatments significantly affected both marital and sexual satisfaction after treatment was terminated, as well as during the treatment itself (Pepe and Byrne, 1991).

Treatment of Infertility

Partners older than 35 should see a doctor after 6 months of unsuccessful attempts to conceive. Younger couples can wait as long as a year. Older couples need help sooner because of physical and psychological factors that work against conception the longer treatment is postponed. Also, some methods are not available to couples after they reach a certain age.

Treatment for infertility will depend on the cause. Surgical and hormonal treatments are most common. The partners will also probably be instructed in fertility awareness methods (described earlier in the chapter) so that they can have intercourse when there is the greatest likelihood that the woman is ovulating. If these treatment methods are not successful, the couple may want to consider alternative means of conception that have become available through recent breakthroughs in medical technology.

Alternative Means of Conception

Artificial insemination is the injection of sperm into the woman's vagina or uterus for the purpose of inducing pregnancy (Cushner, 1986). **Homologous insemination** (or artificial insemination–husband, AIH), is artificial insemination using the man's sperm. His sperm is collected, frozen, and stored until a sufficient quantity is available; then it is thawed and injected. AIH is usually chosen to try to resolve problems with the man's sperm (such as

a low sperm count), but the rate of conception is only about 5%. **Heterologous insemination** (or artificial insemination–donor, AID), is more effective (Tagatz, Bigson, Schiller, and Nagel, 1980).

In vitro fertilization (**IVF**) involves removing an egg cell from a woman, fertilizing it with sperm in the laboratory, growing it for 3 or 4 days, and then implanting one or more of the subsequent blastocysts (preembryos) in the uterine wall. Up to four blastocysts may be returned to the womb, since using multiple blastocysts increases the chance of pregnancy. With in vitro fertilization, there is about a 25% pregnancy rate. IVF offers the reward of a biological child, but it entails extremely high financial, emotional, and physical costs (L. S. Williams, 1992). The procedure is used when the fallopian tubes are blocked, so that the sperm can't reach the ovum. The procedure is opposed by those who feel it is immoral in that it tampers with nature.

Cryopreservation, or the freezing of blastocysts, is fast becoming commonplace as a way of augmenting in vitro fertilization. Cryopreservation makes it possible to store the extra blastocysts (preembryos) for later use in the event that earlier attempts at implantation are unsuccessful. Cryopreservation fur-

This photo shows families attending a twenty-fifth anniversary reunion of in vitro fertilization. These babies are living examples of the success of in vitro fertilization. Louise Brown, front center, was the first female born through in vitro.

ther allows for the possibility of blastocyst adoption. It is estimated that frozen blastocysts may be kept potentially viable for 600 years and perhaps even 10,000 years (J. N. Edwards, 1991).

Embryo transplant, in comparison to IVF, is relatively simple, less invasive, and more successful, because the embryo is over 14 days developed. This method has the added advantage of being nonsurgical; the transfer from donor to recipient is accomplished by a specially designed catheter. The use of the procedure need not be confined to infertile women. It can allow fertile women who are concerned about adverse genetic transmissions to bear a child (J. N. Edwards, 1991).

In a **gamete intrafallopian transfer** (**GIFT**), the egg and sperm are inserted directly into the fallopian tube, where normal conception takes place. "GIFT is what nature really does, with a little help from us," says Dr. Ricardo Asch, professor of gynecology and obstetrics at the University of California at Irvine (Ubell, 1990). The success rate is 40%—double that of in vitro fertilization.

In an **ovum transfer,** a volunteer female donor is artificially inseminated with sperm from the infertile woman's partner. The **zygote** (fertilized egg cell) is removed after 5 days and transplanted to the mother-to-be, who carries the child during pregnancy (Dunn, Ryan, and O'Brien, 1988).

A **surrogate mother** agrees to be inseminated with the semen of the father-to-be, to carry the fetus to term, and to give the child to the couple along with all rights. There are many unresolved legal questions relating to the rights of the child and to the legitimacy of surrogate agreements. Sometimes the surrogate mother changes her mind and decides not to give up the child. Surrogate mothers give three reasons for serving in this capacity: (1) compassion and a desire to help a childless couple, (2) enjoyment of pregnancy, and (3) money. In one study, half of surrogate mothers were married and already had children of their own (Sobel, 1981).

The Adoption Option

The number of adoptions per year in the United States increased steadily over the decades and reached a peak of 175,000 in 1970. About half of those who petition for adoption are related to the child they wish to adopt. Among women who have ever married, adoption is more common among Whites than among Blacks or Hispanics, among those with at least a high school education, and

among those in higher income brackets. In 2001, many adoptions were from foreign countries, with the largest number being infant girls from China. Russia provides almost as many adoptive children to the United States, and smaller numbers come from South Korea, Guatemala, Ukraine, Romania, Vietnam, and other countries (Congressional Coalition on Adoption Institute, 2002). Interracial adoptions of minority children in the United States have declined because of the influence of minority group advocates and social workers who are concerned about identity problems in the children.

Because there are long waiting periods to adopt a child through established agencies, some adoptive parents turn to independent sources: the mother herself or an agent (usually a lawyer) specializing in open adoption. In **open adoption,** the birth mother

artificial insemination   Injection of sperm into the woman's vagina or uterus for the purpose of inducing pregnancy.

homologous insemination   Artificial insemination by using the sperm of the man. Also called artificial insemination–husband (AIH).

heterologous insemination   Artificial insemination by using the sperm of a donor. Also called artificial insemination–donor (AID).

in vitro fertilization (IVF)   Removing the egg cell from the mother, fertilizing it with the partner's sperm in the laboratory, and then implanting the fertilized egg in the uterine wall.

embryo transplant   The process of removing an embryo from the uterus of a donor and implanting it into the uterus of another woman.

gamete intrafallopian transfer (GIFT)   The process of inserting sperm cells and an egg cell directly into the fallopian tube, where fertilization is expected to occur.

ovum transfer   The process of artificially inseminating a volunteer female with sperm from an infertile woman's partner and removing the zygote after 5 days and transplanting it to the mother-to-be, who carries the child during pregnancy.

zygote   A fertilized egg cell.

surrogate mother   A woman who agrees to be artificially inseminated with the semen of a father-to-be, to carry the fetus to term, and then to give the child to the couple along with all parental rights.

open adoption   A system of adoption in which the birth mother is permitted to meet and play an active role in selecting the adoptive parents and to maintain some form of contact with her child depending on the agreement reached.

is permitted to meet and play an active role in selecting the adoptive parents. She may continue to have contact with her child and the adoptive parents after her child has been placed, depending on the agreement. Open adoption is usually expensive, involving lawyer fees and birth expenses. Six states forbid private adoptions, but other states, such as California and Texas, support them. Many authorities claim that open adoption eases the pain for the birth mother and is in the best interests of the child (Kallen, Griffore, Popovich, and Powell, 1990). Other specialists claim the opposite, saying that it is not in the child's best interests to tell him or her of the adoption unless asked, much less let the child know who the birth mother and biological father are. Some states have laws allowing adoptees to get copies of their original birth certificates.

Family practitioners in North America once believed that successful adoption outcomes required complete severance of adopted children's biological ties. Original birth records were sealed, and adoptees received little background biological information. Although many people now challenge this view, thousands of adoptees have been raised under this secrecy rule. Recently, increasing numbers of adoptees have searched for and contacted their birth mother. These reunions have created an unforeseen social event called the adoption reunion, which can pose several problems. Birth mothers may not have told others that they had had the child. They may marry, have another child, and pretend their second child is their first. Keeping the secret can create anxiety in birth mothers over the years; then the existence of a child they gave up for adoption is revealed. Mothers and children can't help but wonder whether they will be accepted by the other person. Some birth mothers and some adopted children are glad that they have had the reunion; others are not satisfied with the contact outcome (March, 1997).

Until the 1970s, adoption in the United States was shrouded by secrecy and stigma. Members of the adoption triad (adoptive parents, birth parents, and adopted child) were protected from one another in the belief that all benefited from confidentiality. Birth mothers allowed their parental rights to be terminated, transferring those rights to adoption agencies, which then placed the children with adoptive parents. Adoptive parents and birth parents never met, and adopted children usually were not given the opportunity to meet their birth parents. This secrecy was the result of the stigma that the culture

had placed upon adoption: Birth parents had children out of wedlock, and so adopted children were "illegitimate." In recent decades, there have been noticeable changes in the confidentiality rules once commonplace in agency-facilitated adoptions. Adoption practices now lie on a continuum of openness that allows for different levels of communication between adoptive parents and birth parents. In confidential adoptions, there is no communication between the adoptive family and the birth parents. In fully disclosed, or open, adoptions, the adoptive family and the birth parents maintain direct, ongoing communication. In mediated adoptions, communication between the adoptive family and the birth parents is relayed through a third party without the exchange of identifying information.

Many adoptive families move along the continuum throughout their life cycle, making significant changes in levels of openness. For example, adoptions that begin as confidential may evolve into relationships involving direct correspondence and full disclosure. Conversely, some adoptions move in the opposite direction, decreasing in openness over time. Changes in adoption openness are potentially stressful to the family system; they are often a response to one or more members' dissatisfaction with the current level of openness. For example, a child can become unhappy with the lack of information regarding his or her background. Lack of basic genealogical or background information interferes with the process of developing a coherent identity and sense of self. Adoptive parents, too, can be dissatisfied with their ability to provide the child with a birth history and related information. Consequently, changes in adoption openness are often made in response to a problem or an issue the family needs to address.

The very act of increasing adoption openness can be stressful. When a family moves toward more openness, it must extend its boundaries to include someone often perceived as threatening. The media sometimes portray birth parents as attempting to reclaim adopted children if given the opportunity. And adopted children may be portrayed as being very upset if their birth parents do not measure up to their idealized image. Once an adoption reunion takes place, the birth parents and the adopted child must arrive at some arrangement whereby they maintain contact in a manner satisfactory to all concerned. Continuing to negotiate boundaries that maintain a level of comfort for all members of the triad requires significant skill. Experience has shown that relationships work best when they evolve over time, with any changes in openness being mutually determined by all parties involved (Mendenhall, Grotevant, and McRoy, 1996).

An important consideration is how the adoptive parents feel about having adopted children and how the adoptees themselves turn out. As in other families, the family environment is a crucial factor in adoptees' adjustment (Stein and Hoopes, 1986). Although school and behavior problems are more prevalent in adopted children during the elementary years, most adopted children do not show any such problems, especially by adolescence (Brodzinsky, Schechter, Braff, and Singer, 1984). In a study of adoptive parents and their adolescents, parents acknowledged disadvantages of adoption yet reported that their lives and those of their children were no different from those of biological families (Kaye and Warren, 1988). The adolescents themselves acknowledged disadvantages of adoption even less than their parents. Some adoptees become aware of negative reactions to them because others characterize their parents as different from the norm. Secrecy about biological kinship ties prevents adoptees from being able to respond to others' questions about their parents. After a reunion with birth parents, adoptees generally have a higher perception of self and feel more socially acceptable (March, 1995).

TO PARENT OR NOT TO PARENT

Couples today can decide when to have children, how many children to have, and even whether to have children. These choices have become possible because of adequate means of contraception and changing social norms.

In a 2000 population survey, an examination of lifetime birth expectations of all married women ages 18–34 revealed that the number of births to date was 2.1 per woman and that 48% did not expect any future births (U.S. Bureau of the Census, 2002). Among those surveyed, 9.3% expected to have no children at all. Having children is still favored over not having children, although the number of children desired is declining.

Delayed Parenthood

In recent decades, the timing of the birth of the first child has been delayed. In 2000, the median age for

women at first birth was 25, compared to 22.0 in 1972. Birthrates for women in their thirties increased 2% in 2000 to 94.1 per 1,000, up 67% since its low in 1975. In 2000, the proportion of all first births to women 30 and older was 24% compared to just 5% in 1975 (U.S. Bureau of the Census, 2002). In 2000, 13% of U.S. births were to women 35 and older, up from 8.9% in 1990 and 4.6% in 1980 (Centers for Disease Control and Prevention, 2002a). This delay in parenthood may be attributed to delayed marriage, financial considerations, increased pressure for women to get more education and get started in a career, and desire for personal development. However, according to one study, there were no differences in marital adjustment or self-esteem between delayed childbearers and those having children at younger ages (Roosa, 1988).

The long-term effect of delaying first birth is decreasing fertility, because women who delay childbearing end up having fewer children. The effect is positive for many families. Partners have more time to adjust to marriage before becoming parents. They are usually more emotionally mature, stable, and responsible. Late childbearers are more settled in jobs and careers and more likely to have greater insight, own their own homes, and have more savings. They are usually better able to handle the competing demands of work and parenthood. Thus, a new stage appears to be developing: a transition stage between marriage and parenthood during which partners are free to pursue personal development, to build a stable marriage, and to become financially secure before taking on the responsibility of children.

The trend toward delayed parenthood may or may not be accompanied by increased health risks. Assuming adequate health care during pregnancy, childbirth, and the postpartum period, infants born to women ages 30–35 appear to be just as healthy at birth as those born to younger women (Witwer, 1990a). However, there does seem to be greater risk of spontaneous abortions, chromosomal abnormalities, and multiple gestations among women over 30 than among those younger. If the mother is 35 or older, the infant is at higher risk for low birth weight and infant death during the first year than if the mother is younger (Tough et al., 2002).

Reasons for Having Children

The arguments couples give for having children are very personal ones (Neal, Groat, and Wicks, 1989):

In a recent survey, the larger proportion of women who had their first baby after age 30 were highly educated, professional women in dual-career marriages.

My life would not be complete without having children. Children help you feel fulfilled. I never felt like an important person until I became a parent.

I've always wanted a family of my own. When you have children, it gives you someone to do things with, to provide companionship, fun, and love.

I think I'd be very lonesome if I and my spouse were all alone. Life could get pretty boring.

I don't think you really become a mature adult until you have children. I know I never really grew up until after the kids were born. You learn responsibility and to think of someone besides yourself. It helps us to be better people.

Unless you have children, people think there's something wrong with you. I think it's only natural to feel you want to be a parent and that you can be a good one too.

I've always wanted someone to love and who loves me.

I think children help to bring you together and to have something in common. It gives you something to work for.

Children are a part of you. When you're gone, they're still here, an extension of you, carrying on your life and family.

I think one of the reasons for marriage is to have children. It's part of finding spiritual fulfillment. (Author's counseling and teaching notes)

Couples who desire children recognize that there are disadvantages, but for them the advantages far outweigh the negative factors (Goldsteen and Ross, 1989). They'd rather have children than extra money to spend or extra time for leisure, travel, or new interests and hobbies. They put having children before being able to come and go as they wish, having an orderly household, working full-time, or being alone with their spouse.

Choosing a Child-Free Marriage

While the vast majority of couples want to have children, voluntary childlessness is increasing. According to census data, childlessness among all women 40 to 44 years old increased from 10 percent in 1980 to 19 percent in 1998; among ever-married women, childlessness doubled from 7 percent in 1980 to 14 percent in 1998 (Bachu, 1999). Women who were more educated, engaged in managerial and professional occupations, and lived in families with highest income experienced the highest levels of childlessness (Bachu, 1999).

The increase in women choosing to remain child-free is often explained by social changes, namely, more access to better contraceptives, more women having careers and participating in the paid workforce, and the adoption of more feminists' ideas—but those are not the only reasons. Gillespie (2003) examined why some women choose not to become mothers. She interviewed 25 voluntarily child-free individuals ranging in age from 21 to 50. She found that personal freedom and the ability to develop relationships with other adults were two of the primary attractions to remaining child-free, as well as a fundamental rejection of the activities associated with mothering. The participants did not view motherhood as necessarily natural and fulfilling, instead, they saw it in terms of what losses they would experience and sacrifices they would make if they had children. Some participants perceived motherhood in terms of a loss of free time, energy, and identity and described the nurturing and caring roles associated with motherhood as unfulfilling. In sum, motherhood included demands, hard work, responsibilities, and sacrifices to their well-being that they were not prepared to make (Gillespie, 2003).

Having children means readjusting one's lifestyle to take into account their needs and activities. A mother from Ann Arbor, Michigan, commented, "Suddenly I had to devote myself to the child totally. I was under the illusion that the baby was going to fit into my life, and I found that I had to switch my life and my schedule to fit him" (Author's counseling notes). It's a simple fact that without children there is no childwork and less housework. Childlessness allows partners more freedom to do what they please.

However, choosing to be child-free is still negatively stereotyped (Park, 2002) and seen by some as deviant, unfeminine, and unhealthy (Gillespie, 2000). But feminism has helped redefine gender roles and present women with more choices. Gillespie (2003) suggests that "a trend to remain child-

free and an articulation of the lack of desire for motherhood create new possibilities to forge a childfree femininity" (p. 134).

Effects of Children on Parents' Happiness

One of the motherhood and marital myths is that married women with children are happier than women in childless couples. Children can have either a positive or a negative effect on individual psychological well-being depending on the situation (Goldsteen and Ross, 1989; Menaghan, 1989).

The effect on marriage of having children is variable. As discussed in Chapter 8, marital satisfaction is at its lowest ebb during the child-rearing years (Schumm and Bugaighis, 1986). Couples who expect that the presence of children will solve their marital problems are in for a rude awakening. Having children usually aggravates marital tensions.

Judging from the thousands of cases of child abuse in the United States each year, large numbers of people should not become parents. Many people have neither the interest nor the aptitude to be parents; the resultant performance of the parental role is at best marginally competent and at worst blatantly irresponsible.

One of the arguments people offer for having children is that they don't want to be alone in their old age. There is some evidence that widows who are childless report a lower sense of well-being than those who are not (Beckman and Houser, 1982).

For many people, one reason for having children is to perpetuate the family. From their older relatives, the children learn family history, values, and traditions to pass on to future generations.

It is helpful if prospective mates choose each other partially on the basis of their desire to have children or not.

However, friendship with people of the same age is far more important to the happiness of older adults. The decision to have children should not be based on the assumption that parenthood will lead to psychological rewards in old age.

The Decision to Have or Not to Have Children

The decision to have children is an important one. It is helpful if prospective spouses can choose each other partially on the basis of whether they want children (Callan, 1983; Oakley, 1985). Couples who are trying to decide whether they want children can find various types of help (Skovholt and Thoen, 1987). Couples who search for information and thoroughly discuss alternatives before making parenthood decisions are more likely to make decisions they can live with afterward than are those couples who never really consider the alternatives.

A QUESTION OF POLICY

EMBRYOS

Policy issues surrounding abortion and fertility have been at the forefront of political debate for the last 30 years and show no sign of abating. Intensely personal, and in the case of abortion, intensely controversial, these issues revolve around the core of what it means to be human and how we can control the creation of human life. For many people, policies governing abortion and fertility have a huge impact on their lives as individuals and within families.

Abortion and fertility treatment are complicated issues with many different sides. One of the fundamental questions behind the arguments is: When does life begin? On one side is a movement defining the moment of conception as the beginning of life, and abortion in all cases as murder. On another side is the belief that the fertilized egg does not yet have the information to make life and should not be considered human (Swomley, 2002). Still others believe that regardless of when life begins, it is a woman's choice (and not the government's) to control what happens to her own embryo.

The debate becomes even more complicated when we examine current fertility treatments. Many people do not understand that fertility treatments also raise questions regarding the beginning of life. Today, many women seek professional assistance for infertility. A woman may receive a series of hormonal treatments that cause her to produce multiple eggs, which are removed and then fertilized with sperm. Typically, many eggs are fertilized because some may not be viable. Multiple fertilized eggs are implanted in the womb in the hope that at least one will be successful. If several embryos appear to be viable, the woman may be asked to selectively abort one or more to increase the survival probability of the other(s) as well as to reduce the complications associated with multiple births. If not all embryos are implanted, they may be frozen for later use in case the pregnancy is not successful. Embryos are typically retained for 5 years, then discarded. The discarded embryos have never been placed in the mother's womb, and their disposal is not viewed as abortion. The public policy question becomes whether or not these embryos have the same status as the ones in the womb.

QUESTIONS TO CONSIDER:

Does an embryo have a set of rights independent of the mother and deserve the protection of the state? Why or why not?

Is the status of an embryo dependent on how it was formed? That is, does it matter whether a woman became pregnant from rape, incest, casual sex, consensual sex within a committed relationship, or in vitro fertilization? Explain.

What would be an appropriate policy to regulate the use of frozen fertilized embryos from fertility clinics?

What rights does a father have with regard to the embryo?

What kinds of genetic screening should doctors be allowed to carry out before fertilizing an egg?

What would the societal implications be if all abortions were deemed illegal?

SUMMARY

1. Family planning means having children by choice and not by chance; it means having the number wanted when they are wanted. Family planning is used to protect the health of the mother and children, to reduce the negative psychological impact and stress of parenthood, to maintain the well-being of the marriage and the family and its quality of life, and to avoid contributing to global overpopulation.

2. Oral contraceptives are effective, convenient, and easy to use. They are of several types: combination pills containing estrogen and progestin, the minipill (progestin only), and the emergency contraceptive pill (hormonal pills taken in large doses postcoitally). RU-486, the "abortion pill," is a new option.

3. Combination pills have a number of positive health effects: They reduce the risk of benign breast disease, ovarian cysts, iron-deficiency anemia, PID, ectopic pregnancy, rheumatoid arthritis, and endometrial and ovarian cancer. Overall, if women are under 50, don't smoke, and are in good health, they can use oral contraceptives with only a very small risk.

4. Birth control pills do not protect against sexually transmitted diseases.

5. Other hormonal contraceptives include progestin implants, progestin injections, contraceptive rings and patches, and intrauterine systems.

6. Contraceptive foam, suppositories, creams, jellies, and film are vaginal spermicides that are used to prevent conception by blocking the entrance to the uterus and by immobilizing and killing the sperm.

7. Mechanical contraceptive devices include the IUD, condom, diaphragm, and cervical cap.

8. Methods of birth control without devices include various fertility awareness techniques, which rely on limiting intercourse to the so-called safe period of the month, when the woman can't get pregnant (there is really no completely safe period); coitus interruptus (withdrawal); and various means of noncoital stimulation. Douching has no value as a contraceptive technique.

9. Sterilization is the most popular contraceptive method among married women, with the pill second and the condom third.

10. Treatment for infertility will depend on the causes. Surgical and hormonal treatments are most common. The couple may also be instructed in fertility awareness methods to enhance the possibility of conception.

11. Alternative means of conception include artificial insemination (either AIH or AID), in vitro fertilization (IVF), embryo transplant, gamete intrafallopian transfer (GIFT), ovum transfer, and surrogate mothers.

12. In open adoption, the birth mother is permitted to meet and play an active role in selecting the new parents and to have a role in her child's life after placement.

13. At one time, adoption was shrouded in secrecy and stigma: The adoptive parents and adopted child were prevented from knowing the birth history of the child. Adoption practices now lie on a continuum of openness, allowing for different levels of communication between adoptive parents, birth parents, and child. Adoption reunions are not without risk, since either the birth and adoptive parents or the child may be hurt.

14. The crucial factor in how adopted children turn out is the family environment in which they are brought up.

15. Couples today can decide when to have children, how many children to have, and even whether to have children.

16. The number of children desired by U.S. families is declining, with most couples wanting no more than two.

17. More women are delaying parenthood so that they can complete their education, get established in their jobs, have more time to adjust to marriage, and have greater opportunity for personal freedom before having their first baby.

18. The arguments for having children are very personal ones: to make life complete, to have a family of one's own, to avoid boredom, to feel like a mature adult, to meet society's expectations, to have someone to love and to be loved by, to have something to share with one's spouse, or to find spiritual fulfillment. Moreover, society, friends, and parents still put a great deal of pressure on couples to have children.

19. Women who want to remain childless are more likely to be well educated, urban, less traditional in their gender roles, upwardly mobile, and professional; they are also more likely to marry at a later age than women who want children.

20. There are a number of arguments against having children, such as world overpopulation and restrictions on personal freedom. Without children, there is less work at home, more opportunity for self-fulfillment, less strain on the marriage, less worry and tension, less expense, and fewer obstacles to the pursuit of a career.

21. Having children is not a guarantee of personal or marital happiness, especially for those who lack the interest or aptitude for parenthood.

22. The decision to have children is one that couples should thoughtfully consider.

KEY TERMS

family planning	emergency contraceptives	intrauterine system (IUS)
oral contraceptives	progestin implant	spermicides
combination pills	progestin injection	intrauterine device (IUD)
placebo	vaginal contractive ring	condom
minipill	contraceptive patch	diaphragm

cervical cap

sterilization

vasectomy

castration

tubal ligation

laparoscopy

rhythm method

douching

coitus interruptus

abortion

artificial insemination

homologous insemination

heterologous insemination

in vitro fertilization (IVF)

embryo transplant

gamete intrafallopian transfer (GIFT)

ovum transfer

zygote

surrogate mother

open adoption

QUESTIONS FOR THOUGHT

1. Do you believe in family planning? Why or why not?

2. What are the pros and cons of using the usual birth control pill containing a combination of estrogen and progestin?

3. Would you want to use a spermicide as a contraceptive? Which ones would you use or not use? Why?

4. Assume you are an unmarried person; which of the following types of contraception would you use: condom, diaphragm, or oral contraception? Explain the reasons for your preference.

5. Assume you are married and have all the children you want; would you consider sterilization for yourself (vasectomy if you are a man, tubal ligation if you are a woman)? Explain the reasons for your decision.

6. For you, what is the basic issue, if any, in judging the morality of abortion? Explain.

SUGGESTED READINGS

Critchlow, D. T. (1999). *Intended Consequences: Birth Control, Abortion, and the Federal Government in Modern America.* New York: Oxford University Press. Takes a comprehensive look at the debate over birth control and abortion in America, both before and after the pill and *Roe v. Wade.*

Feeney, J. A., Hohaus, L., Noller, P., and Alexander, R. P. (2001). *Becoming Parents: Exploring the Bonds Between Mothers, Fathers, and Their Infants.* New York: Cambridge University Press. Explores questions that many new parents ask themselves.

Foge, L. (1999). *The Third Choice: A Woman's Guide to Placing a Child for Adoption.* Berkeley, CA: Creative Arts Book. Provides a guide for birth mothers considering adoption and discusses pregnancy, birth, relinquishment, and grief and recovery.

McFarlane, D. R. (2000). *The Politics of Fertility Control: Family Planning and Abortion Policies in the American States.* New York: Chatham House. Discusses the political controversy surrounding fertility control and the reasons the debate is so important.

Shanley, M. L. (2001). *Making Babies, Making Families: What Matters Most in an Age of Reproductive Technologies, Surrogacy, Adoption, and Same Sex and Unwed Parents.* Boston: Beacon Press. Focuses on the need for new family laws that reflect the changing nature of the family today.

Siegel, J. E., and McCormick, M. C. (2000). *Prenatal Care: Effectiveness and Implementation.* Cambridge: Cambridge University Press. Evaluates the effectiveness of prenatal care interventions and discusses the issue from a broader perspective of public and long-term health issues.

Winstein, M. (1999). *Your Fertility Signals: Using Them to Achieve or Avoid Pregnancy Naturally.* St. Louis: Smooth Stone Press. Explains ovulation and the natural methods of temperature and other signals to reduce or eliminate the need for contraceptives.

LEARNING OBJECTIVES

After reading the chapter, you should be able to:

- Describe the signs and symptoms of pregnancy, discuss the use of pregnancy tests, and calculate the birth date.

- Discuss the emotional reactions to prospective parenthood and pregnancy and the developmental tasks of pregnancy.

- Understand basic facts about prenatal medical and health care, some of the minor side effects and major complications of pregnancy, and the issues of sexual relations and mental health during pregnancy.

- Identify the stages of prenatal development.

- Discuss prepared childbirth and the Lamaze method of natural childbirth.

- Understand basic information about labor, options for delivery, induced or accelerated labor, the use of anesthesia, and cesarean sections.

- Discuss the following topics in relation to postpartum care, decisions, and adjustments: care of the newborn, bonding, rooming in, breast- versus bottle-feeding, postpartum adjustments, and returning to work.

Pregnancy and Childbirth

Most couples want to have children sometime in their lives. But expectant parents are faced with a number of important questions: How does a couple know if the woman is pregnant? How can the birth date be calculated? What are some typical reactions to parenthood and pregnancy, and what major adjustments do men and women face? What do they need to know to protect the health of the baby? What are the possible complications of pregnancy? How can couples prepare themselves for the experience of childbirth? What happens during labor and childbirth itself? What about the use of anesthesia? What about natural childbirth methods? What about induced, or accelerated, labor? Or delivery by cesarean section? What do couples need to know before and after the baby is born? These are some of the important questions discussed in this chapter.

PREGNANCY

Most women suspect they are pregnant before medical tests confirm the fact. They can feel subtle changes in their body, and they begin to think about the changes in their life that a baby will bring. And they wonder how their partner will react to the news.

Signs and Symptoms of Pregnancy

One of the first questions the prospective mother asks is, "How do I know for certain that I'm pregnant?" The signs and symptoms of pregnancy can be divided into three categories. **Presumptive signs** indicate a possibility of pregnancy. They are the first signs that are noticed by the woman, but they are subjective and may be caused by conditions other than pregnancy, so she may only assume pregnancy from them. The presumptive signs are (1) cessation of menstruation, (2) morning sickness (nausea and possibly vomiting at any time of day), (3) an increase in the size, tenderness, and fullness of the breasts, along with a darkening of the areolas (the ring around the nipple), (4) frequent urination, (5) quickening, or the feeling of fetal movement by the mother, and (6) overpowering sleepiness.

Probable signs of pregnancy are more objective than are presumptive signs, since they must be interpreted by the physician. Some of them occur later in pregnancy than the presumptive signs, but they still are not absolute proof. The probable signs include (1) a positive pregnancy test, (2) darkening of vaginal tissues and of cervical mucous membranes (the so-called Chadwick's sign), (3) softening of cervical tissue (the Hegar's sign), (4) enlargement of the abdomen and uterus, (5) mapping of the fetal outline manually, (6) intermittent contractions of the uterus, and (7) an increase in the basal body temperature (from 98.8° F to 99.9° F for more than 16 days).

Positive signs of pregnancy are indisputable, since no other condition except pregnancy causes them. There are six of them. The examiner can (1) feel the fetus move, (2) hear the fetal heartbeat, (3) get an electrical tracing of the fetal heart, (4) detect a doubling of HCG levels, (5) map the fetal outline by means of special ultrasonic equipment, and (6) detect the fetal skeleton by X-ray. When any of these signs are discovered, the mother and her physician *know* she is pregnant. Because of the dangers of radiation to the developing fetus, doctors use X-rays only in rare circumstances.

Tests for Pregnancy

The sooner the woman knows she is pregnant, the earlier she can begin prenatal care. Since most women don't want to wait several months to determine if they are pregnant, pregnancy tests are administered. The two basic categories of tests are biologic and immunologic. There are numerous types of tests in each category, but all are based on detecting the presence of **human chorionic gonadotropin (HCG),** which is secreted by the placenta. In the older biologic tests, a woman's urine was administered to test animals such as mice, frogs, toads, or rabbits. If HCG was present in the urine, it caused ovulation in female animals. Pregnancy was detected by killing the animal and examining the ovaries. The disadvantages were that pregnancy could not be detected until 4–6 weeks after the last menstrual period and that many animals were killed.

The immunologic tests are easier to perform and yield results more quickly. They involve adding the woman's urine to anti-HCG chemicals to see the reaction. The immunologic tests are easier to administer than the biologic tests, but they are not 100% accurate, especially in the first few weeks of pregnancy. They can give either false positive or false negative readings. Furthermore, these tests will not detect ectopic pregnancies. A woman with a negative test who does not menstruate within another week should repeat the test.

Home pregnancy tests sold under various brand names are immunologic tests designed to measure the presence of HCG. These tests are convenient and relatively inexpensive. Manufacturers claim 99% accuracy when the tests are performed correctly.

Calculating the Birth Date

The duration of the pregnancy is ordinarily estimated at 280 days, or 40 weeks, from the beginning of the last period. Of course, these are average figures. One study showed that 46% of women had their babies either the week before or the week after the calculated date, and 74% within a 2-week period before or after the date. Occasionally, pregnancy is prolonged more than 2 weeks beyond the calculated date; usually, an error in calculation is involved. At the most, 4% of pregnancies actually last 2 weeks or more beyond the average time (Guttmacher, 1983).

The expected date of birth may be calculated using **Naegele's formula** as follows: subtract 3 months from the first day of the last menstrual period and then add 7 days. Thus, if the date of the first day of the last period was November 16, subtracting 3 months gives the date August 16, and adding 7 days gives the birth date as August 23. This is really a shortcut for counting 280 days from any fixed date. In other words, a woman ordinarily delivers her baby 9 months and 7 days after the first day of her last menstrual period (Guttmacher, 1983).

Emotional Reactions to Pregnancy

Becoming a parent can be one of the most exciting and meaningful experiences in life (Cowan and Cowan, 1995). How men or women react to prospective parenthood depends on a number of factors. A very important one is whether the pregnancy is planned (Snowden, Schott, Awalt, and Gillis-Knox, 1988). Do the partners want a child at this time? Do they feel ready to accept the responsibilities? Are the mother and father of appropriate ages?

Another important factor is the status of the couple's relationship. Do they have a harmonious relationship? (The more stressful the relationship, the more difficulty the couple will have adjusting to parenthood.) Are they married? If not, how do they feel about raising a child out of wedlock? Does the woman want to be a single or unmarried par-

ent? Does the woman want to bear his child? Does the man want her to bear his child? Will they assist each other in the rearing of the child? Will he accept responsibilities as a father? Will she as a mother? How will the child affect their relationship? Unpartnered women have been found to experience greater psychological risk and more complications during their pregnancies because of inadequate social support (Liese, Snowden, and Ford, 1989).

May (1982) studied 100 expectant fathers and their partners to determine what factors were important to a subjective sense of readiness for pregnancy and fatherhood. She found four factors that were most important to these men:

1. Whether they had intended to be a father at some time in their lives.
2. Stability in the couple's relationship.
3. Relative financial security.
4. A sense of closure to the childless period of their lives; in other words, they had to feel they had achieved most of the goals they wanted to accomplish before fatherhood.

presumptive signs Signs by which a woman presumes she is pregnant. These include cessation of menstruation; morning sickness; an increase in the size, tenderness, and fullness of the breasts, along with a darkening of the areolas; frequent urination; quickening, or the feeling of fetal movement by the mother, and overpowering sleepiness.

probable signs Signs detected by the examining physician that indicate pregnancy is probable. These include a positive pregnancy test; darkening of vaginal tissues and of cervical mucous membranes; softening of the cervical tissue; enlargement of the abdomen and uterus; mapping of the fetal outline manually; intermittent contractions of the uterus, and an increase in the basal body temperature.

positive signs Signs of pregnancy detected by the physician that indicate positively that the woman is pregnant. These include feeling the fetus move; hearing the fetal heartbeat; getting an electrical tracing of the fetal heart; detecting a doubling of HCG levels; mapping the fetal outline by means of special ultrasonic equipment; and detecting the fetal skeleton by X-ray.

HCG (human chorionic gonadotropin) A hormone produced by the placenta that, if present in the mother's urine, is an indication of pregnancy.

Naegele's formula A method of calculating the expected date of birth by subtracting 3 months from the first day of the last period and adding 7 days.

How does a woman know when she might be pregnant? What signs may tell her that she is? Signs of pregnancy can be detected, interpreted, and confirmed by a physician.

The timing of the pregnancy was extremely important to the men in this study, just as it is important to women.

Pregnancy affects the man and the woman differently. The woman has to carry the child for 9 months, accompanied by varying degrees of physical discomfort or difficulties and sometimes by anxiety about impending childbirth. Many women want to be mothers but hate the period of pregnancy. One woman commented, "I don't like being pregnant. I feel like a big toad. I'm a dancer, used to being slim, and can't believe what I look like from the side. I avoid mirrors" (Boston Women's Health Book Collective, 1998, p. 440). Other women are extremely happy during pregnancy. As one woman noted, "I was excited and delighted. I really got into eating well, caring for myself, getting enough sleep. I liked walking through the streets and having people notice my pregnancy" (Boston Women's Health Book Collective, 1998, p. 440).

Part of the woman's reaction to her pregnancy depends on the reaction of her partner to her and her changing figure. One study emphasized that a woman accepts her pregnancy when it brings her closer to her partner but rejects pregnancy when she feels it serves to distance her from her partner. The woman's reaction to pregnancy is also strongly related to the financial and emotional support and help she receives from her partner.

PRENATAL CARE

Ordinarily, the fetus is well protected in its uterine environment, but the expectant mother needs to take special care of herself during pregnancy. Pregnancy can be exhausting and pregnant women need extra rest and nutrition. Good prenatal care is essential to maintain the health of the expectant mother and child.

The Importance of Prenatal Care

Time is of the essence with prenatal care, because the first 3 months of fetal development are crucial to the health of the child. Furthermore, inadequate prenatal nutrition increases the likelihood of low birth weight and infant death (Jamieson and Buescher, 1992). Babies of poor women seem to be at special risk for low birth weight (R. Turner, 1992b). Young maternal age is also a very high risk factor for poor pregnancy outcome. In both cases, part of the reason is inadequate prenatal care (S. S. Brown, 1989).

Data in the 1988 National Survey of Family Growth (NSFG) were obtained from 8,450 women ages 15–44 (of whom 63% were White, 33% Black, and 4% members of other groups). The interviews covered the women's fertility history and intentions, contraceptive use, and prenatal care, as well as socioeconomic and demographic characteristics. Ninety-eight percent of the respondents obtained prenatal care, but only 65% initiated care within the first trimester. Census data have shown that 82.5% of mothers began prenatal care in the first trimester, while 3.9% of mothers did not begin prenatal care until the third trimester or had no care at all (U.S. Bureau of the Census, 1999a). Most of the women who get little or no prenatal care lack health insurance coverage (Klitsch, 1990b). Young women are significantly less likely than older women to receive early prenatal care. Teenagers are more likely to delay care until at least the fifth month or to receive no care at all. Additionally, women who intended to become pregnant are more likely to seek early care than are women whose pregnancies were unwanted (Hollander, 1995c). Women who do not want anyone to know about the pregnancy have significantly higher odds of receiving inadequate prenatal care (C. Cook, Selig, Wedge, and Gohn-Baube, 1999).

Data from other studies indicate the importance of family structure and its effect on prenatal care. Hispanic married women living with the father of the expected child are substantially more likely to receive adequate prenatal care than are women of other groups. Hispanic women living alone or with their mother are significantly more likely to receive inadequate prenatal care (Albrecht, Miller, and Clarke, 1994).

Initial visits to the doctor include a complete physical examination. It is helpful if the prospective father goes along, because he needs to be involved. The physician will take a complete medical history, perform various tests, and make recommendations regarding nutrition, health care during pregnancy, sexual relations, potential minor complications, and danger signs to watch for in avoiding major complications. Many expectant mothers are concerned about too much weight gain, but too little weight gain can be just as harmful, resulting in underweight infants and premature birth (Witwer, 1990b). Low birth weight seems to run in families. That is, infants whose mothers were below normal weight at birth or infants who have a low-birth-weight sibling are more likely to have low birth weight themselves (Mahler, 1996b).

Because the baby receives his or her nutrients and oxygen from the mother's bloodstream via the placenta and umbilical cord, everything the mother consumes affects the fetus. If the mother's diet is nutritionally inadequate, the baby will not receive vital nutrients, and the mother's health will also suffer. Rest and moderate exercise are also important to the well-being of both the pregnant woman and the fetus. Pregnant women need more sleep and rest because the energy demands on their body are so great. Moderate exercise won't harm the fetus, which is cushioned by the amniotic fluid, and toned-up muscles will aid delivery and help the woman regain her nonpregnant shape afterward.

Minor Side Effects of Pregnancy

No pregnancy is without some discomfort. Expectant mothers may experience one or several of the following discomforts to varying degrees and at various times during pregnancy: nausea (morning sickness), heartburn, flatulence, hemorrhoids, constipation, shortness of breath, backache, leg cramps, uterine contractions, insomnia, minor vaginal discharge, and varicose veins. Because of the physical

Home pregnancy tests are convenient and relatively inexpensive. Most home pregnancy test kits advise women to see their physician after they have examined the results of the test.

The woman's reaction to pregnancy is strongly related to the emotional support and help she receives from her partner.

and hormonal changes in their body, expectant mothers also often experience lethargy and mood swings.

Major Complications of Pregnancy

Major complications arise only infrequently, but when they do they present a more serious threat to the health and life of the baby than do the minor discomforts already mentioned. For example, pernicious vomiting is prolonged and persistent vomiting. One patient in several hundred suffers from this condition to such an extent that hospitalization is required.

Toxemia is characterized by waterlogging of connective tissue (edema), as indicated by swollen limbs and face or rapid weight gain, protein in the urine, headache, and blurring of vision. The placenta may not grow properly and may not be able to provide adequate oxygen and nourishment to the baby. Treatment for mothers experiencing toxemia includes rest and possibly medication to reduce high blood pressure. Toxemia is more common in first pregnancies and is linked to a family history of the condition. If toxemia goes unchecked, it can lead to convulsions (eclampsia), which can be very dangerous for both mother and child (Pasquariello, 1999).

Spontaneous abortion, or miscarriage, may be indicated by vaginal bleeding. Spontaneous abortion is fairly common, occurring in one out of every five or six pregnancies, often before the 12th week. Early miscarriage can be nature's way of screening out future problems, indicating an irregularity in development (Boston Women's Health Book Collective, 1998). About 85% of all first-trimester miscarriages are due to genetic abnormalities of the fetus. The primary causes of second-trimester miscarriages are maternal factors, including structural problems of the uterus, acute infections, cervical abnormalities, hormonal imbalances, environmental toxins, and undue stress (Boston Women's Health Book Collective, 1998). Almost all women who have had a miscarriage will be able to go on to have successful pregnancies, and 70% of women who have had two miscarriages will be able to carry subsequent pregnancies to term.

Abruptio placentae, the premature separation of the placenta from the uterine wall, happens in about 1 out of every 200 pregnancies, usually in the third trimester. In **placenta previa,** the placenta is growing partly over or all the way over the opening to the cervix (Remez, 1992a). Painless bleeding occurs from week 28 because the placenta is partially or completely blocking the baby's exit by covering the cervix. In cases of heavy bleeding, a premature delivery by cesarean section may be required. If the placenta is still covering the cervix after the 38th week, a cesarean section is needed, but sometimes vaginal birth is possible if the placenta only extends close to the cervix (Pasquariello, 1999). Women who smoke during the first two trimesters of pregnancy are almost three times as likely as women who do not to have their pregnancy complicated by placenta previa (Rind, 1992a).

Ectopic pregnancy occurs when the fertilized ovum attaches itself and grows somewhere other than the uterus. It may be a **tubal pregnancy,** with the ovum attached to the wall of the fallopian tube and growing there rather than within the uterus. Or the pregnancy may be situated in the ovary, abdomen, or cervix. Figure 12.1 shows possible implantation sites; all such pregnancies have to be terminated by an operation. Data indicate that the number of such pregnancies has been climbing steadily. This may be due to a number of factors: the postponement of childbearing, during which time the fallopian tubes age; previous abortion; pelvic inflammatory disease (PID); sexually transmitted diseases; frequent douching with commercial preparations; or previous surgery. Any condition that affects the fallopian tubes and impedes transport of the fertilized ovum will contribute to an ectopic pregnancy ("Increasing Rates," 1984, p. 14). In spite of the increase in such pregnancies, the mortality rates have fallen, indicating that women are getting prompter and better treatment ("Annual Ectopic Totals," 1983).

Rh incompatibility is determined during an initial prenatal exam. The Rh factor is a protein found in the blood. Because some of a baby's red blood cells cross the placenta and enter the mother's bloodstream during pregnancy and delivery, an Rh-negative mother will develop antibodies to the blood cells of an Rh-positive baby. If she has another Rh-positive baby, the antibodies in her blood will pass through the placenta and destroy the baby's red blood cells, possibly causing jaundice, anemia, mental retardation, and even death. Fortunately, a

toxemia A serious complication of pregnancy characterized by waterlogging of connective tissue (edema).

abruptio placentae The premature separation of the placenta from the uterine wall.

placenta previa A complication of pregnancy in which the placenta grows partly or all the way over the opening to the cervix, usually causing abruptio placentae.

ectopic pregnancy Attachment of the blastocyst and growth of the embryo in any location other than inside the uterus.

tubal pregnancy A type of ectopic pregnancy in which attachment of the blastocyst and growth of the embryo occur in the fallopian tube.

Rh incompatibility A condition in which the mother has Rh-negative blood and the fetus has Rh-positive blood or vice versa.

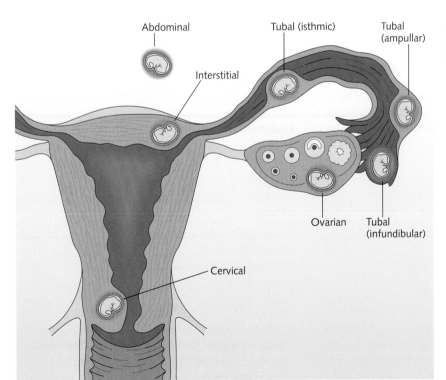

Abdominal

Interstitial

Tubal (isthmic)

Tubal (ampullar)

Ovarian

Tubal (infundibular)

Cervical

Figure 12.1 Possible Implantation Sites for Ectopic Pregnancy

serum called anti-Rh gamma globulin was developed in the 1960s. When administered to an Rh-negative mother within a few hours of giving birth to an Rh-positive baby, it prevents the development of antibodies. Or it may be given at about week 28 of the pregnancy, in which case the antibodies are gradually destroyed (Berkow, 1987). If tests of the amniotic fluid (amniocentesis) reveal that the fetus may already be affected, intrauterine blood transfusions may be given into the fetal abdominal cavity.

Sexual Relations during Pregnancy

Pregnancy is a major life transition and generally results in a change in sexual activity. Most researchers studying sexuality during pregnancy have reported a decrease in sexual desire and frequency of sexual intercourse from the first to the third trimester, with a sharp decline in the frequency of coitus from the second to the third trimester (Hyde, DeLamater, and Plant, 1996). However, a classic study by Masters and Johnson (1966) found a marked increase in sexual interest in the second trimester, followed by a decline in the third trimester. These findings were substantiated by a longitudinal study of couples expecting their first child. The women reported a decrease in sexual desire, frequency, and satisfaction throughout pregnancy, but most commonly in the third trimester. Among the men, this decrease was common only during the third trimester (Bogren, 1991).

Many reasons have been given for this decline in sexual interest during pregnancy, including chronic exhaustion, the feeling of being less sexually attractive, physical discomfort associated with intercourse, concern for the pregnancy, and fear of causing harm to the fetus by intercourse or orgasm (Bogren, 1991). However, most doctors believe that sexual intercourse causes no harm to the fetus, although many recommend curtailing sexual intercourse in the last 4 weeks of pregnancy. There are several conditions that may make intercourse late in pregnancy unsafe, including a previous miscarriage, some dilation of the cervix, vaginal or uterine bleeding, rupture of the bag of water, and premature labor.

Mental Health

Most expectant mothers experience some stress during pregnancy. A moderate amount of stress has no harmful effect on the fetus, but prolonged nervous and emotional disturbance of the mother is associ-

ated with low birth weight, infant hyperactivity, feeding problems, irritability, and digestive disturbances (Istvan, 1986). Women who experience stressful events during pregnancy appear to be at increased risk for premature delivery (Mahler, 1996c). Rini, Dunkel-Schetter, Wadhwa, and Sandman (1999) studied prenatal psychosocial predictors of infant birth weight and length. They found that women with more resources had higher-birth-weight babies, whereas those reporting more stress had shorter gestations. Factors such as being married, having higher income and education, and giving birth for the first time were associated with lower stress. Emotional disturbance may also have negative effects on the mother herself. Women who suffer from pernicious vomiting during pregnancy have been found to be under considerable emotional stress, usually because of conflict between wanting and not wanting the unborn child.

There is a close relationship between severe emotional trauma and spontaneous abortion (Berkow, 1987). Women who are prone to bearing premature infants may show similar emotional distress. Emotional disturbance has also been shown to be related to difficult and prolonged labor and to physical complications of pregnancy such as toxemia.

Pregnancy is not always the euphoric, blissful experience that romantic literature describes. It can be a happy, healthful time, but it can also be a period of stress and anxiety, especially for the immature and unprepared. That is why preparation for childbirth and for parenthood is so important.

PRENATAL DEVELOPMENT

Prenatal development takes place during three periods:

1. **The germinal period**—from conception to implantation (attachment to the uterine wall), about 14 days.

2. **The embryonic period**—from 2 weeks to 8 weeks after conception.

3. **The fetal period**—from 8 weeks through the remainder of the pregnancy.

The mother's experience of the pregnancy changes from period to period as the baby grows inside her. All of the major body structures are formed during the first two periods, the time when

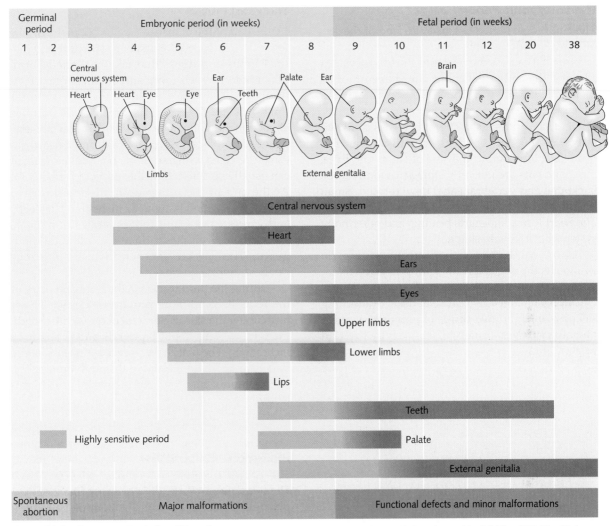

Figure 12.2 Sensitive Periods of Development (*Note:* From *Human Development: A Life-Span Approach* by F. P. Rice, 1992, New York: Macmillan.)

the baby is most vulnerable to harmful drugs, environmental pollutants, and radiation (see Figure 12.2). By the end of the fourth or fifth month, the mother can usually feel fetal movement. The last several months of pregnancy are most uncomfortable for the mother because the growing fetus crowds her internal organs and strains the muscles of her back.

The Germinal Period

The fertilized ovum, called a zygote, is propelled down the fallopian tubes by hairlike cilia. About 30 hours after fertilization, the process of cell division begins. One cell divides into two, two into four, and

so on. Every time the cells divide, they become smaller, allowing the total mass, called the blastula, to pass through the fallopian tubes.

Three to 4 days after fertilization, the newly formed **blastocyst** begins to attach itself to the inner lining of the uterus in a process called implantation. Implantation is complete about 10 days after the blastula enters the uterus.

blastocyst The mass of cells 3 to 4 days after fertilization takes place that grows into an embryo.

The Embryonic Period

The embryonic period begins at the end of the second week, with the embryo developing around the layer of cells across the center of the blastocyst. At 18 days, the embryo is about one-sixteenth of an inch long. During its early weeks, the human embryo resembles those of other vertebrate animals, as Figure 12.3 illustrates. The embryo has a tail and traces of gills, both of which soon disappear. The head develops before the rest of the body. Eyes, nose, and ears are not yet visible at 1 month, but a backbone and vertebral canal have formed. Small buds that will develop into legs and arms appear. The heart forms and starts beating, and other body systems begin to take shape.

Hormonal changes in the mother's body begin as soon as the egg is fertilized and may be accompanied by sleepiness, fatigue, and emotional upset. Hormonal changes also cause nausea, or morning sickness, in about two-thirds of pregnant women. Morning sickness usually disappears by the 12th week.

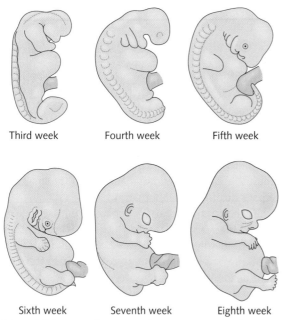

Third week   Fourth week   Fifth week

Sixth week   Seventh week   Eighth week

Figure 12.3 Development of Human Embryo from the Third Week to Eighth Week after Conception (*Note:* From *Human Development: A Life-Span Approach* by F. P. Rice, 1992, New York: Macmillan.)

The Fetal Period

By the end of the embryonic period (2 months), the fetus has developed the first bone structure and distinct limbs and digits that take on human form. Major blood vessels form, and internal organs continue to develop. By the end of the first trimester (one-third the length of pregnancy), the fetus is about 3 inches long; most major organs are present, the head and face are well formed, and a heartbeat can be detected with a stethoscope. Fetal movement can usually be detected by the fourth or fifth month. At the end of the fifth month, the fetus weighs about 1 pound and is about 12 inches long. It sleeps and wakes, sucks, and moves its position. Eyes, eyelids, and eyelashes form at the end of the sixth month. The eyes are light-sensitive, and the fetus can hear uterine sounds.

During the third trimester, the head and body of the fetus become more proportionate. Fat layers form under the skin. By the end of the eighth month, the fetus weighs about 5 pounds and is about 18 inches long. The nails have grown to the ends of the fingers and toes by the end of the ninth month. The skin becomes smoother and is covered with a protective waxy substance called vernix caseosa. The baby is ready for delivery.

PREPARED CHILDBIRTH

The term **prepared childbirth,** as used here, means physical, social, intellectual, and emotional preparation for the birth of a baby. Physical preparation involves the mother's taking care of her body to provide the optimal physical environment for the growing fetus and physically conditioning her body so that she is prepared for labor and childbirth. Prepared childbirth also involves social preparation of the home, partner, and other children so that the proper relationships exist within the family in which the child will be growing up. Prepared childbirth involves intellectual preparation: obtaining full knowledge and understanding of what the process of birth entails and what to expect before, during, and after delivery, including adequate instruction in infant and child care. Finally, prepared childbirth involves psychological and emotional conditioning to keep fear, anxiety, and tension to a minimum and to make the process as pleasant and pain-free as possible.

Prepared childbirth does not exclude drugs and medication during labor and delivery, if the mother desires to use them. In other words, the focus is not just on unmedicated childbirth (often referred to as natural childbirth, when in fact all childbirth is natural), but on whether the woman, her partner, and her family are really prepared for the experience of becoming parents.

The Lamaze Method

One of the most popular childbirth training methods is the **Lamaze method,** which originated in Russia and was introduced to the Western world in 1951 by Fernand Lamaze (1970), a French obstetrician (Samuels and Samuels, 1996). The important elements of the Lamaze method include the following:

- Learning about birth, including the importance of relaxing uninvolved muscles.

- Exercising to get in good physical condition.

- Learning controlled breathing and ways to relax the muscles and release muscular tension. These techniques are useful in pain prevention, which can minimize the need for pain-relieving drugs.

- Offering emotional support to the woman during labor and delivery, primarily by teaching the

man how to coach her during the process. The importance of the partners' relationship and communication are emphasized. In this method as well as other prepared childbirth methods, the attendance of the father or another support person in childbirth education classes and during labor and delivery is essential. Research has shown that the presence of a supportive companion or labor coach during labor lessens women's need for obstetric intervention (R. Turner, 1991).

An important feature of the Lamaze method is that the mother is taught that she can be in control during the experience of childbirth (Felton and Segelman, 1978).

prepared childbirth   Physical, social, intellectual, and emotional preparation for the birth of a baby.

Lamaze method   A popular childbirth training and delivery method in which the woman comes to be in control of the childbirth experience by getting in good physical shape, learning controlled breathing and muscle relaxation techniques, and receiving emotional support from her partner.

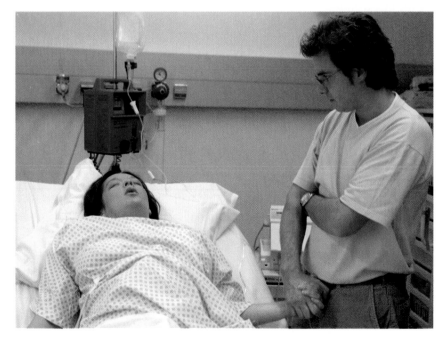

Expectant fathers are encouraged to attend birth preparation classes and to act as coaches during labor and delivery. Fathers who are present at delivery tend to show more interest in their infants and to talk to them more than do fathers who are not present.

The Use of Ultrasounds

There are many cultural variations surrounding pregnancy and childbirth. One study examined the prenatal and childbirth experiences of Japanese couples living in the United States. One striking difference found between Japanese and American couples involved the use of fetal sonograms, or ultrasounds. Japanese women are accustomed to receiving an ultrasound at each prenatal visit to ensure normal fetal development. In Japan, it has become almost a ritual for the first pictures in a baby photo album to be a series of fetal sonogram pictures. Japanese couples having a baby in the United States expressed concern and anxiety over not having regular sonograms. Ultrasound pictures gave them peace of mind and assurance at each prenatal visit that the baby was developing normally (Yeo, Fetters, and Maeda, 2000).

Interestingly, health insurance does not cover the cost of prenatal care or childbirth in Japan, so parents must pay the full cost themselves, including every ultrasound examination. However, ultrasounds are relatively inexpensive in Japan, so couples can afford to pay for them. In the United States, health insurance typically covers an ultrasound, but the cost is very high. This prevents most Japanese couples in the United States from being able to afford multiple ultrasounds. The Japanese parents' need for seeing the development of their child through multiple ultrasounds, whether to fulfill emotional or cultural needs, often goes unmet in the United States (Yeo et al., 2000).

LABOR AND DELIVERY

Real **labor** consists of rhythmic contractions that recur at fixed intervals, usually about 15–20 minutes apart at first and decreasing to 3- to 4-minute intervals when labor is well under way. In addition, the total length of each muscular contraction increases from less than half a minute to more than a minute. One sign that labor is about to begin or has already begun is the discharge of the blood-tinted mucus plug that has sealed the neck of the uterus. The plug is dislodged from the cervix and passes out of the vagina as a pinkish discharge known as **show.** Its appearance may anticipate the onset of labor by a day or more, or it may indicate that dilation has already begun (Berkow, 1987).

Sometimes the first indication of the impending labor is the rupture of the **bag of water (amniotic sac),** followed by a gush or leakage of watery fluid from the vagina. In one-eighth of all pregnancies, especially first pregnancies, the membrane ruptures *before* labor begins. When this happens, labor usually will commence in 6–24 hours if the woman is within a few days of term; 80% go into labor within 48 hours. If she is not near term, labor may not commence for 30–40 days or longer. This delay is actually necessary, because the longer the fetus has to develop completely, the greater the chance of the baby being born healthy. When the membrane rup-

tures more than 24 hours prior to labor, there is an increase in the risk of infection. It is important at this stage to guard against infection by not taking baths, refraining from sexual intercourse, and remaining well rested and hydrated. Practitioners or physicians may also advise monitoring body temperature while waiting for labor to begin to make sure there is no infection (Boston Women's Health Book Collective, 1998). About half the time, however, the bag of water doesn't rupture until the last hours of labor.

The Duration of Labor

Bean (1974) reported a study of 10,000 women who delivered at a Baltimore hospital. The study showed the total length of labor of each woman, from the onset of the first contraction until the expulsion of the afterbirth. The median number of hours of labor for primiparous women (first labor) was 10.6; for multiparous women (all labor subsequent to the first), it was 6.2. One woman in 100 may anticipate that her first child will be born following less than 3 hours of labor, while 1 woman in 9 requires more than 24 hours.

The physician will give instructions as to when he or she wants to be notified. Most want to be called as soon as rhythmic contractions are established. The physician will also determine when the mother should go to the hospital or birthing center.

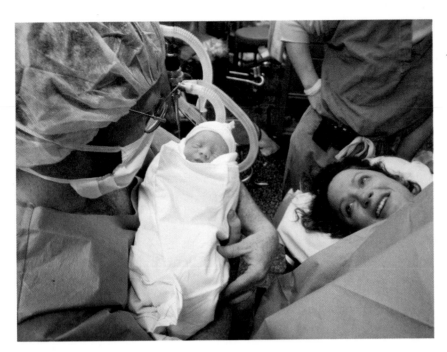

The second stage of labor ends with the birth of the baby. Within the next few minutes, the baby's physical condition will be carefully evaluated.

Stages of Labor

The actual process of labor can be divided into three phases. The first stage is the dilation stage, during which the force of the uterine muscles pushing on the baby gradually opens the mouth of the cervix, which increases from less than four-fifths of an inch in diameter to 4 inches. This phase takes longer than any other. There is nothing the mother can do to help except relax as completely as possible to allow the involuntary muscles to do their work.

The second stage begins upon completion of dilation and ends with the birth of the baby. It involves the passage of the baby through the birth canal. During the phase when hard contractions begin, the mother alternately pushes and relaxes to help force the baby through the birth canal. After the baby is delivered and tended to, the obstetrician again turns his or her attention to the mother for the third stage of labor.

The third stage involves the passage of the placenta, or afterbirth. The mother may be kept in the delivery room for an hour or so after delivery while her condition is checked. When her condition is considered normal, she is usually placed in a recovery room for a while before being returned to her own room.

The Use of Anesthesia

Anesthesia used to alleviate pain in childbirth can be divided into two categories: general anesthesia and local or regional anesthesia. General anesthesia affects the whole body by acting on the central nervous system. It can slow or stop labor and lower maternal blood pressure. It crosses the placental barrier and affects the fetus as well as the mother, decreasing the responses of the newborn infant. Local or regional anesthesia blocks pain in specific areas and has minimal effect on the fetus.

Induced, or Accelerated, Labor

There are various reasons physicians sometimes induce labor with drugs: Rh blood problems, diabetes, toxemia, an overdue baby, ruptured membranes,

---

labor   Rhythmic muscular contractions of the uterus that expel the baby.

show   Blood-tinged mucus that is passed when the mucus plug is expelled; an early sign of labor.

bag of water (amniotic sac)   Sac containing the fluid in which the fetus is suspended.

Options for Delivery

In the early 1900s, about 95% of babies were born at home. Birthing was a family event. By the 1950s, that ratio had been reversed, with 95% of babies being born in hospitals. The switch was at the urging of physicians, who prefer delivery in the sterile, well-equipped, more convenient hospital setting. In the 1970s, the "medicalization" of childbirth began to be criticized. Some expectant parents and some medical practitioners objected to the rigidity, impersonality, and expense of hospital delivery practices. They felt that family members should have the choice of being present during delivery and that women should have more control over the childbirth process. These dissatisfactions led to the development of new options for delivery. In some states, nurse-midwives, rather than physicians, provide prenatal care and often assist in or perform routine deliveries. Some hospitals now provide alternatives to sterile and impersonal delivery rooms.

Birthing rooms are lounge-type, informal, cheerful rooms within the hospital itself. Medical equipment is available but unobtrusive. Both labor and delivery take place in the birthing room, attended by the father and medical personnel. The mother is encouraged to keep her baby with her after delivery to encourage bonding.

Birthing centers offer an alternative to the traditional hospital setting. They are separated from but near a hospital, offering a low-tech, homelike environment with the medical backup of the hospital. They provide complete prenatal and delivery services and emphasize childbirth as a family-centered event, giving both parents maximum involvement. They also focus on the emotional and social components of childbirth. The parents learn about infant care while still in the center.

Some couples opt for home birth. Supervised by a physician or nurse-midwife, home births are less expensive than hospital deliveries. At home, a woman can labor and give birth in a comfortable environment, surrounded by loved ones. Statistics show that home birth is as safe as hospital birth for low-risk women with adequate prenatal care and a qualified attendant. Typically, the midwife interviews the pregnant woman to determine if a high-risk situation exists (diabetes, blood disorders, **breech birth, transverse birth,** multiple births). If a high-risk situation does exist or may develop, the midwife and family decide whether home birth is a viable option. Occasionally, there will be complications during home delivery. A midwife is trained to recognize the early stages of complications and to take the appropriate action. Transport to the hospital during the course of the birthing process may be necessary for the health of either the baby or the mother. Some midwives require the mothers to preregister at a nearby hospital in case any complications arise.

Each type of delivery has advantages and disadvantages, which the couple must weigh carefully. The overriding consideration, however, must be the health and well-being of mother and baby.

and labor that stops too soon. Physicians also want to ensure that trained personnel will be available, especially in remote areas. In 1978, the FDA recommended against elective induction (that which is solely for the woman's or physician's convenience). Risks of induced labor include internal hemorrhaging, uterine rupture, hypertension, oxygen deprivation to the fetus, premature birth, and excessive labor pain (Berkow, 1987).

Cesarean Section

Medical complications may require a **cesarean section,** which is direct removal of the fetus by incision of the abdomen and uterine wall. Some medical indications of the need for a cesarean include a small pelvic opening, difficult labor, breech or other malpresentation, placenta previa, heart disease, diabetes, or a sexually transmitted disease in the mother. Although cesareans are major surgery, the risk of maternal death is less than 2%. It is regarded as one of the safest of all abdominal surgeries. However, the cesarean section rate quadrupled between 1970 and the 1980s, to a rate that some authorities felt was too high because not all the cesareans performed were justified or necessary ("C-section Rates," 1989; Ryan, 1988). Today, the cesarean section is the most common operation performed in the United States. In 1968, there were an average of 5% of cesarean sections; that figure rose to 25% in 1987 and dropped to 22% in 1999 (National Center for Health Statistics, 2000b). There used to be an attitude of "once a cesarean, always a cesarean." Current understanding is that at least three-quarters of women who have had a previous cesarean section may be able to have a subsequent vaginal delivery (Remez, 1994). Another reason is the introduction of programs to augment and induce labor (Hollander, 1996e).

THE POSTPARTUM PERIOD

Just as prospective parents have a number of decisions to make about the delivery of the baby, so new parents have a number of decisions to make about the period right after the birth. Different physicians and hospitals have different policies about the amount of contact between the parents and the newborn, about how long the hospital stay should be, and about when and whether to start breastfeeding. Because caring for a newborn can be exhausting and challenging for new parents, planning ahead for the postpartum period can make the transition easier for both the parents and the infant.

Care of the Newborn

As soon as the baby emerges, the most important task is to get him or her breathing, if he or she does not do so on his or her own. The physician or midwife swabs or suctions the nose and mouth with a rubber bulb to remove any mucus. The **umbilical cord** is clamped in two places—about 3 inches from the baby's abdomen—and cut between the clamps. There are no nerve endings in the cord, so neither the infant nor the mother feels the procedure. Drops of an antibiotic or silver nitrate are put in the infant's eyes to prevent bacterial infection, since the infant could be blinded by gonorrhea bacteria if the mother is infected. An exemption may sometimes be obtained if the physician is certain there is no gonorrhea.

One minute after delivery and again at 5 minutes, the baby is evaluated by a widely used system developed by pediatrician Virginia Apgar and called the **Apgar score.** The test assigns values for various signs and permits a tentative, rapid diagnosis of the baby's physical condition. The five signs of the baby's condition at birth that are measured are heart rate, respiratory effort, muscle tone, reflex response (response to breath test and to skin stimulation of the feet), and color. Each sign is given a score of 0, 1, or 2 (Greenberg, Bruess, and Sands, 1986). Thus, the maximum score on the scale is 10, which is rare. A score of 0 may indicate neonatal death. A score of 1–3 indi-

cates that the infant is very weak; 4–6, moderately weak; and 7–10, in good condition.

Parent–Infant Contact and Bonding

There is some evidence that parent–infant contact during the early hours and days of life is important for bonding (M. Klaus and Kennel, 1982). Studies at Case Western Reserve University in Cleveland confirmed the traditional belief that the emotional bonds between mother and infant are strengthened by intimate contact during the first hours of life. This is referred to as **bonding.**

Rooming-In

To avoid separating newborns from their parents, most hospitals are equipped with **rooming-in** facilities, where the baby is cared for most of the time by the mother in her own room or in a room the mother shares with several others. One advantage to rooming-in is that the new father and siblings can share in the baby's care, so that child care is family-centered from the beginning. Another advantage is that new mothers can learn much about infant care while still in the hospital, thus reducing the anxiety and even panic that may occur if they are given the total responsibility all at once upon their return home. Most mothers return home on the second day after birth.

breech birth When the buttocks or feet are the first part of the baby to pass through the vagina.

transverse birth When the shoulder and arm of the baby are the first parts seen at the opening of the vagina.

cesarean section Removal of the fetus by incising the abdominal and uterine wall.

umbilical cord The hollow cord connecting the circulation system of the fetus to the placenta.

Apgar score A widely used system to evaluate the physical condition of the newborn, named after the originator, Virginia Apgar.

bonding Development of emotional attachment between the mother and newborn immediately after birth.

rooming-in Method of postpartum care in which the mother and father care for their newborn themselves in an area of the hospital assigned to them.

Breast- versus Bottle-Feeding

One of the questions every mother faces is whether to breast-feed her baby. If the decision to breast-feed is made during pregnancy, the mother can massage her nipples and toughen them for the experience. One consideration is how the mother feels about nursing. Both bottle- and breast-fed babies do well emotionally, depending on the parents' relationship with their child. Each child needs physical contact and warmth, the sound of a pleasant voice, and the sight of a happy face. A warm, accepting mother who is bottle-feeding her baby helps her infant feel secure and loved. The important thing is the total parent–child relationship, not just the method of feeding.

Whatever type of milk is given has to be of sufficient quantity and has to agree with the baby. Most doctors would agree that there is usually nothing nutritionally better for the baby than mother's milk, provided the supply is adequate (Eiger and Olds, 1987). Babies less frequently develop allergies to the mother's milk and have a lower incidence of intestinal infections and a lower incidence of crib death (Palti, Mansbach, Pridan, Adler, and Palti, 1984). Mother's milk also contains antibodies that protect the baby against infectious diseases. Sometimes, however, the mother's supply is not adequate, or her nipples become so cracked and sore that nursing becomes too painful. Because of the effort involved, nursing mothers may become excessively fatigued by 3 months postpartum. Such problems can usually be overcome. One way is to supplement the breast with a bottle (Spock and Rothenberg, 1985). Most nutritionists feel that babies are ready for supplementary solid foods at 6 months of age, and earlier in many cases. It is important also that the nursing mother watch her diet carefully, since the baby receives necessary nutrients from her. Furthermore, drugs taken by her may be passed along to the baby in her milk. AIDS may also be transmitted (M. F. Rogers, 1985).

Beyond the benefits to the baby, women who breast-feed reduce their risk of breast cancer. Results of a Mexican case-control study suggested that the longer the woman breast-feeds, the lower her risk may be (Hollander, 1996c).

Some women find breast-feeding to be a challenge, and they become very upset if they can't manage it; others really want to breast-feed. Many mothers do not breast-feed their babies because they have full-time employment outside the home. Women who are employed part-time are more likely to breast-feed and to breast-feed longer than are women employed full-time, suggesting that conflicts between breast-feeding and working at a job vary according to the intensity of the employment (Lindberg, 1996).

Each mother should follow her best instincts and do what she really wants to do and what seems best for the baby. If needed, mothers can receive support and advice from La Leche League, which has chapters all over the world and which gives advice and help to breast-feeding mothers. Overall, after two decades of decline, there has been a definite increase in the percentage of mothers who are breast-feeding their babies, especially among middle- and upper-class mothers (Eiger and Olds, 1987).

Postpartum Adjustments

The period following childbirth is one of conflicting feelings. The long period of pregnancy is over, which is a source of feelings of relief. If the baby is wanted and healthy, considerable happiness and elation are felt. Within several days after delivery, however, the woman may experience various degrees of "baby blues," or postpartum depression, characterized by feelings of sadness and by tears, depression, insomnia, irritability, and fatigue (Hopkins, Marcues, and Campbell, 1984).

These feelings have numerous causes (Pfost, Stevens, and Matejcak, 1990). Biological factors, including genetics, variation in hormone levels, diminished thyroid activity, and sleep deprivation, may play a role (Albright, 1993). The mother may have been under emotional strain while she anxiously awaited her baby. Once the tension is over, a letdown occurs, resulting in feelings of exhaustion and depression. Childbirth itself may impose considerable physical strain on her body, which requires a period of rest and recovery. Following childbirth, there is a rapid decline in levels of estrogen and progesterone in the bloodstream, which may have a negative effect on her. Research has found that the best predictor of postpartum depression is the level of depression during pregnancy. For example, chronic stressors such as frequent conflict with support network members, maternal health problems, and lack of social support have been

One advantage of rooming-in arrangements is the new father's opportunity to share in the baby's care from the very beginning.

linked to postpartum depression (Seguin, Potvin, St-Denis, and Loiselle, 1999). Apparently, some postpartum depression is a current manifestation of previously existing depression (Albright, 1993).

After the birth, the mother feels the strain of wanting to do everything right in caring for the baby. One young mother remarked, "I never imagined that one small baby would require so much extra work. I'm exhausted" (Author's counseling notes). If the mother does not have much help from her partner, or if the partner continues to make personal demands on her, she may become exhausted from a lack of sleep, from the physical and emotional strain of caring for the baby, from the work around the house, and from caring for other children, in addition to attending to her partner's needs. Clearly, she needs help and understanding and a great deal of social support. Conscientious partners who do everything they can to assist are also affected by a lack of sleep, interference with regular work, and the strains imposed on them.

The experience of rearing a child can be more negative than, more positive than, or similar to what was expected prior to the child's birth. Perhaps the most important opportunity for divergence between expectations about and experiences with child rearing occurs after the birth of the first child. This discrepancy between expectations and experiences may affect the ease of new parents' adjustment to parenthood. One study of a sample of 473 married, middle-class, White women pregnant with their first child indicated that the women expected things to be better at 1 year postbirth than they actually were. The discrepancy significantly affected the ease of their adjustment to motherhood. Adjustment was more difficult when parenting expectations exceeded experiences in the mother's relationship with her spouse, her sense of physical well-being, her sense of maternal competence, and her maternal satisfaction. In addition, high expectations regarding child care assistance from spouse and support from extended family were associated with more difficult periods of adjustment (Kalmuss, Davidson, and Cushman, 1992).

Returning to Work

Among the considerations following childbirth are whether the mother or father will return to work and, if so, the timing of that return. One study found that close to 20% of women interrupted their paid work for 1 month or less after giving birth, 53% had begun to work by the 6th month, and 61%

had returned to work by the beginning of the 12th month. Financial considerations seemed to play an important role in the timing of the women's return to employment after childbirth. In particular, women from families that owned a home and therefore had to make mortgage payments and those with higher tax rates, as well as women who worked during pregnancy, returned to work sooner. Higher family income from sources other than the woman's earnings had the opposite effect: The women were more likely to stay home longer. Access to quality nonparental child care was also an important consideration. The decision to return to work requires adequate provision for care of the child while the parent is absent (Joesch, 1994).

The Family and Medical Leave Act of 1993 enables parents to take time off from work without pay and without losing their job. Parents can take up to 12 weeks of unpaid family leave providing they do not work in a company with fewer than 50 employees. They are entitled to return to work without penalty. The act lengthens the break from employment to some degree, since health benefits are covered by the employer during the leave. More important, the law guarantees the same or a comparable position upon return from leave, reducing the cost associated with finding a new job and thus lowering the cost of staying at home (Monroe, Garand, and Teeters, 1995).

Sexual Relations after Childbirth

What about sexual interest and activity after childbirth? There is little consistency in the research findings on the time when most people resume sexual activity following childbirth (Reamy and White, 1987). In one study, Kenney (1973) found that at 4 weeks postpartum 75% of women had returned their sexual activity to prepregnancy levels. Grudzinskas and Atkinson (1984) interviewed 328 women at 5–7 weeks after childbirth and found that only 50% had resumed intercourse. Masters and Johnson (1966) reported that all 101 women they studied had resumed sexual intercourse 6–8 weeks after childbirth. Hyde et al. (1996) studied 570 women and 550 of their partners and found that on average couples resumed sexual intercourse approximately 7 weeks postpartum. Interestingly, breast-feeding women reported significantly less sexual activity and less sexual satisfaction after childbirth than women who were not breast-feeding—a finding that has been reported by other researchers as well. There are three possible explanations for this. First, breast-feeding causes significant biological changes in the body. Estrogen production is suppressed, which decreases vaginal lubrication, making intercourse uncomfortable. And high levels of prolactin, coupled with decreased levels of testosterone, may contribute to reduced sexual desire. Second, breast-feeding mothers may have their needs for intimate touching met by breast-feeding and thus show less interest in sexual expression with their partner. Third, breast-feeding mothers may be fatigued from the drain on their bodies and the responsibility of feeding. Of course, it may be a combination of all three of these factors (Hyde et al., 1996).

A QUESTION OF POLICY

EMBRYONIC STEM CELLS

Research using embryonic stem (ES) cells has been touted as the most important medical breakthrough of the century and has the potential to provide cures for diseases and disorders that afflict millions of Americans. Considered "human clay," ES cells, by the nature of their plasticity, have the ability to change into any tissue type of the body—such as, but not limited to, brain, kidney, heart, and liver. Adult stem cells also possess plasticity, but they do not appear to have the same unlimited potential as ES cells to form an array of specialized mature cell types on command. Research using ES cells is a very complicated and controversial issue, and it is beyond the scope of this book to discuss all the ethical, political, and legal angles of the stem-cell debate. However, we feel it is one of the most important emerging public policy issues of the new millennium and expect families to be grappling with it for years to come.

ES cells could be used in cell-replacement therapies to replace damaged or diseased tissue. In addition, ES cells could be used in uncovering the mechanisms of genetic diseases, and in generating sources of normal and impaired tissues for use in drug discovery. Their potential importance in the advancement of medical treatments and cures is not at the center of the debate, however; rather, the controversy surrounds where ES cells come from.

One source of ES cells is in vitro fertilization (IVF) clinics. Typically, these clinics have thousands of frozen embryos that are regularly discarded after a set period of time. These embryos have come from couples who have, more than likely, been successful at having a baby with IVF and no longer need the embryos. Surplus cells are frozen in case the IVF was not successful and another embryo would need to be implanted. Most couples who use IVF techniques opt for having more than one egg fertilized at a time, then frozen, because often the first attempt at pregnancy is not successful and a new embryo needs to be implanted in the woman's uterus. It saves time, cost, and physical stress to retrieve multiple eggs, fertilize them, and store them for potential later use. (For a more in-depth discussion of these procedures, see Kiessling and Anderson, 2003).

The conservative argument is that these frozen embryos are life and should not be used for medical research or medical treatment, and ultimately should be adopted. The case of frozen embryos raises a whole new issue of ethical debate, but the reality currently is that the majority of these embryos are being thrown away. In August 2001, President George W. Bush approved the use of 78 lines of ES cells for science—but scientists find this insufficient because many of the cell lines were not handled properly, making them vulnerable to viruses and other contaminating proteins. Scientists doing research on ES cells want access to discarded frozen embryos from fertility clinics to advance medical treatments.

QUESTIONS TO CONSIDER:

Should scientists be allowed to use frozen embryos for medical research? Why or why not? Would your response be any different if you or a family member were suffering from an incurable disease that had the potential to be cured through the use of stem cells?

If the use of frozen embryos for science is unethical, is it also unethical to discard these frozen embryos? Discuss.

What are the ethical issues surrounding in vitro fertilization techniques using frozen embryos to help increase the chances of a couple having a baby?

Why is the practice of freezing, storing, and discarding embryos in fertility clinics not nearly as controversial as the use of these frozen embryos for science?

Who should determine the future outcome of frozen embryos?

SUMMARY

1. The signs and symptoms of pregnancy can be divided into three categories: presumptive signs, probable signs, and positive signs. Suspicions of pregnancy can also be confirmed by a pregnancy test, the most common of which are immunologic tests.

2. The birth date can be calculated by using Naegele's formula, a short way of counting 280 days from the beginning of the last menstrual period.

3. How men and women react to prospective parenthood and pregnancy depends on a large number of factors, including their desire and readiness to be parents and the status of their relationship. The timing of the pregnancy is extremely important. Some women hate being

pregnant; others are extremely happy during pregnancy. Part of the woman's reaction to pregnancy depends on the reaction of her mate to her and her changing figure. The developmental tasks of pregnancy for a couple consist of developing an emotional attachment to the fetus; solving practical issues, such as financial and living arrangements; resolving dependency issues in relation to each other; and resolving the relationships with their parents.

4. Couples are wise to get good prenatal care as soon in the pregnancy as possible. Women may experience minor discomforts early in pregnancy. Major complications such as pernicious vomiting, toxemia, threatened spontaneous abortion, placenta previa, ectopic pregnancy, Rh incompatibility, and certain illnesses require expert medical help. Sexual relations usually continue during pregnancy up until the later part of the third trimester. The mental health of the mother is also important during pregnancy since her emotional state affects the pregnancy, the childbirth experience, and the emotions of the child.

5. Prenatal development takes place during three periods: the germinal period, the embryonic period, and the fetal period.

6. Couples can prepare themselves for childbirth; physical, social, intellectual, and emotional preparation for the baby is necessary. Preparations may include learning about birth, exercising to get in good physical condition, learning relaxation techniques and proper breathing, and preparing the man to give emotional support and help to the woman during labor and delivery. The most popular prepared childbirth method is the Lamaze method.

7. Couples may want to consider all factors before deciding where to give birth, whether in a hospital, at home, or at a birthing center.

8. Labor may be divided into three stages: dilation, childbirth, and passage of the afterbirth. Anesthesia may be general, which affects the mother's whole body and that of the baby, or local or regional, which blocks pain locally or regionally and doesn't have as much negative effect on the fetus. Induced, or accelerated, labor and cesarean sections are warranted only if sufficient medical reasons are present.

9. Remarkable advances have been made in saving the lives of preterm or small-for-gestational-age babies.

10. Bonding between parent and child is more likely if parents maintain intimate contact with their infant from the time of birth. Rooming in allows the mother and the father to have this contact and to take care of the baby themselves.

11. Either breast- or bottle-feeding, properly done, may meet both the physical and the emotional needs of the baby. However, breast-feeding offers several medical benefits to both the child and the mother.

12. Postpartum blues are common.

13. Adjustments to parenthood depend partly on the degree to which actual experiences coincide with expectations.

14. Among the considerations following childbirth are whether the parent will return to work and, if so, the timing of the return.

KEY TERMS

presumptive signs	ectopic pregnancy	bag of water (amniotic sac)
probable signs	tubal pregnancy	breech birth
positive signs	Rh incompatibility	transverse birth
human chorionic gonadotropin (HCG)	blastocyst	cesarean section
	prepared childbirth	umbilical cord
Naegele's formula	Lamaze method	Apgar score
toxemia	labor	bonding
abruptio placentae	show	rooming-in
placenta previa		

QUESTIONS FOR THOUGHT

1. How can a woman determine whether she is pregnant?
2. What are some major and minor side effects of pregnancy?
3. What are the usual effects on sexual relations of being pregnant?
4. If you were having a baby, or your partner were having a baby, would you consider the Lamaze method of childbirth? Why or why not?
5. What are your views on bottle-feeding versus breast-feeding? Explain the reasons for your views.
6. If you were having a baby, or your partner were having a baby, would you consider a home birth? Why or why not?

SUGGESTED READINGS

Boston Women's Health Book Collective. (1998). *The New Our Bodies, Ourselves.* New York: Touchstone/Simon & Schuster. Represents an updated edition of a classic.

Freedman, L. H. (1999). *Birth as a Healing Experience: The Emotional Journey of Pregnancy Through Postpartum.* Binghamton, NY: Harrington Park Press. Examines the emotional and spiritual aspects of pregnancy and the postpartum period and discusses consequences of cesarean sections and other medical interventions.

Goldberg, R. (2003). *Ever Since I Had My Baby.* New York: Three Rivers Press. Focuses on understanding, treating, and preventing the most common physical after-effects of pregnancy and childbirth.

Kitzinger, S. (2003). *The New Pregnancy and Childbirth: Choices and Challenges.* London: Dorling Kindersley. Examines the many different choices and challenges presented to families today when having a baby.

Lanham, C. (1999). *Pregnancy After a Loss: A Guide to Pregnancy After a Miscarriage, Stillbirth or Infant Death.* Berkeley, CA: Berkeley Publishing Group. Provides guidance for devastated couples dealing with a subsequent pregnancy.

Lowdermilk, D., and Perry, S. (2004). *Maternity and Women's Health Care.* St. Louis, MO: Mosby. Provides an overview of health issues and bodily changes during pregnancy.

Otte, T. (2000). *The Illustrated Guide to Pregnancy and Birth.* Los Angeles: Lowell House. Represents a standard parents' guide to pregnancy, birth, and newborn care.

Spencer, P. (1999). *Parenting Guide to Pregnancy and Childbirth.* New York: Ballantine Books. Answers the typical questions of parents-to-be.

Stoppard, M. (1999). *The New Parent.* North York, Ontario: Elan. Serves as a practical guide to being a first-time parent and addresses the needs of working and stay-at-home parents, single parents, and adoptive or stepparents.

LEARNING OBJECTIVES

After reading the chapter, you should be able to:

- Understand that philosophies and emphases in child rearing change over the years; that men and women differ in their views, as do parents and children; and that cultural and biological differences and life circumstances differences in children require varying methods as well.

- Discuss parental roles in meeting children's needs and the importance of sharing responsibilities, including paternal involvement in child rearing.

- Identify the basic emotional needs of children.

- Describe some of the basic considerations in fostering children's cognitive and intellectual growth, meeting their emotional needs, and socializing and disciplining them.

- Discuss the following in relation to one-parent families: occurrence, unmarried teenage mothers, family structure and children's adjustments, special issues for the female-headed family, special issues for the male-headed family, and family work.

Parent–Child Relationships

Being a parent has many rewards and pleasures. For some people, living childless—even with a loving partner—is unthinkable. They want children as a creative expression of themselves: to love and to be loved by them. They find their own lives enriched by having children.

But parenting is not an easy task. New parents soon learn that taking care of an infant involves long hours of physical labor and many sleepless nights. One mother commented, "No one told me a baby wakes up four or five times a night." Parents soon learn that their life as a couple isn't the same. They don't have the same freedom of movement and the opportunities to do what they want to do. Parenting is an ongoing 24-hour-a-day job 7 days a week for years and, once begun, is irrevocable. You can't give the baby back. A baby changes things. In fact, the baby changes everything, so parents should give considerable thought to the responsibilities involved. If they devote themselves to learning how to be the best possible parents, they and their children are better able to enjoy the experience (Vukelich and Kliman, 1985).

 ## PHILOSOPHIES OF CHILD REARING

Most parents have idealized notions of the best way to raise children, but the reality may not coincide with the ideal (Dressel and Clark, 1990). Child-rearing philosophies—like fashions—seem to go in cycles. Yesterday's parents, feeling their own parents were too strict, turned to self-demand schedules, child-centered homes, progressive education, and more indulgent concepts of child rearing (Alwin, 1990). Now some parents are worried that today's children are too spoiled and are reacting to what they feel has been overpermissiveness. Child-rearing philosophies change from one generation to the next and parents often have to sort out conflicting advice (Dail and Way, 1985). What is important is the quality of the parent–child relationship and the overall climate of the family setting, not necessarily the particular philosophy of child rearing that the parents follow.

Parental Differences

Parents often differ in their basic philosophies of child rearing, a situation that can create marital conflict and confusion for the child. Each parent may feel that the way he or she was reared is the right way and that other methods will not be as effective. Mothers and fathers convey their parenting beliefs to their children by means of their parenting practices. When these children are grown, their parenting behavior may be patterned after their own parents' practices (Simons, Beaman, Conger, and Chao, 1992). Or parents may repudiate the methods by which they were reared and resolve to do differently with their own children (Reis, Barbara-Stein, and Bennett, 1986). Differences between fathers and mothers are common (Coleman, Ganong, Clark, and Madsen, 1989). Fathers tend to emphasize intellectual development more and social development less than mothers do. Both mothers and fathers emphasize intellectual development more for boys than for girls. Moreover, fathers tend to be less sensitive than mothers to their infant's communications and respond slowly or nonappropriately to their infant's signals (McGovern, 1990). Some research suggests that fathers in our culture tend to be stricter disciplinarians, while mothers tend to be more nurturing (Starrels, 1994). The point is that parents differ in their parenting philosophies and capabilities. Some parents know a lot about child development; others know little (Glascoe and MacLean, 1990).

Parent–Child Differences

Several studies have shown that children and parents have overlapping but different perceptions of their relationship and of each other's behavior; that is, children's reports of their parents' behavior may not agree with how the parents perceive themselves. From a developmental point of view, parent–child agreement can be seen as one of the characteristics of effective parenting. People's thoughts and actions often are based on their definition of a situation. Children are influenced by their perceptions of parental attitudes and behaviors rather than by actual parental attitudes. When perceptions are not in agreement, misunderstandings and disagreements result. One of the challenges of child rearing is to communicate so that children and parents can better understand each other and can come to some sort of mutual agreement on child-rearing practices (Tein, Roosa, and Michaels, 1994).

In 1971, Bengtson and Kuypers hypothesized that differences in perceptions of closeness between generations reflect the developmental perspectives of parents and adult children. They argued that parents, heavily invested in their children, emphasize continuity between generations. The young adult children, striving for independence, emphasize the differences, reflecting their needs for autonomy and individuation. This phenomenon is referred to as developmental stake. More recently, Giarrusso, Stallings, and Bengtson (1995) proposed a revision of developmental stake theory, suggesting that the term **intergenerational stake** better represents family perceptions of closeness. In their reconceptualization, the emphasis shifts from a focus on individual development to life course concerns that characterize each generation. Moreover, this reconceptualization extends the focus on young adults and middle-aged parents to include middle-aged adults and their aging parents. Intergenerational stake, or the divergence in perceptions of closeness between generations, appears to be greatest among young adults and then later in the life course.

Cultural Differences

Cultural differences also play an important role in philosophies of child rearing. One study examined the beliefs about child rearing, intelligence, and education among parents from different ethnic backgrounds. Immigrant parents from Cambodia, Mexico, the Philippines, and Vietnam and U.S.-born Anglo-American and Mexican American parents responded to questions about what is most important for first- and second-graders to learn in school and what characterizes an intelligent child. Immigrant parents rated conformity to external standards as more important than development of autonomous behavior. In contrast, U.S.-born parents favored autonomy over conformity. Parents from all groups except Anglo-Americans indicated that noncognitive characteristics, such as motivation, social skills, and practical school skills, were as important as or more important than cognitive characteristics, such as problem-solving skills, verbal ability, and creative ability. Thus, parents from different cultural backgrounds have different ideas about what it means to be intelligent, what kind of skills children need in order to do well in school, and what practices will promote their children's development (Okagaki and Sternberg, 1993).

Using data from the National Survey of Families and Households, a study of cultural variations in parenting among White, African American, His-

panic, and Asian American mothers and fathers, researchers assessed parents in terms of parenting attitudes, behaviors, and involvement. However, even taking differences in socioeconomic status into consideration, the researchers found more similarities than differences between and among the four parenting groups. Among the various cultural groups, White parents placed less general emphasis on the children's exercising self-control and succeeding in school than did African American, Hispanic, and Asian American parents (Julian, McKenry, and McKelbey, 1994).

Life Circumstances

Not only is family background important in the way parents relate to their children, but life circumstances also affect parent–child relationships (Pittman, Wright, and Lloyd, 1989). The level of marital satisfaction has a significant effect on parenting practices (Simons, Whitbeck, Conger, and Melby, 1990), as does the level of parental mental health and self-esteem. Parents who experience a great deal of stress in their lives, such as economic stress, often have more difficulty being patient and relaxed with their children. One study found that African American and Hispanic mothers who were on welfare were less emotionally and verbally responsive to their children, spanked them more, and were generally more likely to impose restrictions and punishment than were those not on welfare (Philliber and Graham, 1981). However, welfare was not the cause per se; rather, it was the overall frustration of their lives that affected the quality of parenting. These parenting behaviors are found more frequently among parents with less education and lower maternal age. Other studies have shown that more mothers than fathers feel the stress of parenting, primarily because of the heavier burden and greater responsibilities placed on them (Dodson, 1998; Scott and Alwin, 1989). The total circumstances of parents' lives influence the quality of parenting. The quality of family relationships in the parents' families of origin also has both direct and

intergenerational stake Family members' perceptions of closeness, especially as they relate to life course concerns that characterize each generation.

Cultural Conflict and Acculturation

Cultural pride and values are important to families, but many cultural groups feel that they are faced with a dilemma: whether to accommodate themselves to the Anglo-American world and learn to compete in it or to retain traditional customs and values and live apart (Markstrom-Adams, 1990).

In a study of 109 reservation and urban American Indian parents and children, Stubben (1998) found that 95% identified that cultural values are very important to their family, but many of these traditional values are at odds with the dominant culture. Native American culture is oriented to the present and is not concerned with time or the future; White culture is future-oriented, concerned with time and planning ahead. Native Americans see human life as being in harmony with nature; Whites seek conquest over nature. Native American life is group-oriented and emphasizes cooperation; White society emphasizes individualism and competition (Stubben, 2001). Glover (2001) described the traditional Native American values to be generosity, respect for elders, respect for all creation, harmony, and individual freedom; she explained that it is "difficult to separate these values and describe each individually because they are interwoven, interconnected, and related to Native American spirituality and tribalism" (p. 214). In Native American culture, all things are respected and have a spiritual nature such as children, the earth and creatures from the land, sea and sky (Glover, 2001). It is important to honor through harmony and balance what is thought to be a very sacred connection with the energy of life (Garrett and Wilbur, 1999). As everything is intimately connected biologically, spiritually, and emotionally, a person is connected to families, households, and communities (Glover, 2001).

Another example of the acculturation dilemma is the comparison of traditional Chinese values with Western urban industrial values. Confucianism has been a major influence on the Chinese family for more than 2,000 years. The philosophy stresses the importance of filial piety, respect and obedi-ence toward parents and older generations, family obligations, harmonious relationships, parental control, and emotional restraint. These concepts, in essence, are the basis of traditional Chinese family life. Confucian beliefs emphasize specific expectations of behavior with regard to age, gender, and birth order. There is a protocol in place based on obedience and respect that dictates that women defer to men, sons defer to fathers, and younger brothers defer to older ones. Respect follows an upward pattern from young to old and from female to male, with the elderly male being the most revered and having the most power (Wu, 2001). This protocol is designed to preserve family harmony and minimize the level of conflict within a family.

Chinese Americans teach children to conform to the wishes of their parents, the elderly, teachers, and people of higher status. Traditional approaches of child rearing feature authoritarian methods: a strict interpretation of good and bad behavior, limitation of social interaction, firm discipline involving physical punishment, expectation of obedience and conformity, and the absence of overt parental praise. Chinese children are also taught emotional restraint and are less likely than American children to be praised by their parents for their good behavior or school performance. Traditional Chinese families do not typically give rewards to their children (Uba, 1994). Emphasis is traditionally placed more on self-discipline than on external control, with the idea being that behavior is based on one's internal morality rather than on fear of being punished or the expectation of reward (Wu, 2001; Uba, 1994).

As in many other cultures, Chinese American parents often struggle to maintain traditional values while living among Western values, and it becomes a difficult balance (Wu, 2001). However, Nieto (1996) believes that when people can be part of two different cultures, they afford themselves the advantage of seeing things from different perspectives and becoming comfortable in a variety of situations.

indirect influences on their psychological and physical health. These, in turn, influence the parents' relationships with their own children (Harvey, Curry, and Bray, 1991).

Another life circumstance affecting parenting is maternal age at first birth. The older a mother is when she has her first child, the more likely she is to give praise and physical affection to her child. The younger a mother at first birth, the more likely she is to criticize her child and use physical punishment (Conger, McCarty, Yang, Lahey, and Burgess, 1984). When pregnancy occurs in the early teen years, it may have long-term negative consequences for the young mother's social, psychological, and material well-being and for her child. Teenage fathers often are not involved in the care of their children, particularly when they are not married to the mother. Common obstacles to teenage father involvement is a strained relationship with the child's mother (W. Allen and Doherty, 1996) and a disinterest in child rearing (Rhein et al., 1997). Teen fatherhood is related to a variety of risk factors, such as low educational performance, risky sexual behavior, and drug use (Thornberry, Smith, and Howard, 1997). Because of immaturity and life circumstances, many teenage parents have a great deal of difficulty meeting their children's total needs.

Other life circumstances are sociolcultural background and generational differences. For example, among Mexican American families there are important intergenerational differences in child-rearing practices related to variations in the sociocultural backgrounds of families. Parents who are first- or second-generation immigrants, especially mothers, are very similar in their socialization practices. Foreign-born mothers stress earlier autonomy, productive use of time, and strict obedience more than do mothers of third-generation adolescents. Immigrant parents generally emphasize socialization practices that revolve around issues of responsibility. This approach is characterized by an expectation of earlier self-reliance and adherence to family rules within an open parent–child relationship; it resembles an authoritative parenting. In contrast, U.S.-born parents, particularly mothers, emphasize socialization practices that revolve around expressions of concern. This approach is characterized by emotional support and the expectation of proper behavior at home and in school (Buriel, 1993).

Differences in Children

Biological influences play a much larger role in child-rearing practices than is sometimes admitted. For example, there are biological bases for intelligence and personality (B. C. Miller, 1993). For this reason, no one method of child rearing can be considered best for all children. Children are individuals; what works for one may not work for another. Some children want close attachments with parents, for example, while others do not (Rosen and Rothbaum, 1993). Some children are more difficult to raise than others (Simons et al., 1990). Children who are temperamentally easy to raise have a positive effect on healthy family functioning (Stoneman, Brody, and Burke, 1989).

PARENTAL ROLES

Although all children are different, they all go through the same developmental stages and have the same basic growth needs. No matter what child-rearing strategy the parents follow, they must meet these needs.

Meeting Children's Needs

The parental role sounds simple: to meet the needs of children so that they can grow (Amato and Ochiltree, 1986). Within all children are the seeds of growth, that is, a natural inclination to develop to maturity. Parents don't have to teach children to grow physically, for example. The tendency to grow is so strong that only by extreme physical deprivation can parents prevent physical development, and even then some development takes place. The parental task is to discover the physical needs of the child and to fulfill those needs.

Similarly, the parental task is to fulfill emotional needs so that children become emotionally secure and stable people. If children's needs for love, affection, security, understanding, and approval are met, they are more likely to develop positive feelings. But if their emotional needs are unmet, children may become fearful, hostile, insecure, anxious, and rejecting.

The quality of children's attachment to their parents has been studied extensively. For example, children's early positive attachments show themselves later in more frequent, sociable, and positive interactions with parents and peers. Conversely, children with insecure attachments are more likely to cling to their parents, interact negatively with them and with their peers, and show signs of anxiety around their parents. Children form secure attachments to their parents through positive, reciprocal interactions over time. When attachments with parents are severed by separation, children feel threatened, which can be detrimental to their self-esteem and interpersonal relations (Bullock, 1993).

Children also have social needs. They are naturally gregarious, and they want to be with others, generally like other people, and ordinarily try to please them and be accepted by them. But these natural tendencies are unsophisticated. Children want to make friends but don't know how to relate; they want others to like them but don't know how to please. Their need, therefore, is for socialization—to

The parental role sounds so simple—to meet the needs of children so they can grow. In what ways does a child need to grow? What must parents do to satisfy all of the child's needs?

build on their normal desire to belong and to relate by learning group mores, customs, manners, and habits so that they can fit into the group. The parental task is to provide their children with the necessary opportunities for socialization so that they can become a part of society. Furthermore, certain parental practices, such as a high degree of parental affection and authoritative child rearing, may stimulate a child's positive orientation toward others and influence the child's acceptance by a peer group. In other words, parental reactions to their child's need for help are related to their child's prosocial behavior and social confidence (Dekovic and Janssens, 1992).

The capacity for intellectual growth is also inborn. Children are born naturally curious: They want to learn about everything, and they desire a variety of new experiences by which this learning can take place. The parental role is to encourage cognitive growth and to fulfill these intellectual needs by providing sensory stimulation and a variety of learning experiences. Parents facilitate intellectual growth by providing opportunities for observation, reading, conversation, and contact with others and with the natural world. When a child's environment is stimulating, curiosity is encouraged, and his or her cognitive development will proceed very rapidly. But if a child's surroundings are sterile, unchanging, and uninteresting, or if

his or her human contacts and experiences are limited, growth will stop or slow down because of intellectual deprivation.

According to a study of the children of White, Black, and Hispanic adolescent mothers, the early home environment and the mother's level of education seem to be the most important influences on cognitive attainment among their children (S. Edwards, 1992b). Parental encouragement in response to children's grades and support for children's autonomy also help children to be intrinsically motivated and to perform better in school (Ginsburg and Bronstein, 1993).

Children have the capacity to grow morally as well as intellectually. They are born trusting and become mistrusting only when they learn that they cannot depend on people around them. They are born with a capacity to develop a conscience and to distinguish different moral values. But their ability is only a potential one; it has to be developed through educated reasoning, imitation of the example of others, and simple trial and error. The parental role here is to fulfill their children's moral needs for trust and for values to live by.

Sometimes, of course, children's needs aren't met because parents either can't or won't fulfill them. The children do not receive proper food and rest; they are not loved or socialized; and they are deprived intellectually and spiritually. When this happens, growth stops or slows down, and the children become physically, emotionally, socially, intellectually, or morally limited. Growth takes place when needs are fulfilled; development is delayed because of deprivation.

Sharing Responsibilities

In many societies, the man's primary family role is that of economic provider. Traditionally, women assume responsibility for the day-to-day care and supervision of children and are more likely to provide children with emotional and physical comfort. Yet children benefit if both parents share in meeting their needs (Atkinson, 1987). The needs of dependent children are not easily met by the mother or father alone, especially if there is more than one child. Having only one parent to fulfill the role of both parents is exhausting and potentially overwhelming.

Every parent brings strengths and weaknesses to the role. Like most mothers, the best fathers are almost indispensable (S. M. H. Hanson and Bozett, 1987). One mother related:

> I do an awful lot for the children, but there are some things that John can do better. He can put the baby to bed, rock her, and get her to sleep a lot more calmly and easily than I can. I'm too impatient. He teaches our oldest son how to fish, roller skate, and play baseball. I never could do those things. And John is very affectionate. He hugs and kisses Maurine and holds her. I do too, but not like John. She is in seventh heaven when she is in his arms. You don't have to tell me that my children need their father. I know they do. (Author's counseling notes)

Closeness to their fathers adds to children's happiness and life satisfaction and minimizes psychological stress. Closeness to stepfathers also contributes to children's well-being. Overall, these findings indicate that fathers are important figures in the lives of children and young adults (Amato, 1994b). Moreover, the fathers also benefit from caring for their children, and paternal involvement also increases marital satisfaction (Ishii-Kuntz, 1994; Kalmijn, 1999).

Despite these benefits, fathers with preschool children participate, on average, in only 26% of child care activities (Ishii-Kuntz, 1994). Other studies indicate that in two-parent families in which the mother is not employed fathers spend about 20–25% as much time as the mothers do in child

care activities. In two-parent families with employed mothers, the level of paternal engagement is substantially higher. But this does not necessarily mean that fathers are doing more; it may mean that mothers are doing less. Fathers are proportionally more involved when mothers are employed, but their level of involvement in absolute terms may not differ significantly. Other studies have found that fathers spend much more time on child care when there are younger children in the family and that they are more involved with their sons than with their daughters, particularly when the children are of school age (Ishii-Kuntz, 1994).

Although middle-class fathers take a more active role than lower-class fathers, the major responsibilities for child care still fall most heavily on the mother. However, many fathers wish to increase the time they spend with their children, but numerous cultural, occupational, family, and personal barriers may stand in their way. For example, some fathers are too consumed with achieving economic success to pay much attention to their children (LaRossa and Reitzes, 1993). At least when residing in the home, fathers are more involved in the rearing of their children than were fathers a generation or two ago. The gap between men's and women's participation in child rearing appears to be shrinking. As a result, today's fathers report feeling closer to their children than their own fathers were to them. Social attitudes toward fathering have also shifted. Perhaps more than ever before, fathers are acknowledged as important to the intellectual and emotional well-being of their offspring. Not surprisingly, research supports the notion that fathers can enhance their children's social, emotional, and cognitive development (Woodworth, Belsky, and Crnic, 1996).

There is increasing recognition that fathers can and should participate in child rearing and that if they do not their children miss much, and they themselves miss out on a chance for self-actualization (Barnett and Baruch, 1987). One observation of child care in public places, such as parks, revealed that 43% of the children had men as the primary caregiver (Amato, 1989). Some of the men may have been noncustodial fathers, but all were taking children on excursions and participating in their children's growth and development. Concurrently, demographers are noting that a small but growing number of fathers are limiting their work hours to spend more time with their children. Others are leaving the workforce entirely and becoming stay-at-home fathers so that their children receive consistent in-home care and so that they can enjoy and participate in their children's growth and development.

In sum, there have been increases over time in the average degree of paternal involvement with children. However, mothers continue to spend more time with their children than do fathers and to take responsibility for most of their day-to-day care, regardless of their employment status. Many working women, therefore, are engaged in a second shift of taking care of their family after returning from a day of paid work (Ishii-Kuntz, 1994). At the same time, the father's involvement is increasingly recognized as a benefit to the child and the father and to marital harmony.

Parents' employment and responsibilities outside the home sometimes result in their children becoming **latchkey children:** unsupervised youngsters who care for themselves before or after school, on weekends, and during holidays while the parents work. It is estimated that 5 million children in the United States ages 5–13 are home regularly without direct adult supervision while the parents work (Tirozzi, 1998). They commonly carry keys to let themselves in their homes—hence the term *latchkey children.* Some parents cite benefits of self-care: independence, self-reliance, less stereotyped gender-role views of mothers, peer interaction, greater participation in household duties, and greater ability to care for self. Other parents believe that such claims reflect attempts to ease parents' guilty feelings.

Numerous studies emphasize the negative aspects of self-care. Children frequently mention that they experienced fear and apprehension at being left alone (Council for Children, 1984). Overall, the environmental context is the single most important factor in how well latchkey children adjust to self-care. Whether the children are in a relatively safe, crime-free setting or in an environment in which the potential for crime is higher makes a difference in fear levels (B. E. Robinson, Rowland, and Coleman, 1986).

Contrary to popular opinion, most latchkey children are not the children of low-income single parents who cannot afford stable child care arrangements (Cain and Hofferth, 1989). Most are older, White, middle-class children who live in suburban or rural areas. More than 28 million school-age children have both parents or their only parent in the workforce (Chaddock, 1999), and these parents are usually still at work when the school day ends. Because of this, most Americans (93%) want school-based after-school programs in their community. In response to parents' demands, Congress in 1997 set aside $1 million to fund pilot after-school programs. The subsequent demand was so great that Congress increased the sum to $40 million in 1998 and to $200 million in 1999 (Chaddock, 1999). By 2002, $1 billion was allocated, but despite continued higher authorization amounts, the amount actually given to after-school programs is decreasing (Afterschool Alliance, 2003).

FOSTERING COGNITIVE AND INTELLECTUAL GROWTH

The word **cognition** (derived from the Latin *cognoscere,* "to know") refers to the process of becoming acquainted with the world and objects in it, including ourselves. We do this by taking in information through the senses of vision, touch, taste, hearing, and smell; processing this information; and acting on it. This process goes on constantly, so an infant is developing cognitively all the time.

Parental Contributions

Parents can assist their children's cognitive development in several ways. One way is by providing secure human relationships from which exploration can take place. Cognitive development proceeds faster when the child feels emotionally secure.

In addition to providing a secure base, parents can enhance cognitive development by offering a stimulating and intellectually rich environment (Parks and Smeriglio, 1986). This means talking and singing to babies; playing music; offering objects that vary in shape, texture, size, and color; propping babies up so that they can see more; taking them places so as to expose them to a variety of sights, sounds, and people; and offering playthings to look at, hold, squeeze, suck, bite, taste, smell, hear, and examine. It means offering toddlers playthings they can climb onto, crawl under, push, pull, drag, ride, swing, jump on, float, and splash with.

Compared with children who receive stimulation, children who are environmentally deprived do much more poorly on IQ tests because of cognitive delays. With this in mind, the Head Start program was created. Head Start is a federally funded program offering early education, health care, social services, and nutrition to children from low-income families. The goal of the Head Start program is to compensate for this cultural deprivation by offering an environment rich in sensorimotor experiences. Head Start does help, and there has been some effort to extend it to younger children. Specifically, intervention by age 18 months is recommended for infants who are markedly environmentally deprived.

Language Development and Cultivation

In the beginning, human babies produce vowel-like sounds that are expressions of emotional distress or comfort. Between 9 and 12 months, babies show that they understand words and respond and adjust to them. For example, a baby may open his or her mouth in response to the word *cracker* or accept a glass of water in response to the word *drink.* The median age for uttering the first word is 11 months. By 12 months, the average vocabulary is two words. Between 12 and 18 months, babies begin to combine words. The earliest sentences are usually two words: a noun and a verb, such as "Daddy gone."

Language development has a definite connection to environment and human relationships. Parents who read stories to their children and talk to them enable them to produce significantly more sounds and thus to learn to talk earlier than do other infants. Both the amount and the warmth of the vocalization of parents with their infants are related to their children's vocalization. Furthermore, communication skills that parents teach their children have a definite effect on the children's peer acceptance. In other words, there is a positive relationship between children's popularity in their peer group and their communication skills (Burleson, Della, and Applegate, 1992).

Education Defining and Modeling

As children get older, parents serve as models and definers of their children's educational aspirations and attainment (J. Cohen, 1987). Parents transmit their educational values to their children. Parents who are well educated serve as examples of what they hope their children will achieve. Those who take an interest in their children's schooling are teaching them that education is important and that they are expected to do well. In his study of parents as educational models and definers, J. Cohen (1987) found that mothers and fathers were about equal in

their modeling influence, although whichever parent had more education tended to have more influence. Because of their higher levels of education, white-collar parents were usually more effective educational models than were blue-collar parents.

MEETING EMOTIONAL NEEDS

The basic emotional needs of children are for security, trust, love, and affection, as well as self-esteem. The psychoanalyst Erik Erikson (1959) concluded that developing trust is the basic **psychosocial task** during the first year of life. If infants are well-handled, nurtured, and loved, they develop trust and security and a basic optimism. Badly handled, they become insecure and mistrustful. Overall, infant affect (positive emotion) is positively correlated with the quality of the home environment in which they are brought up (Luster, Boger, and Hannan, 1993).

During the first year of life, parents can best meet these emotional needs by fostering their children's feelings of dependency, helping them feel totally secure. This is accomplished in several ways. The home environment is important. If it is fairly relaxed and free of tension and anxiety, if it is a pleasant, happy place, children develop a feeling of well-being merely by living there. The emotional tone that parents convey is also important. Warm, loving, pleasant parents who are themselves calm and relaxed convey these feelings to their children. Being able to depend on parents for need fulfillment, whether it be for food when hungry or for comfort when upset, also develops infants' sense of security and trust. Physical contact and closeness are also important. Infants feel secure when held close to their parent's warm body, when they can feel their hand on their parent's face, or when they feel the comfort of loving

latchkey children Unsupervised children who care for themselves before or after school, on weekends, or during holidays while their parents work. They commonly carry keys to let themselves in the house or apartment.

cognition Literally, the act of knowing; the act of becoming acquainted with the world and the objects, people, and conditions in it.

psychosocial task The skills, knowledge, functions, and attitudes individuals need to acquire at different periods in their lives.

344 Chapter 13 *Parent–Child Relationships*

QUESTIONS FOR THOUGHT

1. What are the basic emotional needs of children? Do these match with what you remember as your needs as a child?

2. What are the needs of children for socialization and discipline? Do you believe in spanking children? Why or why not?

3. What are some strategies for single parents, both mothers and fathers, to manage their many responsibilities?

4. What are some things parents can do to promote their children's emotional and intellectual development?

SUGGESTED READINGS

Bigelow, B. J., Tesson, G., and Lewko, J. H. (1996). *Learning the Rules: The Anatomy of Children's Relationships*. New York: Guilford Press. Examines what relationships mean to children and how children manage them.

Blankenhorn, Z. (1995). *Fatherless: Confronting Our Most Urgent Social Problem*. New York: Basic Books. Argues that father absence causes all major social problems and that only one type of fatherhood can serve children.

Borkowski, J. G., Ramey, S. L., and Bristol-Power, M. (2002). *Parenting and the Child's World: Influences on Academic, Intellectual, and Social-Emotional Development*. Mahwah, NJ: Lawrence Erlbaum. Describes when, where, and how parenting matters and the major antecedents and moderators of effective parenting.

Cicchetti, D., Rappaport, J., Sandler, I., and Weissberg, R. (2000). *The Promotion of Wellness in Children and Adolescents*. Washington, DC: CWLA Press. Examines the complicated issues of encouraging child and adolescent wellness in American society.

Cicirelli, B. G. (1995). *Sibling Relationships Across the Life Span*. New York: Plenum. Discusses the influence of lifelong sibling relationships and gives up-to-date reviews of research literature.

Crittenden, A. (2001) *The Price of Motherhood: Why the Most Important Job in the World Is Still the Least Valued*. New York: Metropolitan Books. Reviews current social scientific literature on motherhood.

Daly, K. (1996). *Families and Time*. Thousand Oaks, CA: Sage. Explores the family's use of time.

Deutsch, F. M. (1999). *Halving It All: How Equally Shared Parenting Works*. Cambridge, MA: Harvard University Press. Describes how shared parenting is enacted in the handling of the details of everyday life.

Dodson, L. (1999). *Don't Call Us Out of Name: The Untold Lives of Women and Girls in Poor America*. Boston: Beacon Press. Gives poor women's stories of work, family, and poverty and their demeaning experiences with the social service system.

Dongen, M., van Frinking, G., and Jacobs, M. (Eds.). (1995). *Changing Fatherhood: An Interdisciplinary Perspective*. Amsterdam: Thesis. Examines fatherhood from many perspectives.

Harkness, S., and Super, C. M. (Eds.). (1996). *Parents' Cultural Belief Systems: Their Origins, Expressions, and Consequences*. New York: Guilford Press. Focuses on the beliefs parents have about children.

Luster, T., and Okagaki, L. (Eds.). (1993). *Parenting: An Ecological Perspective*. Hillsdale, NJ: Lawrence Erlbaum. Explores social networks and their influence upon families.

Murray, S. A. (1994). *Beating the Devil Out of Them: Corporal Punishment in American Families*. New York: Lexington Books. Summarizes 30-plus years of research on the occurrence and effects of violence inflicted on children.

Phoenix, A., Woollett, A., and Lloyd, E. (Eds.). (1991). *Motherhood: Meanings, Practices, and Ideologies*. London: Sage. Offers essays on motherhood.

Rivdens, J. (1994). *Mothers and Their Children: A Feminist Sociology of Child Rearing*. London: Sage. Argues for the need to reexamine caregiving principles.

Rossi, A., and Rossi, P. (1990). *Of Human Bonding: Parent-Child Relations Across the Life Course*. New York: Aldine de Gruyter. Examines how relations between children and parents vary across the life course.

Sigel, I. E., McGillicudy, D. E., Lisi, A. V., and Goodnow, J. J. (Eds.). (1992). *Parental Belief Systems: The Psychological Consequences for Children* (2nd ed.). Hillsdale, NJ: Lawrence Erlbaum. Discusses parental cognition.

Wood, B., and Beck, R. J. (1994). *Home Rules*. Baltimore: Johns Hopkins University Press. Focuses on parental expectations for children.

Wrigley, J. (1995). *Other People's Children: An Intimate Account of the Dilemmas Facing Middle-Class Parents and the Women They Hire to Raise Their Children*. New York: Basic Books. Discusses in-home caregivers and parents' relationships with them.

Yablonsky, L. (1990). *Fathers and Sons: The Most Challenging of All Family Relationships*. New York: Gardner Press. Reports the results of surveys and interviews with fathers and sons.

Zucchino, D. (1997). *The Myth of the Welfare Queen*. New York: Touchstone Books. Portrays a year in the lives of two women as they navigate the patchwork of federal and state programs to support their families.

LEARNING OBJECTIVES

After reading the chapter, you should be able to:

- Understand that family-of-origin experiences continue to exert an influence after marriage.

- Discuss the causes of and alternatives to parental disapproval of mate choice.

- Identify some of the effects of positive and negative identification with parents and the way these affect a person in adulthood.

- Understand the realities of care provided by families to their elderly family members.

- Discuss important considerations relating to intergenerational bonds—in particular, mother–grown daughter relationships and father-son support

- Discuss important issues in relation to conflicts between parents and adult children.

- Summarize some of the basic information about relationships with in-laws, including the relationship of in-law adjustment to marital happiness and the causes of and alternatives to in-law conflict.

- Identify considerations in living with extended families during middle age.

- Discuss relationships with grandparents: how grandparents are different today than in former generations, what grandparents can do for grandchildren, how adolescents and young adults relate with grandparents, what grandchildren can do for grandparents, and how grandparents parent their

Parents and Extended Family Relationships

The couple relationship in marriage does not exist in isolation. Not only do the spouses continue to maintain relationships with their own parents, but each has also acquired a whole new set of in-laws. How the spouses relate to their own parents and to their parents-in-law has important influences on their marriage and their children.

In this chapter, we are concerned with these extended family relationships and their effect on the couple. We are also concerned with some special situations: problems created by parental disapproval of choice of partner, positive and negative parental identification, interdependence between generations, mother–daughter relationships, and conflict between parents and adult children.

Special attention is given to in-law and grandparent relationships. What kinds of in-laws and grandparents do people like? What are important roots of conflict? What are some special considerations when couples live with in-laws or grandparents? What are some positive aspects of such relationships? What can grandparents do for children, and what can children do for grandparents? In answering all these questions, this chapter emphasizes working out harmonious relationships among generations.

PARENT–ADULT CHILD RELATIONSHIPS

The relationship a child experienced with his or her parents while growing up continues to exert a profound influence on that person as an adult. If the relationship with the parents has been satisfying, pleasant emotional reactions and memories are carried into adulthood. However, disruptive relationships involving frustration, deprivation, fear, or hurt produce unpleasant emotional experiences and memories that reemerge from time to time, producing varying amounts of stress. In some cases, time moderates the distress; in others, parent–child misunderstandings emerge and influence the family relationships across the life span.

When Parents Disapprove of Choice of Partner

Parent–young adult child relationships become particularly important in the mate selection process. Parental influence may begin when the adolescent first starts dating (M. P. Johnson and Milardo, 1984). The parents are appropriately interested in their child's choice of friends and dating partners. The key to maintaining a harmonious relationship and to continuing dialogue with their adolescent lies in how they express that concern. If the parents object to the choice, the couple are sometimes pushed into each other's arms for comfort and solace. This "Romeo and Juliet" effect may result in a hasty, poor partner choice that would not have been made if the relationship had been allowed to evolve or dissolve naturally.

Parental objections are usually based on one or more of the following reasons:

- **The parents don't like the person their son or daughter has chosen:** "He's rude." "She's crude." "He's impolite." "She has a bad reputation." "He's not a very nice person." "She's too domineering." These objections are based on dislike of the other person's personality.

- **The parents feel the other person has a problem:** "He drinks too much." "She's too emotional." "He can't hold a steady job." "She can't get along with anybody."

- **The other person is different from the parent's family:** "Her family are rather common people." "He's not educated." "She's not of our faith." "Why couldn't he have picked some nice Italian (or Irish, Jewish, African American, or Latino) girl?"

- **There is a significant age difference:** "She's too young." "He's too old for her."

- **The person has been married once or more before:** "This is his third time around." "She has three children by a previous marriage. Why does he want to get stuck with her?"

- **They're in too much of a hurry:** "They've only known each other for three months." "They don't even know each other." "We don't even know him (her)."

Some families would object no matter whom their son or daughter selected. Such families may be possessive of their offspring and unwilling to let them leave home or grow up. Or they want to keep their children home to help the family. An only daughter who was still at home was expected to care for her widowed mother. She explained:

The relationship a child experiences with his or her parents while growing up continues to exert a profound influence on that person as an adult.

I had to take my mother into consideration. No, I couldn't do anything. She had to be my prime concern. . . . So there was just no question about it. . . . It was my responsibility because my older brother was married, and my other brother was in school, so I was elected. (Allen and Pickett, 1987, p. 522)

Parental disapproval may be expressed in a number of ways. Parents who object before marriage may not be able to back off after the wedding, so they continue to object and criticize, exerting an adverse influence. Parents may come between the partners by taking sides in disputes. For the children's part, choosing a spouse in opposition to parental acceptance may be indicative of problems in the parent–young adult relationship, which may find disruptive expression in the marriage. Furthermore, the selection of a partner to whom parents object is often motivated by a desire to rebel against parental values, a motivation that impairs judgment in choosing a partner.

Of course, young adults can try to get their parents to like their partner. If objections are based on lack of knowledge, given time and opportunity to get acquainted, some parents end up approving. But parents are not always wrong. If there are serious differences, this may be a warning signal to go slowly, to take more time and not rush into marriage. Premarital counseling may also help the couple clarify issues.

The time to resolve problems is before marriage, if possible, or else troublesome issues will carry over into the marriage. One woman explained,

When my husband was courting me, I tried in every way to get his parents to like me, but they would never accept me. They seemed to resent everything I did. I knew I was going to have in-law problems after marriage, and we certainly did. (Author's counseling notes)

Children's Identification with Parents

As we have seen, in healthy families, children form close emotional attachments to parents. In the process, gender-role socialization takes place. That is, girls learn what it is like to be a spouse and mother, and boys learn what it is like to be a spouse and father. Each child also forms expectations of what traits and behaviors to expect from the opposite sex based on the role models they have observed. This identification, particularly with parents, influences marital expectations and behavior. However, identification may be positive or negative.

Positive identification is the attachment of the child to images of desired loving behavior. In this situation, the young adult child seeks to duplicate family-of-origin relationships in his or her own marriage. Such situations become troublesome when the spouse is not like the beloved parent—for example, when the woman cannot be like her spouse's mother or the man like his spouse's father. As one man said, "I'm not like your father, so don't expect me to be." The man who expects his partner to play the same role in their marriage that his mother did in hers is suggesting, "I can only love you if you're like my mother." People may develop unrealistic expectations from the example set by their own parents.

Negative identification results in an effort to avoid being like the parent. In situations of negative identification, differences rather than similarities underlie spouse selection and facilitate marital harmony. For example, a man reared by a demanding mother might always be wary lest a female dominate him. A woman may avoid men who drink because, as a child, she was frightened when her father came home drunk. She may find her partner's restraint particularly appealing. In marriage, two personalities interact. How they deal with the partner's conscious and unconscious needs will partly determine the success of the marriage.

Interdependence between Generations

For many years, the myth grew that elderly people were alienated from their families, especially from their adult children, that families did not care for their elderly relatives, and that children had abandoned their elderly parents to institutions for care. Families as primary social units were believed to be dying out, or at least were seen as irresponsible toward elderly members. The myth was substantiated by the decrease in family size and the geographical mobility of families (understood as widening the generation gap), the development of an advanced society that supported nonworking members, and the proliferation of nursing homes and hospitals to care for chronically ill and frail elderly persons.

We now know that the myth is indeed just that. While independence and autonomy remain a cultural ideal, families are typified by interdependence. Interdependence refers to cooperation between persons and groups; one benefits from the contributions of others even as they contribute to one's own well-being. Families tend to maintain varying degrees of interdependence throughout the life course. The flow of resources typically is from the older generations to the younger ones even when elderly members are receiving some form of assistance. Families were and still are a major source of help to the elderly. Families often go to great lengths to care for their elderly members and do not lightly enter into decisions to institutionalize them. They also maintain strong bonds with older members and visit the older relatives who are institutionalized and mentally or physically impaired. Nevertheless, the myth constituted a serious indictment of families. Only after several decades of research on the part of gerontologists was this myth laid to rest (High, 1991).

Bengtson (2001) sees an increasing importance placed on multigenerational bonds and the diversity of intergenerational family styles; he proposes that "relations across more than two generations are becoming increasingly important to individuals and families in American society; that they are increasingly diverse in structure and functions; and that in the early 21st century, these multigenerational bonds will not only enhance but in some cases replace nuclear family functions, which have been so much the focus of sociologists during the 20th century" (p. 2). Silverstein and Bengtson (1997) identified five types of intergenerational relationships, with most being strong, positive, and mutually supportive. They found that 25% of family generational relationships were tight-knit or emotionally and psychically close and supportive; 25% were sociable, with high levels of affinity; 16% were obligatory, with low levels of attachment and mutual exchange of help, but with potential for future support; 16% were intimate but distant, with promise of possible future support; and only 17% were detached with low levels of connectedness.

Research has shown that some late-life events are associated with increased intergenerational involvement. Using data from the National Survey of Families and Households, Roan and Raley (1996) examined the effects of mothers' widowhood on intergenerational relations. Their longitudinal analysis revealed that coresidence was not common but that adult children were more likely to coreside with their mothers if their mothers were widowed. Moreover, the mothers' widowhood increased intergenerational contact because parents and adult children shared their grief and offered mutual support. Although Blacks were less likely to provide financial assistance to kin, they had a higher likelihood than Whites of coresiding with or frequently contacting kin.

Despite social changes such as geographic mobility, divorce, and women's participation in the labor force, adult children, especially daughters, remain the most reliable source of instrumental social support for their parents. There are two major reasons for support: (1) the ties of affection and (2) the sense of responsibility. Strong affectional ties are powerful motivating factors in providing support. Daughters are more likely to be directly motivated to act by feelings of emotional intimacy. Sons are more inclined to help parents out of a sense of obligation regardless of the quality of their relationship.

Dependence between generations is not limited to what the middle-aged generation does for the older generation, however. It includes the contributions that the older generations make to younger family members as well. These contributions are sizable and take the form of shared meals, loans for household appliances and furnishings, transfers of deeds and titles, and bargain-rate sales of homes, businesses, and vehicles. Some grandparents cosign loans for their children and grandchildren or save money for the grandchildren's tuition. Others provide child care or other services that allow the parents to work or do other things. Gifts are also common. Overall, more resources flow down the generations than flow up.

The social support patterns between middle-aged parents and their adult children differ according to marital status. Parents in first marriages are more likely overall than parents in other marital situations to report giving support. Middle-income widows are also inclined to help their children financially through gifts, loans, and asset transfers (Eggebeen, 1992). Giving social support to children, whether reciprocated or not, is associated with better psychological well-being than is only receiving social support from children. Parents benefit psychologically by being able to give support as well as receive it (Marks, 1995).

Mother–Daughter Relationships

Parental and filial sentiment and responsibility persist into adulthood, with the mother–daughter relationship the most enduring and active of intergenerational bonds. Typically, married daughters see their mothers more often than sons do (Guinzburg, 1983), and maternal grandparents see their grandchildren more than paternal grandparents do. L. R. Fischer (1983) found that the mother–daughter bond becomes even closer after the daughter has a baby. Living nearby is associated with less conflict between daughters and mothers, but more conflict with mothers-in-law. Daughters are much more likely to ask their mothers than their mothers-in-law for child-rearing advice. Daughters with children, compared with those without children, are more likely to have more contact with their mothers—more telephone contact with mothers both near and far and more visits with near mothers (L. R. Fischer, 1983).

Daughters invest time and money in their aging mothers, giving significant aid both to dependent mothers and to mothers who are self-sufficient. The aid is generally tailored to the elderly mothers' needs (Guberman, Maheu, and Maille, 1992; Walker and Pratt, 1991). Moreover, daughters are more likely than sons to adjust their visiting or helping behavior in accordance with the contributions of their siblings (Spitze and Logan, 1991).

When there is strain in the mother–daughter relationship, it is usually because of the mother's criticism of the daughter: her weight, temper, or past

positive identification The attachment of a child to positive images of desired loving behavior.
negative identification The effort on the part of the child not to be like the parent.

and present behavior. Mothers also sometimes criticize their daughters for home management issues, such as the way the daughter keeps house or cooks. Mothers also like to give their daughters advice on child rearing—what to feed a child or how to toilet-train a child. Sometimes the mother's criticism focuses on the daughter's partner. However, in L. R. Fischer's (1983) study, 42% of daughters reported no sources of irritation or annoyance with their mothers. Generally, mothers and daughters report strong, positive feelings in their relationship, although these feelings are stronger for mothers than for daughters. Most mothers praise daughters while discussing their faults or choose not to discuss their faults at all (Fingerman, 1996).

An investigation of the sources of tension between aging mothers and adult daughters revealed some interesting findings (Fingerman, 1996). One source of tension in the mother–daughter relationship is conflicting ideas of inclusion and exclusion. Most mothers and daughters consider the other person important in their life, yet mothers seem to feel closer to their daughters emotionally than daughters feel to their mothers. Mothers are more likely to name their daughter as their preferred confidante or the person with whom they most enjoy spending time. Differences in sources of tension may stem from these differences in emotional investment. If daughters find their mother intrusive, their complaints may be related to their mother's investment in the relationship. Daughters feel intruded on, whereas mothers feel excluded.

Another major source of conflict is concern about mothers' well-being. Tension may arise from discrepancies in perceptions of the mothers' needs. Daughters are often concerned about their elderly mothers' self-care—for example, the mother's exerting herself unnecessarily or her refusal to get a flu shot. Daughters are solicitous about their mothers' physical well-being regardless of the mothers' actual health status.

Similarity in education and values between mothers and daughters enhances communication, intimacy, and understanding (Welsh and Stewart, 1995). Not surprisingly, well-educated mothers are more likely to react favorably to their married daughters' return to school than are less educated mothers, and well-educated mothers are consistently more likely to be used as confidantes (Suitor, 1987). Less educated mothers are more likely to express disapproval of their daughters' pursuit of an education. One daughter whose mother had only an elementary education reported:

> She doesn't care for [my going to school]. She feels I should be home where I belong. . . . I wouldn't have any trouble if I was home here all of the time. (Wouldn't have any trouble with what sorts of things?) Marriage, kids, any problems. She attributes anything that goes wrong [to my being away from home]. . . . I'm married, so my husband should feed me and clothe me and I should sit home and have dinner ready on the table. (Suitor, 1987, p. 439)

Other factors affect mother–daughter attachments. One of these is the aid pattern between the two generations. L. Thompson and Walker (1984) identified four basic patterns of aid exchange between mothers and daughters:

1. **Mother-dependent:** The flow of assistance is greater from daughter to mother than from mother to daughter.

2. **High-reciprocity:** Mother and daughter exchange high levels of aid.

3. **Low-reciprocity:** Mother and daughter exchange low levels of aid.

4. **Daughter-dependent:** The flow of assistance is greater from mother to daughter than from daughter to mother.

Research suggests that aid patterns may be developmental, changing as the mother and daughter age and change. Researchers studied two sets of mother–daughter relationships: (1) young adult women (students) and their middle-aged mothers, and (2) these same middle-aged women and their mothers. They found that the typical aid patterns from parent to child continue until the elderly parent is unable to contribute. Among younger pairs, the daughter-dependent pattern is the model, but it is the least typical pattern among older pairs. As mothers get older, they come to depend more and more on their daughters for assistance, which sometimes causes role strain for the daughters, particularly if they work full-time in addition to taking care of their own households and families (Scharlach, 1987). Another study investigated the emotional strain associated with caregiving as experienced by both Black and White daughters. Because extended Black families typically help in the caregiving for elderly relatives, Black daughters reported less role strain overall, but the caregiver's personal and social life is a predictor of stress in both groups (Mui, 1992).

The aid patterns also are significantly related to the degrees of mother–daughter attachment. In general, among young pairs, those most materially dependent (usually the younger daughters) report lower levels of attachment. In other words, middle-aged mothers usually provide more aid and report more positive evaluations of attachment than their daughters, who may be rebelling against parental authority. Among older pairs, high reciprocity of aid is most conducive to attachment for both mothers and daughters, and high material interdependence is associated with high emotional interdependence. However, among all groups, the need to maintain independence continues throughout life. The ability to give aid remains more important to attachment than receiving aid (L. Thompson and Walker, 1984). In the most satisfying arrangement, the mother–daughter relationship is mutual and interdependent (Boyd, 1989). Even the aid patterns in intergenerational caregiving between mothers and daughters may be perceived as reciprocal. Mothers report that they are

not uncomfortable with their dependence on their daughters because of their earlier contribution to their children. Daughters, too, note the importance of their mothers in their lives, especially in providing emotional support. In turn, the daughters are willing to provide assistance to their mothers (Walker, Pratt, Martell, and Martin, 1991).

Conflict between Parents and Adult Children

Conflict can arise when the adult children do not follow socially approved behavior that the parents have taught. Even after the children are grown and have left their parents' home, the elderly parents still expect their offspring to live according to the way the parents want them to live. C. B. Fisher, Reid, and Melendez (1989) asked 55 elderly adults to describe situations that provoked anger between them and their adult children, who were now living separately. Figure 14.1 shows the major sources of conflict. Parents were most angry at their adult children for failure to live up to role expectations: failure to act like a good spouse or parent or a successful professional. The second greatest source of parental dismay was failure of adult children to conform to

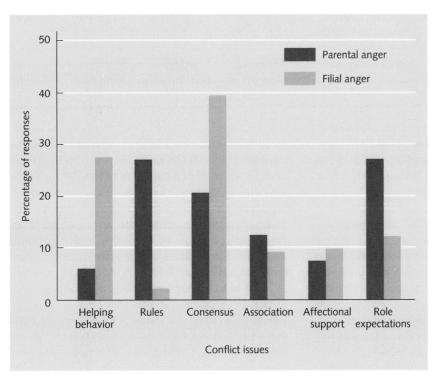

Figure 14.1 Distribution of Conflict Issues between Parents and Adult Children (*Note:* From "Conflict in Families and Friendships of Later Life" by C. B. Fisher, J. D. Reid, and M. Melendez, 1989, *Family Relations, 38*, p. 85.)

social rules as taught by parents: meeting family obligations within the adult child's own family, such as helping the spouse with chores; coming home to the family instead of socializing with colleagues after work; keeping appointments; and following rules of behavior, such as those relating to drinking, drug taking, or reckless driving. More than 20% of adult parents also were upset over failure to reach consensus on values and opinions. Some elderly parents expressed disappointment as well over the extent of their contact with adult children, affectional support, and helping behavior.

Adult children were most angry at the lack of consensus with parents and at the lack of help their parents gave them; they were unhappy to a lesser extent with differences in role expectations and were disappointed by failure to provide empathy, fairness, respect, love, or trust or by infrequent contact. It is apparent that these elderly parents and their adult children still had certain expectations of each other (C. B. Fisher et al., 1989).

Parent–Adult Child Relationships and Psychological Functioning

Adult children's lives can affect their parents' well-being. Parents continue to worry about their children no matter how old the children are. When the children have marital problems, financial difficulties, health problems, vocational difficulties, or other problems, their parents are bound to be affected. For example, the marital conflict of adult children is related to higher levels of anger, sadness, and pessimism in mothers (E. J. Hall and Cummings, 1997).

Parents remain heavily invested in their children's lives throughout the life course. All parents hope that their children will grow up and establish themselves as successful, functioning adults. If the children do not do so, parents become concerned and upset. Children who have not successfully negotiated leaving their parents' home and who have not become independent serve as a reminder that parents have not achieved their task of socialization. Generally, parents whose adult children have mental, physical, or stress-related problems experience greater depression than parents of children who do not have these problems (Pillemer and Suitor, 1991).

The relationships between adult children and their parents have psychological consequences for the younger generation, too. Sons whose relationships with their parents are positive have lower levels of psychological distress than do sons whose

relationships are negative. It is important to note that positive relationships with mothers and with fathers are significant predictors of adult sons' psychological distress. The more positive the relationships with their mothers or fathers, the lower the level of distress (Barnett, Marshall, and Pleck, 1992).

Similarly for daughters, having a positive relationship with a parent is associated with a high sense of well-being and low levels of distress. Distress is often conditioned by family-role patterns. For example, having a poor relationship with one's mother is associated with psychological distress, particularly among daughters who are single or childless (Barnett, Kibria, Baruch, and Pleck, 1991). Thus, the quality of the relationships between adult children and their parents is associated with the psychological functioning of both generations (Umberson, 1992).

IN-LAWS

In-law disagreements are most common in the early years of marriage. Some young couples are able to work out their relationships with in-laws, including the spouse's parents, siblings, and other relatives, so that good accommodations are reached. Others settle into a permanent state of friction with their in-laws. This friction may not break up the marriage, but it can cause unhappiness (L. R. Fischer, 1983).

Successful In-Law Relationships

One study longitudinally examined the influence of in-laws on marital success among couples who were married on average for 20 years (Bryant, Conger, and Meehan, 2001). The researchers found that in-laws are influential in the overall success of the marriage, even beyond the first few years. Even after an average of 20 years of marriage, unhappiness and conflict with in-laws led to decreased perceptions of marital success. The influence of in-laws thus continues far beyond the early years of marriage, and perhaps vulnerability to the opinions and behaviors of those who are close to them never ends (Bryant et al., 2001).

One of the most comprehensive studies on in-laws was reported in the book *In-laws: Pro and Con* by Duvall (1954). Her study is an old one, but it is still a rich source of relevant information and shows that in-law problems are not a new phenomenon. Her findings form the basis for the discussion that follows.

Many couples have a fine relationship with each partner's family. How important are in-laws to marital success?

About one-fourth of all couples in Duvall's study had a very fine relationship with their in-laws. Couples give the following reasons for liking their in-laws:

- "They are the kind of people we admire: sincere, interesting, young in spirit, good-natured, pleasant and fun, generous, tolerant, and understanding."
- "They do many things to help us" (Goetting, 1990). "They take care of the baby." "They help us when we're sick or when my husband is away." "They give us so many things, like furniture, clothes, and money."
- "They are more like parents to me than my own parents." Orphans and people who are estranged from their own parents may be especially close to their in-laws.
- "They are the parents of my spouse, who is a fine person."
- "We're in-laws ourselves so we can appreciate what it means." Such couples objected to stereotyped prejudices against in-laws, which they felt were unfair.

The Roots of Conflict

The literature on family and couple therapy often cites in-laws as a significant source of stress in couples' relationships (Bryant et al., 2001). There are many reasons for in-law conflicts. While spouses are almost obligated to form family relationships with in-laws, "rarely is this forced relationship a natural match of kindred spirits" (Berg-Cross, 1997, p. 177). Sometimes the problem is with the parents-in-law, but more frequently it is with the partners themselves, who in many cases are more critical of their in-laws than the in-laws are of them.

In-law relationships often are described as ambiguous, and this ambiguity stems from the fact that married couples belong to three different families: the new family of the couple plus both partners' family of origin (Byrant et al., 2001). In-law relationships can cause hostility and stress between spouses who have emotional and psychological loyalties to their own family (Globerman, 1996; Horsley, 1997). It takes time for young partners to shift their primary loyalties from parents to each other. If the marriage is to succeed, however, their first loyalty must be to each other. For a healthy marital relationship, it is very important that the new family develop a strong and autonomous bond, particularly during the first few years of marriage (Jorgenson, 1994). As Timmer and Veroff (2000) report that low levels of conflict with in-laws among newlyweds predicts marital happiness for both husbands and wives.

Some parents create problems because they resent the person their son or daughter married. Some parents find it hard to accept a son- or daughter-in-law who comes from a different national, religious,

Adult Child Contact with Elderly Black Parents

Feelings of affection and frequency of contact are reciprocally linked; that is, the more parents and children see each other, the greater affection they will have for each other, and vice versa (Lawton, Silverstein, and Bengtson, 1994). Older African Americans are highly involved in a network of family support. They are often considered the backbone of the Black family system. Older women, in particular, fill familial support roles and have a very important role in intergenerational assistance. Elderly Black parents are also more likely than elderly parents of other groups to live in extended families.

However, the literature on the Black elderly has largely ignored issues of gender. The mother–daughter bond is said to be particularly salient among Blacks, as it is among Whites; a few studies have reported on the influence of gender on the interaction between parents and children.

A study of 575 Black respondents examined gender differences and levels of contact with children among Black middle-aged and elderly persons. Men, especially those who lived alone, experienced substantially fewer visits and phone calls per year than did women. This means there was a subgroup of Black men who were not currently married, who lived alone, who were less involved with their children, and whose needs for both contact and assistance were unmet (Spitze and Miner, 1992).

A later study based on the National Survey of Black Families examined gender differences in relation to intergenerational patterns of support. Four hundred and eighty-seven young adult fathers and mothers cited grandmothers as the person to whom they turn for parenting support. Mothers are more likely to seek both help with child care and advice, whereas fathers are more likely to seek assistance with child care only. As has been found in other studies of grandparenthood, residential proximity is fundamental to contact between generations (Hunter, 1997).

---

economic, or social background. Others resent anyone a son or daughter married because the person "is not the right one" or "is not good enough." In these cases, the intolerance of the parents is the primary problem.

Parents may have difficulty adjusting to the "loss" of their child and create problems by being overprotective and meddling. Sometimes the dependent child encourages this overprotection and continues to look to parents rather than to their spouse for guidance. In such cases, the spouse rightly feels left out and finds it unbearable to have to play second fiddle to the in-laws.

LIVING WITH PARENTS OR IN-LAWS

Coresidence by parents and adult children is not uncommon. The U.S. Census Bureau (2002) reports that about 18 million adults ages 18–34 live with their parents, up from about 12.5 million in 1970. Research has indicated that coresidence typically reflects the housing needs of adult children rather than the caregiving needs of parents, and that it does not generally have negative effects on parent–adult child relationships (R. A. Ward and Spitze, 1992). When adult children live with their parents, it's usually because of the adult children's needs and circumstances (R. A. Ward, Logan, and Spitze, 1992). Most young couples do not want to live with either partner's parents after marriage, but the younger they are when they get married, the greater the likelihood that they will do so for a while, since they cannot afford living quarters of their own. This "doubling" sometimes adds to the stress of family relationships (Kleban, Brody, Schoonover, and Hoffman, 1989).

Effects of Coresidence

Coresident young adults give, receive, and perceive more support from their parents than nonresident adult children but report significantly less affectionate relationships with their parents. The effects of coresidence are more positive when the children are older, employed, or in school (L. K. White and Rogers, 1997).

According to the National Survey of Families and Households, parental satisfaction with the presence of adult children (ages 19–34) in the home was highly related to parent–adult child conflict and to the level of positive social interaction between parent and child. The negative consequences of dependency are also influenced by the children's marital and parental status. Parents whose adult children move back home after marital breakups report more negative effects of coresidence than do parents of never-married children. Also, supporting adult children who are unemployed and who are continually financially dependent becomes more burdensome as the share of adult children's basic needs paid for by parents increases. Supporting grandchildren as well as adult children exerts additional negative influence on parental experiences (Aquilino, 1991). However, many parents are highly satisfied with the coresident living arrangement and describe mostly positive relationships with their adult children.

Sources of Stress

The type of living arrangement affects the amount of stress. If doubling up takes place under one roof but in two separate apartments or living quarters, the situation is not any more stressful than if the two families lived next door to each other. But when families live in the same house or apartment and share living space, the likelihood of conflict is greater. Some families even end up sharing the same sleeping quarters. If at all possible, it is helpful if each couple has at least one room they can call their own and to which they can retreat, when necessary, for privacy.

When it is not possible to be completely separate, conflict is less likely if families develop a clear understanding of financial and household obligations ahead of time. Who is to pay for what, and how much? What household and yard work are family members expected to do? The division of household labor and responsibilities is a particularly challenging area for coresiding families. In the National Survey of Families and Households, adult children reported doing substantial amounts of weekly housework; parents reported doing lower amounts. Adult children did more housework in one-parent households than in two-parent households and did increasing amounts with age. Daughters spent somewhat more time on household work than did sons. Also, when a parent was in poor health, the adult children did more housework. Some adult children might have been doing extra housework that they themselves generated, so they were probably not relieving their parents of any substantial amount of housework in exchange for living in the house (Spitze and Ward, 1995).

Another potentially stressful situation is created when parents and adult children share responsibilities for a family business. A study of two-generation farm families revealed differences in family satisfaction between the older generation and their married sons and daughters-in-law (Weigel and Weigel, 1990). The older generation held most of the power over decision making and money. Very often, the younger generation supplied labor but had very little control, as well as consistently lower income. The older generation wanted more family togetherness, while the younger generation wanted more independence, freedom, and equality. The overlapping of work and family roles creates a special dilemma for family members who not only live together or close by but also work together.

Extended Families during Middle Age

Living in an extended household sometime during middle age is not a rare phenomenon in the United States. About one-third of White women and two-thirds of Black women will live with their parents at some time as they pass through middle age (Beck and Beck, 1989). Usually, the arrangement is temporary, but middle-aged people may be called on to help an aging parent or one or more adult children through a crisis or period of need. These middle-aged individuals have been termed the "sandwich generation" because they simultaneously help their parents and their children.

GRANDPARENTS

Recent demographic trends have contributed to a rise in the number of grandparents and to fewer grandchildren per grandparent. For most, grandparenthood begins in middle age and spans several decades, lasting well into the grandchild's adulthood. More people living longer means that adults today can expect to share their role as grandparent with other grandparents and that some can expect to be great-grandparents (Szinovacz, 1998).

Today's grandparents are usually much different from the stereotypic image. For example, the modern grandmother is far less likely to be wrapped in her shawl, rocking idly before the fireplace. She is more apt to be youthful, vigorous, alert, and energetic, with plenty of ideas and enthusiasm. She's also

Many elderly people will give up their independence and share a residence with an adult child. One advantage, confirmed by research, is the unique emotional attachments between grandparents and grandchildren.

likely to be employed. In one national study, one-third of grandmothers who were babysitting were also jobholders themselves (Aldous, 1995).

Today's grandparents are different from previous cohorts in a number of ways. Increasingly, each generation of grandmothers and grandfathers will span a greater range of ages because of teen births and delayed parenthood (Szinovacz, 1998). Improved nutrition and medical care have made it possible for people to stay healthier longer. As discussed in Chapter 1, the life expectancy of today's woman in the United States is 79; of today's man it is 74.

Modern grandparents have a chance to be younger in mind and spirit. Many middle-income grandparents can, if they so choose, keep up in appearance, taste, vitality, and knowledge with their children and children-in-law. They can continue to think creatively and to take refresher courses in their fields of knowledge. Modern mass media and increasing opportunities for adult education in the community help middle-aged and older citizens keep up with modern trends and ideas. Moreover, grandparents are motivated by their grandchildren to send e-mail, view films, visit websites, and read books, keeping them current with new ideas and technology. Many grandparents also learn a great deal by traveling.

Finally, modern grandparents are different from the grandparents who preceded them because they are more likely to have intergenerational lineages. Today, grandparents may have living parents and even grandparents. When the age at first birth is during early adolescence for a number of generations in a row, intergenerational lineages are more likely. Although not numerous, grandmothers can be in their late twenties and have living mothers and grandmothers (Burton, 1995; C. Stack, 1974). Conversely, when young adults delay the age of first birth, the time between generations increases, and intergenerational lineages are less likely (Szinovacz, 1998).

What Grandparents Can Do for Grandchildren

There has been an increasing recognition of the importance of grandparents (Whitveck, Hoyt, and Huck, 1993). In fact, social scientists have referred to grandparents as central to family dynamics and as a valuable family resource (Ingersoll-Dayton and Neal, 1991). The emotional attachments between grandparents and grandchildren have been described as unique because the relationship is exempt from the psycho-emotional intensity and responsibility that exist in the parent–child relationship (Barranti, 1985). However, the relationship between grandchildren and grandparents is mediated by the parents. Usually, the connections with the maternal grandparents are stronger than those with the paternal grandparents. However, if the parents align more closely with the paternal grandparents, the grandchildren are likely to do so as well (Chan and Elder, 2000). The relationship between grandparents and grandchildren also is influenced by changes in family life, such as a move or a divorce. Following a parental divorce or separation, contact between grandchildren and maternal grandparents often increases or at least is maintained, while contact with paternal grandparents often declines (King and Elder, 1995).

Grandparents can do a number of things for children (Denham and Smith, 1989). For example, they can help children feel secure and loved (Kivett, 1993). Children can never have too much of the right kind of love—love that helps them grow and develop and that eliminates anxiety, tension, and emotional pain. Love that adds security and trust, that accepts and understands, is always needed. The role of modern grandparents is associated less with authority and power and more with warmth and affection (Wilcoxon, 1987). Many grandparents continue to play an important role in the lives of grandchildren even after the parents have divorced (Gladstone, 1988; C. L. Johnson and Barer, 1987).

Grandparents can play a crucial role during family transitions, such as divorce. They are a source of family continuity and stability. Because of their function in maintaining the family system, grandparents may be seen as "family watchdogs." Although they usually play a relatively passive role in the family, during crisis grandparents often become actively involved in the family. A large percentage of divorced adult children, for example, are dependent on their parents for help. Contact between grandchildren and grandmothers usually increases after the separation or divorce of an adult child. In addition, grandmothers report that they provide more support (babysitting, teaching family history and tradition, giving advice) after the separation or

Grandparents can be important in the lives of adolescents and young adults. Research shows that grandparents share family history and help the young understand their parents.

Grandparents Who Parent Their Grandchildren

In recent years, we have seen a dramatic increase in the number of grandparents serving as primary caregivers to their grandchildren and great-grandchildren. According to the U.S. Census Bureau (2002), 5.6 million grandparents live with their grandchildren, and 42% of those grandparents are the primary caregivers for the children. More grandmothers (62%) than grandfathers (38%) take full responsibility for their grandchildren. The media refer to some grandparents as the "silent saviors," "the second line of defense," and "the safety net." These terms are used to describe grandparents who thought their child-rearing days were over and who now find themselves raising their children's children. In interviews with 114 grandparents who provided daily care to their grandchildren, researchers identified three categories of caregiving: (1) custodial grandparents, whose grandchildren live with them and with whom they have a legal relationship; (2) grandparents whose grandchildren live with them but with whom there is no legal relationship; and (3) grandparents whose grandchildren do not live with them but for whom they provide day care.

As a group, the grandparents who provided care to grandchildren were solvers of what seemed to be insoluble problems. Custodial grandparents attempted to provide a stable environment for their grandchildren, sometimes when their own children were drug- and alcohol-addicted. Grandparents, especially day care grandparents, attempted to provide their grandchildren with a stable day care environment when parents worked and day care costs were prohibitive. Grandparents evidenced strength in the face of adversity and coped with their situations, apparently because they felt they must.

As discussed in Chapter 1, grandchildren altered their caregivers' lives, both positively and negatively, especially when they lived with their caregivers. Caregivers responsible for a child's daily personal and legal (decision-making) care felt profoundly the effect of providing such care. Granted the legal right to the grandchild by the court, custo-dial grandparents assumed the responsibility for both the daily care of the grandchild and decision making for the child's upbringing. In essence, they assumed the functions typically linked to parenthood. Although rearing grandchildren sometimes seemed burdensome, almost two-thirds of the custodial grandparents reported having more of a purpose for living because of providing care to their grandchild; the grandchild kept them active and "in shape."

The living-with grandparents assumed some, if not all, of the daily physical care for the grandchild, but they did not have legal custody. There were at least two categories of living-with grandparents: those who had the grandchild's parents living with them and those who did not. These grandparents never knew when the grandchild's parents would take the grandchild back, and they had no way of protecting the child from an unsuitable or even dangerous parent.

A three-generational household raised other issues. Grandparents reported feeling that they walked a thin line in trying to provide a stable environment for their grandchildren without overstepping parental boundaries. The parent retained decision-making responsibilities but often left the grandparent with the physical care of the grandchild. Such a relationship gave the grandparent great responsibility without any authority. These grandparents also reported a strain between their beliefs about what grandparenting would be like and how it actually was.

Day care grandparents assumed responsibility for the regular care of their grandchildren and assumed no legal responsibility. Although these grandparents arranged their schedules around their grandchild's day, they were least affected by their caregiving role because the children went home at the end of the day. Some day care grandparents were thrilled to be taking care of their grandchildren; others resented the assumption that they wished to spend their days in this way. Of the three categories, however, these grandparents tended to function more according to our societal definition of grandparents than of parents (Jendrek, 1993).

divorce (Ingersoll-Dayton and Neal, 1991; Purnell and Bagby, 1993). They play an even more important role in families in which there are unwed teenage mothers. One study found that babies were more secure when their grandmothers took over responsibility for their care and gave directions to the teenage mother (Oyserman, Radin, and Benn, 1993).

Grandparents can help children learn to know, trust, and understand other people. Children can learn that their grandmother's arms can be just as comforting as their mother's. They can discover that their grandfather's house is a safe and happy home away from home. They learn how to be flexible and to adjust to the ways their grandmother thinks, feels, and behaves, which are different from the ways their mother does.

Grandparents help children to bridge the gap between the past and the present, to give children a sense of history. Most children enjoy hearing grandparents talk about what life was like when they were growing up. By sharing their rich heritage with children, grandparents give them a deeper, broader foundation upon which to base their own lives and to build new knowledge (P. Martin, Hagestad, and Diedrich, 1988). This knowledge about their cultural and family heritage helps adolescents' identity development.

Grandparents can provide children with experiences and supervision that their parents do not have time or money to provide. In this sense, the grandparent acts as a surrogate parent (Presser, 1989). This is especially important given the increase in one-parent families and the increase in time spent at work.

Grandparents can give children a sense of values and a philosophy of life that is the result of years of living. Valuable life experiences and lessons need to be shared; in this regard, grandparents play the traditional role of valued elder.

Grandparents may play the role of arbitrator between their adult children and grandchildren. Grandparents may be the negotiators between the young and the middle-aged regarding behaviors and values. They may serve as interpreters in helping each generation understand the other's perspective, and they may provide a refuge for both adult children and grandchildren (Ingersoll-Dayton and Neal, 1991).

Finally, grandparents can give children a wholesome attitude toward old age. In Western culture especially, in which youthfulness is almost worshipped, children need to know and learn to respect their elders. Older people who have lived rich, fruitful, meaningful lives are a good example for children. They are role models for the future role of grandparent, for aging, and for family relationships.

Adolescents, Young Adults, and Grandparents

Grandparents can be important in the lives of adolescents and young adults (G. E. Kennedy, 1990). They can tell adolescents and young adults about the family history and help them understand their parents. Grandparents also function as confidants and provide outlets when parent–teen relations become tense. By observing grandparents and talking with them, adolescents are better able to understand the behavior and attitudes of their parents.

Research on the relationship between college-age men and women and their grandparents revealed that, when there is high contact between generations, the maternal grandmother–granddaughter bond is the strongest (Uhlenberg and Hammill, 1998). In addition, maternal grandmothers describe a closer relationship with grandchildren than do grandfathers. Grandfathers often have a narrower view of what they have to offer children than do grandmothers and perceive granddaughters as not needing or wanting their advice. However, paternal grandfathers and grandsons have a more intense bond than do maternal grandfathers and grandsons (Kivett, 1985).

What Grandchildren Can Do for Grandparents

The grandparent–grandchild relationship is not a one-way street, with benefits flowing only from grandparent to grandchild (Ashton, 1996). Grandchildren can enhance the lives of their grandparents in several ways (Baranowski, 1983). First, grandchildren are a source of biologic continuity and living evidence that the family will endure. All individuals wish a part of themselves to survive after death, and grandchildren are in a perfect position to play this part. In a sense, grandchildren allow a grandparent to glimpse his or her own immortality. Second, grandparents' self-concept is enhanced by playing the role of mentor, historian, and resource person. Third, the lives of some older people are enhanced by the presence of grandchildren. Grandchildren can help keep grandparents up-to-date by introducing them to the new ideas, customs, and traditions of the younger generation. Finally, grandchildren who have grown past early childhood can provide a variety of types of assistance to help grandparents maintain an independent lifestyle. Adolescents can help their grandparents with lawn care, household chores, and other tasks related to maintaining a home. Such help plays a crucial role in enabling older adults to stay in their homes as long as possible.

LEARNING OBJECTIVES

After reading the chapter, you should be able to:

- Understand that conflict is inevitable in family relationships.

- Identify the sources of conflict in the family: personal, physical, interpersonal, and situational or environmental.

- Discuss the effects of conflict on children.

- Discuss methods of dealing with conflict.

- Describe the meaning of family crises and the definable stages of coping with one.

- Understand the reasons for infidelity and the crisis it creates.

- Discuss the crisis of economic distress, the effects on individuals and family relationships, and means of coping with it.

- Describe the crisis of violence and abuse in the family; the factors related to violence; the facts about spouse abuse and child abuse, including sexual abuse; and the treatment for spouse and child abuse.

- Describe the stages of grief and people's reactions during each stage.

Conflict, Family Crises, and Crisis Management

A certain amount of conflict and discord is a normal part of every relationship. Two people will never agree on everything. Tensions build up and misunderstandings occur in the process of living. The numerous decisions that couples must make and the disappointments, frustrations, and adjustments they must face will result, at some time, in a hurt look, an angry word, or a more overt quarrel. Some couples have more conflict than others, and some are able to deal with it more constructively than others, but the potential for conflict is present in every human relationship. In fact, those partners who are the closest to each other and have the greatest potential for satisfaction in their relationship also have the greatest potential for conflict.

How conflict is managed, rather than how much conflict there is, distinguishes satisfied from dissatisfied couples (E. Jones and Gallois, 1989). Although some conflict may be inevitable, that does not mean it is always desirable or helpful. Conflict can destroy love and even an otherwise good marriage. But it can also relieve tensions, clear the air, and bring two people closer together than ever before. It depends on the total circumstances, the focus of the conflict, the way it is handled, and the ultimate outcome.

In this chapter, we look closely at conflict—its causes, its functions in marriage, some ways couples deal with it, and its effects on children. After looking at conflict, we discuss typical patterns of family adjustment to crises and describe the processes of adjustment. In addition, we discuss four major crises that families may face: infidelity, economic distress, violence and abuse, and death.

CONFLICT AND CHILDREN

When children are involved, conflict necessitates additional considerations. How are children affected by conflict? Are older children and adolescents affected to the same extent as younger children? Should parents quarrel in front of the children? Is it best to try to hide marital problems from them? These are all questions of great significance for families' and children's well-being.

The Family Environment

When the family environment is characterized by positive affect—love, warmth, faith, trust, consideration, and empathy—children thrive. Such an environment helps them feel good about themselves and know that they are loved and wanted. Conversely, researchers have found that child-rearing environments in which interpersonal relations are characterized by anger and conflict place children at risk for the development of behavioral and emotional problems (Jaycox and Repetti, 1993).

A general family atmosphere of anger and discord has a greater impact on children than marital discord. Some parents who have discordant marriages may maintain the image of a harmonious relationship and keep their disputes hidden from their children. However, children are very observant, and it is impossible for them to escape a general climate of anger and conflict in the home. The effects of conflict on children are less if they can withdraw when their parents are fighting, even if they cannot withdraw completely from a negative home environment.

Interparent Conflict

Exposure to interparent conflict is a source of stress for children and is predictive of problems in child adjustment (Kerig, 1996). The more disruptive of family functioning parental conflicts are, the more likely they are to be perceived by children as stressful and to reduce children's reliance on the family as a safe emotional environment in which their needs can be met. Consistent with this, empirical evidence has confirmed that children who perceive their parents' fights as frequent and intense also have a higher incidence of maladjustment and behavior problems.

Quarrels between parents that are directly related to their children, such as disagreements about child-rearing practices, have a more negative impact on parenting and child development than quarrels that are not related to the children. Children begin to see themselves as a source of conflict and to blame themselves for their parents' difficulties. As a result, they are more disturbed than if the conflict does not involve them. Furthermore, parents who quarrel with each other may take out their anger on their children. Sometimes older children are drawn into the argument and try to take sides or to keep their parents from fighting. Failure to achieve peace is disturbing to them, and, here again, children blame themselves for not being able to do anything about their family's difficulties.

Moreover, the effects of family conflict are heightened by direct exposure to conflict and ag-

Some conflict and discord may be a normal part of every relationship. Research suggests that couples who are closer and have the greatest potential for satisfaction in their relationship also have the greatest potential for conflict.

gression. Ninety two-parent families with a child 9–13 years of age participated in a study which showed that repeated conflict in the family sensitized children to interparent aggression, with the result that subsequent conflict affected them more than if it had not been experienced so frequently before. Consistent with a sensitization hypothesis, interparent physical aggression during the previous year was related to child withdrawal and anxiety (Gordis, Margolin, and John, 1997). Children who are exposed to interparent aggression tend to have a higher incidence of emotional and behavioral problems (M. J. Rogers and Holmbeck, 1997).

Marital conflicts that include physical aggression seem to be especially distressing to children and to have a lasting effect on how they react to subsequent interadult conflicts. Tensions between spouses may become intertwined with tensions among other family members, especially the children. Dysfunctional families are characterized by the spread of tensions from one subsystem to another, particularly from the parents to the children (Margolin, Christensen, and John, 1996).

Older Children and Adolescents

Frequent or intense conflict between parents is often associated with a wide range of indicators of adolescent maladjustment, including negative acting-out behavior, emotional upset, and poor academic performance (Buehler, Krishnakumar, Anthony,

Tittsworth, and Stone, 1994). An analysis of the effects of marital and parent–child conflict on older children and on grandmothers indicated that older children reported relatively intense, defensive, and emotional reactions (anger, fear) to the conflict. Grandmothers reported feeling sad because of the conflict, but they did not feel a sense of threat as did the older children (Hall and Cummings, 1997). One investigation showed that tense family conflict may increase adolescent suicidal ideation. That is, adolescents may be more likely to think about suicide when they experience tension in the family (Shagle and Barber, 1993).

SOURCES OF CONFLICT

Conflict may have its origin in (1) personal sources, (2) physical sources, (3) interpersonal sources, or (4) situational or environmental sources.

Personal Sources

Personal sources of conflict are those that originate within the individual when inner drives, instincts,

personal sources of conflict   Those that originate within the individual when inner drives, instincts, and values pull against one another.

and values pull against each other. The conflict is not with one's partner but with oneself, and tensions arise from the internal battle. As a result of these inner tensions, the individual has disagreements or gets into quarrels in situations that heighten that tension. Consider this case:

> Mr. M. was brought up by parents who rejected him and made him feel unwanted and unloved as a child. As a result, he became the kind of man who was afraid to show love for his wife or to let her get close to him. He needed her and wanted her attention and companionship; but whenever she tried to develop a close, loving, intimate relationship, he became anxious and fearful and would end up rejecting her or pushing her away. She was very hurt and became frustrated and angry, which, in turn, made him mad. They always ended up in a fight when they started getting close to each other. (Author's counseling notes)

In this example, the man had deep-seated fears of being too distant, but also anxiety about being too close (Israelstam, 1989).

Irrational fears and anxieties and neurotic needs can be the basic sources of spousal friction. For example, a spouse who has a deep-seated fear of losing his or her partner becomes extremely jealous, even for only superficial contacts. Emotional illness is another source of friction and arguments. For example, when a spouse is depressed, the couple may experience disruptive and hostile behavior when the partners interact with each other (Schmaling, Whisman, Fruzzetti, and Truax, 1991). Premarital depression is also associated with subsequent deterioration of marital relationships (Beach and O'Leary, 1993). Even emotionally healthy men and women have mood swings that influence their behavior.

The basic cause of personal conflicts lies deep within the psyche of the individuals involved. Usually, the anxieties have their origins in childhood experiences and early family relationships. For this reason, troubles that arise in marriage because of these previous experiences are difficult to deal with. Permanent solutions can be found when the internal tensions within the individual are relieved.

Physical Sources

Physical sources of conflict are inner tensions having a physical origin. Physical fatigue is one such source. Fatigue causes irritability, emotional upset,

impatience, distorted reasoning, and a low tolerance for frustration. It causes people to say and do things that they wouldn't say or do ordinarily. Hunger, overwork, and a low level of blood sugar are also potential sources of tension. A painful headache may be just as much a source of conflict as a serious disagreement.

Interpersonal Sources

Interpersonal sources of conflict are those that occur in relationships between people. All couples have marital problems, but unhappily married people are more likely to complain of neglect and lack of love, affection, sexual satisfaction, understanding, appreciation, and companionship than are the happily married. Furthermore, their self-image suffers; their spouse may magnify their faults, belittle their efforts, and make false accusations. They feel worthless, and the complaints become the focus of the conflict that ensues. Lack of communication, inability to resolve differences, and withdrawal from each other also perpetuate the difficulties (Dhir and Markman, 1984).

The intimate interaction patterns and relationships between partners far outweigh other major sources of conflict. Couples begin to feel hurt, resentful, and frustrated when the partners are not meeting each other's sociopsychological needs. Relationships with kin, the community, or others outside the family do not affect the partners as much as their relationship with each other does. They expect that their sociopsychological needs for understanding, communication, love, affection, and companionship will be met. If those needs are not met, the couple may become dissatisfied and discontented.

It is difficult to sort out the cause and effect of conflict because of the interrelationship of multiple problems. Marriage counselors know that the problems couples complain about in the beginning of counseling may be only symptoms of the focal point of conflict. The real causes of difficulties often run much deeper. For example, a spouse's lack of sexual interest may be correlated with quarreling, lack of communication, dislike of the partner, mental health problems, infidelity, or general alienation. Sometimes, the couple may not realize the basic reasons for the difficulties. These causes often are found in the psyche of one of the individuals or in the pattern of the couple's interpersonal relationship.

Racism

Cultural strains among minority families often include racism. Many families face the difficult task of raising their children to have positive self-concepts in a society in which racist attitudes, negative media images, and stereotypes are all too common (A. Thomas and Speight, 1999). For example, S. Hill (2001) has noted, "Too often, racist depictions of African Americans undermine the confidence and self-esteem of children and threaten their success and well-being" (p. 498). Studies have found that a positive racial identity is related to increased psychological health, self-esteem, and achievement, while a negative racial identity is linked to low self-esteem, problems with psychological adjustment, low school achievement, and high rates of school dropout, teenage pregnancy, gang involvement, eating disorders, drug abuse, and involvement in crime. Due to the potential consequences of a negative racial identity, it is important that people from minority groups develop a positive sense of self that includes feelings of racial pride (A. Thomas and Speight, 1999).

Some families choose to address racism by socializing children to acknowledge the fact that we live in a society with oppressive and racist beliefs, and by teaching them to try to work within it. One study reported that nearly all African American parents felt that racial socialization is important in preparing their children to cope with the reality of racism (A. Thomas and Speight, 1999). Parents gave both their boy and girl children messages of racial pride and self-pride; the importance of achievement, moral values, and family; and the need to overcome negative social messages and racism. However, boys were given more messages on overcoming racism, whereas girls were encouraged to pursue an education and become financially independent (A. Thomas and Speight, 1999). Parents believed that these strategies might help mitigate the cultural strains of racism.

Situational or Environmental Sources

Situational or environmental sources of conflict include things such as living conditions, societal pressures on family members, cultural strains among minority group families, such as discrimination and assimilation (Vega, Kolody, and Valle, 1988), and unexpected events that disturb family functioning. A study in Sweden showed that disharmonious mother–child and father–child relations increased as the children grew older, with the disharmony peaking in late childhood (Stattin and Klackenberg, 1992).

Sometimes a marital relationship remains in a state of relative equilibrium until some traumatic event occurs to disrupt the relationship. Sometimes a long-standing marriage suddenly becomes conflictual. For example, one man could not work through his feelings of isolation and deprivation following the death of his father, so he felt he had been an undutiful son and withdrew from his spouse and family while he struggled with his guilt and neediness. In this instance, a specific event triggered the conflict, although the seeds of tension were already present in the relationship. Unexpected events such as unemployment, change of jobs, disaster, illness, pregnancy, death, or a forced separation or move may be enough to trigger a cri-

sis. Couples who are emotionally insecure or unstable usually have far more difficulty coping than do other couples. Couples characterized by high levels of tension have even more conflict when their time together increases because of vacations, retirement, illness, or reduced hours of employment.

METHODS OF DEALING WITH CONFLICT

It is not the existence of conflict per se that is problematic for the family, but the methods of managing and resolving the conflict. The methods discussed in this section include avoidance, ventilation and catharsis, and constructive and destructive arguments. As we discussed in Chapter 10, some couples

physical sources of conflict Inner tensions having a physical origin, such as fatigue, hunger, or a headache.

interpersonal sources of conflict Those tensions that occur in the relationships between people.

situational or environmental sources of conflict These include living conditions, societal pressures, cultural strains, and unexpected events.

have a lot of conflict but keep it under control and resolve their tensions and problems. Other couples are unable to minimize tension or solve anything, so small problems grow into big ones.

Avoidance

Some couples try to deal with conflict through **avoidance.** That is, they try to prevent conflict by avoiding the people, situations, and issues that stimulate it. The following comments illustrate avoidance techniques: "My husband really growls when he gets up in the morning, so it's better if we don't say anything," and "My wife is very sensitive about her kinky hair, so I never say anything" (Author's counseling notes). In each case, the couple is trying to avoid conflict.

In some instances, however, couples try to avoid discussing controversial issues even though they are important in the marriage. In these cases, keeping quiet might be counterproductive; the couple avoids conflict but also fails to resolve the problem (Bowman, 1990). Partners who never address important issues in their efforts to avoid controversy gradually withdraw from each other. Gradual disengagement and alienation occur when partners stop communicating with and caring about each other. As a result, there is increased loneliness, less reciprocity in attempting to settle issues, a loss of intimacy, and a decline in other forms of interaction, such as sexual intercourse.

One of the most common complaints of women is that their spouse won't talk to them about problems. These men seek to prevent conflict by avoiding issues. As a result, the women become even more frustrated and either exert pressure in efforts to confront their spouse with the problem or withdraw more and more. The problems are not solved.

Sometimes, however, temporarily avoiding conflict is the wisest choice. Positive solutions can be found only after intense negative feelings have subsided and people can think straight. Thus, upset individuals might want to engage in physical activity, go to a movie, visit a neighbor, or discuss things with a counselor before confronting the problem.

Ventilation and Catharsis

The opposite of avoiding conflict is ventilating it. **Ventilation** means expressing negative emotions and feelings. This concept has been used in psychotherapy for years. It involves encouraging people who are upset to talk out or to act out their feelings to get them in the open; only then can the individuals scrutinize their feelings, understand them, and channel them in less destructive directions. This therapeutic approach, which emphasizes the importance of "letting it out," is based on the

Stressful living conditions or unexpected events that disturb family functioning affect every member of the family, not just the adults. The more children in a family, the more strain, stress, and conflict are naturally introduced.

idea of **catharsis,** or draining off negative emotions and feelings so that they can be replaced by more positive ones. This assumes that people have a tendency toward aggression that cannot be bottled up. If they attempt to repress this tendency, it will only result in a more destructive expression at some later time. Therefore, it is better to let out the aggression through a series of minor confrontations than to let negative feelings accumulate until they become a potential relationship bomb.

This approach to dealing with conflict can be helpful psychotherapy for people with feelings of hostility and emotional problems. But venting one's hostilities on the psychiatrist's couch, in the counseling center, or in other psychotherapeutic environments, and in the presence of a trained therapist, is far different from doing the same in one's own home, where the hostilities are directed toward one's spouse or children. In therapy, an adult may express hostilities toward a family member verbally, or a child may express them physically, in the presence of the therapist, but not actually in the physical presence of the person. Telling a therapist "I hate my spouse" is far different from actually telling the spouse "I hate you." In the first instance, the hostilities may have been drained off harmlessly, such that when the individual gets back home he or she feels less hateful; but in the second instance, even though the individual feels better, the spouse feels worse and will usually retaliate in some fashion. This may result in an increase of hostile feelings between the two people.

Almost no research supports the idea of catharsis in the family and some shows the reverse; that is, opportunities to observe or to give vent to anger, hostility, and violence tend to produce greater subsequent levels of aggression and violence (Tavris, 1982). The reason is that the family is an intimate, closely confined group, with members intensely involved with one another. If excessive hostility is directed at other family members, they feel angry, hurt, or misunderstood. If this reactive emotion is not dealt with, additional disagreements arise and tension mounts, sometimes to intolerable levels. Furthermore, family members can't get away from the source of friction without splitting up the family, even if only temporarily. Of course, tolerance for verbal aggression ranges widely. What one person finds to be excessive aggression may be completely

acceptable behavior to another. Of critical importance here is the fact that when verbal aggression becomes excessive it can lead to physical aggression (Phelps, Meara, Davis, and Patton, 1991).

One study of over 5,000 couples found that men and women engaged in about equal amounts of verbal aggression toward their partners. This aggression tended to decrease with age and with increasing numbers of children in the family and to increase with alcohol abuse and the use of other drugs. Socioeconomic status and race were not found to be related to verbal aggression (Straus and Sweet, 1992).

What about more intellectual, rational approaches to problem solving? Evidence suggests that families that take the calm, rational, intellectual, emotion-suppressing approach have much lower levels of physical violence. This is even more true for working-class families than for middle-class families. Intellectual approaches that observe "civility" and "etiquette" in interpersonal relationships are more helpful in the long run in promoting marital harmony and stability and in resolving conflicts (M. J. Martin, Schumm, Bugaighis, Jurich, and Bollman, 1987).

Constructive Conflicts

A distinction must be made between conflicts that are constructive and those that are destructive. **Constructive arguments** are those that attack the problems, stick to the issues, and lead to a more complete understanding and to consensus, compromise, or other acceptable solutions to the problem. They minimize negative emotions, foster respect and confidence, and bring a couple closer together.

---

avoidance   Method of dealing with conflict by avoiding the people, situations, and issues that stimulate it.

ventilation   The process of airing, or expressing, negative emotions and feelings.

catharsis   Venting negative emotions to rid oneself of them so that they can be replaced by more positive ones.

constructive arguments   Arguments that stick with the issues, that attack the problem and not the other person, that employ rational methods, and that result in greater understanding, consensus, compromise, and closeness between two people.

They take place in a nonhostile, trusting atmosphere in which honest disagreements may be discussed and understood and in which the argument progresses according to fair rules. They involve a low level of negative verbal responses.

Destructive Conflicts

Destructive arguments are those that attack the other person rather than the problem. They seek to shame, belittle, or punish the other person through name calling or by attacking sensitive issues in a spirit of ill will, hatred, revenge, or contempt (Halford, Hahlweg, and Dunne, 1990). They frequently rely on criticism and negative personal comments in attempts to influence the other person. Destructive arguments are characterized by a lack of genuine communication and by suspicion, and they often rely on interpersonal strategies that involve threat or coercion. The argument brings up many side issues, and it seeks to relieve the attacker's own tensions at the expense of the other person. Destructive arguments elevate tension levels; increase resentment and hostility toward the other person; undermine confidence, trust, friendship, and affectionate feelings; result in loss of companionship; and engender greater alienation. One of the characteristics of destructive arguments is the way they get off the track and raise irrelevant issues.

FAMILY CRISES

A **crisis** may be defined as a drastic change in the course of events; it is a turning point that affects the trend of future events. It is a time of instability, necessitating decisions and adjustments. Sometimes the crisis develops because of events outside the family: a hurricane, earthquake, flood, war, economic depression, or plant closure. At other times a crisis occurs within the family system: divorce, alcoholism, the loss of a family member, or conflict that erupts in violence (Weigel, Weigel, and Blundall, 1987). Internal crises tend to demoralize a family, increasing resentment, alienation, and conflict. Sometimes a crisis develops out of a series of smaller external and internal events that build up to the point at which family members can't cope. Broderick (1984) explained:

> Even small events, not enough by themselves to cause any real stress, can take a toll when they come one after another. First an unplanned pregnancy, then a move, then a financial problem that results in having to borrow several thousand dollars, then the big row with the new neighbors over keeping the dog tied up, and finally little Jimmy breaking his arm in a bicycle accident, all in three months, finally becomes too much. (p. 310)

Broderick calls this situation **crisis overload.**

During a family crisis, families go through three stages—onset, disorganization, and reorganization—before reaching a new level of organization (Boss, 1987; Lavee, McCubbin, and Patterson, 1985; Walker, 1985). The new level may be higher or lower than the level before the crisis.

Stage 1: Onset

The first stage is the onset of the crisis and the increasing realization that a crisis has occurred (see Figure 15.1). An initial reaction may include disbelief. Family members may define a situation differently; what is a major crisis to one person may not be to another. One spouse, for example, may be on the verge of asking for a divorce; the other may refuse to accept the fact that there is a problem, believing that the spouse is "making too big a deal out of it." The first step, therefore, is to define the problem and gradually accept that a crisis exists—for example, gradually recognizing and accepting a child's disability. The impact of the crisis will depend on the nature of the precipitating event and the interpretation and cognitive perception of it, the degree of hardship and stress the crisis produces, and the resources available to handle the problem.

Stage 2: Disorganization

The second stage is a period of disorganization. Shock and disbelief may make it impossible to function or to think clearly in the beginning (see Figure 15.1). "I don't know what I'm going to do" is a common reaction. The period of disorganization may last for only a few hours, or it may stretch into days or weeks. During this period, the family's normal functioning is disrupted. Tempers are short, loyalties are strained, tension fills the air, friction increases, and family morale declines. Child and spouse abuse is more likely to develop during the time of maximum disorganization than at any other time.

When the volcano Mount Saint Helens erupted on May 18, 1980, thousands of people felt the stress.

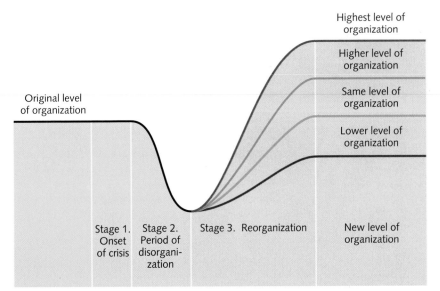

Original level of organization

Highest level of organization

Higher level of organization

Same level of organization

Lower level of organization

Stage 1. Onset of crisis

Stage 2. Period of disorganization

Stage 3. Reorganization

New level of organization

Figure 15.1 Family Adjustment to a Crisis

Associated Press reports from Washington after the eruption indicated that, locally, criminal assaults rose 25%, suicide threats and attempts doubled, and the number of cases of battered women increased 45% (Blumenthal, 1980). The situation was particularly stressful because of the violence of the explosion (500 times the force of the atom bomb dropped on Hiroshima) and the uncertainty of subsequent explosions. People did not know what would happen next or how long the catastrophe would last. The effects of stress were delayed, however. The greatest increase in spouse abuse cases did not occur until about 30 days after the major eruption.

Other studies have shown that the use of alcohol and other drugs sharply increases during times of stress and may lead to a deeper level of disorganization or serve to handicap the individual's and family's capacity to bounce back from the crisis (Anisman and Merali, 1999; J. Miller, Turner, and Kimball, 1981).

Stage 3: Reorganization

The third stage is one of gradual reorganization during which family members try to take remedial action (see Figure 15.1). If the crisis is a financial one, family members may borrow money, sell the family car, or cash in some savings. Other family members may get temporary employment to help out, or a former wage earner may start drawing unemployment. If the financial crisis persists, the stock of resources

begins to run out. The family has to think about taking out a second mortgage, selling the house, or moving to another neighborhood.

Once the family hits bottom, things may begin to improve. The unemployed wage earner gets a new job, and bills are gradually paid off; the family begins to recoup its emotional and physical resources. Eventually, after a period that may range from days to months, the family is reorganized at a new level. Sometimes the new level is not as satisfactory as the old; at other times the level of organization is superior to the old. For example, in the case of a financial crisis, family money management improves or total income is higher, or both. At any rate, the level is high enough and stable enough to mark the end of the period of crisis.

Crisis theory, such as that just described, is helpful as a model for understanding what happens

---

destructive arguments　Arguments that attack the other person rather than the problem; that increase resentment and hostility and undermine trust, friendship, and affectionate feelings; that result in greater alienation; and that do not solve the problem.

crisis　A drastic change in the course of events; a turning point that affects future events.

crisis overload　A series of crises occurring one after another until they become more than a person can handle.

Families who experience crises, such as the loss of their home due to a natural disaster, will pass through the predictable stages of disbelief, disorganization, and reorganization before they begin rebuilding their lives.

when families have various kinds of crises. While this theory can be applied to a wide variety of crises, we have selected four types for detailed discussion here: (1) infidelity, (2) economic distress, (3) violence and abuse, and (4) death and grief.

THE CRISIS OF INFIDELITY

The majority of Americans still enter marriage expecting and committed to sexual fidelity. Americans place a high value on sexual exclusiveness as important to a healthy marriage. The National Health and Social Life Survey found that 80% of married women and 65–85% of married men of every age reported that they had no partners other than their spouse while married (Michael, Gagnon, Laumann, and Kolata, 1994). Ninety percent of married adults had had only one sex partner in the previous 12 months. These figures reflect the fact that a large majority of married Americans are faithful; here we will discuss those who are not.

Reasons for Infidelity

Why do adults become involved in extramarital affairs even though they say they don't believe in them? There are a variety of reasons.

Emotional Need   For some people, extramarital affairs represent an effort to fulfill emotional needs.

Affairs are an expression of personality problems. A woman may unconsciously seek an older father figure (who is already married) to comfort her and love her and to replace the father whom she lost in childhood or who rejected her as a child. A man may want an older woman who will mother him because he never felt loved and cared for by his mother while he was growing up.

Extramarital affairs can be an important validation of attractiveness and self-esteem. Affairs may result from fear about one's self-worth or sexual attractiveness. The affairs become an attempt to feel better about oneself. More generally, infidelity may be a symptom of emotional difficulties in the individual and an attempt to resolve these difficulties.

Unresolved Marital Problems   Infidelity can also be a symptom of unresolved problems in the marriage itself. These problems build up year after year and are not successfully addressed. An affair encourages a spouse to divert energy away from the marital relationship (Pittman, 1993).

Unresolved issues can include the lack of communication, the efforts of one person to dominate the other, the failure to show affection, and the lack of social life and companionship. People repress their feelings because they don't like to be upset and frustrated all the time. Eventually, they shut off their positive feelings of warmth and affection as well. The marital partners may be at a stalemate, unable to either revive the marriage or end it. However, they are still vulnerable and will respond to those people who fulfill the needs not being met in their primary relationship. In these situations, a spouse may cultivate a marital arrangement—that is, participate in an affair that meets some immediate needs without disrupting the marriage further (Pittman, 1993).

If hostility builds up between marital partners, an extramarital affair becomes a way of balancing the animosity felt toward a spouse or a way of getting even for the hurts suffered in the marriage. Most people are not interested in extramarital relationships when everything is going smoothly in their marriage. For this reason, an affair can be a symptom of problems rather than the problem itself, even though it sometimes stabilizes but usually compounds the difficulties.

Ambivalence about Marriage   Single people who are ambivalent about getting married may seek sexual partners who are already married because they feel "safer" knowing they won't have to make a permanent commitment. They escape the responsibilities of being a spouse but gain the benefits of having a lover.

Pleasure and Excitement   Some people have affairs simply because they want the excitement of sexual variety. Other people enjoy the sense of competition with a married spouse, and the married person's unavailability only serves to increase the challenge. They like the excitement of illicit sex. There is risk, of course. One is the possibility that they might become emotionally involved whether they intended to or not. To other people, a one-night stand provides excitement and freedom from the responsibilities of an emotional commitment. The risks here include the possibility of AIDS or another sexually transmitted disease and the negative effects on the marriage because marital vows have been violated.

A new relationship may seem more exciting than an old one, primarily because it is different. But once the initial flush of intense emotions declines, the lovers may feel empty unless something deeper has developed in the meantime.

Permissive Values   Some individuals don't really see anything wrong with extramarital sex—as long as their spouses don't find out or it doesn't hurt anyone. Some people have numerous partners before marriage and continue to do so afterward be-

cause permissiveness is a part of their value system. One married man became involved with another woman with whom he continued to have sex. He couldn't understand why his spouse was so upset when she found out. As far as he was concerned, he ought to have been allowed to have both a spouse and a mistress.

Affairs as Crises for Married People

Extramarital affairs have varying effects on married people and their marriages. Both men and women have affairs, and some marriages are never the same afterward. A sense of betrayal and the ensuing distrust are common. One woman remarked, "I don't know if I can ever trust him again. Every time he's out of town I wonder what he is doing and who he's with" (Author's counseling notes). Another woman commented, "All I can think of is that he was doing this with that other woman. I can't give myself to him" (Author's counseling notes). In such cases, extramarital affairs may be a major factor in precipitating divorce.

Sometimes, however, the crisis of an affair stimulates the couple to finally accept the fact that their marriage is in deep trouble and that they need help. One woman explained:

> I've been trying to tell my husband for years that I was unhappy in our marriage, but he didn't listen. Now, I've met someone else, and for the first time my husband is listening and is willing to go to a marriage counselor. (Author's counseling notes)

In this case, the affair had a positive value.

Some marriages are not affected very much by an affair. One of the spouses is having an affair, but the other doesn't care. These are often marriages in which the emotional bonds between the spouses are already broken, so the extramarital relationship is simply evidence of the fractured marriage. These people have either lost or never had a meaningful relationship with each other. In still other marriages, the spouses may agree that one or both of them has the freedom to have affairs. And in some situations, one spouse discovers that the other has been unfaithful but chooses not to confront the situation because they have children and do not want to divorce or separate for their sake.

Affairs that are most threatening to the marriage are ongoing ones that include emotional involvement, as well as sexual relations. Women are much more likely than men to be emotionally invested in the relationship (Penn, Henandez, and Bermudez, 1997). People who believe that they have fallen deeply in love don't want to give up the affair, which seems meaningful and exciting. One person involved in an affair remarked, "I haven't felt like this for years. I can't give up something that makes me feel alive again" (author's counseling notes). Of course, what people don't realize in the beginning is that the intense emotional excitement will pass. If the relationship is to endure, the couple needs to have many other things going on in the relationship.

From many points of view, extramarital relationships become a crisis in the marriage that requires considerable effort to resolve.

THE CRISIS OF ECONOMIC DISTRESS

Many families have to face the crisis of economic distress due to employment instability or uncertainty; underemployment; declining income due to demotion, cutbacks, or retirement; or the inability to earn an adequate income because of lack of education and skills, disability, or health problems (Chilman, 1991). Economic distress has profound effects on individual and family functioning. In this section, we will examine some of these effects.

Types of Economic Distress

The effects of an economic crisis depend on the type of crisis and its duration. For example, a permanent closure of one's office or plant is more stressful than a temporary cut in hours.

Employment Instability Even during prosperous times, the unemployment rate in the United States hovers at around 5% of the labor force. During periods of recession, the percentage increases considerably. As of 2003, the overall unemployment rate was 6%. The rates are always highest among minority groups and among both males and females under 20 years of age (U.S. Bureau of the Census, 2000). During recessions, unemployment rates are usually higher in the construction and agricultural industries. People with the least education and seniority have the highest rates of attrition (U.S. Bureau of the Census, 2000).

The effect of unemployment on individuals and families depends partly on how long it lasts, whether it involves permanent job displacement or a temporary layoff, whether other comparable or replacement jobs are readily available, and whether there is more than one wage earner in the family. Young couples and single mothers with a number of children, especially young children, are most affected by unemployment. Many have minimal skills and resources, so they have to turn to others for help.

Employment Uncertainty Some families feel the stress of employment uncertainty for long periods of time (Wilson, Larson, and Stone, 1993). For example, when a corporation like General Motors announces that it is closing an assembly plant, families may wait for months to learn whether the plant to be closed is in Michigan or Texas. Individuals and families wait while the armed services decide which base to close. Workers in a particular plant are told to expect layoffs but don't know which workers will be let go. Those already unemployed endure the uncertainty of not knowing where and when they will find another job (Voydanoff, 1990).

Underemployment Underemployment is also a source of economic distress. It may involve working at a job below one's skills and training or working fewer hours or at lower pay than one would like. During recessions, many white-collar workers—even those at middle-management levels—and highly skilled blue-collar workers are laid off and forced to accept whatever type of employment they can find.

Declining Income Another source of economic distress is a decline in personal or family income due to a demotion, cut in hours and pay, declining sales or profits (D. R. Johnson and Booth, 1990), forced retirement (Hanks, 1990), or divorce or widowhood (Choi, 1992). Adverse economic changes require families to adjust to a lower income by changing their lifestyle, reducing their consumption, or increasing their income by changing jobs or by having another family member go to work (Elder, Conger, Foster, and Ardelt, 1992). Typically, the custodial parent and children experience a decline in income following divorce, whereas the noncustodial parent enjoys an increase. Noncustodial parents often do not share a fair proportion of their earnings with their former spouse to help support the children (Weitzman, 1985), and women whose marriages fail face increasing odds of becoming poor (Arendell, 1987; L. A. Morgan, 1989). Farm families typically have varied and uncertain incomes from year to year and in poor crop years are faced with a substantial financial crisis of undetermined duration (Meyer and Lobao, 1997).

Effects on Individuals and on Family Relationships

Economic distress has a significant effect on the individuals and families involved. Unemployment and employment uncertainty are associated with depression, anxiety, psychophysiological distress, and mental hospital admissions (Dooley, Catalano, and Rook, 1988; Ensminger and Celentano, 1988). The level of economic status affects mortality; the advent of poverty, for example, increases the hazard of dying for both men and women (Zick and Smith, 1991a). Men's unemployment is associated with increased psychological distress for their spouses (Liem and Liem, 1988). In fact, women show more anxiety and depression when their spouse is unemployed than when they are unemployed themselves (Voydanoff and Donnelly, 1989a). Some studies show that unemployment lowers self-esteem, which, in turn, is related to a lower level of self-mastery and to an increase in depression (Perrucci, Perrucci, Targ, and Targ, 1988; Shamir, 1986).

The effect of economic distress on families is extensive and wide ranging. For one thing, families need a minimum level of income and employment stability to function. Without it, many find themselves subject to separation and divorce (Liem and Liem, 1988). In a study of farm families, D. R. Johnson and Booth (1990) found that economic hardships were strongly related to thoughts about divorce. One study of White, middle-class couples found that those who were under economic pressure had lower marital quality because of an increase in hostility and a decrease in warmth among family members (Lorenz, Conger, Simon, Whitbeck, and Elder, 1991). Other studies have shown that income loss and economic strain are negatively associated with marital quality and family satisfaction due to financial conflicts, the man's psychological instability, marital tensions and hostility, and lack of warmth and support (Conger et al., 1990). Mount-

ing economic pressure makes men more irritable and short-tempered, increasing their hostility in the marital relationship and causing them to behave more punitively in their parent role (Elder et al., 1992; McLoyd, 1989). These patterns are repeated in farm families. Those with employed wives had higher debt loads than did those with nonemployed wives; the women also worked longer hours in all production (including paid work, farm production, and household production) and were less satisfied with their marital relationships. Not surprisingly, the men had lower levels of life satisfaction (Godwin, Draughn, Little, and Marlowe, 1991).

A study of 429 inner-city families traced the effects of economic pressure on the emotional status and parenting behavior of African American and Anglo-American parents. Family hardship and strong economic pressure diminished the sense of parental competency among both Blacks and Whites. Parents became depressed and demoralized under economic pressure and lost confidence in their parenting ability. Black parents suffered more emotional distress than did White parents. One possible explanation is that the African American families had fewer economic resources to begin with, so any economic distress directly diminished their confidence in their ability to effectively meet their children's needs (Elder, Eccles, Ardelt, and Lord, 1995).

Problems within marriage can also spill over to work, resulting in loss of income. One study found that marital distress is associated with work loss—particularly among men in their first 10 years of marriage. Based on the average earnings of participants, work loss associated with marital problems translated into a loss of approximately $6.8 billion per year. Preventing marital problems may thus result in important psychological and economic benefits for society (Forthofer, Markman, Cox, Stanley, and Kessler, 1996).

Coping with Economic Distress

Individuals and families use various strategies in coping with economic distress. Avoidance coping involves keeping one's feelings to oneself, refusing to believe the economic crisis is real, and eating, drinking, and smoking to relieve tensions. Avoiding the problem may allow more positive interaction with one's spouse and fewer arguments about finances and partially lessen the impact of financial distress (Wilhelm and Ridley, 1988); however, it doesn't solve the problem. Instead of ignoring or avoiding the problem, families are better served in the long run by developing skills in conflict management and problem solving. A more positive approach is to cut back on expenditures wherever possible and postpone major purchases, such as a new car or orthodontic treatment (Elder et al., 1992). Selling property or possessions is sometimes necessary. Some families rent rooms, take in boarders, or supply child care for others. Many families have to borrow from savings or life insurance policies. Finding part-time or temporary employment may be possible. Teenagers or other family members may have to go to work. Other families start small businesses at home. Skills such as sewing or carpentry can be tapped to earn additional income. Generally, married men spend significantly less time unemployed than do single men, probably because of the realization that they need income to help support their families (Teachman, Call, and Carver, 1994).

Before their resources are exhausted, families may turn to relatives, friends, coworkers, neighbors, self-help groups, human service professionals, or helping agencies. A study of African American families revealed that both family and nonkin were important sources of emergency assistance (R. J. Taylor, Chatters, and Mays, 1988). Major types of support may include money, goods, services, emotional support, babysitting, transportation, job-hunting aid, and advice and feedback. There are also many types of social and government programs designed to help people who are in financial distress. However, many families find these sources of help frustrating and humiliating to access and use, so they avoid them as much as possible (Dodson, 1998).

Instead, family members frequently seek the social support of relatives and friends as they try to cope with economic distress. External support can reduce the stress of individuals, but it may also generate costs for the persons involved. These contrasting effects may be operating in families with unstably employed men whose spouses seek emotional support outside the immediate family. In theory, for example, the woman's support from external sources reduces her stress, but it can also affirm the man's sense of failure as a breadwinner and evoke more negativity on his part in family relationships. In families headed by a man with an unstable work history, the woman's support from relatives and friends is positively associated with the man's negativity

toward his spouse (E. B. Robertson, Elder, Skinner, and Conger, 1991).

THE CRISIS OF VIOLENCE AND ABUSE

Family violence generally refers to any rough or extended use of physical force or aggression or of verbal abuse by one family member toward another. Violence may or may not result in the physical injury of another person. Thus, a man who throws and breaks dishes, destroys furniture, or punches out walls when he is angry may not injure his spouse or children, but he is certainly being violent. Family violence is not easily defined, however, because there are disagreements over what use of force, if any, is appropriate, and because there is often a discrepancy between spouses' perceptions of family violence.

Attitudes toward violence have a significant effect on whether people act violently toward a spouse or children. In our society, men are more often socialized to accept violence. Early in their lives, boys are encouraged to behave belligerently and aggressively and to use physical force (Scher and Stevens, 1987). The legitimation of violence increases the probability that violence will occur in relationships (K. R. Williams, 1992).

In Sweden, a parent can be imprisoned for a month for striking a child; in contrast, many Americans believe that spanking children is normal and necessary, and even good. In fact, as we saw in Chapter 13, a high percentage of families use corporal punishment to discipline their children. But many spankings verge on beatings.

Some men and women believe that it is acceptable for spouses to hit each other under some circumstances. Most spouse beaters deny they have beaten anyone—"I just pushed her around a little bit, but I didn't really hurt her" is a common assertion—yet many have in fact badly injured the other person. Even civil authorities hesitate to interfere in family quarrels because of the different beliefs about legitimate force and illegitimate violence in the family. As violence continues, however, public tolerance seems to be declining, and people are demanding preventive and remedial action (Gross and Robinson, 1987).

Some writers argue that there are two distinct forms of couple violence taking place within fami-

Violence may or may not result in physical injury of another person. Family violence refers to any rough or extended use of physical force or aggression or of verbal abuse by one family member toward another.

lies. Data gathered from women's shelters suggest that some families suffer from occasional outbursts of violence from either spouse (common couple violence), while other families are terrorized by systematic male violence (patriarchal terrorism; M. P. Johnson, 1995). It must not be assumed that common couple violence is unimportant. Suggesting that only severe, repeated violence counts as a problem seems to come disturbingly close to normalizing minor violence. There is evidence that minor violence is associated with depression and poor family functioning. It is also associated with a greater risk of severe future assaults (Hamby, Poindexter, and Gray-Little, 1996).

Spouse abuse and *child abuse* are more limited and specific terms than *family violence*; they usually refer to acts of violence that have a high probability of injuring the victim. An operational definition of **child abuse,** however, may include not only physical assault that results in injury but also malnourishment, abandonment, neglect (defined as the failure to provide adequate physical and emotional care), emotional abuse, and sexual abuse (Finkelhor and Araji, 1986; Hodson and Skeen, 1987). Sexual abuse by a relative is incest (J. A. Nelson, 1986). **Spouse abuse** may include not only battering but sexual abuse and marital rape as well. Violence often starts during courtship and continues after marriage (Bernard, Bernard, and Bernard, 1985; Flynn, 1987; Make-

peace, 1987). Studies of both victims and perpetrators of courtship violence reveal a higher likelihood of violence among minority groups and among people without strong religious beliefs or affiliations or infrequent church attendance, people with very low or very high income, people who experience social stress or isolation, people from disrupted homes, people who have had emotionally distant and harsh parenting, people who start dating early, and people who have problems with school, employment, or substance abuse (Makepeace, 1987).

Factors Related to Violence

Family violence is a multifaceted phenomenon that can best be understood from a multidisciplinary perspective. Indeed, no single theory or discipline

family violence Any rough or extended use of physical force or aggression or verbal abuse by one family member toward another.

child abuse May include not only physical assaults on a child but also malnourishment, abandonment, neglect, emotional abuse, and sexual abuse.

spouse abuse Physical or emotional mistreatment of one's spouse.

has been adequate in explaining it (McKenry, Julian, and Gavazzi, 1995).

Family violence may be related to stress of one kind or another. When stressors are uncontrollable, unpredictable, or chronic, the likelihood of substance abuse increases (Anisman and Merali, 1999). Although alcohol and drug use may initially be used to decrease the anxiety of stressful life events, substance use itself can become a stressful event and violence may follow. One study found that male partners' unemployment and drug or alcohol use were associated with increased risk for physical, sexual, and/or emotional abuse (Coker, Smith, McKeown, and King, 2000).

Unplanned pregnancies and premarital pregnancies can also cause emotional stress and place a strain on the limited financial resources of both the mother and the father. Women report being the victims of beatings before and after the birth of their child. Attacks during pregnancy are especially brutal, with women being kicked or punched in the stomach.

Financial problems, unemployment, or job dissatisfaction that men perceive as evidence of incompetency in fulfilling their role as provider are linked to child abuse and woman beating. Social isolation also raises the risk that severe violence will be directed at children or spouses (Coley and Beckett, 1988). Families who lack close personal friendships and who are poorly integrated into the community lack support networks during times of stress. They also are less influenced by the social expectations of friends and family. Certainly, an abusive man will discourage his spouse from becoming friendly with neighbors out of embarrassment or fear of discovery, and this isolation increases her vulnerability and compounds her problem.

Despite violent family histories, men who develop strong attachments to and perceive threats of negative sanction from significant others (partners, friends, relatives) are less likely to be violent with their female partner. The last thing abusers want is for other people to know about their abuse (Lackey and Williams, 1995). This indicates that abusive behavior can be modified or changed.

Domestic violence is found among families of all socioeconomic and ethnic groups (Hampton, Gelles, and Harrop, 1989). Physical abuse between spouses occurs in middle- and upper-class marriages, but it seems more frequent among lower-class families (Lockhart, 1987). This may be due partly to the underreporting of violence among middle- and upper-class families. Furthermore, lower-class women are more dependent economically on their spouses and so feel locked into an abusive relationship. Middle- and upper-class families have many more resources to mediate stress, such as greater financial resources, better access to contraception and abortion and to medical and psychological personnel, and more opportunities to utilize babysitters, nursery schools, and camps to provide relief from family responsibilities.

Spousal incompatibility with respect to status contributes to marital dissatisfaction and to violence. Couples in which the woman's educational attainments are low relative to the man's experience a high incidence of spousal violence. Similarly, couples in which the woman is more successful than the man also experience marital dissatisfaction and a high incidence of spousal violence. Either extreme creates tensions.

A lot of family violence is related to alcohol and drug abuse. Some people are not abusive until they are under the influence. A question arises: Do they lose control because of the alcohol or drugs, or do they drink or take drugs to give them an excuse for their abusive behavior? Either one or both may be true.

Family violence is more likely in divorced and remarried households than in first-time marriages (Kalmuss and Seltzer, 1989). The cumulative stress of experiencing multiple family transitions heightens the risk of family conflict (Kalmuss and Seltzer, 1989). However, even though conflict and violence are more likely, they are not inevitable (Heyman, O'Leary, and Jouriles, 1995).

Spouse Abuse

Spouse abusers may seem to be ordinary citizens in other aspects of their lives, but a positive social facade frequently conceals disturbing personality characteristics. Spouse abusers have been described as having Jekyll-and-Hyde personalities. They typically have poor self-images, which they express by being violent (Goldstein and Rosenbaum, 1985). Excessive jealousy and alcohol or drug abuse are also common among abusers. Because they are insecure individuals who do not feel good about themselves, abusers typically seek a partner who is passive and compliant, whom they can bully, and whom they can blame for all of their own problems. Their abused partner becomes their scapegoat, because the abusers cannot accept responsibility for their own actions.

Controlled studies indicate that men who physically abuse their spouses are characterized by generalized aggressive tendencies, impulsive and defiant personality styles, an external locus of control, type A behavior, rigid authoritarian attitudes, a traditional-role identity, and low self-esteem and self-concepts. They perceive their spouse as less physically attractive than do men in distressed but nonabusive marriages. Abusers report lower levels of marital satisfaction and significant problems in communication. Anger, verbal attacks, and withdrawal appear to dominate the problem-solving interactions in abusive marriages. Abusive relationships have also been found to be associated with sexual dysfunction. Abusive men evidence significantly lower relationship closeness and less sexual assertiveness and sexual satisfaction in their marriages than do nonabusive men. They demonstrate more negative attitudes toward sex and greater sexual preoccupation (Hurlbert and Apt, 1991). In addition, they have very negative attitudes toward women and lower levels of rational thinking (Eisikovits, Edleson, Guttmann, and Sela-Amit, 1991).

One study of American couples conservatively documented that one in every eight men had committed a violent act against his spouse during the preceding year. A comprehensive review of another study revealed the reported rate of woman abuse in the United States to be between 11% and 22% (Hoffman, Demo, and Edwards, 1994).

Abusers are not only males. A number of studies indicate that women, particularly those who are younger, inflict more verbal and physical aggression than men (Morse, 1995; O'Leary et al., 1989; Stets, 1990; Swinford, DeMaris, Cernkovich, and Giordano, 2000). However, these studies highlight the importance of distinguishing between the frequency of aggressive acts and the severity. The greater average strength and size of men enable them to do more injury. Women are likely to use violence against men in self-defense, causing physical harm or injury in retaliation against their spouse. A woman who kills her spouse is often reacting to his abuse (Goetting, 1987). Women use violence predominantly in self-defense, whereas males use violence predominantly to intimidate their partner (Flynn, 1990).

Figure 15.2 shows the primary tactics and behaviors male abusers manifest to get and maintain control in relationships. Battering is an intentional act used to gain power and control over another person. Physical abuse is only one part of a whole system of abusive behavior that an abuser uses against his partner. Violence includes not only the acts of physical aggression but also patterns of oppression occurring over time, including events leading up to and following the use of force itself. The most widely held theory of the pattern or cycle of violence outlines at least three phases—the tension-building phase, the acute battering phase, and the loving contrition phase—that ensnare women in a web of punishment and deceit (Wolf-Smith and LaRossa, 1992).

In trying to understand abuse of women, people often wonder, What about those who are abused? What are they like, and why do they allow themselves to be mistreated? These questions denigrate the victim and assume that she is lacking in some way. Women from any background can find themselves in abusive relationships. The onset of abuse is insidious and intermittent, leaving the woman with mixed messages and an unclear picture of her situation. Some abused women have experienced childhood abuse, which has been shown to elevate the probability that they will become the victims of domestic assault. Women subjected to abusive parenting tend to develop hostile, rebellious orientations and are likely to affiliate with and marry men with similar characteristics who engage in a variety of deviant behaviors, including violence toward their spouse (Simons, Johnson, Beaman, and Conger, 1993). Yet whether or not the woman comes from an abusive family history, she becomes confused about herself and her partner. Sometimes her partner is nice to her and says he loves her and needs her; at other times he is abusive. He tries to make her feel that the reason he becomes violent and abusive is that she has done something wrong. She comes to feel that he's abusing her to try to make her a better person. She comes to accept the blame for what happens and to feel that it is her fault (B. Andrews and Brewin, 1990). She does not want to be hurt (she's not a masochist), so she searches for the right way to behave so that her partner will be consistently loving. She feels that he's good and she's bad. She doesn't confront him or question his behavior. Her security depends on his approval, so she acts compliant and renounces her own wishes. She gives up her freedom if he demands that she quit her job or give up her activities, interests, and friends. Every part of her life is affected by his control. Her self-confidence and self-esteem continue to diminish

Figure 15.2 Control Chart
This chart uses the wheel as a symbol of the relationship of physical abuse to other forms of abuse. Each spoke represents a tactic used to control or gain power, which is the hub of the wheel. The rim that surrounds and supports the spokes is physical abuse. It holds the system together and gives it strength. (*Note:* From Domestic Abuse Intervention Project [202 E. Superior Street. Duluth, Minnesota 55802. 218-722-2781.] All rights reserved.

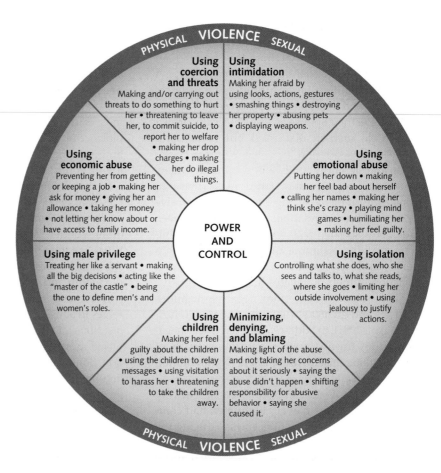

PHYSICAL **VIOLENCE** SEXUAL

Using coercion and threats
Making and/or carrying out threats to do something to hurt her • threatening to leave her, to commit suicide, to report her to welfare • making her drop charges • making her do illegal things.

Using intimidation
Making her afraid by using looks, actions, gestures • smashing things • destroying her property • abusing pets • displaying weapons.

Using economic abuse
Preventing her from getting or keeping a job • making her ask for money • giving her an allowance • taking her money • not letting her know about or have access to family income.

Using emotional abuse
Putting her down • making her feel bad about herself • calling her names • making her think she's crazy • playing mind games • humiliating her • making her feel guilty.

POWER AND CONTROL

Using male privilege
Treating her like a servant • making all the big decisions • acting like the "master of the castle" • being the one to define men's and women's roles.

Using isolation
Controlling what she does, who she sees and talks to, what she reads, where she goes • limiting her outside involvement • using jealousy to justify actions.

Using children
Making her feel guilty about the children • using the children to relay messages • using visitation to harass her • threatening to take the children away.

Minimizing, denying, and blaming
Making light of the abuse and not taking her concerns about it seriously • saying the abuse didn't happen • shifting responsibility for abusive behavior • saying she caused it.

PHYSICAL **VIOLENCE** SEXUAL

because he makes her feel that she is a bad person and everything is her fault. She doesn't leave him because she hopes things will change, she feels that if she just tries harder everything will be all right, she's afraid she'll lose his love, and she's fearful of what he might do to her (DeMaris and Swinford, 1996; Forward, 1986). Women who remain in abusive relationships report that there is little or no change in the frequency or severity of abuse or the amount of love and affection expressed, and they often report that their relationship is not as bad as it could be (Herbert, Silver, and Ellard, 1991).

Child Abuse

Early studies attempted to show that abusive parents suffered from mental or emotional illness, that the reason people abused their spouse or children was that they suffered from psychoses, neuroses, or psychopathic problems of one kind or another. More recent research has shown that child abusers are not necessarily emotionally ill. However, they usually exhibit more psychological problems than other parents do. Abusive behavior can be triggered by the child's irritating behavior, which the parents neither expect nor understand. They often have negative concepts of self, which they project onto the child. When parents feel negative about themselves, the abuse is magnified. Once begun, abuse continues because of the parents' continuing lack of knowledge about children and parenting and their growing contempt for themselves. Abusive parents see themselves as unworthy people and so allow the abuse to continue as a method of validating their unworthiness.

Abuse of children may also be a spillover from stress and conflict in the parents' lives. Financial difficulties or a lack of parenting skills result in a high level of stress, with the child becoming the target of parental frustration. Repeated incidences of abuse result in reduced feelings of personal control, with

Spouses Who Abuse

Spouses who abuse their partners tend to share both characteristics and tactics.

Characteristics of an Abusive Spouse

- High rates of violence in childhood, both as victim and perpetrator
- A resort to violent means more readily than by nonabusive spouse
- Jealousy
- Marital maladjustment
- A tolerant attitude toward spousal abuse
- Impulsive behavior
- Anger that is greater in duration, intensity, and frequency than that in nonabusive spouse
- Abandonment anxiety
- Sleep disturbance
- Depression

Tactics of an Abusive Spouse

- Social isolation
- Verbal abuse
- Emotional abuse
- Economic dependence
- Intermittent undermining
- Manipulation
- Intense anger and demandingness

Abusive behavior increases in severity in relation to the characteristics just listed. The tactics are usually employed intermittently. This keeps the victims on guard, wary of when the next round of abuse will occur and never knowing how severe the next attack will be. However, abused individuals have seen and experienced enough to be afraid. In fact, the fear can become so intense that it is almost disabling (Dutton and Haring, 1999; Hanson, Cadsky, Harris, and Lalonde, 1997).

outcomes no longer contingent upon one's own efforts (Kugler and Hanson, 1988). Very young, single, poor parents are particularly prone to child abuse, since their immaturity and inexperience and inability to cope create feelings of helplessness and anger that they are not able to control (Young and Gately, 1988).

Parent–child interaction is reciprocal; one affects the other. Children with certain characteristics have a greater potential for being recipients of parental abuse than do others. Those who are hardest to take care of and who provoke the greatest stress in the parents are most likely to be abused. The same is true for those who are perceived to be different, such as premature babies and those of low birth weight, who are more likely to be restless and fretful and who require intensive care, and children who have physical disabilities or whose development is delayed. Parents with more children than their resources can adequately support are more likely to abuse them (Zuravin, 1991). If there is a lack of emotional-attachment behavior between parents and child, the child is more likely to be abused. Some evidence suggests that children who live with one or more nonbiological parents are at greater risk for violence and abuse than are children who are cared for by biological parents (Gelles and Harrop, 1991). In families characterized by extreme battering, substantial variability exists in the level of aggression directed toward children. Some children in such families are not physically victimized by the parents at all; others are beaten frequently and severely. In families characterized by extreme battering, boys are more often victims of aggression than are girls (Jouriles and Norwood, 1995).

Child abuse takes two main forms: attack and neglect (Gelles and Conte, 1990). The effects caused by parents who physically attack and hurt their children may be devastating both emotionally and physically. The battered child may suffer fractures, lacerations, burns, hemorrhages, and bruises to the brain or internal organs.

The negative effects of child abuse are compounded because abuse has a detrimental effect on children's emotional and social relationships. Because abused children are likely to exhibit a higher level of negative behavior and to be behaviorally disturbed, less socially competent (Trickett, 1993), more aggressive, and less cooperative, they are likely to be less well liked by their peers (Haskett and Kistner, 1991; Salzinger, Feldman, and Hammer, 1993). Teachers may view them as disturbed. Abused children have more discipline referrals and suspensions and often perform poorly academically (Eckenrode, Laird, and Doris, 1993).

Adults who were abused as children may show increased use of alcohol and drugs and higher incidence of HIV infection than adults who were not abused. Apparently, they engage in self-destructive behavior that reflects very low self-esteem (Allers and Benjack, 1991).

Other research indicates that not only is the child who is abused affected, but his or her siblings are affected as well (Jean-Gilles and Crittenden, 1990). Moreover, abused children who have adjustment problems in adolescence are more likely to perpetuate violence in their adult intimate relationships (Swinford et al., 2000). The potential for emotional rehabilitation of abused children depends on the

REPORT CHILD ABUSE.
CALL (415) 431-5133.

Bay Area Child Abuse Councils

Whether verbal or physical, child abuse is usually due to the parents' inability to cope with the frustrations of their lives and to their lack of knowledge about children and parenting. For their own sake and for the sake of their children, abusive parents need to be encouraged to seek out the many kinds of help available to them.

damage done. There are cases of battered children blossoming into happy people after being adopted by loving parents. However, if the abuse was sexual, residual trauma may continue to plague even older adults and disrupt their ability to function (Allers, Benjack, and Allers, 1992).

Treatment for Spouse and Child Abuse

Those who have been abused may exhibit psychological symptoms such as **posttraumatic stress disorder** (severe stress reactions that occur after a person has suffered a trauma) and high levels of depression, avoidance, and anxiety, as well as showing borderline psychotic and passive-aggressive behavior patterns. Many of the aftereffects of trauma hamper an individual's ability to function in relationships. Common problems include an inability to trust, difficulty in sharing emotions, sexual dysfunction, poor parenting skills, a hot-tempered personality, and an aversion to members of the opposite sex (Busby, Steggell, Glenn, and Adamson, 1993).

Crisis shelters (Berk, Newton, and Berk, 1986), transition houses, hot-line services, police intervention teams, the legal system, trained social service workers, family therapy services and teams (Gelles and Maynard, 1987), and many other organizations are involved in dealing with abuse. Considerable progress has been made in treating both the abused and the abusive, and every effort ought to be made to get professional help for these people.

Authorities, such as medical personnel, and the general public are being encouraged to report cases of child or spouse abuse so that intervention can begin as soon as possible. The natural inclination of people not to interfere allows much abuse to go unreported and untreated. However, in recent years, the media have focused increasing attention on spouse and child abuse. Based on reports alleging child abuse and neglect, the U.S. Census Bureau reported 87,480 cases of sexual abuse in 2000 and 862,455 child victims of maltreatment in total (U.S. Bureau of the Census, 2002).

Sexual Abuse of Children

One of the myths concerning child sexual abuse is that child molesters are usually unknown to their victims. In fact, the opposite is true. In 80–90% of the cases, the offender is someone in the child's immediate family whom the child loves and trusts (England and Thompson, 1988). Because of its prevalence and importance, the discussion of sexual abuse of children here will focus on incest, after brief discussions of child abuse symptoms and pedophilia.

Symptoms of Child Sexual Abuse It is important that adults recognize symptoms of child sexual abuse (Banyard and Williams, 1996). Child sexual abuse may be a causative factor in many severe disorders, including dissociative, anxiety, eating, and affective disorders, and sexual and substance abuse problems. It may also be a contributing factor in many other conditions, such as paranoid, obsessive-compulsive, and passive-aggressive disorders. Many studies have found sexual abuse victims to have high levels of anxiety and depression, suicidal tendencies, and difficulty with intimate relationships. Mood disturbances (depression, guilt, and low self-esteem) are frequent. Depression is the most common symptom, and victims tend to be more self-destructive and suicidal than are nonabused depressed individuals. They can suffer from anxiety attacks and phobias and experience sleep and appetite disturbances. They may suffer from all kinds of somatic disorders, especially gastrointestinal problems. They may have significantly more medical complaints than nonabused persons, especially of chronic pelvic pain, headaches, backaches, skin disorders, and genitourinary problems (Ratican, 1992).

Pedophilia One type of child sexual abuse is called **pedophilia.** The *Diagnostic and Statistical Manual of Mental Disorders* of the American Psychiatric Association (1994) defines pedophilia as "recurrent, intense sexually arousing fantasies, sexual urges, or behaviors involving sexual activity with a prepubescent child or children (generally age 13 or younger)" and lasting over a period of at least 6 months. All pedophiles are child sexual abusers, but not every person who is involved in the sexual abuse of children is a pedophile. The true pedophile can be sexually aroused only by sexual activity with children, whereas other adults who sexually abuse children may not find the activity a primary source of sexual arousal and may have other motivations.

Incest: Definition and Offenders **Incest** is sexual activity between people who are closely related. The relationships that are forbidden by law vary from state to state. Most social scientists consider all forms of sexual contact, sexual exploitation, and sexual overtures initiated by any adult who is

blood-related or surrogate family to the child as incest. In other words, the abuse is considered incestuous if the adult shares a primary relationship with the child, whether they are related or not.

In the United States, incest occurs in one in six families; about 100,000 new cases are reported each year. Perpetrators are members of the victims' nuclear and extended families (Gilgun, 1995). The most prevalent form of incest is between siblings, not parent–child, grandparent–grandchild, or stepparent–stepchild, as is often supposed.

Brother–Sister Incest Some brother–sister sexual activity involves sexual play while both are young. In other cases, an older sibling is involved with a young child in sexually exploitative behavior. In a study of 796 college students who had experienced sibling incest, one-fourth said that the sexual contacts were exploitative (Finkelhor, 1980). Occasionally, blackmail is involved: The older sibling threatens to tell the parents something the younger sibling has done unless he or she allows sexual contact.

Reactions to brother–sister sexual contact are varied. With increased sibling age differential, the chances of exploitative relationships increase. Occasional experiences are less significant than a series of incidents over years. When an older sibling blackmails, bribes, or forces a younger one to comply, the victim's reactions are quite negative. When it involves mutual consent of siblings of similar age, the participants may realize that parents would disapprove and so feel guilty, but few long-term effects result.

Father–Daughter Incest Much of the research has focused on father–daughter relationships. Such incest usually takes place in unhappy and disorganized family contexts. In most cases, the spouses' sexual relationship is unsatisfactory, so the man turns to his daughter for affection and sex, often initiating the relationship when the daughter begins to mature. In

---

posttraumatic stress disorder Severe stress reactions that occur after a person has suffered a trauma.

pedophilia A sexual perversion in which a person's primary or exclusive method of achieving sexual arousal is by fantasizing about or engaging in sexual activity with prepubertal children.

incest Sexual activity between two people who are closely related.

these cases, the sexual abuse of his daughter is not basically a sexual problem, but rather represents the sexual expression of nonsexual problems, such as depression, low self-esteem, and feelings of inadequacy (Gelles and Conte, 1990).

The incestuous contact is usually premeditated and initiated by the father and passively tolerated by the daughter. The father begins by cuddling, hugging, and kissing his daughter, which both may enjoy. The contact expands to include touching (such as feeling the daughter's buttocks or breasts), playful wrestling, prolonged kissing, or genital caressing. It usually takes place without any force being used and may develop into full intercourse.

Long-term effects on the victim can be severe. The girl may carry a burden of guilt, shame, bitterness, anger, and low self-esteem for years. She may be at greater risk for divorce or low marital satisfaction than women who have not been sexually abused (Gelster and Feinauer, 1988).

Another of the serious aspects of parent–child incest was revealed in a study of incestuous fathers and stepfathers who were in treatment: 49% of them also abused children outside of the family, and 18% of them were raping adult women at the same time they were abusing their own children (Abel, Becker, Cunningham-Rathner, Mittlemen, and Rouleau, 1988).

Father–daughter incest may continue over many years, until the daughter is old enough to understand, resist, or leave home. She may tell her mother, another family member, or a friend, but she rarely goes to the police.

Intervention   Intervention is difficult in cases of incest, partly because authorities are seldom made aware of the problem. Most states require professionals who may come in contact with it to report cases of suspected sexual abuse. Treatment of sexual abusers is difficult at best, and the professionals who treat them need specialized training (Priest and Smith, 1992).

THE CRISIS OF DEATH AND GRIEF

Another type of family crisis is death. Death, especially of a spouse, child, or other close relative, is among life's most stressful events. It creates considerable physical, mental, and emotional stress and tension, which may take a long time to subside.

No matter the circumstances surrounding a person's death, it still comes as a shock. In fact, people who have watched loved ones suffer through chronic illness before dying are sometimes affected as much as or more than those whose loved ones died after a short illness.

Many people grieve in a similar way, and understanding the way grief typically works can help people through a difficult mourning process. Most people experience a feeling of shock or numbness after first learning of a death. They may appear unemotional as they carry out funeral plans and make other necessary arrangements. As reality sinks in and the business of the funeral is over, many people break down and begin a process of mourning. Grief can be expressed emotionally, physically, and psychologically. Crying may be a physical expression of grief, whereas depression may be a psychological expression. Numbness, disbelief, denial, anger, confusion, shock, sadness, yearning, humiliation, despair, and guilt are all part of the process. Mourning is personal and may last months or years, but it is important for the bereaved person to allow himself or herself to grieve (Coleman and Ganong, 2002). Many people experience loneliness and despair while grieving, but the weeks and months following the death of a loved one can also be a time of personal growth (Neimeyer, Prigerson, and Davis, 2002).

Hiltz (1998) described three stages of grief. The first is a short period of shock during which the surviving family members are stunned and immobilized with grief and disbelief. The second is a period of intense suffering during which individuals experience intense physical and emotional symptoms. Physical reactions may include disturbed sleep, stomach upset and loss of appetite, weight loss, loss of energy and muscular strength, and shortness of breath or tightness in the chest (Rosenbloom and Whittington, 1993). Emotional reactions may include anger, guilt, depression, anxiety, and preoccupation with thoughts of the deceased. During this stage of intense grief, people need to talk with friends or family about their loss. But since grief and death are uncomfortable subjects, this opportunity is often denied, and recovery from the loss is more difficult and prolonged. Finally, in the third stage, there is a gradual reawakening of interest in life.

One common reaction to bereavement is to purify the memory of the deceased by mentally downplaying that person's negative characteristics. The bereaved tend to remember the good things about the deceased and to forget negative traits or events. If this idealization continues, it can prevent the formation of new intimate friendships. Extended bereavement can result in a sentimentalized, nostalgic, and morose style of life.

Men and women may respond differently to bereavement. Men find it more difficult to express grief, but they can accept the reality of death more quickly. Women are better able to continue working during bereavement than are men. After the death of a spouse, men are more apt to describe their loss as the loss of part of themselves; women may frame their loss in terms of being deserted, abandoned, and left to fend for themselves.

The negative impact of bereavement and the loss of a loved one cannot be overstated. Damage to the self accompanies widowhood, for example, if the

The emotional impact of an unexpected death, such as that of a young mother, is gauged by how alive and distinctive the person was at the time of death. Responsibilities often shift suddenly and heavily onto surviving family members.

spouse was important in the life of the partner. The degree and duration of this damage depend on the intensity of the involvement with the departed and the availability of significant others. Daughters who were caregivers to their elderly mothers compared their bereavement feelings at 2 months and 6 months following the mother's death. During this period, the daughters reported decreases in feelings of emotional shock, anger, and helplessness. But bereavement feelings are often complex and sometimes contradictory. For example, daughters reported feeling relatively high levels of psychological strength in coping with their mother's death while simultaneously reporting feelings of shock, anger, and guilt.

Clearly, the loss of a parent, particularly a mother for whom the daughter had been caring, involves significant distress (Pratt, Walker, and Wood, 1992). The death of a family member often affects the health and well-being of other family members. It also affects the structure and dynamics of the family, including the relationships between survivors, possibly leading to increased closeness or to strain in these relationships.

One of the most common deaths faced by adults is the death of a parent. Demographers report that the death of a father is most likely to occur when adult children are ages 35–54 and that the death of a mother is most likely to occur when they are ages 45–64. The death of a parent is a common life transition for adults and may be a significant predictor of change in marital quality. It may affect adult children's marital relationships, which, in turn, affect individuals' well-being. The death of a parent may place a great deal of strain on many marital relationships. The decline in marital quality may occur because the partner fails to provide emotional support, cannot comprehend the significance and meaning of the loss, or is disappointed by the bereaved individual's slow recovery. Some partners feel imposed on by the continuing stress and depression of the bereaved person. Compared with nonbereaved individuals, people who have recently experienced the death of a mother express a greater decline in social support from their partner and an increase in their partner's negative behavior. Those who have recently experienced the death of a father express a greater increase in relationship strain and frequency of conflict and a greater decline in relationship harmony.

The period following a parent's death may be a time when individuals are in particular need of

CHAPTER 16

LEARNING OBJECTIVES

After reading the chapter, you should be able to:

- Summarize social and demographic factors that increase individual probability of divorce.

- Summarize the causes of divorce as identified by divorced men and women.

- Describe the process of disaffection.

- Describe the important factors to consider in making a decision about whether to get divorced.

- Discuss marriage counseling, marriage enrichment, and structured separation as alternatives to divorce.

- Discuss ways to get divorced—no-fault divorce and mediation—in terms of property and finances, child support, legal fees, and children.

- Understand the major adjustments that adults make after divorce.

- Discuss the following in relation to children and divorce: child custody, child support, visitation rights, and the reactions of children.

The Family and Divorce

The United States has one of the highest divorce rates in the world. The divorce rate surged during the 1960s and 1970s as the baby boomers came of age. Rates of divorce declined slightly during the 1980s and were stable but high through the 1990s (J. R. Goldstein, 1999). While the divorce rate appears to have stabilized and may be declining slightly, it remains high (Heaton, 2002). Demographers estimate that about 40% of first marriages will end in divorce (National Marriage Project, 2000). The National Center for Health Statistics (2002) reports that 12% of marriages end after 3 years, 20% end after 5 years, 33% end after 10 years, and 43% end after 15 years. After 10 years, 32% of White women's first marriages have dissolved, 34% of Hispanic women's marriages have dissolved, and 47% of black women's first marriages have dissolved. Asian women have the lowest divorce rate with 20% of first marriages ending after 10 years of marriage.

The increasing numbers of divorced people have resulted in numerous books on the subject—books that discuss everything from do-it-yourself divorce to divorce as a creative experience. With the books has come increasing interest in examining divorce laws, which in their old forms created much suffering for millions of couples and their children. Most state legislatures have now changed their laws and encourage reconciliation counseling, divorce mediation, and no-fault divorce.

All of the statistics, laws, court cases, and individual efforts involve human beings: parents and children who are trying to make the best of difficult situations, each in his or her own way. We need, therefore, to take a careful look at the facts and causes of divorce, at our divorce laws, and at children's reaction to divorce and its effects on them. We also need a more sympathetic understanding of what couples go through and how they struggle to adjust following a divorce.

PROBABILITY OF DIVORCE: SOCIAL AND DEMOGRAPHIC FACTORS

In looking at divorce rates, let us examine first those social and demographic factors that increase or decrease the probability of divorce. Divorce rates vary from group to group and relate to factors such as age at marriage, religion, occupation, income, edu-

Divorce is a stressful and troubling experience for everyone involved.

cation, ethnicity, geographic area, and parental divorce (Glick, 1990; Lester, 1999). These factors will not pinpoint which individuals are going to get divorced, but they do indicate statistical probabilities for different groups. Let's look at some of the more important social and demographic correlates of divorce and separation in the United States.

Marital Age

Age at first marriage is one of the most important predictors of marital success: People who marry quite young are more likely to divorce than are those who wait until they are older (Heaton, 2002; Teachman, 2002). In fact, T. C. Martin and Bumpass (1989) concluded that age at marriage is the strongest predictor of divorce in the first 5 years of marriage and that the negative effects of youthful marriage last far into marriage.

Data from the 2002 National Survey of Families and Households show that after 10 years of marriage, 48% of first marriages of brides under age 18 have ended in divorce or legal separation, compared with only 24% of those to brides at least age 25 at marriage (Bramlett and Mosher, 2002). Women in the youngest category are twice as likely to experience marital break up within 10 years than women the oldest age category. This difference is the largest among White women, while there is virtually no difference by age at marriage among Hispanic women (see Figure 16.1).

As discussed in Chapter 1, the age at first marriage has been increasing since the mid-1950s. This relative delay in marrying is a result of people staying in school longer, women entering the workforce in greater numbers, and rates of cohabitation increasing dramatically. Because more people are older today when they experience their first marriage, we may continue to see a slight decline in the divorce rate.

Religion and Socioeconomic Status

Frequency of attendance at religious services is correlated strongly and negatively with divorce or separation. That is, those who attend church regularly are less likely to divorce or separate. Religious teachings can be powerful factors in motivating

couples to try to make their marriage succeed. The 2002 National Survey of Families and Households indicated that the higher the importance attached to religion, the lower the likelihood of marital breakup (Bramlett and Mosher, 2002). Wineberg (1994) found that those who had strong religious beliefs were more likely to reconcile when difficulties arose and that religion was strongly correlated with the success of their reconciliation.

Socioeconomic status includes education, income, and occupation. Figure 16.2 shows the relationships between education level and divorce rate. Studies show that rates of divorce or separation are higher at lower socioeconomic levels. Overall, the National Center for Health Statistics (2002) stated that other individual characteristics of women that are associated with a greater probability of marital dissolution include lower education, lower family income, not working at the beginning of marriage, working full-time as opposed to working part-time, having no religious affiliation, and already having one child or more at the start of the marriage.

Geographic Area

Divorce rates vary across different regions of the country. Divorce rates are highest in the South and next highest in the West. Figure 16.3 shows the differences. Divorce rates also tend to be higher in

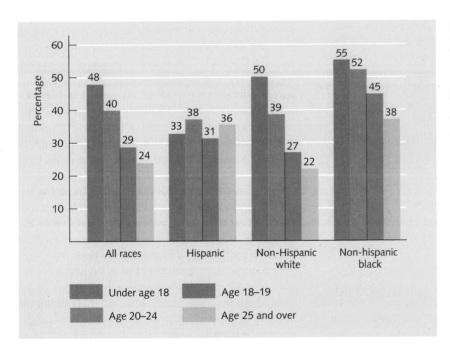

Figure 16.1 Probability That the First Marriage Breaks Up within 10 Years by Race/Ethnicity and Age at the Beginning of the Marriage: United States, 1995 (*Note:* From the National Center for Health Statistics, 2000. [Table 21, p. 55].)

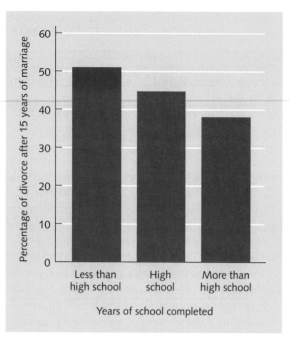

Figure 16.2   Percentage of Ever-Married People Who Have Ever Been Divorced or Legally Separated, by Years of School Completed (*Note:* Adapted from National Center for Health Statistics, 2000 [Table 21, p. 55].)

large cities and lower in small cities or rural areas, even when adjusted for other variables such as ethnic, religious, and socioeconomic differences. This is explained partly by the higher levels of residential mobility among people in large cities and urban areas than among people in small cities and rural areas. Rapid economic growth, demographic changes (birth rates, death rates, proportion of elderly), and employment rates are all correlated with divorce rates (Lester, 1997, 1999). Overall, the National Center for Health Statistics (2002) reported that first marriages are more likely to be disrupted in communities with higher unemployment, lower median family income, and a higher percentage of families living below poverty level or receiving public assistance. First marriages are also more likely to be disrupted in central cities and in communities with a lower percentage of college-educated members, a higher crime rate, and a higher percentage of women never married.

Parental Divorce

It is commonly believed that people whose parents are divorced are more susceptible to divorce themselves. A longitudinal study of the intergenerational transmission of divorce found that prior to 1975 people from divorced families were 2.5 times more likely to divorce than were those from intact families; by 1995, however, the likelihood of divorce for the children of divorced parents had fallen to less than 50% (Wolfinger, 1999), with divorce more likely for girls than for boys from divorced families (Amato, 1996). Much of this difference is attributable to the tendency of girls from divorced families to marry younger and to have less education (Feng, Giarrusso, Bengston, and Frye, 1999).

If both spouses experienced parental divorce, their risk of divorce is increased. The risk of divorce is particularly high if parental divorce occurred when the spouses were 12 years of age or younger. Spouses whose parents divorced are more likely to have problems with anger, jealousy, hurt feelings, communication, infidelity, and so on. As children, they may have been exposed to poor models of behavior and may not have learned the skills and attitudes that facilitate successful functioning within their married role. Therefore, they may be more likely to become divorced themselves (Amato, 1996) or to have more negative intimate relationships (van-Schaick and Stolberg, 2001). After examining national longitudinal data that spanned almost 20 years, Amato and DeBoer (2001) concluded that parental divorce approximately doubled the odds that offspring would see their own marriages end in divorce. They suggested that offspring with divorced parents have an elevated risk of divorcing because they hold a comparatively weak commitment to the idea of an enduring marriage. Amato and Booth (2001) reported that parental behaviors most likely to predict problematic marriages for offspring include jealousy, being domineering, getting angry easily, being critical, being moody, and not talking to the spouse.

However, even though research shows that parental divorce increases the likelihood of offspring divorce, Teachman (2002) found from examining the childhood living experiences of 4,947 children that living apart from both parents, irrespective of the reason, is associated with an increased risk of divorce. In particular, he found that children who were born to a mother who was not married and who did not experience parental divorce or death experienced a very high rate of divorce. He found that neither the number of transitions in childhood living arrangements nor parental remarriage affected the risk of an

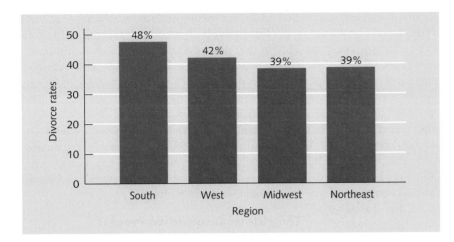

Figure 16.3 Divorce Rates by Region, after 15 Years of Marriage (*Note:* Data from National Center for Health Statistics, 2000 [Table 21, p. 56].)

offspring's marriage ending in divorce, and he suggested that "there is strong evidence that children who were born out of wedlock (and who did not experience parental divorce or death) are as likely, if not more likely than children of divorce to see their own marriages dissolve" (p. 728).

The Presence of Children

The risk of marital dissolution is highest among childless couples, probably because they are not constrained to stay together by the presence of children (Heaton, 1990). There are differences in the risk of marital dissolution depending on the ages and number of children. The likelihood of marital dissolution decreases as the number of children rises to a maximum of four. Once couples have five or more children, the likelihood of marital dissolution increases. The rates of divorce are relatively low when the youngest child is under age 3 but rise sharply when that child reaches the mid-teens and decline substantially after he or she reaches age 17. Thus, children's stabilizing effect on marriage is strongest when they are very young or when they have reached adulthood. One of the most interesting findings is that parents of sons are less likely to divorce than are parents without sons (S. P. Morgan, Lye, and Condran, 1988). This is attributed to the father's greater involvement with sons than with daughters (Seccombe and Lee, 1987). Other research has found that, if the family includes at least one son, fathers spend increased time with their children. If there is more paternal involvement in family life, through either the father's investing more time with the children or doing household chores, the woman has a

greater perception of fairness in the relationship and is more satisfied with the marriage (Kalmij, 1999; Katzev, Warner, and Acock, 1994).

CAUSES OF MARITAL BREAKUP

Social and demographic factors indicate the probability of divorce, but they don't reveal the actual causes of marital breakup. Causes may be determined by studying people who are divorcing in order to find out their perceptions of the reasons their marriages have failed.

Spouses' Perceptions

The research on divorce and marital satisfaction indicates two critical times in a marriage when divorce is most likely: (1) the first 7 years of marriage, during which half of all the divorces occur, and (2) at midlife, when people often have young teenage children. The latter period has been described by some researchers as possibly the lowest point in marital satisfaction during the life course (see, for example, Adelman, Chadwick, and Baerger, 1996; Orbuch, House, Mero, and Webster, 1996). Gottman and Levenson (2000) studied the predictors of divorce in these two critical periods of a marriage. They found that different sets of variables predicted early divorce and later divorce. Negative affect during conflict (for example, criticism, contempt, defensiveness) predicted early divorcing, but it did not predict later divorcing. By contrast, the lack of positive affect in discussing the events of the day (for example, being excited or showing interest in what a spouse had to say) predicted later divorcing, but it did not predict early divorcing. Thus, it could be the case that marriages characterized by criticism, contempt, and intense fighting dissolve sooner than do those without positive affect. In marriages without positive affect, people may stay together but become emotionally detached and postpone divorce until their loneliness becomes unbearable and they no longer feel the need to remain married for the sake of the children (Gottman and Levenson, 2000).

Indeed, showing positive affect may be one of the most important aspects of a successful marriage. Gigy and Kelly (1992) found that the most common reasons for divorcing, cited by nearly 80% of all men and women in their study, were a gradual growing apart, a loss of a sense of closeness, and a lack of feelings of being loved and appreciated. Severe and intense fighting was cited by only 40% of the couples. Dolan and Hoffman (1998) found that, regardless of women's socioeconomic status, lack of emotional support and incompatibility were the most frequently cited determinants of divorce. Gottman and Levenson (2000) suggest, "Perhaps changing the affective nature of the way couples discuss such mundane topics as the events of their day, in which they either make an emotional connection upon reunion or fail to do so, could affect the way they resolve conflict, and possibly the future course of the marriage" (p. 743).

One longitudinal study of 95 newlywed couples examined how couples' perception of their marital bond predicted which marriages stayed together and which marriages ended in divorce (Carrere et al., 2000). Specifically, the researchers examined the explanations spouses gave for the behavior within the relationship, the perceived stability of the marriage, whether spouses remembered negative events or positive ones, how each spouse described and talked about his or her partner in telling a story, and how spouses' selectively attended to positive or negative aspects of the marriage and qualities of their partner. Through examining these variables, they predicted with 87.4% accuracy those couples whose marriage remained intact or divorced at 4–6 years of marriage and 81% accuracy at 7–9 years. This study supports the relationship between perceptions and marital outcome.

In another study of newlywed couples, Huston, Caughlin, Houts, Smith, and George (2001) found

that disillusionment—such as an abatement of love, a decline in overt affection, a lessening of the conviction that one's spouse is responsive, and an increase in ambivalence—determines which couples will divorce and which will have a stable marriage. It is not surprising that spouses who are zestful and take a positive attitude toward life are more likely to maintain a happy marriage (Veroff, Douvan, Orbuch, and Acitelli, 1998), and those who are moody, emotionally unstable, and have high levels of negativity have lower levels of marital happiness (Caughlin, Huston, and Houts, 2000).

The Marital Disaffection Process

The loss of intimacy and love is a major component of marital dissolution (Kersten, 1990). Kingsbury and Minda (1988) identified marital disaffection as an indicator of whether couples plan to continue or terminate their relationship. Marital disaffection involves the gradual loss of emotional attachment, a decline in caring, emotional estrangement, and an increasing sense of apathy and indifference. Positive feelings are replaced over time by neutral or even negative feelings. However, it is important to emphasize that mutual disaffection is the result of other problems in the relationship, rather than the initial cause. Spouses report they want a divorce because they don't love each other, but falling out of love is usually a consequence of years of unresolved tensions in the relationship.

One of the most revealing descriptions of the development of marital disaffection is given by Kersten (1990), who divides the process into three phases: (1) a beginning phase, (2) a middle phase, and (3) an end phase. The beginning phase is characterized by increased disappointment, disillusionment, and feelings of hurt and anger. One partner's (or both partners') thoughts begin to center on the other partner's negative traits because that partner's behavior is not what was expected. The partners are still optimistic about the future of their marriage and attempt to solve the problems by asserting their feelings or by attempting to please their spouse.

During the middle phase, anger and hurt increase in frequency and intensity. Spouses expect their partner to behave in certain negative ways, and apathy increases. Some partners begin to weigh whether to stay in or leave the marriage as they sort out factors relating to the children, finances, or religion. Attempts to please the partner decrease, but problem-solving attempts (such as entering a drug treatment program) increase.

During the end phase, anger again is the most frequent feeling. Feelings of trust decline, and apathy and a sense of helplessness increase. The following is a typical expression of apathy: "I've just put up with the same behavior so long now—I just want out because I don't see him ever changing. . . . It's too late to rekindle the feelings. . . . I don't want to try" (Kersten, 1990, p. 261). The most frequent thoughts during this stage concern wanting to end the marriage and determining exactly how it can be dissolved. However, there may still be some ambivalence. Before this stage, counseling is infrequently pursued, but now many couples seek marital therapy in a last attempt to save the marriage or to get assistance in leaving it.

Basic to the dissolution of the relationship is the perception that the costs of staying together outweigh the rewards. Partners focus on the negative traits of their spouse, so it is very difficult to change their feelings. To do so requires the partner to make drastic changes. Sometimes changes are made and feelings do become positive again, but it takes a lot of hard work. If the marriage is dissolved, the disaffected spouse continues to focus on the negative traits of the ex-spouse, convincing him- or herself that dissolution was justified (Kersten, 1990).

THE DIVORCE DECISION

The decision to divorce is a difficult one for most people. Few couples are able to make such a decision easily and quickly; rather, they usually agonize for months or years before finally deciding. Even then, the partners may change their mind a number of times, repeatedly separating and then moving back together. Many couples file a petition for divorce, only to withdraw it. Others even go to court and then change their mind at the last minute.

From a counselor's point of view, it's hard to predict who will or will not get divorced. Some couples have relatively minor problems but give up easily. Other couples seem to be likely candidates for divorce but through intense effort and motivation overcome all obstacles and end up with a good marriage. The outcome depends partially on the motivation and commitment of the partners.

There are, of course, some couples who never divorce, but not necessarily because the two people love each other or are compatible. Consider this case:

> Mr. and Mrs. P. have been married 43 years. He's 79 and she's 76. They absolutely hate each other. They say and do horrible things to each other. They constantly criticize each other and are in chronic conflict. They have no companionship, never share any social activities together. He's gay, has male lovers on the side, and never has intercourse with her. He's intellectual, verbal, and artistic. She's none of these things. He's a dreamer, she's practical. The only reason they give for living together is to have two Social Security checks instead of one. (Author's counseling notes)

According to exchange theory, reconciliation is more likely when the costs of divorce are high, the barriers to getting out of the marriage are great, and the alternatives are few. Levinger (1979) proposed a three-factor theory of marital cohesion, identifying three basic considerations in deciding whether to remain married:

1. **Satisfaction with or attractions of the marriage.** These are the forces that strengthen the marriage bond. They may include sexual fulfillment, emotional bonding, care, concern, and need (even neurotic need) for each other. Attractions may also include socioeconomic rewards: a better income, an improved standard of living, superior social status, a nice house, more economic security, or the need for the physical services that a spouse can provide.

2. **Barriers to getting out of the marriage.** These are the forces that prevent marriage breakdown. In one study, three perceived barriers were cited most often by participants as being very important: (1) the possibility of children suffering (50.1%), (2) the threat of losing a child (46%), and (3) religious beliefs (41.4%). About 33% of married individuals felt that their dependence on their spouse was very important in keeping their marriage intact, while 31% cited their spouse's dependence on them as very important. While married couples perceived financial security to be important, it was not important enough to keep them from divorcing (Knoester and Booth, 2000). When the perceived barriers were analyzed as to how well they actually deter divorce,

only two decreased the odds of divorce: (1) the importance of religious beliefs and (2) dependence on one's spouse. When responses were separated by gender, it became evident that women rank perceived dependence on their spouse and religious beliefs as more essential barriers to divorce and that men rank more highly the threat of losing a child and the influence of family and friends. Responses to other barriers did not differ significantly between women and men. Neither of the perceived barriers that involve children were found to be deterrents to divorce. Overall, although many people perceive certain barriers to divorce and value them as important, these barriers apparently do not keep couples together (Knoester and Booth, 2000).

3. **The attractiveness of alternatives to the marriage.** These include an evaluation of personal assets: sexual attractiveness, appearance, age, and other factors that influence the possibilities of remarrying, if desired. Individuals with high socioeconomic status marry spouses of the same status. Attractive men and men with high socioeconomic status marry women who are the most attractive. People with high self-esteem and a sense of personal competence are more likely to feel that they can get along on their own (Dreman, Orr, and Aldor, 1989). Spouses with good education, high income, and intelligence realize that even if they are cut off from their spouse's earning power they still are capable of living the good life.

A powerful motivating force in divorce is the desire to leave one's spouse to marry another person. A person who is involved in an ongoing emotional and sexual relationship outside of marriage may not be as hesitant about getting a divorce as a person who has no one else on the side. While an extramarital affair is often a result of an unhappy marriage, it also may be the added incentive to terminate the marriage.

A fourth factor affects the decision to stay married or get divorced. This factor was not discussed by Levinger (1979), but it is an important one: the intensity of the emotional pain generated by an unhappy marriage. Some people don't really believe in divorce, but they can't tolerate the unhappiness of the marriage any longer. One man explained:

> I've remained in the marriage for twenty-eight years because I didn't believe in divorce and because I didn't want to desert my children. But I can't take it any longer. My wife hates me and takes every occasion to let me know she does. She tells me she hopes I'll die so she can collect my life insurance. There is no love, companionship, or anything positive left in our relationship. (Author's counseling notes)

A woman commented:

> You can't imagine what it was like being married to my alcoholic husband. He was completely irresponsible. I did literally everything around the house, yard, and in raising our five children. Yet, he wouldn't admit that he had an alcohol problem. (Author's counseling notes)

In these situations, there was no question in the minds of the individuals that divorce was the only acceptable course.

One of the most debated questions is whether or not couples should stay together for the sake of the children. Some social scientists believe the answer is yes, unless abuse is occurring in the relationship, because many marriages that end in divorce can be salvaged. Booth and Amato (2001) studied national longitudinal data from parents and their adult children to examine the way in which the amount of marital conflict influences the impact of divorce on children. They found that many marriages that end in divorce are low-conflict. Divorces in these low-conflict marriages can be very damaging to children as children can be unaware of the unhappiness and be completely shocked when their parents do divorce. Booth and Amato (2001) also found that high-conflict marriages that end in divorce appear to have a neutral or even beneficial effect on children: "Presumably, escape from a high-conflict marriage benefits children because it removes them from an aversive, stressful home environment. In contrast, a divorce that is not preceded by a prolonged period of overt discord may represent an unexpected, unwelcome, and uncontrollable event, an event that children are likely to experience as stressful" (p. 210). Booth and Amato noted that two categories of children are most at risk for future psychological problems: those who grow up with parents who stay married but remain conflicted and hostile, and those whose parents are in low-conflict marriages and divorce anyway.

However, not everyone agrees that couples should stay together when they are in low-conflict marriages. Some studies show that 5- and 6-year-olds perceive their parents' low-conflict marriages to be high in conflict. Other research shows that boys raised in two-parent families where the parents were very cold to each other have a harder time showing intimacy than those raised in divorced families (Coontz, 2001).

In reality though, very few marriages are happy or unhappy all the time. Waite and Gallagher (2000) found that couples who rank in the lowest percentile on marital satisfaction but who don't divorce often say they are very happy 5 years later. Using the National Survey on Families and Households data, they found that 64% of those who said they were unhappy but stayed together reported they were happy 5 years later and another 25% reported improvement in their marriage. Interestingly, almost 75% of the spouses of those who reported to be unhappily married reported for themselves that they were happy in their marriages. Thus, perception varies within a marriage as to whether or not it is a happy one (Waite and Gallagher, 2000).

ALTERNATIVES TO DIVORCE

When spouses are dissatisfied with their marriage, they might consider marriage counseling, marriage enrichment programs, and separation.

Marriage Counseling

Some couples need to consider that there may be alternatives to divorce. One important alternative is marriage counseling. Couples cannot be expected to live together unhappily, but breaking up the marriage may not always be the best or only option. Divorce often substitutes one set of problems for another. Another option is to see if, with professional help, the unhappy marriage can become a satisfying one. Couples are often skeptical about the outcome of counseling—especially if they have never been to a counselor before or if they have had unhappy experiences with therapists. Not all therapists are equally competent. One summary of the efficacy of marital and family therapy found that therapy involved beneficial outcomes in about two-thirds of the cases, that there is a greater chance of a positive outcome when spouses are treated together rather than individually, and that positive results typically occur in treatments of short dura-

tion—from 1 to 20 sessions (Piercy and Sprenkle, 1990). Analysis of the effects of marital and family therapy indicated very definitely that it works (Shadish, Ragsdale, Glaser, and Montgomery, 1995). Other research has indicated that marital therapy is effective, at least in the short term, in reducing marital conflicts. In addition, research has shown marital therapy to be effective over the long term in promoting marital stability, reducing marital conflicts, and preventing divorce (Bray and Jouriles, 1995; Pinsof and Wynne, 1995).

Marriage therapy or counseling has become a growing business as more people have grown to feel comfortable asking for help with their relationships. Therapists have benefited from years of research documenting the underlying variables in a strong and happy marriage versus an unhappy one (Fowers, 2000; Gottman and Silver, 1999). In addition, some states require **conciliation counseling** before a divorce may be granted. Florida has implemented a 3-day waiting period for marriage licenses if couples do not seek premarital education. Some states are trying to create a 60-day waiting period for a marriage license unless the couple has received 4 hours of premarriage education or counseling. In addition, some states provide incentives and subsidies for premarital education and require marriage education in high school (Hawkins, Nock, Wilson, Sanchez, and Wright, 2002).

Marriage Enrichment

Marriage enrichment programs combine education with group discussion to assist couples in improving marital communication, relationships, and problem solving. Programs are conducted in groups shortly before or after the wedding or any number of years after it. The central purpose of such programs is preventive: to address issues before they become unmanageable conflicts (Guerney and Maxson, 1990; Mace, 1987).

One such program, the Prevention and Relationship Enhancement Program (PREP), was designed to teach partners skills and ground rules for

conciliation counseling Marriage counseling ordered by the court in which spouses try to decide whether they want to dissolve their marriage or agree to try to solve their problems.

countant if many assets are involved. Settlements that are agreed on do not become binding until approved by the court. One advantage of a mediated settlement is that the partners are more likely to comply with decisions that are made jointly than with financial judgments that are ordered by the court against the will of the couple. Disputes regarding child custody and visitation rights and responsibilities ideally are settled on the basis of the best interests of the children. Research has shown that people who use divorce mediation have better relationships with their ex-spouses, are generally more satisfied with the outcomes of divorce, have less need for relitigation, and feel more satisfied with the process and the results (Marlow and Sauber, 1990). They also report better relationships with their children (R. Beck and Blank, 1997).

The process of no-fault divorce requires less extensive litigation (many couples file without benefit of attorneys), reduces legal expenses, and makes a "friendly" divorce easier than under the old adversary system. It has partially removed from the legal process the punitive element of moral condemnation that pervaded divorce for centuries.

Some other changes bring up further questions. One of the changes has been an increase in the percentage of men who have filed the petition once they no longer had to make public accusations against their spouse. At the same time, with the threat of reprisals removed, spousal support has been awarded less frequently, for shorter periods of time, and for smaller amounts. In addition, household property and furniture are less likely to be awarded exclusively to the woman, and attorney's fees are more likely to be paid by both spouses. Fewer women are awarded full custody, and joint custody arrangements have increased. The effect on child support payments to the custodial parent has been variable. Overall, the loss of bargaining power by the woman has resulted in a less favorable financial settlement to many women, particularly older homemakers. Those who do not have substantial earning power of their own are affected greatly, with many having to reduce their standard of living significantly because of inadequate support from their ex-spouse. So, although no-fault divorce has many advantages, it has also created some inequities and contributed to economic hardship for many custodial parents and their children.

ADULT ADJUSTMENTS AFTER DIVORCE

The problems of adjustment after divorce may be grouped into a number of categories: (1) getting over the emotional trauma of divorce, (2) dealing with the attitudes of society, (3) loneliness and the problem of social readjustment, (4) adjustments of the noncustodial spouse, (5) finances, (6) realignment of responsibilities and work roles, (7) contacts with the ex-spouse, and (8) kinship interaction.

Disputes over custody may need to be solved by employing a mediator. Child custody and visitation rights issues resolved in mediation seem to have more positive outcomes than court-imposed determinations.

Emotional Trauma

Under the best circumstances, divorce is an emotionally disturbing experience. Under the worst conditions, it may result in a high degree of shock and disorientation. Divorce is often an emotional crisis triggered by a sudden loss. The process of divorce may involve emotional turmoil before and during the divorce, the shock and crisis of separation, mourning as the relationship is laid to rest, and disruption as one attempts to regain balance and reorganize. A drawn-out and bitter legal battle tends to heighten the emotional trauma of divorce. In these cases, the actual divorce decree comes as a welcome relief from a long period of pain.

The trauma is greater when one spouse wants the divorce and the other doesn't, when the idea comes unexpectedly, when one spouse continues to be emotionally attached to the other after the divorce, or when friends and family disapprove.

For most couples, the decision to divorce is viewed as an end-of-the-rope decision that is reached, on average, over a period of about 2 years. One spouse usually wants a divorce more than the other, and spouses who want the marriage to end are likely to view divorce differently than those who would like the marriage to continue (Emery, 1994). Wang and Amato (2000) found that spouses who wanted and initiated the divorce exhibited less attachment to their ex-spouse and better overall divorce adjustment. Thus, the partner who leaves experiences less postdivorce distress than the partner who is left (Emery, 1994).

Most studies reveal that during the pre- and postseparation periods both men and women report a decline in psychological adjustment (Doherty, Su, and Needle, 1989; Gove and Shin, 1989). The early postseparation period is the hardest time for some, as they struggle to come to grips with the loss of their spouse and with the personal cost that loss entails. The time of greatest trauma for others is at the time of final separation. After that comes a long period of realization that the relationship is over emotionally as well as legally. An examination of the relationship between divorce and psychological stress in adult women showed that stress and depression increased significantly soon after the divorce and then diminished over the next 3 years, although not to the same levels reported by married women (Lorenz et al., 1997). The fact that physical health is poorer, alcohol consumption is higher, (Mastekaasa, 1994), and the suicide rate is much greater for divorced men and women than for married people indicates that getting divorced can be traumatic (S. Stack, 1990).

Societal Attitudes toward Divorce

Part of the trauma of divorce stems from the attitudes of society toward divorce and divorced persons. In the eyes of some, divorce reflects moral failure or personal inadequacy. It takes a lot of courage to let it be known publicly that one has failed. "Friends," one woman remarked bitterly, "they drop you like a hot potato." However, negative attitudes are lessening as divorce becomes more common. One reason is that people today who recall their parents' marriage as being unhappy or who experienced parental divorce have more accepting attitudes toward the possibility of their own and other people's divorce (Amato and Booth, 1991).

In general, people who hold negative attitudes toward divorce are likely to view their own divorce as a moral failure. People who hold positive, accepting attitudes toward divorce when they are married report less attachment to the ex-spouse following divorce and better postdivorce adjustment than do people who hold negative, rejecting attitudes (Wang and Amato, 2000).

Loneliness and Social Readjustment

Even if two married people did not get along, at least they knew that someone else was in the house. After divorce, they begin to realize what it is like to live alone. This adjustment is especially hard on those without children or those whose children are living with the other spouse. Holidays can be particularly difficult.

Numerous authorities suggest that the friendship and companionship of other people are among the most essential ingredients for a successful readjustment after divorce, so getting involved with others is important. Finding new relationships that are positive and supportive helps undo the psychological injury caused by the divorce. Several studies have shown that social network size is a significant predictor of postdivorce adjustment: the more friends one has, the better one adjusts (Coysh,

Johnston, Tschann, Wallerstein, and Kline, 1989; De-Garmo and Forgatch, 1999).

The strongest predictor of divorce adjustment seems to be involvement in an intimate relationship. People with a new dating (or cohabiting) partner report better overall adjustment, less attachment to their ex-spouse, and a more positive outlook on life (Wang and Amato, 2000). Remarriage also leads to better overall adjustment and a more positive appraisal of life (Marks and Lambert, 1998; Wang and Amato, 2000). Remarriage is likely to help people adjust not only by providing a confidant and a regular sexual partner but also by increasing economic security (A. D. Shaprio, 1996).

There seems to be some difference in the social readjustment of divorced people according to their age at the time of divorce, with older individuals having a more difficult time adjusting than do younger individuals (Wang and Amato, 2000). Older women in particular have a hard time readjusting. Fewer women than men over age 40 at the time of divorce remarry. Many women have inadequate income to support themselves and their children. Many people are moderately or severely lonely and depressed shortly after a divorce. Among people who do not remarry, loneliness represents one of the grave consequences of divorce.

Adjustments to Custody Arrangements

Adjustments to custody arrangements vary. Caring parents miss their children and often seek every opportunity to be with them. They often suffer from anxiety and guilt that they can't be with their children more and do more for them. Other parents virtually abandon their children, never seeing, calling, or writing them or remembering holidays and birthdays. A third category of parents would like to see their children more often but are prevented from doing so by geographical distance or other circumstances. Overall, research shows that divorce reduces the closeness between noncustodial parents and their children and that there are fewer contacts between older divorced parents and their adult offspring later in life (Cooney and Uhlenberg, 1990).

King and Heard (1999) studied family interactions following divorce, based on 1,565 responses from divorced mothers to the National Survey of Families and Households. They considered father visitation, mother satisfaction with the visitation,

and the parental conflict that surrounds the visitation. Overall, they found that mothers prefer involved fathers even if some conflict occurs as a result. Only a small number of mothers were content to have the fathers relatively absent from involvement with them and the children. Interestingly, this study did not find an association between father involvement and child well-being, nor was conflict a predictor of child outcomes. Instead, mother satisfaction appeared to play an influential role in child outcomes: Child well-being suffered when mothers were dissatisfied, whatever the arrangements.

Shapiro and Lambert (1999) examined the National Survey of Families and Households to identify the effects of divorce on the quality of the father-child relationship over time. Father well-being was also observed. They found that divorced fathers with custody perceive poorer relationship quality with their children than do continuously married fathers. Fathers with joint physical custody (coresident) continue daily involvement with their children but usually have to fight to get it. They feel more in control, and the role of father is likely to be highly salient to them. Nonresident fathers perceive the poorest relationships, have the least contact with their children, and probably feel a loss of control. However, both coresident and nonresident fathers experience higher levels of depression and unhappiness than continuously married fathers (A. D. Shapiro and Lambert, 1999).

G. Stone (2002) explored the role that varying types of social support have on the psychological well-being of nonresidential fathers following divorce. He found that the psychological well-being of nonresidential fathers was associated with a combination of support factors that included support from the father's workplace, support from the father's new intimate partner, support from the father's former spouse, and support from the father's former in-laws. Interestingly, the most important variable for fathers was the level of support they reported from their workplace. This suggests that the workplace for fathers is an important place for receiving support and encouragement to enhance their psychological well-being after a divorce. Unfortunately, many workplaces are not father-friendly. Levine and Pittinsky (1997) suggest that several important changes must occur in the workplace: valuing fatherhood and the importance of fathers in children's lives; offering father education and training programs;

encouraging fathers' participation in their children's schools; supporting fathers who need to stay home when a child is ill; and allowing flextime and flexible work hours to help meet the demands of parenthood. Often, workplaces are more mother-friendly than father-friendly.

Finances

In spite of some advances, women still earn less income than males, given the same occupation, education, experience, and hours. Furthermore, the mother still ends up with primary custody of the children in 85% of cases. Some mothers receive only a little or irregular support from their ex-spouse. Although most divorced mothers work, their incomes are lower, and mothers with custody of their children often experience serious economic hardship (A. D. Shapiro, 1996). In a study of divorcees, 71% said that financial difficulties were their major problem (Amato and Partridge, 1987). Even if the marriage is disrupted after the children have left home, the economic position and lifestyle of women are seriously eroded (L. A. Morgan, 1989).

It is estimated that divorced women with custody of the children experience a 71% decline in family income in the year immediately following the divorce (Glick, 1990). While men may also experience a decline in income, it is usually not to the same degree as women. As stated before, most children live with their mothers after a divorce. Even though the court may mandate a father to pay child support, many women do not actually receive the full amount awarded to them, and some women receive no financial support from their ex-spouse to help with the cost of raising their children.

Many divorced female retirees also find themselves struggling financially. According to government data, 22% of divorced female retirees live in poverty compared to 18% of widows. This situation will probably become more serious because the number of retirement-age women will increase by 84% in the next 20 years to 9.6 million (U.S. Bureau of the Census, 1999a). Part of this problem stems from divorce settlements that do not take into account retirement and pension benefits for women. Also, many women negotiate to keep the house and primary custody of the children in the divorce settlement, but the house becomes too costly to maintain on their own income and thus becomes a financial drain, preventing them from saving for re-

tirement. Many women do not get a share of their ex-spouse's pension benefits or retirement plans, and women who have stayed at home to raise a family typically have no pension plan of their own. Imagine a scenario in which a couple decides that the woman will stay home to raise the children while the man will work outside the home. After 20 years of this arrangement, they decide to divorce. She is forced to go to work outside of the home at age 45, while he maintains his job status and has a 20-year jump on his retirement savings. Given their uneven work history and lower salaries than men, older women are particularly vulnerable to poverty in later life.

Realignment of Responsibilities and Work Roles

The divorced parent with custody of the children is faced with the prospect of an overload of work. Now one parent must perform all the family functions that were formerly shared by two people. She or he also has to readjust the parenthood role to include taking over functions formerly fulfilled by the noncustodial parent. As a consequence, less time is devoted to the children, they listen less, and there are often more problems controlling and guiding them. So, whether male or female, the solo parent has to fulfill all family functions and may have little relief from that responsibility.

Contacts with the Ex-Spouse

Understandably, many partners are so angry at their spouse when they divorce that they carry these feelings through the divorce process and sometimes for many years after. This anger needs to be dealt with both for the partner's sake and for the children's so that the children are not exposed to it unendingly and are not drawn into the fight between their parents (Isaacs and Leon, 1988a).

The more upsetting the divorce has been and the more vindictive the spouse, the less the other person wants to have any postdivorce contact. This is particularly true in cases of remarriage. Most second wives or husbands object to contacts with former spouses, because this usually leads to resentment and conflicts, especially if a bitter ex-spouse tries to cause trouble for the new couple.

When contacts are maintained, it is usually in relation to the children or support money or both

(Bloom and Kindle, 1985). When the children have problems, both parents need to be involved and to correspond or talk to each other about the problems. In this case, an amicable relationship helps them work things out and makes things easier on the children (Tschann, Johnston, and Wallerstein, 1989). Sometimes, however, couples have to turn to the courts to settle disputes after the divorce.

Most postdivorce disputes are related to visitation rights and child support. Some communities have "Father's Day" in court, when fathers are taken to task for not making support payments on time. Other disputes may occur if a former spouse seeks to reduce spousal support payments or to increase them.

Some spouses have difficulty breaking emotional attachments following divorce. This increases the subjective stress experienced. The greater the attachment, the more difficulty spouses have in adjusting to divorce.

In contrast to these situations, some couples remain friends. One woman commented:

> My former husband and I get along better now than when we were married. He came over for dinner the other night; I cooked, and we had a pleasant evening. It's strange, but when we were married, we fought all the time. Now we are really good friends. (Author's counseling notes)

Kinship Interaction

Both divorced men and women rely on kin in times of divorce, especially for practical support but also for social-emotional support to relieve psychological distress. Most parents are active in easing the strains in the lives of their divorcing adult children and their grandchildren (C. L. Johnson, 1988). Men are more likely to rely on kin in the early stages of divorce, and women over longer periods of time (Gerstel, 1988).

Divorce is a multigenerational process that affects parents and other kin, as well as the divorcing couple and their children (Ferreiro, Warren, and Konanc, 1986). Positive support from parents can have an important effect on the divorcing person's adjustment. Helpful behavior includes the following:

- **Emotional support.** This involves listening, showing empathy, and affirming love and affection.
- **Child care.** This might mean occasional babysitting or taking the grandchildren for weekends.

- **Good, rational advice.** Examples include being able to talk over decisions with parents.
- **Respect for autonomy and regression.** Divorcing people have contrasting needs. Some want autonomy in decision making; others want to regress to dependency for a while (Lesser and Comet, 1987).

The effects of divorce differ between adult sons and daughters. In general, divorced daughters with child custody have more contact with parents and receive more help from parents than do married daughters. Sons, by contrast, have more contact with parents and receive more babysitting help when they are married than they do in other situations (Spitze, Logan, Deane, and Zerger, 1994).

Overall, continued contact with former in-laws after divorce is not frequent. Women are more likely than men to maintain ties with ex-kin. Most of the positive relationships with ex-kin involve grandchildren, with custodial parents maintaining more contact than noncustodial parents. Relationships with ex-kin that are not sustained tend to end abruptly after separation, with little chance of subsequent resumption (Ambert, 1988a).

CHILDREN AND DIVORCE

There has been growing concern over the number of children exposed to parental divorce. Several studies indicate that children from divorced families are referred to mental health facilities at least as frequently as and sometimes more often than their counterparts from intact families. Furthermore, custodial parents are virtually unanimous in reporting that their children evidence emotional and behavioral difficulties both at school and at home following divorce. There is a need to discuss the whole subject of children and divorce in more detail (P. M. Lee, Picard, and Blain, 1994).

Child Custody

The term **custody** refers to both legal custody (who holds decision-making rights) and physical custody (where the children will live). In **sole legal custody,** the noncustodial parent forfeits the right to make decisions about the children's health, education, or religious training; in effect, the custodial parent is given control over child rearing. In **joint legal custody,** custody is shared between the two parents, with parental rights and obligations left as they were during the marriage. There are advantages and disadvantages to both arrangements.

Traditionally, sole custody of the children has been granted to the mother unless it can be established that she is unfit. It is not surprising that mothers tend to be more satisfied than fathers with custody arrangements. As more mothers have physical custody and thus primary control of their children, fathers' access to their children can be significantly reduced, leading fathers to feel distant from their parental roles (Madden-Derdich and Leonard, 2002). However, more and more men are becoming custodial parents as courts are taking into consideration the best interests of the child and awarding joint custody—in which both parents are responsible—more often. Studies show that joint custody has advantages for some children by maintaining an ongoing involvement with both parents, and that children in joint physical or legal custody are better adjusted than children in sole-custody settings (Bauserman, 2002).

In cases of custody dispute, a mediator may be employed or a child development expert appointed to investigate the family situation and to recommend custody arrangements to the court. The wishes of older children are usually taken into consideration in deciding with whom they will reside.

In cases of joint custody, the children typically reside with one parent and visit the other often. Children have access to both parents, and both are responsible for the welfare of the children. Important decisions are made jointly. Joint custody fathers are more likely to be actively involved in parenting than are noncustodial fathers (Bowman and Ahrons, 1985). Joint custody also takes the pressure off one parent to assume total responsibility. Some research indicates that joint custody increases parental self-esteem, lessens depression, diminishes anxiety, and ameliorates parents' feelings of disruption (Coysh et al., 1989).

Joint custody arrangements require maturity and forbearance on the part of both parents; otherwise, numerous squabbles create continual tension (Lowery and Settle, 1985). Bringing together two people who want to be apart and who don't get along can perpetuate all the squabbles of the unhappy marriage. Some parents also experience great stress when they interact with social institutions, family, and friends. For example, the desire of both parents to receive school announcements, report cards, or results of doctor's examinations commonly meets with resistance. Friends and family members may view a friendly relationship as deviant and pressure the ex-spouses not to have anything to do with each other. There is general agreement, however, that joint custody, if desired and amicably managed by both parents, is a good solution to a difficult problem.

Child Support

Providing for continued support of children is one of the obligations of parenthood. Under law, this is an obligation of both the mother and the father, whether the parents are married or not. Since 85% of custodial parents are women, child support awards are the most common mechanism by which noncustodial fathers are required to transfer economic resources to their children. These transfers are often very critical to the well-being of the children.

As the number of single-parent families has risen, so has the importance of collecting child support as a public policy issue. According to 2000 U.S. Census Bureau data, 31% of all children under age 18 resided in single-parent homes, and 26% of single-parent families (compared to 6% of married-couple families) lived below the poverty line. The poverty rate for custodial mothers (28.7%) was more than twice as high as that for custodial fathers (11%). Approximately 59% of the 13.5 million custodial parents had child support awards (62% of custodial mothers and 39% of custodial fathers) (Grall, 2002). Often custodial parents are not awarded child support payments because the other parent is judged unable to pay. Seventy percent of the mothers and 57% of the fathers with awards received at least a portion of the money (Scoon-Rogers, 1999). It is estimated that only a quarter of custodial parents receive the full amount awarded (Lino, 2000).

custody A term that refers to both legal custody (the parent's right to make decisions regarding the welfare of the child) and physical custody (the parent's right to have the child living with him or her).

sole legal custody Situation in which the noncustodial parent forfeits the right to make decisions about the children's health, education, or religious training.

joint legal custody Custody shared by both parents, both of whom are responsible for child rearing and for making decisions regarding the child.

There are essentially three systems for determining the amount of child support awards: (1) specifying a straight percentage of the noncustodial parent's income based on the number of dependent children; (2) calculating support according to the combined income of both parents, with each paying the percentage that is their share of the combined income; and (3) taking both parents' incomes into consideration but allowing for exemptions such as taxes, work-related expenses, or new dependents of a noncustodial parent. Investigators have concluded that many noncustodial parents can afford to pay substantially more child support than is awarded under any of these three systems (Klitsch, 1989).

In an attempt to establish fairer standards for child support obligations, federal lawmakers passed legislation requiring that each state establish standards for determining child support, and judges who deviate from this standard must provide grounds, in writing, for doing so. This legislation gave the courts less discretion than they previously had held, but it has still resulted in widely varying standards from state to state (Klawitter, 1994). Coleman, Ganong, Killian, and McDaniel (1999), in studying child support obligations, found little agreement about how much money parents should pay for child support, with a large discrepancy between what states recommended and what parents thought was fair. Many parents felt that there should be a reduction in the father's obligation if the mother remarried but not if only the father remarried. Thus, a reduction of financial support appears to relate mostly to the mother's perceived increased income, and not to additional financial responsibilities assumed by the father (Coleman et al., 1999).

The legal system has three approaches to promote compliance with support orders. The deterrence-based approach uses legal punishment to ensure payment of support. It can be either specific, which involves punishing an individual who is delinquent in payment in order to prevent future delinquency, or general, which involves punishing offenders in order to discourage others from becoming delinquent (Sorensen and Halpern, 1999). These punishments include interception of tax refunds, liens on property, and jail time. There is some statistical evidence that the deterrence-based approach does increase child support payments (Sorensen and Halpern, 1999).

Another approach is based on compliance. Rather than relying on punishment after the fact, this approach intervenes before the law is broken (A. J.

Reiss, 1984). The compliance approach uses random checking, or checking of potential offenders, resulting in funds being withheld from earnings before a child support payment is missed. This approach has also been shown to have a positive effect on payments (Sorensen and Halpern, 1999).

Finally, the consensus-based approach relies not on fear of punishment or on payment regulation, but on societal acceptance and concurring norms. There are two strategies for establishing the proper norm: (1) enforcing the law consistently until behavior changes and (2) using the media to convince the public that the norm has merit. Establishing standards for determining child support and encouraging judges to use consistent criteria when awarding child support are two examples of the consensus-based approach.

Studies have shown that compliance with support orders is positively affected by both income withholding and the father's perception of fairness. They have also revealed that, once a parent feels that the order is fair, withholding no longer has an impact on compliance, and that withholding does not reduce compliance among those who perceive the order to be fair. These results suggest that policymakers should focus on improving perceptions of fairness while continuing to promote income withholding in efforts to improve compliance (Lin, 2000).

Making regular child support payments is very important to children's welfare. It lets the children know that they are cared for by both parents. It better enables the children to have the necessities of life, to live in better neighborhoods and housing, and to have adequate food, clothing, and education. It prevents the children from being penalized because of the actions of parents. They need to be loved and nurtured by both parents, regardless of their parents' marital status.

Visitation Rights

Ordinarily, visitation rights are granted to the noncustodial parent. These rights may be unlimited—allowing visitation at any time—or they may be restrictive—limiting visitation only to specific times. The majority of parents not living with their children had joint custody or visitation privileges. If the parents had an agreement for child support, 85% had visitation or joint custody. If there was no agreement in child support due, 67% had visitation or shared custody (Grall, 2002). A vindictive spouse can make life miserable by managing to be away with the children when it's time for the other parent to visit, by poisoning the children's minds against the other parent, by refusing to allow the children to phone or write, or by using visitation rights as a club to wield over the other parent's head.

According to the provisions of the Uniform Marriage and Divorce Act of 1979,

(A) A parent not granted custody of the child is entitled to reasonable visitation rights unless the court finds, after a hearing, that visitation would endanger the child's physical health or significantly impair his [or her] emotional development.

(B) The court may modify an order granting or denying visitation rights whenever modification would serve the best interests of the child; but the court shall not restrict a parent's visitation rights unless it finds that the visitation would endanger a child's physical health or significantly impair his [or her] emotional development. (Cited in R. L. Franklin and Hibbs, 1980, p. 289)

Although increased visitation is believed to reflect a good noncustodial parent–child relationship, this association is mediated by the postdivorce parental relationship.

Reactions of Children

Using national longitudinal data to examine parent–child relationships before and after parental divorce, researchers found that parents report escalating problems in their relationships with their children as early as 8–12 years prior to divorce. The low quality of the parents' marriage largely accounted for this association. Low quality in the parents' marriage when children were 10 years old on average was a predictor of low parental affection for the children when they were 18 years old. Divorce further eroded affection between fathers and children, indicating that the quality of the parents' marriage had both direct and indirect long-term consequences for parent–child affection.

Why should low marital quality translate into problematic parent–child relations? Marital discord may preoccupy and distract parents, leaving them emotionally unavailable and unable to deal with their children's needs. It also may cause parents to be irritable and hot-tempered in dealing with their children. At the same time, marital discord may increase children's behavior problems, making them

more difficult to manage. The result could be a situation in which parent–child relationships spiral downward (Amato and Booth, 1996).

The conflict and difficulties that lead to divorce are set in motion well before the family separates. The roughly 2 years that follow disruption have been described as a "crisis period" characterized by dramatic changes in children's day-to-day lives. Consequently, any effects of divorce on children may reflect not only the stress of the breakup and its aftermath but also dysfunctional family processes, marital conflict, or problems children have prior to the breakup (Booth, 1999; B. R. Morrison and Cherlin, 1995).

A growing number of clinicians emphasize that children perceive divorce as a major negative event that stimulates painful emotions, confusion, and uncertainty. Some clinicians feel that the majority of children regain psychological equilibrium within a year or so and resume a normal curve of growth and development (Hetherington and Stanley-Hagen, 1999). Two studies show no significant association between adult self-esteem and the experience of parental divorce as a child. However, both studies show a lowered sense of power in later life, primarily because of lower educational attainment (Amato, 1988; Glenn and Kramer, 1985).

Other researchers feel that, for a substantial portion of children, the upheaval in their lives will interfere with normal social-emotional growth. This view is substantiated by Judith Wallerstein in a 25-year study of 60 divorced families, involving 130 children, living in Marin County, California (Wallerstein and Lewis, 1998). Wallerstein found that 10 years after divorce, half the women and one-third of the men were still so angry at their former spouse that this anger colored their relationship with their children. The children in her study had memories of abandonment, terror, and loneliness. They felt that they had been denied the basic security with which to grow and that they had lost their childhood by feeling compelled to assume responsibility for their parents' well-being. And the effects of divorce did not disappear over time, but instead appeared to be cumulative. High levels of alcohol abuse, promiscuity, and delinquency showed up 10–15 years after the parents' divorce. Half the children entered adulthood as underachieving, self-deprecating young men and women. Financial support for college was often missing, as few fathers offered consistent financial support throughout childhood and toward higher education. Overall, Wallerstein concluded

Children often perceive divorce as a major negative event that stimulates painful emotions, confusion, and uncertainty.

from decades of research that divorce causes serious harm to children who experience it.

Wallerstein's sample (Wallerstein and Lewis, 1998) came from an affluent area during years of rapid social change in the United States. There was no control group with which to compare findings. No study was done of how tension prior to divorce affected children. So whether these findings can be applied to other children from divorced families is not certain.

The effects of divorce on children depend on many variables: whether divorce improves or reduces the quality of parenting, whether divorce improves or worsens the emotional atmosphere of the home, whether the divorce is amicable or bitter, what the effect of divorce is on the parents, and what custody and living arrangements are worked out.

In the time immediately surrounding the divorce, children may go through a period of mourning and grief, and the mood or feeling may be one of sadness and dejection. One 7-year-old described divorce as "when people go away" (F. P. Rice, 1979).

Other common reactions are a heightened sense of insecurity. Children feel that "if you really loved me, you wouldn't go away and leave me." Some become very afraid that their custodial parent will also leave, and the child may become very possessive of that parent. One mother remarked, "Since the divorce, Tommy has been very upset when I go to work or when he goes to school. I think he's afraid that he'll come home and not find me there" (F. P. Rice, 1979, p. 304).

Another common reaction of children is to blame themselves. If the children are a major source of conflict for the couple, the children may feel they are responsible. Some children think that the departing parent is abandoning them because they haven't been "good boys or girls." Yet another common reaction is for children to try to bring their parents together. They wish that everyone could live together and be happy. The longing for a reunited family may go on for a long time, until children fully understand the realities of the situation and the reason for the separation.

Children have other adjustments to make. They need to adjust to the absence of one parent, often one on whom they depended deeply for affection and for help. One teenage girl remarked, "The hardest thing for me was to get used to living without my father. I never really realized how much I needed him until he left" (Author's counseling notes).

Older children may also be required to assume more responsibility for family functioning: cooking, housekeeping, even earning money to support the family. This is usually a maturing experience for them, but it's also a difficult adjustment. Some children, used to having everything, have a difficult time realizing that money is short and that they can't buy the clothes and other things they used to.

Children of divorce may also have a more difficult time developing good relationships with their siblings as adults. In a study of sibling relationship quality among young adults who had experienced childhood parental divorce, Riggio (2001) found that individuals who experienced parental divorce between 8 and 19 years of age experienced significantly fewer positive feelings toward the sibling in adulthood. They also recalled fewer positive feelings, beliefs, and behaviors toward the sibling in childhood compared to individuals who experienced parental divorce before the age of 8 years and compared to individuals from intact families.

Research consistently finds that children whose parents are separated or divorced are more likely to have behavioral problems (for a review of this literature see Amato, 2001, or Reifman, Villa, Amans, Rethinam, and Telesca, 2001). However, children in intact families with high levels of parental conflict also have high levels of problem behaviors. Thus, while divorce is clearly disruptive to children, living with two quarreling parents appears to be equally problematic. Increasingly, researchers conclude that parental conflict poses a greater threat to children's well-being than does family structure per se (C. Buehler et al., 1998; Wandewater and Lansford, 1998).

Of course, special adjustments are necessary for children of divorced parents. For example, when the parent caring for the children begins to date again and to become emotionally involved with another person, the children must share their parent with another adult. If the parent remarries, as the majority do, the children are confronted with readjustment to a stepparent and perhaps stepsiblings.

Some parents attend programs with their children designed to help children cope with divorce. One study conducted focus groups for children to talk about their problems and feeling about being caught in the middle of their parents' disputes, parents not keeping them informed, and complications arising when parents' new partners enter the family. Children expressed that the best way a friend could help them cope with divorce was by discussing it, provided the friend had also been through a divorce (Hans and Fine, 2001).

Other research has found that short coping programs can help ease the pain in children's lives caused from divorce. One longitudinal study interviewed 249 divorced families that included custodial mothers and their adolescent children. In a 6-year follow-up, they found that an 11-week program designed to strengthen a mother's parenting skills and her child's ability to cope after a divorce made a significant difference in the overall well-being of the child. For example, adolescents in the study who had participated in the program compared to those who did not showed fewer mental health problems, had less alcohol and drug use, had fewer sexual partners, and showed fewer externalizing problems such as acting out. Thus, it appears that programs designed to help families cope with the changes and challenges that are inevitable with a divorce can be very helpful.

In conclusion, it is important to note that divorced and blended families have some of the same forms of resiliency as intact families (Rodgers and Rose, 2002). In a study that examined factors outside families that may contribute to the resiliency of adolescents who have experienced divorce, Rodgers and Rose (2002) found that while parents are of primary importance to the well-being of children, peers, schools, and neighbors also are important for adolescents coping with divorce: "In the end, optimal adolescent development appears to be a product of relationships both within and outside of families" (p. 1036). While children of divorce may have a difficult time in the beginning, most learn to adjust and do well.

A QUESTION OF POLICY

SINGLE-PARENT FAMILIES

There are many different types of single-parent families—from wealthy older widowers to poor young teenage mothers. There are also many different types of concerns—from children growing up in poverty to the belief that single-parent families deprive children of a vital need to be raised by both a mother and a father.

One thing most people do agree on is that children growing up in poverty are disadvantaged, and single-parent families, most of which are headed by women, have a high rate of poverty (as discussed in Chapter 9). One public policy that has been put into place to address the economic difficulties of many single-mother families is the collection of child support from what are typically described as "deadbeat dads." As discussed in the text, federal law mandates that noncustodial fathers pay child support, and one means of collecting this support is to garnish wages. However, because fathers typically remarry and form new families, some argue that this policy merely takes money from one child to

LEARNING OBJECTIVES

After reading the chapter, you should be able to:

- Identify trends relating to remarriage and stepfamilies.

- Discuss various factors in relation to remarriage: types of remarried families, divorce and success in remarriage, courtship and mate selection in remarriage, finances, and remarriage and marital satisfaction.

- Describe differences between primary families and stepfamilies.

- Discuss the major challenges in stepparent–stepchild relationships.

- Identify the effects on children of parents' cohabiting before remarriage.

- Discuss basic information about stepsibling relationships.

Coming Together: Remarriage and Stepparenting

According to the cultural ideal, marriage lasts until "death do us part." Historically, this marital commitment was largely borne out, and most marriages ended with the death of a spouse, often when young children were still present (Glick, 1976). As life expectancy has increased and as cultural norms for divorce and remarriage have changed, more marriages are ended by divorce than by death. Whether the marriage ends by divorce or death, remarriage and the formation of stepfamilies have become quite common (Coontz, 2000).

Today, approximately 46% of all marriages are remarriages, and the largest proportion of the remarried population is divorced people who have married other divorced people. In fact, approximately two-thirds of people who divorce each year remarry eventually. Furthermore, remarriage occurs fairly quickly. Fifty-four percent of divorced women remarry within 5 years, and 75 percent of divorced women remarry within 10 years (National Center for Health Statistics, 2002). The median interval between divorce and remarriage is 3 years for women and 4.5 years for men (U.S. Bureau of the Census, 2002).

Spouses who initiate the divorce tend to remarry more quickly than those who do not initiate the divorce, but this differential diminishes after about 3 years of being separated (Sweeney, 2002). From studying the National Survey of Families and Households, Sweeney (2002) finds evidence that the initiator status is a stronger predictor of remarriage among relatively older women than among younger women, which suggests that older women may be more willing to stay in an unhappy marriage until the likelihood of finding a better relationship is good.

Remarriage rates vary by ethnic background. Blacks remarry more slowly than Whites or Hispanics. For example, after 5 years of divorce, the probability of remarriage is 58% for White women, 44% for Hispanic women, and 32% for Black women. The probability for remarriage after 10 years of being divorced is 70% for White women, 68% for Hispanic women, and 49% for Black women (National Center for Health Statistics, 2002).

Fifteen percent of remarriages have ended in divorce after 3 years and almost 25% after 5 years. Second marriage disruption is more likely for women under age 25 at remarriage than for women at least age 25 at remarriage. After 10 years of re-marriage, the probability of divorce is 47% for women who were under age 25 at remarriage and 34% for women at least age 25 at remarriage. Women who have children at the time of remarriage are also more likely to experience a divorce than women who do not have any children. Divorce in remarriages is also more likely in families with low income, low education, and high unemployment (National Center for Health Statistics, 2002).

Vital questions are: To what extent are remarriages successful? How might couples increase the chances of success? What special challenges do remarrieds face? Also, how do primary families differ from stepfamilies? How are stepmother and stepfather roles defined? What challenges do stepparents face? What are the reactions and adjustments of different stepchildren? What do we need to know about stepsibling relationships? What is it like growing up in a stepfamily?

REMARRIAGE

Remarried families (sometimes called binuclear families) may be grouped into categories according to family configuration. Couples with one remarried spouse include families with (1) no children, (2) children-in-common only, (3) her children (stepfather families), (4) his children (stepmother families), (5) children-in-common plus her children (natural parent plus stepfather), (6) children-in-common plus his children (natural parent plus stepmother), and (7) children of both spouses (two stepparents—either the man or the woman had a child out of wedlock). Couples with two remarried spouses include families with (1) no children, (2) children-in-common only, (3) her children (stepfather families), (4) his children (stepmother families), (5) children-in-common plus her children (natural parent plus stepfather), (6) children-in-common plus his children (natural parent plus stepmother), (7) children of both spouses (two stepparents), (8) children-in-common plus their children (natural parents plus two stepparents), (9) custodial children of the mother plus relationships with the father's children on a noncustodial basis, and (10) custodial children of the father plus relationships with the mother's children on a noncustodial basis.

Family relationships can become quite complicated in remarriages when one or both spouses bring

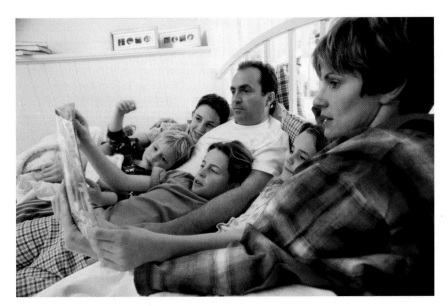

Family relationships can become quite complicated in remarriages when one or both spouses bring children from a previous marriage and the remarried couple then have children of their own.

children from a previous marriage, especially since half of all women who remarry will bear a child with their new spouse (Wineberg, 1990). Children may have natural parents plus stepparents, both natural siblings and stepsiblings, both natural grandparents and stepgrandparents, and natural aunts and uncles plus step-aunts and step-uncles, not to mention cousins and other relatives. Adult spouses relate to each other, to their own natural parents and grandparents, to their new parents-in-law and grandparents-in-law, and to their new brothers- and sisters-in-law. They may also continue to relate to their former parents- and grandparents-in-law, to their former brothers- and sisters-in-law, and to other family members. It is no wonder that family integration is sometimes challenging.

Divorce and Success in Remarriage

The majority of survey studies have revealed that the probability of divorce is slightly greater in remarriages than in first marriages (Booth and Edwards, 1992). This means that half the children whose parents divorce and remarry will experience a second parental divorce (Coleman and Ganong, 1990).

From one point of view, remarriage should be more successful than first marriage. Remarrieds are older, more mature and experienced, and often highly motivated to make their marriage work. One study showed that, relative to other couples, spouses in remarried and stepfather families reported higher relationship quality and stronger motivations to be in the relationship (Kurdek, 1989a). According to self-reports of remarried couples, differences in marital satisfaction or quality of the marital relationship are rarely found, and when they are, they tend to be small in magnitude (Ganong and Coleman, 1994). Overall, research has shown that remarriages are just as happy as first marriages, with little difference in partners' well-being (Demo and Acock, 1996b; Ihinger-Tallman and Pasley, 1997). While spouses in long-established stepfamilies view their marital relationship as just as happy as their first marriage, they also view their second marriage as more egalitarian in terms of housework and child care (Hetherington, 1999a), more open and pragmatic, and less romantic, and they are more willing to confront conflict (Hetherington et al., 1992). Although the risk of divorce is higher for remarried couples, many eventually establish strong, positive marital relationships and an adaptive, well-functioning parenting environment (Hetherington and Stanley-Hagan, 1999).

For some couples, remarriage introduces challenges that were not present in their first marriage. The biggest challenge can be children. Remarried couples with children from prior marriages are more likely to divorce than are remarried couples without stepchildren (Tzeng and Mare, 1995). Since mothers still most often get custody, their children are likely living with her and her new spouse, who becomes a stepfather. A divorced parent and the children may be a "closed system" of social interaction, which is difficult for a new stepparent to enter. In general, men more often feel excluded in the face of spouse–child relationships than do women (Hobart, 1987). The man's children are usually living with his ex-spouse, creating family ties with her household, and the potential for conflict and resentment. The woman's ex-spouse as noncustodial father usually sees his children, so he has contact with both his ex-spouse and her new partner, also allowing the possibility of conflict and problems. Being a stepparent is a far more difficult task than being a biological parent, because children often have difficulty accepting a substitute parental figure. The spouse of a noncustodial parent must try to develop a friendly relationship with stepchildren from visits. All of the adults are coparenting, with three or four parent figures as opposed to two. The children are continually reacting to and dealing with growing up in two households, with three or four adult figures, and with two or more models of relationship patterns with the opposite sex. Both adults and children must contend with the attitudes and influences of other family members. Thus, blending families can be complicated and challenging.

Stepsibling relationships can also pose challenges. Sometimes there is competition between the new spouse's and the partner's children. They each may become jealous of the time and attention their own parent gives to the stepchildren. However, researchers have found that most adolescents view their custodial parent's remarriage as positive (E. Anderson, Greene, Hetherington, and Clingempeel, 1999). The most frequent word that adolescents used to describe their reactions to remarriage was *happy,* followed by *satisfied* and *pleased.* Mothers also rated the reaction of their adolescents to their remarriage as positive. One reason given by adolescents who viewed their custodial parents' remarriages as positive was that their family had fewer money problems (E. Anderson et al., 1999).

Courtship and Mate Selection in Remarriage

There are a number of ways that courtship and mate selection in remarriage are different from those in first marriage. For one thing, the two people typically are older. Overall, people who remarry are likely to be more emotionally mature and more experienced than when they married the first time around. For another thing, the majority have children. The median ages of two children at the time of remarriage are 6 and 8 years. This means that a custodial parent may evaluate a potential mate in terms of his or her potential as a stepparent (Church, 1999).

Sometimes ex-spouses and families become involved in the courtship of the couple. In some situations, the ex-spouse may try to break up the relationship, turn the children against the new partner, exert a negative influence on family members so that they won't accept the newcomer, and create jealousy and tension between the new partners. If family members liked the first spouse and sympathize with him or her, they may have a difficult time accepting the newcomer (Kurdek, 1989b). Potential mates of formerly married people are often introduced to other family members only after there is some assurance of commitment by the couple. The announcement of the new involvement may come as a surprise, with family members not having enough time or exposure to get used to the new relationship. New partners enter a family system that has an established history, and there are no guidelines for how they should fit in. Consequently, there may be several false starts in attempting to build relationships with the family, the children, and possibly the ex-spouse.

There are differences in the length of courtship among remarrieds. Generally, the length of the courtship before the second marriage is similar to that before the first marriage. That is, people with very brief courtships the first time around have very brief courtships before remarrying. However, age is an important variable. Males over 30 experience second courtships about half as long as those of younger males. At all ages, women with lower income and education marry sooner than women with higher income and education, whereas men with higher income and education marry sooner than those with lower income and education (Glick, 1990). The median number of years between divorce and remarriage is about 3 years for women and 4½ years for men, although this varies by age, race/ethnicity, the presence and number of children, and income (Lampard and Peggs, 1999; Wineberg, 1999). During the period of emotional turmoil before and after a divorce, people are very vulnerable to the attention of others who are nice to them. Sexual intimacy usually

Successful Remarriages

How are happily remarried couples able to succeed? Many factors enter in, of course, but couples who succeed seem to have five factors in common.

The first factor is that the partners have given themselves time to get to know each other well. Like any marriage, remarriages are more complete if each member of the couple really knows the other well beforehand.

Second, happily married couples resist the many pressures to remarry before they are ready. These pressures stem from society itself and from friends and relatives who can't tolerate others being unmarried for very long and who fix them up with dates. And then there are the pressures of loneliness and the need for love and companionship.

Remarriage is also sometimes used as a reparative measure—to try to make it up to the children for the hurts and anguish caused by the death of the other parent or by divorce. Such motivations may backfire; instead of helping the children, a troubled marriage or a difficult stepparent relationship may actually make the situation worse.

Not all reasons for remarriage are desirable. Some divorced people remarry on the rebound as a way of hurting their former spouse by showing that they are still desirable. Remarriage can also become a reenactment of an earlier, neurotic relationship that, although unhealthy, nevertheless supplied certain needs. The partners must sort out what they most seek in their relationship and be certain that they are not pressured into marriage for the wrong reasons or before they are ready.

Third, partners are able to discuss every aspect of their relationship before marriage. If they haven't done so before, then they do so afterward.

Fourth, partners have learned from past mistakes. Before remarriage, they need to ask themselves: Do I understand what went wrong the first time? What were the underlying causes of my marital problems? Have I gained insight into the shortcomings, and am I able to overcome them?

Finally, partners put their marriage first. These couples have learned that the basis for sound parent–child relationships is a sound marriage. The partners' primary loyalty is to each other, and secondarily to their children.

There will be numerous forces inside and outside their homes that will be trying to pull couples apart. Unless their bond is secure, the marriage can be broken. Immature children and stepchildren may try to weaken their bond, as may ex-spouses. Even other family members who resent the divorce or the remarriage may try to sow seeds of distrust or suspicion between the partners.

The happier the remarriage, the more secure and loving will be the environment in which children are reared.

commences early in a relationship, which tends to intensify the emotional involvement and the feeling of being in love. However, parents may hesitate to cohabit or to begin a partnered relationship if they feel it will negatively affect their children (Lampard and Peggs, 1999).

There may also be subtle psychological influences at work in the spouse selection process. Some people want to marry a person who they believe resembles a spouse to whom they were married before. When people are divorced by a spouse against their will and remain emotionally attached to that spouse, or when a former spouse has died, they may seek another spouse who reminds them of their former one. Of course, no two people are alike, so trouble arises in the remarriage when one or both spouses discover that their new mate is *not* like their former spouse or when they try to pressure their new mate to be like the former one.

Even if people don't like some characteristics of a former spouse, they may seek out a new spouse with similar traits, because the reasons they were initially attracted to that type of person still exist. Consider this example:

> Joe was brought up by a very domineering mother whom he rebelled against. His first wife, Joan, reminded him of his mother. He and his wife fought frequently; the conflict became so upsetting that Joe divorced her. He vowed never to have anything to do with that kind of woman again. But a year later, he was remarried to the same kind of woman all over again. Even though he rebelled against that kind of woman, it was the only type of relationship he knew.

It brought him a sense of security. It was the one norm that he patterned his subsequent relationships after. (Author's counseling notes)

Carrying Expectations from One Marriage to Another

Remarried couples face many of the same expectations as first-married couples. But in addition to these expectations, remarried couples usually have other expectations unique to their status as people who have been married more than once. One expectation is that being married to the second spouse is going to be similar in some ways to being married to the first one. However, these expectations may be not only unrealistic but also unfair to the second spouse. One result is that spouses replicate the mistakes of their first marriage in remarriage, because they expect that the situation will be the same (Kalmuss and Seltzer, 1986).

One potential problem is rooted in pain experienced in the previous marriage. People who were married before remember all too well the problem behaviors of their former spouse, such as alcohol abuse, extramarital affairs, belittling comments, violent outbursts, rancorous arguments, irresponsibility, selfishness, and a lack of love and affection. As a result, these people enter a second marriage with a real fear that the problems and hurts they experienced before will happen again. This fear may make them oversensitive to anything their new partner does or says that reminds them of the difficulties they had before. One man explained his feelings:

> My first wife hated sex and rejected me most of the time over the many years of our marriage. As a result, I'm very sensitive to anything that my second wife does which seems to be rejection. If she's tired or sick and doesn't feel like intercourse, I'm hurt by her lack of desire, even though she really doesn't mean to reject me. Actually, she's very affectionate, and loves to make love. I even had trouble accepting that. I couldn't believe that she really liked it. Gradually, though, I accepted the fact that she really wanted me, so that now I'm not upset by those rare occasions when she is not willing. (Author's counseling notes)

Sensitivity to many forms of behavior develops. One woman became very sensitive to criticism because her first spouse had frequently berated her, especially in relation to her role as a mother. She became upset whenever her second spouse made suggestions for changing some of her methods of handling the children. The last thing she wanted was similar treatment from this man. Many other examples could be given. In each case, the reaction of the remarried person is quite understandable, but it can create problems if it is so extreme that it interferes with the new spousal relationship.

Another problem in remarriage involves confusion over role expectations. This confusion arises

Many different motivations may be involved when there are large age discrepancies between spouses, and many of these marriages are quite successful. In fact, overall, there are no significant differences in marital quality among couples from various age groups.

because of the difficulty in sorting out what one's second spouse expects from what one's first spouse required. Both men and women in remarriages tend to base some of their expectations of spousal roles on the role performance of former spouses, even if the first marriage was quite unhappy. This is unfair to the current spouse, who may not be at all like the former spouse. The key is to relate to one's spouse as a unique individual, not as a person whom one expects to be like someone else.

Problems may also arise when people want their new partner to play a role completely different from that played by the former spouse. This happens when a person has developed an intense dislike of things a former spouse did and, consequently, expects the second spouse to behave in a completely different manner. This can lead to some interesting behavior. Here is one such example:

Ann was first married to a husband who expected her to wait on him hand and foot. To keep the peace, she did so for 25 years, even though she became more and more resentful of having to do so. Finally she could stand it no longer and got a divorce. She vowed that she never wanted anything to do with that type of man again.

Hank was first married to a wife who never assumed any responsibility for the house, the children, or for earning income. He did virtually everything for the whole family, because he couldn't stand a dirty house, unkempt children, and living in poverty. After 25 years he grew to resent it and divorced his wife. He vowed he would never marry that type of woman again.

Ann and Hank met and fell in love. Ann was very impressed that Hank was the kind of man who had always done everything at home. At last, she would be married to the kind of husband she had always wanted. Hank was delighted when he found out that Ann had waited on her husband for all those years. At last, he would have a wife who would do things for him for a change.

But in the beginning, both Ann and Hank were very much disappointed. Hank became resentful because Ann asked him to do the same things he had resented doing for his first wife. Ann was disillusioned because she found out that Hank expected her to serve him just as she had done for her first husband. It took some time before they each understood the feelings and needs of the other and before they

learned to compromise in meeting those needs. (Author's counseling notes)

It can be quite unfair to expect one's spouse to fulfill needs that were not met in a previous marriage, but one naturally might want important needs met that were not fulfilled before. The key is *mutual* fulfillment, not a situation in which one person does all the giving and the other does all the receiving.

Finances

Financial problems can be particularly bothersome for remarried couples (Mason, Skolnick, and Sugarman, 1998). A divorced father who remarries usually has to pay child support. If he is also helping to support his new wife's children, there is a double financial burden, particularly if her ex-spouse does not keep up with child support payments. However, for a female-headed single-parent family, remarriage is one of the fastest routes out of economic hardship (Zill, Morrison, and Coiro, 1993). In general, women benefit more from remarriage than do men (Ozawa and Yoon, 2002).

Fishman (1983) described the two basic economic patterns that stepfamilies adopt: (1) "Common-pot" families pool all their resources for household expenses, whereas (2) "two-pot" families safeguard individual resources for personal use or for their biological children. Fishman found that a common-pot system unifies the stepfamily, while the two-pot economy encourages biological loyalties and personal autonomy. The common-pot approach is illustrated in Figure 17.1. In the fictional Becker-Robinson stepfamily, Mike and Fran live together with his two children and her three children. Fran works full-time, and Mike owns a shoe store. They bought a house in both their names. All earnings are pooled together in a joint account. Fran receives sporadic child support from her ex-spouse, which she puts in the common pot. Resources of time, services, goods, and cash are distributed according to individual family members' needs, not biological relationship. This is not always simple to do. Sacrifices are necessary, and tensions arise. For example, Fran's daughter Ann is going to college, and her expenses come from the common pot. This means that the money is not available for other things (Fishman, 1983).

In the two-pot approach, each marital partner contributes a specific amount to the ongoing maintenance of the household, but children are supported

Figure 17.1 The Common-Pot Approach (*Note:* From "The Economic Behavior of Stepfamilies" by B. Fishman, 1983, *Family Relations, 32,* pp. 359–366. Copyright © 1983 by the National Council on Family Relations. Reprinted by permission.)

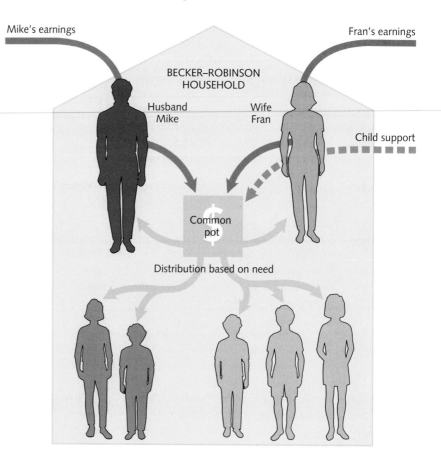

by their biological parents. This approach is illustrated in Figure 17.2. In the fictional Marshall-Linton stepfamily, Harry and Sheila live together with Sheila's three children. She receives $200 a week in child support. Harry's older daughter, Greta, is away at college; his younger daughter, Ginny, lives with her mother and new stepfather. Ginny visits regularly; Greta's visits are sporadic. Harry gives Sheila $50 per week for his share of food and small expenses. The house is in Harry's name, and he pays the fixed expenses—mortgage, gas, and electric. He also sends his ex-spouse a monthly stipend for Ginny's support and pays for Greta's college expenses. Sheila adds the $200 a week she gets for child support to the $50 Harry gives her and deposits the money in her personal account. Out of this, she runs the house and pays for clothes and incidentals for her children and herself. Harry and Sheila have no joint checking or savings account. Obviously, in this two-pot system, the financial arrangement indicates a tenuous bond in the marriage. Harry's ex-spouse was a

"spendaholic" who was always buying and who left him and sued for alimony and divorce. He is fearful to trust another woman again. Sheila tries to be a good spouse. She is a homebody who does not spend much on herself, but Harry still criticizes her when she does spend. The bond between them is weak.

These examples illustrate that a financial commitment to a new spouse comes slowly; and still more slowly, if at all, comes financial commitment to stepchildren. The challenge for each stepfamily is to build the interpersonal bonds, sense of group commitment, and economic system that meet both family and individual needs and that reflect family members' commitment to one another (Fishman, 1983).

Relationships with the Ex-Spouse

In reality, divorced people seldom have affectionate feelings toward the former spouse but rather usually have a long list of complaints. However, individuals who divorce typically have to develop a

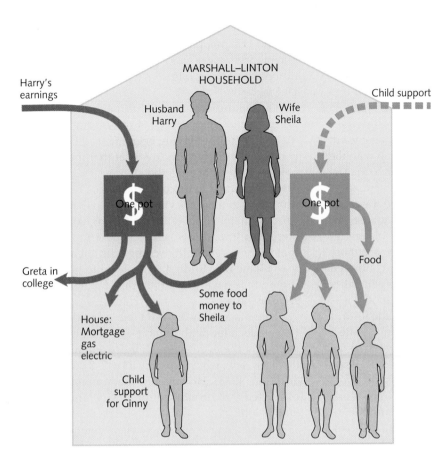

Figure 17.2 The Two-Pot Approach (*Note:* From "The Economic Behavior of Stepfamilies" by B. Fishman, 1983, *Family Relations, 32,* pp. 359–366. Copyright © 1983 by the National Council on Family Relations. Reprinted by permission.)

new relationship with the ex-spouse when children are involved. This new relationship can be a difficult one, particularly in the early stages of divorce as ex-spouses deal with feelings of ambivalence, anger, attachment, and remorse, as well as sometimes fighting viciously and even reconciling passionately (Masheter, 1997).

Even when ex-spouses seem to hate each other, they probably have developed an emotional attachment that does not end when the marriage ends. In the first stages of separation, signs of continued attachment between ex-spouses, such as continually calling the other person or needing to know his or her whereabouts, are not uncommon. Four actions characteristic of continued attachment are (1) spending a lot of time thinking about the former relationship, (2) wondering what the ex-partner is doing, (3) doubting that the divorce really happened, and (4) feeling that one will never recover from the marital breakup (Kitson, 1982). Preoccupation with the ex-spouse is usually characteristic of a problematic rela-

tionship with the individual (Masheter, 1997), which often includes hostility, particularly among depressed women (Thabes, 1997). Partners often blame each other for their hurt feelings and feel justified in their aggression and hostility. In a longitudinal study, Ambert (1988b) concluded that postdivorce harmony is rare, although after 6 years most divorced people—especially nonparents—have rather indifferent feelings toward their ex-spouse. Particularly after remarriage, interaction between the ex-spouses tends to decrease (D. H. Christensen and Rettig, 1995).

Buunk and Mutsaers (1999) examined how the nature of one's relationship with a former spouse is related to satisfaction in remarriage by focusing on three aspects of the relationship with the ex-spouse: attachment, hostility, and friendship. After 6 years of remarriage, on average, there was little continued attachment to or friendship with the ex-spouse, although there were still feelings of hostility, particularly when children were involved. In general, positive feelings toward the ex-spouse were quite rare. The relationship with the ex-spouse was more positive among the more highly educated and among those who did not have children from the former marriage. Continued attachment to the ex-spouse was especially problematic in relation to current marital satisfaction. Men who still felt attached to a former spouse reported that their current spouse had problems with the relationship with the ex-spouse. The more attached men still felt to the former spouse, the less happy the second marriage. In addition, the more their current spouse reported feelings of continued attachment to a former spouse, the less happy these women were. One possible reason for this gender difference is that women are more sensitive about their spouse's feelings of continued attachment than are men. Among women, hostility toward and/or friendship with a former spouse was dependent on their current spouse's attitude toward this type of relationship. These findings may reflect a higher interpersonal sensitivity of women to the attitudes of their spouse, but they may also indicate that women express their hostility toward their former spouse more so than do men, which may make their current spouse develop a negative attitude toward the friendship with that former spouse (Buunk and Mutsaers, 1999).

In general, relationships between ex-spouses seem to reach a low level of intensity after a number of years, with most remarried individuals not feeling a need to maintain a close relationship with the former spouse. This suggests that most individuals eventually get over the severe hostility characteristic of many relationships between ex-spouses during the initial stages of separation (Buunk and Mutsaers, 1999).

STEPFAMILIES

Many couples expect stepfamily relationships to be similar to those of primary families, and they may be disappointed, surprised, and bewildered if they find differences (Bray and Berger, 1993). Research suggests that expecting or forcing a stepfamily to be like a traditional biological family can lead to new problems or exacerbate existing ones (Bray and Berger, 1993). Stepfamilies need to recognize that building a sense of family takes time, that family boundaries must be flexible to accommodate exist-

ing ties to noncustodial parents and extended family, and that stepparents cannot replace biological parents and may need to develop a separate, nontraditional parenting role (Hetherington and Stanley-Hagan, 1999).

Disappointment may occur if stepparents have unrealistically high expectations of themselves and their new family. Having been married before and been parents before, they expect that they will be able to step right into the stepparent role. They may be shocked to discover that their stepchildren don't take to them the way they do to their biological parents. This may cause feelings of anxiety, anger, guilt, and low self-esteem. They may feel that there is something wrong with them, or they may blame the children. They need to realize that it may take several years to develop satisfactory relationships.

There is usually an initial period of disequilibrium associated with divorce and remarriage, followed by the eventual restabilization of the new family system, which typically takes 2–3 years (Hetherington, 1989). However, some researchers have estimated that restabilization in stepfamilies may take as long as 5–7 years (Cherlin and Furstenberg, 1994). After stepfamilies have been together for 5 or more years, restabilization seems to have taken place, and it is then that we see more similarities than differences in the ways in which families function. Thus, in long-term stable stepfamilies, relationship patterns become more like those in nondivorced families (Bray and Kelly, 1998). This transition or restabilization is somewhat dependent on family history. Children whose parents had a highly conflictual marital relationship show a decrease in behavioral problems following divorce, whereas those from families with little conflict experience an increase in problems following divorce (Amato, Loomis, and Booth, 1995).

Parents and stepparents sometimes enter into their new family with a great deal of guilt and regret over their failed marriage. They feel sorry for their children, whom they have put through an upsetting experience. This has several effects. Usually, parents and stepparents tend to be overindulgent, are not as strict as they might otherwise be, and have more trouble guiding and controlling the children's behavior (Amato, 1987). Often, they try to buy the children's affection and cooperation. One stepfather reported:

Stepfamilies in Cultural Context

There are many cultural differences in how stepfamilies are perceived and how they function. As stated previously in the text, culture shapes and instructs most family patterns. Berger (2000) examined the differences in stepfamilies in two different countries: the United States and Israel. He found that American stepfamilies see themselves as being more different from biological nuclear families, whereas Israeli stepfamilies see themselves as being more similar to nuclear families. American stepfamilies reported lower levels of functioning on psychological measures than Israeli stepfamilies, and they were much more likely to view therapy as a means for working out problems in stepfamilies. Only a small minority of Israeli stepfamilies considered therapy an option for family problems.

Berger (2000) attributes these differences to a fundamental difference in culture: American culture places emphasis on individuality, personal freedom, and personal happiness; Israeli culture places more emphasis on collectivity, compli-

ance with social norms, and strong social controls that regulate unconventional behavior. Interestingly, American stepfamilies were much more comfortable with being seen as different than were Israeli stepfamilies. The Israeli emphasis on conformity may stigmatize nonconventional family configurations and contribute to the tendency of stepfamilies in Israel to pass for nonstepfamilies. The American emphasis on personal happiness and satisfaction may contribute to reported lower levels of functioning because of the difficulty in meeting unrealistic personal expectations. For example, the belief that adjustment will occur quickly, love and caring will develop instantaneously, working hard prevents problems, and personal happiness will be met are unrealistic measures for success in stepfamilies. Consequently, American stepfamilies give themselves a lower rating, compared to Israeli stepfamilies, on levels of family satisfaction and personal satisfaction because of higher expectations for personal happiness, which have been shaped by culture.

I would get angry at something my stepdaughter did and feel guilty afterward, so I'd take her to the store and buy her a present. One day after a similar episode, she asked, "What are you going to buy me today?" I realized she had caught on very quickly and had learned how to use my guilt to her own advantage. (Author's counseling notes)

Stepparents' roles are ill-defined (Church, 1999; Mason et al., 1998), and state laws give almost no recognition to the parental role of residential stepparents (Mason, Harrison, Svare, and Wolfinger, 2002). Stepparents have no legal decision-making authority in their stepchildren's lives. Dependent benefits, including medical insurance and death benefits, sometimes exclude stepchildren, and in the event of death or divorce, there is not recognition of inheritance, visitation, or custody rights for stepparents; nor is there an obligation of child support or continuation of dependent benefits (Mason et al., 2002).

Yet stepparents take on a lot of parenting tasks in a stepfamily and often are primary caregivers. One study examined data from the National Survey of Families and Households along with in-depth interviews with 27 married couples in which at least one partner had children from a former relationship (Mason et al., 2002). They found that stepparents function like biological parents on caregiving tasks. For example, stepparents and biological parents put in a similar number of hours per week on parental tasks such as transporting children and helping with homework. They give advice, set and enforce rules, and economically contribute to the well-being of their stepchildren. The majority of stepparents believe it is false to state that stepparents don't have the full responsibility of being a parent (Mason et al., 2002).

Efforts to try to be parents may be rejected by older children. Stepparents can't be mere friends; as responsible adults, they need to make a contribution to the lives of stepchildren. Clinicians advise stepparents to focus initially on nurturing stepchildren and developing feelings of affection before attempting to discipline. Too often, stepparents do not spend enough time building trust and friendships before they start disciplining, which typically leads to resistance and negative reactions from stepchildren (Visher and Visher, 1996).

Stepparents must attempt to deal with children who have already been socialized by another set of parents. Stepparents may not agree with the way

433

during the first year of adjustment to remarriage (E. Anderson et al., 1999).

While children in stepfamilies experience higher rates of negative outcomes than children in biological families (Crosbie-Burnett and Giles-Sims, 1994), many children get along very well with their stepparents. Communication with stepparents is the key and is an important predictor of well-being in children in stepfamilies (W. E. Collins, Newman, and McKenry, 1995). In fact, most stepchildren view their stepparents positively, although usually not as positively as children view their biological parents (Hetherington and Jodl, 1994).

It is important to remember that, while stepchildren may show more behavioral problems, they are not necessarily suffering from a mental or behavioral disorder (Bray, 1999). Studies have found that 70–80% of children in stepfamilies function in the nonclinical range (not suffering from mental or behavioral disorders) and only 20–30% in the clinical range (suffering from such disorders) (Bray, 1999). In contrast, 85–90% of children in nondivorced families function in the nonclinical range. Although statistically the risk is double, most children in stepfamilies seem to function normally (Bray, 1999). And while problems may reemerge or develop in late adolescence and adulthood, the percentage of children who experience severe, lasting problems is relatively small (Hetherington and Stanley-Hagan, 1999). Thus, most children in divorced families and stepfamilies do not develop behavioral problems, are quite resilient through all the transitions, and become competent and well-adjusted individuals (Emery and Forehand, 1996). Also, many studies do not consider length of time in a family when comparing children of first-married families and stepfamilies. Studies often compare long-established nondivorced families to stepfamilies in early stages of family formation, with negative conclusions drawn about stepfamilies (Hetherington and Clingempeel, 1992).

Most family scholars who study divorce and remarriage today conclude that what happens inside a family is more important than family type or structure in influencing children's adjustment (Amato, 1994a; Avenevoli, Sessa, and Steinberg, 1999; Demo and Acock, 1996a; Zill, 1994). Children appear to be at greater risk for behavioral problems when they grow up in highly conflictual first marriages, more so than in well-functioning, supportive single-parent or remarried families (Amato, 1993). Children, regardless of the family structure (nondi-vorced nuclear families, single-parent families, stepfamilies), exhibit greater well-being, achievement, socially responsible behavior, and social competence and fewer behavior problems when they are raised in a loving, harmonious, supportive family environment (E. Anderson et al., 1999; Hetherington, 1999b; Hetherington and Stanley-Hagan, 1999).

Facilitating Bonds between Stepparents and Stepchildren

Most stepparents want to get along with their stepchildren, but, as stated previously, this relationship can be difficult and problematic. Recent research has examined the challenges faced by stepparents in developing bonds with stepchildren, and some common styles and strategies have emerged.

One study revealed three common patterns of behavior among stepparents in forming a relationship with their stepchild: (1) nonseekers of affinity with children, (2) early affinity seekers, and (3) continuous affinity seekers (Ganong, Coleman, Fine, and Martin, 1999). Affinity-seeking strategies are intentional actions by people who are trying to get other people to like them or feel positive toward them. Nonseekers were not mean or neglectful, but they mainly interacted with the children in order to become closer to the parent, not to win the children's affection. They did very little or nothing intentionally to get their stepchildren to like them and usually did not think a lot about this. Early seekers pursued a relationship with the children prior to living with them. Although they sought to bond with the children, they had other motivations, such as getting the children to respond to their discipline as they filled a new role of replacement parent. These stepparents stopped seeking affinity soon after they began living with the stepchildren. Continuous affinity seekers actively pursued the children's affection early in the relationship and continued to do so after the remarriage. They deliberately tried to get their stepchildren to like them and purposefully engaged in activities that stepchildren liked to do. Stepparents who were affinity seekers also described themselves as liking children in general. None of the nonseekers described themselves in this way. Stepparents who were continuous affinity seekers had the strongest bonds with their stepchildren because it was important to them to continue working on the relationship after becoming a stepfamily (Ganong et al., 1999).

Certain characteristics of both stepparents and stepchildren have been found to contribute to the development of a close relationship. Personality appears to be an important characteristic of successful stepparents. Stepparents who are successful at establishing a close relationship with their stepchildren tend to be more laid back and less eager to establish control or fill a role as a disciplinarian. Although they make attempts to become friends with their stepchildren, they have less need to be in control of the relationship and do not need to have a friendship develop immediately (Ganong et al., 1999). Overall, the friendship style of stepparenting seems to be the most successful in facilitating bonding with stepchildren (Erera-Weatherley, 1996). As for stepchildren, those who have something in common with their stepparent and those who want the stepparent to function as a parent experience a stronger bond with the stepparent. Stepchildren who think the stepparent had something to do with their parents' separating and remaining separated typically reject the stepparent's attempts at bonding (Ganong et al., 1999).

Common activities stepparents use to get their stepchildren to like them include doing fun things as a family, going on family outings, playing games, nonverbally expressing feelings, spending money on things the stepchildren want, and spending time talking together. Although stepchildren may have fun doing things as a family, group activities do not necessarily offer many opportunities for stepparents and stepchildren to interact directly with each other. One-on-one activities, such as playing board games, going fishing, and having conversations between just the stepparent and stepchild, appear to be the most effective means for bonding (Ganong et al., 1999).

Cohabiting with a New Partner

One of the issues that many divorced people face is whether to live together with a new partner before remarriage. If either partner has children, the effects on them need to be considered. Isaacs and Leon (1988b) studied the adjustment of children of divorced mothers under four different circumstances: (1) The mother remarried, (2) she lived with a partner but was not remarried, (3) she was seriously involved but not living with a partner, and (4) she was not seriously involved. The children whose mothers were not remarried but were living with their new partner had substantially more behavioral problems than did any of the other groups.

The most well-adjusted group was children whose mothers were not involved, followed by those whose mothers had remarried. This suggests that divorced parents should take children into consideration when deciding the degree of commitment and the living arrangement.

Co-parents and Parenting Coalitions

An ideal for cooperative postdivorce parenting is co-parenting by divorced parents and a parenting coalition when there are more than two parenting adults after remarriage (Visher and Visher, 1989). In **co-parenting,** the two divorced parents cooperate rather than compete in the task of raising their children. In a **parenting coalition,** the biological parents (now divorced and remarried) plus the stepparents cooperate in rearing their own children and any stepchildren. The children have contact with both of their parents and with their stepparents.

There are a number of advantages to these kinds of cooperative parenting. The children's needs, as well as the needs of adults, can be met more adequately than if there is continued antagonism between adults. The children are not caught in a web of hostility, and their chances of becoming messengers between two households are greatly reduced, as is their fear of losing a parent. The power struggles between households are lessened as well. The children's self-esteem is enhanced, so they are easier to be with. Not only that, but the parents' responsibilities are lessened since the task of rearing the children is shared.

Frequently, adults are not aware of the pain they are causing their children by their hostile behavior. If they decide to control the anger, the children benefit from the new atmosphere of cooperation (Visher and Visher, 1989). However, despite evidence that a positive relationship is beneficial for children's adjustment and well-being, most ex-spouses do not get along well, which results in many nonresidential fathers eventually withdrawing and having limited or no contact with their children (Hetherington and Jodl, 1994). In contrast to fathers, nonresidential

co-parenting Two divorced parents cooperating rather than competing in the task of raising their children.

parenting coalition The biological parents (now divorced and remarried) plus the stepparents, who cooperate in rearing their own children and any stepchildren.

In a stepfamily, instead of obtaining one new brother or sister at a time, a child may get several at once. The child may also be confronted with the parent's having to share attention with stepsiblings.

mothers are almost twice as likely to remain in contact with their children following divorce, and stepmothers and biological mothers are more likely to get into competitive relationships that lead to loyalty conflicts in children (Hetherington and Jodl, 1994). It is important to remember that mothers have been referred to as the gatekeepers to relationships of other people with their children. This is especially noticeable in children's relations with both noncustodial fathers and stepfathers (Hetherington and Stanley-Hagan, 1999).

STEPSIBLING RELATIONSHIPS

Sibling relationships in stepfamilies that are warm and supportive are associated with greater social competence and responsibility in children, whereas sibling rivalry and aggression are associated with antisocial behavior (Hetherington and Jodl, 1994). The term **sibling rivalry** refers to the competition of brothers and sisters for the attention, approval, and affection of parents. The problem arises be-

sibling rivalry   The competition of brothers and sisters for the attention, approval, and affection of parents.

cause of envy and fear that one brother or sister is receiving more physical or emotional care and benefits from parents.

Sibling rivalry is often exaggerated in the stepfamily. Instead of obtaining one new brother or sister, a child may get several all at once. And the stepsiblings may not be helpless infants, but children of similar or older ages who can be very demanding of the child's own parent. From the children's point of view, a tendency to be jealous is quite understandable. The children may have become used to living with one parent and to seeking out that parent for help, comfort, and advice. Then they are confronted with their parent's turning his or her attention to a new spouse and stepchildren. Stepsiblings may also be forced to share living quarters, and even their own bedroom, as well as all other spaces such as bathrooms and playrooms. They may find their toys broken, their things messed up, their clothes borrowed, and so on. However, on average, relationships among stepsiblings are less contentious than among biologically related siblings, particularly in adolescence. This may be due to ambiguity in the stepsibling role and to the lack of connection and involvement among many stepsiblings. It is also possible that children can more easily understand that a different relationship exists with their siblings based on biological relatedness of parent and child (Hetherington and Stanley-Hagan, 1999).

About half of all women who remarry give birth in their second marriage (Wineberg, 1990). Sibling rivalry in the blended family becomes more complex than in the biological family. Biological parents may have a tendency to show preferential treatment, either favoring their own offspring or overcompensating for the absence of biological ties and favoring their stepchildren (Hobart, 1987).

The initial reactions of stepsiblings or future stepsiblings to one another are not always indicative of the degree of problems in the future. Children who seem suspicious and distant from one another at first can grow into loyal and trusting friends. Stepsiblings have been known to become very proud of one another. Younger children often idolize older stepsiblings, who may become very protective of younger stepsiblings. Learning to share with one another and to live with others who have not been part of one's immediate family is a broadening, enriching experience and helps children, who

otherwise tend to be egocentric and selfish, to share and to be tolerant of others. It is easier to build positive relationships when the children are young. Generally, younger children are more trusting and accepting than older children and more flexible in making adjustments. Also, families with harmonious relationships between the spouses show less sibling rivalry than do families in which the marriage is troubled, indicating the effect of the total marriage on the children in the family.

Some couples who have children of their own report that having a baby improves stepsibling relationships. One study reported that the birth of a new sibling in stepfamilies was universally positive, with none of the children in the sample rating it as negative (E. Anderson et al., 1999). The new baby can serve as a bond between the two groups of children. It gives them something in common and something to care for besides themselves and can unite them around a mutual interest.

A QUESTION OF POLICY

STEPFAMILY RIGHTS

As stated in the chapter, stepparents have no legal rights to their stepchildren if a legal adoption has not occurred. If the marriage ends, regardless of how many years they were the stepparent, they may have no custody rights, legal responsibility for child support, or visitation rights with the child. Basically, the relationship of the stepparent to the stepchild is legally terminated upon the divorce from or death of the custodial parent.

The legal standing of stepchildren would be improved by adoption, but the stepparent can only adopt if the noncustodial natural parent has relinquished his or her parental rights. Even when noncustodial parents offer no child support and are absent from the child's life, they rarely are willing to give up parental rights. Mason (2003) believes that "federal and state policies affecting families and children, as well as policies governing private sector employee benefits, insurance and other critical areas of everyday life, may need to be adapted to address the concerns of modern stepfamilies" (p. 97). The

American Bar Association Family Law Section is working on legislative reforms regarding stepparents' legal rights to discipline, to provide child support, to receive visitation and custody rights. As one can imagine, there is a lot of controversy surrounding these issues.

QUESTIONS TO CONSIDER:

Should stepchildren receive the survivor and death benefits that a natural child would if the stepparent dies? Should this be based on the number of years a family relationship was established? Discuss.

How can a will protect the interests of a stepfamily given the fact that the stepchild has no inheritance rights if his or her stepparent dies?

What happens to the relationship between stepparent and stepchild in the case of a divorce? What responsibility, if any, does the stepparent have to the child?

What policy should be in place for stepchildren who have been economically and emotionally dependent on a stepparent for many years?

SUMMARY

1. Marrying more than once has become quite common. The majority of divorced people also have children; when they remarry, new stepfamilies are created.

2. Remarried families may have one or two remarried spouses, each with or without children. Family relationships and integration become quite complicated and difficult in reconstituted families.

3. The probability of divorce is slightly greater in remarriages than in first marriages, but successful remarrieds state that their new marriage is better than their first marriage. Overall, research indicates few differences in marital satisfaction between first marriages and remarriages.

4. Remarriage introduces some complexity not present in first marriage. The biggest challenge is children. Relationships with ex-spouses and stepsiblings can also pose problems.

5. Courtship and mate selection in remarriage are different from those in first marriage. The couple is older. The majority of remarrieds have children. Ex-spouses and family members may become involved in the courtship of the couple. Some people want to marry someone like their ex-spouse, or they try to pressure their new mate to be like the former one.

6. Couples carry expectations from one marriage to another. One expectation is that being married to a second spouse is going to be similar in some ways to marriage to the first spouse. One result is that spouses replicate the mistakes of their first marriage in remarriage or have real apprehension that the problems and hurts that they experienced before will happen again. This fear makes them oversensitive and reminds them of the difficulties they had before.

7. Another challenge may arise because of confusion over role expectations and enactment. A person may desire a spouse to play a role similar to or completely different from the one played by a former spouse.

8. Financial problems may emerge in remarriage because of the necessity of supporting both the new family and the children from the previous family.

9. Some remarrieds pool all of their resources in a "common pot," distributing them according to each individual family member's needs. Other remarrieds use a "two-pot" system in which each partner contributes a specific amount to the ongoing maintenance of the household, with the children supported by their biological parents.

10. Individuals who divorce typically have to develop a new relationship with the former spouse when children are involved. This new relationship is often a difficult one, particularly in the early stages of divorce, as ex-spouses deal with feelings of ambivalence, anger, attachment, and remorse, as well as sometimes viciously fighting and passionately reconciling. In general, relationships between ex-spouses seem to reach a low level of intensity after a number of years, with most remarried individuals not feeling a need to maintain a close relationship with the former spouse.

11. In the short term, there is less conflict in remarriages than in first marriages, but conflict increases as new problems arise.

12. In successful remarriages, spouses give themselves time to know each other well, resist the many pressures to remarry before they are ready, discuss every aspect of their relationship before marriage, have learned from past mistakes, and put their marriage first.

13. Many couples expect stepfamily relationships to be like those of primary families. Many are disappointed, because stepfamily and primary family relationships are not the same.

14. Part of the problem of living in a stepfamily is that positive roles of stepparents are not clearly defined.

15. Most family scholars who study divorce and remarriage today conclude that what happens inside a family is more important than family type or structure in influencing children's adjustment. Children, regardless of the family structure, exhibit greater well-being, higher achievement, more socially responsible behavior and social competence, and fewer behavioral problems when they are raised in a loving, harmonious, supportive family environment.

16. Overall, the friendship style of stepparenting seems to be the most successful in facilitating bonding with stepchildren.

17. Children whose mothers cohabit with their new partner before marriage have more behavior problems than those whose mothers are not living with a boyfriend, whose mothers are remarried, or whose mothers are not involved in a relationship.

18. Stepchildren are all individuals. They can't all be treated alike any more than can all biological children or stepparents be treated alike.

19. Co-parenting by divorced parents involves co-operating in the task of raising the children. A parenting coalition involves the biological parents and the stepparents in raising their own children and any stepchildren. Co-parenting and parenting coalitions after divorce are advantageous to children and parents alike.

20. Sibling rivalry refers to the competition of siblings for the attention, approval, and affection of parents. The situation is often aggravated in the stepfamily.

21. Couples can be encouraged by the fact that the initial reactions of stepsiblings or future stepsiblings to one another are not always indicative of the degree of problems in the future. Many become very close and loyal friends. Couples report that having a baby of their own improves stepsibling relationships, although it can also lead to sibling rivalry.

KEY TERMS

co-parenting   parenting coalitions   sibling rivalry

QUESTIONS FOR THOUGHT

1. If you were divorced at age 30 with two school-age children in your custody, would you want to remarry? Why or why not? If you did remarry, what are some of the problems you would be most likely to encounter? If you did not remarry, what are some of the problems you would be most likely to encounter?

2. What do you believe would be the differences between being a parent and being a stepparent as far as relationships with children are concerned?

3. If you divorced, what sorts of things would you try to do that would be in the best interests of your children?

4. If you divorced and wanted to remarry, what would you do to ensure that your remarriage was successful?

SUGGESTED READINGS

Bray, J. H., and Kelly, J. (1999). *Stepfamilies: Love, Marriage, and Parenting in the First Decade*. New York: Broadway Books. Gives guidelines for problem solving in stepfamilies.

Cath, S. H., and Shopper, M. (2001). *Stepparenting: Creating and Recreating Families in America Today*. Hillsdale, NJ: Analytic Press. Examines the adult experience of divorce.

Kirkness Norwood, P., and Wingender, T. (1999). *The Enlightened Stepmother: Revolutionizing the Role*. New York: Morrow/Avon. Helps individuals prepare for the role for which most women are overwhelmingly unprepared.

Pryor, J., and Rodgers, B. (2001). *Children in Changing Families: Life After Parent Separation*. Malden, MA: Blackwell. Offers insights into why some children survive change in families better than others.

Shomberg, E. F. (1999). *Blending Families: A Guide for Parents, Step-Families, Step-Grandparents and Everyone Building a Successful New Family*. New York: Berkely Publishing Group. Focuses on the complexity of intergenerational stepfamilies.

Thoele, S. P. (1999). *Courage to Be a Stepmom: Finding Your Place Without Losing Yourself*. Berkeley, CA: Wildcat Canyon Press. Addresses the emotions felt by stepmothers and offers suggestions for meeting individuals' needs while building relationships with stepchildren.

Glossary

abortion The expulsion of the fetus. Can be either spontaneous or induced.

abruptio placentae The premature separation of the placenta from the uterine wall.

affective sensitivity Empathy, or the ability to identify with the feelings, thoughts, and attitudes of another person.

affinity A relationship formed by marriage without ties of blood.

AIDS Acquired immunodeficiency syndrome; a sexually transmitted disease caused by the human immunodeficiency virus (HIV) and characterized by irreversible damage to the body's immune system and, eventually, death.

androgyny A blending of male and female characteristics and roles; especially, a lack of gender-typing with respect to roles.

Apgar score A widely used system to evaluate the physical condition of the newborn, named after the originator, Virginia Apgar.

artificial insemination Injection of sperm into the woman's vagina or uterus for the purpose of inducing pregnancy.

attachment theory Theory suggesting that early interactions with parents lead to the formation of attachments that reflect children's perceptions of their own self-worth and their expectations about intimate relationships.

autonomy The assertion of independence and self-will.

avoidance Method of dealing with conflict by avoiding the people, situations, and issues that stimulate it.

bag of water (amniotic sac) Sac containing the fluid in which the fetus is suspended.

bargaining The process by which two parties decide what each will give and receive in arriving at a decision.

bilateral descent Inheritance is passed through both the male and the female line.

binuclear family An original family divided into two families by divorce.

blastocyst The mass of cells 3–4 days after fertilization takes place that grows into an embryo.

blended, or reconstituted, family A family formed when a widowed or divorced person, with or without children, marries another person who may or may not have been married before and who may or may not have children.

B-love Term used by Maslow for Being-love, which is love for the very being and uniqueness of another person.

body language Posture, facial expression, still or tense muscles, blushing, panting, tears, sweating, shivering, increased pulse rate, thumping heart, and other bodily reactions that convey feelings and reactions.

bonding Development of emotional attachment between the mother and newborn immediately after birth.

breech birth When the buttocks or feet are the first part of the baby to pass through the vagina.

castration Removal of the testicles.

catharsis Venting negative emotions to rid oneself of them so that they can be replaced by more positive ones.

cervical cap A small, thimble-shaped, rubber barrier that fits over the cervix and prevents the sperm from entering the uterus.

cesarean section Removal of the fetus by incising the abdominal and uterine wall.

child abuse May include not only physical assaults on a child but also malnourishment, abandonment, neglect, emotional abuse, and sexual abuse.

chlamydia A family of infections caused by a bacterium leading to nongonococcal urethritis and epididymitis in men, and cervical infections and pelvic inflammatory disease (PID) in women.

coercive power The threat of physical force or other types of punishment to force compliance.

cognition Literally, the act of knowing; the act of becoming acquainted with the world and the objects, people, and conditions in it.

cognitive developmental theory A theory suggesting that gender roles and identities cannot be learned until children reach a certain stage of intellectual development.

cohabiting family Two people of the opposite sex who are living together and sharing sexual expression and who are committed to their relationship without formal legal marriage.

cohort A group of people born during the same period of time.

coitus interruptus Withdrawal of the penis from the vagina prior to ejaculation; used as an attempt at birth control.

combination pills Oral contraceptives containing both estrogen and progestin.

common-law marriage A marriage by mutual consent, without a license, recognized as legal under certain conditions by some states.

communication A message one person sends and another receives.

companionate love A low-key emotion with feelings of affection and deep attachment.

compatibility The capability of living together in harmony.

conciliation counseling Marriage counseling ordered by the court in which spouses try to decide whether they want to dissolve their marriage or agree to try to solve their problems.

condom A latex rubber sheath worn over the penis to prevent sperm from being ejaculated into the vagina; also prevents venereal disease.

conflict theory A theory that family conflict is normal and that the task is not to eliminate conflict but to learn to control it so that it becomes constructive.

consanguinity The state of being related by blood; having descended from a common ancestor.

conscious love Rational, reasoning love.

constructive arguments Arguments that stick with the issues, that attack the problem and not the other person, that employ rational methods, and that result in greater understanding, consensus, compromise, and closeness between two people.

consummate love A term used by Sternberg to describe love as a combination of intimacy, passion, and commitment.

contraceptive patch A patch applied weekly to either the buttocks, abdomen, upper torso, back, or outer upper arm that releases hormones every 24 hours to prevent pregnancy.

co-parenting Two divorced parents cooperating rather than competing in the task of raising their children.

corporal punishment Physical or bodily punishment with the intention of inflicting pain but not injury for the purpose of correction or control.

crisis A drastic change in the course of events; a turning point that affects future events.

crisis overload A series of crises occurring one after another until they become more than a person can handle.

culture The sum total of ways of living, including the values, beliefs, aesthetic standards, linguistic expressions, patterns of thinking, behavioral norms, and styles of communication a group of people has developed to ensure its survival in a particular physical and human environment.

cunnilingus Stimulation of the female genitals with the mouth.

custody A term that refers to both legal custody (the parent's right to make decisions regarding the welfare of the child) and physical custody (the parent's right to have the child living with him or her).

date rape The forcing of involuntary sexual compliance on a person during a voluntary, prearranged date or after a couple meets informally in a social setting.

dating A courting practice in which two people meet and participate in activities together in order to get to know each other.

dependent love Love that one develops for someone who fulfills one's needs.

destructive arguments Arguments that attack the other person rather than the problem; that increase resentment and hostility and undermine trust, friendship, and affectionate feelings; that result in greater alienation; and that do not solve the problem.

developmental tasks Growth responsibilities that arise at various stages of life.

diaphragm A thick, dome-shaped latex rubber cap that is stretched over a collapsible metal ring, designed to cover the cervical opening to prevent sperm from entering the uterus.

discipline A means by which socialization takes place; the process of instruction in proper conduct or action.

D-love Term used by Maslow for Deficiency-love, which develops when another person meets one's needs.

dopamine A neurotransmitter that functions in the parts of the brain that control emotions and bodily movement.

double-bind communication Conflicting messages sent when verbal messages and body language don't agree.

douching Squirting liquid containing vinegar or another substance into the vagina; sometimes used to try to wash out sperm after intercourse.

dual-career family Also called dual-professional family; a subtype of the dual-earner family in which there are two career-committed partners, both of whom are trying to fulfill professional roles that require continuous development.

dual-earner family A family in which both spouses are in the paid labor force.

ectopic pregnancy Attachment of the blastocyst and growth of the embryo in any location other than inside the uterus.

ego resiliency (ER) The generalized capacity for flexible and resourceful adaptation to stressors.

embryo transplant The process of removing an embryo from the uterus of a donor and implanting it into the uterus of another woman.

emergency contraceptives Oral contraceptives taken after intercourse to prevent unwanted pregnancy.

endogamy Marriage within a particular group.

endorphins Chemical neurotransmitters that have a sedative effect on the body.

equity theory A subcategory of exchange theory holding that people seek a fair and balanced exchange in which the partners can mutually give and take what is needed.

erotic love Sexual, sensuous love.

ethnicity The way people define themselves as part of a group through similarities in ancestry and cultural heritage.

evolutionary theories Theories suggesting that genetic heritage is more important than social learning in the development of gender roles.

exchange theory The theory that people choose relationships in which they can maximize their benefits and minimize their costs.

exogamy Marriage outside of a particular group.

expert power Power that is given because a person is considered superior in knowledge of a particular subject.

expressive role The role of the family in meeting the emotional and social needs of family members.

extended family An individual, possibly a partner, any children you might have, and other relatives who live in the household or nearby.

extradyadic sexual activity Sexual activity outside the dyadic, or couple, relationship.

familism Emphasis on the needs of the family above those of the individual.

family Any group of people united by ties of marriage, blood, or adoption, or any sexually expressive relationship, in which (1) the adults cooperate financially for their mutual support, (2) the people are committed to one another in an intimate interpersonal relationship, (3) the members see their individual identities as importantly attached to the group, and (4) the group has an identity of its own.

family developmental theory A theory that divides the family life cycle into phases, or stages, over the life span and emphasizes the developmental tasks that need to be accomplished by family members at each stage.

family life cycle The phases, or stages, of the family life span, each of which is characterized by changes in family structure, composition, and functions.

family of origin The family into which you are born and in which you are raised.

family of procreation The family you establish if you have children of your own.

family planning Having children by choice and not by chance; having the number of children wanted at the time planned.

family violence Any rough or extended use of physical force or aggression or verbal abuse by one family member toward another.

feedback Response to the message another has sent and disclosure of one's own feelings and ideas.

fellatio Stimulation of the male genitals with the mouth.

femininity Personality and behavioral characteristics of a female according to culturally defined standards of femaleness.

feminist theory Theory (or perspective) that focuses on male dominance in families and society and examines how gender differences are related to power differentials between men and women.

feminization of poverty The trend toward increasing proportions of women, regardless of ethnicity or age, living in poverty.

filtering process A process by which mates are sorted by filtering out ineligibles according to various standards.

flextime A company policy that allows employees to choose the most convenient hours for them to work during the day, selected from hours designated by the employer.

friendship love A love based on common concerns and interests, companionship, and respect for the partner's personality and character.

gamete intrafallopian transfer (GIFT) The process of inserting sperm cells and an egg cell directly into the fallopian tube, where fertilization is expected to occur.

gaslighting The process by which one person destroys the self-confidence, perception, and sense of reality of another person.

gay or lesbian family Two people of the same sex who are living together and sharing sexual expression and commitment.

gender Personality traits and behavior that characterize one as masculine or feminine.

gender identity A person's personal, internal sense of maleness or femaleness, which is expressed in personality and behavior.

gender role A person's outward expression of maleness or femaleness in a social setting.

gender-role congruence Agreement between partners' gender-role expectations and their performance.

gender schema theory A theory suggesting that people have very definite ideas about how males and females should look and behave, based on the framework of logic and ideas used to organize information and make sense of it.

gender stereotypes Assumed differences, norms, attitudes, and expectations about men and women.

generational transmission The process by which one generation passes knowledge, values, attitudes, roles, and habits on to the next generation.

gonorrhea A sexually transmitted disease caused by the bacterium Neisseria gonorrheae.

hepatitis B A highly contagious sexually transmitted disease that affects the liver. It can cause extreme illness or even death.

herpes simplex A sexually transmitted disease caused by a virus that can produce cold sores or fever blisters on the mouth or face (oral herpes) and similar symptoms in the genital area (genital herpes).

heterogamy The selection of a partner who is different from oneself.

heterologous insemination Artificial insemination by using the sperm of a donor. Also called artificial insemination–donor (AID).

homogamy The selection of a partner who is similar to oneself.

homologous insemination Artificial insemination by using the sperm of the man. Also called artificial insemination–husband.

hooking up Engaging in sexual behavior—from kissing to having intercourse—without emotional involvment.

human chorionic gonadotropin (HCG) A hormone produced by the placenta that, if present in the mother's urine, is an indication of pregnancy.

human papillomavirus (HPV) Any of a group of viruses that infect the skin. There are more than 70 types of HPV; 30 of these are sexually transmitted and cause genital warts.

hypergamous union Marriage in which the woman marries upward on the social ladder.

hypogamous union Marriage in which the woman marries beneath herself on the social ladder.

ideal mate theory A theory that people tend to marry someone who fulfills their fantasy of what an ideal mate should be like, based partly on early childhood experiences.

imaging The process of playacting to present oneself in the best possible manner.

implementation power Power that sets decisions in motion.

incest Sexual activity between two people who are closely related.

informational power Power acquired because of extensive knowledge of a specific area.

instrumental role The role of the family in meeting the needs of society or the physical needs of family members.

intergenerational stake Family members' perceptions of closeness, especially as they relate to life course concerns that characterize each generation.

interpersonal sources of conflict Those tensions that occur in the relationships between people.

intrauterine device (IUD) A device that is inserted into the uterus and worn there as a means of preventing pregnancy.

intrauterine system (IUS) A contraceptive device that is inserted into the uterus and releases very small amounts of progestin continuously for up to 5 years.

in vitro fertilization (IVF) Removing the egg cell from the mother, fertilizing it with the partner's sperm in the laboratory, and then implanting the fertilized egg in the uterine wall.

involuntary stable (permanent) singles Never-marrieds and previously marrieds who wanted to marry, who have not found a mate, and who have more or less accepted being single.

involuntary temporary singles Never-marrieds and previously marrieds who have actively been seeking a mate but have not found one.

joint legal custody Custody shared by both parents, both of whom are responsible for child rearing and for making decisions regarding the child.

labor Rhythmic muscular contractions of the uterus that expel the baby.

Lamaze method A popular childbirth training and delivery method in which the woman comes to be in control of the childbirth experience by getting in good physical shape, learning controlled breathing and muscle relaxation techniques, and receiving emotional support from her partner.

laparoscopy Sterilization procedure whereby a tubular instrument is passed through the abdominal wall and the fallopian tubes are severed and/or closed.

latchkey children Unsupervised children who care for themselves before or after school, on weekends, or during holidays while their parents work. They commonly carry keys to let themselves in the house or apartment.

legitimate power Power that is bestowed by society on men and women as their right according to social prescription.

limerence A term used by Tennov (1979) to describe the intense, wildly emotional highs and lows of being in love.

machismo Spanish for "manhood"; masculinity.

marital adjustment The process of modifying, adapting, and altering individual and couple patterns of behavior and interaction to achieve maximum satisfaction in the relationship.

marital adjustment tasks Areas of concern in marriage in which adjustments need to be made.

masculinity Personality and behavioral characteristics of a male according to culturally defined standards of maleness.

matriarchal family A family in which the mother is head of the household with authority over other family members.

matrilineal descent Inheritance that is traced through the female line.

matrilocal residence A residential pattern in which newlyweds reside with or near the woman's family.

minipill An oral contraceptive containing progestin only.

Naegele's formula A method of calculating the expected date of birth by subtracting 3 months from the first day of the last period and adding 7 days.

narcissistic love Love of self; selfish, self-centered love.

needs theories Theories of mate selection proposing that we select partners who will fulfill our own needs—both complementary and instrumental.

negative affect reciprocity A pattern of communication in unhappy couples whereby partners respond negatively to each other's statements.

negative identification The effort on the part of the child not to be like the parent.

neolocal residence A residential pattern in which newlyweds leave their parents' home and reside in a new location of their choice rather than with either family.

no-fault divorce A legal approach that eliminates fault as a precondition for access to courts and recognizes the right of individuals to petition for divorce on the grounds of irretrievable breakdown of the marriage or irreconcilable differences.

noncontingent reinforcement Unconditional approval of another person.

norepinephrine A hormone secreted by the adrenal glands that has a stimulating effect on blood pressure and acts as a neurotransmitter.

norms See *social norms.*

nuclear family A father, a mother, and their children.

observational modeling The process by which children observe, imitate, and model the behavior of others around them.

open adoption A system of adoption in which the birth mother is permitted to meet and play an active role in selecting the adoptive parents and to maintain some form of contact with her child depending on the agreement reached.

oral contraceptives Birth control pills taken orally (by mouth).

orchestration power The power to make the important decisions that determine family lifestyle.

ovum transfer The process of artificially inseminating a volunteer female with sperm from an infertile woman's partner and removing the zygote after 5 days and transplanting it to the mother-to-be, who carries the child during pregnancy.

parental identification and modeling The process by which the child adopts and internalizes parental values.

parent image theory A theory of mate selection that a person is likely to marry someone resembling his or her parent of the opposite sex.

parenting coalition The biological parents (now divorced and remarried) plus the stepparents, who cooperate in rearing their own children and any stepchildren.

patriarchal family A family in which the father is head of the household with authority over other family members.

patrilineal descent Inheritance that is traced through the male line.

patrilocal residence A residential pattern in which a newlywed couple resides with or near the man's family.

pedophilia A sexual perversion in which a person's primary or exclusive method of achieving sexual arousal is by fantasizing about or engaging in sexual activity with prepubertal children.

personal sources of conflict Those that originate within the individual when inner drives, instincts, and values pull against one another.

physical sources of conflict Inner tensions having a physical origin, such as fatigue, hunger, or a headache.

placebo A pill that has no pharmacological effect.

placenta previa A complication of pregnancy in which the placenta grows partly or all the way over the opening to the cervix, usually causing abruptio placentae.

polyandrous family A woman married to more than one husband.

polygamous family A single family unit based on the marriage of one person to two or more mates.

polygynous family A man married to more than one woman.

positive identification The attachment of a child to positive images of desired loving behavior.

positive signs Signs of pregnancy detected by the physician that indicate positively that the woman is pregnant.

postparental years The period between the last child leaving home and the spouses' retirement; also called the empty-nest years.

posttraumatic stress disorder Severe stress reactions that occur after a person has suffered a trauma.

power In intimate relationships, the ability to influence one's partner to get what one wants.

power processes The ways in which power is applied.

prepared childbirth Physical, social, intellectual, and emotional preparation for the birth of a baby.

presumptive signs Signs by which a woman presumes she is pregnant.

probable signs Signs detected by the examining physician that indicate pregnancy is probable.

progestin implant A capsule containing progestin that is implanted under the skin and can remain in place for several years to prevent pregnancy.

progestin injection An injection of progestin to prevent pregnancy.

propinquity In mate selection, the tendency to choose someone who is geographically near.

psychosocial task The skills, knowledge, functions, and attitudes individuals need to acquire at different periods in their lives.

pubic lice Parasitic insects occupying hairy regions of the body that suck blood from their human hosts, causing itching. Known informally as "crabs."

reciprocal parent–child interaction The influence of the parent on the child and the child on the parent so that each modifies the behavior of the other.

Rh incompatibility A condition in which the mother has Rh-negative blood and the fetus has Rh-positive blood or vice versa.

rhythm method A method of birth control whereby the couple have intercourse only during those times of the menstrual cycle when the woman is least likely to get pregnant.

rites of passage Ceremonies by which people pass from one social status to another.

roles See *social roles.*

romantic love A profoundly tender or passionate affection for another person, characterized by intense feelings and emotion.

rooming-in Method of postpartum care in which the mother and father care for their newborn themselves in an area of the hospital assigned to them.

sandwich generation Middle-aged adults caught between caregiving for their children and for their elderly parents.

scabies A parasitic infection of mites that burrow into the skin, lay eggs, and cause itching.

scapegoating Blaming someone else for every bad thing that happens.

selfism A personal value system that emphasizes that the way to find happiness is through self-gratification and narcissism.

serotonin A chemical neurotransmitter that has a stimulating effect on the body and can produce a feeling of intense pleasure.

sexually transmitted disease (STD) Disease transmitted through sexual contact.

show Blood-tinged mucus that is passed when the mucus plug is expelled; an early sign of labor.

sibling rivalry The competition of brothers and sisters for the attention, approval, and affection of parents.

single-parent family A parent (who may or may not have been married) and one or more children.

situational or environmental sources of conflict These include living conditions, societal pressures, cultural strains, and unexpected events.

socialization The process by which people learn the ways of a given society or social group so that they can function within it.

social learning theory A theory that suggests that parents act as role models for their children and that children learn to imitate their parents' behavior, attitudes, and perceptions.

social learning theory of gender identity A theory emphasizing that boys develop "maleness" and girls develop "femaleness" through exposure to scores of influences—including parents, peers, television, and schools—that teach them what it means to be a man or a woman in their culture.

social norms Expectations for behavior as one performs social roles.

social roles Culturally defined social positions such as mother, grandparent, supervisor, or student.

social structure/cultural theories Theories suggesting that most of the differences between male and female gender roles are established because of the status, power, and division of labor in a given society.

sole legal custody Situation in which the noncustodial parent forfeits the right to make decisions about the children's health, education, or religious training.

spermicides Chemicals that are toxic to sperm and used as a contraceptive in the form of foam, suppository, cream, jelly, or film.

spouse abuse Physical or emotional mistreatment of one's spouse.

steady dating Dating one person exclusively.

stepfamily A remarried man and/or woman plus children from a former marriage.

sterilization The process of rendering a person infertile, by performing either a vasectomy in the male or tubal ligation in the female.

structural-functional theory A theory that emphasizes the function of the family as a social institution in meeting the needs of society.

structured separation A time-limited approach in which partners terminate cohabitation, commit themselves to regularly scheduled therapy with a therapist, and agree to regular interpersonal contact—with a moratorium on a final decision either to reunite or to divorce.

surrogate mother A woman who agrees to be artificially inseminated with the semen of a father-to-be, to carry the fetus to term, and then to give the child to the couple along with all parental rights.

symbolic interaction theory A theory that describes the family as a unit of interacting personalities communicating through symbols.

syphilis A sexually transmitted disease caused by the spirochete bacterium *Treponema pallidum.* It can be fatal if not treated.

systems theory A theory that emphasizes the interdependence of family members and how those members affect one another.

theory A tentative explanation of facts and data that have been observed.

theory of primary interest and presumed competence The theory that the person who is most interested in, most involved with, and best qualified to make a particular choice will be more likely to do so.

toxemia A serious complication of pregnancy characterized by waterlogging of connective tissue (edema).

transgendered People who feel their biological sex does not match their gender identity.

transsexual A transgendered person who seeks to live as a member of the opposite sex with the help of hormones and surgery.

transverse birth When the shoulder and arm of the baby are the first parts seen at the opening of the vagina.

tubal ligation Female sterilization by severing and/or closing the fallopian tubes so that the ovum cannot pass down the tube.

tubal pregnancy A type of ectopic pregnancy in which attachment of the blastocyst and growth of the embryo occur in the fallopian tube.

umbilical cord The hollow cord connecting the circulation system of the fetus to the placenta.

unconditional positive regard Acceptance of another person as he or she is.

vaginal contraceptive ring A flexible, transparent ring that is inserted into the vagina and releases a combination of estrogen and progestin continuously at a low dose for 1 month.

vasectomy Male sterilization whereby the vas deferens are cut and tied to prevent the sperm from being ejaculated out of the penis.

ventilation The process of airing, or expressing, negative emotions and feelings.

voidable marriage A marriage that can be set aside by annulment under certain prescribed legal circumstances.

void marriage A marriage considered invalid in the first place because it was illegal.

voluntarily childless family A couple who decide not to have children.

voluntary stable (permanent) singles Never-marrieds and previously marrieds who choose to be single.

voluntary temporary singles Never-marrieds and previously marrieds who are not opposed to the idea of marriage but are not currently seeking mates.

work–family spillover The extent to which participation in one domain (e.g., work) impacts participation in another domain (e.g., family).

zygote A fertilized egg cell.

Bibliography

Abbey, A., Andrews, F. M., and Halman, L. J. (1994). Psychosocial predictors of life quality. *Journal of Family Issues, 15,* 253–271.

Abbey, A., Ross, L. T., Mcduffie, D., and Mcauslan, P. (1996). Alcohol and dating risk factors for sexual assault among college women. *Psychology of Women Quarterly, 20*(1), 147–169.

Abbott, D. A., and Brody, G. H. (1985). The relation of child age, gender, and number of children to the marital adjustment of wives. *Journal of Marriage and the Family, 47,* 77–84.

Abel, G. G., Becker, J., Cunningham-Rathner, J., Mittlemen, M., and Rouleau, J. L. (1988). Multiple paraphiliac diagnosis among sex offenders. *Bulletin of the American Academy of Psychiatry and Law, 16,* 153–168.

Abell, E., Clawson, M., Washington, W. N., Bost, K. K., and Vaughn, B. E. (1996). Parenting values, attitudes, behaviors, and goals of African American mothers from a low-income population in relation to social and societal context. *Journal of Family Issues, 17,* 593–613.

Abell, E., and Gecas, B. (1997). Guilt, shame, and family socialization. *Journal of Family Issues, 18,* 99–123.

Abelman, R., and Pettey, G. R. (1989). Child attributes as determinants of parental television-viewing mediation. *Journal of Family Issues, 10,* 251–266.

Abortion doesn't impair the ability of women to become pregnant. (1985). *Family Planning Perspectives, 17,* 39, 40.

Abortion Law Homepage. (2000, April 10). Partial-birth abortion laws. Retrieved from http://members.aol.com/abtrbng/pbal.htm

Abramson, P. R. (1983). Woman attracted to man she couldn't be happy with. *Medical Aspects of Human Sexuality, 17,* 141.

Acitelli, L. K. (2001). Maintaining and enhancing a relationship by attending to it. In J. H. Harvey and A. Wenzel (Eds.), *Close relationships: Maintenance and Enhancement* (pp. 153–167). Mahwah, NJ: Erlbaum.

Ackard, D. M., and Neumark-Sztainer, D. (2002). Date violence and date rape among adolescents: Associations with disordered eating behaviors and psychological health. *Child Abuse and Neglect, 26*(5), 455–473.

Adamcyzk-Robinette, S. L., Fletcher, A. C., and Wright, K. (2002). Understanding the authoritative parenting–early adolescent tobacco use link: The mediating role of peer tobacco use. *Journal of Youth and Adolescence, 31*(4), 311–318.

Adams, R. G. (1985). People would talk: Normative barriers to cross-sex friendships for elderly women. *The Gerontologist, 25,* 605–611.

Adelman, P. K., Chadwick, K., and Baerger, D. R. (1996). Marital quality of Black and White adults over the life course. *Journal of Social and Personal Relationships, 13,* 361–384.

Afterschool Alliance. (2003). Closing the door on afterschool programs: An analysis of how the proposed cut to the 21st century community learning centers program will affect children and families in every state. Retrieved May 19, 2003, from http://afterschoolalliance.org

Agocha, V., and Cooper, M. (1999). Risk perceptions and safer-sex intentions: Does a partner's physical attractiveness undermine the use of risk-relevant information? *Personality and Social Psychology Bulletin, 25*(6), 746–759.

Ahmeduzzaman, M., and Roopnarine, J. L. (1992). Sociodemographic factors, functioning style, social support, and fathers' involvement with preschoolers in African-American families. *Journal of Marriage and the Family, 54,* 699–707.

Ahn, N. (1994). Teenage childbearing and high school completion: Accounting for individual heterogeneity. *Family Planning Perspectives, 26,* 17–21.

Ahrons, C. R., and Rodgers, R. (1987). *Divorced Families: A Multidisciplinary View.* New York: Norton.

Aizcorbe, A. Kennickell, A., and Moore, K. (2003). Recent changes in the U.S. family finances: Evidence from the 1998 and 2001 survey of consumer finances. *Federal Reserve Bulletin,* January 2003, 1–32.

Ahuvia, A. C., and Adelman, M. B. (1992). Formal intermediaries in the marriage market: A typology and review. *Journal of Marriage and the Family, 54,* 452–463.

Albrecht, S. L., Miller, N. K., and Clarke, L. L. (1994). Assessing the importance of family structure in understanding birth outcomes. *Journal of Marriage and the Family, 56,* 987–1003.

Albright, A. (1993). Postpartum depression: An overview. *Journal of Counseling and Development, 7,* 316–320.

Aldous, J. (1977). Family interaction patterns. *Annual Review of Sociology* (pp. 105–135). Palo Alto, CA: Annual Review.

Aldous, J. (1987). New views on the family life of the elderly and near-elderly. *Journal of Marriage and the Family, 49,* 227–234.

Aldous, J. (1995). New views of grandparents in intergenerational context. *Journal of Family Issues, 16,* 104–122.

Aldous, J., Ganey, R., Trees, S., and Marsh, L. C. (1991). Families and inflation: Who was hurt in the last high-inflation period? *Journal of Marriage and the Family, 53,* 123–134.

Alexander, P. C., and Lupfer, S. L. (1987). Family characteristics and long-term consequences associated with sexual abuse. *Archives of Sexual Behavior, 16,* 235–245.

Al-Krenawi, A., and Graham, J. R. (1998). Divorce among Muslim Arab women in Israel. *Journal of Divorce and Remarriage, 29,* 103–119.

Allan, G. (1985). *Family Life.* Oxford: Basil Blackwell.

Allen, A., and Thompson, T. (1984). Agreement, understanding, realization, and feeling understood as predictors of communicative satisfaction in marital dyads. *Journal of Marriage and the Family, 46,* 915–921.

Allen, K. R., and Pickett, R. S. (1987). Forgotten streams in the family life course: Utilization of qualitative retrospective interviews in the analysis of lifelong single women's family careers. *Journal of Marriage and the Family, 49,* 517–526.

Allen, S., and Hawkins, A. (1999). Maternal gatekeeping: Mothers' beliefs and behaviors that inhibit greater father involvement in family work. *Journal of Marriage and the Family, 61*(1), 199–212.

Allen, W., and Doherty, W. (1996). The responsibilities of fatherhood as perceived by African American teenage fathers. *Families in Society, 77*(3), 142–155.

Allers, C. T., and Benjack, K. J. (1991). Connections between childhood abuse and HIV infection. *Journal of Counseling and Development, 70,* 309–313.

Allers, C. T., Benjack, K. J., and Allers, N. T. (1992). Unresolved childhood sexual abuse: Are older adults affected? *Journal of Counseling and Development, 71,* 14–17.

Allgeier, A. R., Allgeier, E. R., and Rywick, T. (1981). Orientations toward abortion: Guilt or knowledge? *Adolescence, 16,* 273–280.

Althaus, F. (1991). Young adults choose alternatives to marriage, remain single longer. *Family Planning Perspectives, 23,* 45–46.

Althaus, F. (1992). Study finds low condom breakage rate, ties most slippage to improper use. *Family Planning Perspectives, 24,* 191–192.

Althaus, F. (1995). Most vasectomies are performed in urology practices by physicians using ligation and local anesthesia. *Family Planning Perspectives, 27,* 220–221.

Althaus, F. (1997). Women who use barrier methods with spermicide may have higher risks of urinary tract infections. *Family Planning Perspectives, 29,* 48–49.

Alwin, D. F. (1990). Cohort replacement and changes in parental socialization values. *Journal of Marriage and the Family, 52,* 347–360.

Amato, P. R. (1987). Family process in one-parent, stepparent, and intact families: The child's point of view. *Journal of Marriage and the Family, 49,* 327–337.

Amato, P. R. (1988). Long-term implications of parental divorce for adult self-concept. *Journal of Family Issues, 9,* 201–213.

Amato, P. R. (1989). Who cares for children in public places? Naturalistic observation of male and female caregivers. *Journal of Marriage and the Family, 51,* 981–990.

Amato, P. R. (1993). Children's adjustment to divorce: Theories, hypothesis, and empirical support. *Journal of Marriage and the Family, 55,* 23–38.

Amato, P. R. (1994a). The implications of research findings on children in stepfamilies. In A. Booth and J. Dunn (Eds.), *Stepfamilies: Who Benefits? Who Does Not?* (pp. 81–87). Hillsdale, NJ: Erlbaum.

Amato, P. R. (1994b). Father–child relations, mother–child relations, and offspring's psychological well-being in early adulthood. *Journal of Marriage and the Family, 56,* 1031–1042.

Amato, P. R. (1996). Explaining the intergenerational transmission of divorce. *Journal of Marriage and the Family, 58,* 628–640.

Amato, P. R. (2000). Diversity within single parent families. In D. H. Demo and K. R. Allen (Eds.), *Handbook of family diversity* (pp.149–172). London: Oxford University Press.

Amato, P. R. (2001). Children of divorce in the 1990s: An update of the Amato and Keith (1991) meta-analysis. *Journal of Family Psychology, 15*(3), 355–370.

Amato, P. R., and Booth, A. (1991). The consequences of divorce for attitudes toward divorce and gender roles. *Journal of Family Issues, 12,* 306–322.

Amato, P. R., and Booth, A. (1996). A perspective study of divorce in parent–child relationships. *Journal of Marriage and the Family, 58,* 356–365.

Amato, P. R., and Booth, A. (2001) The legacy of parents' marital discord: Consequences for children's marital quality. *Journal of Personality and Social Psychology, 81*(4), 627–638.

Amato, P. R., and DeBoer, D. D. (2001). The transmission of marital instability across generations: Relationship skills or commitment to marriage? *Journal of Marriage and the Family, 63*(4), 1038–1051.

Amato, P. R., and Gilbreth, J. G. (1999). Nonresident father and children's well-being: A meta-analysis. *Journal of Marriage and Family, 61,* 557–573.

Amato, P. R., and Keith, N. (1991). Parental divorce and the well-being of children: A meta-analysis. *Psychology Bulletin, 110,* 26–46.

Amato, P. R., Loomis, L. S., and Booth, A. (1995). Parental divorce, marital conflict, and offspring well-being during early adulthood. *Social Forces, 73*(3), 895–915.

Amato, P. R., and Ochiltree, G. (1986). Family resources and the development of child competence. *Journal of Marriage and the Family, 48,* 47–56.

Amato, P. R., and Partridge, S. (1987). Women and divorce with dependent children: Material, personal, family, and social well-being. *Family Relations, 36,* 316–320.

Ambert, A. (1988a). Relationships with former in-laws after divorce: A research note. *Journal of Marriage and the Family, 50,* 679–686.

Ambert, A. (1988b). Relationship between ex-spouses: Individual and dyadic perspectives. *Journal of Social and Personal Relationships, 5,* 327–346.

American Psychiatric Association. (1994). *Diagnostic and Statistical Manual of Mental Disorders* (4th ed.). Washington, DC: American Psychiatric Association.

American Social Health Association. (2000, April). Untreated chlamydia can lead to infertility; routine testing is critical, especially for young women. Retrieved from http://www.ashastd.org/press/040100.html

American Social Health Association. (2003). STD statistics. Retieved May 2, 2003, from http://www.ashastd.org/stdfaqs/statistics.html

The American Society for Aesthetic Plastic Surgery (2002). Percent of change in select procedures: 1997–2001. Retrieved November 17, 2002, from http://www.surgery.org/stats_html_pages/percent_change_2001.html

Anderson, E., Greene, S., Hetherington, E., and Clingempeel, W. (1999). The dynamics of parental remarriage. In E. M. Hetherington (Ed.), *Coping with Divorce, Single Parenting, and Remarriage: A Risk and Resiliency Perspective* (pp. 295–319). Mahwah, NJ: Erlbaum.

Anderson, S. A. (1986). Cohesion, adaptability, and communication: A test of an Olson circumplex model hypothesis. *Family Relations, 35,* 289–293.

Anderson, S. A., Russell, C. S., and Schumm, W. R. (1983). Perceived marital quality and family life cycle categories: A further analysis. *Journal of Marriage and the Family, 45,* 127–139.

Andersson, L., and Stevens, N. (1993). Associations between early experiences with parents and well-being in old age. *Journal of Gerontology, 48,* P109–P116.

Andre, T., Whigham, M., Hendrickson, A., and Chambers, S. (1999). Competency beliefs, positive affect, and gender stereotypes of elementary students and their parents about science versus other school subjects. *Journal of Research in Science Teaching, 36*(6), 719–747.

Andrews, B., and Brewin, C. R. (1990). Attributions of blame for marital violence: A study of antecedents and consequences. *Journal of Marriage and the Family, 52,* 757–776.

Andrews, F. M., and Halman, L. J. (1992). Infertility and subjective well-being: The mediating roles of self-esteem, internal control, and interpersonal conflict. *Journal of Marriage and the Family, 54,* 408–417.

Anisman, H., and Merali, Z. (1999). Understanding stress: Characteristics and caveats. *Alcohol Research and Health, 23,* 241–249.

Annual ectopic totals rose steadily in 1970s but mortality rates fell. (1983). *Family Planning Perspectives, 15,* 85, 86.

Ansbacher, R., and Adler, J. P. (1988). Infertility workshop and sexual stress. *Medical Aspects of Human Sexuality, 22,* 55–63.

Anson, O. (1989). Marital status and women's health revisited: The importance of a proximate adult. *Journal of Marriage and the Family, 51,* 185–194.

Aquilino, W. S. (1991). Predicting parents' experiences with coresident adult children. *Journal of Family Issues, 12,* 323–342.

Aquilino, W. S. (1994). Later life parental divorce and widowhood: Impact on young adults' assessment of parent–child relations. *Journal of Marriage and the Family, 56,* 908–922.

Arendell, T. J. (1987). Women and the economics of divorce in the contemporary United States. *Signs, 13,* 121–135.

Aron, A. Norman, C. C., Aron, E. M. McKenna, C., and Heyman, R. E. (2000). Couples' shared participation in novel and arousing activities and experienced relational quality. *Journal of Personality and Social Psychology, 78,* 273–284.

Arp, D. H., Arp, C. S., Stanley, S. M., Markman, H. J., and Blumberg, S. L. (2000). *Fighting for Your Empty Nest Marriage: Reinventing Your Relationship When the Kids Leave Home.* San Francisco: Jossey-Bass/Pfeiffer.

Arthur, N. M. (1990). The assessment of burnout: A review of three inventories useful for research and counseling. *Journal of Counseling and Development, 69,* 186–189.

Ashton, V. (1996). A study of mutual support between Black and White grandmothers and their adult grandchildren. *Journal of Gerontological Social Work, 26,* 87–100.

Atkinson, A. M. (1987). Fathers' participation and evaluation of family day care. *Family Relations, 38,* 146–151.

Avenevoli, S., Sessa, F. M., and Steinberg, L. (1999). Family structure, parenting practices, and adolescent adjustment: An ecological examination. In E. M. Hetherington (Ed.), *Coping with Divorce, Single Parenting, and Remarriage: A Risk and Resiliency Perspective* (pp. 65–90). Mahwah, NJ: Erlbaum.

Axelson, L. J., and Dail, P. W. (1988). The changing character of homelessness in the United States. *Family Relations, 37,* 463–469.

Baber, K. M., and Allen, K. R. (1992). *Women and Families: Feminist Reconstructions.* New York: Guilford Press.

Bachrach, C. A., London, R. A., and Maza, P. L. (1991). On the path to adoption: Adoption seeking in the United States, 1988. *Journal of Marriage and the Family, 53,* 705–718.

Bachu, A. (1999). Is childlessness among American women on the rise? *Population Division Working Paper No. 37.* Retrieved June 6, 2003, from http://www.census.gov/population/www/documentation/twps0037/twps0037.html

Backover, A. (1991). Native Americans: Alcoholism, FAS puts a race at risk. *Guidepost, 37,* 1–9.

Bahr, S. J., Chappell, C. B., and Leigh, G. K. (1983). Age at marriage, role enactment, role consensus, and marital satisfaction. *Journal of Marriage and the Family, 45,* 795–803.

Baize, H., and Schroeder, J. (1995). Personality and mate selection in personal ads: Evolutionary preferences in a public mate selection process. *Journal of Social Behavior and Personality, 10,* 517–536.

Baley, R. K. (1995). Black–White differences in kin contact and exchange among never married adults. *Journal of Family Issues, 16,* 77–103.

Balkwell, C. (1985). An additudinal correlate of the timing of a major life event: The case of morale in widowhood. *Family Relations, 34,* 577–581.

Bancroft, J., Sherwin, B. B., Alexander, G. M., Davidson, D. W., and Walker, A. (1991). Oral contraceptives, androgens, and the sexuality of young women: II. The role of androgens. *Archives of Sexual Behavior, 20,* 121–135.

Bandura, A. (1976). *Social Learning Theory.* Englewood Cliffs, NJ: Prentice-Hall.

Bane, M. J. (1997, January/February). Welfare as we might know it. *American Prospect, 30.* Retrieved June 30, 2000, from http://www.prospect.org/archives/30/fs30bane.html

Bank, L., Forgatch, M. S., Patterson, G. R., and Fetrow, R. A. (1993). Parenting practices of single mothers: Mediators of negative contextual factors. *Journal of Marriage and the Family, 55,* 371–384.

Banyard, L., and Williams, L. N. (1996). Characteristics of child sexual abuse as correlates of women's adjustment: A prospective study. *Journal of Marriage and the Family, 58,* 853–865.

Baranowski, M. D. (1983). Strengthening the grandparent–grandchild relationship. *Medical Aspects of Human Sexuality, 17,* 106–126.

Barber, B. K., and Thomas, D. L. (1986). Dimensions of fathers' and mothers' supportive behavior: The case for physical affection. *Journal of Marriage and the Family, 48,* 783–794.

Barich, R. R., and Bielby, D. D. (1996). Rethinking marriage. *Journal of Family Issues, 17,* 139–169.

Barnes, S. L. (2001). Stressors and strengths: A theoretical and practical examination of nuclear, single-parent, and augmented African American families. *Families in Society, 82*(5), 449–460.

Barnett, R. C., and Baruch, G. K. (1987). Determinants of fathers' participation in family work. *Journal of Marriage and the Family, 49,* 29–40.

Barnett, R. C. and Hyde J. S. (2001). Women, men, work, and family: An expansionist theory. *American Psychologist, 56*(10), 781–796.

Barnett, R. C., Kibria, N., Baruch, G. K., and Pleck, J. H. (1991). Adult daughter–parent relationships and their associations with daughters' subjective well-being and psychological distress. *Journal of Marriage and the Family, 53,* 29–42.

Barnett, R. C., Marshall, N. L., and Pleck, J. H. (1992). Adult son–parent relationships and their associations with sons' psychological distress. *Journal of Family Issues, 13,* 505–525.

Barranti, C. C. R. (1985). The grandparent–grandchild relationship: Family resource in an era of voluntary bonds. *Family Relations, 34,* 343–352.

Barrett, A. (1999). Social support and life satisfaction among the never married. *Research on Aging, 21*(1), 46–72.

Barrow, J. C., and Moore, C. A. (1983). Group interventions with perfectionistic thinking. *The Personnel and Guidance Journal, 61,* 612–615.

Barth, R. (2003). Abusive and neglecting parents and the care of their children. In M. A. Mason, A. Skolnick, and S. D. Sugarman (Eds.), *All Our Families* (pp. 265–284). New York: Oxford University Press.

Bassoff, E. S. (1984). Relationships of sex-role characteristics and psychological adjustment in new mothers. *Journal of Marriage and the Family, 46,* 449–454.

Battaglia, D. M., Datteri, D., and Lord, C. (1998). Breaking up is (relatively) easy to do: A script for the dissolution of close relationships. *Journal of Social and Personal Relationships, 15*(6), 829–845.

Baumeister, R., and Bratslavsky, E. (1999). Passion, intimacy, and time: Passionate love as a function of change in intimacy. *Personality and Social Psychology Review, 3*(1), 49–67.

Baumeister, R., Wotman, S., and Stillwell, A. (1993). Unrequited love: On heartbreak, anger, guilt, scriptlessness, and humiliation. *Journal of Personality and Social Psychology, 64*, 377–394.

Baumrind, D. (1996). Parenting: Discipline controversy revisited. *Family Relations, 45*, 405–414.

Baur, P. A., and Okun, M. A. (1983). Stability of life satisfaction in late life. *The Gerontologist, 23*, 261–265.

Bauserman, R. (2002). Child adjustment in joint-custody versus sole-custody arrangements: A meta-analytic review. *Journal of Family Psychology, 16*(1), 91–102.

Baxter, L. A. (1984). Trajectories of relationship disengagement. *Journal of Social and Personal Relationships, 1*, 29–48.

Baxter, L. A. (1990). Dialectical contradictions in relationship development. *Journal of Social and Personal Relationships, 7*, 69–88.

Baxter, L. A., Braithwaite, D. O., and Nicholson, J. H. (1999). Turning points in the development of blended families. *Journal of Social and Personal Relationships, 16*(3), 291–313.

Baxter, L. A., and Montgomery, B. M. (1997). Rethinking communication in personal relationships from a dialectical perspective. In S. Duck (Ed.), *Handbook of Personal Relationships* (pp. 325–349). New York: Wiley.

Baxter, L. A., and Simon, E. P. (1993). Relationship maintenance strategies and dialectical contradictions in personal relationships. *Journal of Social and Personal Relationships, 10*, 225–242.

Beach, S. R. H., and O'Leary, K. B. (1993). Dysphoria and marital discord: Are dysphoric individuals at risk for marital maladjustment? *Journal of Marital and Family Therapy, 19*, 355–368.

Bean, C. (1974). *Methods of Childbirth.* New York: Dolphin.

Beck, J. G., Bozman, A. W., and Qualtrough, T. (1991). The experience of sexual desire: Psychological correlates in a college sampling. *The Journal of Sex Research, 28*, 443–456.

Beck, R., and Blank, N. (1997). Broadening the scope of divorce mediation to meet the needs of children. *Mediation Quarterly: Journal of the Academy of Family Mediators, 14*(3), 179–185.

Beck, R. W., and Beck, S. H. (1989). The incidence of extended households among middle-age Black and White women: Estimates from a 15-year panel study. *Journal of Family Issues, 10,* 147–168.

Becker, P. E. (1999, November). Scaling back: Dual-earner couples' work–family strategies. *Journal of Marriage and the Family, 61,* 995–1007.

Becker, P. E., and Moen, P. (1999). Scaling back: Dual-earner couples' work–family strategies. *Journal of Marriage and the Family, 61,* 995–1007.

Beckman, L., Harvey, S., Satre, S., and Walker, M. (1999). Cultural beliefs about social influence strategies of Mexican immigrant women and their heterosexual partners. *Sex Roles, 40*(11/12), 871–892.

Beckman, L. J., and Houser, B. B. (1982). The consequences of childlessness on the social-psychological well-being of older women. *Journal of Gerontology, 37,* 243–250.

Bell, R. A., Daly, J. A., and Gonzalez, M. C. (1987). Affinity-maintenance in marriage and its relationship to women's marital satisfaction. *Journal of Marriage and the Family, 49,* 445–454.

Bell, W., and Garner, J. (1996). Kincare. *Journal of Gerontological Social Work, 25,* 11–20.

Belsky, J. (1992). Medically indigent women seeking abortion prior to legalization: New York City, 1969–1970. *Family Planning Perspectives, 24,* 129–134.

Belsky, J., and Rovine, M. (1990). Patterns of marital change across the transition to parenthood: Preparing to three years postpartum. *Journal of Marriage and the Family, 52,* 5–19.

Belsky, J., Youngblade, L., Rovine, M., and Volling, B. (1991). Patterns of marital change and parent–child interaction. *Journal of Marriage and the Family, 53,* 487–498.

Bem, S. L. (1985). Androgyny and gender schema theory: A conceptual and empirical integration. In T. B. Sonderegger (Ed.), *Nebraska Symposium on Motivation: Psychology of Gender* (pp. 179–226). Lincoln: University of Nebraska Press.

Benazon, N., Wright, J., and Sabourin, S. (1992). Stress, sexual satisfaction, and marital adjustment in infertile couples. *Journal of Sex and Marital Therapy, 18,* 273–284.

Benedikt, M. (1999). *Values.* Austin: University of Texas Press.

Bengtson, V. L. (2001). Beyond the nuclear family: The increasing importance of multigenerational bonds. *Journal of Marriage and Family 63,* 1–16.

Bengtson, V. L., and Kuypers, J. A. (1971). Generational differences and the developmental stake. *Aging and Human Development, 2,* 249–260.

Benin, M., and Keith, D. M. (1995). The social support of employed African-American and Anglo mothers. *Journal of Family Issues, 15,* 275–297.

Benson, M. J., Arditti, J., Reguero DeAtiles, J. T., and Smith, S. (1992). Intergenerational transmission: Attributions in relationships with parents and intimate others. *Journal of Family Issues, 13,* 450–464.

Benson, M. J., Larson, J., Wilson, S. M., and Demo, D. H. (1993). Family of origin influences on late adolescent romantic relationships. *Journal of Marriage and the Family, 55,* 663–672.

Berardo, D. H., Shehan, C. L., and Leslie, G. R. (1987). A residue of tradition: Jobs, careers, and spouses' time in housework. *Journal of Marriage and the Family, 49,* 381–390.

Berg-Cross, L. (1997). *Couples therapy.* Thousand Oaks, CA: Sage.

Berger, R. (2000). Stepfamilies in cultural context. *Journal of Divorce and Remarriage, 33,* 111–130.

Berghout-Austin, A. M., Salehi, M., and Leffler, A. (1987). Gender and developmental differences in children's conversations. *Sex Roles, 16*(9/10), 497–510.

Bergner, R. M. (2000). Love and barriers to love: An analysis for psychotherapists and others. *American Journal of Psychotherapy, 54*(1), 1–17.

Berk, R. A., Newton, P. J., and Berk, S. F. (1986). What a difference a day makes: An empirical study of the impact of shelters for battered women. *Journal of Marriage and the Family, 48,* 481–490.

Berkow, R. (Ed.). (1987). *The Merck Manual* (15th ed.). Rahway, NJ: Merck, Sharp and Dohme Research Laboratories.

Berman, W. H. (1988). The relationship of ex-spouse attachment to adjustment following divorce. *Journal of Family Psychology, 1,* 312–328.

Bernard, J. L., Bernard, S. L., and Bernard, M. L. (1985). Courtship violence and sex-typing. *Family Relations, 24,* 573–576.

Berry, R. E., and Williams, F. L. (1987). Assessing the relationships between quality of life and marital income satisfaction: A path analytic approach. *Journal of Marriage and the Family, 49,* 107–116.

Beutell, N. J., and Greenhaus, J. H. (1980). Some sources and consequences of interrole conflict among married women. *Proceedings of the Annual Meeting of the Eastern Academy of Management, 17,* 2–6.

Bianchi, S., Milkie, M., Sayer, L., and Robinson, J. (2000). Is anyone doing the housework? Trends in the gender division of household labor. *Social Forces, 79,* 191–228.

Birnbaum, C. (2000, October/November). The love and sex survey 2000. *Twist,* pp. 54–56.

Blackwell, D. L., and Lichter, D. T. (2000). Mate selection among married and cohabiting couples. *Journal of Family Issues, 21*(3), 275–302.

Blair, S. L. (1993). Employment, family, and perceptions of marital quality among husbands and wives. *Journal of Family Issues, 14,* 189–212.

Blaisure, K. R., and Allen, K. R. (1995). Feminists and the ideology and practice of marital equality. *Journal of Marriage and the Family, 57,* 5–19.

Blee, K. M., and Tickamyer, A. R. (1995). Racial differences in men's attitudes about women's gender roles. *Journal of Marriage and the Family, 57,* 21–30.

Bloom, B. L., and Kindle, K. R. (1985). Demographic factors in the continuing relationships between former spouses. *Family Relations, 34,* 375–381.

Blum, R. W., Resnick, N. C., and Stark, T. (1990). Factors associated with the use of court bypass by minors to obtain abortions. *Family Planning Perspectives, 22,* 158–160.

Blumenthal, L. (1980, July 25). Upsurge in violence, stress, blamed in eruptions. *Seattle Times,* p. 1.

Blumstein, P., and Schwartz, P. (1983). *American Couples: Money, Work, Sex.* New York: Morrow.

Bode, J. (1987). Testimony before the U.S. House of Representatives select committee on Children, Youth, and Families. In *The Crisis of Homelessness: Effects on Children and Families.* G. Miller (Chair). Washington, DC: U.S. Government Printing Office.

Bogenschneider, K. (2002). *How Policymaking Affects Families and What Professionals Can Do.* Mahwah, NJ: Erlbaum.

Bogren, L. Y. (1991). Changes in sexuality in women and men during pregnancy. *Archives of Sexual Behavior, 20,* 35–45.

Bohannan, P. (1984). *All the Happy Families.* New York: McGraw-Hill.

Bohannon, J., and White, P. (1999). Gender role attitudes of American mothers and daughters over time. *Journal of Social Psychology, 139*(2), 173–179.

Boland, J. P., and Follingstad, D. R. (1987). The relationship between communication and marital satisfaction: A review. *Journal of Sex and Marital Therapy, 13,* 286–313.

Bond, J. T., Galinsky, E., and Swanberg, J. E. (1998). *The 1997 National Study of the Changing Workforce.* New York: Families and Work Institute.

Booth, A. (1999). Causes and consequences of divorce: Reflections on recent research. In R. Thompson and P. Amato (Eds.), *The Postdivorce Family: Children, Parenting, and Society* (pp. 29–48). Thousand Oaks, CA: Sage.

Booth, A., and Amato, C. R. (1994). Parental gender role nontraditionalism and offspring outcomes. *Journal of Marriage and the Family, 56,* 865–877.

Booth, A., and Amato, P. R. (2001). Parental predivorce relations and offspring postdivorce well-being. *Journal of Marriage and the Family, 63*(1), 197–212.

Booth, A., and Edwards, J. M. (1985). Age at marriage and marital instability. *Journal of Marriage and the Family, 47,* 67–75.

Booth, A., and Edwards, J. N. (1992). Starting over. Why remarriages are more unstable. *Journal of Family Issues, 13,* 174–179.

Boss, P. G. (1987). Family stress. In M. B. Sussman and S. K. Steinmetz (Eds.), *Handbook of Marriage and the Family* (pp. 695–723). New York: Plenum.

Boston Women's Health Book Collective. (1998). *Our Bodies, Ourselves for the New Century: A Book by and for Women.* New York: Touchstone Books.

Botwin, M. D., Buss, D. M., and Shackelford, T. K. (1997). Personality and mate preference: Five factors in mate selection and marital satisfaction. *Journal of Personality, 65,* 108–136.

Bowen, G. L., and Chapman, M. B. (1996). Poverty, neighborhood danger, social support, and the individual adaptation among at-risk youth in urban areas. *Journal of Family Issues, 17,* 641–666.

Bowen, G. L., and Orthner, D. K. (1983). Sex-role congruency and marital quality. *Journal of Marriage and the Family, 45,* 223–230.

Bowlby, J. (1977). The making and breaking of affectional bonds. *British Journal of Psychiatry, 130,* 201–210.

Bowman, M. E., and Ahrons, C. R. (1985). Impact of legal custody status on fathers' parenting postdivorce. *Journal of Marriage and the Family, 47,* 481–488.

Bowman, M. L. (1990). Coping efforts and marital satisfaction: Measuring marital coping and its correlates. *Journal of Marriage and the Family, 52,* 463–474.

Boxer, A. M., and Cohler, B. J. (1989). The life course of gay and lesbian youth: An immodest proposal for the study of lives. *Journal of Homosexuality, 17*(3/4), 315–355.

Boyd, C. J. (1989). Mothers and daughters: A discussion of theory and research. *Journal of Marriage and the Family, 51,* 291–301.

Boyum, L. A., and Parke, R. D. (1995). The role of emotional expressiveness in the development of children's social competence. *Journal of Marriage and the Family, 57,* 593–608.

Brackbill, R. M., Sternberg, M. R., and Fishbein, M. (1999, January/February). Where do people go for treatment of sexually transmitted diseases? *Family Planning Perspective, 31*(1), 10–15.

Bradsher, J. E., Longino, C. F., Jr., Jackson, D. J., and Zimmerman, R. S. (1992). Health and geographic mobility among the recently widowed. *Journal of Gerontology, 47,* S261–S268.

Bramlett, M. D., and Mosher, W. D. (2002). Cohabitation, marriage, divorce, and remarriage in the United States.

National Center for Health Statistics. *Vital Health Stat, 23*(22), 1–94.

Brand, E., Clingempeel, W. G., and Bowen-Woodward, K. (1988). Family relationships and children's adjustment in stepmother and stepfather families. In E. M. Hetherington and J. D. Arasteh (Eds.), *Impact of Divorce, Single-Parenting, and Stepparenting on Children* (pp. 299–324). Hillsdale, NJ: Erlbaum.

Bray, J. (1999). Stepfamilies: The intersection of culture, context, and biology. *Monographs of the Society for Research in Child Development, 64*(4), 210–218.

Bray, J. H., and Berger, S. H. (1993). Developmental issues in stepfamilies. Research project: Family relationships and parent–child interactions. *Journal of Family Psychology, 7,* 76–90.

Bray, J. H., and Hetherington, E. M. (1993). Families in transition: Introduction and overview. *Journal of Family Psychology, 7,* 3–8.

Bray, J. H., and Jouriles, E. N. (1995). Treatment of marital conflict and prevention of divorce. *Journal of Marital and Family Therapy, 21,* 461–473.

Bray, J. H., and Kelly, J. (1998). *Stepfamilies: Love, Marriage, and Parenting in the First Decade.* New York: Broadway Books.

Brayfield, A. (1995). Juggling jobs and kids: The impact of employment schedules on fathers' caring for children. *Journal of Marriage and the Family, 57,* 321–332.

Brennen, R. T., Barnett, R. C., and Gareis, K. C. (2001). When she earns more than he does: A longitudinal study of dual-earner couples. *Journal of Marriage and the Family, 63,* 168–182.

Brindis, C., Starbuck-Morales, S., Wolfe, A. L., and McCarter, B. (1994). Characteristics associated with contraceptive use among adolescent females in school-based family planning programs. *Family Planning Perspectives, 26,* 160–164.

Broderick, C. B. (1984). *Marriage and the Family* (2nd ed.). Englewood Cliffs, NJ: Prentice-Hall.

Broderick, C. B., and Smith, J. (1979). The general systems approach to the family. In W. R. Burr, R. Hill, F. I. Nye, and I. L. Reiss (Eds.), *Contemporary Theories About the Family* (Vol. 2, pp. 112–129). New York: Free Press.

Brody, C. J., and Steelman, L. C. (1985). Sibling structure and parental sex-typing of children's household tasks. *Journal of Marriage and the Family, 47,* 265–273.

Brody, G. H., Stoneman, D., Flor, D., and McCrary, C. (1994). Religion's role in organizing family relationships: Family process in rural, two-parent African-American families. *Journal of Marriage and the Family, 56,* 878–888.

Brody, L., Copeland, A., Sutton, L., Richardson, D., and Guyer, M. (1998). Mommy and daddy like you best:

Perceived family favoritism in relation to affect, adjustment and family process. *Journal of Family Therapy, 20*(3), 269–291.

Brodzinsky, D., Schechter, D., Braff, A., and Singer, L. (1984). Psychological and academic adjustment in adopted children. *Journal of Consulting and Clinical Psychology, 52,* 582–590.

Broman, C. L. (1993). Race differences in marital well-being. *Journal of Marriage and the Family, 55,* 724–732.

Broman, C. L. (2001). Work stress in the family life of African Americans. *Journal of Black Studies, 31*(6), 835–846.

Bronfenbrenner, U. (1975). Liberated women: How they're changing American life. Interview conducted for *U.S. News & World Report,* p. 49.

Bronstein, P., Klauson, J., Stoll, M. F., and Abrams, C. L. (1993). Parenting behavior and children's social, psychological, and academic adjustment in diverse family structures. *Family Relations, 42,* 268–276.

Brown, G., Van Ummersen, C., and Phair, J. (2002). *Breaking the Barriers: Presidential Strategies for Enhancing Career Mobility.* Washington, DC: American Council on Education.

Brown, L. M., and Gilligan, C. (1992). *Meeting at the Crossroads: Women's Psychology and Girls' Development.* New York: Random House.

Brown, S. L., and Booth, A. (1996). Cohabitation versus marriage: A comparison of relationship quality. *Journal of Marriage and the Family, 58,* 668–678.

Brown, S. S. (1989). Drawing women into prenatal care. *Family Planning Perspectives, 21,* 73–80.

Brubaker, T. H. (1990). Families in later life: A burgeoning research area. *Journal of Marriage and the Family, 52,* 959–981.

Brumberg, J. J. (1997). *The Body Project: An Intimate History of American Girls.* New York: Vintage Books.

Bryant, C. M., Conger, R. D., and Meehan, J. M. (2001). The influence on in-laws on change in marital success. *Journal of Marriage and the family, 63*(3), 614–626.

Bryant, Z. L., and Coleman, M. (1988). The Black family as portrayed in introductory marriage and family textbooks. *Family Relations, 37,* 255–259.

Bryson, K. R., and Casper, L. M. (1999, May). Coresident grandparents and grandchildren. (*Current Population Reports,* Series P23-198). Washington, DC: U.S. Bureau of the Census.

Buehler, C., Krishnakumar, A., Anthony, C., Tittsworth, S., and Stone, G. (1994). Hostile interparental conflict in youth maladjustment. *Family Relations, 43,* 409–416.

Buehler, C., Krishnakumar, A., Stone, G., Anthony, C., Pemberton, S., Gerard, J., and Barber, B. K. (1998). In-

terparental conflict styles and youth problem behaviors: A two-sample replication study. *Journal of Marriage and the Family, 60,* 119–132.

Buehler, R., Griffin, D. W., and Ross, M. (1995). It's about time: Optimistic predictions in work and love. In W. Stroebe and M. Hewstone (Eds.), *European Social Review of Psychology, Vol. 6* (pp. 1–32). Chichester, UK: Wiley.

Bulcroft, K., and O'Connor, M. (1986). The importance of dating relationship on quality of life for older persons. *Family Relations, 35,* 397–401.

Bulcroft, R. A., and Bulcroft, K. A. (1993). Race differences in attitudal and motivational factors in the decision to marry. *Journal of Marriage and the Family, 55,* 338–355.

Bullock, J. R. (1993). Children's loneliness and their relationships with family and peers. *Family Relations, 42,* 46–49.

Bumpass, L. L., and Lu, H-H. (2000). Trends in cohabitation and implications for children's family contexts in the U.S. *Population Studies, 54,* 29–41.

Bumpass, L. L., Martin, T. C., and Sweet, J. A. (1991). The impact of family background and early marital factors on marital disruption. *Journal of Family Issues, 12,* 22–42.

Bumpass, M. F., Crouter, A. C., McHale, S. M. (1999). Work demands for dual-earner couples: Implications for parents' knowledge about children's daily lives in middle childhood. *Journal of Marriage and the Family, 61,* 465–475.

Burden, D. S. (1986). Single parents and the work setting: The impact of multiple job and homelife responsibilities. *Family Relations, 35,* 37–43.

Burgess, E. W., and Locke, H. J. (1953). *The Family: From Institution to Companionship.* New York: American Book.

Buriel, R. (1993). Child-rearing orientations in Mexican-American families: The influence of generation and sociocultural factors. *Journal of Marriage and the Family, 55,* 987–1000.

Burleson, B., and Denton, W. (1997). The relationship between communication skill and marital satisfaction: Some moderating effects. *Journal of Marriage and the Family, 59,* 884–902.

Burleson, B. R., Della, J. G., and Applegate, J. L. (1992). Effects of maternal communication in children's social-cognitive and communication skills on children's acceptance by the peer group. *Family Relations, 41,* 264–272.

Burr, J., and Mutchler, J. (1999). Race and ethnic variation in norms of filial responsibility among older persons. *Journal of Marriage and the Family, 61*(3), 674–687.

Burt, M., Aron, L. Y., Douglas, T., Valente, J., Lee, E., and Iwen, B. (1999, December 7). *Homelessness: Programs and the People They Serve: Findings from the National Sur-*

vey of Homeless Assistance Providers and Clients. Washington, DC: Urban Institute. Retrieved June 30, 2000, from http://www.urban.org/ housing/homeless/ homeless.html

Burton, L. M. (1995). Intergenerational patterns of providing care in African American families with teenage childbearers: Emergent patterns in an ethnographic study. In V. L. Bengtson, K. W. Schaie, and L. M. Burton (Eds.), *Adult Intergenerational Relations: Effects of Societal Change* (pp. 79–98). New York: Springer.

Burton, L. M., Dilworth-Anderson, P., and Merriwether-de-Vries, C. (1995). Contest and surrogate parenting among contemporary grandparents. *Marriage and Family Review, 20,* 349–366.

Busby, T. M., Steggell, G. L., Glenn, E., and Adamson, D. W. (1993). Treatment issues for survivors of physical and sexual abuse. *Journal of Marital and Family Therapy, 19,* 377–392.

Buscaglia, L. (1982). *Living, Loving, and Learning.* New York: Fawcett Columbine.

Buss, D. M., and Schmitt, D. P. (1993). Sexual strategies theory: An evolutionary perspective on human mating. *Psychological Bulletin, 2,* 204–232.

Buunk, B. P., and Mutsaers, W. (1999). The nature of the relationship between remarried individuals and former spouses and its impact on marital satisfaction. *Journal of Family Psychology, 13*(2), 165–174.

Byers, E. S. (1988). Effects of sexual arousal on men's and women's behavior in sexual disagreement situations. *The Journal of Sex Research, 25,* 235–254.

Cain, V. S., and Hofferth, S. L. (1989). Parental choice of self-care for school-age children. *Journal of Marriage and the Family, 51,* 65–77.

Callan, V. J. (1983). Childlessness and partner selection. *Journal of Marriage and the Family, 45,* 181–186.

Callan, V. J. (1987). The personal and marital adjustment of mothers and of voluntarily and involuntarily childless wives. *Journal of Marriage and the Family, 49,* 847–856.

Camasso, M. J., and Roche, S. E. (1991). The willingness to change to formalized child care arrangements: Parental considerations, cost and quality. *Journal of Marriage and the Family, 53,* 1071–1082.

Cameron, S., and Collins, A. (1998). Sex differences in stipulated preferences in personal advertisement. *Psychological Reports, 82,* 119–123.

Campbell, N. L., and Moen, P. (1992). Job–family role strain among employed single mothers of preschoolers. *Family Relations, 41,* 205–211.

Canli, T., Desmond, J. E., Zhao, Z., and Gabrieli, J. D. (2002). Sex differences in the neural basis of emotional memories. *Proceedings National Academy of Science USA, 99*(16), 10789–10794.

Caplan, P. J. (1986, October). Take the blame off mother. *Psychology Today, 20,* 70–71.

Carlson, C., Uppal, S., and Prosser, E. C. (2000). Ethnic differences in processes contributing to the self-esteem of early adolescent girls. *Journal of Early Adolescence, 20*(1), 44–67.

Carrere, S., Buehlman, K. T., Gottman, J. M., Coan, J. A., and Ruchstuhl, L. (2000). Predicting marital stability and divorce in newlywed couples. *Journal of Family Psychology, 14*(1), 42–58.

Carstensen, L. L., Gottman, J. M., and Levenson, R. W. (1995). Emotional behavior in long-term marriage. *Psychology and Aging, 10,* 140–149.

Carter, S., and Sokol, J. (1987). *Men Who Can't Love.* New York: M. Evans.

Casper, L. M. (1997, September). My daddy takes care of me! Fathers as care providers. (*Current Population Reports: Household Economic Studies,* Series P70-59). Washington, DC: U.S. Bureau of the Census.

Casper, L. M., and Bianchi, S. M. (2002). *Continuity and Change in the American Family.* Thousand Oaks, CA: Sage.

Casper, L. M., and Bryson, K. R. (1998). *Co-Resident Grandparents and Their Grandchildren: Grandparent Maintained Families.* (Population Division Working Paper No. 26). Washington, DC: U.S. Bureau of the Census.

Cates, W. (1999). Estimates of the incidence and prevalence of sexually transmitted diseases in the United States. *Sexually Transmitted Disease, 26,* s2–s7.

Caughlin, J. P., Huston, T. L., and Houts R. M. (2000). How does personality matter in marriage? An examination of trait anxiety, interpersonal negativity and marital satisfaction. *Journal of Personality and Social Psychology, 78,* 326–336.

Ceglian, C. P., and Gardner, S. (1999). Attachment style: A risk for multiple marriages? *Journal of Divorce and Remarriage, 31,* 125–139.

Center for Drug Evaluation and Research. (2000, September 30). Mifepristone questions and answers. Retrieved from http://www.fda.gov/cder/drug/infopage/ mifepristone/mifepristone-qa.htm

Centers for Disease Control and Prevention. (2001). Youth risk behavior surveillance, 2001. *Morbidity and Mortality Weekly Report* June 28, 2002/51(SS04), 1–64. Retrieved November 7, 2002, from http://www.cdc.gov/ nccdphp/dash/yrbs/2001/index.htm

Centers for Disease Control and Prevention. (2002a). Births to women 35 and older. http://www.cdc.gov/nchs/ data/nvsr51/nvsr51_02.pdf (Accessed May 1, 2003).

Centers for Disease Control and Prevention. (2002b). *Tracking the Hidden Epidemics: Trends in STDs in the United States 2000.* Washington, DC: Department of Health and Human Services.

Centers for Disease Control and Prevention. (2003a). Advancing HIV Prevention: New strategies for a changing epidemic—United States, 2003. *Morbidity and Mortality Weekly Report, 52,* 1–2.

Centers for Disease Control and Prevention. (2003b) HIV/AIDS update, A glance at the HIV epidemic Retrieved May 1, 2003, from http://www.cdc.gov/hiv/pubs/facts.htm

Cere, D. (2000). *The Experts' Story of Courtship: A Report to the Nation.* New York: Institute for American Values.

Chaddock, G. (1999). Learning: K–12: Say goodbye to "latch-key" kids. *Christian Science Monitor, 91*(245), 14.

Chan, C. G., and Elder, G. H. (2000). Matrilineal advantage in grandchild–grandparent relations. *The Gerontologist, 40,* 179–190.

Chatters, L. M., Taylor, R. J., and Neighbors, H. W. (1989). Size of informal helper network mobilized during a serious personal problem among Black Americans. *Journal of Marriage and the Family, 51,* 667–676.

Cheng, C. (1999). Gender-role differences in susceptibility to the influence of support availability on depression. *Journal of Personality, 67*(3), 439–467.

Cherlin, A. J. (1996) *Public and Private Families: An Introduction.* New York: McGraw-Hill.

Cherlin, A., and Furstenberg, F. F. (1994). Stepfamilies in the United States: A reconsideration. In J. Blake and J. Hagen (Eds.), *Annual Review of Sociology* (pp. 359–381). Palo Alto, CA: Annual Reviews.

Chilman, C. (1991). Working poor families: Trends, causes, effects, and suggested policies. *Family Relations, 40,* 191–198.

Chiriboga, D. A. (1982). Adaptation to marital separation in later and earlier life. *Journal of Gerontology, 37,* 109–114.

Choi, N. G. (1992). Correlates of the economic status of widowed and divorced elderly women. *Journal of Family Issues, 13,* 38–54.

Christensen, A., and Heavey, C. L. (1990). Gender, power, and marital conflict. *Journal of Personality and Social Psychology, 59,* 73–85.

Christensen, A., and Jacobson, N. (2000). *Reconcilable Differences.* New York: Guilford Press.

Christensen, D. H., and Rettig, K. D. (1995). The relationship of remarriage to post-divorce coparenting. *Journal of Divorce and Remarriage, 24,* 73–88.

Christmon, K. (1990). Parental responsibility of African-American unwed adolescent fathers. *Adolescence, 25,* 645–654.

Church, E. (1999). Who are the people in your family? Stepmothers' diverse notions of kinship. *Journal of Marriage and Divorce, 31,* 83–105.

Civic, D. (1999). The association between characteristics of dating relationships and condom use among heterosexual young adults. *AIDS Education and Prevention, 11*(4), 343–352.

Clark, C., Shaver, P., and Abrahams, M. (1999). Strategic behaviors in romantic relationship initiation. *Personality and Social Psychology Bulletin, 25*(6), 707–720.

Clark P. G., Siviski, R. W., and Weiner, R. (1986). Coping strategies of widowers in first year. *Family Relations, 35,* 425–430.

Clark, S. C. (2001). Work cultures and work/family balance. *Journal of Vocational Behavior, 58*(3), 348–365.

Clarkberg, M., and Moen, P. (2001). Understanding the time-squeeze: Married couples' preferred and actual work-hour strategies. *American Behavior Scientist, 44*(7), 1115–1136.

Clarke, S. C. (1995, July 14). Advanced report of final marriage statistics, 1989 and 1990. *Monthly Vital Statistics Report, 43*(12).

Clark-Nicolas, P., and Gray-Little, B. (1991). Effect of economic resources on marital quality in Black married couples. *Journal of Marriage and the Family, 53,* 645–655.

Clemens, A. W., and Axelson, L. J. (1985). The not-so-empty nest: The return of the fledgling adult. *Family Relations, 34,* 259–264.

Cohan, C. L., and Kleinbaum, S. (2002). Toward a greater understanding of the cohabitation effect: Premarital cohabitation and marital communication. *Journal of Marriage and the Family, 64,* 180–192.

Cohen, D., Dent, C., and MacKinnon, D. (1991). Condom skills education and sexually transmitted disease reinfection. *The Journal of Sex Research, 28,* 139–144.

Cohen, J. (1987). Parents as educational models and definers. *Journal of Marriage and the Family, 49,* 339–351.

Cohen, O., and Savaya, R. (1997). Broken glass: The divorced woman in Muslim Arab society in Israel. *Family Process, 36,* 225–245.

Cohen, O., and Savaya, R. (2003a). Adjustment to divorce: A preliminary study among Muslim Arab citizens of Israel. *Family Process, 42,* 269–290.

Cohen, O., and Savaya, R. (2003b). Perceptions of the societal image of Muslin Arab divorced men and women in Israel. *Journal of Social and Personal Relationships, 20,* 193–202.

Cohn, D. A., Silver, D. H., Cowan, C. P., Cowan, P. A., and Pearson, J. (1992). Working models of childhood attachment and couple relationships. Journal of Family Issues, 13, 432–449.

Coke, M. M. (1992). Correlates of life satisfaction among elderly African-Americans. *Journal of Gerontology, 49,* P316–P320.

Coker, A. L., Harlap, S., and Fortney, J. A. (1993). Oral contraceptives and reproductive cancers: Weighing the risks and benefits. *Family Planning Perspectives, 25,* 17–21.

Coker, A. L., McKeown, R. E., Sanderson, M. Davis, K. E., Valois, R. F., and Huebner, E. S. (2000). Severe dating violence and quality of life among South Carolina high school students. *American Journal of Preventive Medicine, 19,* 220–227.

Coker, A. L., Smith, P. H., McKeown, R. E., and King, M. J. (2000). Frequency and correlates of intimate partner violence by type: physical, sexual, and psychological battering. *American Journal of Public Health 2000, 90*(4), 553–559.

Coleman, L. M., Antonucci, T. C., Adelmann, P. K., and Crohan, S. E. (1987). Social roles in the lives of middle-aged and older Black women. *Journal of Marriage and the Family, 49,* 761–771.

Coleman, M., and Ganong, L. H. (1990). Remarriage and stepfamily research in the 1980s: Increased interest in an old family form. *Journal of Marriage and the Family, 52,* 925–940.

Coleman, M., and Ganong, L. H. (1991). Remarriage and stepfamily research in the 1980s. In A. Booth (Ed.), *Contemporary Families: Looking Forward, Looking Back* (pp. 192–207). Minneapolis: National Council on Family Relations.

Coleman, M. and Ganong, L. (2002). Resilience and families. *Family Relations, 51,* 101–102.

Coleman, M., Ganong, L. H., Clark, J. M., and Madsen, R. (1989). Parenting perceptions in rural and urban families: Is there a difference? *Journal of Marriage and the Family, 51,* 329–335.

Coleman, M., Ganong, L. H., and Fine, M. (2000). Reinvestigating remarriage: Another decade of progress. *Journal of Marriage and the Family, 62*(4), 1288–1307.

Coleman, M., Ganong, L. H., Killian, T., and McDaniel, A. K. (1999). Child support obligations: Attitudes and rationale. *Journal of Family Issues, 20*(1), 46–68.

Coles, R. L., (2002). Black single fathers: Choosing to parent full-time. *Journal of Contemporary Ethnography 31*(4), 411–439.

Coley, S. M., and Beckett, J. O. (1988). Black battered women: A review of empirical literature. *Journal of Counseling and Development, 66,* 266–270.

Collins, C., Hartman, C., and Sklar, H. (1999). *Divided Decade: Economic Disparity at the Century's Turn.* Boston: United for a Fair Economy.

Collins, N. L., and Read, S. J. (1994). Cognitive representations of attachment: The structure and function of working models. In K. Bartholomew and D. Perlman (Eds.), *Advances in Personal Relationships, Vol. 5: Attachment Processes in Adulthood* (pp. 53–90). London: Jessica Kingsley.

Collins, P. H. (1987). The meaning of motherhood in Black cultural and Black mother/daughter relationships. *Sage: A Scholarly Journal on Black Women, 4,* 3–10.

Collins, W. A., and Sroufe, L. A. (1999). Capacity for intimate relationships: A developmental construction. In W. Furman, B. Bradford Brown, and C. Fiering (Eds.), *The Development of Romantic Relationships in Adolescence* (pp. 125–147). Cambridge, UK: Cambridge University Press.

Collins, W. E., Newman, B. M., and McKenry, P. C. (1995). Intrapsychic and interpersonal factors related to adolescent psychological well-being in stepmother and stepfather families. *Journal of Family Psychology, 9,* 433–445.

Coltrane, S. S., and Ishii-Kuntz, M. (1992). Men's housework: A life course perspective. *Journal of Marriage and the Family, 54,* 43–57.

Coltrane, S. (2000). Research on household labor: Modeling and measuring the social embeddedness of routine family work. *Journal of Marriage and the Family 62*(4), 1208–1233.

Conger, R. D., Conger, K. J., Elder, G. H., Lorenz, R. O., Simons, R. L., and Whitbeck, L. B. (1992). A family process model of economic hardship and adjustment of early adolescent boys. *Child Development, 63,* 526–541.

Conger, R. D., Elder, G. H., Jr., Lorenz, F. O., Conger, K., Simons, R. L., Whitbeck, L. B., Huck, S., and Melby, J. N. (1990). Linking economic hardship to marital quality and instability. *Journal of Marriage and the Family, 52,* 643–656.

Conger, R. D., McCarty, J. A., Yang, R. K., Lahey, B. B., and Burgess, R. L. (1984). Mother's age as a predictor of observed maternal behavior in three independent samples of families. *Journal of Marriage and the Family, 46,* 411–424.

Congressional Coalition on Adoption Institute. Adoption Education. (2002). Retrieved February 27, 2003, from http://www.ccainstitute.org/adoptionstatistics.shtml

Consortium of Social Science Associations. (1999, March 12). *Is Welfare Reform Working? The Impact of Economic Growth and Policy Changes: Executive Summary, COSSA*

Congressional Seminar. Washington, DC: COSSA. Retrieved June 30, 2000, from http://members.aol.com/socscience/welfareseminar.htm

Cook, C., Selig, K., Wedge, B., and Gohn-Baube, E. (1999). Access barriers and the use of prenatal care by low-income, inner-city women. *Social Work, 44*(2), 129–139.

Cook, E. P. (1985). Androgyny: A goal for counseling. *Journal of Counseling and Development, 63*, 567–571.

Coombs, R. H., and Landsverk, J. (1988). Parenting styles and substance use during childhood and adolescence. *Journal of Marriage and the Family, 50*, 473–482.

Cooney, T. M., and Hogan, D. P. (1991). Marriage in an institutionalized life course: First marriage among American men in the 20th century. *Journal of Marriage and the Family, 53*, 178–190.

Cooney, T. M., Pedersen, F. A., Indelicato, S., and Palkovitz, R. (1993). Timing of fatherhood: Is "on-time" optimal? *Journal of Marriage and the Family, 55*, 205–215.

Cooney, T. M., and Uhlenberg, P. (1990). The role of divorce in men's relations with their adult children after mid-life. *Journal of Marriage and the Family, 52*, 677–688.

Cooney, T. M., and Uhlenberg, P. (1991). Changes in work-family connections among highly educated men and women, 1970 to 1980. *Journal of Family Issues, 12*, 69–90.

Coontz, S. (2000). Historical perspectives on family studies. *Journal of Marriage and the Family, 2*, 283–297.

Coontz, S. (2000, June). Inventing today's families. Paper presented at the annual conference of the American Family Therapy Association, San Diego, CA.

Coontz, S. (2001, June 21). Council on contemporary families, *USA Today*, p. 8D.

Cotton, S., Antill, J. K., and Cunningham, J. D. (1989). The work motivations of mothers with preschool children. *Journal of Family Issues, 10*, 189–210.

Council for Children. (1984). *Taking Action for Latchkey Children.* Charlotte, NC: Council for Children.

The court edges away from Roe v. Wade. (1989). *Family Planning Perspectives, 21*, 184–187.

Court reaffirms Roe but upholds restrictions. (1992). *Family Planning Perspectives, 24*, 174–185.

Cousins, P. C., and Vincent, J. P. (1983). Supportive and adversive behavior following spousal complaints. *Journal of Marriage and the Family, 45*, 679–682.

Cowan, C. C., and Cowan, P. A. (1995). Intervention leads to transition to parenthood. *Family Relations, 44*, 412–423.

Cowan, P., and Cowan, C. P. (2003). New families: Modern couples as new pioneers. In M. A. Mason, A. Skolnick, and Sugarman S. D. (Eds.), *All Our Families* (pp. 196–219). New York: Oxford University Press.

Coysh, W. S., Johnston, J. R., Tschann, J. M., Wallerstein, J. S., and Kline, M. (1989). Parental postdivorce adjustment in joint and sole physical custody families. *Journal of Family Issues, 10*, 52–71.

Craig, M. E., Kalichman, S. C., and Follingstad, D. R. (1989). Verbal coercive sexual behavior among college students. *Archives of Sexual Behavior, 18*, 421–434.

Crispell, D. (1996, July). Empty nests are getting fuller. *The Numbers News.* Retrieved July 17, 2000, from http://www.demographics.com/ publications/fc/96_nn/9607_nn/9607NN11.htm

Crnic, K. A., and Booth, C. L. (1991). Mothers' and fathers' perceptions of daily hassles of parenting across early childhood. *Journal of Marriage and the Family, 53*, 1042–1050.

Crohan, S. E. (1996). Marital quality and conflict that crossed the transition to parenthood in African-American and White couples. *Journal of Marriage and the Family, 58*, 933–944.

Crosbie-Burnett, M., and Giles-Sims, J. (1994). Adolescent adjustment of stepparenting styles. *Family Relations, 43*, 394–399.

Crouter, A. C., Bumpas, M. F., Head, M.R., and McHale, S. M. (2001). Implications of overwork and overload for the quality of men's family relationships. *Journal of Marriage and the Family, 63*(2), 404–416.

Crouter, A. C., Helms-Erikson, H., Updegraff, K., and McHale, S. M. (1999). Conditions underlying parents' knowledge about children's daily lives in middle childhood: Between and within family comparisons. *Child Development, 70*, 246–259.

Crystal, S., and Beck, P. (1992). A room of one's own: SRO and the single elderly. *The Gerontologist, 32*, 684–692.

C-section rates remain high, but postcesarean vaginal births are rising. (1989). *Family Planning Perspectives, 21*, 36–37.

Csikszentmihalyi, M. (1999, October). If we are so rich, why aren't we happy? *American Psychologist*, 821–827.

Csikszentmihalyi, M., and Schneider, B. (2000). *Becoming Adult: How Teenagers Prepare for Work.* New York: Basic Books.

Curran, D. (1983). *Traits of a Healthy Family.* New York: Ballantine Books.

Cushman, L. F., Romero, D., Kalmuss, D., Davidsong, A. R., Heartwell, S., and Rubin, M. (1998). Condom use among women choosing long-term hormonal contraception. *Family Planning Perspectives, 30*(5), 240, 243.

Cushner, I. M. (1986). Reproductive technologies: New choices, new hopes, new dilemmas. *Family Planning Perspectives, 18*, 129–132.

Dail, P. W., and Way, W. L. (1985). What do parents observe about parenting upon prime time television? *Family Relations, 34,* 491–499.

Dalla, R. L., and Gamble, W. C. (1997). Exploring factors relating to parenting competence among Navaho teenage mothers: Dual techniques of inquiry. *Family Relations, 46,* 113–121.

Dandeneau, N. L., and Johnson, F. N. (1994). Facilitating intimacy: Interventions and effects. *Journal of Marital and Family Therapy, 20,* 17–33.

Darling, N., Dowdy, B. B., VanHorn, M. L., and Caldwell, L. L. (1999). Mixed-sex settings and the perception of competence. *Journal of Youth and Adolescence, 28*(4), 461–480.

Darney, P. D. (1990). Acceptance and perceptions of NORPLANT among users in San Francisco, U.S.A. *Studies in Family Planning, 21,* 152.

Davidson, J. (1989). Longevity blooms with younger grooms. *Psychology Today, 21,* 72.

Davies, L. (1995). A closer look at gender and distress among the never married. *Women and Health, 23,* 13–30.

Davis, K. E. (1985). Near and dear: Friendship and love compared. *Psychology Today, 19,* 22–30.

Davis-Brown, K., Salamon, S., and Surra, C. A. (1987). Economic and social factors in mate selection: An ethnographic analysis of an agriculture community. *Journal of Marriage and the Family, 49,* 41–55.

Day, J. C., and Newburger, E. C. (2002, July). The big payoff: Educational attainment and synthetic estimates of work-life earnings. *Current Population Reports,* Series P23-210). Washington, DC: U.S. Bureau of the Census, Economics and Statistics Administration.

Deacon, S. (1999). Explore your family: An experiential family-of-origin workshop. *Family Therapy, 26*(2), 87–102.

Deater-Deckard, K., and Scarr, S. (1996). Parenting stress among dual-earner mothers and fathers: Are there gender differences? *Journal of Family Psychology, 10*(1), 45–59.

Deaux, K., and Major, B. (1987). Putting gender into context: An interactive model of gender-related behavior. *Psychological Review, 94,* 369–389.

DeGarmo, D. S., and Forgatch, M. S. (1999). Contexts as predictors of changing maternal parenting practices in diverse family structures. In E. M. Hetherington (Ed.), *Coping with Divorce, Single Parenting, and Remarriage: A Risk and Resiliency Perspective* (pp. 227–252). Mahwah, NJ: Erlbaum.

DeGarmo, D. S., and Kipson, G. C. (1996). Identity relevance and disruption as predictors of psychological stress for widowed and divorced women. *Journal of Marriage and the Family, 58,* 983–997.

Dekovic, M., and Gerris, J. R. M. (1992). Parental reasoning complexity, social class, and child-rearing behaviors. *Journal of Marriage and the Family, 54,* 675–685.

Dekovic, M., and Janssens, J. M. A. M. (1992). Parents' child-rearing style and child's sociometric status. *Developmental Psychology, 28,* 925–932.

DeMaris, A., and Swinford, S. (1996). Female victims of spousal violence. *Family Relations, 45,* 98–106.

DeMeis, D. K., and Perkins, H. W. (1996). "Super moms" of the nineties. *Journal of Family Issues, 17,* 777–792.

Demo, D. H. (1992). Parent–child relations: Recent changes. *Journal of Marriage and the Family, 54,* 104–117.

Demo, D. H., and Acock, A. C. (1993). Family diversity and the division of domestic labor. How much have things really changed? *Family Relations, 42,* 323-331.

Demo, D. H., and Acock, A. C. (1996a). Family structure, family process, and adolescent well-being. *Journal of Research on Adolescence, 6*(4), 457–488.

Demo, D. H., and Acock, A. C. (1996b). Singlehood, marriage, and remarriage. *Journal of Family Issues, 17,* 388–407.

Denham, T. E., and Smith, C. W. (1989). The influence of grandparents and grandchildren: A review of the literature and resources. *Family Relations, 38,* 345–350.

Depaulo, B. (2001, October 23). Singleness is not the same as not settled. *USA Today,* p. D2.

Desmarais, S., and Curtis, J. (1999). Gender differences in employment and income experiences among young people. In J. Barling and E. Kelloway (Eds.), *Young Workers' Varieties of Experiences* (pp. 59–88). Washington, DC: American Psychological Association.

deTurck, M. A., and Miller, G. R. (1986). The effect of husbands' and wives' social cognition on their marital adjustment, conjugal power and self-esteem. *Journal of Marriage and the Family, 48,* 715–724.

Dhir, K. S., and Markman, H. J. (1984). Application of social judgment theory to understanding and treating marital conflict. *Journal of Marriage and the Family, 46,* 597–610.

Dionne, E. J., Jr. (1989, August 3). Poll finds ambivalence on abortion persists in U.S. *New York Times,* p. 1.

Dodson, L. (1998). *Don't Call Us Out of Name: The Untold Lives of Women and Girls in Poor America.* Boston: Beacon Press.

Doe v. Bolton, 410 U.S. 179 (1973).

Doherty, W. J. (2001). *Take Back Your Marriage: Sticking Together in a World That Pulls Us Apart.* New York: Guilford Press.

Doherty, W. J., Su, S., and Needle, R. (1989). Marital disruption and psychological well-being. *Journal of Family Issues, 10,* 72–85.

Dolan, M. A., and Hoffman, C. D. (1998). Determinants of divorce among young women: A reexamination of critical influences. *Journal of Divorce and Remarriage, 28*(3/4), 97–106.

Donovan, C. (1997). Confronting the hidden epidemic: The Institute of Medicine's report on sexually transmitted diseases. *Family Planning Perspectives, 29,* 87–89.

Donovan, C., and Klitsch, N. (1995). Oral contraceptive users may be at some increased risk of cervical carcinoma. *Family Planning Perspectives, 27,* 134–136.

Donovan, P. (1994). Condom breaks and slips occur more often among less experienced users. *Family Planning Perspectives, 26,* 283–284.

Dooley, D., Catalano, R., and Rook, K. S. (1988). Personal and aggregate unemployment and psychological symptoms. *Journal of Social Issues, 47,* 107–123.

Dorfman, L. T., and Heckert, D. A. (1988). Egalitarianism in retired rural couples: Household tasks, decision making, and leisure activities. *Family Relations, 37,* 73–78.

Dorfman, L. T., and Mertens, C. E. (1990). Kinship relations in retired rural men and women. *Family Relations, 39,* 166–173.

Dowling, C. (1983). The relative explosion. *Psychology Today, 17,* 54–59.

Downey, G., Lebolt, A., and Rincon, C. (1998). Rejection sensitivity and children's interpersonal difficulties. *Child Development, 69,* 1074–1091.

Downie, J., and Coates, R. (1999). The impact of gender on parent–child sexuality communication: Has anything changed? *Sexual and Marital Therapy, 14*(2), 109–121.

Doyle, J. A. (1985). *Sex and Gender.* Dubuque, IA: Brown.

Dreman, S., Orr, E., and Aldor, R. (1989). Competence or dissonance? Divorcing mothers' perceptions of sense of competence and time perspective. *Journal of Marriage and the Family, 51,* 405–415.

Dressel, P. L. (1980). Assortive mating in later life. *Journal of Family Issues, 1,* 379–396.

Dressel, P. L., and Clark, A. (1990). A critical look at family care. *Journal of Marriage and the Family, 52,* 769–782.

Dubroff, L. M., and Papalian, M. M. (1982, June). Syphilis and gonorrhea in pregnant patients. *Medical Aspects of Human Sexuality, 16,* 85–90.

Duck, S. W. (1982). A topography of relationship disengagement and dissolution. In S. W. Duck (Ed.), *Personal Relationships. 4: Dissolving Personal Relationships* (pp. 1–29). London: Academic Press.

Duncan, S., Box, T., and Silliman, B. (1996). Racial and gender effects on perceptions of marriage preparation programs among college-educated young adults. *Family Relations, 45,* 80–90.

Dunn, P. C., Ryan, I. J., and O'Brien, K. (1988). College students' acceptance of adoption and five alternative fertilization techniques. *Journal of Sex Research, 24,* 282–287.

Dupre, A. R., Hampton, H. L., Morrison, H., and Meeks, G. R. (1993). Sexual assault. *Obstetrical and Gynecological Survey, 48,* 640–648.

Dusky, L. (2003, Spring). Harvard stumbles over rape reporting. *Ms.* pp. 39–40.

Dutton, D., and Aron, A. P. (1974). Some evidence of heightened sexual attraction under conditions of high anxiety. *Journal of Personal and Social Psychology, 30,* 510–517.

Duvall, E. M. (1954). *In-Laws: Pro and Con.* New York: Association Press.

Duvall, E. M. (1977). *Marriage and Family Development* (5th ed.). Philadelphia: Lippincott.

Dwyer, J. W., and Coward, R. T. (1991). A multivariate comparison of the involvement of the adult sons versus daughters in care of impaired parents. *Journal of Gerontology, 46,* S259–S269.

Dyk, P. A. H. (1990). Healthy family sexuality: Challenge and assessment. *Family Relations, 39,* 216–220.

Eckenrode, J., Laird, N., and Doris, J. (1993). School performance and disciplinary problems among abused and neglected children. *Developmental Psychology, 29,* 53–62.

Edwards, J. N. (1987). Changing family structure and youthful well-being. *Journal of Family Issues, 8,* 355–372.

Edwards, J. N. (1991). New conceptions: Biosocial innovations and the family. *Journal of Marriage and the Family, 53,* 349–360.

Edwards, S. (1992a). Among high-risk adults, men with more than four partners, women older than 19 used condoms less. *Family Planning Perspectives, 24,* 283–284.

Edwards, S. (1992b). Early environment and mothers' intellectual ability affect cognitive attainment of adolescents' children. *Family Planning Perspectives, 24,* 89–90.

Edwards, S. (1994). Women who have undergone a tubal sterilization have a reduced risk of contracting ovarian cancer. *Family Planning Perspectives, 26,* 90–91.

Eggebeen, D. J. (1988). Determinants of maternal employment for White preschool children: 1960–1980. *Journal of Marriage and the Family, 50,* 149–159.

Eggebeen, D. J. (1992). Family structure and intergenerational exchanges. *Research on Aging, 14,* 427–447.

Eggebeen, D. J., and Hawkins, A. J. (1990). Economic need and wives' employment. *Journal of Family Issues, 11,* 48–66.

Ehrensaft, M., Langhinrichsen-Rohling, J., Heyman, R., O'Leary, K., and Lawrence, E. (1999). Feeling controlled in marriage: A phenomenon specific to physically aggressive couples. *Journal of Family Psychology, 13*(1), 20–32.

Eiger, M. S., and Olds, S. W. (1987). *The Complete Book of Breastfeeding.* New York: Workman.

Eisikovits, Z. C., Edleson, J. L., Guttmann, E., and Sela-Amit, M. (1991). Cognitive styles and socialized attitudes of men who batter: Where should we intervene? *Family Relations, 40,* 72–77.

Eitzen, D. S., and Zinn, M. B. (2000). The missing safety net and families: A progressive critique of the new welfare legislation. *Journal of Sociology and Social Welfare, 27*(1), 53–72.

Ekman, P., Levenson, R. W., and Friesen, W. V. (1983). Autonomic nervous system activity distinguishes among emotions. *Science, 221,* 1208–1210.

Elder, G. H., Conger, R. D., Foster, E. M., and Ardelt, M. (1992). Families under economic pressure. *Journal of Family Issues, 13,* 5–37.

Elder, G. H., Jr., Eccles, J. S., Ardelt, M., and Lord, S. (1995). Inner-city parents under economic pressure: Perspectives on strategies of parenting. *Journal of Marriage and the Family, 57,* 771–784.

Elliot, F. R. (1986). *The Family: Change or Continuity?* Atlantic Highlands, NJ: Humanities Press International.

Emery, R. E. (1994). *Renegotiating Family Relationships: Divorce, Child Custody, and Mediation.* New York: Guilford Press.

Emery, R. E. (1995). Divorce mediation: Negotiating agreements and renegotiating relationships. *Family Relations, 44,* 377–383.

Emery, R. E., and Forehand, R. (1996). Parental divorce and children's well-being: A focus on resilience. In R. J. Haggerty, L. R. Sherrod, N. Garmezy, and M. J. Rutter (Eds.), *Stress, Risk, and Resilience in Children and Adolescents: Processes, Mechanisms, and Interventions* (pp. 64–99). New York: Cambridge University Press.

Engle, G., Olson, K. R., and Patrick, C. (2002). The personality of love: Fundamental motives and traits related to components of love. *Personality and Individual Differences, 32*(5), 839–853.

England, L. W., and Thompson, C. L. (1988). Counseling child sexual abuse victims: Myths and realities. *Journal of Counseling and Development, 66,* 370–373.

Enns, C. Z. (1988). Dilemmas of power and equality in marital and family counseling: Proposal for a feminist perspective. *Journal of Counseling and Development, 67,* 242–248.

Ensminger, M. E., and Celentano, D. D. (1988). Unemployment and psychiatric distress. *Social Science Medicine, 27,* 239–247.

Entwisle, D. R., and Alexander, K. L. (1996). Family type and children's growth in reading and math over the primary grades. *Journal of Marriage and the Family, 58,* 341–355.

Erera-Weatherley, P. I. (1996). On becoming a stepparent: Factors associated with the adoption of alternative stepparenting styles. *Journal of Divorce and Remarriage, 25*(3/4), 155–174.

Erikson, E. H. (1959). *Identity and the Life Cycle.* New York: International Universities Press.

Erkut, S., Fields, J., Sing, R., and Marx, F. (1996). Diversity in girls' experiences: Feeling good about who you are. In B. Leadbeater and N. Way (Eds.), *Urban Girls.* New York: New York University Press.

Essex, M. J., and Nam, S. (1987). Marital status and loneliness among older women: The differential importance of close family and friends. *Journal of Marriage and the Family, 49,* 93–106.

Fass, P. S. (1977). *The Damned and the Beautiful.* New York: Oxford University Press.

Feeney, J. A. (1999a). Issues of closeness and distance in dating relationships: Effects of sex and attachment style. *Journal of Social and Personal Relationships, 16*(5), 571–590.

Feeney, J. A. (1999b). Romantic bonds in young adulthood: Links with family experiences. *Journal of Family Studies, 5*(1), 25–46.

Feeney, J. A., and Noller, P. (1991). Attachment style and verbal descriptions of romantic partners. *Journal of Social and Personal Relationships, 8,* 187–215.

Feeney, J. A., and Noller, P. (1996). *Adult Attachment.* Thousand Oaks, CA: Sage.

Feingold, A., and Mazzella, R. (1998). Gender differences in body image are increasing. *Psychological Science, 9*(3), 190–195.

Feldman, C. M. (1997). Childhood precursors of adult interpartner violence. *Clinical Psychology: Science and Practice, 4,* 307–334.

Feldman, S. S., Mont-Reynaud, R., and Rosenthal, D. A. (1992). When East moves West: Acculturation of values of Chinese adolescents in the United States and Australia. *Journal of Research on Adolescence, 2,* 147–173.

Feldman, S. S., Wentzel, K. R., and Gehring, T. M. (1989). A comparison of the views of mothers, fathers, and preadolescents about family cohesion and power. *Journal of Family Psychology, 3,* 39–60.

Felson, R. B., and Zielinski, M. A. (1989). Children's self-esteem and parental support. *Journal of Marriage and the Family, 51,* 727–735.

Felton, G., and Segelman, F. (1978). Lamaze childbirth training and changes in belief about personal control. *Birth and Family Journal, 5,* 141–150.

Feng, D., Giarrusso, R., Bengtson, V. L., and Frye, N. (1999). Intergenerational transmission of marital quality and marital instability. *Journal of Marriage and the Family, 61,* 451–463.

Ferree, M. M. (1990). Beyond separate spheres: Feminism and family research. *Journal of Marriage and the Family, 52,* 866–884.

Ferree, M. M. (1991). The gender division of labor in two-earner marriages. *Journal of Family Issues, 12,* 158–180.

Ferreiro, B. W., Warren, N. J., and Konanc, J. T. (1986). ADAP: A divorce assessment proposal. *Family Relations, 35,* 439–449.

Field, D. (1999). Continuity and change in friendships in advanced old age: Findings from the Berkeley Older Generational Study. *International Journal of Aging and Human Development, 48,* 325–346.

Fields, J., and Casper, L. M. (2001). America's Families and Living Arrangements: March 2000. Current Population Reports, P20-537, U.S. Census Bureau, Washington, DC.

Filsinger, E. E., and Thoma, S. J. (1988). Behavioral antecedents of relationship stability and adjustment: A five-year longitudinal study. *Journal of Marriage and the Family, 50,* 785–795.

Fincham, F. D., and Bradbury, T. N. (1992). Assessing attributions in marriage: The relationship attribution measure. *Journal of Personality and Social Psychology, 62,* 457–468.

Finding Answers and Support for Herpes. (1999). Research Triangle Park, NC: American Social Health Association. Retrieved from http://www.ashastd.org/herpes/hrc/educate.html

Fine, M., and Hovestadt, A. J. (1984). Perceptions of marriage and rationality by levels of perceived health in the family of origin. *Journal of Marriage and Family Therapy, 10,* 193–195.

Fine, M. A., and Kurdek, L. A. (1995). Relation between marital quality and (step)parent–child relationship quality for parents and stepparents in stepfamilies. *Journal of Family Psychology, 9*(2), 216–223.

Fine, M. A., McKenry, P. C., Donnelly, B. W., and Voydanoff, P. (1992). Perceived adjustment of parents and children: Variations by family structure, race, and gender. *Journal of Marriage and the Family, 54,* 118–127.

Fine, M. A., Voydanoff, P., and Donnelly, B. W. (1993). Relations between parental control and warmth and child well-being in stepfamilies. *Journal of Family Psychology, 7,* 222–232.

Fingerhut, L. A., Makuc, D., and Kleinman, J. C. (1987). Delayed prenatal care and place of first visit: Differences by health insurance and education. *Family Planning Perspectives, 19,* 212–214.

Fingerman, K. L. (1996). Sources of tension in the aging mother and adult daughter relationship. *Psychology and Aging, 11,* 591–606.

Finkelhor, D. (1980). Sex among siblings: A survey on prevalence, variety, and effects. *Archives of Sexual Behavior, 9,* 171–194.

Finkelhor, D., and Araji, S. (1986). Explanations of pedophilia: A four factor model. *The Journal of Sex Research, 22,* 145–161.

Finkelhor, D., Mitchell, K., and Wolak, J. (2000). *Online Victimization: A Report on the Nation's Youth.* Washington, DC: National Center for Missing and Exploited Children.

Finlay, B. A. (1981). Sex differences in correlates of abortion: Attitudes among college students. *Journal of Marriage and the Family, 43,* 571–581.

Firestone, J., Harris, R., and Lambert, L. (1999). Gender role ideology and the gender based differences in earnings. *Journal of Family and Economic Issues, 20*(2), 191–215.

Firestone, J., and Shelton, B. A. (1988). An estimation of the effect of women's work on available leisure time. *Journal of Family Issues, 9,* 478–495.

Fischer, J. L., Sollie, D. L., Sorell, G. T., and Green, S. K. (1989). Marital status and career stage influence on social networks of young adults. *Journal of Marriage and the Family, 51,* 521–534.

Fischer, L. R. (1983). Mothers and mothers-in-law. *Journal of Marriage and the Family, 45,* 187–192.

Fischman, J. (1986). Women and divorce: Ten years after. *Psychology Today, 20,* 15.

Fisher, C. B., Reid, J. D., and Melendez, M. (1989). Conflict in families and friendships of later life. *Family Relations, 38,* 83–89.

Fisher, P. A., and Fagot, B. I. (1993). Negative discipline in families. A multidimensional risk model. *Journal of Family Psychology, 7,* 250–254.

Fishman, B. (1983). The economic behavior of stepfamilies. *Family Relations, 32,* 359–366.

Fitzgerald, B. (1999). Children of lesbian and gay parents: A review of the literature. *Marriage and Family Review, 29*(1), 57–75.

Fletcher, G., Simpson, J., Thomas, G., and Giles, L. (1999). Ideals in intimate relationships. *Journal of Personality and Social Psychology, 76*(1), 72–89.

Floge, L. (1989). Changing attitudes toward family issues in the United States. *Journal of Marriage and the Family, 51,* 873–893.

Floyd, F. J. (1988). Couples' cognitive/affective reactions to communication behaviors. *Journal of Marriage and the Family, 50,* 523–532.

Floyd, F. J., Hanes, S. N., Doll, E. R., Winemiller, D., Lemsky, C., Burgy, T. M., Werle, M., and Heilman, N. (1992). Assessing retirement satisfaction and perceptions of retirement experiences. *Psychology and Aging, 7,* 609–621.

Flynn, C. P. (1990). Relationship violence by women: Issues and implications. *Family Relations, 39,* 194–198.

Folk, K. F., and Beller, A. H. (1993). Part-time work, child-care choices for mothers of preschool children. *Journal of Marriage and the Family, 55,* 146–157.

Forrest, J. D. (1986). The end of IUD marketing in the United States: What does it mean for American women? *Family Planning Perspectives, 18,* 52–57.

Forste, R., Tanfer, K., and Tedrow, L. (1995). Sterilization among currently married men in the United States, 1991. *Family Planning Perspectives, 27,* 100–122.

Forthofer, M. S., Markman, H. J., Cox, M., Stanley, S., and Kessler, R. C. (1996). Associations between marital distress and work loss in a national sample. *Journal of Marriage and the Family, 58,* 597–605.

Forward, S. (1986). *Men Who Hate Women: The Women Who Love Them.* New York: Bantam Books.

Foshee, V. A., Linder, G. F., Bauman, K. E., Langwick, S. A., Arriaga, X. B., Heath, J. L., McMahon, P. M., and Bangdiwala, S. (1996). The safe dates project: Theoretical basis, evaluation design, and selected baseline findings. *American Journal of Preventive Medicine, Supplement, 12*(5), 39–47.

Fossett, M. A., and Kiecolt, K. J. (1993). Mate availability and family structure among African-Americans in U.S. metropolitan areas. *Journal of Marriage and the Family, 55,* 288–302.

Foster, D., Klinger-Vartabedian, L., and Wispe, L. (1984). Male longevity and age differences between spouses. *Journal of Gerontology, 39,* 117–120.

Foster, S. E., Vaughn, R. D., Foster, W. H. and Califano, J. A., Jr. (2003). Alcohol consumption and expenditures for underage drinking and adult excessive drinking. *Journal of the American Medical Association, 289*(8), 989–995.

Fowers, B. J. (2000). *The Myth of Marital Happiness.* San Francisco: Jossey-Bass.

Fowers, B. J., Montel, K. H., and Olson, D. H. (1996). Predicting marital success for premarital couple types based on PREPARE. *Journal of Marital and Family Therapy, 22,* 103–119.

Fowers, B. J., and Olson, D. H. (1986). Predicting marital success with PREPARE: A predictive validity study. *Journal of Marital and Family Therapy, 12,* 403–413.

Fowers, B. J., and Olson, D. H. (1989). ENRICH marital inventory: A discriminant validity and cross-validation assessment. *Journal of Marital and Family Therapy, 15,* 65–79.

Fowler, C. R. (1982). How to destroy marriage. *Medical Aspects of Human Sexuality, 16,* 16–31A.

Francome, C. (1992). Irish women who seek abortions in England. *Family Planning Perspectives, 24,* 265–268.

Frank, N. L., Poindexter, A. N., Johnson, N. L., and Bateman, L. (1992). Characteristics and attitudes of early contraceptive implant acceptors in Texas. *Family Planning Perspectives, 24,* 209–213.

Franklin, D. L., Smith, S. E., and McMiller, W. E. C. (1995). Correlates of marital status among African-American mothers in Chicago neighborhoods of concentrated poverty. *Journal of Marriage and the Family, 57,* 141–152.

Franklin, R. L., and Hibbs, "B." (1980). Child custody in transition. *Journal of Marital and Family Therapy, 6,* 285–291.

Franzwa, G., and Lockhart, C. (1998). The social origins and maintenance of gender: Communication styles, personality types and grid-group theory. *Sociological Perspectives, 41*(1), 185–208.

Fredericks, C. (1999). HIV testers and non-testers at a university student health center: A study of college student sexual risk-taking. (Doctoral dissertation, University of Southern California, 1999). *Dissertation Abstracts International, 60,* 2-A.0346.

Freud, S. (1953). *Three Essays on the Theory of Sexuality* (Standard ed.). Vol. 7. London: Hogarth, 1953.

Freudenberger, H. J. (1987). Today's troubled men. *Psychology Today, 21,* 46–47.

Friedman, P. (2000, April). The earned income tax credit. *Welfare Information Network Issue Notes, 4*(4). Retrieved April 9, 2003, from www.welfareinfo.org

Fromm, E. (1956). *The Art of Loving.* New York: Harper & Row.

Fuligni, A., Burton, L., Marshall, S., Perez-Febles, A., Yarrington, J., Kirsh, L., and Merriwether-DeVries, C. (1999). Attitudes toward family obligations among American adolescents with Asian, Latin American, and European backgrounds. *Child Development, 70*(4), 1030–1044.

Gabrel, C., and Jones, A. (2000). The National Nursing Home Survey: 1997 summary. *Vital Health and Statistics, 13*(147).

Gage, M. G., and Christensen, D. H. (1991). Parental roles, socialization and transition to parenthood. *Family Relations, 40,* 332–337.

Galambos, N. L., and Silbereisen, R. K. (1989). Role strain in West German dual-earner households. *Journal of Marriage and the Family, 51,* 385–389.

Galinsky, E. (1999). *Ask the Children: What America's Children Really Think about Working Parents.* New York: Morrow.

Galinsky, E., and Bond, J. T. (1998). *The 1998 Business Work-Life Study: A Sourcebook.* New York: Families and Work Institute.

Galinsky, E., and Johnson, A. A. (1998). *Reframing the Business Case for Work-Life Initiatives.* New York: Families and Work Institute.

Galliher, R. V., Rostosky, S. S., Welsh, D. P., and Kawaguchi, M. C. (1999). Power and psychological well-being in late adolescent romantic relationships. *Sex Roles, 40,* 689–710.

Galvin, K. M., and Brommel, B. J. (1986). *Family Communication: Cohesion and Change* (2nd ed.). Glenview, IL: Scott, Foresman.

Ganong, L. H., and Coleman, M. (1994). *Remarried Family Relationships.* Thousand Oaks, CA: Sage.

Ganong, L. H., Coleman, M., Fine, M., and Martin, P. (1999). Stepparents' affinity-seeking and affinity-maintaining strategies with stepchildren. *Journal of Family Issues, 20*(3), 299–327.

Garcia, E. C. (2001). Parenting in Mexican American families. In N. B. Webb (Ed.), *Culturally Diverse Parent–Child and Family Relationships: A Guide for Social Workers and Other Practitioners* (pp. 157–179). New York: Columbia University Press.

Garcia, S., and Khersonsky, D. (1997). They are a lovely couple: Further examination of perceptions of couple attractiveness. *Journal of Social Behavior and Personality, 12*(2), 367–380.

Garfinkel, I., and McLanahan, S. S. (1986). *Single Mothers and Their Children.* Washington, DC: Urban Institute.

Garner, D. M. (1997, January/February). Body image. *Psychology Today,* 32–84.

Garrett, M. T., and Wilbur, M. P. (1999). Does the worm live in the ground? Reflections on Native American spirituality. *Journal of Multicultural Counseling and Development, 27*(4), 193–206.

Gary, L., Beatty, L. A., and Berry, G. L. (1986). Strong Black families: Models of program development for Black families. In S. Van Zandt et al. (Eds.), *Family Strengths 7: Vital Connections* (pp. 453–468). Lincoln, NE: Center for Family Strengths.

Gates, G. J. and Sonenstein, F. L. (2000). Heterosexual genital sexual activity among adolescent males: 1988 and 1995. *Family Planning Perspectives, 32*(6), 295–297 and 304.

Gayles, G. (1984). The truths of our mother's lives: Mother–daughter relationships in Black women's fiction. *Sage: A Scholarly Journal on Black Women, 1,* 8–12.

Gazmararian, J. A., et al. (1995). The relationship between pregnancy intendedness and physical violence in mothers of newborns. *Obstetrics and Gynecology, 85,* 1031–1038.

Gelles, R. J., and Conte, J. R. (1990). Domestic violence and sexual abuse of children: A review of research in the eighties. *Journal of Marriage and the Family, 52,* 1045–1058.

Gelles, R. J., and Harrop, J. W. (1991). The risk of abusive violence among children with nongenetic caregivers. *Family Relations, 40,* 78–83.

Gelles, R. J., and Maynard, P. E. (1987). A structural family systems approach to intervention in cases of family violence. *Family Relations, 36,* 270–275.

Gelster, K. L. P., and Feinauer, L. L. (1988). Divorce potential and marital stability of adult women sexually abused as children compared to adult women not sexually abused as children. *Journal of Marital and Family Therapy, 14,* 269–277.

Gerstel, N. (1988). Divorce and kin ties: The importance of gender. *Journal of Marriage and the Family, 50,* 209–219.

Giarrusso, R., Stallings, M., and Bengtson. V. L. (1995). *The "Intergenerational Hypothesis" Revisited: Parent–Child Differences in Perceptions of Relationships 20 Years Later.* New York: Springer.

Gibbs, J. (1996). Health compromising behaviors in urban early adolescent females: Ethnic and socioeconomic variations. In B. Leadbeater and N. Way (Eds.), *Urban Girls.* New York: New York University Press.

Gigy, L., and Kelly, J. B. (1992). Reasons for divorce: Perspectives of divorcing men and women. *Journal of Divorce and Remarriage, 18,* 169–187.

Gilbert, N. (2003). Working families; Hearth to market. In M. A. Mason, A. Skolnick, and S. D. Sugarman (Eds.), *All Our Families* (pp. 220–243). New York: Oxford University Press.

Giles, D. (1994). Summer resorts: Black resort towns are enjoying a renaissance thanks to buppies and their families. *Black Enterprise, 25,* 90–91.

Giles-Sims, J., Straus, M. A., and Sugarman, D. B. (1995). Child, maternal, and family characteristics associated with corporal punishment. *Family Relations, 44,* 170–176.

Gilgun, J. F. (1995). We shared something special: The moral discourse of incest perpetrators. *Journal of Marriage and the Family, 57,* 265–281.

Gill, G. K. (1998). The strategic involvement of children in housework: An Australian case of two-income families. *International Journal of Comparative Sociology, 39,* 301–314.

Gillespie, R. (2000). Disbelief, disregard and deviance as discourses of voluntary childlessness. *Women's Studies International Forum, 23,* 223–234.

Gillespie, R. (2003). Understanding the gender identity of voluntarily childless women. *Gender and Society, 17*(1), 122–136.

Ginsburg, G. S., and Bronstein, P. (1993). Family factors related to children's intrinsic/extrinsic motivational orientation and academic performance. *Child Development, 64,* 1461–1474.

Gist, J. and Figueiredo, C. (2002). *Deeper in Debt: Trends among Midlife and Older Americans.* (Available from AARP Public Policy Institute, 601 E Street, NW, Washington, DC 20049).

Gladow, N. W., and Ray, M. P. (1986). The impact of informal support systems on the well-being of low income single parents. *Family Relations, 35,* 123–125.

Gladstone, J. W. (1988). Perceived changes in grandmother–grandchild relations following a child's separation or divorce. *The Gerontologist, 28,* 66–72.

Glascoe, F. P., and MacLean, W. E. (1990). How parents appraise their child's development. *Family Relations, 39,* 280–283.

Glass, J. (1992). Housewives and employed wives: Demographic and attitudinal change, 1972–1986. *Journal of Marriage and the Family, 54,* 559–569.

Glenn, N. D. (1991). The recent trend in marital success in the United States. *Journal of Marriage and the Family, 53,* 261–270.

Glenn, N. D. (1999). Further discussion of the effects of no-fault divorce on divorce rates. *Journal of Marriage and the Family, 61,* 800–802.

Glenn, N. D., and Kramer, K. B. (1985). The psychological well-being of adult children of divorce. *Journal of Marriage and the Family, 47,* 905–912.

Glenn, N. D., and Marquardt, E. (2001). *Hooking Up, Hanging Out, and Hoping for Mr. Right: College Women on Dating and Mating Today.* New York: Institute for American Values.

Glenn, N. D., and McLanahan, S. (1982). Children and marital happiness: A further specification of the relationship. *Journal of Marriage and the Family, 44,* 63–72.

Glenn, N. D., and Weaver, C. N. (1988). The changing relationships of marital status to reported happiness. *Journal of Marriage and the Family, 50,* 317–324.

Glick, P. C. (1976). Updating the life cycle of the family. *Journal of Marriage and the Family, 39,* 5–13.

Glick, P. C. (1990). American families: As they are and were. *Sociology and Social Research, 74,* 139–145.

Globerman, J. (1996). Motivations to care: Daughters and sons-in-law caring for relatives with Alzheimer's disease. *Family Relations, 45,* 37–45.

Glover, G. (2001). Parenting in Native American Families. In N. B. Webb (Ed.), *Culturally Diverse Parent–Child and Family Relationships: A Guide for Social Workers and Other Practitioners.* New York: Columbia University Press.

Godwin, D. D., Draughn, P. S., Little, L. F., and Marlowe, J. (1991). Wives' off-farm employment, farm family economic status, and family relationships. *Journal of Marriage and the Family, 53,* 389–402.

Goetting, A. (1987). Homicidal wives. *Journal of Family Issues, 8,* 332–341.

Goetting, A. (1990). Patterns of support among in-laws in the United States. *Journal of Family Issues, 11,* 67–90.

Gold, M. A., Schein, A., and Coupey, S. M. (1997). Emergency contraception: A national survey of adolescent health activity. *Family Planning Perspectives, 29,* 15–19.

Goldberg, S. B. (2003, Spring). For a woman to get that federal court nomination, does she have to be Scalia in a skirt? *Ms.,* pp. 42–46.

Goldberg, W. A., Greenberger, E., Hamill, S., and O'Neil, R. (1992). Role demands in the lives of employed single mothers with preschoolers. *Journal of Family Issues, 13,* 312–333.

Goldscheider, F. K., and Goldscheider, C. (1989). Family structure and conflict: Nest-leaving expectations of young adults and their parents. *Journal of Marriage and the Family, 51,* 87–97.

Goldsteen, K., and Ross, C. E. (1989). The perceived burden of children. *Journal of Family Issues, 10,* 504–526.

Goldstein, C., and Rosenbaum, A. (1985). An evaluation of the self-esteem of maritally violent men. *Family Relations, 34,* 425–428.

Goldstein, J. R. (1999). The leveling of divorce in the United States. *Demography, 36,* 409–414.

Goldstein, L. H., Diener, N. L., and Mangelsdorf, S. C. (1996). Maternal characteristics and social support across the transition to motherhood: Associates with maternal behavior. *Journal of Family Psychology, 10,* 60–71.

Gollub, E. L., Stein, D., and El-Sadr, W. (1995). Short-term acceptability of the female condom among staff and patients at New York City Hospital. *Family Planning Perspectives, 27,* 155–158.

Good, G. E., and Mintz, L. B. (1990). Gender role conflict and depression in college men: Evidence for compounded risk. *Journal of Counseling and Development, 69,* 17–21.

Gordis, E. B., Margolin, G., and John, R. S. (1997). Marital aggression, observed parental hostility, and child behavior during triadic family interaction. *Journal of Family Psychology, 11,* 76–89.

Gordon, M. (1981). Was Waller ever right? The rating and dating complex reconsidered. *Journal of Marriage and the Family, 43,* 67–76.

Gottfried, A. E., Gottfried, A. W., Killian, C., and Bathurst, K. (1999). Maternal and dual-earner employment. In M. Lamb (Ed.), *Parenting and Child Development in "Nontraditional" Families* (pp. 15–37). Mahwah, NJ: Erlbaum.

Gottman, J. M. (1994). *What Predicts Divorce? The Relationship Between Marital Process and Marital Outcomes.* Hillsdale, NJ: Erlbaum.

Gottman, J. M. (1998). Psychology and the study of marital processes. *Annual Review of Psychology, 49,* 169–197.

Gottman, J. M. (2000a). *Seven Principles of Marriage.* New York: Crown.

Gottman, J. M. (2000b). Decade review: Observing marital interaction. *Journal of Marriage and the Family, 62*(4), 927–947.

Gottman, J. M., Coan, J., Carrere, S., and Swanson, C. (1998). Predicting marital happiness and stability from newlywed interaction. *Journal of Marriage and the Family, 60*(1), 5–22.

Gottman, J. M., and Levenson, R. W. (1988). The social psychophysiology of marriage. In P. Noller and M. A. Fitzpatrick (Eds.), *Perspective on Marital Interaction* (pp. 182–200). Philadelphia: Multilingual Matters.

Gottman, J. M., and Levenson, R. W. (1992). Marital processes predictive of later dissolution: Behavior, physiology, and health. *Journal of Personality and Social Psychology, 63,* 221–233.

Gottman, J. M., and Levenson, R. W. (2000). The timing of divorce: Predicting when a couple will divorce over a 14-year period. *Journal of Marriage and the Family, 62,* 737–745.

Gottman, J. M., and Porterfield, A. (1981). Communicative competence in the nonverbal behavior of married couples. *Journal of Marriage and the Family, 43,* 817–824.

Gottman, J. M., and Silver, N. (1999). *The Seven Principles for Making Marriage Work.* New York: Crown.

Gove, W. R., and Shin, H. (1989). The psychological well-being of divorced and widowed men and women. *Journal of Family Issues, 10,* 122–144.

Graefe, D. R. and Lichter, D. T. (1999). Life course transitions of American Children: Parental cohabitation, marriage and single motherhood. *Demography, 36*(2), 205–217.

Grall, T. (September, 2000). Custodial mothers and fathers and their child support. (*Current Population Reports* Series P 60–217). Washington. DC: U.S. Bureau of the Census.

Gralinski, J. H., and Kopp, C. B. (1993). Everyday rules for behavior: Mothers' requests to young children. *Developmental Psychology, 29,* 573–584.

Grant-Vallone, E. J., and Donaldson, S. I. (2001). Consequences of work-family conflict on employee well-being over time. *Work and Stress, 15*(3), 214–226.

Granvold, D. K., and Tarrant, R. (1983). Structured marital separation as a marital treatment method. *Journal of Marital and Family Therapy, 2,* 189–198.

Graves, K. L., and Leigh, B. C. (1995). The relationship of substance use with sexual activity among young adults in the United States. *Family Planning Perspectives, 27,* 18–22.

Gray-Little, B., Baucom, D., and Hamby, S. (1996). Marital power, marital adjustment, and therapy outcome. *Journal of Family Psychology, 10*(3), 292–303.

Green, G. (1964). *Sex and the College Girl.* New York: Dial.

Green, K. L., Cameron, R., Polivy, J., Cooper, K., Liu, L., Leiter, L., and Heatherton, T. (1997). Weight dissatisfaction and weight loss attempts among Canadian adults. *Canadian Medical Association Journal, 157,* S17–S25.

Greenberg, B. S., Eastin, M., Hofschire, L., Lachlan, K., and Brownell, K. (in press). How commercial television treats obesity and other body types. *American Journal of Public Health.*

Greenberg, J. S., Bruess, C. E., and Sands, D. W. (1986). *Sexuality: Insights and Issues.* Dubuque, IA: Brown.

Greenberger, E., and O'Neil, R. (1990). Parents' concerns about their child's development: Implications for fathers' and mothers' well-being and attitudes toward work. *Journal of Marriage and the Family, 52,* 621–635.

Greenblat, C. (1983). The salience of sexuality in the early years of marriage. *Journal of Marriage and the Family, 45*(2), 289–299.

Greenstein, T. N. (1996). Husbands' participation in domestic labor: Interactive effects of wives' and husbands' gender ideology. *Journal of Marriage and the Family, 68,* 585–595.

Greif, G. L. (1986). Mothers without custody and child support. *Family Relations, 35,* 87–93.

Gringlas, M., and Weinraub, M. (1995). The more things change . . . Single parenting revisited. *Journal of Family Issues, 16,* 29–52.

Gross, D. R., and Robinson, S. E. (1987). Ethics, violence, and counseling: Hear no evil, see no evil, speak no evil? *Journal of Counseling and Development, 65,* 340–344.

Grossman, R. A., and Grossman, B. D. (1994). How frequently is emergency contraception prescribed? *Family Planning Perspectives, 26,* 270–271.

Grudzinskas, J. G., and Atkinson, L. (1984). Sexual function during the puerperium. *Archives of Sexual Behavior, 13*, 85–91.

Guberman, N., Maheu, P., and Maille, C. (1992). Women as family caregivers: Why do they care? *The Gerontologist, 32*, 607–617.

Guelzow, M. G., Bird, G. W., and Koball, E. H. (1991). An exploratory path analysis of the stress process for dual-career men and women. *Journal of Marriage and the Family, 53*, 151–164.

Guerney, B., and Maxson, P. (1990). Marital and family enrichment research: A decade review and look ahead. *Journal of Marriage and the Family, 52*, 1127–1135.

Guinzburg, S. (1983). Mothers and married sons. *Psychology Today, 17*, 14.

Gutmann, M. C. (1996). *The Meanings of Macho: Being a Man in Mexico City.* Berkeley: University of California Press.

Guttmacher, A. F. (1983). *Pregnancy, Birth, and Family Planning* (Revised and updated by I. H. Kaiser). New York: New American Library.

Gwinnell, E. (1998). *Online Seductions: Falling in Love with Strangers on the Internet.* New York: Kodansha International.

Hackel, L. S., and Ruble, D. N. (1992). Changes in the marital relationship after the first baby is born: Predicting the impact of expectancy disconfirmation. *Journal of Personality and Social Psychology, 62*, 944–957.

Haddock, S. A., Ziemba, S. J., Schindler Zimmerman, T., and Current, L. R. (2001). Ten adaptive strategies for family and work balance: Advice from successful families. *Journal of Marital and Family Therapy, 27*(4), 445–458.

Haggstrom, G. W., Kanouse, D. E., and Morrison, P. A. (1986). Accounting for the educational shortfalls of mothers. *Journal of Marriage and the Family, 48*, 175–186.

Hahn, B. A. (1993). Marital status in women's health: The effect of economic marital acquisitions. *Journal of Marriage and the Family, 55*, 495–504.

Haley, J. (1982). Restoring law and order in the family. *Psychology Today, 16*, 61–69.

Halford, W. K., Hahlweg, K., and Dunne, M. (1990). The cross-cultural consistency of marital communication associated with marital distress. *Journal of Marriage and the Family, 52*, 487–500.

Hall, E. J., and Cummings, E. M. (1997). The effects of marital and parent–child conflicts on other family members: Grandmothers and grown children. *Family Relations, 46*, 135–143.

Hall, L. D., Walker, A. K., and Acock, A. T. (1995). Gender and family work in one-parent households. *Journal of Marriage and the Family, 57*, 685–692.

Hall-Eston, C., and Mullins, L. (1999). Social relationship, emotional closeness, and loneliness among older meal program participants. *Social Behavior and Personality, 27*(5), 503–517.

Hamby, S. L., Poindexter, D. C., and Gray-Little, V. (1996). Four measures of partner violence: Construct similarity and classification differences. *Journal of Marriage and the Family, 58*, 127–139.

Hamer, J., & Marchioro, K. (2002). Becoming custodial dads; Exploring parenting among low-income and working-class African American fathers. *Journal of Marriage and Family, 64*(1), 116–129.

Hamilton, K., and Waller, G. (1993). Media influences on body size estimation in anorexia and bulimia. *British Journal of Psychiatry, 162*, 837–840.

Hampson, R. B., Beavers, W. R., and Hulgus, Y. (1990). Cross-ethnic family differences: Interactional assessment of White, Black, and Mexican-American families. *Journal of Marital and Family Therapy, 16*, 307–319.

Hampton, R. L., Gelles, R. J., and Harrop, J. W. (1989). Is violence in Black families increasing? A comparison of national survey rates. *Journal of Marriage and the Family, 51*, 969–980.

Hanks, R. S. (1990). The impact of early retirement incentives. *Journal of Family Issues, 11*, 424–437.

Hans, J. D., and Fine, M. A. (2001). Children of divorce: Experiences of children whose parents attended a divorce education program. *Journal of Divorce and Remarriage, 36*(1/2), 1–26.

Hansen, G. L. (1987). Extradyadic relations during courtship. *Journal of Sex Research, 23*, 382–390.

Hanson, S. L. (1992). Involving families and programs for pregnant teens: Consequences for teens and their families. *Family Relations, 41*, 303–311.

Hanson, S. M. H., and Bozett, F. W. (1987). Fatherhood: A review and resources. *Family Relations, 36*, 333–340.

Hardesty, C., and Bokemeier, J. (1989). Finding time and making do: Distribution of household labor in nonmetropolitan marriage. *Journal of Marriage and the Family, 51*, 253–267.

Hardy, G., Orzek, A., and Heistad, S. (1984). Learning to live with others: A program to prevent problems in living situations. *Journal of Counseling and Development, 63*, 110–112.

Hargrave, T. D., and Sells, J. N. (1997). The development of a forgiveness scale. *Journal of Marital and Family Therapy, 23*, 21–62.

Haring-Hidore, M., Stock, W. A., Okun, M. A., and Witler, R. A. (1985). Marital status and subjective well-being: A research synthesis. *Journal of Marriage and the Family, 47,* 947–953.

Harned, M. S. (2001). Abused women or men? An examination of the context and outcomes of dating violence. *Violence and Victims, 16*(3), 269–285.

Harris, K. F., and Marmer, J. K. (1996). Poverty, paternal involvement, and adolescent well-being. *Journal of Family Issues, 5,* 614–640.

Harris, K. M., and Morgan, S. P. (1991). Fathers, sons, and daughters: Differential paternal involvement in parenting. *Journal of Marriage and the Family, 53,* 531–544.

Hart, C. H., DeWolf, D. M., Wozniak, P., and Burts, D. C. (1992). Maternal and paternal disciplinary styles: Relations with preschoolers' playground behavioral orientations and peer status. *Child Development, 63,* 879–892.

Harvey, D. M., Curry, C. J., and Bray, J. H. (1991). Individuation and intimacy in intergenerational relationships and health: Patterns across two generations. *Journal of Family Psychology, 5,* 204–236.

Harvey, S. M., Beckman, L. J., Sherman, C., and Petitti, D. (1999). Women's experience and satisfaction with emergency contraception. *Family Planning Perspectives, 31*(5), 237–240, 260.

Haskett, M. E., and Kistner, J. A. (1991). Social interactions and peer perceptions of young physically abused children. *Child Development, 62,* 979–990.

Hatch, L. R., and Bulcroft, K. (1992). Contact with friends in later life: Disentangling the effects of gender and marital status. *Journal of Marriage and the Family, 54,* 222–232.

Hatch, R. C., James, D. E., and Schumm, W. R. (1986). Spiritual intimacy and marital satisfaction. *Family Relations, 35,* 539–545.

Hatcher, R. A., Trussell, J., Stewart, F., Cates, W., Stewart, G. K., Guest, F., and Kowal, D. (1998). *Contraceptive Technology* (17th ed.). New York: Ardent Media.

Hatcher, R. A., Zieman, M., Watt, A. P., Nelson, A., Darney, P. A., and Pluhar, E. (1999). *A Pocket Guide to Managing Contraception.* Tiger, GA: Bridging the Gap Foundation.

Hatfield, E., & Rapson, R. (1995). *A World of Passion: Cross Cultural Perspectives on Love and Sex.* New York: Allyn & Bacon.

Hattery, A. J. (2001). Tag-team parenting: Costs and benefits of utilizing nonoverlapping shift work in families with young children. *Families in Society, 82*(4), 419–427.

Hawkins, A. J., Nock, S. L., Wilson, J. C., Sanchez, L., and Wright, J. D. (2002). Attitudes about covenant marriage and divorce: Policy implication from a three-state comparison. *Family Relations, 51*(2), 166–175.

Hazan, C., and Shaver, P. (1987). Romantic love conceptualized as an attachment process. *Journal of Personality and Social Psychology, 52,* 511–524.

Heaton, T. B. (1990). Marital stability throughout the child-rearing years. *Demography, 27,* 55.

Heaton, T. B. (2002). Factors contributing to increasing marital stability in the United States. *Journal of Family Issues, 23,* 392–409.

Heaton, T. B., and Albrecht, S. L. (1991). Stable unhappy marriages. *Journal of Marriage and the Family, 53,* 747–758.

Heaton, T. B., and Jacobson, C. K. (1994). Race differences in changing family demographics in the 1980s. *Journal of Family Issues, 15,* 290–308.

Heaton, T. B., and Pratt, E. L. (1990). The effects of religious homogamy on marital satisfaction and stability. *Journal of Family Issues, 11,* 191–207.

Heidrich, S. N., and Ryff, C. D. (1993). Physical and mental health in later life: The self-system as mediator. *Psychology and Aging, 8,* 327–338.

Heilbrun, A. B., and Loftus, M. P. (1986). The role of sadism and peer pressure in the sexual aggression of male college students. *Journal of Sex Research, 22,* 320–332.

Heintz-Knowles, K. E. (2001). Balancing acts: Work–family issues on prime-time TV. In J. Bryant and J. A. Bryant (Eds.), *Television and the American Family* (pp. 177–206). Mahwah, NJ: Erlbaum.

Henggeler, S. W., Edwards, J. J., Hanson, C. L., and Okwumabua, T. H. (1988). The psychological functioning of wife-dominant families. *Journal of Family Psychology, 2,* 188–211.

Henley, N., and Freeman, J. (1995). The sexual politics of interpersonal behavior. In J. Freeman (Ed.), *Women: A Feminist Perspective* (5th ed., pp. 79–91). Mountain View, CA: Mayfield.

Henretta, J. C., Chan, C. G., and O'Rand, A. M. (1992). Retirement reason versus retirement process: Examining the reasons for retirement typology. *Journal of Gerontology, 47,* S1–S7.

Henshaw, S. K. (1998). Unintended pregnancy in the United States. *Family Planning Perspectives, 30*(1), 24–29, 46.

Henshaw, S. K. (1992). Abortion trends in 1987 and 1988: Age and race. *Family Planning Perspectives, 24,* 85–86.

Henshaw, S. K., and Kost, K. (1996). Abortion patients in 1994–1995: Characteristics in contraceptive use. *Family Planning Perspectives, 28,* 140–158.

Herbert, T. B., Silver, R. C., and Ellard, J. H. (1991). Coping with an abusive relationship: I. How and why do women stay? *Journal of Marriage and the Family, 53,* 311–325.

Herdt, G. (1992). *Gay Culture in America: Essays from the Field.* Boston: Beacon Press.

Herold, E. S., and Way, L. (1988). Sexual self-disclosure among university women. *The Journal of Sex Research, 24,* 1–14.

Herrigan, J., and Herrigan, J. (1973). *Loving Free.* New York: Grosset & Dunlap.

Hetherington, E. M. (1989). Coping with family transitions: Winners, losers and survivors. *Child Development, 60,* 1–14.

Hetherington, E. M. (1993). An overview of the Virginia longitudinal study of divorce and remarriage with a focus on early adolescence. *Journal of Family Psychology, 7,* 1–18.

Hetherington, E. M. (1997). Teenaged childrearing and divorce. In S. Luthar, J. A. Burack, D. Cicchetti, and J. Weisz (Eds.), *Developmental Psychopathology: Perspective on Risk and Disorders* (pp. 350–373). New York: Cambridge University Press.

Hetherington, E. M. (1998). Social capital and the development of youth from nondivorced, divorced, and remarried families. In A. Collins (Ed.), *Relationships as Developmental Contexts: The 29th Minnesota Symposium on Child Psychology.* Mahwah, NJ: Erlbaum.

Hetherington, E. M. (1999a). Family functioning in non-stepfamilies and different kinds of stepfamilies: An integration. *Monographs of the Society for Research in Child Development, 64*(4), 184–191.

Hetherington, E. M. (1999b). Family functioning and the adjustment of adolescent siblings in diverse types of families. *Monographs of the Society for Research in Child Development, 64*(4), 1–25.

Hetherington, E. M., and Clingempeel, W. G. (1992). Coping with marital transitions. *Monographs of the Society for Research in Child Development, 57*(2/3), Chicago: University of Chicago Press.

Hetherington, E. M., Clingempeel, W. G., Anderson, E. R., Deal, J., Stanley-Hagan, M., Hollier, E. A., and Lindner, M. (1992). Coping with marital transitions: A family systems perspective. *Monographs of the Society for Research in Child Development, 57*(2/3).

Hetherington, E. M., and Henderson, S. H. (1997). Fathers in stepfamilies. In M. E. Lamb (Ed.), *The Role of the Father in Child Development* (3rd ed., pp. 212–226). New York: Wiley.

Hetherington, E. M., and Jodl, K. M. (1994). Stepfamilies as settings for child development. In A. Booth and J. Dunn (Eds.), *Stepfamilies: Who Benefits? Who Does Not?* (pp. 55–79). Hillsdale, NJ: Erlbaum.

Hetherington, E. M., and Stanley-Hagan, M. M. (1999). Stepfamilies. In M. Lamb (Ed.), *Parenting and Child Development in "Nontraditional" Families* (pp. 137–159). Mahwah, NJ: Erlbaum.

Heyman, R. E., O'Leary, K. D., and Jouriles, E. M. (1995). Alcohol and aggressive personality styles: Potentiators of serious physical aggression against wives? *Journal of Family Psychology, 9,* 44–57.

Heyman, R. E., Sayers, S. L., and Bellack, A. S. (1994). Global marital satisfaction versus marital adjustment: An empirical comparison of three measures. *Journal of Family Psychology, 8,* 432–446.

Hickman, G. P., Bartholomae, S., and McKenry, P. C. (2000). Influence of partnering style on the adjustment and academic achievement of traditional college freshman. *Journal of College Student Development, 41*(1), 41–54.

Higginbottom, S. F., Barling, J., and Kelloway, E. K. (1993). Linking retirement experience and marital satisfaction: A mediational model. *Psychology and Aging, 8,* 508–516.

High, D. M. (1991). A new myth about families of older people? *The Gerontologist, 31,* 611–618.

Hill, E. J., Hawkins, A. J., Ferris, M., and Weitzman, M. (2001). Finding an extra day a week: The positive influence of perceived job flexibility on work and family life balance. *Family Relations, 50*(1), 49–57.

Hill, M. (1988). Class, kinship density, and conjugal role segregation. *Journal of Marriage and the Family, 50,* 731–741.

Hill, S. A. (2001). Class, race, and gender dimensions of child rearing in African American families. *Journal of Black Studies, 31,* 494–508.

Hiller, D. V., and Dyehouse, J. (1987). A case for banishing dual-career marriages from research literature. *Journal of Marriage and the Family, 49,* 787–795.

Hillis, S. D. (1999). Women who are sterilized at age 30 or younger have increased odds of regret. *Family Planning Perspectives, 93*(6), 889–895.

Hiltz, S. R. (1978). Widowhood: A roleless role. *Marriage and Family Review, 1,* 1–10.

Hite, S. (1981). *The Hite Report: A Nationwide Study of Female Sexuality.* New York: Dell.

Ho, G., Bierman, R., Beardsley, L. (1998). Natural History of cervicovaginal papillomavirus infection in young women. *New England Journal of Medicine, 338*(7), 423–428.

Hobart, C. (1987). Parent–child relations and remarried families. *Journal of Family Issues, 8,* 259–278.

Hodson, D., and Skeen, P. (1987). Child sexual abuse: A review of research and theory with implications for family life educators. *Family Relations, 36,* 215–221.

Hofferth, S., Brayfield, A., Deich, S., and Holcomb, P. (1991). *The National Childcare Survey, 1990.* Washington, DC: Irving Institute Press.

Hofferth, S. L. (1985). Updating children's life course. *Journal of Marriage and the Family, 47,* 93–115.

Hoffman, K. L., Demo, D. H., and Edwards, J. N. (1994). Physical wife abuse in a non-Western society: An integrated theoretical approach. *Journal of Marriage and the Family, 56,* 131–146.

Hoge, D. R., Petrillo, G. H., and Smith, E. I. (1982). Transmission of religious and social values from parents to teenage children. *Journal of Marriage and the Family, 44,* 569–580.

Holahan, J., and Wang, M. (2003). Changes in health care coverage 2000–2001. (Kaiser Family Foundation: The Kaiser Commission on Medicaid and the Uninsured, publication no. 4089. Retrieved April 21, 2003, from http://www.kff.org

Hollander, D. (1995b). Improvements in neonatal care have increased survival rates for very low birth weight infants. *Family Planning Perspectives, 27,* 182–183.

Hollander, D. (1995c). Young, minority, and disadvantaged women exhibit least favorable pregnancy-related health behavior. *Family Planning Perspectives, 27,* 259–260.

Hollander, D. (1996a). Barrier methods may protect some women against cervical chlamydia, but pill use does not affect risk. *Family Planning Perspectives, 28,* 37–38.

Hollander, D. (1996b). Conception may take a long time among women who smoke. *Family Planning Perspectives, 28,* 181–182.

Hollander, D. (1996c). Long-term breast feeding, especially a first child, lowers breast cancer risks. *Family Planning Perspectives, 25,* 239.

Hollander, D. (1996d). Monthly probability of conception is highest during the six days ending on the day of ovulation. *Family Planning Perspectives, 28,* 127–128.

Hollander, D. (1996e). Programs to bring down cesarean rates proved to be successful. *Family Planning Perspectives, 28,* 182–184.

Hollander, D. (1997). 1995 U.S. fertility rates were lower than any since the mid 1980s. *Family Planning Perspectives, 29,* 47–48.

Holman, T. B., and Burr, W. R. (1980). Beyond the beyond: The growth of family theories in the 1970s. *Journal of Marriage and the Family, 42,* 729–741.

Holman, T. B., and Dao Li, B. (1997). Premarital factors influencing perceived readiness for marriage. *Journal of Family Issues, 18,* 124–144.

Holman, T. B., and Jacquart, M. (1988). Leisure-activity patterns and marital satisfaction: A further test. *Journal of Marriage and the Family, 50,* 69–77.

Holman, T. B., Larson, J. H., and Harmer, S. L. (1994). Premarital couples: The development and predictive validity of a new premarital assessment instrument: The Preparation for Marriage Questionnaire. *Family Relations, 43,* 46–52.

Holman, T. B., Larson, J., Stahmann, R., and Carroll, J. (2001). General principles, implications, and future directions. In T. B. Holman (Ed.), *Premarital Prediction of Marital Quality or Breakup* (pp. 191–222). New York: Kluwer Academic/Plenum.

Holmes, E. R., and Holmes, L. D. (1995). *Other Cultures, Elder Years.* Thousand Oaks, CA: Sage.

Honeycutt, J. M. (1986). A model of marital functioning based on an attraction paradigm and social-penetration dimension. *Journal of Marriage and the Family, 48,* 651–667.

Hoopes, D. S. (1979). Intercultural communication concepts and the psychology of intercultural experiences. In M. Pusch (Ed.), *Multicultural Education: A Cross-Cultural Training Approach* (pp. 3–33). La Grange Park, IL: Intercultural Press.

Hopkins, J., Marcues, M., and Campbell, S. B. (1984). Postpartum depression: A critical review. *Psychological Bulletin, 95,* 498–515.

Horn, L., Chang Wei, C., and Berker, A. (2002). *What Students Pay for College: Changes in Net Price of College Attendance between 1992–93 and 1999–2000.* Washington, D.C.: U.S. Department of Education, National Center for Education Statistics.

Horning, L. E., and Rouse, K. A. G. (2002). Resilience in preschoolers and toddlers from low-income families. *Early Childhood Education Journal, 29*(3) 155–159.

Horowitz, R. (1983). *Honor and the American Dream.* New Brunswick, NJ: Rutgers University Press.

Horsley, G. (1997). In-laws: Extended family therapy. *American Journal of Family Therapy, 25,* 18–27.

Horwitz, A. D., White, H. R., and Howell-White, S. (1996). Becoming married and mental health: A longitudinal study of cohorts of young adults. *Journal of Marriage and the Family, 58,* 895–907.

Houser, B. B., and Berkman, S. L. (1984). Aging parent/mature child relationships. *Journal of Marriage and the Family, 46,* 245–299.

Houts, R. M., Robins, E., and Huston, T. L. (1996). Compatibility and the development of premarital relationships. *Journal of Marriage and the Family, 58,* 7–20.

Howes, C., and Hamilton, C. E. (1992). Children's relationships with caregivers: Mothers and child-care teachers. *Child Development, 63,* 859–866.

Howes, C., Phillips, D. A., and Whitebook, M. (1992). Thresholds of quality: Implications for the social development of children in center-based child care. *Child Development, 63,* 449–460.

Hoyt, M. F. (1986). Neuroticism and mate selection. *Medical Aspects of Human Sexuality, 20,* 11.

Hubacher, D., Lara-Ricalde, R., Taylor, D. J., Guerra-Infante, F., and Guzman-Rodriguez, R. (2001). Use of copper intrauterine devices and the risk of tubal infertility among nulligravid women. *New England Journal of Medicine, 345*(8), 561–567.

Hughes, M. (1989). Parenthood and psychological well-being among the formerly married. *Journal of Family Issues, 10,* 463–481.

Hunsley, J., Pinsent, C., Lefedvre, M., James-Tanner, S., and Vito, D. (1995). Assessment of couples, marriages, and families: Construct of validity of the short forms of the Dyadic Adjustment Scale. *Family Relations, 44,* 231–237.

Hunter, A. (1997). Counting on grandmothers: Black mothers' and fathers' reliance on grandmothers for parenting support. *Journal of Family Issues, 18,* 251–269.

Hurlbert, D. F., and Apt, C. (1991). Sexual narcissism and the abusive male. *Journal of Sex and Marital Therapy, 17,* 279–292.

Hurst, C. E., and Guldin, D. A. (1981). The effects of intra-individuals and inter-spouse status inconsistency on life satisfaction among older persons. *Journal of Gerontology, 36,* 112–121.

Huston, T. L., Caughlin, J. P., Houts, R. M., Smith, S. E., and George, L. J. (2001). The connubial crucible: Newlywed years as predictors of marital delight, distress, and divorce. *Journal of Personality and Social Psychology, 80*(2), 237–252.

Hyde, J., DeLamater, J., and Plant, E. (1996). Sexuality during pregnancy and the year postpartum. *Journal of Sex Research, 32*(2), 143–151.

Hyde, J. S., Essex, M. J., Clark, R., and Klein, M. H. (2001). Maternity leave, women's employment, and marital incompatibility. *Journal of Family Psychology, 15*(3), 476–491.

Ihinger-Tallman, M., and Pasley, K. (1997). Stepfamilies in 1984 and today: A scholarly perspective. *Marriage and Family Review, 26*(1/2), 19–40.

Increasing rates of ectopic pregnancies. (1984). *Medical Aspects of Human Sexuality, 18,* 14.

Ingersoll-Dayton, B., and Neal, M. B. (1991). Grandparents in family therapy: The clinical research study. *Family Relations, 40,* 264–271.

Isaacs, M. B., and Leon, G. (1988a). Divorce, disputation, and discussion: Communication styles among reunited separated spouses. *Journal of Family Psychology, 1,* 298–311.

Isaacs, M. B., and Leon, G. (1988b). Remarriage and its alternatives following divorce: Mother and child adjustment. *Journal of Marriage and Family Therapy, 14,* 163–173.

Ishii-Kuntz, M. (1994). Paternal involvement and perceptions toward fathers' roles: A comparison between Japan and the United States. *Journal of Family Issues, 15,* 30–48.

Ishii-Kuntz, M., and Lee, G. R. (1987). Status of the elderly: An extension of the theory. *Journal of Marriage and the Family, 49,* 413–420.

Israelstam, K. V. (1989). Interacting individual belief systems in marital relationships. *Journal of Marriage and Family Therapy, 15,* 53–63.

Istvan, J. (1986). Stress, anxiety, and birth outcomes: A critical review of the evidence. *Psychological Bulletin, 100,* 331–348.

Jackson, J., and Berg-Cross, L. (1988). Extending the extended family: The mother-in-law and daughter-in-law relationship of Black women. *Family Relations, 37,* 293–297.

Jacobs, J.A., and Gerson, K. (1998). Who are the overworked Americans? *Review of Social Economy 56,* 442–459.

Jacobs, J.A., and Gerson, K. (2001). Overworked individuals or overworked families? Explaining trends in work, leisure, and family time. *Work and Occupations, 28*(1), 40–63.

Jacoby, S. (1999). Great sex: What's age got to do with it? *Modern Maturity, 42*(5), 40–45, 91.

Jagger, E. (2001). Marketing Molly and Melville: Dating in a postmodern, consumer society. *Sociology, 35*(1), 39–57.

Jamieson, D. J., and Buescher, P. A. (1992). The effect of family planning participation on prenatal care use and low birth rate. *Family Planning Perspectives, 24,* 214–218.

Jarrett, R. L. (1996). Welfare stigma among low-income, African-American single mothers. *Family Relations, 25,* 368–374.

Jarvis, C. (2001) *The Marriage Sabbitical: The Journey that Brings You Home.* Cambridge, Mass.: Perseus Publishing.

Jaycox, L. H., and Repetti, R. L. (1993). Conflict in families and the psychological adjustment of preadolescent children. *Journal of Family Psychology, 7,* 344–355.

Jean-Gilles, M., and Crittenden, P. M. (1990). Maltreating families: A look at siblings. *Family Relations, 39,* 323–329.

Jedlicka, D. (1984). Indirect parental influences on mate choice: A test of the psychoanalytic theory. *Journal of Marriage and the Family, 46,* 65–70.

Jendrek, M. P. (1993). Grandparents who parent their grandchildren: Effects on lifestyle. *Journal of Marriage and the Family, 55,* 609–621.

Joe, T., and Yu, P. (1984). *The "Flip-Side" of Black Families Headed by Women: The Economic Status of Black Men.* Washington, DC: Center for the Study of Social Policy.

Joesch, J. M. (1991). The effect of price of child care on AFDC mothers' paid work behavior. *Family Relations, 40,* 161–166.

Joesch, J. M. (1994). Children and the timing of women's paid work after child birth: A further specification of the relationship. *Journal of Marriage and the Family, 56,* 429–440.

Johansen, A. S., Leibowitz, A., and Waite, L. J. (1996). The importance of childcare characteristics—the choice of care. *Journal of Marriage and the Family, 58,* 759–772.

John, D., Shelton, D. A., and Luschen, K. (1995). Race, ethnicity, gender, and perceptions of fairness. *Journal of Family Issues, 16,* 357–379.

Johnson, C. L. (1988). Postdivorce reorganization of relationships between divorcing children and their parents. *Journal of Marriage and the Family, 50,* 221–231.

Johnson, C. L., and Barer, B. M. (1987). Marital instability and changing kinship networks of grandparents. *The Gerontologist, 27,* 330–335.

Johnson, C. L., and Troll, L. (1992). Family functioning in late, late life. *Journal of Gerontology, 47,* S66–S72.

Johnson, C. L., and Troll, L. (1996). Family structure and the timing of transitions from 70 to 103 years of age. *Journal of Marriage and the Family, 58,* 178–187.

Johnson, D. R., Amoloza, T. O., and Booth, A. (1992). Debility and developmental change in marital quality: A three-wave panel analysis. *Journal of Marriage and the Family, 54,* 582–594.

Johnson, D. R., and Booth, A. (1990). Rural economic decline and marital quality: A panel study of farm marriages. *Family Relations, 39,* 159–165.

Johnson, M. P. (1995). Patriarchal terrorism in common couple violence: Two forms of violence against women. *Journal of Marriage and the Family, 57,* 283–294.

Johnson, M. P., and Milardo, R. M. (1984). Network interference in pair relationships: A social psychological recasting of Slater's theory of social regression. *Journal of Marriage and the Family, 46,* 893–899.

Jones, E., and Gallois, C. (1989). Spouses' impressions of rules for communication in public and private marital conflicts. *Journal of Marriage and the Family, 51,* 957–967.

Jones, E. F., and Forrest, J. D. (1992). Contraceptive failure rates based on the 1988 NSFG. *Family Planning Perspectives, 24,* 12–19.

Jorgensen, S. R. (1986). *Marriage and the Family: Development and Change.* New York: Macmillan.

Jorgenson, J. (1994). Situated address and the social construction of "in-law" relationships. *Southern Communication Journal, 59,* 196–204.

Jouriles, E. N., and Norwood, W. B. (1995). Physical aggression toward boys and girls in families characterized by the battering of women. *Journal of Family Psychology, 9,* 69–78.

Judiesch, M. K., and Lyness, K. S. (1999). Left behind? The impact of leaves of absence on managers' career success. *Academy of Management Journal, 42,* 641–651.

Julian, P. W., McKenry, P. C., and McKelbey, M. W. (1994). Cultural variations in parenting. *Family Relations, 43,* 30–37.

Julian, T., McKenry, R., Gavazzi, S., and Law, J. (1999). Test of family of origin structural models of male verbal and physical aggression. *Journal of Family Issues, 20*(3), 397–423.

Jupiter Media Matrix. (2002). Jupiter Research: Dating and Personals. Retrieved May 16, 2003, from http://www.jupitermediamatrix.com

Kagan, N., and Schneider, J. (1987). Toward the measurement of affective sensitivity. *Journal of Counseling and Development, 65,* 459–464.

Kahn, J. G., Brindis, C. D., and Glei, D. A. (1999). Pregnancies averted among U.S. teenagers by the use of contraceptives. *Family Planning Perspectives, 31*(1), 29–34.

Kaiser Family Foundation. (2001, August). Sexsmarts: Sexually transmitted disease. Retrieved December 11, 2002 from http://www.kff.org/content/2001/3148/SummaryofFindings.pdf

Kallen, D. J., Griffore, R. J., Popovich, S., and Powell, V. (1990). Adolescent mothers and their mothers view adoption. *Family Relations, 39,* 311–316.

Kalmijn, M. (1999). Father involvement in childrearing and the perceived stability of marriage. *Journal of Marriage and the Family, 61,* 409–421.

Kalmuss, D., Davidson, A., and Cushman, L. (1992). Parenting expectations, experiences, and adjustment to parenthood: A test of the violated expectations framework. *Journal of Marriage and the Family, 54,* 516–526.

Kalmuss, D., and Seltzer, J. A. (1986). Continuity of marital behavior in remarriage: The case of spouse abuse. *Journal of Marriage and the Family, 48,* 113–120.

Kalmuss, D., and Seltzer, J. A. (1989). A framework for studying family socialization over the life cycle. *Journal of Family Issues, 10*, 339–358.

Kalmuss, D. S., and Namerow, P. P. (1994). Subsequent child-bearing among teenage mothers: The determinants of a closely spaced second birth. *Family Planning Perspectives, 26*, 149–153.

Kaplan, L., and Hennon, C. B. (1992). Remarriage education: A personal reflections program. *Family Relations, 41*, 127–134.

Karavasilis, L., Doyle, A. B., and Markiewicz, D. (2003). Associations between parenting style and attachment to mother in middle childhood and adolescence. *International Journal of Behavioral Development, 27*(2), 153–164.

Kass, A. A., and Kass, L. (2000). *Wing to Wing, Oar to Oar: Readings on Courting and Marrying.* Notre Dame, IN: University of Notre Dame Press.

Katzev, A. R., Warner, R. L., and Acock, A. C. (1994). Girls or boys? Relationship of child gender to marital instability. *Journal of Marriage and the Family, 56*, 89–100.

Kaye, K., and Warren, S. (1988). Discourse about adoption in adoptive families. *Journal of Family Psychology, 1*, 406–433.

Keenan, J., Gallup, G., Goulet, N., and Kulkarni, M. (1997). Attributions of deception in human mating strategies. *Journal of Social Behavior and Personality 12*(1), 45–52.

Keith, P. M. (1986). Isolation of the unmarried in later life. *Family Relations, 35*, 389–395.

Keith, P. M., and Nauta, A. (1988). Old and single in the city and the country: Activities of the unmarried. *Family Relations, 37*, 79–83.

Keith, P. M., and Schafer, R. B. (1985). Role behavior, relative deprivation, and depression among women in one- and two-job families. *Family Relations, 34*, 227–233.

Kelley H. H., and Thibaut, J. W. (1978). *Interpersonal Relations: A Theory of Interdependence.* New York: Wiley-Interscience.

Kelley, P. (1992). Healthy stepfamily functioning. *Families in Society, 73*, 579–587.

Kelly, R. F., and Voydanoff, P. (1985). Work/family role strain among employed parents. *Family Relations, 34*, 367–374.

Kennedy, G. E. (1990). College students' expectations of grandparent and grandchild role behaviors. *The Gerontologist, 30*, 43–48.

Kennedy, J. (1999). Romantic attachment style and ego identity, attributional style, and family of origin in first-year college students. *College Student Journal, 33*(2), 171–180.

Kenney, J. A. (1973). Sexuality of pregnant and breastfeeding women. *Archives of Sexual Behavior, 2*, 215–229.

Kenny, D. A., and Acitelli, L. K. (1994). Measuring similarity in couples. *Journal of Family Psychology, 8*, 417–431.

Kercher, K., Kosloski, K. D., and Normoyle, J. B. (1988). Reconsideration of fear of personal aging and subjective well-being in later life. *Journal of Gerontology, 43*, P170–P172.

Kerig, P. K. (1996). Assessing the links between interparental conflict and child adjustment: The conflict and problem-solving scales. *Journal of Family Psychology, 10*, 454–473.

Kerr, M., Stattin, H., and Trost, K. (1999). To know you is to trust you: Parents' trust is rooted in child disclosure of information. *Journal of Adolescence, 22*, 737–752.

Kersten, K. K. (1990). The process of marital disaffection: Intervention at various stages. *Family Relations, 39*, 257–265.

Kestelman, P., and Trussell, J. (1991). Efficacy of the simultaneous use of condoms and spermicides. *Family Planning Perspectives, 23*, 226–227.

Kiessling, A., and Anderson, S. (2003). *Human Embryonic Stem Cells: An Introduction to the Science and Therapeutic Potential.* Sudbury, MA: Jones and Bartlett.

Kilpatrick, A. C. (1982). Job change in dual-career families: Danger or opportunity. *Family Relations, 31*, 363–368.

Kilty, K. M., and Behling, J. H. (1985). Predicting the retirement intentions and attitudes of professional workers. *Journal of Gerontology, 40*, 219–227.

Kilty, K. M., and Behling, J. H. (1986). Retirement financial planning among professional workers. *The Gerontologist, 26*, 525–530.

King, T., and Bannon, E. (2002). At what cost? The price that working students pay for a college education. (The State PIRGs' Higher Education Project). Retrieved November 7, 2002, from http://www.pirg.org/highered/atwhatcost4-16-02.pdf

King, V., and Elder, G. H. (1995). American children view their grandparents: Linked lives across three rural generations. *Journal of Marriage and the Family, 57*, 165–178.

King, V., and Heard, H. E. (1999). Nonresident father visitation, parental conflict, and mother's satisfaction: What's best for child well-being? *Journal of Marriage and the Family, 61*, 385–396.

Kingsbury, N. M., and Minda, R. B. (1988). An analysis of three expected intimate relationship states: Commitment, maintenance, and termination. *Journal of Social and Personal Relationships, 5*, 405–422.

Kinnunen, U., Gerris, J., and Vermulst, A. (1996). Work experiences and family functioning among employed fathers of children of school age. *Family Relations, 45,* 449–455.

Kinston, W., Loader, P., and Miller, L. (1987). Quantifying the clinical assessment of family health. *Journal of Marriage and Family Therapy, 13,* 49–67.

Kipnis, D. (1984). The view from the top. *Psychology Today, 18,* 30–36.

Kipp III, S. M., Price, D. V., and Wohlford, J. K. (2002). Unequal opportunity: Disparities in college access among the 50 states. *Lumina Foundation for Education New Agenda Series, 4*(3).

Kitson, G. C. (1982). Attachment to the spouse in divorce: A scale and its applications. *Journal of Marriage and the Family, 44,* 379–393.

Kivett, V. R. (1985). Grandfathers and grandchildren: Patterns of association, helping, and psychological closeness. *Family Relations, 34,* 565–571.

Kivett, V. R. (1993). Racial comparisons in the grandmother role. *Family Relations, 42,* 165–172.

Klagsbrun, F. (1985). *Married People Staying Together in the Age of Divorce.* New York: Bantam Books.

Klaus, H. (1984). Natural family planning. *Medical Aspects of Human Sexuality, 18,* 59–70.

Klaus, M., and Kennel, J. (1982). *Parent–Infant Bonding* (2nd ed.). St. Louis: Mosby.

Klawitter, M. (1994). Child support awards and the earnings of divorced non-custodial fathers. *Social Service Review, 68,* 351–368.

Kleban, M. H., Brody, E. M., Schoonover, C. B., and Hoffman, C. (1989). Family help to the elderly: Perceptions of sons-in-law regarding parent care. *Journal of Marriage and the Family, 51,* 303–312.

Klebanov, P. K., Brooks-Gunn, J., and Duncan, G. J. (1994). Does neighborhood and family poverty affect mothers' parenting, mental health, and social support? *Journal of Marriage and the Family, 56,* 441–455.

Klein, D. M., and White, J. M. (1996). *Family Theories: An Introduction.* Newbury Park, CA: Sage.

Kleiner, H. S., Hertzog, J., and Targ, D. B. (1998). *Grandparents Acting as Parents.* Paper presented at the national satellite video conference Grandparents Raising Grandchildren: Implications for Professionals and Agencies, Purdue University Cooperative Extension Service.

Klepinger, D. A., Lundberg, S., and Plotnick, R. T. (1995). Adolescent fertility and the educational attainment of young women. *Family Planning Perspectives, 27,* 23–28.

Klitsch, M. (1988a). FDA approval ends cervical cap's marathon. *Family Planning Perspectives, 20,* 137–138.

Klitsch, M. (1988b). The return of the IUD. *Family Planning Perspectives, 20,* 19–40.

Klitsch, M. (1989). Noncustodial fathers can probably afford to pay far more child support than they now provide. *Family Planning Perspectives, 21,* 278–279.

Klitsch, M. (1990). Women who lack health insurance coverage are more likely to bear seriously ill newborns. *Family Planning Perspectives, 22,* 415.

Klitsch, M. (1992). Abortion experience does not appear to reduce women's self-esteem or psychological well-being. *Family Planning Perspectives, 24,* 282–283.

Klitsch, M. (1996). New generation of progestins may raise oral contraceptive users' risk of blood clots. *Family Planning Perspectives, 28,* 33–34.

Klohnen, E. C., Vandewater, E. A., and Young, A. (1996). Negotiating the middle years: Ego-resiliency and successful midlife adjustment in women. *Psychology and Aging, 11,* 431–442.

Kniveton, B., and Day, J. (1999). An examination of the relationship between a mother's attitude toward the sex education of her children and her perception of her own parent's view. *Emotional and Behavioral Difficulties, 4*(2), 32–37.

Knoester, C., and Booth, A. (2000). Barriers to divorce. *Journal of Family Issues, 21,* 78–99.

Knox, D., Daniels, V., Sturdivant, L., and Zusman, M. E. (2001). College student use of the Internet for mate selection. *College Student Journal, 35*(1), 158–160.

Kosmin, B. A., Mayer, E., and Keysar, A. (2001). *American Religious Identification Survey.* New York: City University of New York, Graduate Center. Retrieved January 7, 2003, from http://www.gc.cuny.edu./studies/aris index.htm

Kost, K., Forrest, D., and Harlap, S. (1991). Comparing health risks and benefits of contraceptive choices. *Family Planning Perspectives, 23,* 54–61.

Kramarow, E., Lentzner, H., Rooks, R., Weeks, J., and Saydah, S. (1999). *Health, United States, 1999: Health and Aging Chartbook.* Hyattsville, MD: National Center for Health Statistics.

Krause, N., and Baker, E. (1992). Financial strain, economic values, and somatic symptoms in later life. *Psychology and Aging, 7,* 4–14.

Krissman, K. (1990). Social support and gender role attitude among teenage mothers. *Adolescence, 49,* 709–716.

Krotz, J. L. (1999, July/August). Getting even. *Working Woman, 24*(7), 42–46.

Kugler, K. E., and Hanson, R. O. (1988). Relational competence and social support among parents at risk of child abuse. *Family Relations, 37,* 238–332.

Kuhlthau, K., and Mason, K. O. (1996). Market child-care versus care by relatives. *Journal of Family Issues, 17,* 561–578.

Kurdek, L. A. (1989a). Relationship quality for newly married husbands and wives: Marital history, stepchildren, and individual-preference predictors. *Journal of Marriage and the Family, 51,* 1053–1064.

Kurdek, L. A. (1989b). Social support and psychological distress in first-married and remarried newlywed husbands and wives. *Journal of Marriage and the Family, 51,* 1047–1052.

Lackey, C., and Williams, K. R. (1995). Social bonding and a succession of partner violence across generations. *Journal of Marriage and the Family, 57,* 295–305.

Laird, J. (1993). Lesbian and gay families. In R. Walsh and L. D. Wynne (Eds.), *Normal Family Processes* (pp. 282–328). New York: Guilford Press.

Lamaze, F. (1970). *Painless Childbirth.* Chicago: Regnery.

Lamb, M. (1998). Cybersex: Research notes on the characteristics of the visitors to online chat rooms. *Deviant Behavior: An Interdisciplinary Journal, 19,* 121–135.

Lambert, J., and Thomasson, G. (1997). Mormon American families. In M. K. DeGenova (Ed.), *Families in Cultural Context* (pp. 85–108). Mountain View, CA: Mayfield.

Lampard, R., and Peggs, K. (1999). Repartnering: The relevance of parenthood and gender to cohabitation and remarriage among the formerly married. *British Journal of Sociology, 50,* 443–465.

Landers, A. (1985, June 11). Is affection more important than sex? *Family Circle.*

Landry, D. J., and Forrest, J. E. (1995). How old are U.S. fathers? *Family Planning Perspectives, 27,* 159–161.

LaRossa, R., and Reitzes, D. C. (1993). Continuity and change in middle-class fatherhood, 1925–1939: The culture-conduct connection. *Journal of Marriage and the Family, 55,* 455–468.

Larsen, A. S., and Olson, D. A. (1989). Predicting marital satisfaction using PREPARE: A replicator's study. *Journal of Marital and Family Therapy, 15,* 311–322.

Larson, J. H., Crane, D. R., and Smith, C. W. (1991). Morning and night couples: The effect of wake and sleep patterns on marital adjustment. *Journal of Marital and Family Therapy, 17,* 53–65.

Larson, J. H., and Holman, P. D. (1994). Premarital predictors of marital quality and stability. *Family Relations, 43,* 228–237.

Larzelere, R. E., Amberson, T. G., and Martin, J. A. (1992). Age differences in perceived discipline problems from 9 to 48 months. *Family Relations, 41,* 192–199.

Larzelere, R. E., and Meranda, J. A. (1994). The effectiveness of parental discipline with toddler misbehavior: The different levels of child distress. *Family Relations, 43,* 480–488.

Lau, S., and Pun, K. (1999). Parental evaluations and their agreement: Relationship with children's self-concepts. *Social Behavior and Personality, 27*(6), 639–650.

Lauer, J., and Lauer, R. (1985). Marriages made to last. *Psychology Today, 19,* 22–26.

Lavee, Y., McCubbin, H. I., and Patterson, J. M. (1985). The double ABCX model of family stress and adaptation: An empirical test by analysis of structural equations with latent variables. *Journal of Marriage and the Family, 47,* 811–825.

Lavee, Y., Sharlin, S., and Katz, R. (1996). The effect of parenting stress of marital quality. *Journal of Family Issues, 17,* 114–135.

Lavine, H., Sweeney, D., and Wagner, S. (1999). Depicting women as sex objects in television advertising: Effects on body dissatisfaction. *Personality and Social Psychology Bulletin, 25*(8), 1049–1058.

Lawton, L., Silverstein, M., and Bengtson, B. (1994). Affection, social contact, and geographic distance between adult children and their parents. *Journal of Marriage and the Family, 56,* 57–68.

Lee, G. R. (1988a). Marital intimacy among older persons. *Journal of Family Issues, 9,* 273–284.

Lee, G. R. (1988b). Marital satisfaction in later life: The effects of nonmarital roles. *Journal of Marriage and the Family, 50,* 775–783.

Lee, G. R., Seccombe, K., and Shehan, C. L. (1991). Marital status and personal happiness: An analysis of trends and data. *Journal of Marriage and the Family, 53,* 839–844.

Lee, P. M., Picard, F., and Blain, M. D. (1994). A methodological and substantive review of intervention outcome studies for families undergoing divorce. *Journal of Family Psychology, 8,* 3–15.

Leigh, G. K., Holman, T. B., and Burr, W. R. (1984). An empirical test of sequence in Murstein's SVR theory of mate selection. *Family Relations, 33,* 225–231.

LeMasters, E. E. (1957). *Modern Courtship and Marriage.* New York: Macmillan.

Leshner, A. I. (2000). *Anabolic Steroid Abuse* (NIH publication no. 00-3721). Wasington, DC: U.S. Department of Health and Human Services, National Institute of Health.

Lesser, E. K., and Comet, J. J. (1987). Help and hindrance: Parents of divorcing children. *Journal of Marital and Family Therapy, 13,* 197–202.

Lester, D. (1997). Correlates of worldwide divorce rates. *Journal of Divorce and Remarriage, 26,* 215–219.

Lester, D. (1999). Regional differences in divorce rates: A preliminary study. *Journal of Divorce and Remarriage, 30,* 121–124.

Levant, R. F., Slattery, S. C., and Loiselle, J. E. (1987). Fathers' involvement in housework and child care with school-age daughters. *Family Relations, 36,* 152–157.

Levine, J. A., and Pittinsky, T. L. (1997). *Working Fathers: New Strategies for Balancing Work and Family.* Reading, MA: Addison-Wesley.

Levinger, G. (1979). A social psychological perspective on marital dissolution. In G. Levinger and O. C. Moles (Eds.), *Divorce and Separation* (pp. 37–60). New York: Basic Books.

Levinson, D. (1988). Family violence in cross-cultural perspective. In V. B. Van Hasselt, R. L. Morrison, A. S. Bellack, and M. Hersen (Eds.), *Handbook of Family Violence* (pp. 435–455). New York: Plenum.

Levinson, D. J. (1978). *The Seasons of a Man's Life.* New York: Ballantine Books.

Lewis, K. G., and Moon, S. (1997). Always single and single again women: A qualitative study. *Journal of Marital and Family Therapy, 23,* 115–134.

Lewis, R. A., Volk, R. J., and Duncan, S. F. (1989). Stresses on fathers and family relationships relative to rural youth leaving and returning home. *Family Relations, 38,* 174–181.

Li, Q. (1999). Teachers' beliefs and gender differences in mathematics: A review. *Educational Research, 451*(1), 63–76.

Liang, J. (1982). Sex differences in life satisfaction among the elderly. *Journal of Gerontology, 37,* 100–108.

Lichter, D. T., Anderson, R. M., and Hayward, M. D. (1995). Marriage markets and marital choice. *Journal of Family Issues, 16,* 412–431.

Liebowitz, M. R. (1983). *The Chemistry of Love.* Boston: Little, Brown.

Liem, R., and Liem, J. H. (1988). Psychological effects of unemployment on workers and their families. *Journal of Social Issues, 44,* 87–105.

Liese, L. H., Snowden, L. R., and Ford, L. K. (1989). Partner status, social support, and psychological adjustments during pregnancy. *Family Relations, 38,* 311–316.

Lin, I. (2000). Perceived fairness and compliance with child support obligations. *Journal of Marriage and the Family, 62,* 388–398.

Lincoln, R. (1984). The pill, breast, and cervical cancer, and the role of progestogens in arterial disease. *Family Planning Perspectives, 16,* 55–63.

Lind, P., and Connole, H. (1985). Sex differences in behavioral and cognitive aspects of decision control. *Sex Roles, 12*(7/8), 813–823.

Lindberg, L. D. (1996). Women's decisions about breast feeding and maternal employment. *Journal of Marriage and the Family, 58,* 239–251.

Lino, M. (2000, March). *Expenditures on Children by Families, 1999 Annual Report.* (Miscellaneous publication no. 1528–1999). Washington, DC: U.S. Department of Agriculture, Center for Nutrition Policy and Promotion.

Lino, M. (2001, March). *Expenditures on Children by Families, 2000 Annual Report.* (Miscellaneous publication no. 1528–2000). Washington, DC: U.S. Department of Agriculture, Center for Nutrition Policy and Promotion.

Linz, D. (1989). Exposure to sexually explicit materials and attitudes toward rape: A comparison of study results. *The Journal of Sex Research, 26,* 50–84.

Lips, H. M. (1991). *Women, Men, and Power.* Mountain View, CA: Mayfield.

Lips, H. M. (1997). *Sex and Gender: An Introduction* (3rd ed.). Mountain View, CA: Mayfield.

Lloyd, S. A., and Cate, R. M. (1984). Predicting premarital relationship stability: A methodological refinement. *Journal of Marriage and the Family, 46,* 71–76.

Lockhart, L. L. (1987). A reexamination of the effects of race and social class on the incidence of marital violence: A search for reliable differences. *Journal of Marriage and the Family, 49,* 603–610.

Long, E. C., Angera, J. J., and Carter, S. J. (1999). Understanding the one you love; a longitudinal assessment of an empathy training program for couples in romantic relationships. *Family Relations, 48*(3) 235–242.

Longmore, M. A., Manning, W. D., and Giordano, P. C. (2001). Preadolescent parenting strategies and teens' dating and sexual initiation: A longitudinal analysis: *Journal of Marriage and the Family, 63*(2), 322–335.

Loomis, L. S., and Booth, A. (1995). Multigenerational caregiving and well-being: The myth of the beleaguered sandwich generation. *Journal of Family Issues, 16,* 131–148.

Lopata, H. Z. (1993). The interweave of public and private: Women's challenge to American society. *Journal of Marriage and the Family, 55,* 176–190.

Lopez, F. G., and Thurman, C. W. (1993). High-trait and low-trait angry college students: A comparison of family environments. *Journal of Counseling and Development, 71,* 524–527.

Lorenz, F. O., Conger, R. D., Simon, R. L., Whitbeck, L. B., and Elder, G. H., Jr. (1991). Economic pressure and marital quality: An illustration of the method variance problem and the causal modeling of family processes. *Journal of Marriage and the Family, 53,* 375–388.

Lorenz, F. O., Simons, R. L., Conger, R. D., Elder, G. H., Jr., Johnson, C., and Chao, W. (1997). Married and recently divorced mothers' stressful events and distress: Tracing change across time. *Journal of Marriage and the Family, 59,* 219–232.

Lowe, G. D., and Witt, D. D. (1984). Early marriage as a career contingency: The prediction of educational attainment. *Journal of Marriage and the Family, 46,* 689–698.

Lowery, C. R., and Settle, S. A. (1985). Effects of divorce on children: Differential impact on custody and visitation patterns. *Family Relations, 34,* 455–463.

Luster, T., Boger, R., and Hannan, K. (1993). Infant affect and home environment. *Journal of Marriage and the Family, 55,* 651–661.

Lutwak, N. (1985). Fear of intimacy among college women. *Adolescence, 77,* 15–20.

MacDermid, S., Huston, R. L., and McHale, S. M. (1990). Changes in marriage associated with transition to parenthood: Individual differences as a function of sex-role attitudes and changes in the division of household labor. *Journal of Marriage and the Family, 52,* 475–486.

MacDermid, S., Jurich, J., Myers-Walls, J., and Pelo, A. (1992). Feminist teaching: Effective education. *Family Relations, 41*(1), 31–38.

MacDonald, T., and Ross, M. (1999). Assessing the accuracy of predictions about dating relationships: How and why do lovers' predictions differ from those made by observers. *Personality and Social Psychology Bulletin, 25*(1), 1417–1419.

MacDonald, W. L., and DeMaris, A. (1996). Parenting stepchildren and biological children. *Journal of Family Issues, 17,* 5–25.

Mace, D. (1987). Three ways of helping married couples. *Journal of Marriage and Family Therapy, 13,* 179–185.

Mace, D., and Mace, V. (1974). *We Can Have Better Marriages If We Really Want Them.* Nashville: Abingdon.

Mace, D., and Mace, V. (1980). Enriching marriages: The foundation stone of family strength. In N. Stinnett et al. (Eds.), *Family Strengths: Positive Models for Family Life.* Lincoln: University of Nebraska Press.

MacEwen, K. E., and Barling, J. (1991). Effects of maternal employment experiences on children's behavior via mood, cognitive difficulties, and parenting behavior. *Journal of Marriage and the Family, 53,* 635–644.

Madden-Derdich, D. A., and Leonard, S. A. (2002). Shared experiences, unique realities: formerly married mothers' and fathers' perceptions of parenting and custody after divorce. *Family Relations, 51*(1), 37–45.

Maddock, J. W. (1989). Healthy family sexuality: Positive principles for educators and clinicians. *Family Relations, 38,* 130–136.

Mahler, K. (1996a). Completed, premarital pregnancies more likely among cohabiting women than among singles. *Family Planning Perspectives, 28,* 179–180.

Mahler, K. (1996b). Risk of low birth weight rises among infants with mother and siblings with low birth weight. *Family Planning Perspectives, 28,* 129–130.

Mahler, K. (1996c). Stress during pregnancy may lead to premature delivery, but birth weight appears unaffected. *Family Planning Perspectives, 28,* 292–297.

Major, V. S., Klein, K. J., and Ehrhart, M. G. (2002). Work time, work interference with family, and psychological distress. *Journal of Applied Psychology, 87*(3), 427–436.

Makepeace, J. M. (1987). Social factor and victim-offender differences in courtship violence. *Family Relations, 36,* 87–91.

Make the cover a sales tool. (1998, March 1). *Folio: The Magazine for Magazine Management.* Retrieved from http://www.foliomag.com/content/plus/1998/19980301.htm#3

Malamuth, N. M. (1989a). The attraction to sexual aggression scale: Part one. *The Journal of Sex Research, 26,* 26–49.

Malamuth, N. M. (1989b). The attraction to sexual aggression scale: Part two. *The Journal of Sex Research, 26,* 324–354.

Malinak, R., and Wheeler, J. (1985). Endometriosis. *Female Patient, 6,* 35–36.

Malkin, A. R., Wornian, K., and Chrisler, J. C. (1999). Woman and weight: Gendered messages on magazine covers. *Sex Roles, 40*(7/8), 647–655.

Mancini, J. A., and Orthner, D. K. (1988). The context and consequences of family change. *Family Relations, 37,* 363–366.

Mann, J. (1994). *The Difference: Growing up Female in America.* New York: Warner Books.

Manning, R. D. (2000). *Credit Card Nation.* New York: Basic Books.

Manning, W. D. (2002). The implication of cohabitation for children's well-being. In A. Booth and A. C. Crouter (Eds.), *Just Living Together: Implications for Children, Families, and Public Policy.* Hillsdale, NJ: Erlbaum.

March, K. (1995). Perception of adoption as social stigma: motivation, search and reunion. *Journal of Marriage and the Family, 57,* 653–660.

March, K. (1997). The dilemma of adoption reunion: Establishing open communication between adoptees and their birth mothers. *Family Relations, 26,* 99–105.

Marchbanks, P. A., McDonald, J. A., Wilson, H. G., Folger, S. G., Mandel, M. G., Daling, J. R., et al. (2002). Oral contraceptives and the risk of breast cancer. *New England Journal of Medicine, 346*(26), 2025–2032.

Marcus, I. M. (1983). The need for flexibility in marriage. *Medical Aspects of Human Sexuality, 17,* 120–131.

Margolian, L. (1991). Abuse and neglect in nonparental child care: A risk assessment. *Journal of Marriage and the Family, 53,* 694–704.

Margolin, G., Christensen, A., and John, R. S. (1996). The continuance and spillover of everyday tensions in distressed and nondistressed families. *Journal of Family Psychology, 10,* 304–321.

Margolin, G., Talovic, S., Fernandez, V., and Onorato, R. (1983). Sex role considerations and behavior marital therapy: Equal does not mean identical. *Journal of Marital and Family Therapy, 9,* 131–145.

Margolis, M. (1984). *Mothers and Such: Views of American Women and Why They Changed.* Berkeley: University of California Press.

Marks, N. F. (1995). Midlife marital status differences in social support relationships with adult children and psychological well-being. *Journal of Family Issues, 16,* 5–28.

Marks, N. F., and Lambert, J. D. (1998). Marital status continuity and change among young and midlife adults. *Journal of Family Issues, 19,* 652–686.

Markstrom-Adams, C. (1990). Coming-of-age among contemporary American Indians as portrayed in adolescent fiction. *Adolescence, 25,* 225–237.

Marlow, L., and Sauber, S. R. (1990). *The Handbook of Divorce Mediation.* New York: Plenum.

Marshall, S. K., and Markstrom-Adams, C. (1995). Attitudes on interfaith dating among Jewish adolescents. *Journal of Family Issues, 16,* 787–811.

Martin, B. (1990). The transmission of relationship difficulties from one generation to the next. *Journal of Youth and Adolescence, 19,* 181–199.

Martin, M. J., Schumm, W. R., Bugaighis, M. A., Jurich, A. P., and Bollman, S. R. (1987). Family violence and adolescents' perceptions of outcomes of family conflict. *Journal of Marriage and the Family, 49,* 165–171.

Martin, P., Hagestad, G. O., and Diedrich, P. (1988). Family stories: Events (temporarily) remembered. *Journal of Marriage and the Family, 40,* 533–541.

Martin, T. C., and Bumpass, L. L. (1989). Recent trends in marital disruption. *Demography, 26,* 37–51.

Masheter, C. (1997). Healthy and unhealthy friendship and hostility between ex-spouses. *Journal of Marriage and the Family, 59,* 463–475.

Maslow, A. H. (1962). *Toward a Psychology of Being.* Princeton, NJ: Van Nostrand.

Maslow, A. H. (1970). *Motivation and Personality* (2nd ed.). New York: Harper & Row.

Mason, M. A. (2003). The modern American stepfamily: Problems and possibilities. In M. A. Mason, A. Skolnick, and S. D. Sugarman (Eds.), *All Our Families* (pp. 96–116). New York: Oxford University Press.

Mason, M. A., Harrison-Jay, S., Svare, G. M., and Wolfinger, N. H. (2002). Stepparents: De facto parents or legal strangers? *Journal of Family Issues, 23*(4), 507–522.

Mason, M. A., Skolnick, A., and Sugarman, S. D. (Eds.). (1998). *All Our Families: New Policies for a New Century.* New York: Oxford University Press.

Mastekaasa, A. (1992). Marriage and psychological well-being: Some evidence on selection into marriage. *Journal of Marriage and the Family, 54,* 901–911.

Mastekaasa, A. (1994). Psychological well-being and marital disillusion: Selection effects. *Journal of Family Issues, 15,* 208–228.

Masters, W. H., and Johnson, V. E. (1966). *Human Sexual Response.* Boston: Little, Brown.

Mattessich, P., and Hill, R. (1987). Life cycle and family development. In M. B. Sussman and S. K. Steinmetz (Eds.), *Handbook of Marriage and the Family* (pp. 437–469). New York: Plenum.

Matthews, S. H., and Rosner, T. T. (1988). Shared filial responsibility: The family as the primary caregiver. *Journal of Marriage and the Family, 50,* 185–195.

May, K. A. (1982). Factors contributing to first-time father's readiness for fatherhood: An exploratory study. *Family Relations, 31,* 353–361.

Maynard, F. (1974). Understanding the crises in men's lives. In C. E. Williams and J. F. Crosby (Eds.), *Choice and Challenge* (pp. 135–144). Dubuque, IA: Brown.

Maynard, R., and Rangaragan, A. (1994). Contraceptive use and repeat pregnancies among welfare-dependent teenage mothers. *Family Planning Perspectives, 26,* 198–205.

Mazur, A. (1986). U.S. trends in feminine beauty and over-adaptation. *The Journal of Sex Research, 22,* 281–303.

McCabe, M. P. (1987). Desired and experienced levels of premarital affection and sexual intercourse during dating. *The Journal of Sex Research, 23,* 23–33.

McCabe, M. P. (1999). The interrelationship between intimacy, relationship functioning, and sexuality among men and women in committed relationships. *Canadian Journal of Human Sexuality, 8*(1), 31–38.

McCandless, N. J., Lueptow, L. B., and McClendon, M. (1989). Family economic status and adolescent sex-typing. *Journal of Marriage and the Family, 51,* 627–635.

McCarthy, G. (1999). Attachment style and adult love relationships and friendships: a study of a group of women at risk of experiencing relationship difficulties. *British Journal of Medical Psychology, 72,* 305–321.

McCarthy, G., and Taylor, A. (1999). Avoidant/ambivalent attachment style as a mediator between abusive childhood experiences and adult relationship difficulties. *Journal of Child Psychology and Psychiatry and Allied Discipline, 40,* 465–477.

McFee, R. B., Turano, J. A., and Roberts, S. (2001) Risk factors for dating violence in adolescents. *Journal of the American Medical Association, 286*(22), 2813.

McGovern, M. A. (1990). Sensitivity and reciprocity in the play of adolescent mothers and young fathers with their infants. *Family Relations, 339,* 427–431.

McHale, S. M., and Crouter, A. C. (1992). You can't always get what you want: Incongruence between sex-role attitudes and family work roles and its implications for marriage. *Journal of Marriage and the Family, 54,* 537–547.

McKenry, P. C., Julian, T. W., and Gavazzi, S. M. (1995). Toward a biopsychosocial model of domestic violence. *Journal of Marriage and the Family, 57,* 307–320.

McLanahan, S., and Adams, J. (1987). Parenthood and psychological well-being. *Annual Review of Sociology, 13,* 237–257.

McLanahan, S., and Sandefur, G. (1994). *Growing Up with a Single Parent: What Hurts, What Helps.* Cambridge, MA: Harvard University Press.

McLeod, J. D., and Eckberg, D. A. (1993). Concordance for depressive disorders and marital quality. *Journal of Marriage and the Family, 55,* 733–746.

McLoyd, V. C. (1989). Socialization and development in a changing economy: The effects of paternal job and income loss on children. *American Psychologist, 44,* 293–302.

McLoyd, V. C., and Wilson, L. (1992). Telling them like it is: The role of economic and environmental factors in single mothers' discussion with their children. *American Journal of Community Psychology, 20,* 419–444.

McNeely, C., Shew, M., Beuhring, T., Sieving, R., Miller, B., and Blum, R. (2002). Mothers' influence on the timing of the first sex among 14 and 15 year olds. *Journal of Adolescent Health, 31*(3), 256–265.

McQuillian, G. M. (2000, September). *Implications of a National Survey for STDs: Results from the NHANES Survey.* Presentation at 2000 Infectious Disease Society of America Conference, New Orleans, LA.

Mead, M. (1950). *Sex and Temperament in Three Primitive Societies.* New York: Merton Books.

Mederer, H. J., and Weinstein, L. (1992). Choice and constraints in a two-person career. *Journal of Family Issues, 13,* 334–350.

Meehan, P. J., Saltzman, L. E., and Sattin, R. W. (1991). Suicides among older United States residents: Epidemiologic characteristics and trends. *American Journal of Public Health, 81,* 1198–1200.

Meeks, S., Arnkoff, D. B., Glass, C. R., and Notarius, C. I. (1986). Wives' employment status, hassles, communication and relational efficacy: Intra- versus extra-relationship factors and marital adjustment. *Family Relations, 34,* 249–255.

Meer, J. (1985). Flex-time and sharing. *Psychology Today, 19,* 74.

Menaghan, E. G. (1989). Psychological well-being among parents and nonparents. *Journal of Family Issues, 10,* 547–565.

Menaghan, E. G., and Parcel, T. L. (1991). Determining children's home environments: The impact of maternal characteristics in current occupational and family conditions. *Journal of Marriage and the Family, 53,* 417–431.

Mendenhall, P. J., Grotevant, H. D., and McRoy, R. G. (1996). Adoptive couples: Communication and changes made in openness levels. *Family Relations, 45,* 223–229.

Messer, A. A. (1983). Continuation in adult life of parent–child relationships: Effect on marriage. *Medical Aspects of Human Sexuality, 17,* 28–43.

Meyer, K., and Lobao, L. (1997). Farm couples in crisis politics: The importance of household, spouse, and gender in responding to economic decline. *Journal of Marriage and the Family, 59,* 204–218.

Michael, R. T., Gagnon, J. H., Laumann, E. O., and Kolata, G. (1994). *Sex in America.* Boston: Little, Brown.

Milkie, M.A., and Peltola, P. (1999). Playing all roles: Gender and the work–family balancing act. *Journal of Marriage and the Family, 61,* 476–490.

Miller, B. C. (1993). Families, science, and values: Alternative views of parenting effects in adolescent pregnancy. *Journal of Marriage and the Family, 55,* 7–21.

Miller, B. C., and Heaton, T. B. (1991). Age at first sexual intercourse and the timing of marriage and childbirth. *Journal of Marriage and the Family, 53,* 719–732.

Miller, J., Turner, J. G., and Kimball, E. (1981). Big Thompson flood victims: One year later. *Family Relations, 30,* 111–116.

Miller, J. E. (1991). Birth intervals and perinatal health: An investigation of three hypotheses. *Family Planning Perspectives, 23,* 62–70.

Miller, K. J., Gleaves, D. H., Hirsch, T. G., Green, B. A., Snow, A. C., and Corbett, C. C. (2000). Comparisons of body image dimensions by race/ethnicity and gender in a university population. *International Journal of Eating Disorders, 27*(3), 310–316.

Mills, R. J., Grasmick, H. G., Morgan, C. T., and Wenk, D. (1992). The effects of gender, family satisfaction, and economic strain on psychological well-being. *Family Relations, 41,* 440–445.

Minkler, M. (1998). Intergenerational households headed by grandparents: Demographic and sociological contexts. In *Grandparents and Other Relatives Raising Children: Background Papers for Generations United's Expert Symposium* (pp. 3–18). Washington, DC: Generations United.

Minton, H. L., and McDonald, G. J. (1983/1984). Homosexual identity formation as a developmental process. *Journal of Homosexuality, 9*(2/3), 65–77.

Mirowsky, J., and Ross, C. E. (1987). Belief in innate sex roles: Sex stratification versus interpersonal inference in marriage. *Journal of Marriage and the Family, 49,* 527–540.

Mishel, L., Bernstein, and Boushey, H. (2003). *The State of Working America 2002–03,* Ithaca, NY: Cornell University Press.

Mitchell, B. A., and Gee, E. M. (1996). "Boomerang kids" and mid-life parental marital satisfaction. *Family Relations, 45,* 442–448.

Moen, P. (1991). Transitions in mid-life: Women's work and family roles in the 1970s. *Journal of Marriage and the Family, 53,* 135–150.

Molder, C., and Tolman, R. (1998). Gender and contextual factors in adolescent dating relationships. *Violence Against Women, 4,* 180–194.

Monroe, C. A., Garand, J. C., and Teeters, H. (1995). Family leave legislation in the U.S. House. *Family Relations, 44,* 46–55.

Montgomery, M. J., and Sorell, G. T. (1997). Differences in love attitudes across family life stages. *Family Relations, 46,* 55–61.

Mookherjee, H. N. (1997). A comparative assessment of life satisfaction in the United States: 1978–1988. *Journal of Social Psychology, 132,* 407–409.

Moore, K. A., Peterson, J. L., and Furstenberg, F. F. (1986). Parental attitudes and the occurrence of early sexual activity. *Journal of Marriage and the Family, 48,* 777–782.

Moore, S., and Leung, C. (2002). Young people's romantic attachment styles and their associations with well-being. *Journal of Adolescence, 25,* 243–255.

Morgan, L. A. (1989). Economic well-being following marital termination. *Journal of Family Issues, 10,* 86–101.

Morgan, S. P., Lye, D., and Condran, G. (1988). Sons, daughters, and the risk of marital disruption. *American Journal of Sociology, 90,* 1053–1077.

Morrison, B. R., and Cherlin, A. J. (1995). The divorce process and young children's well-being: A prospec-

tive analysis. *Journal of Marriage and the Family, 57,* 800–812.

Morrison, D. R., and Lichter, D. T. (1988). Family migration and female employment: The problem of underemployment among migrant married women. *Journal of Marriage and the Family, 50,* 161–172.

Morse, B. J. (1995). Beyond the Conflict Tactics Scale: Assessing gender differences in partner violence. *Violence and Victims, 10,* 251–272.

Moss, B. F., and Schwebel, A. I. (1993). Marriage and romantic relationships. Defining intimacy in romantic relationships. *Family Relations, 42,* 31–37.

Moss, N. E., and Abramowitz, S. I. (1982). Beyond deficit-filling and developmental stakes: Cross-disciplinary perspectives on parental heritage. *Journal of Marriage and the Family, 44,* 357–366.

Mui, A. C. (1992). Caregivers' strain among Black and White caregivers: A role theory perspective. *The Gerontologist, 32,* 203–212.

Mullis, R. L., and McKinley, K. (1989). Gender-role orientation of adolescent females: Effects on self-esteem and locus of control. *Journal of Adolescent Research, 4,* 506–516.

Mupinga, E. E., Garrison, M. E. B., and Pierce, S. H. (2002). An exploratory study of the relationships between family functioning and parenting styles: The perceptions of mothers of young grade school children. *Family and Consumer Sciences Research Journal, 31*(1), 112–129.

Murdock, G. P. (1949). *Social Structure.* New York: Macmillan.

Murstein, B. I. (1980). Mate selection in the 1970s. *Journal of Marriage and the Family, 42,* 777–792.

Myers, D. G. (2000). Hope and happiness. In J. E. Gillham (Ed.) *The science of optimism and hope: Research essays in honor of Martin E. P. Seligman. Laws of life symposia series* (pp. 323–336). Philadelphia, PA: Templeton Foundation Press.

Myers, D. G. (2000). The funds, friends, and faith of happy people. *American Psychologist, 55*(1), 56–67.

Myers, S. M., and Booth, A. (1996). Men's retirement and marital quality. *Journal of Family Issues, 17,* 336–357.

Nakonezny, P. A., Shull, R. D., and Rodgers, J. L. (1995). The effect of no-fault divorce law on the divorce rate across the 50 states and its relation to income, education, and religiosity. *Journal of Marriage and the Family, 57,* 477–488.

Namerow, P. B., Kalmuss, D. S., and Cushman, L. F. (1993). The determinants of young women's pregnancy-resolution choices. *Journal of Research on Adolescence, 3,* 193–215.

National Center for Health Statistics. (2000). *National Vital Statistics Reports, 48,* 14.

National Center for Health Statistics. (2002). Marriage and Divorce. Retrieved January 6, 2003, from http://www.cdc.gov/nchs/fastats/marriage.htm

National Center for Injury Prevention and Control. Dating Violence Fact Sheet. (2002, September). Retrieved from http://www.cdc.gov.ncipc/factsheets/datviol.htm

National Committee on Pay Equity. (1998). *The Wage Gap by Education.* (Fact sheet). Retrieved August 21, 2000, from http://feminist.com/ fairpay/f_education.htm

National Marriage Project. (2000). *The state of our unions: The social health of marriage in America, 2000.* New Brunswick, NJ: Rutgers University.

National Women's Health Resource Center. (1998). *Women and Sexually Transmitted Diseases (STDs).* Retrieved February 14, 1998, from http://www.healthywomen.org/qa/std.html#1

Neal, A. G., Groat, H. T., and Wicks, J. W. (1989). Attitudes about having children: A study of 600 couples in the early years of marriage. *Journal of Marriage and the Family, 51,* 313–328.

Neal, J., and Frick-Horbury, D. (2001). The effects of parenting styles and childhood attachment patterns on intimate relationships. *Journal of Instructional Psychology, 28*(3), 178–183.

Neimeyer, R. S., Prigerson, H. G., and Davis, B. (2002). Mourning and meaning. *American Behavioral Scientist, 46*(2), 235–251.

Nellie Mae. (2000). Research and information. Retrieved May 8, 2003, from http://www.nelliemae.com/library/research_8.html

Nelson, C., and Keith, J. (1990). Comparisons of female and male early adolescent sex role attitude and behavior development. *Adolescence, 25,* 183–204.

Nelson, J. A. (1986). Incest: Self-report findings from a nonclinical sample. *The Journal of Sex Research, 22,* 463–477.

Nelson, M. B. (2002/2003, December/January). And now they tell us women don't really like sports? *Ms.* pp. 32–36.

Nelson, W. P., and Lavant, R. F. (1991). An evaluation of a skills' training program for parents and stepfamilies. *Family Relations, 40,* 291–296.

New Survey Reveals Americans Underestimate Their Risk for Contracting Genital Herpes. (2000). Research Triangle Park, NC: American Social Health Association. Re-

trieved from http://www.ashastd.org/press/042600.html

Nieto, S. (1996). *Affirming Diversity: The Sociopolitical Context of Multicultural Education* (2nd ed.). New York: Longman.

Nock, S. L. (1995). Commitment and dependency in marriage. *Journal of Marriage and the Family, 57,* 503–514.

Nock, S. L., and Kingston, P. W. (1988). Time with children: The impact of couple's work-time commitments. *Social Forces, 67,* 59–85.

Nordenberg, T. (1999, July/August). Chlamydia's quick cure. *FDA Consumer Magazine.* Retrieved July 25, 2000, from http://www.fda.gov/fdac/ features/1999/499_std.html

Norton, A. J., and Glick, P. G. (1986). One-parent families: A social and economic profile: *Family Relations, 35,* 9–13.

Norton, A. J., and Moorman, J. E. (1987). Current trends in marriage and divorce among American women. *Journal of Marriage and the Family, 49,* 3–14.

Nugent, J. K. (1991). Cultural and psychological influences on the father's role in infant development. *Journal of Marriage and the Family, 53,* 475–485.

Nye, F. I. (1978). Is choice and exchange theory the key? *Journal of Marriage and the Family, 40,* 219–233.

Oakley, D. (1985). Premarital childbearing decision making. *Family Relations, 34,* 561–563.

Ohannesian, C. M., and Crockett, L. J. (1993). A longitudinal investigation of the relationship between educational investment and adolescent sexual activity. *Journal of Adolescent Research, 8,* 167–182.

Okagaki, L., and Sternberg, R. J. (1993). Parental beliefs in children's school performance. *Child Development, 64,* 36–56.

O'Kelly, C. G., and Carney, L. S. (1986). *Women and Men in Society: Cross-Cultural Perspectives on Gender Stratification.* Belmont, CA: Wadsworth.

Okraku, I. O. (1987). Age and attitudes toward multigenerational residence, 1973 to 1983. *Journal of Gerontology, 42,* 280–287.

O'Leary, K. D., Barling, J., Arias, I., Rosenbaum, A., Malone, J., and Tyree, A. (1989). Prevalence and stability of physical aggression between spouses: A longitudinal analysis. *Journal of Consulting and Clinical Psychology, 57,* 263–268.

Oles, P. K. (1999). Toward a psychological model of midlife crisis. *Psychological Reports, 84,* 1059–1069.

Olson, D. (2000). *Empowering Couples: Building on Your Strengths.* Minneapolis: Life Innovations.

Olson, D. H., Fournier, D. G., and Druckman, J. M. (1982). *PREPARE-ENRICH Counselors Manual* (Rev. ed.). Available from PREPARE-ENRICH, P.O. Box 1363, Stillwater, OK 74076.

Olson, D. H., McCubbin, H. I., Barnes, H., Larsen, A., Muyen, M., and Wilson, M. (1983). *Families: What Makes Them Work.* Beverly Hills, CA: Sage.

Olson, S. L., and Banyard, B. (1993). "Stop the world so I can get off for a while": Sources of daily stress in the lives of low-income single mothers of young children. *Family Relations, 42,* 50–56.

O'Neil, R., and Greenberger, E. (1994). Patterns of commitment to work and parenting: Implications for role strain. *Journal of Marriage and the Family, 56,* 101–118.

Orbuch, T. L., House, J. S., Mero, R. P., and Webster, P. S. (1996). Marital quality over the life course. *Social Psychology Quarterly, 59,* 162–171.

Ortega, S. T., Whitt, H. P., and William, J. A. (1988). Religious homogamy and marital happiness. *Journal of Family Issues, 9,* 224–239.

Orth-Gomer, K. (2001). Women and heart disease: New evidence for psychosocial, behaviorial, and biological mediators of risk and prognosis. *International Journal of Behavioral Medicine, 8*(4), 251–269.

Orthner, D. K., and Neenan, P. A. (1996). Children's impact on stress and employability of mothers in poverty. *Journal of Family Issues, 17,* 667–687.

Osmond, M. W., and Thorne, B. (1993). Feminist theories: The social construction of gender in families and society. In P. G. Boss, W. J. Doherty, R. LaRossa, W. R. Schumm, and S. K. Steinmetz (Eds.), *Source of Family Theories and Methods* (pp. 591–622). New York: Plenum.

Oyserman, D., Radin, N., and Benn, R. (1993). Dynamics in a three-generational family: Teens, grandparents, and babies. *Developmental Psychology, 29,* 564–572.

Ozawa, M. N., and Yoon H. S. (2002). The economic benefit of remarriage: Gender and income class. *Journal of Divorce and Remarriage, 36*(3/4), 21–39.

Paasch, K. M., and Teachman, J. D. (1991). Gender of children and receipt of assistance from absent fathers. *Journal of Family Issues, 12,* 450–466.

Paden, S. L., and Buehler, C. (1995). Coping with the dual-income lifestyle. *Journal of Marriage and the Family, 57,* 101–110.

Palti, H., Mansbach, I., Pridan, H., Adler, B., and Palti, Z. (1984). Episodes of illness in breast-fed and bottle-fed infants in Jerusalem. *Journal of Medical Sciences, 20,* 395–399.

Papp, P. (1983). *The Process of Change.* New York: Guilford Press.

Parachini, A. (1987, August 19). Condoms fail government tests. *Portland Press Herald.*

Park, K. (2002). Stigma management among the voluntarily childless. *Sociological Perspectives, 45*(1), 21–45.

Parks, P. L., and Smeriglio, V. L. (1986). Relationships among parenting knowledge, quality of stimulation in the home, and infant development. *Family Relations, 35,* 411–416.

Pasquariello, P. (1999). *Book of Pregnancy and Child Care.* New York: Wiley.

Patterson, C. J. (1992). Children of lesbian and gay parents. *Child Development, 63,* 1025–1043.

Patterson, C. J., and Redding, R. (1996). Lesbian and gay families with children: Implications of social science research for policy. *Journal of Social Issues, 52*(3), 29–50.

Pawlowski, B., and Dunbar, R. (1999). Withholding age as putative deception in mate search tactics. *Evolution and Human Behavior, 20*(1), 53–69.

Penn, C. D., Hernandez, S. L., and Bermudez, J. M. (1997). Using a cross-cultural perspective to understand infidelity in couples therapy. *The American Journal of Family Therapy, 25,* 169–185.

Pepe, M. B., and Byrne, T. J. (1991). Women's perceptions of immediate and long-term effects of failed infertility treatment on marital and sexual satisfaction. *Family Relations, 40,* 303–309.

Perrewe, P. L., and Hochwater, W. A. (2001). Can we really have it all? The attainment of work and family values. *Current Directions in Psychological Science, 10*(1), 29–33.

Perrucci, C. C., Perrucci, R., Targ, D. B., and Targ, H. R. (1988). *Plant Closings.* New York: Aldine de Gruyter.

Perry, B. (1995). Step-parenting: How vulnerable are step-children? *Educational and Child Psychology, 12*(2), 58–70.

Peterson, G. W., and Rollins, B. C. (1987). Parent–child socialization. In M. B. Sussman and S. K. Steinmetz (Eds.), *Handbook of Marriage and the Family* (pp. 471–507). New York: Plenum.

Peterson, R. R., and Gerson, K. (1992). The determinants of responsibility for childcare arrangements among dual-earner couples. *Journal of Marriage and the Family, 54,* 527–536.

Petitti, D. B. (1992). Reconsidering the IUD. *Family Planning Perspectives, 24,* 33–35.

Pfost, K. S., Stevens, M. J., and Matejcak, A. J., Jr. (1990). A counselor's primer on postpartum depression. *Journal of Counseling and Development, 69,* 148–151.

Phelps, R. E., Meara, N. M., Davis, K. L., and Patton, M. J. (1991). Blacks' and Whites' perceptions of verbal aggression. *Journal of Counseling and Development, 69,* 345–350.

Philliber, S. G., and Graham, E. H. (1981). The impact of age of mother on mother–child interaction patterns. *Journal of Marriage and the Family, 43,* 109–115.

Pictman, J. S., and Blanchard, D. (1996). The effects of work history and timing of marriage on the division of household labor: A life-force perspective. *Journal of Marriage and the Family, 58,* 78–90.

Piercy, F. P., and Sprenkle, D. H. (1990). Marriage and family therapy: A decade review. *Journal of Marriage and the Family, 52,* 1116–1126.

Pill, C. J. (1990). Stepfamilies: Refining the family. *Family Relations, 39,* 186–193.

Pillemer, K., and Suitor, J. J. (1991). "Will I ever escape my children's problems?" Effects of adult children's problems on elderly parents. *Journal of Marriage and the Family, 53,* 585–594.

Pina, D. L., and Bengston, D. L. (1993). The division of household labor and wives' happiness: Ideology, employment and perceptions of support. *Journal of Marriage and the Family, 55,* 901–912.

Pinhas, L., Toner, B. B., Ali, A., Garfinkel, P. E., and Stuckless, N. (1999). The effects of the ideal of female beauty on mood and body satisfaction. *International Journal of Eating Disorders, 25*(2), 223–226.

Pinsof, W. M., and Wynne, L. C. (1995). The efficacy of marital and family therapy: An empirical overview, conclusion, and recommendation. *Journal of Marital and Family Therapy, 21,* 585–613.

Pipher, M. (1994). *Reviving Ophelia: Saving the Selves of Adolescent Girls.* New York: Ballantine Books.

Pipher, M. (1996). *The Shelter of Each Other. Rebuilding Our Families.* New York: Grosset/Putnam Books.

Pittman, F. (1993). Beyond betrayal: Life after infidelity. *Psychology Today, 26,* 32–38+.

Pittman, J. F., Wright, C. A., and Lloyd, S. A. (1989). Predicting parenting difficulties. *Journal of Family Issues, 10,* 267–286.

Planned Parenthood of Southeastern Pennsylvania v. Casey, 60 U.S. L. W. 4795 (1992).

Pleck, J. (1997). Paternal involvement: Levels, sources, and consequences. In M. E. Lamb (Ed.), *The Role of the Father in Child Development* (3rd ed., pp. 66–103). New York: Wiley.

Poehlman, E. T., Melby, T. L., and Badylak, S. F. (1991). Relation of age and physical exercise status on metabolic rate in younger and older healthy men. *Journal of Gerontology, 46,* B54–B58.

Ponzetti, J. L. (1990). Loneliness among college students. *Family Relations, 39,* 336–340.

Pope, G., Olivardia, R., Gruber, A., and Borowiecki, J. (1999). Evolving ideals of male body image as seen through action toys. *International Journal of Eating Disorders, 26*(1), 65–72.

Popenoe, D., and Whithead, B. D. (2002). *Sex without Strings: Relationships without Rings.* Piscataway, NJ: The National Marriage Project, Rutgers.

Popenoe, D., and Whithead, B. D. (2002a). *Should We Live Together? What Young Adults Need to Know about Cohabitation before Marriage.* New Brunswick, NJ: Rutgers University Publications, National Marriage Project.

Potts, M. (1988). Birth control methods in the United States. *Family Planning Perspectives, 20,* 288–297.

Powlishta, K. K., and Maccoby, E. E. (1990). Resource utilization in mixed-sex dyads: The influence of adult presence and task typ. *Sex Roles, 23*(5/6), 223–240.

Pratt, C. C., Walker, A. A., and Wood, D. L. (1992). Bereavement among former caregivers to elderly mothers. *Family Relations, 41,* 278–283.

Pratto, F. (1996). Sexual politics: The gender gap in the bedroom, the cupboard, and the cabinet. In D. M. Buss and N. M. Malamuth (Eds.), *Sex, Power, Conflict: Evolutionary and Feminist Perspectives.* New York: Oxford University Press.

Presser, H. B. (1989). Some economic complexities of child care provided by grandmothers. *Journal of Marriage and the Family, 51,* 581–591.

Presser, H. B. (2000, February). Nonstandard work schedules and marital instability. *Journal of Marriage and the Family, 62,* 93–110.

Priest, R., and Smith, A. (1992). Counseling adult sex offenders: Unique challenges and treatment paradigms. *Journal of Counseling and Development, 71,* 27–32.

Purnell, M., and Bagby, B. H. (1993). Grandparents' rights. Implications for family specialists. *Family Relations, 42,* 173–178.

Pyke, K., and Coltrane, F. (1996). Entitlement, obligation, and gratitude in family work. *Journal of Family Issues, 17,* 60–82.

Querido, J. G., Warner, T. D., and Eyberg, S. M. (2002). Parenting styles and child behavior in African American families of preschool children. *Journal of Clinical Child and Adolescent Psychology, 31*(2), 272–277.

Quinn, P., and Allen, K. R. (1989). Facing challenges and making compromises: How single mothers endure. *Family Relations, 38,* 390–395.

Quinn, W. H. (1983). Personal and family adjustment in later life. *Journal of Marriage and the Family, 45,* 57–73.

Rachlin, V. C. (1987). Fair vs. equal role relations in dual-career and dual-earner families: Implications for family interventions. *Family Relations, 36,* 187–192.

Raley, E. K. (1995). Black-White differences in kin contact and exchange among never married adults. *Journal of Family Issues, 16*, 77–103.

Rank, M. R. (1987). The formation and dissolution of marriages in the welfare population. *Journal of Marriage and the Family, 49*, 15–20.

Rank, M. R., and Hirschl, T. A. (1999). The likelihood of poverty across the American adult life span. *Social Work, 44*(3), 201–216.

Rankin-Esquer, L. A., Burnett, C. K., Baucom, D. H., and Epstein, M. (1997). Autonomy and relatedness in marital functioning. *Journal of Marital and Family Therapy, 23*, 175–190.

Ratican, K. L. (1992). Sexual abuse survivors: Identifying symptoms and special treatment considerations. *Journal of Counseling and Development, 71*, 33–40.

Raup, J. L., and Myers, J. E. (1989). The empty nest syndrome: Myth or reality. *Journal of Counseling and Development, 68*, 180–183.

Read, J. G., and Bartkowski, J. P. (2000). To veil or not to veil? A case study of identity negotiation among Muslim women in Austin, Texas. *Gender and Society, 14*(3), 395–417.

Reamy, K. J., and White, S. E. (1987). Sexuality in the puerperium: A review. *Archives of Sexual Behavior, 16*, 165–186.

Reed, J. P. (1975). The current legal status of abortion. In J. G. Well (Ed.), *Current Issues in Marriage and the Family* (pp. 200–208). New York: Macmillan.

Regan, P. C. (1998). Minimum mate selection standards as a function of perceived mate value, relationship context, and gender. *Journal of Psychology and Human Sexuality, 10*, 53–73.

Regan, P. C., and Berscheid, E. (1997). Gender differences in characteristics desired in a potential sexual and marriage partner. *Journal of Psychology and Human Sexuality, 9*, 25–37.

Regan, P. C., and Dreyer, C. (1999). Lust? Love? Status? Young adults' motives for engaging in casual sex. *Journal of Psychology and Human Sexuality, 11*(1), 1–24.

Reifman, A., Villa, L. C., Adams, J. A., Rethinam, V., and Telesca, T. Y. (2001). Children of divorce in the 1990s: A meta-analysis. *Journal of Divorce and Remarriage, 36*(1/2), 27–36.

Reik, T. A. (1957). *Of Love and Lust.* New York: Straus & Cudahy.

Reinisch, J. M., and Beasley, R. (1990). *The Kinsey New Report on Sex.* New York: St. Martin's Press.

Reinisch, J. M., Hill, C. A., Sanders, S. A., and Ziemba-Davis, M. (1995). High-risk sexual behavior at a Midwestern university: A confirmatory survey. *Family Planning Perspectives, 27*, 79–82.

Reis, J., Barbara-Stein, L., and Bennett, S. (1986). Ecological determinants of parenting. *Family Relations, 35*, 547–554.

Reise, S. P., and Wright, T. M. (1996). Personality traits, cluster B personality disorders, and sociosexuality. *Journal of Research in Personality, 30*, 128–136.

Reiss, A. J., Jr. (1984). Selecting strategies of social control over organizational life. In K. Hawkins and J. M. Thomas (Eds.), *Enforcing Regulation.* Boston: Kluwer-Nijhoff.

Reiss, I. L. (1980). *Family Systems in America* (3rd ed.). New York: Holt, Rinehart & Winston.

Reker, G. T., Peacock, E. J., and Wong, P. T. P. (1987). Meaning and purpose in life and well-being: A life-span perspective. *Journal of Gerontology, 42*, 44–49.

Remez, L. (1992a). Abruptio placentae rates increase significantly in U.S. from 1979 to 1987. *Family Planning Perspectives, 24*, 143–144.

Remez, L. (1994). Vaginal delivery after cesarean is successful nearly 75% of the time. *Family Planning Perspectives, 26*, 240.

Remez, L. (1996). Early implant removals most often requested because of side effects. *Family Planning Perspectives, 28*, 35–37.

Remez, L. (2000). Oral sex among adolescents: Is it sex or is it abstinence? *Family Planning Perspectives, 32*(6), 298–304.

Renshaw, D. C. (1984). Touch hunger—a common marital problem. *Medical Aspects of Human Sexuality, 18*, 63–70.

Repetti, R. L., and Wood, J. (1997). Effects of daily stress at work on mothers' interaction with preschoolers. *Journal of Family Psychology, 11*, 90–108.

Requests for reversal of tubal sterilization linked with young age at surgery and marital disruption. (1984). *Family Planning Perspectives, 16*, 139–140.

Reschobsky, J. D., and Newman, S. J. (1991). Home upkeep and housing quality of older home owners. *Journal of Gerontology, 46*, S288–S297.

Rexroat, C., and Shehan, C. (1987). The family life cycle and spouses' time in housework. *Journal of Marriage and the Family, 49*, 737–750.

Rhein, L., Ginsburg, K., Schwartz, D., Pinto-Martin, J., Zhao, H., Morgan, A., and Slap, G. (1997). Teen father participation in child rearing: Family perspectives. *Journal of Adolescent Health, 21*(4), 244–252.

Rice, F. P. (1979). *Working Mother's Guide to Child Development.* Englewood Cliffs, NJ: Prentice-Hall.

Rice, F. P. (1986). *Adult Development and Aging.* Boston: Allyn & Bacon.

Rice, F. P. (1993). *The Adolescent: Development, Relationships, and Culture* (7th ed.). Boston: Allyn & Bacon.

Richards, L. N., and Schmiege, C. J. (1993). Problems and strengths of single-parent families. Implications for practice and policy. *Family Relations, 42,* 277–285.

Richardson, B., and Kilty, K. N. (1992). Retirement intentions among Black professionals: Implications for practice with older Black adults. *The Gerontologist, 32,* 7–16.

Ridgeway, C., and Smith-Lovin, L. (1999). The gender system and interaction. *Annual Review of Sociology, 25,* 191–215.

Riggio, H. R. (2001). Relations between parental divorce and the quality of adult sibling relationships. *Journal of Divorce and Remarriage, 36*(1/2), 67–82.

Rind, P. (1991). Depression and anxiety decrease after abortion, regardless of method. *Family Planning Perspectives, 23,* 237–238.

Rind, P. (1992a). Smoking and pregnancy nearly triple women's risk of placenta previa. *Family Planning Perspectives, 24,* 47–48.

Rind, P. (1992c). Tubal sterilization may confer some protection against ovarian cancer. *Family Planning Perspectives, 24,* 44–45.

Rini, C., Dunkel-Schetter, C., Wadhwa, R., and Sandman, C. (1999). Psychological adaptation and birth outcomes: The role of personal resources, stress, and sociocultural context in pregnancy. *Health Psychology, 18*(4), 333–345.

Risman, B. J. (1986). Can men "mother"? Life as a single father. *Family Relations, 35,* 95–102.

Roan, C. L., and Raley, R. K. (1996). Intergenerational coresidence and contact: A longitudinal analysis of adult children's response to their mother's widowhood. *Journal of Marriage and the Family, 58,* 708–717.

Roberto, K. A., and Scott, J. P. (1986). Equity considerations in the friendships of older adults. *Journal of Gerontology, 41,* 241–247.

Roberts, T. W. (1992). Sexual attraction and romantic love: Forgotten variables in marital therapy. *Journal of Marital and Family Therapy, 18,* 357–364.

Roberts, D. (2002). *Shattered Bonds: The Color of Child Welfare.* New York: Basic Books.

Robertson, E. B., Elder, G. H., Jr., Skinner, M. L., and Conger, R. D. (1991). The costs and benefits of social support in families. *Journal of Marriage and the Family, 53,* 403–416.

Robertson, J. F., and Simons, R. L. (1989). Family factors, self-esteem and adolescent depression. *Journal of Marriage and the Family, 51,* 125–138.

Robinson, B. E., Rowland, B. H., and Coleman, M. (1986). Taking action for latchkey children and their families. *Family Relations, 35,* 473–478.

Robinson, J. P., Godbey, G., and Jacobson, A. J. (1999). *Time for Life: The Surprising Ways Americans Use Their Time.* University Park: Pennsylvania State University Press.

Robinson, L. C., and Blanton, P. W. (1993). Marital strengths in enduring marriages. *Family Relations, 42,* 38–45.

Rodgers, B. (1996). Social and psychological wellbeing of children from divorced families: Australian research findings. *Australian Psychologist, 31,* 174–182.

Rodgers, K. B., and Rose, H. A. (2002). Risk and resiliency factors among adolescents who experience marital transitions. *Journal of Marriage and Family, 64*(4), 1024–1037.

Rodman, H. (1991). Should parental involvement be required for minors' abortions? *Family Relations, 40,* 155–160.

Roe v. Wade, 410 U.S. 113 (1973).

Rogers, M. F. (1985). AIDS in children: A review of the clinical, epidemiological and public health aspects. *Pediatric Infectious Disease, 4,* 230–236.

Rogers, M. J., and Holmbeck, G. N. (1997). Effects of interparental aggression on children's adjustment: The moderating role of cognitive appraisal and coping. *Journal of Family Psychology, 11,* 125–130.

Rogers, S. J. (1996). Mothers' work hours and marital quality: Variations by family structure and family size. *Journal of Marriage and the Family, 58,* 606–617.

Rogers, S. J. (1999, February). Wife's income and marital quality: Are there reciprocal effects? *Journal of Marriage and the Family, 61,* 123–132.

Rogler, L. H., and Procidano, M. E. (1989a). Egalitarian spouse relations and wives' marital satisfaction in intergenerationally linked Puerto Rican families. *Journal of Marriage and the Family, 51,* 37–39.

Rogler, L. H., and Procidano, M. E. (1989b). Marital heterogamy and marital quality in Puerto Rican families. *Journal of Marital and Family Therapy, 51,* 363–372.

Rohner, R. P., Kean, K. J., and Cournoyer, D. E. (1991). Effects of corporal punishment, perceived caregiver warmth, and cultural beliefs on the psychological adjustment of children in St. Kitts, West Indies. *Journal of Marriage and the Family, 53,* 681–693.

Rook, K., Dooley, D., and Catalano, R. (1991). Stress transmission: The effects of husbands' job stressors on the emotional health of their wives. *Journal of Marriage and the Family, 53,* 165–177.

Roosa, M. W. (1988). The effect of age in the transition to parenthood: Are delayed childbearers a unique group? *Family Relations, 37,* 322–327.

Rosen, K. H., and Stith, S. M. (1993). Intervention strategies for treating women in violent dating relationships. *Family Relations, 42,* 427–433.

Rosen, K. S., and Rothbaum, F. (1993). Quality of parental caregiving and security of attachment. *Developmental Psychology, 29,* 358–367.

Rosenbloom, C. A., and Whittington, F. J. (1993). The effects of bereavement on eating behaviors and nutrient intakes in elderly widowed persons. *Journal of Gerontology, 48,* S223–S229.

Ross, C. E., and Huber, J. (1985). Hardship and depression. *Journal of Health and Social Behavior, 26,* 312–327.

Ross, C. E., Mirowsky, J., and Goldstein, K. (1990). The impact of family on health: The decade in review. *Journal of Marriage and the Family, 52,* 1059–1078.

Ross, C. E., and Van Willigen, M. D. (1996). Gender, parenthood, and anger. *Journal of Marriage and the Family, 68,* 572–584.

Roy, L., and Sawyers, J. K. (1986). The double-bind: An empirical study of responses to inconsistent communications. *Journal of Marital and Family Therapy, 12,* 395–402.

Rubin, Z., Hill, C. T., Peplau, L. A., and Dunkel-Schetter, C. (1980). Self-disclosure in dating couples: Sex roles and the ethic openness. *Journal of Marriage and the Family, 42,* 305–317.

Rubinstein, R. L., Alexander, B. B., Goodman, M., and Luborsky, M. (1991). Key relationships of never-married, childless older women: A cultural analysis. *Journal of Gerontology, 5,* S270–S277.

Ruble, D. N., and Brooks-Gunn, J. (1982). The experience of menarche. *Child Development, 53,* 1557–1566.

Rusbult, E., Olsen, N., Davis, J. L., and Hannon, P. A. (2001). Commitment and relationship maintenance mechanisms. In J. H. Harvey and A. Wenzel (Eds.), *Close Relationships: Maintenance and Enhancement* (pp. 87–113). Mahwah, NJ: Erlbaum.

Ryan, K. J. (1988). Giving birth in America, 1988. *Family Planning Perspectives, 20,* 298–301.

Sabatelli, R. M., and Cecil-Pigo, E. F. (1985). Relational interdependence and commitment in marriage. *Journal of Marriage and the Family, 47,* 931–937.

Sahlstein, E. M., and Baxter, L. A. (2001). Improving commitment in close relationships: A relational dialectics perspective. In J. H. Harvey and A. Wenzel (Eds.), *Close Relationships: Maintenance and Enhancement* (pp. 115–132). Mahwah, NJ: Erlbaum.

Salzinger, S., Feldman, R. S., and Hammer, M. (1993). The effects of physical abuse on children's social relationships. *Child Development, 64,* 169–187.

Samuels, M., and Samuels, N. (1996). *The New Well Pregnancy Book.* New York: Simon & Schuster.

Sanchez, L., and Kane, E. W. (1996). Women's and men's constructions of perceptions of household fairness. *Journal of Family Issues, 17,* 358–387.

Sandfort, J. R., and Hill, M. S. (1996). Assisting young, unmarried mothers who become self-sufficient: The effects of different types of early economic support. *Journal of Marriage and the Family, 58,* 311–326.

Santee, B., and Henshaw, S. K. (1992). The abortion debate: Measuring gestational age. *Family Planning Perspectives, 24,* 172–173.

Santelli, J. S., Davis, M., Celentano, B. D., Crump, D., and Burwell, L. T. (1995). Combined use of condoms with other contraceptive methods among inner-city Baltimore women. *Family Planning Perspectives, 27,* 74–78.

Sarason, I. G. (1981). *The Revised Life Experiences Survey.* Unpublished manuscript, University of Washington.

Sarvis, B., and Rodman, H. (1974). *The Abortion Controversy.* New York: Columbia University Press.

Sauer, L. E., and Fine, M. A. (1988). Parent–child relationships in stepparent families. *Journal of Family Psychology, 1,* 434–451.

Sawyer, R. G., and Pinciaro, P. J. (1998). College students' knowledge and attitudes about Norplant and Depo Provera. *American Journal of Health Behavior, 22*(3), 163–171.

Scanzoni, J. (1987). Families in the 1980s. *Journal of Family Issues, 8,* 394–421.

Schaninger, C. M., and Buss, W. C. (1986). A longitudinal comparison of consumption and finance handling between happily married and divorced couples. *Journal of Marriage and the Family, 48,* 129–136.

Scharlach, A. E. (1987). Role strain in mother–daughter relationships in later life. *The Gerontologist, 27,* 627–631.

Scher, M., and Stevens, M. (1987). Men and violence. *Journal of Counseling and Development, 65,* 351–355.

Schlenker, J. A., Caron, S. L., and Halteman, W. A. (1998). A feminist analysis of *Seventeen* magazine: Content analysis from 1945–1995. *Sex Roles, 38*(1/2), 135–149.

Schmaling, K. B., Whisman, M. A., Fruzzetti, A. E., and Truax, P. (1991). Identifying areas of marital conflict: Interactional behaviors associated with depression. *Journal of Family Psychology, 5,* 145–157.

Schoen, R., and Weinick, R. M. (1993). Partner choices in marriage and cohabitations. *Journal of Marriage and the Family, 55,* 408–414.

Schoen, R., and Woolridge, J. (1989). Marriage choices in No. Carolina and Virginia, 1969–71 and 1979–81. *Journal of Marriage and the Family, 51,* 465–481.

Schumm, W. R., Barnes, H. L., Bollman, S. R., Jurich, A. P., and Bugaighis, M. A. (1986). Self-disclosure and marital satisfaction revisited. *Family Relations, 34,* 241–247.

Schumm, W. R., and Bugaighis, M. A. (1986). Marital quality over the marital career: Alternative explanations. *Journal of Marriage and the Family, 48,* 165–168.

Schwartz, P. (2000). *Everything You Know about Love and Sex Is Wrong: Twenty-five Relationship Myths Redefined to Achieve Happiness and Fulfillment in Your Intimate Life.* New York: Penguin Putnam.

Schwartz, R., and Schwartz, L. J. (1980). *Becoming a Couple.* Englewood Cliffs, NJ: Prentice-Hall.

Schwarz, J. E. (1998). The hidden side of the the Clinton economy. *The Atlantic Monthly, 282*(4), pp. 18–21.

Scoon-Rogers, L. (1999, March). Child support for custodial mothers and fathers: 1995. (*Current Population Reports,* Series P60-196). Washington, DC: U.S. Bureau of the Census.

Scott, J., and Alwin, D. F. (1989). Gender differences in parental strain: Parental role or gender role? *Journal of Family Issues, 10,* 482–503.

Sears, H. A., and Galambos, N. L. (1992). Women's work conditions and marital adjustment in two-earner couples: A structural model. *Journal of Marriage and the Family, 54,* 789–797.

Seccombe, K., and Ishii-Kuntz, M. (1991). Perceptions of problems associated with aging: Comparisons among four older-age cohorts. *The Gerontologist, 31,* 527–533.

Seccombe, K., and Lee, G. (1987). Female status, wives' autonomy, and divorce. A cross-cultural study. *Family Perspectives, 20,* 241–249.

Secondi, G. (2002). Biased childhood sex ratios and the economic status of the family in rural China. *Journal of Comparative Studies, 33,* 215–235.

Seguin, L., Potvin, L., St-Denis, M., and Loiselle, J. (1999). Socio-environmental factors and postnatal depressive symptomatology: A longitudinal study. *Women and Health, 29*(1), 57–72.

Serbin, L. A., Sprafkin, C., Elman, M., and Doyle, A. (1982). The early development of sex-differentiated patterns of social influence. *Canadian Journal of Behavioral Science, 14,* 350–363.

Sexton, C. S., and Perlman, D. S. (1989). Couples' orientation, gender role orientation, and perceived equity as determinants of married power. *Journal of Marriage and the Family, 51,* 933–941.

Sexuality Information and Education Council of the United States (SIECUS). (2002, April). Ideology triumphs over sound public health policy. Retrieved April 9, 2003, from http://www.siecus.org

Shadish, W. R., Ragsdale, K., Glaser, R. R., and Montgomery, L. M. (1995). The efficacy and effectiveness of marital and family therapy: A perspective from meta-analysis. *Journal of Marital and Family Therapy, 21,* 345–360.

Shagle, S. C., and Barber, B. K. (1993). Effects of family, marital, and parent–child conflict on adolescent self-derogation and suicidal ideation. *Journal of Marriage and the Family, 55,* 964–974.

Shamir, B. (1986). Self-esteem and the psychological impact of unemployment. *Social Psychology Quarterly, 49,* 61–72.

Shanas, E. (1979). The family as a social support system in old age. *The Gerontologist, 19,* 169–174.

Shapiro, A. D. (1996). Explaining psychological distress in a sample of remarried and divorced persons. *Journal of Family Issues, 17,* 186–203.

Shapiro, A. D., and Lambert, J. D. (1999). Longitudinal effects of divorce on the quality of father–child relationship and on father's psychological well-being. *Journal of Marriage and the Family, 61,* 397–408.

Shapiro, D. L., and Levendosky, A. A. (1999). Adolescent survivors of childhood sexual abuse: The mediating role of attachment style and coping in psychological and interpersonal functioning. *Child Abuse and Neglect, 23,* 1175–1191.

Shehan, C. L., Berardo, F. M., Bera, H., and Carley, S. M. (1991). Women in age-discrepant marriages. *Journal of Family Issues, 12,* 291–305.

Sheinberg, M., and Penn, P. (1991). Gender dilemmas, gender questions, and the gender mantra. *Journal of Marriage and Family Therapy, 17,* 33–44.

Shelton, B. (1992). *Women, Men and Time.* New York: Greenwood Press.

Sherman, A. (1999, August 22). *Extreme Child Poverty Rises Sharply in 1997.* Washington, DC: Children's Defense Fund.

Sherwin, R., and Corbett, S. (1985). Campus sexual norms and dating relationships: A trial analysis. *The Journal of Sex Research, 21,* 258–274.

Siegel, J. M. (1995). Looking for Mr. Right? *Journal of Family Issues, 16,* 194–211.

Signorielli, N. (1998, February). Television and the perpetuation of gender-role stereotypes. *AAP News,* 7–10.

Signorielli, N., and Bacue, A. (1999). Recognition and respect: A content analysis of prime-time television characters across three decades. *Sex Roles, 40*(7/8), 527–544.

Silber, T. (1980). Abortion in adolescence: The ethical dimension. *Adolescence, 15,* 461–474.

Silberstein, L. R., Striegel-Moore, R. H., Timko, C., and Rodin, J. (1988). Behavioral and psychological implications of body dissatisfaction: Do men and women differ? *Sex Roles, 19,* 219–232.

Silliman, B., and Schumm, W. (1995). Client interests in premarital counseling: A further analysis. *Journal of Sex and Marital Therapy, 21*(1), 43–56.

Silverman, J. G., Raj, A., Mucci, L. A., and Hathaway, J. E. (2001). Dating violence against adolescent girls and associated substance use, unhealthy weight control, sexual risk behavior, pregnancy, and suicidality. *Journal of the American Medical Association, 286*(5), 572–579.

Silverstein, M., and Bengston, V. L. (1997) Intergenerational solidarity and the structure of adult child–parent relationships in American families. *American Journal of Sociology, 103,* 429–460.

Silverstein, M., and Chen, X. (1999). The impact of acculturation in Mexican American families on the quality of the adult grandchild–grandparent relationship. *Journal of Marriage and the Family, 61,* 188–198.

Silverstein, M., Chen, X., and Heller, K. (1996). Too much of a good thing? Intergenerational social support and the psychological well-being of older parents. *Journal of Marriage and the Family, 58,* 970–982.

Simenauer, J., and Carroll, D. (1982). *Singles: The New Americans.* New York: Simon & Schuster.

Simons, R. L., Beaman, J., Conger, R. D., and Chao, W. (1992). Gender differences in the intergenerational transmission of parenting beliefs. *Journal of Marriage and the Family, 54,* 823–836.

Simons, R. L., Beaman, J., Conger, R. D., and Chao, W. (1993a). Childhood experience, conceptions of parenting, and attitudes of spouse as determinants of parental behavior. *Journal of Marriage and the Family, 55,* 91–106.

Simons, R. L., Beaman, J., Conger, R. D., and Chao, W. (1993b). Stress, support, and antisocial behavior trait as determinants of emotional well-being and parenting practices among single mothers. *Journal of Marriage and the Family, 55,* 385–398.

Simons, R. L., Johnson, C., Beaman, J., and Conger, R. D. (1993). Explaining women's double jeopardy: Factors that mediate the association between harsh treatment as a child and violence by a husband. *Journal of Marriage and the Family, 55,* 713–723.

Simons, R. L., Whitbeck, L. B., Conger, R. D., and Melby, J. N. (1990). Husband and wife determinants of parenting: A social learning and exchange model of parental behavior. *Journal of Marriage and the Family, 52,* 375–392.

Simpson, J. A., Ickes, W., and Orina, M. (2001). Empathic accuracy and preemptive relationship maintenance. In J. Harvey and A. Wenzel (Eds.), *Close Romantic Relationships: Maintenance and Enhancement* (pp. 27–46). Mahwah, NJ: Erlbaum.

Skovholt, T. M., and Thoen, G. A. (1987). Mental imagery and parenthood decision making. *Journal of Counseling and Development, 65,* 315, 316.

Small, A., Teagno, L., and Selz, K. (1980). The relationship of sex role to physical and psychological health. *Journal of Youth and Adolescence, 9,* 305–314.

Smith, C. J., Noll, J. A., and Bryant, J. B. (1999). The effect of social context on gender self-concept. *Sex Roles, 40*(5/6), 499–512.

Smith, D. E. (1993). The standard North American family: SNAF as an ideological code. *Journal of Family Issues, 14,* 50–65.

Smith, D. S. (1985). Wife employment and marital adjustment: A cumulation of results. *Family Relations, 34,* 483–490.

Smith, P., and Beaujot, R. (1999). Men's orientation toward marriage and family roles. *Journal of Comparative Family Studies,* 471–487.

Smith, T. W. (1994). *The Demography of Sexual Behavior.* Menlo Park, CA: Kaiser Family Foundation.

Snowden, L. R., Schott, T. L., Awalt, S. J., and Gillis-Knox, J. (1988). Marital satisfaction in pregnancy: Stability and change. *Journal of Marriage and the Family, 50,* 325–333.

Snyder, D. K., Velasquez, J. M., and Clark, B. L. (1997). Parental influence on gender and marital role attitudes: Implication for intervention. *Journal of Marital and Family Therapy, 23,* 191–201.

Sobel, D. (1981, June 29). Surrogate mothers: Why women volunteer. *New York Times,* p. B5.

Society for Human Resource Management. (2001). Society for Human Resource Management benefit survey. Retrieved May 18, 2003, from http://www.shrm.com

Sollie, D. L., and Kaetz, J. F. (1992). Teaching university-level family studies courses: Techniques and outcomes. *Family Relations, 41,* 18–24.

Sollie, D. L., and Scott, J. P. (1983). Teaching communication skills: A comparison of videotape feedback methods. *Family Relations, 32,* 503–511.

Solomon, J. C., and Marx, J. (1995). To grandmother's house we go: Health and school adjustment of children raised solely by grandparents. *The Gerontologist, 35,* 386–394.

Somers, M. D. (1993). A comparison of voluntarily child-free adults and parents. *Journal of Marriage and the Family, 55,* 643–650.

Sonenstein, F. L., Pleck, J. H., and Ku, L. C. (1989). Sexual activity, condom use and AIDS awareness among adolescent males. *Family Planning Perspectives, 21,* 152–158.

Sorensen, E., and Halpern, A. (1999). Single mothers and their child support receipt: How well is child support enforcement doing? Unpublished manuscript. Washington, DC: Urban Institute.

South, S. J. (1991). Sociodemographic differentials in mate selection preferences. *Journal of Marriage and the Family, 53,* 928–940.

South, S. J. (1993). Racial and ethnic differences in the desire to marry. *Journal of Marriage and the Family, 55,* 357–370.

South, S. J. (1995). Do you need to shop around? *Journal of Family Issues, 16,* 432–449.

South, S. J., and Lloyd, K. M. (1992). Marriage opportunities and family formation: Further implications of imbalanced sex ratios. *Journal of Marriage and the Family, 54,* 440–451.

Spencer, M. B., Dobbs, B., and Swanson, D. P. (1988). African American adolescents: Adaptational processes and socioeconomic diversity in behavioral outcomes. *Journal of Adolescence, 11,* 117–137.

Spitze, G. (1988). Women's employment and family relations: A review. *Journal of Marriage and the Family, 50,* 595–618.

Spitze, G., and Logan, J. R. (1991). Sibling structure and intergenerational relations. *Journal of Marriage and the Family, 53,* 871–884.

Spitze, G., Logan, J. R., Deane, G., and Zerger, S. (1994). Adult children's divorce and intergenerational relationships. *Journal of Marriage and the Family, 56,* 279–293.

Spitze, G., Logan J. R., and Robinson, J. (1992). Family structure and changes in living arrangements among elderly non-married parents. *Journal of Gerontology, 47,* 289–296.

Spitze, G., and Miner, S. (1992). Gender differences in adult child contact among Black elderly parents. *The Gerontologist, 32,* 213–218.

Spitze, G., and Ward, R. (1995). Household labor in intergenerational households. *Journal of Marriage and the Family, 57,* 355–361.

Spitzer, B., Henderson, K., and Zivian, M. (1999). Gender differences in population versus media body sizes: A comparison over four decades. *Sex Roles, 40*(7/8), 545–565.

Spock, B., and Rothenberg, M. B. (1985). *Dr. Spock's Baby and Child Care.* New York: Pocket Books.

Sprecher, S. (1985). Sex differences in bases of power in dating relationships. *Sex Roles, 12,* 449–462.

Sprecher, S., Metts, A., Burleson, G., Hapfield, E., and Thompson, A. (1995). Domains of expressive interaction in intimate relationships: Associations with satisfaction and commitment. *Family Relations, 44,* 203–210.

Sprey, J. (1988). Current theorizing on the family: An appraisal. *Journal of Marriage and the Family, 50,* 875–890.

Stacey, J. (2003). Gay and lesbian families: Queer like us. In M. A. Mason, A. Skolnick, and S. D. Sugarman (Eds.), *All Our Families* (pp. 144–169). New York: Oxford University Press.

Stack, S. (1990). New micro-level data on the impact of divorce on suicide, 1959–1980: A test of two theories. *Journal of Marriage and the Family, 52,* 119–127.

Stack, S., and Wasserman, R. (1995). The effect of marriage, family, and religious ties on African-American suicide ideology. *Journal of Marriage and the Family, 57,* 215–222.

Stafford, L., and Canary, D. J. (1991). Maintenance strategies and romantic relationship type, gender and relational characteristics. *Journal of Social and Personal Relationships, 8,* 217–242.

Stafford, L., and Reske, J. R. (1990). Idealization and communication in long distance premarital relationships. *Family Relations, 39,* 274–289.

Stanley, S. M., and Markman, H. J. (1992). Possessing commitment in personal relationships. *Journal of Marriage and the Family, 54,* 595–608.

Stanley, S. M., Markham, H. J., and Blumberg, S. (2001) *Fighting for your marriage.* San Francisco, CA: Jossey-Bass.

Stanley, S. M., Markman, H. J., St. Peters, M., and Leber, B. D. (1995). Strengthening marriages and preventing divorce. New directions in prevention research. *Family Relations, 44,* 392–401.

Stanley, S. M., Whitton, S. W., and Markman, H. (2000). *Maybe I Do: Interpersonal Commitment and Premarital and Non-marital Cohabitation,* unpublished manuscript, University of Denver.

Starrels, M. E. (1994). Gender differences in parent–child relations. *Journal of Family Issues, 15,* 148–165.

Starrels, M. E., Bould, S., and Nicholas, L. J. (1994). The feminization of poverty in the United States. *Journal of Family Issues, 15,* 590–607.

Stattin, H., and Klackenberg, G. (1992). Discordant family relations in intact families: Developmental tendencies over 18 years. *Journal of Marriage and the Family, 54,* 940–956.

Stegman, M. A., Quercia, R. G., and McCarthy, G. (2000, June). Housing America's working families. *New Century Housing, 1*(1). Retrieved July 6, 2000, from http://www.nhc.org/affiliates/chprpt.pdf

Stein, L., and Hoopes, J. (1986). *Identity Formation in the Adopted Child.* New York: Child Welfare League of America.

Stein, P. (Ed.). (1981). *Single Life: Unmarried Adults in Social Context.* New York: St. Martin's Press.

Steinberg, L., and Silverberg, S. B. (1987). Influences on marital satisfaction during the middle stages of the family life cycle. *Journal of Marriage and the Family, 49,* 751–760.

Stephen, T. D. (1985). Fixed-sequence and circular-causal models of relationship development: Divergent views on the role of communication in intimacy. *Journal of Marriage and the Family, 47,* 955–963.

Stephens, M. A. P., Franks, M. N., and Townsend, A. L. (1994). Stress and rewards in women's multiple roles: Case of women in the middle. *Psychology and Aging, 9,* 45–52.

Sternberg, R. (1986). A triangular theory of love. *Psychological Review 93,* 119–135.

Sternberg, R., and Barnes, M. (Eds.). (1988). *The Psychology of Love.* New Haven, CT: Yale University Press.

Sternberg, R. J. (1998). *Cupid's Arrow: The Course of Love Through Time.* Cambridge: Cambridge University Press.

Stets, J. E. (1990). Verbal and physical aggression in marriage. *Journal of Marriage and the Family, 52,* 501–514.

Stets, J. E. (1992). Interactive processes in dating aggression: A national study. *Journal of Marriage and the Family, 54,* 165–177.

Stets, J. E., and Henderson, D. A. (1991). Contextual factors surrounding conflict resolution while dating: Results from a national study. *Family Relations, 40,* 29–36.

Stevens, G., and Schoen, R. (1988). Linguistic intermarriage in the United States. *Journal of Marriage and the Family, 50,* 267–279.

Stinnett, N., and DeFrain, J. (1985). *Secrets of Strong Families.* Boston: Little, Brown.

Stinnett, N., Knorr, B., DeFrain, J., and Rowe, G. (1981). How strong families cope with crises. *Family Perspective, 15,* 159–166.

Stohs, J. H. (1994). Alternative ethics in employed women's household labor. *Journal of Family Issues, 15,* 550–561.

Stoller, E. P. (1985). Exchange patterns in the informal support networks of the elderly: The impact of reciprocity on morale. *Journal of Marriage and the Family, 47,* 335–342.

Stone, G. (2002). Nonresidential father postdivorce well-being: The role of social supports. *Journal of Divorce and Remarriage, 36*(3/4) 139–150.

Stone, R. I. (1999). Long-term care: Coming of age in the 21st Century. In R. Butler, L. Grossman, and M. Oberlink (Eds.), *Life in an Older America* (pp. 4973). New York: Twentieth Century Fund.

Stoneman, Z., Brody, G. H., and Burke, M. (1989). Sibling temperaments and maternal and paternal perceptions of marital, family, and personal functioning. *Journal of Marriage and the Family, 51,* 99–113.

Storaasli, R. D., and Markman, H. J. (1990). Relationship problems in the early stages of marriage. *Journal of Family Psychology, 4,* 80–98.

Storey, W. (2000). Children in married and common law relationships: Legal differences. *Parents News Magazine.*

Strate, J. M., and Dubnoff, S. J. (1986). How much income is enough? Measuring the income adequacy of retired persons using a survey based approach. *Journal of Gerontology, 41,* 393–400.

Straus, M. A. (2001). *Beating the Devil out of Them: Corporal Punishment in American Families and Its Effects on Children.* New Brunswick, NJ: Transaction.

Straus, M. A., and Donnelly, D. (1993). Corporal punishment of teenage children in the United States. *Youth and Society, 24,* 419–442.

Straus, M. A., and Sweet, S. (1992). Verbal/symbolic aggression in couples: Incidence rates and relationships to personal characteristics. *Journal of Marriage and the Family, 54,* 346–357.

Straus, M. A., and Yodanis, C. L. (1996). Corporal punishment in adolescence and physical assaults on spouses in later life: What accounts for the link? *Journal of Marriage and the Family, 58,* 825–841.

Strong, B., Wilson, S., Robbins, M., and Johns, T. (1981). *Human Sexuality* (2nd ed.). Minneapolis: West.

Strouse, J. S. (1987). College bars as social settings for heterosexual contacts. *The Journal of Sex Research, 23,* 374–382.

Stryker, S. (1972). Symbolic interaction theory: A review and some suggestions for comparative family research. *Journal of Comparative Family Studies, 3,* 17–32.

Stubben, J. D. (1998). Culturally competent substance abuse prevention research among rural Native American communities. *Rural Substance Abuse: State of Knowledge and Issues* (National Institute on Drug Abuse Research Monograph Series No. 168, pp. 459–483).

Stubben, J. D. (2001). Working with and conducting research among American Indian families. *American Behavioral Scientist, 44*(9), 1466–1481.

Stull, D. E., and Scarisbrick-Hauser, A. (1989). Never-married elderly: A reassessment with implications for long-term care policy. *Research on Aging, 11,* 124–139.

Sue, D. (1997). Counseling strategies for Chinese Americans. In C. C. Lee (Ed.), *Multicultural Issues in Counseling: New Approaches to Diversity* (2nd ed., pp. 173–187). Alexandria, VA: American Counseling Association.

Sugarman, D. B., and Hotaling, G. T. (1989) Dating violence: Prevalence, context and risk markers. In M. A. Pirog-Good and J. E. Stets (Eds.), *Violence in Dating Relationships* (pp. 3–32). New York: Praeger.

Sugarman, S. D. (2003). Single-parent families. In M. A. Mason, A. Skolnick, and S. D. Sugarman (Eds.), *All Our Families* (pp. 14–39). New York: Oxford University Press.

Suitor, J. J. (1987). Mother–daughter relations when married daughters return to school: Effects of status similarity. *Journal of Marriage and the Family, 49*, 435–444.

Suitor, J. J. (1991). Marital quality and satisfaction with the division of household labor across the family life cycle. *Journal of Marriage and the Family, 53*, 221–230.

The Supreme Court upholds parental notice requirements. (1990). *Family Planning Perspectives, 22*, 177–181.

Surra, C. A. (1990). Research theory on mate selection and premarital relationships in the 1980s. *Journal of Marriage and the Family, 52*, 844–865.

Surra, C. A., and Hughes, D. K. (1997). Commitment processes and an account of the development of premarital relationships. *Journal of Marriage and the Family, 59*, 5–21.

Sweeney, M. M. (2002). Remarriage and the nature of divorce: Does it matter which spouse chose to leave? *Journal of Family Issues, 23*(3), 410–440.

Swinford, S. P., DeMaris, A., Cernkovich, S. A., and Giordano, P. C. (2000). Harsh physical discipline in childhood and violence in later romantic involvements: The mediating role of problem behaviors. *Journal of Marriage and the Family, 62*, 508–519.

Swomley, J. M. (2002). Abortion is not immoral. In M. E. Williams (Ed.), *Abortion: Opposing Viewpoints.* San Diego, CA: Greenhaven Press.

Sykes, M. (2000). "Late-term" confusion, "partial-birth" lies. *Pro-Choice Views.* Retrieved from http://pro choice.about.com/newsissues/prochoice/library/blla tetermconfusion.htm

Szinovacz, M., and Harpster, P. (1993). Employment status, gender-role attitudes, and marital dependence in later life. *Journal of Marriage and the Family, 55*, 927–940.

Szinovacz, M. E. (1998). Grandparents today: A demographic profile. *The Gerontologist, 38*, 37–52.

Tagatz, G., Bigson, M., Schiller, P., and Nagel, T. (1980). Artificial insemination utilizing donor semen. *Minnesota Medicine, 63*, 539–541.

Tanfer, K. (1987). Patterns of premarital cohabitation among never-married women in the United States. *Journal of Marriage and the Family, 49*, 483–497.

Tanfer, K. (1994). Knowledge, attitudes, and intentions of American women regarding their hormonal implant. *Family Planning Perspectives, 26*, 60–65.

Tannen, D. (1982). *You Just Don't Understand: Women and Men in Conversation.* New York: Morrow.

Tannen, D. (1994). *Talking Nine to Five: How Women's and Men's Conversational Styles Affect Who Get Heard, Who Get Credit, and What Gets Done at Work.* New York: Morrow.

Tavris, C. (1982). Anger diffused. *Psychology Today, 16*, 25–29.

Taylor, M. A., and Shore, L. M. (1995). Predictors of planned retirement age: An adaptation of Beehr's model. *Psychology and Aging, 10*, 76–83.

Taylor, R. J. (1985). The extended family as a source of support to elderly Blacks. *The Gerontologist, 25*, 488–495.

Taylor, R. J. (1986). Receipt of support from family among Black Americans: Demographic and familial differences. *Journal of Marriage and the Family, 48*, 67–77.

Taylor, R. J., Chatters, L. M., and Mays, V. M. (1988). Parents, children, siblings, in-laws, and non-kin as sources of emergency assistance to Black Americans. *Family Relations, 37*, 298–304.

Taylor, R. J., Chatters, L. M., Tucker, M. B., and Lewis, E. (1990). Developments in research on Black families: A decade review. *Journal of Marriage and the Family, 52*, 993–1014.

Teachman, J. D. (2002). Childhood living arrangements and the intergenerational transmission of divorce. *Journal of Marriage and Family, 64*(3), 717–729.

Teachman, J. D., Call, B. R. A., and Carver, K. P. (1994). Marital status in the duration of joblessness among White men. *Journal of Marriage and the Family, 56*, 415–428.

Teachman, J. D., and Polonko, K. (1990). Negotiating divorce outcomes: Can we identify patterns in divorce settlements? *Journal of Marriage and the Family, 52*, 129–139.

Tein, J., Roosa, M. W., and Michaels, M. (1994). Agreement between parent and child reports on parental behaviors. *Journal of Marriage and the Family, 56*, 341–355.

Tennov, D. (1979). *Love and Limerence: The Experience of Being in Love.* New York: Stein & Day.

Teti, D. M., and Lamb, M. E. (1989). Socioeconomic and marital outcomes of adolescent marriage, adolescent childbirth, and their co-occurrence. *Journal of Marriage and the Family, 51*, 203–212.

Teti, D. M., Lamb, M. E., and Elster, A. B. (1987). Long-range socioeconomic and marital consequences of adolescent marriage in three cohorts of adult males. *Journal of Marriage and the Family, 49*, 499–506.

Tew, S., and Kirchgaessner, C. (1999). *About One in 10 Women Using Contraceptives Experience an Accidental Pregnancy.* (News release). New York: Alan Guttmacher Institute.

Thabes, V. (1997). Survey analysis of women's long-term, postdivorce adjustment. *Journal of Divorce and Remarriage, 27,* 163–175.

Thomas, A., and Speight, S. (1999). Racial identity and racial socialization attitudes of African American parents. *Journal of Black Psychology, 25*(2), 152–170.

Thompson, J. K., and Heinberg, L. J. (1999). The media's influence on body image disturbance and eating disorders: We've reviled them, now can we rehabilitate them? *Journal of Social Issues, 55*(2), 339–353.

Thompson, K. M., Wonderlich, S. A., Crosby, R. D., and Mitchell, J. E. (2001). Sexual violence and weight control techniques among adolescent girls. *International Journal of Eating Disorders, 29,* 166–176.

Thompson, L. (1991). Family work. Women's sense of fairness. *Journal of Family Issues, 12,* 181–196.

Thompson, L., and Walker, A. J. (1984). Mothers and daughters: Aid patterns and attachment. *Journal of Marriage and the Family, 46,* 313–322.

Thompson, L., and Walker, A. J. (1995). The place of feminism in family studies. *Journal of Marriage and the Family, 57*(4), 847–865.

Thompson, R., and Zuroff, D. (1999). Development of self-criticism in adolescent girls: Roles of maternal dissatisfaction, maternal coldness, and insecure attachment. *Journal of Youth and Adolescence, 28*(2), 197–210.

Thomson, E., McLanahan, S. S., and Curtin, R. D. (1992). Family structure, gender, and parental socialization. *Journal of Marriage and the Family, 54,* 368–378.

Thornberry, T., Smith, C., and Howard, G. (1997). Risk factors for teenage fatherhood. *Journal of Marriage and the Family, 59*(3), 505–522.

Tichenor, V. J. (1999). Status and income as gendered resources: The case of marital power. *Journal of Marriage and the Family, 61,* 638–650.

Tiedje, L. B., Wortman, C. B., Downey, G., Emmons, C., Biernat, M., and Lang, E. (1990). Women with multiple roles: Role compatibility perceptions, satisfaction, and mental health. *Journal of Marriage and the Family, 52,* 63–72.

Tiesel, J. W., and Olson, D. H. (1992). Preventing family problems: Troubling trends and promising opportunities. *Family Relations, 41,* 398–403.

Tiggle, R. B., Peters, M. D., Kelley, H. H., and Vincent, J. (1982). Correlational and discrepancy indices of understanding and their relation to marital satisfaction. *Journal of Marriage and the Family, 44,* 209–216.

Timko, C., and Moos, R. H. (1991). A typology of social climates in group residential facilities for older people. *Journal of Gerontology, 46,* S160–S169.

Timmer, S., and Veroff, J. (2000). Family ties and the discontinuity of divorce in black and white newlywed couples. *Journal of Marriage and Family 62,* 349–361.

Tirozzi, G. (1998). *Non-School Hours: Mobilizing School and Community Resources.* Washington, DC: U.S. Government Printing Office.

Tooke, W., and Camire, L. (1991). Patterns of deception in intersexual and intrasexual mating strategies. *Ethnology and Sociobiology, 12,* 345–364.

Tornstam, L. (1992). Loneliness in marriage. *Journal of Social and Personal Relationships, 9,* 197–217.

Tough, S., Newburn-Cook, C., Johnson, D. W., Svenson, L. W., Rose, S., and Belik, J. (2002). Delayed childrearing and its impact on population rate changes in lower birth weight, multiple birth, and preterm delivery. *Pediatrics, 109*(3), 399–403.

Townsend, J. M. (1998). *What Women Want—What Men Want: Why the Sexes Still See Love and Commitment So Differently.* New York: Oxford University Press.

Trends in the HIV and AIDS Epidemic. (1998, December). Atlanta: Centers for Disease Control and Prevention. Retrieved from http://www.cdc.gov/hiv/stats/trends98.pdf

Trent, K., and South, S. J. (1989). Structural determinants of the divorce rate: A cross-societal analysis. *Journal of Marriage and the Family, 51,* 391–404.

Trent, K., and South, S. J. (1992). Sociodemographic status, parental background, childhood family structure, and attitudes toward family formation. *Journal of Marriage and the Family, 54,* 427–439.

Trepanier-Street, M. L., Romatowski, J. A., and McNair, S. (1990). Development of story characters in gender-stereotypic and non-stereotypic occupational roles. *Journal of Early Adolescence, 10,* 496–510.

Trickett, P. K. (1993). Maladaptive development of school-aged, physically abused children: Relationships with child-rearing context. *Journal of Family Psychology, 7,* 134–147.

Trotter, R. J. (1986). The three faces of love. *Psychology Today, 20,* 46–54.

Trovato, F., and Lauris, G. (1989). Marital status and mortality in Canada: 1951–1981. *Journal of Marriage and the Family, 51,* 907–922.

Trussell, J., and Grummer-Strawn, L. (1990). Contraceptive failure of the ovulation method of periodic abstinence. *Family Planning Perspectives, 22,* 65–75.

Trussell, J., Warner, D. L., and Hatcher, R. A. (1992). Condom slippage and breakage rates. *Family Planning Perspectives, 24,* 20–23.

Trzcinski, E., and Finn-Stevenson, M. (1991). In response to arguments against mandated parental leave: Findings from the Connecticut survey of parental leave policies. *Journal of Marriage and the Family, 53,* 445–460.

Tschann, J. M., Johnston, J. R., and Wallerstein, J. S. (1989). Resources, stressors, and attachment as predictors of adult adjustment after divorce: A longitudinal study. *Journal of Marriage and the Family, 51,* 1033–1046.

Tuan, M. (1999). Neither real Americans nor real Asians? Multigenerational Asian ethnics navigating the terrain of authenticity. *Qualitative Sociology, 22*(2), 105–125.

Tucker, M. B., and Taylor, R. J. (1989). Demographic correlates of relationship status among Black Americans. *Journal of Marriage and the Family, 51,* 655–665.

Turkel, A. R. (1998). All about Barbie: Distortions of a transitional object. *Journal of the American Academy of Psychoanalysis, 26*(1), 165–177.

Turner, C. F., Rogers, S. M., Miller, H. G., Miller, W. C., Gribble, J. N., Chromy, J. R., et al. (2002). Untreated gonococcal and chlamydial infection in a probability sample of adults. *Journal of the American Medical Association, 287*(6), 726–733.

Turner, R. (1990). Delays in conception found among women who had used the pill. *Family Planning Perspectives, 22,* 139–140.

Turner, R. (1991). Companion during labor lessens women's need for obstetric intervention. *Family Planning Perspectives, 23,* 238–239.

Turner, R. (1992). Underweight births are equally likely among poor Blacks and Whites. *Family Planning Perspectives, 24,* 95–96.

Turner, R. (1993). Condom use is low among U.S. heterosexuals at risk of HIV infection; 15% of population has at least one risk factor. *Family Planning Perspectives, 25,* 43–44.

Turner, R. H. (1970). *Family Interaction.* New York: Wiley.

Tyrer, L. B. (1984). Precautions in diaphragm use. *Medical Aspects of Human Sexuality, 18,* 243, 247.

Tzeng, J. M. (1992). The effects of social economic heterogamy and changes on marital disillusion for first marriages. *Journal of Marriage and the Family, 54,* 609–619.

Tzeng, J. M., and Mare, R. D. (1995). Labor market and socioeconomic effects on marital stability. *Social Science Research, 24,* 329–351.

Uba, L. (1994). *Asian Americans: Personality patterns, identity, and mental health.* New York: Guilford.

Ubell, E. (1990, January 14). You don't have to be childless. *Parade Magazine,* pp. 14, 15.

Uhlenberg, P., and Hammill, B. G. (1998). Frequency of grandparent contact with grandchildren sets: Factors that make a difference. *The Gerontologist, 38,* 276–285.

Ulbrich, P. M., Coyle, A. T., and Llabre, M. M. (1990). Involuntary childlessness and marital adjustment: His and hers. *Journal of Sex and Marital Therapy, 16,* 147–158.

Umberson, D. (1987). Family status and health behaviors: Social control as a dimension of social integration. *Journal of Health and Social Behavior, 23,* 306–319.

Umberson, D. (1992). Relationships between adult children and their parents: Psychological consequences with both generations. *Journal of Marriage and the Family, 54,* 654–674.

Umberson, D. (1995). Marriage as support or strain? Marital quality following the death of a parent. *Journal of Marriage and the Family, 57,* 709–723.

Umberson, D., and Gove, W. R. (1989). Parenthood and psychological well-being. *Journal of Family Issues, 10,* 440–462.

U.S. General Accounting Office. (2001). Consumer finance: College students and credit cards. Retrieved from May 9, 2003, from http://www.gao.gov/new.items/d01773.pdf

U.S. Bureau of the Census (1998). *Statistical Abstract of the United States, 1998.* Washington, DC: U.S. Government Printing Office.

U.S. Bureau of the Census. (1999a). *Statistical Abstract of the United States, 1999* (118th ed.). Washington, DC: U.S. Government Printing Office.

U.S. Bureau of the Census (2000). *Statistical Abstract of the United States, 2000.* Washington, DC: U.S. Government Printing Office.

U.S. Bureau of the Census (2001). *Statistical Abstract of the United States, 2001.* Washington, DC: U.S. Government Printing Office.

U.S. Bureau of the Census (2002). *Statistical Abstract of the United States, 2002.* Washington, DC: U.S. Government Printing Office.

U.S. Department of Health and Human Services. (2000, September 30). FDA approves Mifepristone for the termination of early pregnancy. Retrieved from http://www.fda.gov/bbs/topics/NEWS/NEW00737.html

Usui, W. M., Keil, T. J., and Durig, K. R. (1985). Socioeconomic comparisons and life satisfaction of elderly adults. *Journal of Gerontology, 40,* 110–114.

Vaillant, C. O., and Vaillant, G. E. (1993). Is the U-curve of marital satisfaction an illusion? A 40-year study of marriage. *Journal of Marriage and the Family, 55,* 230–239.

Vanderkooi, L., and Pearson, J. (1983). Mediating divorce disputes: Mediator behavior, styles, and roles. *Family Relations, 32,* 557–566.

Vannoy, D. (1991). Social differentiation, contemporary marriage, and human development. *Journal of Family Issues, 12,* 251–267.

Vannoy, D., and Philliber, W. W. (1992). Wife's employment and quality of marriage. *Journal of Marriage and the Family, 54,* 387–398.

van-Schaick, K., and Stolberg, A. L. (2001). The impact of paternal involvement and parental divorce on young adults' intimate relationships. *Journal of Divorce and Remarriage, 36*(1/2), 99–122.

Vega, W. A., Kolody, B., and Valle, R. (1988). Marital strain, coping, and depression among Mexican-American women. *Journal of Marriage and the Family, 50,* 391–403.

Ventura, S. J., Martin, J. A., Curtin, S. C., Mathews, T. J., and Park, M. M. (2000). Births: Final data for 1998. *National Vital Statistics Reports, 48*(3). Hyattsville, MD: National Center for Health Statistics.

Veroff, J., Douvan, E., Orbuch, T. L., and Acitelli, L. K. (1998). Happiness in stable marriages: The early years. In T. N. Bradbury (Ed.), *The Developmental Course of Marital Dysfunction* (pp. 152–179). New York: Cambridge University Press.

Vinje, D. (1996). Native American economic development on selected reservations: A comparative analysis. *American Journal of Economics and Sociology, 55,* 427–442.

Visher, E. B., and Visher, J. S. (1989). Parenting coalition after remarriage: Dynamics and therapeutic guidelines. *Family Relations, 38,* 65–70.

Visher, E. B., and Visher, J. S. (1990). Dynamics of successful stepfamilies. *Journal of Divorce and Remarriage, 14,* 3–12.

Visher, E. B., and Visher, J. S. (1996). *Therapy with Stepfamilies.* New York: Brunner/Mazel.

Volling, B. L., and Belsky, J. (1991). Multiple determinants of father involvement during infancy in dual-earner and single-earner families. *Journal of Marriage and the Family, 53,* 461–474.

Voydanoff, P. (1988). Work role characteristics, family structure demands, and work/family conflict. *Journal of Marriage and the Family, 50,* 749–761.

Voydanoff, P. (1990). Economic distress and family relations: A review of the eighties. *Journal of Marriage and the Family, 52,* 1099–1115.

Voydanoff, P. (2002). Linkages between the work–family interface and work, family, and individual outcomes; An integrative model. *Journal of Family Issues, 23*(1), 138–164.

Voydanoff, P., and Donnelly, B. W. (1989a). Economic distress and mental health. *Lifestyles, 10,* 139–162.

Voydanoff, P., and Donnelly, B. W. (1989b). Work and family roles and psychological stress. *Journal of Marriage and the Family, 51,* 923–932.

Voydanoff, P., Donnelly, B. W. (1999). Multiple roles and psychological distress: The intersection of the paid worker, spouse, and parent roles with the role of the adult child. *Journal of Marriage and the Family, 61,* 725–738.

Vuchinich, S., Hetherington, E. M., Vuchinich, R. A., and Clingempeel, W. G. (1991). Parent and child interaction and gender differences in early adolescents' adaptation to stepfamilies. *Developmental Psychology, 27,* 618–626.

Vukelich, C., and Kliman, D. S. (1985). Mature and teenage mothers' infant growth expectations and use of child development information sources. *Family Relations, 34,* 189–196.

Wade, J. C., and Brittan-Powell, C. (2001). Men's attitudes toward race and gender equity: The importance of masculinity ideology, gender-related traits, and reference group identity dependence. *Psychology of Men and Masculinity, 2*(1) 42–50.

Wagstaff, D. A., Kelly, J. A., Perry, M. K., Sikkema, K. J., Solomon, L. J., Heckman, T. G., and Anderson, E. S. (1995). Multiple partners, risky partners, and high HIV risk among low-income urban women. *Family Planning Perspectives, 27,* 241–245.

Waite, L. J. (1995). Does marriage matter? *Demography, 32,* 483–507.

Waite, L. J., and Gallagher, M. (2000). *The Case for Marriage: Why Married People Are Happier, Healthier, and Better Off Financially.* New York: Doubleday.

Walker, A., and Thompson, L. (1984). Feminism and family studies. *Journal of Family Issues, 5*(4), 545–570.

Walker, A. J. (1985). Reconceptualizing family stress. *Journal of Marriage and the Family, 47,* 827–837.

Walker, A. J., and Pratt, C. C. (1991). Daughters' help to mothers: Intergenerational aid versus caregiving. *Journal of Marriage and the Family, 53,* 3–12.

Walker, A. J., Pratt, C. C., Martell, L. K., and Martin, S. S. K. (1991). Perceptions of aid and actual aid in intergenerational caregiving. *Family Relations, 40,* 318–323.

Walker, A. J., Shin, H., and Bird, D. N. (1990). Perceptions of relationship change and caregiver satisfaction. *Family Relations, 39,* 147–152.

Wallace, P. M., and Gotlib, I. H. (1990). Marital adjustment during the transition to parenthood: Stability and predictors of change. *Journal of Marriage and the Family, 52,* 21–29.

Waller, W. (1937). The rating and dating complex. *American Sociological Review, 2,* 727–734.

Wallerstein, J., and Blakeslee, S. (1995). *The Good Marriage: How and Why Love Lasts.* New York: Houghton Mifflin.

Wallerstein, J., and Lewis, J. (1998). The long-term impact of divorce on children: A first report from a 25-year study. *Family and Conciliation Courts Review Special Issue: A Commemoration of the Second World Congress on Family Law and the Rights of Children and Youth, 36*(3), 368–383.

Walsh, W. M. (1992). Twenty major issues in remarriage families. *Journal of Counseling and Development, 70,* 709–715.

Walster, E., and Walster, G. W. (1978). *A New Look at Love.* Reading, MA: Addison-Wesley.

Wampler, K. S., and Powell, G. S. (1982). The Barrett-Lennard Relationship Inventory as a measure of marital satisfaction. *Family Relations, 35,* 539–545.

Wandewater, E. A., and Lansford, J. E. (1998). Influences of family structure and parental conflict on children's well-being. *Family Relations, 47,* 323–330.

Wang, H., and Amato, P. R. (2000). Predictors of divorce adjustment: Stressors, resources, and definitions. *Journal of Marriage and the Family, 62,* 655–668.

Ward, J. (1996). Raising resisters: The role of truth telling in the psychological development of African American girls. In B. Leadbeater and N. Way (Eds.), *Urban Girls.* New York: New York University Press.

Ward, R. A., Logan, J., and Spitze, G. (1992). The influence of parent and child needs on coresidents in middle and later life. *Journal of Marriage and the Family, 54,* 209–221.

Ward, R. A., and Spitze, G. (1992). Consequences of parent–adult coresidence. *Journal of Family Issues, 13,* 553–572.

Ward, S. K., Chapman, K., Cohn, E., White, S., and Williams, K. (1991). Acquaintance rape and the college social scene. *Family Relations, 40,* 65–71.

Warlick, J. L. (1985). Why is poverty after 65 a woman's problem? *Journal of Gerontology, 40,* 751–757.

Warner, R. L., Lee, G. R., and Lee, J. (1986). Social organization, spousal resources, and marital power: A cross-cultural study. *Journal of Marriage and the Family, 48,* 121–128.

Way, N. (1995). "Can't you see the courage, the strength that I have?" Listening to urban adolescent girls speak about their relationships. *Psychology of Women Quarterly, 19*(1), 107–128.

Webster v. Reproductive Health Services, 109 S. Ct. 3040 (1989).

Weigel, D. J., and Weigel, R. R. (1990). Family satisfaction in two generation farm families: The role of stress and resources. *Family Relations, 39,* 449–455.

Weigel, R. R., and Weigel, D. J., and Blundall, J. (1987). Stress, coping, and satisfaction: Generational differences in farm families. *Family Relations, 36,* 45–48.

Weis, D. L., Slosnerick, M., Cate, R., and Sollie, D. L. (1986). A survey instrument for assessing the cognitive association of sex, love, and marriage. *The Journal of Sex Research, 22,* 206–220.

Weishaus, S., and Field, D. (1988). A half century of marriage: Continuity or change? *Journal of Marriage and the Family, 50,* 763–774.

Weisman, C. S., Plichta, S. B., Tirado, D. E., and Dana, K. S. (1993). Comparison of contraceptive implant adopters and pill users in a family planning clinic in Baltimore. *Family Planning Perspectives, 25,* 224–226.

Weiss, B., Dodge, K. A., Bates, J. E., and Pettit, G. S. (1992). Some consequences of early harsh discipline: Child aggression and a maladaptive social information processing style. *Child Development, 63,* 1321–1335.

Weitzman, L. (1985). *The Divorce Revolution: The Unexpected Social and Economic Consequences for Women and Children in America.* New York: Free Press.

Welsh, W. N., and Stewart, A. J. (1995). Relationships between women and their parents: Implications for midlife well-being. *Psychology and Aging, 10,* 181–190.

Westfall, J. M., Main, D. S., and Barnard, L. (1996). Continuation rates among injectable contraceptive users. *Family Planning Perspectives, 28,* 275–277.

Wethington, E., and Kessler, R. C. (1989). Employment, parental responsibility, and psychological distress. *Journal of Family Issues, 10,* 527–546.

Whisman, M. A., and Jacobson, N. S. (1990). Power, marital satisfaction, and response to marital therapy. *Journal of Family Psychology, 4,* 202–212.

Whitaker, D. J., and Miller K. S. (2000). Parent–adolescent discussions about sex and condoms: Impact on peer influences of sexual risk behavior. *Journal of Adolescent Research, 15*(2), 251–273.

White, L., and Rogers, S. J. (2000). *Economic Circumstances and Family Outcomes: A Review of the 90s.* (Working Paper No. 00-03). University Park: Pennsylvania State University.

White, L. K., and Rogers, S. J. (1997). Strong support but uneasy relationships: Coresidence in adult children relationships with parents. *Journal of Marriage and the Family, 59,* 62–76.

Whitveck, L. B., Hoyt, D. R., and Huck, S. M. (1993). Family relationship history, contemporary parent–grandparent relationship quality, and the grandparent–grandchild relationship. *Journal of Marriage and the Family, 55,* 1025–1035.

Wiederman, M., and Hurd, C. (1999). Extradyadic involvement during dating. *Journal of Social and Personal Relationships, 16*(2), 265–274.

Wilcoxon, S. A. (1985). Healthy family functioning: The other side of family pathology. *Journal of Counseling and Development, 63,* 495–499.

Wilcoxon, S. A. (1987). Grandparents and grandchildren. *Journal of Counseling and Development, 65,* 289–290.

Wilcoxon, S. A., and Hovestadt, A. J. (1983). Perceived health and similarity of family of origin experiences as predictors of dyadic adjustment for married couples. *Journal of Marital and Family Therapy, 9,* 431–434.

Wilfley, E. E., and Rodin, J. (1995). Cultural influences on eating disorders. In K. K. Brownell and C. G. Fairburn (Eds.), *Body Images: Development, Deviance, and Change.* New York: Guilford Press.

Wilhelm, M. S., and Ridley, C. A. (1988). Stress and unemployment in rural nonfarm couples: A study of hardships and coping resources. *Family Relations, 37,* 50–54.

Wilkie, J. R., Ferree, M. M., and Ratcliff, K. S. (1998). Gender and fairness: Marital satisfaction in two-earner couples. *Journal of Marriage and the Family, 60,* 577–594.

Wilkinson, D. (1997). American families of African descent. In M. K. DeGenova (Ed.), *Families in Cultural Context.* Mountain View, CA: Mayfield.

Wille, D. E. (1992). Maternal employment: Impact on maternal behavior. *Family Relations, 41,* 273–277.

Williams, J. (2000). *Unbending Gender: Why Family and Work Conflict and What to Do about It.* New York: Oxford University Press.

Williams, K. R. (1992). Social sources of marital violence and deterrence: Testing an integrated theory of assaults between partners. *Journal of Marriage and the Family, 54,* 620–629.

Williams, L., and Jurich, J. (1995). Predicting marital success after five years: Assessing the predictive validity of FOCCUS. *Journal of Marital and Family Therapy, 21,* 141–153.

Williams, L. S. (1992). Adoption actions and attitudes of couples seeking in vitro fertilization. *Journal of Family Issues, 13,* 99–113.

Williams-Deane, M., and Potter, L. S. (1992). Current oral contraceptive use instructions: An analysis of patient package inserts. *Family Planning Perspectives, 24,* 111–115.

Williamson, D. (1991). *The Intimacy Paradox: Personal Authority in the Family System.* New York: Guilford Press.

Willits, F. K., and Crider, D. M. (1988). Health rating and life satisfaction in the later middle years. *Journal of Gerontology, 43,* S172–S176.

Wilson, S. N., Larson, J. H., and Stone, K. L. (1993). Stress among job, insecure workers and their spouses. *Family Relations, 42,* 74–80.

Winch, R. F. (1958). *Mate Selection: A Study of Complementary Needs.* New York: Harper & Row.

Winch, R. F. (1967). Another look at the theory of complementary needs in mate selection. *Journal of Marriage and the Family, 29,* 756–762.

Winch, R. F. (1971). *The Modern Family.* New York: Holt.

Wineberg, H. (1990). Childbearing after remarriage. *Journal of Marriage and the Family, 52,* 31–38.

Wineberg, H. (1994). Marital reconciliation in the United States: Which couples are successful? *Journal of Marriage and the Family, 56,* 80–88.

Wineberg, H. (1999). The timing of remarriage among women who have a failed marital reconciliation in the first marriage. *Journal of Divorce and Remarriage, 30,* 57–69.

Wineberg, H., and McCarthy, J. (1989). Child spacing in the United States: Recent trends and differentials. *Journal of Marriage and the Family, 51,* 213–228.

Witwer, M. (1990a). Advanced maternal age poses no major health risk for first-born infants. *Family Planning Perspectives, 22,* 235–236.

Witwer, M. (1990b). Low rate of weight gain late in pregnancy may signal premature birth. *Family Planning Perspectives, 22,* 92–93.

Witwer, M. (1990c). Oral contraceptive use may protect against PID caused by Chlamydia. *Family Planning Perspectives, 22,* 239–240.

Wolchik, S. A., Sandler, I. N., Millsap, R. E., Plummer, B. A., Greene, S. M., Anderson, E. R., Dawson-McClure, et al. (2002). Six-year follow-up of preventive interventions for children of divorce: A randomized controlled trial. *Journal of the American Medical Association, 288*(15), 1874–1881.

Wolfinger, N. H. (1999). Trends in the intergenerational transmission of divorce. *Demography, 36,* 415–420.

Wolf-Smith, J. H., and LaRossa, R. (1992). After he hits her. *Family Relations, 41,* 324–329.

Woll, S. B., and Cozby, C. P. (1988). Videodating and other alternatives to traditional methods of relationship initiation. In W. H. Jones and D. Perlman (Eds.), *Advances in Personal Relationships* (Vol. 1, pp. 69–108). Greenwich, CT: JAI.

Woodside, D. B., Garfinkel P. E., Lin, E., Goering, P., and Kaplan, A. S. (2001). Comparisons of men with full or partial eating disorders, men without eating disorders, and women with eating disorders in the community. *American Journal of Psychiatry, 158*(4), 570–574.

Woodworth, S., Belsky, J., and Crnic, K. (1996). The determinants of fathering during the child's second and third years of life: A developmental analysis. *Journal of Marriage and the Family, 58,* 679–692.

Wu, S-J. (2001). Parenting in Chinese American families. In N. B. Webb (Ed.), *Culturally Diverse Parent–Child and Family Relationships: A Guide for Social Workers and other Practitioners.* New York: Columbia University Press.

Yeo, S., Fetters, M., and Maeda, Y. (2000). Japanese couples' childbirth experiences in Michigan: Implications for care. *Birth, 27,* 191–198.

Yescavage, K. (1999). Teaching women a lesson. *Violence Against Women 5*(7), 796–812.

Young, G., and Gately, T. (1988). Neighborhood impoverishment and child maltreatment. *Journal of Family Issues, 9,* 240–254.

Young U.S. adults marry considerably later, live with parents longer than counterparts in the 1960s. (1988). *Psychology Today, 20,* 144–145.

Zabin, L. S., Hirsch, M. B., Emerson, M. R., and Raymond, E. (1992). With whom do inner-city minors talk about their pregnancies? Adolescents' communication with parents and parent surrogates. *Family Planning Perspectives, 24,* 148–154.

Zelkowitz, P. (1987). Social support and aggressive behavior in young children. *Family Relations, 36,* 129–134.

Zick, C. D., and Smith, K. R. (1991a). Marital transitions, poverty, and gender differences in mortality. *Journal of Marriage and the Family, 53,* 327–336.

Zick, C. D., and Smith, K. R. (1991b). Pattern of economic change surrounding the death of a spouse. *Journal of Gerontology, 46,* S310–S320.

Zill, N. (1994). Understanding why children in stepfamilies have more learning and behavior problems than children in nuclear families. In A. Booth and J. Dunn (Eds.), *Stepfamilies: Who Benefits? Who Does Not?* (pp. 97–106). Hillsdale, NJ: Erlbaum.

Zill, N., Morrison, D. R., and Coiro, M. J. (1993). Long-term effects of parental divorce and parent–child relationships, adjustment, and achievement in young adulthood. *Journal of Family Psychology, 7*(1), 91–103.

Zimmerman, K., and Cochran, L. (1993). Alignment of family and work roles. *Career Development Quarterly, 41*(4), 344–349.

Zollar, A. C., and Williams, J. S. (1987). The contribution of marriage to the life satisfaction of Black adults. *Journal of Marriage and the Family, 49,* 87–92.

Zuo, J. (1992). The reciprocal relationship between marital interaction and marital happiness: A three-way study. *Journal of Marriage and the Family, 54,* 870–878.

Zuo, J., and Tang, S. (2000). Breadwinner status and gender ideologies of men and women regarding family roles. *Sociological Perspectives, 43*(1), 29–43.

Zuravin, S. J. (1988). Fertility patterns: Their relationship to child physical abuse and child neglect. *Journal of Marriage and the Family, 50,* 983–993.

Zvonkovic, A. M., Greaves, K. M., Schmiege, C. J., and Hall, L. D. (1996). The marital construction of genders through work and family decisions: A qualitative analysis. *Journal of Marriage and the Family, 58,* 91–100.

Zwerling, P. (1989). A gay wedding. In B. Strong and C. DeVault, *The Marriage and Family Experience* (4th ed.). St. Paul, MN: West.

Credits

Index